MW00824216

This collection of interdisciplinary essays is the first to investigate how images in the history of the natural and physical sciences have been used to shape the history of economic thought. The contributors, historians of science and economics alike, document the extent to which scholars have drawn on physical and natural sciences to ground economic ideas, and evaluate the role and importance of metaphors in the structure and content of economic thought. These range from Aristotle's discussion of the division of labor, to Marshall's evocation of population biology, to Hayek's dependence upon evolutionary concepts, and more recently to neoclassical economists' invocation of chaos theory. Resort to such images, the contributors find, is more than mere rhetorical flourish. Rather, appeals to natural and physical metaphors constitute the very subject matter of the discipline and what might be accepted as the "economic."

Natural images in economic thought

Historical Perspectives on Modern Economics

General Editor: Professor Craufurd D. Goodwin, Duke University

This series contains original works that challenge and enlighten historians of economics. For the profession as a whole it promotes better understanding of the origin and content of modern economics.

Other books in the series:

Natural images in economic thought

"Markets read in tooth and claw"

Edited by

PHILIP MIROWSKI
University of Notre Dame

Published by the Press Syndicate of the University of Cambridge
The Pitt Building, Trumpington Street, Cambridge CB2 1RP
40 West 20th Street, New York, NY 10011-4211, USA
10 Stamford Road, Oakleigh, Melbourne 3166, Australia

© Cambridge University Press 1994

First published 1994

Printed in the United States of America

Library of Congress Cataloging-in-Publication Data
Natural images in economic thought : "markets read in tooth and claw"
/ edited by Philip Mirowski.
p.   cm. – (Historical perspectives on modern economics)
Papers presented at the Conference on Natural Images in Economics,
University of Notre Dame, Sept. 1991.
Includes index.
ISBN 0-521-44321-0 – ISBN 0-521-47884-7 (pbk.)
1. Economics – History – Congresses. I. Mirowski, Philip, 1951– .
II. Conference on Natural Images in Economics (1991 : University
of Notre Dame) III. Series.
HB75.N39   1994
330.1 – dc20   93-41164
                                                             CIP

A catalog record for this book is available from the British Library.

ISBN 0-521-44321-0 hardback
ISBN 0-521-47884-7 paperback

Contents

v

Contributors

Timothy L. Alborn is Assistant Professor of History and Social Studies at Harvard University. He works on the relation between scientific culture and the commercial professions in Victorian England.

Randall Bausor earned a Ph.D. in economics from Duke University and is now Associate Professor of Economics at the University of Massachusetts at Amherst. His research concerns the formal modeling of time in economics, the conceptual and philosophical foundations of economic analysis, and the history of twentieth-century economics.

Paul P. Christensen is Assistant Professor of Economics at Hofstra University. His main area of research is the conceptual influences of physical and biological thought on classical economic theory. He has published articles on the influence of Harvey's physiology on the natural philosophy and economics of Thomas Hobbes (*History of Political Economy*, 1989), on the role of energy availability in industrial transformation and technological development, and on the development of an ecological approach to economic production theory.

I. Bernard Cohen is Victor S. Thomas Professor (emeritus) of the History of Science, Harvard University. A past president of the International Union of the History and Philosophy of Science and of the History of Science Society, he is currently researching Newtonian science, the history of computing and information systems, and the interactions between the natural and the social sciences. In collaboration with Anne Whitman, he has produced a new translation of Newton's *Principia*, to be published in 1994 by the University of California Press.

Ivor Grattan-Guinness has both the doctorate (Ph.D.) and higher doctorate (D.Sc.) in the History of Science from London University. He is currently Reader in Mathematics at Middlesex University, England. He was editor of the history of science journal *Annals of Science* from 1974 to 1981 and founder-editor of the journal *History and Philosophy of Logic* from 1980 to 1992. He is a member of the Académie Internationale d'Histoire des Sciences. His latest book is *Convolutions in French Mathematics, 1800–40*, 3 vols. (Basel, 1990). He is editing the *Encyclopaedia of the History and Philosophy of Mathematical Sciences* for Birkhauser and is also working on the history of mathematical logic and the foundations of mathematics from 1870 to 1930.

James P. Henderson is Professor of Economics at Valparaiso University. He holds a Ph.D. degree in economics from Northern Illinois University. He is the Midwest Regional Director for the Association for Social Economics, is on the editorial board of the *Review of Social Economics,* and has served on the Executive Committee of the History of Economics Society. His research interests include William Whewell's contributions to mathematical economics and the ethical and philosophical foundations of Alfred Marshall's economic thought. He is finishing a book on Whewell's economics for Rowman & Littlefield.

Geoffrey M. Hodgson is Lecturer in Economics at the Judge Institute of Management Studies at the University of Cambridge. He has published widely in academic journals and has written several books, including *Economics and Evolution* (Cambridge, 1993), *After Marx and Sraffa* (London, 1991), *Economics and Institutions* (Philadelphia, 1988), and *The Democratic Economy* (Harmondsworth, 1984). He is General Secretary of the European Association for Evolutionary Political Economy.

Michael Hutter has a Dr. rer. pol. from the University of Munich. He is now Professor of Economics, Witten/Herdecke University. His research interests include cultural economics, monetary history and theory, systems theory, and history of economic thought. He is author of *Die Produktion von Recht* (Tübingen, 1989).

Sharon E. Kingsland is Professor of the History of Science at Johns Hopkins University. Her book, *Modeling Nature* (Chicago, 1985), is a history of the use of mathematical models in population ecology in the mid-twentieth century. Her current research is on the history of biology in the United States, especially experimental studies of evolution at the turn of the century.

Arjo Klamer is the author of *Conversations with Economists* (Totawa, NJ, 1984), *The Consequences of Economic Rhetoric* (Cambridge, 1988, edited with Robert Solow and Donald McCloskey), and *The Making of an Economist* (Boulder, 1989, with David Colander). He is Associate Professor of Economics at George Washington University.

Thomas C. Leonard is a graduate student in economics at George Washington University.

Camille Limoges is presently Director of the Research Center for the Social Assessment of Technology (CREST) at the University of Québec at Montréal. He is the author of numerous studies on the history of biology. He is currently working on the dynamics of public technoscientific controversies and on the history of the development of automated instrumentation for biological research and for regulatory purposes.

Claude Ménard is Professor at the University of Québec at Montréal and Director of the Centre d'Analyse Théorique des Organisations et des Marchés, Laboratoire de Microéconomie Appliquée, University of Paris. He is author of *La formation d'une rationalité économique: A. A. Cournot* (Paris, 1978).

Philip Mirowski is Carl Koch Chair of Economics and the History and Philosophy of Science at the University of Notre Dame. He has also taught at the University of Amsterdam, Tufts, Yale, and the University of Massachusetts. He is the author of *Against Mechanism* (Totawa, NJ, 1988) and *More Heat Than Light* (Cambridge, 1989) and the editor of the forthcoming *Ysidro Ycheued: Edgeworth on Chance, Economic Hazard and Statistics* (Savage, MD). He is now at work on the history and theory of the constitution of error in quantitative measurement. "The Realms of the Natural," Chapter 17 of the present volume, was his inaugural lecture for the Koch Chair.

David Chioni Moore, formerly a corporate banker with Citibank and Citicorp in New York, is a Ph.D. candidate in Literature and Critical Theory at Duke University, where he is writing a dissertation on postcolonial cultural theory in a supranational age. His recent work includes "Accounting on Trial: The Critical Legal Studies Movement and Its Lessons for Radical Accounting" (*Accounting, Organizations and Society*, 1991).

James Bernard Murphy received his Ph.D. in philosophy and political science from Yale University in 1990. He is now Assistant Professor of Government at Dartmouth College, where he teaches political theory. His chapter in this volume develops themes from his *Moral Economy of Labor* (New Haven, CT, 1993).

Neil B. Niman is Associate Professor of Economics at the Whittemore School of Business and Economics, University of New Hampshire. While maintaining a long-standing interest in the history of economic thought, he has focused primarily on organizational economics. Recent publications include "Biological Analogies in Marshall's Work" (*Journal of the History of Economic Thought*, 1991) and "The Entrepreneurial Function in the Theory of the Firm" (*Scottish Journal of Political Economy*, 1991).

Theodore M. Porter is Associate Professor of History at the University of California, Los Angeles, and author of *The Rise of Statistical Thinking, 1820–1900* (Princeton, NJ, 1986). His recent work has been concerned mainly with the cultural and political resonances of objectivity. He is writing a book called *The Quantification of Public Life*.

Alexander Rosenberg is the author of six books on the philosophy of social science, the philosophy of biology, and causation, including most recently *Economics: Mathematical Politics or Science of Diminishing Returns?* (Chicago, 1992). He has held fellowships from the American Council of Learned Societies, the National Science Foundation, and the John Simon Guggenheim Foundation. Rosenberg is Professor of Philosophy at the University of California, Riverside.

Margaret Schabas is Associate Professor of Philosophy at York University, Toronto. She is the author of *A World Ruled by Number* (Princeton, NJ, 1990) and numerous articles. Her research examines concepts of nature in classical political economy.

Michael V. White is Senior Lecturer in the Economics Department, Monash University, Clayton, Australia. His principal research is concerned with explaining the appearance of marginalist/neoclassical economics in the nineteenth century, focusing on the work of William Stanley Jevons. He is editing a forthcoming collection of Jevons's uncollected scientific writings.

Acknowledgments

The editor would like to thank the Carl Koch Endowment, the Provost of Notre Dame, and Mike Loux, former dean of the College of Arts and Letters, for supporting the conference "Natural Images in Economics" at the University of Notre Dame in September 1991. The logistics were ably arranged by Sylvia Phillips, without whom the entire project might have prematurely succumbed to entropic degradation. The office of the Reilly Center for Science, Technology, and Values provided assistance, as did Wade Hands, Charles Craypo of the Department of Economics, and the staff at the Center for Continuing Education at Notre Dame. I would like to thank especially the numerous local faculty and invited guests who offered formal comments and informal advice during the conference and would particularly like to single out Arjo Klamer and Avi Cohen for arranging an event not on the printed schedule. Martin Stack provided research assistance and the index for this volume. Last, but not least, I couldn't have done it without you, Pam.

PART I

The Natural and the Social

CHAPTER 1

Doing what comes naturally: four metanarratives on what metaphors are for

PHILIP MIROWSKI

> Science is like fiction, you see. We make up stories, we sketch out narratives, we try to find some pattern beneath events. We are interested observers. And we like to go on with the story, we like to advance, we like to make progress. Even though they are stories told in the dark.
>
> But you have your equations. Your mathematics –
>
> Oh. Mathematics. Mathematics is like language. No one knows where it came from. No one really knows how it works. More horses and fishes. Horses and fishes trapped in signs. . . .
>
> Oh my God, he said. I am sorry.
>
> Don't be sorry. There's nothing to be sorry about. I chose this life.
>
> Ackroyd (1989, 159)

There are two basic types of people in academic circles: those who think all the major issues in their discipline are settled and those who don't. The former type tends to be correlated with those who dabble in applied mathematical pursuits, though like all good generalizations, it has a countable infinity of exceptions, whereas the latter type tends to congregate in departments of history, anthropology, comparative literature, and sociology. The first type of person probably will not like this introduction or, indeed, many of the chapters in this volume.

Whenever one of the former types encounters one of the latter in some professional capacity, perhaps allowing him- or herself to be drawn out concerning his or her basic presuppositions, the resulting dispute often travels along well-worn grooves. "There are more things in heaven and earth than are dreamed of in your philosophy," intones the cornered Ms. Context. "How dare you deny your senses! I defy you to argue I have not kicked this stone or stripped you of your NEH grant!" retorts Mr. Integro-Differential Determinist.

"Suppose that I told you that the simplest intuitive categories, like male and female, are not as rock-solid as you think."

"Oh no. Please don't bring up gender roles and all that. While some of my best friends are feminists, and I can be caught off guard by an elaborate transvestite as much as the next man, in the final analysis seeing is believing. Mankind would have died out as a species long ago if they had listened to you."

"No, wait. I really mean that sex, not gender, can be a historically contested category . . ."

"What is it with you people and your neurotic denial of progress? Haven't you heard that the Iron Curtain has fallen, that deconstruction has fallen out of fashion, and yet science marches onward? I don't care about the Middle Ages or a bunch of superstitious rubes in a flutter over some hermaphrodite. In modern science, we understand perfectly well that sex is a matter of X and Y chromosomes, and the matter can be settled in a few minutes with a microscope."

"Well, then, how do you explain this recent news clipping (Kolata 1992)? It reports, "Scientists say that dozens of birth defects can blur gender and impossibly complicate the search for a simple genetic test to certify someone as female." Moreover, far from being an academic question, it has cropped up numerous times in the testing of female athletes in certification trials in major international sporting events. Imagine – all your life you're a woman, and then, in front of the klieg lights of a TV audience – clang! – you're disqualified, counted out by some faceless white-coated employee in a genetic test lab, who, by the way, couldn't be bothered with all the complex issues involved."

"Leave it to you to root up some obscure anomaly. No truth is perfect; nobody has ever claimed that. None of this matters to me or anyone else wrapped up in surviving everyday life. These little stories of yours are just ignored for the time being in my particular science. Eventually, if there is a problem, that problem will be solved by some scientist, just like we discovered that storks don't bring babies and sunspots don't cause business cycles. I think it would be a great boon to the health of the university if we just corraled all the anthropologists and comp lit specialists and historians and sociologists of science into one big Department of Useless Fictions, set them fighting among themselves, and let the marketplace of ideas take hindmost, don't you?"

Neither Schumpeter nor Hollander nor Stigler nor . . .

Ah yes, the marketplace of ideas: the last refuge of the fin-de-siècle scoundrel. In the long run we are all dead, said an eminent economist;

but he didn't say if there was an injunction to pay off all our debts before we departed. The settler of accounts between the Natural and the Social has always been a deadbeat in the annals of Western economic discourse. A generic Nature has borne too heavy a burden in orthodox histories of economics in the twentieth century, maybe because most economists have thought that all the basic issues were definitively settled.

Take Joseph Schumpeter, for example. He set the tone for the postwar textbook of the "history of economic thought" in his magesterial *History of Economic Analysis*. His objective was to rewrite the history as the narrative of inexorable triumph leading up to the neoclassical orthodoxy, separating out the "science" from the ideology, the historical contingency, vagaries of politics and interdisciplinary influences, and so on. He was a living, breathing contradiction: a worldly philosopher who claimed that "the garb of philosophy is removable" to reveal the timeless doctrine underneath; a polymath who flaunted his own breadth only to dismiss its relevance; a German historicist who ultimately sought to negate history. He was, however, acutely aware of the embarrassing postures his intense self-denial would land him in and struggled mightily with his dark daemon until his death (Allen 1991). The posthumous papers that later were incorporated as early chapters of the *History* attest to this heritage of German-Austrian social thought:

> This history as a whole will answer the question whether there actually has been such uncritical copying of the methods [of mathematical physics] that have meaning only within the particular pattern of science that developed them – apart of course from the programmatic utterances . . . [which] mean next to nothing. (1954, 17)

But the sad fact is that, hundreds of pages later, the question remained woefully unanswered. In the fragment just quoted, he suggests vaguely that mathematics bears no implicit content and writes, "The things we are accused of borrowing are merely the reflexes of the fact that all of us, physicists or economists, have only one type of brain to work with and this brain acts in ways that are to some extent similar." Unhappily, nothing in his massive *History* ventures to describe how physicists' brains, nor indeed the brain of any specific scientist, "work"; and from the sound of it, it was not intellectual history but rather depth psychiatry or neurobiology or perhaps our newfangled cognitive science that was called for in Schumpeter's view to answer the question which apparently motivated his project. The promissory note was never paid in full.

Things have not gotten better in the interim. In texts by George Stigler, Jürg Niehans, Samuel Hollander, Donald Walker, Paul Samuelson, and other leading orthodox economists, the narrative of the triumph of neoclassicism is essentially the same, but now all pretense of breadth, intellectual motivation, and philosophical concern is dispensed with as superfluous. "Science" is treated as a natural kind while Nature calls the tune; rival traditions that interrogated the shape and integrity of the Natural and the Social are summarily banished from the history; and all explanation sports a monotonous sameness, be it yesterday or in the seventeenth century. The heirs of Schumpeter have been living off credit for so long they don't even seem to be aware that there are chronic balance-of-trade problems in the land of social science empire building.

Economics, née political economy, née moral philosophy, has been a prime locus of the hashing out of definitions of both the Natural and the Social in Western culture – hence the inspiration for the present collection of essays. One would think that in the vast library of histories and commentaries on the discipline, which extends well back to the eighteenth century, there would be a wealth of meditations on the uses of Nature in the discussion of Society, if not the obverse; but, in fact, the converse is the case.[1] What we find under the rubric of the "history of economic thought" or "economic methodology" are half-baked assessments of the inexorably cumulative character of a disembodied, self-assured inquiry governed by an ill-defined "scientific method" or else anxieties expressing concern over the legitimate intellectual status of the discipline, purportedly to be assuaged by recourse to some philosopher's stone, be the mason of choice Francis Bacon or Isaac Newton or Immanuel Kant or Georg Hegel or William Whewell or John Stuart Mill or Karl Popper or Thomas Kuhn or Imre Lakatos or (fill in the blank). In the process much of the interesting historical content of the constitution of the object of inquiry gets lost. (We decline to comment here on whether the bulk of the orthodox economics profession, those first sort of people in our rough and ready initial dichotomy, would deem it a world well lost.)

The purpose of this volume is the recovery and revival of the heritage of thought banished by the heirs of Schumpeter. We are not interested in holding up economics to a single abstract yardstick or in drawing a rectilinear curve from any arbitrary text to some modern orthodox topic. Instead, essays in this volume generally ask: What did it mean in a specific historical context for a particular text to lay claim to some variant of a "scientific" status?

Old questions, new answers

The ability to ask certain kinds of questions about the evolution of the discipline has very nearly been lost in many economics departments, and therefore it was the goal of the conference entitled "Natural Images in Economics" at the University of Notre Dame in September 1991 to attempt to revive them. These questions ranged from dauntingly global philosophical issues about the place of economics in the archaeology of knowledge to some relatively parochial historical queries about the exact content of the Natural for a particular text at a particular historical juncture. Some of the questions, arrayed from the lofty to the more mundane, can be surveyed here in an abstract manner.

To begin, there was a danger in an event retailed under the title "Natural Images in Economics" of implicitly taking the Natural/Social distinction as given *a priori* and therefore external to the task of describing the impact of the natural sciences on economic discourse. Happily, the long-neglected question of how and when the separate spheres of Nature and of Society came to assume their modern outlines informs many of the specific narratives contained herein. Innovative research in these areas of the history of science by such figures as Bruno Latour, Ted Porter, Joan Richards, I. B. Cohen, Donna Haraway, Adrian Desmond, and Lorraine Daston can and have provided inspiration for parallel inquiries from the vantage point of the history of economics. But more can be done, and the net can potentially be cast much wider. For instance, the intellectual historian Donald Kelley has written a fascinating book entitled *The Human Measure,* which traces the split between a hermeneutical and naturalist study of society to legal traditions dating from the twelfth century. It opens up the tantalizing possibility that our images of modern science themselves were derived from the model of jurisprudence, so that the subsequent rivalry between the natural and social sciences may be regarded as more of a family feud than the clash of irreconcilable principles (1990, 143, 173). Political economy would then stand in an entirely different relationship to the law than that portrayed by neoclassical imperialists of more recent vintage.[2]

Indeed, one of the conference participants, Margaret Schabas, had earlier asked in another venue whether it makes any sense to maintain a history of economics separate from the disciplinary structures of the history of science.[3] However sanguine one might feel about where inquiries concerning the Natural and the Social might eventually find a home, these are the sorts of long-lost questions encouraged by the reassertion of a historical sensibility represented at this conference. This volume provides tangible evidence that the two previously isolated communities can, at a minimum, get together in the same room (away from home) and find that there is much common basis for discussion. It should be apparent that a fair acquaintance with the history of the sciences (*plural*) is a prerequisite for even broaching the question of the demarcation of the Natural and the Social; and in a world where the polymath is an endangered species, the only practical solution is closer contact between historians of science and historians of economics.

A salutary effect of becoming acquainted with modern history of science is that participating economists would rapidly become sensitized to various ethnographic and literary devices concocted over the centuries to distance ourselves from our unconscious presuppositions concerning the nature of the Natural. For instance, Michael Adas (1989) has bequeathed us an absorbing study of how Western perceptions of superiority over other cultures shifted from a belief in transcendent truths, perhaps inaccessible to but equally valid for all peoples, to a smugness about proprietary technological and scientific artifacts of Western origin; this surely marks a profound watershed in the Natural–Social distinction, one relevant to economistic notions of "development." Simon Schaffer and Steve Shapin (1985) have written a fascinating narrative of the rise of the "experimental form of life" in the context of seventeenth-century English politics. Or again, the foregrounding of the boundaries between what is "us" and "not-us" in the modern social studies of science literature can jolt readers out of our reverie of detachment, what Thomas Nagel has called "the view from nowhere." The topics that might impinge on the history of economic thought could range from the means by which physical and economic concepts have jointly buttressed and constituted one another (Mirowski 1989; Wise 1989–91), to the origins of aperspectival objectivity in Adam Smith's *Theory of Moral Sentiments* (Daston 1992), to the shifting boundaries of what has historically been regarded as human (Sheehan and Sosna 1991); to the role of mathematics in seemingly banishing the dreaded specter of anthropomorphism (Mirowski 1992).

At a somewhat lower level of generality, another currently repressed question concerns the struggle to constitute a separate political economy out of a proposed generic science of society, or out of a single generic science *tout court*. A recurrent theme in Western discourse is the dream of a single unified science. This program from Comte to Carnap mostly centered on "methods," but the reductionist holy grail was never far from sight, holding out the promise of the reduction of economics to psychology, psychology to biology, and biology to physics. Frequently in the narratives in this volume, the protagonists tend to elide the distinction between unification of methods and reductionism in subject matter (or as I. B. Cohen puts it, the distinction between form and function), partly due to the implicit rhetorical strategies of their subjects, but also partly due to the conflicting imperatives of appropriating the trappings of another science in order to constitute political economy as separate and self-sufficient science. The chapters by Michael White and Paul Christensen are especially concerned with this phenomenon, while disputing interpretations of Marshall by Schabas, Niman, Limoges and Ménard would seem to pivot on this issue.

Another question that one could search for in vain in the previous canon of the history of economic thought is that of the relationship of political economy to the protracted, and predominantly Germanic, historicist heritage that had argued the desirability and even necessity of a separate and distinct mode for the study of society. In sociology and anthropology, the doctrine of *Verstehen* and Dilthey's insistence upon a distinction between the *Geisteswissenschaften* and the *Naturwissenschaften* are common currency; but in the economic methodology literature, all that has been tendered are dark hints that the dreaded vampire had a stake driven clean through its heart by Carl Menger in the *Methodenstreit* and then had a few silver bullets pumped into its decrepit frame by Karl Popper. Outside of a brief frisson of interest in Gadamerian hermeneutics (Lavoie 1991), there has been no evidence that economists might actually deem such themes relevant to understanding their own history. Here, the chapters by Michael Hutter and James Murphy are particularly relevant.

Finally, we come to the most finely grained set of questions that have not, until now, engaged the talents of historians of economics: What were the local uses of particular images of the Natural in the constitution of specific economic theories? Perhaps not surprisingly, this is the format that many of the chapters herein have assumed. Historians have always excelled in bringing to life the contingent particularities of the chosen event or singular doctrine, and this gathering was no exception. Pointing out the recourse to biological metaphor or physical analogue is the first step in establishing awareness of the pervasive influence of the Natural on the Social, establishing a baseline from which to construct larger and more complex narratives of their twining twinning exfoliation.

Rather than summarize individual chapters, I shall indicate briefly some ways in which the case studies herein might serve in the construction of more complex narratives of the Natural and the Social. These insights grow out of the uncomfortable experience of witnessing reactions to a book called *More Heat Than Light*. The putative author of this problematic text could not seem to make up his mind whether or not economics ought to imitate physics; whether economists should aspire to be mathematical scientists or literary critics; whether biology or anthropology should constitute the Mecca of economics; whether real physicists are nice guys or pushy parvenus; or even whether any extant economics is a viable intellectual project. To banish this fellow before he spreads discord and drivel thoughout the land, it may clarify matters to lay out all the permutations of possible configurations of the Natural and the Social in Western thought and indicate which ones correlate with potential interpretations of the project embodied in this volume.

Four metaphorical metanarratives

To save space, as well as to placate economists who may have little patience with such distinctions, these four configurations are presented in schematic format in Table 1.1. Some representative names are attached by way of illustration, mainly to signal to philosophers that much more might be said in more self-consciously philosophical contexts. Since we started out in our introductory dialogue positing two basic types of people, and will here allow two states of mind for each type regarding the status of the Natural and the Social, we fashion $2^2 = 4$ broad metanarratives.

I think it fairly transparent that the presuppositions of most neoclassical economists do not venture outside of the ambit of position 1, the only exception being a very few members of the older generation who read German and may have been partisans of position 2a. This clumping of the mass of economic practitioners into more or less a single quadrant cannot be written off completely to herd instincts or severe brainwashing in graduate school, although there is something to be said for each hypothesis (Colander and Klamer 1990). Rather, it is an artifact of the historical genesis of the neoclassical program, as explained in *More Heat Than Light*. In appropriating the formalisms of mid-nineteenth-century energy physics and adapting them to the language of utility and prices, the progenitors and their epigones adopted a certain worldview, one that had to stress the extreme near identity of physics and economics. Veering so close to becoming subsumed in pure identity could be attractive only to a personality who was convinced of a far-reaching unity of science, one necessarily

Table 1.1. *The Natural and the Social*

1. The Natural and the Social are identical in
a. every respect (extreme reductionism)
b. laws (Churchland)
c. epistemic methods (Glymour, Cartwright)
d. metaphorical structure (Schumpeter)
2. The Natural and the Social are disjunct but individually lawlike due to
a. epistemic status (Windelband, Rickert, Weber, Kuhn)
b. ontological status rooted in psychology (Dilthey, Taylor)
c. purposes (Habermas, Dreyfus)
3. The Natural is objectively stable, whereas the Social is patterned on it but is not stable, implying
a. a sociology of collective knowledge (Durkheim, Mannheim)
b. sociology as epistemology (Douglas, Bloor, Shapin)
4. The Natural and the Social are both unstable and hence jointly constructed as mutually supportive
a. out of interests (Latour, Haraway, actant-network theory)
b. out of practices (modern pragmatists, Hacking, Rouse)
c. out of will (Nietzsche, Foucault)

founded on the bedrock of a natural law external to all human endeavor. Perhaps the best example of a neoclassical who understood this with great clarity was Francis Ysidro Edgeworth (see Mirowski 1994). There are still plenty of people who believe that sort of thing today; and those folks surely are convinced that the author of *More Heat* was incapable of making up his mind whether he wanted to assert that the neoclassicals' use of physics was defective, or that the physicists themselves were mistaken about the true conservation principles, or that he was struggling toward some empirical claim about the nature of conservation of economic phenomena. An alternative, and for my money, a more consistent reading of *More Heat* would situate the author as a partisan of position 4b.

Many of the authors who are active partisans of a specific natural metaphor in this volume, such as Ménard and Niman and Grattan-Guinness, should probably be categorized under the rubric of position 1. Advocates of the separate but equal doctrine of position 2 would include James Murphy and Alex Rosenberg, although the latter has been known to take other positions in the past. Partisans of position 3 tend to be located outside of economics (with the notable exceptions of Geoffrey Hodgson and Randall Bausor) and to be critical of the uses made of physical concepts in the past, such as Bernard Cohen, Ted Porter, and Sharon Kingsland. However, the most novel aspect of this volume was to introduce into the discourse, possibly for the first time, advocates of position 4 as rival constructors of alternative narrative histories of economic thought. This group includes David Moore, Tim Alborn, Arjo Klamer, Michael Hutter, and the editor. One advantage of this less-skewed (than normal?) distribution of opinions about tackling the problems of the Natural and the Social was a realization that the terminology of metaphor could be used by all four groups as a vehicle of communication, but that the significance and interpretation of metaphor would vary widely, depending on the presuppositions with which the particular historian sets out.

To indicate the multivalent character of the slippery idea of a Natural metaphor, let us start with a passage that may speak to economists, one frequently quoted nowadays in philosophical circles, from Nietzsche's "Truth and Lie in the Extra-moral Sense":

> What, then, is truth? A mobile army of metaphors, metonyms and anthropomorphisms – in short, a sum of human relations, which have been enhanced, transposed, and embellished poetically and rhetorically, and which after long use seem firm, canonical, and obligatory to a people: truths are illusions about which one has forgotten that this is what they are; metaphors which are worn out and without sensuous power; coins which have lost their pictures and now matter only as metal, no longer as coins. (Kaufmann 1954, 46–7)

For the partisans of some form of identity thesis 1, this quote is an anathema. If someone in economics appropriates a metaphor from (say) physics, it can only be because that person is operationalizing the insight that there is a direct isomorphism of phenomena involved; the metaphor can fail only in not being sufficiently *literal,* which is why the partisans of position 1 typically resist looking into the unfamiliar terminology of metaphors, metonyms, and anthropomorphisms. Utility didn't turn out to be actually a manifestation of potential energy? Too bad, but nice try. Firms don't actually possess anything like a gene? Better luck next time.

Historians occupying position 2, that of separation if not outright quarantine of the Social from the Natural, tend to alight on the phrase "a sum of human relations" to the exclusion of the rest of the quote. For them, recourse to metaphors is the inescapable consequence of interpretation in human social interaction. As Thomas Kuhn has written, "The natural sciences, though they may require what I have called a hermeneutic base, are not themselves hermeneutic enterprises. The human sciences, on the other hand, often are, and may have no alternatives."[4] Thus, it is no big deal for these folks that (say) neoclassical economics is predicated upon an energetics metaphor; descriptions are always parasitic on previous descriptions, interpretations always derive from previous interpretations; the only problem being in this case that the neoclassicals must eventually fess up, confession being good for the soul, thus permitting the reassertion of the Great Dichotomy.

Advocates of position 3 revel in what they regard as the cynicism evident in the Nietzsche quote. For them, metaphors are necessary tools in a multilayered power game; the Natural is predominantly a resource in the furtherance of particular human interests. In this view, when the neoclassicals equated utility with potential energy, they were "really" shoring up their own legitimacy in various ways: making the market appear as a Natural phenomenon, trying to disenfranchise the fuddy-duddy political economists who didn't know the calculus from chicken scratching, fostering the impression of a mechanical interconnection of prices so that special academic expertise would be required for enlightened state intervention. Metaphors for partisans of position 3 are a necessary evil, a kind of false consciousness for the masses. The role of the social anthropologist or historian in this framework is to be a gadfly, nagging all and sundry to testify that their mean lumps of metal were once upon a time freshly minted inflationary coins. I should myself testify that I have dealt in this particular currency in the past, especially when mentioning the Durkheim–Mauss–Douglas thesis (see Chapter 17), but that I should now like to suggest that some aspects of Mary Douglas's later writings are better subsumed under position 4.

The partisans of position 4 love the entire quote from Nietzsche because (beyond the fact that this is the category where he really belongs) his "extra-moral sense" captures the fact of the pervasiveness of metaphor that cannot be matched by any of the other positions. Metaphors here do not come into play solely as literary frills, or as a ghostly hermeneutics suspended above the rock-solid external world, or as weapons in the war of all against all; here, rather, their analysis promises the leveling of all disciplinary pretensions. To quote Richard Rorty, it is "the fantasy that the very idea of hermeneutics should disappear, in the way in which old general ideas do disappear when they lose polemical and contrastive force – when they begin to have universal applicability. My fantasy is of a culture so deeply anti-essentialist that it makes only a sociological distinction between sociologists and physicists, not a methodological or philosophical one" (in Hiley et al. 1991, 71). As a word of warning, we would not be bona fide historians in good standing if we did not continually remind ourselves that this *is* indeed a fantasy, not the reigning state of affairs in any concrete situation. However, it is an exceptionally powerful antidote to the writing of Whig histories and, I would suggest, a cornucopia of strikingly arresting narratives constructed around the device of metaphoric appropriations.

I think we can revise some of Mary Douglas's theses about the functional roles of the Natural and the Social by appending to them the proviso that neither pole provides a timeless Archimedian point for the other, and therefore the very constitution of both poles shifts about skittishly through time. The problem in any coherent narrative, as I tried to suggest in *More Heat,* is where to locate the invariance when confronting pervasive change. Mary Douglas has proposed one solution: "It is naive to treat the quality of sameness, which characterizes members of a class, as if it were a quality inherent in things or as a power of recognition inherent in the mind . . . Institutions bestow sameness" (1986, 58, 63). The invariance relations enter "constructivist" narratives precisely through the dynamics of the process of the naturalization of social thought and through their converse, the "anthropometricization" of natural science. Using Natural metaphors in theories of Society fosters reassuring and graphically concrete images of order, situating humanity squarely at home in "its" universe, while the parallel projection of social concepts onto Nature render what might otherwise be an unintelligible alien world comprehensible and accessible to human desires and purposes. *The identity resides in the process,* and not in any especially stable character of Nature *or* Society. Under these conditions, severe ruptures in physical or social theory can still be assimilated as part and parcel of the "same" project, even though most everything else, from the idiom of the theory to the integrity of the facts, might be inverted or even left behind. But most important, this revised version of the Douglas thesis also explains the persistence of vituperative unresolved disputes over the meaning and primacy of the Natural versus the Social in Western intellectual life. In this view, there are no special ontological or epistemological distinctions that underwrite the Natural–Social duality; the problem of the "Two Cultures" will not be transcended by any concerted program of transdisciplinary education; the vindication of social thought does not await some quantum leap allowing it to catch up to the privileged status of the natural sciences. Instead, the great leveling of essentialisms mentioned by Rorty comes home to roost.

Some brief sketches of how this method of using metaphorical reasoning to construct historical narratives will point in directions toward which this movement might go. Think of this kind of history as a kind of spiral, gyrating back and forth between historically contingent locations of the Natural and the Social, wobbling when the poles themselves shift. Take the interplay of political economy and Darwinian evolution, a topic of much discussion in this volume. To put the sketch crudely, Malthus began his essay by comparing people to animals in order to fix his conception of population pressing upon resources. Darwin, as has often been noted,[5] read Malthus and the political economists, and this (by his own testimony) prompted him to see competition and the division of labor in animal Nature. Darwinism was quite rapidly reprojected back upon society in the form of social Darwinism. Mix two parts social Darwinism with a dash of simple Marshallian microeconomics and you arrive at E. O. Wilson's theory of sociobiology; opt instead for two parts game theory and you get the new population ecology.[6] And since the spiral never stops, mix some elements of the new evolutionary synthesis with varying proportions of population biology and previous economics, and you might end up with either a slightly less mechanistic Marshallianism or else a rejuvenated institutionalism, according to some of the contributors to this volume.

Probability theory is another topic touched on by some of our chapters; it too might be recast as a constructivist spiral narrative. For example, early notions of the probability appeared in legal ("social") contexts concerning the plausibility of evidence and the division of partnership stakes in risky undertakings; quantitative probability was patterned on the model of the fair division of expectations (Daston 1988). When transported to the astronomical context, mathematical "moral" expectation was recast as a "law of error" describing the Natural distribution of observations around a true value. The Gaussian or "normal" distribution was then reflected back onto the Social sphere by Quetelet as errors of approximation to a law-governed *homme moyen* (Porter 1986). Upon reading Herschel's gloss on Quetelet, James Clerk Maxwell transposed the image of order hidden in a seemingly random population back onto Nature by using the same reasoning to derive transport phenomena in the gas laws (Porter 1981). Among others, Francis Ysidro Edgeworth took his cue from Maxwell to describe the ultimate stability of the market in the midst of indeterminateness of contract (Mirowski 1994). In the meantime, probability theory spread in physics from the gas laws to thermodynamics and then to quantum mechanics; from there it was used as justification for the incorporation of probability theory into econometrics. And the spiral ever continues.

It is my contention that just such spiral narratives could organize the otherwise confusing proliferation of "externalist" metaphors documented here for economics, as well as in the history of science literature previously cited for disciplines such as physics, biology, and mathematics. The advocacy of such spirals by historians of economic thought could have some healthy side effects: the liberation from their subordinate status within economics as assistant apologists for an entrenched imperialist campaign against all other varieties of human knowledge; wider access to modern cultural conversations concerning the aims and drawbacks of the present configurations of the sciences (Proctor 1991); initiation of the first serious inquiry concerning the role of mathematics in human discourse and in economics; widened horizons as to what practically constitutes economic discussion outside of academia; and, last but not least, the beginnings of a genuine understanding of the history of orthodox neoclassical economics. And for those still enamored of cost–benefit analysis: What have historians got to lose?

While it is not smart salesmanship to wind up on a downbeat note, it may be prudent to acknowledge that metanarrative 4 is not some sort of universal nostrum for everything that ails economics; nor is it the grand metanarrative that will once and for all silence all other rival narratives. One need only glance at a recent conference volume edited by Andrew Pickering (1992) to observe that partisans of positions 3 and 4 in the science studies community have recently grown violently at odds over the future directions of their specialty. Sociologists of science, there represented by David Bloor and Harry Collins, want to maintain a species of naive realism about Society while pursuing constructivist narratives about Nature, primarily because they believe, "The field of science studies is engaged in a moral struggle to strip science of its extravagant claims to authority. Any move that waffles on this issue appears unethical."[7] By contrast, Bruno Latour, speaking for position 4, wants to utterly demolish all Nature–Society distinctions with his "actant-network theory," treating things, artifacts, and people all as conspiring to spread networks of influence and power, subjecting the lot to some semiotic analysis by means of some canned computer programs. In their debate, it is acknowledged that Collins's work is very good at sniffing out the emergence of controversy, the indefinite negotiation of what will count as facts, and the infinite regress of underdetermination in empirical work, but relatively weak in describing the causes of closure of the indeterminate. Latour, in contrast, is very savvy concerning the slow incremental black boxing of controversy, but relatively weak on why it exists in the first place.

Even the most self-conscious of students of science cannot fully rid themselves of the nasty conundrums associated with Nature and Society; Rorty's fantasy is still very much a fantasy. But that doesn't mean it couldn't be true.

Notes

1. Some exceptions, which are notable by their very absence from the orthodox canons of the history of economic thought, are Foucault (1973), Tribe (1978), and Veblen (1990).
2. "The history of the relation between political economy and jurisprudence (and indeed of political economy itself in any comprehensive way) remains to be written" (Kelley 1990, 257). Lest one think this has a very tenuous relationship to modern concerns, it may be salutary to point out that much of what passes as "policy" analysis, say, about the reform of the U.S. health care system, is in fact only thinly disguised philosophizing about the relationship of Nature to the polity. On this issue, see the fascinating work of Frankford (1992, 1993). Another attempt to sketch the relationship between political economy and jurisprudence is my Chapter 17 in this volume.
3. See Schabas (1992) and the various commentaries that follow it. It is interesting that, as a historian, she does not delve into the possible historical determinants of the great divide that has separated the history of science and history of economics in the past, though this may perhaps have been taken as an obvious corollary of their disciplinary origins.
4. Quoted in Hiley et al. (1991, 23). He then goes on to suggest that "parts of economics and sociology" may have escaped this doom to attain "normal science" status. It just goes to show that if you give a physicist the slightest opportunity, all the old cultural hubris comes roaring out unchecked. At a conference on Kuhn's work at the Massachusetts Institute of Technology on May 18, 1990, Kuhn admitted that more than 50% of the royalties on his book came from it being assigned in social science classes, but then avowed that he rejects the uses made of it there. So much for the intrinsic liberating effect of Kuhnian paradigms! On the misreading of Kuhn as revolutionary, see Fuller (1993).
5. The literature here is vast. Some of the best work is by Robert Young (1985), Adrian Desmond and James Moore (1991), and Silvan Schweber (1980).
6. John Maynard Smith (1990, 36) is wonderfully up front about all this: "But what general sense can one make of the analogies between organism, colony, and human society? . . . if biologists invented pseudoclassical technical terms to replace the obvious colloquial ones, they would be rightly criticized as elitist and obscurantist. . . . If the analogy is so precise that the same mathematical description can be used of the two systems, then it may be possible for workers in one field to borrow mathematics from another, as biologists have borrowed the marginal value theorem and game theory from economists."

7. This is a slightly jaundiced characterization of their project by Bruno Latour (in Pickering 1992, 346). What is significant, however, is that Collins and Yearly acquiesce in this characterization.

References

Ackroyd, Peter. 1989. *First Light.* New York: Grove Weidenfield.

Adas, Michael. 1989. *Machines as the Measure of Men.* Ithaca, NY: Cornell University Press.

Allen, Robert Loring. 1991. *Opening Doors.* New Brunswick, NJ: Transaction.

Blaug, Mark. 1985. *Economic Theory in Retrospect,* 4th ed. Cambridge University Press.

Colander, David, and Klamer, Arjo. 1990. *The Making of an Economist.* Boulder, CO: Westview Press.

Daston, Lorraine. 1988. *Classical Probability in the Age of the Enlightenment.* Princeton, NJ: Princeton University Press.

Daston, Lorraine. 1992. "Objectivity and the Escape from Perspective," *Social Studies of Science,* 22: 597–618.

Desmond, Adrian, and Moore, James. 1991. *Darwin.* London: Michael Joseph.

Douglas, Mary. 1986. *How Institutions Think.* Syracuse, NY: Syracuse University Press.

Foucault, Michel. 1973. *The Order of Things.* New York: Vintage.

Frankford, David. 1992. "Privatizing Health Care: Economic Magic to Cure Legal Medecine," *Southern California Law Review,* 66: 1–98.

Frankford, David. 1993. "Neoclassical Health Economics and the Debate over National Health Insurance," *Law & Social Inquiry,* 18: 351–91.

Fuller, Steve. 1993. "Being There with Thomas Kuhn," *History and Theory,* 36: 241–75.

Hiley, D., Bohman, J., and Shusterman, R., eds. 1991. *The Interpretative Turn.* Ithaca, NY: Cornell University Press.

Kaufmann, Walter, ed. 1954. *The Portable Nietzsche.* New York: Viking.

Kelley, Donald. 1990. *The Human Measure.* Cambridge, MA: Harvard University Press.

Kolata, Gina. 1992. "Who Is Female? Science Can't Say," *New York Times,* Feb. 16.

Lavoie, Don, ed. 1991. *Economics and Hermeneutics.* London: Routledge.

Mirowski, Philip. 1989. *More Heat Than Light: Economics as Social Physics, Physics as Nature's Economics.* Cambridge University Press.

Mirowski, Philip. 1992. "Looking for Those Natural Numbers," *Science in Context,* 5: 165–88.

Mirowski, Philip. 1994. *Ysidro Ycheued: Edgeworth on Chance, Economic Hazard and Statistics.* Savage, MD: Rowman & Littlefield.

Pickering, Andrew, ed. 1992. *Science as Practice and Culture.* Chicago: University of Chicago Press.

Porter, Theodore. 1981. "A Statistical Survey of Gases," *Historical Studies in the Physical Sciences*, (12): 77–114.

Porter, Theodore. 1986. *The Rise of Statistical Thinking*. Princeton, NJ: Princeton University Press.

Porter, Theodore. 1989. "Natural Science and Social Theory," in R. Olby, G. Cantor, and M. Hodge, eds., *Companion to the History of Modern Science*, 1022–43. London: Routledge.

Proctor, Robert. 1991. *Value-Free Science?* Cambridge, MA: Harvard University Press.

Schabas, Margaret. 1992. "Breaking Away: History of Economics as History of Science," *History of Political Economy*, 24: 187–203.

Schaffer, Simon, and Shapin, Steven. 1985. *Leviathan and the Air Pump*. Princeton, NJ: Princeton University Press.

Schumpeter, Joseph. 1954. *A History of Economic Analysis*. New York: Oxford University Press.

Schweber, Silvan. 1980. "Darwin and the Political Economists," *Journal of the History of Biology*, 13: 195–289.

Sheehan, J., and Sosna, M., eds. 1991. *The Boundaries of Humanity*. Berkeley and Los Angeles: University of California Press.

Smith, John Maynard. 1990. "Triumphs of Colonialism," *New York Review of Books*, Sept. 27, 36–7.

Tribe, Keith. 1978. *Land, Labour and Economic Discourse*. London: Routledge.

Veblen, Thorstein. 1990. *The Place of Science in Modern Civilization*. New Brunswick, NJ: Transaction.

Wise, M. Norton. 1989–91. "Work and Waste: Political Economy and Natural Philosophy in Nineteenth Century Britain," *History of Science*, 27: 263–301, 391–449; 28: 221–61.

Young, Robert. 1985. *Darwin's Metaphor*. Cambridge University Press.

CHAPTER 2

So what's an economic metaphor?

ARJO KLAMER and THOMAS C. LEONARD

> Knowing is nothing but working with one's favorite metaphors.
>
> Friedrich Nietzsche
>
> Indeed, as the documents of science pile up, are we not coming to see that whole works of scientific research, even entire schools, are hardly more than the patient repetition, in all its ramifications, of a fertile metaphor?
>
> Kenneth Burke

Until 1983, when Donald McCloskey invited literary criticism to the table of economics, the very notion of metaphor was virtually absent from economic discourse. Arguing in "The Rhetoric of Economics," McCloskey proposed taking metaphor seriously.[1] Since his article appeared in the *Journal of Economic Literature*, metaphor has acquired some currency among economists; its mention is no longer a show-stopping non sequitur.

The currency of the term "metaphor" does not, however, imply a general acceptance of its importance. On the contrary, suspicion and indifference still rule the day, if we may speak metaphorically. The average economist would be unable to locate "metaphor" in the economic lexicon. Many of our colleagues will grant the existence of metaphor, perhaps even conceding its ubiquity, but they then rejoin with the debater's bogey – "So what?"

The suspicion rests, we surmise, on the impression that metaphors introduce ambiguity. The imprecision created by ambiguous meaning is presumably fine for poets, but anathema for scientists. When McCloskey equates economics with poetry because it too relies on metaphors, scientifically minded economists are offended. "What matters is that we, as scientists, write down in a precise way what we mean. Precision is one of the standards by which we measure science. And by

20

that standard, metaphors are nonscientific. If metaphor occurs in economics, so what? – its existence is incidental to the business of doing economics." The "so what?" reply was invoked by Robert Solow (1988) in response to the Klamer–McCloskey rhetorical perspective. According to Solow, the rhetorical perspective had in 1986 yet to advance beyond the " 'look, Ma, a metaphor' stage." A more useful inquiry, he suggests, will examine how metaphors actually work in economics.

Some authors have taken up Solow's "so what?" gauntlet. Klamer (1987) tries to account for the persuasiveness of the individuals-are-rational metaphor by exposing the network of meanings in which that metaphor is embedded. Bicchieri (1988) distinguishes poetic from scientific metaphors and suggests that the latter serve a cognitive function essential to science. Mirowski (1989) argues that neoclassical economics was founded on a nineteenth-century physics metaphor and accuses neoclassical economists of (among other things) violating their appropriated metaphor. And metaphor is the motif in this collection of explorations in the history of economics.

These efforts constitute the beginning of a response to the skeptical "so what?" And while this chapter and those that follow cannot answer decisively, they clearly demonstrate that careful attention to metaphor in economic discourse will deliver unexpected insights. Metaphor proves to be a window for surprising and refreshing vistas of economists and their work.

The original purpose of this chapter was to clear some semantic brush and, in so doing, perhaps clarify the roles that metaphor and other figures play in scientific discourse. To this end, we have added a glossary of terms, which, we hope, will be of use to those less well acquainted with the rhetorical perspective's idiom. Most of what we argue is the plunder of an economic raid into the immense literature spawned by our English, philosophy, and history of science department colleagues.

Brush clearing and clarification are, of course, always precarious (and often quixotic) enterprises. Along the way we found that metaphor takes several guises in economics. McCloskey, Mirowski, and other rhetoricians are right: Economics *is* metaphorical. The skeptics, however, also have a point: Not *all* of economics' metaphors matter. We cannot say, "Metaphor is a metaphor is a metaphor." Some metaphors matter and some don't. By distinguishing among our metaphors, we find that some of the most abstruse ones are unexpectedly important. These metaphors, which we will call constitutive metaphors, matter so profoundly that we argue they can explain much of the confusion and misunderstanding that characterizes discourse within economics and between economics and its lay audiences.

With this conclusion we join ranks with Mirowski, who, in Chapter 1, convincingly argues that fundamental conflicts in what we expect from science prevent us from seeing eye to eye. We play our theme several octaves lower, however, arguing that the conflicts themselves are partly metaphorical in origin. We therefore cannot round up the usual subjects: Neoclassicals are lazy, benighted, antiintellectual, ideologically blinkered, and so on. Instead, we do better to examine economic metaphors, especially those that prevent conversation.

Economic metaphors

As with so many things, we found that language theorists, philosophers, and other students of metaphor begin with Aristotle.[2] The Philosopher's definition is as follows: "[M]etaphor consists in giving the thing a name that belongs to something else; the transference being either from genus to species, or from species to genus, or from species to species, or on grounds of analogy" (Poetica 1457b). Here Aristotle already presages the central claim in the traditional view of metaphor, namely, metaphor as deviation from the meaning of *literal* language. Metaphor is called a *trope,* or "turning" of meaning from the literal to the *figurative:* deviation "from ordinary modes of speech" (Poetics 1458a).[3] When we say that "Johnson is a sparkplug," we do not mean that Johnson is *literally* a sparkplug. The reader understands this in comprehending the implied figurative meaning. "Johnson is a sparkplug" has an intelligible meaning that "Johnson is a socket wrench" does not.[4]

With this gloss in hand, we can gather metaphors without much imagination. A conspicuous example from the economist's bailiwick is <time is money>. (We will sometimes employ brackets to call attention to an expression as metaphorical in some fashion.) The expression is metaphorical because time is not money – as the sentence literally claims. As a matter of fact, the point of a metaphor is precisely that it is *not* taken literally.[5] When <time flies>,[6] money does not likewise take wing. Should your Volvo ever approach relativistic speeds, the cash in your pocket will not "slow down" relative to the funds in your checking account. Somehow, you ignore the literal-minded nonsense and discern the metaphorical meaning of <time is money>: <time is costly in terms of forgone incomes>, or <time imposes an opportunity cost>. Even the inappropriate use of the term "money" (for income) does not impede the metaphorical understanding. <Time is money> has a figurative, nonliteral meaning that is comprehensible: <you get it>.

Other examples readily accumulate. McCloskey (1983, 1985) has already alerted us to many of them. For example, when we say that <GNP is up>, we do not expect our audience to scan the horizon in search of ascending goods and services. Likewise, we do not watch for bloating price tags when it is asserted that <prices are inflated>. Do Alaskans have trouble keeping their <liquid assets> from being frozen? Bubbles, bears, bulls, bliss points, sunspots, cobwebs, and dirty floats all dot the economic landscape. Our most "rigorous" scientific expressions are unabashedly metaphorical. When speaking of <price mechanism>, <transmission mechanism>, <inflation>, <human capital>, <policy instrument>, <multiplier>, and <accelerator>, we do not intend a literal identification with a machine.

Likewise, a literal interpretation is not intended when we refer to the <labor market>. Those who are newly learning economic jargon may associate the expression with an agora or with something like an old-fashioned slave market with actual bidding and haggling. They will, it is hoped, quickly learn that the expression is meant to be figurative. The <labor market> metaphor introduces the most celebrated metaphor of all in economics, namely,

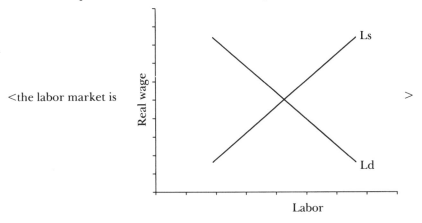

This is not literally true – even if frequent application of this particular metaphor makes the user believe it is. Of course, there are no demand and supply curves in a market. This expression is metaphorical, actually doubly metaphorical. The supply and demand curve diagram is a kind of *icon*, which itself stands in for an elaborate and systematic metaphor on the nature of work in a commercial society. By metaphorically connecting the supply and demand diagram with the notion of a market, and market with work, economists twice give "the thing a name that belongs to something else." If Aristotle is right, <we have a metaphor on our hands>.

Fine. Economic metaphors are everywhere. This should not be surprising; all talk is rife with metaphor. Common talk, for example, is completely permeated with metaphors, as Lakoff and Johnson show in their eminently readable book *Metaphors We Live By* (1980). Yes, <GNP goes up>, to cite just one of their examples, but so does everything else that gets better. Apparently, "up" is associated with "better," or "good," or "happier." Science also abounds with metaphors. For what else is an <energy field> but a metaphor? Newton's corpuscles of light, Maxwell's elastic ether, and contemporary physics's strings are all crucial and famous metaphors in science. The reader will find further examples cited by the philosophers of science Leatherdale (1974), Kuhn (1979), and Hesse (1966, 1980).

So what? Economists may use metaphors, the skeptic might argue, but we can still be precise. Terms, after all, can be defined. A drawing of a labor market can be developed into a mathematical model in which all assumptions are made explicit. Well, true. Nonetheless, there is no way around metaphors in science and hence in economics.

Can we do without metaphor even if we would like to?

Contemporary unease with metaphors in science has a long tradition. Aristotle conceived of logic, rhetoric, and poetry as different realms and, additionally, proposed that language has a different function (and therefore should have a different composition) in each. Metaphorical expression occurs in rhetoric as well as in poetry, but while "similes are useful in prose as well as in verse, [they] must be sparingly used . . . in the same way as metaphors" (Rhetoric 1406b). Metaphor adds "charm" and even <"clearness"> to rhetoric, but such "devices of style" matter far less than substance: "No one uses them in teaching mathematics!" "The language of prose is distinct from poetry" (Rhetoric, 1404a).

Aristotle's functional distinction was taken up with a vengeance by seventeenth-century philosophers, particularly the Empiricists, whose project it was to purge language of its ambiguity and so create for science a <transparent>, semantically fixed language of observation. Consider Locke, who attacked rhetoric, and its "figures," in this famous passage from his *Essay Concerning Human Understanding:*

> If we would speak of Things as they are, we must allow, that the art of Rhetorick, besides Order and Clearness, all the artificial and figurative application of Words Eloquence hath invented, are for nothing else but to insinuate wrong *Ideas,* move the Passions, and thereby mislead the Judgement; and so indeed are perfect cheat. (1975, 508)

Given the rhetorical flourish and exaggeration that was common in the writing of his time, Locke's railing against metaphors is perhaps understandable. Consider the following passage:

> 'Tis evident how much Men love to deceive, and be deceived, since Rhetorick, that powerful instrument of Error and Deceit, has its established Professors, is publickly taught, and has always been in great Reputation: And, I doubt not, but it will be thought great boldness, if not brutality in me, to have said thus much against it. *Eloquence,* like the fair Sex, has too prevailing Beauties in it, to suffer it self ever to be spoken against. And 'tis vain to find fault with those Arts of Deceiving, wherein Men find pleasure to be Deceived. (Locke 1975, 508).

This passage, of course, is Locke's own. His flamboyance and explicitly rhetorical intent are manifest: how metaphorical to equate eloquence and women, or to compare sexual and rhetorical persuasion. Using metaphorical language to condemn metaphor is a <delicious irony.> Does Locke intend the irony or is he innocent of it? Is he wittingly deploying one of the very master tropes he deprecates, or alternatively, does his innocence demonstrate the impossibility of an altogether nonmetaphorical language?

Irony piles upon irony. So let us accept the view that the return to seventeenth-century rhetorical flourish could profitably be avoided in systematic economic or other scientific inquiry. Precision and clarity of expression are no doubt worthy objectives. We might even choose to adopt the ambitious goal of the Royal Society's motto: *Nullius in verba:*

> There is one thing more, about which the Society has been most sollicitous, the manner of their Discourse. . . . They have extracted from all their members, a close, naked natural way of speaking, positive expression; clear senses; a native easiness, bringing all things as near as Mathematical plainnesse as they can. (Cited in Leatherdale 1974, 224)

But *can* we do without metaphor? And if the answer is yes, as a representative economist might argue, what then accounts for the ubiquity of metaphorical speech in our discourse? Is such ubiquity incidental to the purpose of science – weeds always grow faster than flowers – or does metaphor somehow participate in science? Why can't we eliminate the metaphors?

Friedrich Nietzsche's answer remains, characteristically, the strong position 120 years after it was written: Metaphors persist because we cannot think without them. It is not so much that metaphors are cognitive; rather, cognition is metaphorical. Placing metaphor at the very center of knowledge and truth, Nietzsche opens a window on metaphor's larger significance. As on so many other subjects, Nietzsche both anticipated contemporary thinking on metaphor and pushed its implications far beyond the boldest of his intellectual progeny.[7] His most famous passage on metaphor is also the definitive statement of metaphor as the model of knowing and as the essence of language, a view that could not be further from the traditional view:

> What then is truth? A movable host of metaphors, metonymies, and anthropomorphisms: in short, a sum of human relations which have been poetically and rhetorically intensified, transferred, and embellished, and which, after long usage, seem to a people to be fixed, canonical and binding. Truths are illusions which we have forgotten are illusions; they are metaphors that have become worn out and have been drained of sensuous force, coins which have lost their embossing and are now considered as metal and no longer coins. . . . The drive toward the formation of metaphors is the fundamental human drive, which one cannot for a single instant dispense with in thought, for one would thereby dispense with man himself. (Nietzsche 1979, 84–9)

Nietzsche joins the age-old debate and argues that subject and object are inescapably different realms and that metaphor best describes the process by which we come to know the "external" world. By etymology, "metaphor" means "to transfer" or "to carry over," and Nietzsche's epistemology relies on this sense to capture the cognitive bridging of the chasm between subject and object. The world does not seamlessly and without intermediation "in-form" our minds, <like scratches on a tabula rasa>, but we attempt to capture it, ultimately with concepts. Language, then, is also radically metaphorical, a contingent attempt to render things as they are:

> Concerning language: we believe that we know something about the things themselves when we speak of trees, colors, snow and flowers; and yet we possess nothing but a metaphor for things – metaphors which correspond in no way to the original entities. (1979, 83)

> We . . . dare to say "the stone is hard," as if "hard" were something otherwise familiar to us, and not merely a totally subjective stimulation! (82)

All language is irreducibly metaphorical, and therefore so is all our talk about the natural and social worlds. In this view, "literal" and "figurative" are not distinct spheres, but the bounds of a metaphorical continuum. Language begins as metaphor and, only "after long usage," <hardens or freezes> into literality. But even the literal is not true, only more familiar.

How metaphors work

That metaphors have a cognitive and not merely emotive or decorative function is an argument made explicit only after Nietzsche. I. A. Richards (1936) and subsequently Max Black (1962) have been especially influential is developing this view. Figurative speech, especially metaphor, allows us to comprehend in ways that a literal rendering cannot. In some instances, a metaphor is the only way to know, as when we explore natural or social realms that are fundamentally unknown. <Metaphors are markers that orient the discovering wanderer.>

How do metaphors work? The short answer is we don't know. How metaphors work is as mysterious as the process by which we come to recognize metaphorical language. Bound up in language and cognition, a proper theory of metaphor requires a developed theory of semantics and epistemology – vastly beyond the scope of this chapter. An intermediate answer has to rely on the work of students of metaphor.

As Richards and Black pointed out, metaphors make us think by their very nature. When encountering a metaphor, one will, consciously or not, reckon the "associated commonplaces" between two apparently unrelated domains that the metaphor connects. This we can see by investigating the structure of a metaphor.

Let <time is money> be the example. In this metaphor "time" is the subject and "money" the predicate. Richards's terminology dubbed the subject a "tenor" and the predicate a "vehicle." Other designations make the metaphorical subject the "target" domain and the predicate the "import" domain. We will use Black's terminology, which names "time" the *principal subject* of the metaphor and "money" the *subsidiary subject* (Figure 2.1).

If metaphors were undirectional, then "time is money" could be replaced with no loss of content by a literal expression like "time imposes an opportunity cost."[8] In the account that first Richards and then Black gave, the principal and subsidiary subjects interact to create new meaning – insights or semantic resonances that did not exist antecedent to the metaphor. Their perspective is called the interactive model of metaphor. Accordingly, seeing time as money would not only

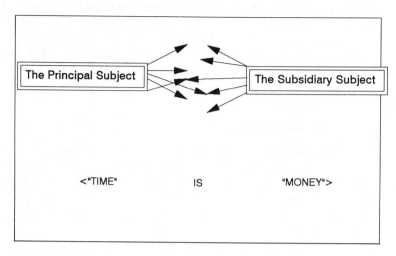

Figure 2.1. The structure of a metaphor. A metaphor consists in giving the principal subject a name that belongs to the subsidiary subject.

affect our notion of time; it also would change our concept of money. The interactive model thus argues that (1) metaphor can convey knowledge, and (2) this cognitive content cannot be achieved in a literal "translation" of (substitution for) the metaphor. Metaphor cannot be reduced to some literal equivalent.

By stating <time is money>, the speaker asks the listener to map certain attributes of the subsidiary subject, money, onto the principal subject, which is time, and vice versa (but not all attributes). There are a great number of associations and attributes that attach to the concept of "money" and could possibly be transferred to "time," such as green paper, golden coins, George Washington, banks, wallets, the central bank, the money multiplier, cost, price, wealth, and richness. The list is virtually endless. Additional uncertainty is introduced because time, too, has many dimensions and related concepts – clock, speed, leisure, calendar, the ticking away of time, and so on – each or all of which could be evoked by "time." So what are the relevant attributes and associated concepts that are evoked by the metaphor?

The metaphor itself does not say. Metaphor does not command, it suggests (see Figure 2.2). Its syntax (or structure) does not reveal its intended meaning, nor does the extrametaphorical meaning of either of its subjects when considered in isolation. Again, the structure

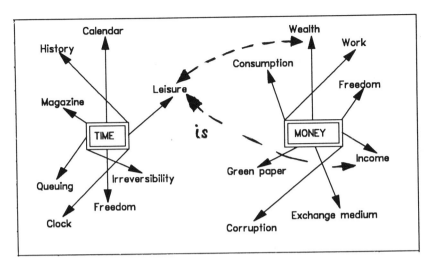

Figure 2.2. The principal and subsidiary subjects in the metaphor
<time is money> have many relevant attributes and associated con-
cepts. The metaphor suggests one connection but leaves open the
possibility for other connections.

of the metaphor and the semantics of its separate subjects do not tell
what dimension or related concept is intended. "Time is money"
could imply that "a clock has a price" or that <a calendar is like
green paper>, but of course, it intends neither of these interpretations. Experimentally, the problem of interpretation is illustrated by
presenting even a common metaphor to young children or to anyone
likewise removed from your "speech community." As children are
wont to do, they will try to reckon a literal meaning. Our field research suggested that children cannot begin to make sense of "time is
money."

Picture two economists who have recently finished a difficult paper
on metaphor, <spending> an afternoon monitoring grass growth
rates – leisure of the theory class. Recklessly, one blurts out, "You
know, time *is* money." Ordinarily, the other economist would glance at
his watch, furrow his brow, and remember the large piles of work back
at the office. However, as an economist, he might instead recognize
the metaphorical play that his colleague intended: Passing time is not
opportunity lost but wealth gained. <Leisure is a normal good>.
Those who <have all the time in the world> are rich. The words are
the same, but the metaphorical meaning is now transformed. Take the

afternoon off, says the metaphor and, in so doing, answer the "American question" of how to be smart *and* rich.

In short, context matters. Meaning depends on where a metaphor (and its utterer) is situated. In the jargon of linguistics, the *pragmatics* of metaphor determine its meaning, as distinct from its syntax or "intrinsic" semantic sense. Because metaphor involves extensive semantic possibilities, it compels the active engagement of the listener. The context of a leisurely afternoon reanimated an old saying without changing the words. A freshly minted metaphor, says Nelson Goodman, "teaches old words new tricks."

Our homely example illustrates the point that metaphor provides cognitive force that cannot always be attained with literal language. By stating that <time is money> when "wealth" or "richness" is the intended association with money, the <metaphor casts the concept of time and money in a different light>, at least for a typical economist. It may set into motion a thought process about the meaning of work, of <spending long hours> at the office instead of conversing with friends and relaxing at home. In other words, a metaphor, if pertinent, affects the way we think not only about the principal and subsidiary subjects, but also about the world beyond the concepts.

This leads to a larger point made by philosophers and literary theorists who have studied metaphor closely: Metaphor is not just a piece of language, but "a process of thought" (Schön 1967, 37). <Time is money> may well result in seeing leisure as forgone income, but such an interpretation is only one unique mapping. A scientific metaphor is propositional; it only invites further inquiry. It does not presuppose or by itself settle the similarities between the principal and subsidiary subjects. The task of interpretation remains. It is this openendedness and lack of explicitness that makes metaphor so useful to scientific inquiry. Mary Hesse expresses the virtue of imprecision:

> A formal, symbolic language can never be a substitute for thought, because the application of a symbolic method to any empirical matter presupposes very careful analysis of the subject matter . . . that the essentials have been grasped and properly expressed in language. In other words, it presupposes that the work of clarification has already been done . . . some necessary overtones of meaning are lost when a word is precisely and uniquely symbolized. The vagueness of living languages as compared with mathematics is the price they pay for their applicability to the world and their capacity for growth. (1955, 88)

Both natural and social phenomena require scientists to consider the extraordinary – the nature of mind, for example, or the character of matter at quantum and cosmological levels. Even less extraordinary realms require figurative speech, as can be confirmed by any macroeconomist who has considered the problem of aggregation. We may attach a name ("the economy") to the unimaginably various and complex activities of a nation's economic life, but we have not thereby ensured that it is a thing. To explain the unfamiliar, scientists inevitably resort to the familiar and the everyday, for what other recourse is there? New concepts do not come to us ready made; their novelty defies our existing language and conceptual schema. Science needs metaphor since it provides the cognitive means to chart the unknown (on this, see Hesse 1955, 1966; Black 1962; Schön 1967).

Cosmological balloons: pedagogical metaphors

Even if metaphors are indispensable to science as vehicles to chart the unknown, it does not follow that *all* metaphors in scientific (economic) discourse are indispensable. Many metaphors in science (and economics) simply serve to illuminate and clarify an exposition and could be omitted without affecting the argumentation as such. We propose to call this class of metaphors in scientific discourse *pedagogical metaphors*.

Effective pedagogical metaphors typically provide mental images (<in our mind's eye>) with which the audience can visualize an otherwise complicated concept. Good teachers are equipped with numerous such metaphors to help their students learn and accept difficult concepts. An example is the <circular flow diagram> that macroeconomists use to demonstrate to students the systematic connectedness of various economic processes.[9] In physics, for example, a metaphor attributed to Arthur Eddington proved to be immensely helpful in elucidating one of the unintuitive propositions of Big Bang theories: The universe expands outward in all directions, but with no center to the explosion. The metaphor proposed seeing the cosmos as a balloon. If galaxies are conceived as dots on the surface of an expanding balloon, then from the perspective of any one galaxy, all the others are moving away in all directions, yet no galaxy is at the center.[10]

Pedagogical metaphors help answer the graduate student's characteristic question, "But what's the intuition?" and the seminar participant's post-Q.E.D. query, "What's the story?" Earthbound economists, confronted with three-dimensional functions and a two-dimensional blackboard, will rely on metaphorical imagery – the surface of the function is a sliced watermelon or a saddle or a cobweb. Note that metaphors of this kind are decidedly *visual*, mental *pictures* that aid in understanding.[11] It is not accidental that our descriptive language here – enlighten, see, view, flash of insight, image, and so on – is doubly metaphorical; it <clearly> embodies vision as a metaphor for knowledge (Schön 1967, 170). These are relatively simple if powerful metaphors.

Accordingly, the pedagogic metaphor is enlisted to help us <see> something that already "exists" and is well understood if not easily grasped. Leatherdale, reworking Alexander Pope's felicitous description, describes this process as " 'what oft was half-apprehended but ne'er before expressed' " (Leatherdale 1974, 100). Pedagogical metaphors in science operate in similar fashion to poetic metaphors. They work with the known, but transmute it. Not surprisingly then, pedagogical metaphors are probably what most scientists or economists think of when metaphor is mentioned. If they have only these metaphors in mind, they are right to conclude that metaphors are helpful but incidental to the course of science.

Human capital: heuristic metaphors

However, scientific discourse depends on other, more influential classes of metaphors. Some metaphors serve to catalyze our thinking, helping to approach a phenomenon in a novel way. We propose to call these thought-propelling metaphors *heuristic metaphors*.

An example of a heuristic metaphor is the metaphor of <human capital>. McCloskey relates the following story:

> One day [agricultural economist Theodore Schultz] interviewed an old and poor farm couple and was struck by how contented they seemed. Why are you so contented, he asked, though very poor? They answer: You're wrong Professor. We're not poor. We've used up our farm to educate four children through college, remaking fertile land and well-stocked pens into knowledge of law and Latin. We are rich. (1990, 13)

Schultz was wrestling with a problem and expressed his flash of insight with the metaphor<human capital>. The metaphor showed him how he could think about an observed phenomenon, in familiar economic terms. The human capabilities of learning, wit, and talent could be seen as physical capital. Problematic areas for the economist – (1) learning and (2) purchases of nonmaterial goods – were connected to the everyday economic concept of physical capital. The metaphor evoked a comparison between the sacrifices that the family made for the education of their children and an investment in a tractor or any other capital goods; human capital is an asset that produces a stream of (psychic) income; and so forth. The metaphor set up an argument by analogy and directed the inquiry into the phenomenon that Schultz encountered.

Note the crucial difference between a pedagogical and a heuristic metaphor. The cosmological balloon and the saddle-shaped function are metaphors that induce us to knock the <heel> of our palm to our foreheads. Ahhhh, of course. Thank you. The pedagogical metaphor's role is typically a cameo. In contrast, a heuristic metaphor is only the beginning of an inquiry. Heuristic metaphors usually will not immediately reveal all possible elaborations. When Schultz thought of <human capital>, he did not perceive its full heuristic power. Nor could he have. Much elaboration was to follow, as can be witnessed in the burgeoning literature on the economics of families, for example. Schumpeter called insight of the kind that Schultz experienced a "preanalytic cognitive act" (1954, 41).

The example of the <human capital> metaphor reinforces the connection between metaphor and thought in science: Metaphor as a way of thinking in new terms. We have seen that metaphor is an essential tool for thinking about the unknown, but it also serves to stimulate novel approaches to the known. Metaphor is cognitive here because its respective subjects interact to create new meaning. Consider again the labor market case.

Imagine a beginning student who wants to understand how work works: what occurs in the workplace between employers and employees, in wage negotiations, on assembly lines, in board rooms – everything related to work. If she is typical, she will be unable to establish what her questions are or even how to designate the tenuously connected phenomena with which she is concerned. Perhaps she has heard about the differential between average remuneration for doctors and nurses, or her uncle is out of work, or she has found that people routinely complain about their jobs. How is she to get a grip on these impressions, anecdotes, experiences? How should she think about her uncle or unhappy working people? A metaphor can help. But there are many metaphors that can do the trick.

If the student finds herself in a sociology class, she will hear about conflicts in the workplace and class struggle. Whether conscious of it or not, she is given the metaphor of <power struggle>. The notion that work can be seen as a <power struggle> enables her to organize her thoughts about the collection of experiences, impressions, and issues that constitute her principal subject. <Work is a power struggle> functions as a heuristic metaphor that gets her started. Thinking in this vein, she will find that what goes on between bosses and their subordinates is high drama, with workers struggling for more power and more meaningful jobs. If she were to pursue this metaphor further, she might find herself in the company of radical economists, sociologists, and political scientists. And slowly she will be able to distinguish patterns in her initially amorphous experiences.

The heuristic metaphor will be different if our student were to wander into a microeconomics lecture. "Power struggle" as a way to organize the complicated nature of work sounds funny or quaint to most economists. It is even a little irksome. The freshman economics student, of course, experiences a similar dissonance when encountering neoclassical economics's double metaphor <work is a market and a market is a geometric diagram>. But the market metaphor is powerful, and our student's as yet unconnected impressions will be organized so she can <see> that wages are set in an impersonal (and decidedly undramatic) marketplace, that job loss is due to movements in demand and supply curves, and that boredom must have its compensations if agents are rational.[12] Thus, the labor market metaphor helps her to <see> what she could not <see> before.

Metaphor begets analogy

Recall our argument that a pedagogical metaphor, unlike its heuristic cousin, illuminates but typically does not lend itself to systematic and sustained development. The "time is money" metaphor, once interpreted, says enough. One could study the phenomenon of money, discuss its creation, and formalize the multiplier process, but all that will be superfluous to the metaphor's limited intent: that we <get the idea> that leisure imposes an opportunity cost or that leisure is valuable. So while the pedagogical metaphor <time is money> did not develop into a scientific analysis, the heuristic <human capital> and <work is a market> metaphors did. The question then arises: Into what does a heuristic metaphor develop? Here the distinction between metaphor and *analogy* will prove to be fruitful.

Many authors, among them McCloskey and Mirowski, use "metaphor" and "analogy" interchangeably. They are close relations. Aristotle, remember, considered analogy as a species of metaphor: "Metaphor consists in giving the thing a name that belongs to something else . . . on grounds of analogy." Yet analogy, even as Aristotle traditionally defined it, is different from metaphor. Whereas a metaphor merely suggests that the principal and subsidiary subjects have attributes in common, an analogy draws explicit parallels between them. According to Aristotle, analogy is based on proportionality, as in "wine-bowl" is to Dionysus as shield is to Ares. By proportionality, Aristotle implies a kind of limited and identifiable relationship between the principal and subsidiary subjects. Note that analogy in this sense is less than a <full-blown> metaphor; saying that "the wine-bowl is the shield of Dionysus" is metaphorical, but to understand it one needs only to grasp the implied proportionality between Dionysus and Ares – nothing else is left to the imagination.

An analogy typically focuses on similarities in relationships. Jevons argued in *The Principles of Science* that "analogy denotes not a resemblance between things, but between the relations of things" (1874/1958, 627). To say that "the atom is a solar system" is to speak metaphorically. When a teacher develops this classic metaphor by drawing the solar system on the blackboard, complete with the sun and elliptically orbiting planets, she proposes an analogy that captures and makes explicit some, though not all, of the "associated commonplaces" suggested by the metaphor. Not all of these correspondences will be appropriate. Gravity does not bind electrons to the atom's nucleus, as it does planets to the sun, nor is the atom's nucleus hot with thermonuclear fusion. Likewise, the solar system's moons and asteroids have no obvious counterpart within the atom. However, less than perfect congruity can also prove to be a virtue, providing insight that a literal rendering cannot achieve. Electrons don't spin on their axes like a planet does, but conceiving of them in this way provides an explanation of an electron's angular momentum and its magnetic field.

Note that the subsidiary subject and, by implication, the principal subject have become systems of relationships. This process inspires the following definition of analogy: Analogy is an expanded metaphor; more precisely, analogy is sustained and systematically elaborated metaphor. Accordingly, in a scientific context, a metaphor becomes heuristic when it stimulates the construction of an analogical system. The mere coinage of a metaphor such as <human capital> does not make science. Science proceeds by taking a fertile metaphor and relentlessly articulating the nature of its subsidiary domains, probing the properties of that terrain, and testing the connections between that domain and the principal domain.

This is what neoclassical economists did with <human capital>; they expanded it into a full-blown analogical system. But not any system will do. Current economic practice prescribes that the (heuristic) metaphor be developed into a model. A model, then, is nothing more and nothing less than an explicitly, most often formally articulated analogy. "Model" once carried the meaning of "scale model," but today, models are analogies where more than a size vector is varied in relationship to the world.

Scale models are figurative in only the narrowest fashion; only one attribute of the thing to be modeled – size – changes. Maps may be thought of as scale models;[13] in fact, maps are a favorite pedagogical metaphor in introductory economics texts that seek to explain abstraction in economic theorizing (on this, see Goldfarb and Griffith 1991). The crucial difference is that scale models (e.g., maps) describe a known reality, whereas scientific models will often describe fundamentally unknown or unknowable aspects of the world. Map makers know precisely which aspects of reality they are omitting or including in their models, but economists typically must select what to characterize with (1) incomplete knowledge and (2) some prior notion of what needs to be explained.

Creating an economic model therefore constitutes reasoning by analogy, as Milton Friedman (1953) argued when he suggested that economists reason "as if." "As if" reasoning defines rational choice as analogous to, for example, a constrained maximization solution technique. No literal meanings are intended. Friedman is clear: Economists are not supposed to lose sight of the analogy's essential if useful fiction. In Black's terms, "there is a willing suspension of ontological disbelief," which may account for the ironic winking and nudging that accompanies "sophisticated" economics (1962, 228).[14] Individual agents don't actually make decisions by employing the techniques of Lagrange and Hamilton to solve a systems of equations; it is useful, however, to see them this way. The argument is meant to be fictitious, as it is when cognitive psychologists argue as if brains were computers. To take either analogy as literal misses the point.

The problem, of course, is that analogies may become elaborate – things in themselves – and eclipse their founding metaphors. Model builders may lose sight of their construct's metaphoricity. Indeed, most economists probably think of their work as making truth statements about the world. In the same breath, however, they will make a watered-down version of Friedman's article their methodological touchstone. Alertness to metaphor reminds us not only that our models are fictions, but that "as if" reasoning – the characteristic mode of economic discourse – is altogether incompatible with a positivist account of economic practice.

Recognizing that some models are useful but witting fictions also has important sociological implications. The act of creating a great metaphor may well be, as Aristotle suggests (*Poetics*, 1459a), the stuff of genius, but in science, metaphor's functional power lies in its "deployability" (Toulmin) – the fertile open-endedness that confers creative power to its interpreters. In science, great metaphors are not born; they are made. The fertility of a scientific metaphor – its potential for subsequent analogical development – is a necessary though not sufficient condition for future success. A successful heuristic metaphor will bear the analogic system only with the aid of a thousand midwives.

The heuristic metaphor, however, usually does not come with instructions that tell which model to develop it into. Take the "labor market." Nothing in that metaphor reveals what form the model might take, nor does it call for a model. One could develop it into a geometrical device like the demand–supply diagram, into a general equilibrium system, into an empirical model, or into a loosely composed Austrian-like analysis. Treating work as a market is only the first (and key) metaphor that leads to supply and demand curves.

Accordingly, many other factors influence the development of a heuristic metaphor into an analogical system. One is reminded of Kuhn's (1962/1970) notions of exemplar and disciplinary matrix; a mixture of tools, strategies, and values determine what the appropriate transformation is. Students who just have finished their introductory microeconomics class will use the basic demand–supply diagram as their exemplar. Graduate students at Minnesota will want to develop a general equilibrium model that makes the structural parameters explicit, and MIT students may want to build models that allow for empirical testing.[15]

The persuasiveness of the analogy is determined by the positive analogies, that is, the attributes and relationships that do correspond. Black, borrowing from topology, talks of the "isomorphism" between the domains. For example, when real wages change as predicted or explained by the model, the analogy is positive.[16] Negative analogies may undermine the persuasiveness of the analogy. The fact that agents do not literally solve Lagrangians is a negative analogy, but it is not fatal to economists concerned principally with prediction. A negative analogy occurs when the predictions of the analogy or model are not met by real events. This outcome is usually more critical and will lead to changes in the analogical construction, depending upon the analogy's connectedness with reality. Economic methodologists make it their profession to investigate the logical characteristics of economic analogies in their search for standards. Their objective, then, is to determine when negative analogies are such that a rejection of the analogy is warranted. That objective has proven elusive mainly because of the complexity of the relationships between the analogical construction and economic reality, as implied by the Duhem–Quine thesis.

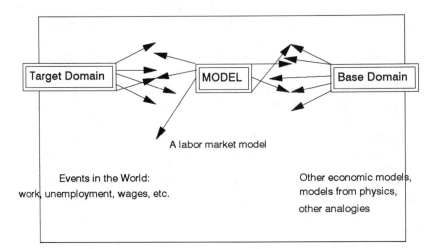

Figure 2.3. A model or analogy is intended to investigate an aspect of the world, which is called the target domain, and does so by borrowing from other models or analogies that make up the base domain.

Analogies (including models) have another quality that is remarkable: They are two sided. On one side, analogies investigate the world, sometimes referred to as the target domain (see Genter 1982). But analogies also have another side, an association that is quite different. A specific model of U.S. labor markets, for example, will also bear some relationship to other models in economics, mathematics, or following Mirowski, physics. The domain from which a specific analogy is borrowed is called the base domain. Figure 2.3 illustrates the two-sidedness of the scientific analogy.

The analogical configuration with which economists work can become an end in itself. Instead of pursuing congruences between the analogy and economic phenomena in the world, economists may work entirely *within* the realm of analogy or only with reference to its base domain, such as analytically related models. This has happened with chess. Although the precise origins of chess are murky, one view is that chess was originally devised to provide instruction to students of war by metaphorically representing war as a game. Today, the connection with war is completely lost. Chess is interesting only as a self-contained game. The original metaphor, <chess is war>, has faded away, eclipsed by the analogic system that is the game of chess.

Thus can metaphors die. "Dead metaphor" is an expression coined by Turbayne (1962). Familiarity and overuse can drain a metaphor of its figurative sense, rendering it literal in impact, as with the once metaphorical terms "skyscraper" and "riverbed." The expression remains, but the incongruity that once alerted us to the metaphor has been eroded by its very currency. The same is true for the heuristic metaphors that create analogies in science. Neoclassical economists almost exclusively focus their research on the characteristics of their models, evidence that their central metaphors are comatose if not actually deceased. The standard question is, "What will happen to the model if we change . . ." The impetus to change economic models almost always derives from developments in other models, not from the nature of its relationship to the world.

Even if the metaphor that underlies an economic model is rhetorically dead, it can be brought back to life. In particular, newcomers to economics and outsiders have the bothersome habit of stumbling over the metaphorical characteristics of economic discourse. Considering significant negative analogies may reanimate metaphors, thereby retarding the process of initiation and conversion. The most commonly heard objection is that the assumptions of the model are unrealistic. It is also sometimes argued that economists have an overly mechanistic and cynical view of the world, supposing that all individuals are calculating and self-interested. These reactions remind economists that their reasoning is inevitably metaphorical and that their metaphors allow for associations that they do not intend.[17] Dead metaphors never actually die. Therefore, "ossified metaphor" may be the better term as it holds open the important possibility of reanimation.

Constitutive metaphors: windows for the implied vision

In addition to pedagogical and heuristic metaphors, there are metaphors of a third kind in economics (and elsewhere in science), *constitutive metaphors*. These metaphors work on an even more fundamental level. Constitutive metaphors are those necessary conceptual schemes through which we interpret a world that is either unknowable (the strong position, per Nietzsche) or at least unknown. To say anything about the world we must characterize it. But because we cannot know literally the nature of the natural and social worlds, we resort to the figurative in characterizing. An antiessentialist epistemology requires metaphor. Schön argues:

> There is a very different tradition associated with the notion of meta-phor, however, – one which treats metaphor as central to the task of accounting for our perspectives on the world: how we think about things, make sense of reality, and set the problems we later try to solve. In this sense, "metaphor" refers both to a certain kind of product – a perspective or frame, a way of looking at things – and to a certain kind of process – a process by which new perspectives on the world come into existence. (1979, 254)

Constitutive metaphors frame a discursive practice in the way that the U.S. Constitution frames U.S. legal discourse. Boyd, who coined the term, defines a constitutive metaphor as one that "constitute[s], at least for a time, an irreplaceable part of the linguistic machinery of a scientific theory: cases in which there are metaphors which scientists use in expressing theoretical claims for which no adequate literal para-phrase is known" (1979, 360).

When we say that a metaphor <frames our thinking>, we mean to say that such metaphors profoundly influence our thinking, what we see and hear. "In discussing the theory of genes, the lecturer may say, 'think of it, if you will, as a kind of code,' when in fact he has no other way of thinking of it" (Schön 1967, 105). Great scientific metaphors typically become entrenched, so that we take them as literally true. But all metaphors start provisionally. Space is Euclidean, and can be thought of only with the metaphor of lines and points, until we think of another way.[18] Usually implicit, constitutive metaphors determine what makes sense and what does not; they will determine, among other things, the effectiveness of pedagogical and heuristic meta-phors. They are essential to our ways of thinking, more so than heuris-tic metaphors. The "human capital" metaphor proved a successful heuristic metaphor, but it succeeded because it resonated with the more fundamental metaphors that constitute neoclassical discourse. When Schultz <saw> <human capital>, he struck the right chord. Had Schultz instead <seen> <moral resolve>, we can guess that the resulting dissonance would have made for a different history. Consti-tutive metaphors, therefore, function as <windows for the implied vision>.

"Constitutive metaphors" are the answer to the question "Where do our heuristic metaphors come from?" On what basis did Paul Samu-elson choose optimization as his heuristic metaphor over, say, satis-ficing or chaos? Was his selection altogether for operational reasons, merely serving the attainment of ever more realistic models? No, of course not. Samuelson's insight recognized optimization as a metaphor compatible with his existing conceptual schema. Like the famous gestalt figures suggest – Wittgenstein's duck-rabbit and the vase versus two faces in profile – what we see depends on what we already know. The constitutive vision is implied in the heuristic metaphors pursued.

Constitutive metaphors, like most fundamental concepts, are hard to specify concretely. Constitutive metaphors are not explicitly stated and marked in the discourse that they constitute. People can talk away entire lives without ever reflecting on the nature of their talk. Accordingly, constitutive metaphors, if they exist at all, can be exposed only by digging into or interpreting the relevant texts, both spoken and written.

Mirowski's *More Heat Than Light* (1989) represents the most ambitious dig for the constitutive metaphors of modern neoclassical discourse as yet. Heeding Borges's assertion that "universal history is the history of a handful of metaphors," Mirowski argues that the Natural has framed the neoclassical thinking about the Social and that thinking about the Natural is framed, in turn, by an analogy with nineteenth-century physics. The dig does not stop there, however, for what constitutes nineteenth-century physics? Could it be the concept of an invariant structure, as Mirowski suggests? This volume attests to the need for further digging and sorting out of metaphors that are merely incidental from those that are constitutive in economics.

The suggestion that a discursive practice revolves around or is framed by constitutive elements is not novel. Thomas Kuhn (1962/ 1970) implied as much with his notion of the "disciplinary matrix," as did Imre Lakatos (1968) with the notion that a "hard core" of unquestioned assumptions constitutes a research program. Yet neither Kuhn's nor Lakatos's conceptual framework explicitly captures the metaphorical character of discourse framing, that is, viewing the principal domain in terms of another domain. More promising in this respect is work by Michel Foucault (*The Order of Things* [1973] and *The Archeology of Knowledge* [1972]) and by Stephen Pepper (*World Hypotheses* [1942]). Foucault and Pepper both make serious attempts to elucidate the metaphors that frame discursive practices.

Pepper's taxonomy of four world hypotheses can perhaps work as a beginning guide to the dig in economic discourse. Those four world hypotheses are "organicism," "mechanism," "formism," and "contextualism." (In case you suspect typos, the strangeness of the names is intended to preempt associations with other more common expressions.) Each hypothesis is characterized by different constitutive metaphors – "root metaphors" Pepper calls them – and generates a distinctive discursive practice.[19]

For example, in terms of the mechanistic world hypothesis, the economy will resemble a machine with a <price mechanism>, <equilibrium>, and <elasticities>. Nature can be seen as a frictionless clockworks, with the social realm isomorphically identical, owing perhaps to some deus ex machina like an invisible hand. With contextualism as the world hypothesis, the economy will have a history in which events are contiguous and human actions are to be understood in context. A contextualist view might allow economics the status of a science like physics, but recognizes that the social realm is embedded in history, so that economics may be arranged like physics, but it cannot be physics. The classical organicist metaphor in economics postulates an entire economy as a living thing, complete with closed, circular flows. Note that living things evolve, an important metaphorical implication (a la Marshall) that may well be at odds with a competing notion of invariance.[20]

Note that the apparently limited number of constitutive (or root) metaphors may help explain Mirowski's notion of metaphor spiraling through history, alighting on the Natural and Social alike: Malthus led to Darwin, who led to social Darwinism, which, with a bit of Marshall, created sociobiology, and so on (Mirowski, Chapter 1, this volume). If the world is unknowable or at least unknown, then we must construct it. What is fascinating is the apparent scarcity of our most elemental conceptual material for construction.

Disagreement or schism?

Constitutive metaphors also help to explain the apparently irreconcilable disagreements among economists and perhaps between economics and its lay audiences. If your constitutive metaphor sees the world as a clockworks and suggests that people don't think but calculate, then thinking about thinking makes little sense. Note that we are not talking about heuristic metaphors here, such as <individuals think by solving constrained optimization problems>. Such hypotheses may well be, as discussed, a useful and *witting* fiction for dealing with a problematic reality. However, a mechanistic constitutive metaphor, we've argued, will determine how we actually see the world. Talk about metaphor and discursive practice will seem altogether misguided and perhaps subversive to an economist who operates under a mechanistic constitutive metaphor. If the world is a frictionless clockworks, then equilibrium prevails everywhere. The notion of disagreements (for economists are part of the world) or discord makes no sense, nor do attempts like this chapter to understand disagreements. To conceive of economics as a discursive practice based on a handful of metaphors would be subversive for such a worldview because it threatens to emphasize rhetorical tools at the expense of fact and logic, a mechanistic world's means of inquiry.

According to the rhetorical perspective, however, disagreements among economists arise not so much because we are misguided or strategic in resistance, or even because we hold different "preferences." Rather, we are subject to clashing constitutive metaphors. Constitutive metaphors are not picked up and discarded like heuristic metaphors or mere preferences; constitutive metaphors are us. A fundamentally changed perspective, say from positivist to rhetorical, requires changing oneself, which is painful and rare. Like Rome and Byzantium, conflicting constitutive metaphors lead not to disagreement, but to schism.

This case illustrates again that metaphors matter and that therefore there is good reason to reflect on the metaphors that constitute economics. We may discover that major disagreements and misapprehension are not the product of stupidity, ignorance, and avarice that we attribute to others, but can be accounted for by conflicting constitutive metaphors. If so – the caveat is that we have as yet merely postulated the existence of constitutive metaphors – contrasting constitutive metaphors may be responsible for the confusion and miscomprehension that we experience in our business.

Moreover, the notion of constitutive metaphors offers a way to decipher the noisy, mixed signals that characterize communication between academic economists and the rest of the world. Communication gaps may be metaphorical in origin: Economists speak of formal metaphors while others rely on organic and contextual metaphors. When discussing trade, for example, lay people and journalists (who are professional lay people) think in dramatic terms; they see <trade wars> and expect <actions> to <retaliate> against <unfair competition>. In contrast, economists think in formal terms about the <impersonal price mechanism>, <comparative advantage>, and <long-run equilibrium>.

Constitutive metaphors may account for differences in the economics of <freshwater and coastal macroeconomists> and for the lack of communication between neoclassical economists and economists of other kinds, such as Marxists, Austrians, post-Keynesians, socio-economists, and institutionalists. Divergent constitutive metaphors may also account for the friction between economic methodologists who focus on the form of economic argument and economic rhetoricians who focus on the context of economic metaphors.

Peroration

Economics is metaphorical, even if some of its metaphors don't matter. Solow's skepticism is thus only partially vindicated; it is true that pedagogical metaphors merely serve to illuminate and are not crucial to the scientific process. Heuristic metaphors are more resistant to skepticism, not just because they are essential to science, allowing new takes on old ideas and a means to confront the wholly new or unfamiliar, but also because (1) they remind us that our models are fictions, and (2) economic practice diverges widely from economic preaching. The metaphors that constitute discourse are unambiguously worthy of study. We argue that they may account for fundamental disagreements within economics and for problems of communication across academic disciplines and with lay audiences. And those disagreements and problems need to be understood by anyone who is serious about intellectual practice. Constitutive metaphors matter unless you are willing to argue that scholars can justifiably be blind to the practice in which they are themselves engaged.

Unearthing constitutive metaphors may not by itself accomplish change, but a statement that <a handful of metaphors constitute discursive practices in economics> could be the heuristic metaphor that leads us to a richer understanding of economics. It compels us to develop a conceptual framework with which we can interpret and characterize alternative discursive practices in economics. The characterization will help us understand.

Saying that economics is metaphorical is no longer taboo, but it is also no longer inconsequential. More exegesis on the literary and pedagogical aspects of metaphor in economics, however useful, will beg the larger questions we have tried to raise. Further research will recognize that arguing <economics is metaphorical> is potentially subversive, if not in the fashion traditionally imagined. By proposing to uncover, identify, and elaborate on the constitutive metaphors of economics, we run the risk of altering them. Max Black proposed that "every science must start with metaphor and end with algebra" (1962, 242). The work that is done in this book suggests that we can profitably stop talking about algebra. When we begin talking about metaphor, science moves.

Glossary of selected terms

Useful references are Abrams (1981) and Lanham (1991).

Allegory: A long or extended metaphor, in which the "left-hand" side of the original metaphor has been lopped off or "forgotten." Examples of allegory are the fables of Lafontaine, Orwell's *Animal Farm,* and perhaps Defoe's *Robinson Crusoe.* An allegory is an expanded metaphor, like analogy, but the expansion comes in the form of a narrative, and it is not systematic. In this sense, allegory belongs more to poetry, as analogy belongs to science. The animals in Orwell's *Animal Farm,* for example, symbolize human types, and the reader is asked to interpret the story allegorically, that is, as corresponding to human society.

Analogy: A sustained and systematically elaborated metaphor, where one system of relationships is joined to another. Analogy makes explicit the ligatures between the principal and subsidiary subjects, specifying only some correspondences among the infinitely many potential commonplace associations suggested by the original metaphor. While allegory continually reminds us of its metaphorical beginnings, and thus prevents a literal reading, analogies are usually less gracious to their original metaphor. An elaborate analogic system may eclipse its founding metaphor, obscuring its parentage as it grows in size and complexity.

Catachresis: The metaphorical use of existing language to fill a gap in the vocabulary. Referring to the support of a table as a "leg," or to the base of a mountain as a "foot," were, at one time, catachrestic acts. John Muth found the need for catachresis when he conceived of expectations that are consistent with the outcome of his model. There was no name for such a phenomenon so he coined the term "rational expectations." (The expression is also metaphorical, because expectations, which usually are thought to be emotional, are given an attribute that appears to belong to another set of phenomena.)

Constitutive metaphor: A metaphor that frames the thinking about its principal subject to the point that the principal subject cannot be considered without it. More broadly, it is the conceptual scheme we use in characterizing a world that is unknowable or unknown. (Note that constitutive metaphors will typically generate or inspire heuristic metaphors.)

Ethos: The character of a person, usually a speaker. The ethos of the speaker influences the nature of the message. Ethos is an important rhetorical device, though not a trope, per se. Students of economics quickly learn to establish the ethos appropriate to a professional economist: Write in an impersonal voice and deploy scientistic language wherever possible. Appeal to the appropriate authorities, that is, economists with an acceptable ethos (not John Kenneth Galbraith, therefore, but serious economists such as Robert Lucas).

Heuristic metaphor: A metaphor that works by motivating inquiry into the principal subject by juxtaposing attributes or relationships of the subsidiary subject. In economics the heuristic metaphor will usually be developed and elaborated into an analogy or model, as with the <human capital> or <work is a market> metaphors. Because heuristic metaphors are not literally true, reasoning *as if* they were implies that economic models are fictions.

Hyperbole: A figure that relies on calculated exaggeration. Aristotle probably considers it a type of metaphor (species to genus), citing "Truly ten thousand good deeds has Ulysses wrought" (Poetics, 1457b), where "ten thousand" represents "many."

Irony: Words that say one thing and mean precisely the opposite, or an unusual incongruity between actual and expected outcomes.

Metaphor: By etymology, meaning to "carry over," a language process whereby attributes of one object (subsidiary subject) are transferred to another (principal subject). In Richards's and Black's accounts, the two subjects then interact to create new meaning. This figurative meaning has cognitive import because it cannot be achieved by some literal equivalent.

Metonymy and synecdoche are metaphorical ways of speaking, and in some schemes they are considered a class of metaphor. But this is not quite correct. Metonymies and synecdoches typically employ a predicate that already belongs to the semantic domain of the implied subject: the "hand" from "all hands on deck" is already related to "body." Metaphor, in contrast, characteristically borrows from another domain that has in principle nothing to do with the principal subject. It is this novel or unexpected juxtaposition of subjects from apparently unrelated domains that gives metaphor its power: <The world is my oyster.> <All the world's a stage.> <Truth is a woman.> <God is a postulate of the ego.> <Trade is war.>

Simple (and oft-cited) metaphors such as these typically link the subject and predicate (metaphors are almost always binary) with a form of the verb "to be," though this is by no means a necessary construction. Metaphors don't require a verb to join the two domains, as evidenced in the following fragments: "stream of consciousness," "skin of the body politic," "this mortal coil," "hard-boiled detective," "music of the spheres," and "ghost in the machine." Metaphor is the most fertile and powerful of all figurative forms precisely because, to use Max Black's term, the "associated commonplaces" are potentially unlimited when two previously unrelated domains are joined.

Metonymy: A figure in which the name of an attribute or adjunct is substituted for that of the thing meant. "Buckingham Palace denied the allegations" or "This department needs some new blood," for example. "Labor supply adjusts to a change in expected real wages" is metonymous, where individuals do the adjusting, not a concept describing an aggregate schedule of hours worked at a given wage.[21] When a student says, "I read Barro over the weekend," he or she is referring metonymously to an article. Consider "The market sailed into uncharted territory today." The whole expression is metaphorical, given the juxtaposition of sailing and a capital market. "The market" is a synecdoche for a price index of selected stocks (say, the Dow–Jones Industrial Average), and "unchartered territory" is metonymous for previously unattained index levels.

Model: An explicitly, and in economics often formally, articulated analogy; a model is typically characterized by *as if* reasoning.

Pedagogical metaphor: Typically employed to clarify difficult, though otherwise understood exposition. It relies on the transparency of resemblances or correspondences between its principal and subsidiary subjects. An example is the <circular flow diagram> of macroeconomics, or the expression <time is money>. Pedagogical metaphors, once interpreted, have served their function; they do not lend themselves to systematic elaboration as do heuristic metaphors.

Poetic metaphor: Deliberate alteration of language to evolve new meaning and achieve emotion in art (T. S. Eliot). Poetic metaphors are not designed for subsequent analogical elaboration and typically exploit the instability of the meaningful connections between their principal and subsidiary subjects.

Pragmatics: The study of the use of language (words, concepts, metaphors).

Rhetoric: The art of "discovering all means of persuasion in any given case," as defined by Aristotle. In the modern definition, rhetoric is viewed as pertaining to all modes of discourse, including scientific discourse. Rhetorical devices include logical operations, metaphors, ethos, and narrative.

Simile: Metaphor that is trivially true, when a metaphorical relationship is made explicit by "like" or "as" constructions. "Time is *like* money," or "Consider a child as a durable good." The traditional view has been that metaphor is merely elliptical or compressed simile, a difference in syntax only. Aristotle's position was that "the simile is also a metaphor; the difference is but slight" (Rhetoric 1406b). But note that the addition of "like" weakens the metaphor. By explicit comparison, <time is *like* money>, the speaker evokes similarities and simultaneously warns for the dissimilarities – as if to suggest that one should not take the comparison too far. Similes are always trivially true because some likeness or similarity can be found between any two subjects. Metaphors may convey a metaphorical truth, but they are almost never literally true. Negative constructions are sometimes exceptions, however, as with "No man is an island unto himself."

Synecdoche (Greek for "taking together"): a figure that occurs when we substitute a part for the whole (see Aristotle's "genus" and "species") or vice versa. "All hands on deck" is an example. "Technical change" in the production function is a synecdoche in the sense that it stands for all the influences that are unaccounted for by the stated factors of production. Synecdoche is probably best considered as a class of metonymous speech.

Trope: A figure of speech in which words are given meanings other than their literal meaning.

Notes

The authors wish to thank Philip Mirowski, Donald McCloskey, and Robert Goldfarb for their helpful criticism. The chapter also benefited from comments by participants in a methodology seminar at George Washington University: Rich Esposito, Cameron Gordon, David Hill, Jack Maher, and Amanda Roberts.

1. Willie Henderson (1982) preceded McCloskey in recognizing the metaphorical nature of economics, though his article met with little fanfare.
2. Aristotle's popularity owes probably more to his famous propensity to produce convenient definitions than to the depth of his treatment of metaphor or to his seniority. Stanford (1972) finds that the word *metaphora* first appears in Isocrates' *Evagoras*.
3. See glossary for the definition of this and other terms.
4. Not everybody agrees that metaphors are tropes. Donald Davidson in particular argues that metaphors have no meaning or sense apart from their literal meaning or sense (in Sachs 1979).
5. McCloskey pointed out the double metaphor in the expression <taking literally>: Nothing is <taken> – it is rather heard or understood, and <literally> means in Latin "by the letters."
6. "Time flies" is no more metaphorical than "Time flows," though most people will take the latter concept as literally true. We will discuss how metaphor is uniquely <well suited> to describe abstract or otherwise extraordinary concepts.
7. On this and what follows, see Paul Cantor in Miall (1982).
8. This traditional view of metaphor Black calls the *substitution* model. The substitution model denies metaphor any nonornamental function.
9. Tim Alborn, however, shows in Chapter 7, this volume, that there is a great deal more to the metaphor than what economists suggest when using it. For instance, it has a complicated history.
10. On this, see Lightman 1989.
11. To <see> this, try to create a successful metaphor for a six-dimensional function or for a complex number.
12. Why, the <labor market> analogy asks, don't bored workers vote with their feet and seek another job?
13. Actually, maps abstract more than size; they also may represent nonspatial ideas – for example, by using colors or shapes.
14. Likewise, Black points out, models as fictions makes explanation impossible, for, as Friedman concedes, *actual* behavior could be anything – satisficing, chaotic, minimizing.
15. The instability of heuristic metaphors is also pointed out by Theodore Porter in Chapter 6, this volume. Some fudging may be needed to get

from nineteenth-century physics to a satisfactory economic model. Of course, this is also the point of Mirowski in *More Heat Than Light* (1989).

16. Mary Hesse furthermore distinguishes neutral analogies, which are analogies that still need to be explored and determined.
17. See Klamer (1987) for an examination of the different associations that can be made with the rationality postulate in economics.
18. We owe this example to McCloskey.
19. Black had similar entities in mind when he referred to "conceptual archetypes" (1962, 241).
20. To assay the universality and robustness of Pepper's categories, try to devise another root metaphor to describe a natural or social system.
21. Indeed, it is metaphorical to view the vastly complex activity of human work as a resource, or input to production (see Lackoff and Johnson 1988, ch. 12).

References

Abrams, M. H. 1981. *A Glossary of Literary Terms*, 4th ed. New York: Holt, Rinehart, & Winston.

Aristotle. 1932. *Rhetoric*. Lane Cooper, ed. New York: Appleton.

Aristotle. 1941. *Basic Works*. Richard McKeon, ed. New York: Random House.

Bennington, Geoff. 1987. "The Perfect Cheat: Locke and Empiricism's Rhetoric." In Andrew E. Benjamin, Geoffrey Cantor, and John R. R. Christie, eds., *The Figural and the Literal*, 103–23. Manchester: Manchester University Press.

Bicchieri, Cristina. 1988. "Should a Scientist Abstain from a Metaphor?" In Arjo Klamer, Donald M. McCloskey, and Robert M. Solow, eds., *The Consequences of Economic Rhetoric*, 100–14. Cambridge University Press.

Black, Max. 1962. *Models and Metaphors*. Ithaca, NY: Cornell University Press.

Boyd, Richard. 1979. "Metaphor and Theory Change: What Is Metaphor For?" In Andrew Ortony, ed., *Metaphor and Thought*, 356–408. Cambridge University Press.

Cantor, Paul. 1982. "Friedrich Nietzsche: The Use and Abuse of Metaphor." In David S. Miall, ed., *Metaphor: Problems and Perspectives*, 71–88. Sussex: Harvester Press.

Cooper, David E. 1986. *Metaphor*. Oxford: Basil Blackwell.

Davidson, Donald. 1979. "What Metaphors Mean." In Sheldon Sacks, ed., *On Metaphor*. Chicago: University of Chicago Press.

Foucault, Michel. 1972. *The Archeology of Knowledge*. New York: Pantheon.

Foucault, Michel. 1973. *The Order of Things*. New York: Vintage.

Friedman, Milton. 1953. *Essays in Positive Economics*. Chicago: University of Chicago Press.

Genter, Derdre. 1982. "Are Scientific Analogies Metaphors?" In David S. Miall, ed., *Metaphor: Problems and Perspectives*, 106–32. Sussex: Harvester Press.

Goldfarb, Robert and William Griffith. 1991. "The 'Theory as Map' Analogy and Changes in Assumption Sets in Economics." In Amitai Etzioni and Paul Lawrence, eds., *Socio-Economics: Towards a New Synthesis*, 105–30. Armonk, NY: Sharpe.

Henderson, Willie. 1982. "Metaphor in Economics." *Economics* (Winter): 147–53.

Hesse, Mary B. 1955. *Science and the Human Imagination*. New York: Philosophical Library.

Hesse, Mary B. 1966. *Models and Analogies in Science*. Notre Dame, IN: University of Notre Dame Press.

Hesse, Mary B. 1980. *Revolution and Reconstruction in the Philosophy of Science*. Bloomington: Indiana University Press.

Hobbes, Thomas. 1968. *Leviathan*. C. B. Macpherson, ed., London: Penguin (First published in 1651).

Jevons, W. Stanley. 1958. *The Principles of Science*. New York: Dover (first published in 1874).

Keynes, John Maynard. 1948. *A Treatise on Probability*. London: Macmillan (first published in 1921).

Klamer, Arjo. 1987. "As If Economists and Their Subjects Were Rational." In John S. Nelson, Allan Megill, and Donald N. McCloskey, eds., *The Rhetoric of Human Inquiry*, 19–33. Madison: University of Wisconsin Press.

Klamer, Arjo. 1990. "Towards the Native's Point of View: The Difficulty of Changing the Conversation." In Don Lavoie, ed., *Economics and Hermeneutics*, 19–33. New York: Routledge.

Klamer, Arjo, and Donald M. McCloskey. 1991. "Accounting as the Master Metaphor of Economics." *European Accounting Review* 1 (May): 145–60.

Klamer, Arjo, Donald M. McCloskey, and Robert M. Solow, eds. 1988. *The Consequences of Economic Rhetoric*. Cambridge University Press.

Kuhn, Thomas. 1970. *The Structure of Scientific Revolutions*. Chicago: University of Chicago Press (first published in 1962).

Kuhn, Thomas. 1979. "Metaphor in Science." In Andrew Ortony, ed., *Metaphor and Thought*, 409–19. Cambridge University Press.

Lakatos, Imre. 1968. "Criticism and the Methodology of Scientific Research Programmes." *Proceedings of the Aristotelian Society* 69: 149–86.

Lakoff, George, and Mark Johnson. 1980. *Metaphors We Live By*. Chicago: University of Chicago Press.

Lanham, Richard A. 1991. *A Handlist of Rhetorical Terms*, 2d edition. Berkeley and Los Angeles: University of California Press.

Leatherdale, W. H. 1974. *The Role of Analogy, Model and Metaphor in Science*. Amsterdam: North Holland.

Lightman, Alan P. 1989. "Magic on the Mind: Physicists Use of Metaphor." *American Scholar* 58: 97–101.

Locke, John. 1975. *An Essay Concerning Human Understanding*. Peter H. Nidditch, ed. Oxford University Press.

McCloskey, Donald N. 1983. "The Rhetoric of Economics." *Journal of Economic Literature* 31 (June): 434–61.

McCloskey, Donald N. 1985. *The Rhetoric of Economics.* Madison: University of Wisconsin Press.

McCloskey, Donald N. 1990. *If You're So Smart: The Narrative of Economic Expertise.* Chicago: University of Chicago Press.

Miall, David S., ed. 1982. *Metaphor: Problems and Perspectives.* Brighton: Harvester.

Mirowski, Philip. 1989. *More Heat Than Light: Economics as Social Physics, Physics as Nature's Economics.* Cambridge University Press.

Nietzsche, Friedrich W. 1979. *Philosophy and Truth: Selections from Nietzsche's Notebooks of the Early 1870s.* Daniel Breazeale, ed. Atlantic Highlands, NJ: Humanities Press.

Ortony, Andrew, ed. 1979. *Metaphor and Thought.* Cambridge University Press.

Pepper, Stephen C. 1942. *World Hypotheses.* Berkeley: University of California Press.

Richards, I. A. 1971. *The Philosophy of Rhetoric.* Oxford University Press (first published in 1936).

Ricoeur, Paul. 1977. *The Rule of Metaphor.* Toronto: University of Toronto Press.

Sachs, Sheldon, ed. 1979. *On Metaphor.* Chicago: University of Chicago Press.

Schön, Donald A. 1967. *The Invention and Evolution of Ideas.* London: Social Science Paperbacks (first published in 1963 as *Displacement of Concepts.* London: Tavistock).

Schön, Donald A. 1979. "Generative Metaphor: A Perspective on Problem-Setting in Social Policy." In Andrew Ortony, ed., *Metaphor and Thought,* 254–83. Cambridge University Press.

Schumpeter, Joseph A. 1954. *History of Economic Analysis.* New York: Oxford University Press.

Simon, Herbert A. 1991. *Models of My Life.* New York: Basic Books.

Solow, Robert M. 1988. "Comments from Inside Economics." In Arjo Klamer, Donald M. McCloskey, and Robert M. Solow, eds., *The Consequences of Economic Rhetoric,* 31–7. Cambridge University Press.

Stanford, W. Bedell. 1972. *Greek Metaphor: Studies in Theory and Practice.* New York: Johnson Reprint (first published in 1936 by Basil Blackwell).

Turbayne, Colin M. 1962. *Myth and Metaphor.* New Haven, CT: Yale University Press.

PART II

Physical metaphors and mathematical formalization

Newton and the social sciences, with special reference to economics, or, the case of the missing paradigm

I. BERNARD COHEN

Newton and the social sciences

An inquiry into the role of Newtonian science or the Newtonian natural philosophy in relation to the social sciences requires at the outset some careful definitions and distinctions. In the present chapter, I am concerned primarily with the social sciences as exemplified by economics and social theory,[1] although my conclusions apply equally to other social sciences such as political science.[2] A common fault of publications that discuss Newton in relation to the social sciences is the failure to make a distinction between some vague and usually unspecified values associated with the name of Newton (often known as "Newtonianism")[3] and a set of specific meanings of Newtonian science and Newtonian philosophy, including what I have called the Newtonian "style."

For more than two centuries, the name of Newton has been invoked by natural scientists and social scientists in expressing the hope that their branch of knowledge might achieve the legitimacy with which Newton endowed rational mechanics. Thus, in the early nineteenth century, the anatomist and paleontologist Georges Cuvier expressed the hope that his science would find "its Newton," but he did not intend that paleontology should take the form of an extended mathematical exercise, nor even that paleontology should become quantitative.[4] Similarly, in the mid-nineteenth century, when the American economist Robert S. Hamilton (1886, 75, as quoted in Bernard and Bernard 1943, 711) expressed the hope that sociology might soon produce its "Principia," he was merely expressing the goal that the "facts and ideas" of this subject would become "methodically arranged, and systematized," so that sociology could learn how "to begin its inquiries properly, how to direct its efforts, or systematize its observations."

In this presentation, I use "Newtonian science" primarily to signify Newton's physics, specifically the physics expounded in his *Principia* (1687, 1713, 1726) and there named by Newton "rational mechanics" and also the experimental natural philosophy set forth in his *Opticks* (1704). Although Newtonian physics embraced both the mathematical science of the *Principia* and the experimental science of the *Opticks,* nearly all writers on Newton and the social sciences refer almost exclusively to that part of Newton's oeuvre that established his greatness and that secured him an enduring place in the highest pantheon of science: the elaboration of modern (Newtonian) rational mechanics and its application to celestial systems. Newton set forth the principles of rational mechanics (laws and definitions) in the first of the three "books" that comprise the *Principia,* and he developed Newtonian gravitational dynamics[5] in relation to the Newtonian system of the world (or Newtonian gravitational cosmology) in the third "book." Newton's experimental natural philosophy was displayed not only in his *Opticks,* but in a number of scientific publications in the *Philosophical Transactions* of the Royal Society of London.[6] We must take note, furthermore, that in the sense just set forth, "Newtonian" rational mechanics does not include considerations of energy and its conservation, virtual displacements or virtual velocities, variational principles, and all the other additions to this subject made by such post-Newtonian figures as Euler, Lagrange, Laplace, Hamilton, Jacobi, and Poincaré.[7] It is my thesis that Newtonian science, in this strict sense of his rational mechanics, did not ever successfully serve the social sciences by offering a useful model for direct emulation or by supplying useful analogies or equations (or their equivalent in proportions or ratios), laws, and concepts. Furthermore, I shall suggest some reasons why Newtonian science (again, in the strict sense) could not have done so. Despite these seemingly negative conclusions, I will show that there has existed a Newtonian paradigm that has not heretofore been fully identified by social scientists and that has served the social sciences.

Analogy, homology, identity, and metaphor: the problem of mismatched homology

In considering the attempts to use Newtonian science or Newtonian natural philosophy in the social sciences, a useful distinction may be made among four levels of discourse and among the different varieties of the Newtonian natural philosophy. The two extremes of the levels of discourse are *identity* and *metaphor,* with *analogy* and *homology* as intermediary.

"Metaphor" has been defined traditionally (e.g., by Aristotle, *Poetics*, 1457b) as the act of assigning the name or the quality of something to something else to which it does not properly or normally belong.[8] Classic examples are the scriptural comparison of life to a pilgrimage and Shakespeare's similar comparison to a stage. A striking metaphor was used by James I soon after gaining the crown of England. "I am the husband," he told Parliament, "and the whole Isle is my lawful wife; I am the head and it is my body" (Cohen, 1993, 30, 86). Such use of metaphor is part of rhetoric, a means of enhancing discourse that transcends the logic of induction and deduction or appeals to the experiential evidence of critical observations and experiment.[9]

Although "analogy" is generally used today to denote many kinds of similarity,[10] in my analysis I use the term in a more restricted sense, one that is somewhat similar to the usage found in the biological sciences. That is, analogy (or analogue) will specifically denote a similarity that centers on an equivalence or likeness of functions or relations or properties. This particular usage also occurs in the physical sciences, as in David Brewster's statement (1843, 181) about waves or undulations as "a property of sound which has its analogy also in light."

I use the term "homology" (along with homologue and homologous) in a biological sense distinct from that of analogy[11] to denote similarity in form as distinguished from similarity in function.[12] This distinction may be seen in an anatomical comparison of the wing of a bird, the foreleg of a quadruped, and the arm of a human being; they are structurally similar but perform quite different functions. The concept of homology may be especially useful in the present context to the degree that it permits an extension from anatomical or structural properties to behavioral ones. It should be noted that structurally equivalent concepts or structurally equivalent laws may have analogous functions.[13]

The four levels of discourse may be illustrated by reference to organismic theories of society. First, identity. Some writers on the subject of the "body politic" have written of the state as if it were actually an organism and not merely like an organism. "What is society?" asked Herbert Spencer in his *Principles of Sociology* (1897, 1:pt. 2, §1); his reply, stated simply and unambiguously, was given in the next section – "an organism." Two others who were of the "identity" persuasion were Johann Caspar Bluntschli (Stark 1962, 61–2), an older contemporary of Spencer's (who even endowed society and its institutions with sex), and Paul von Lilienfeld (Cohen, in press a), one of the foremost organicists of the nineteenth century. Lilienfeld declared that if considering society to be an organism were only a metaphor, he would never have written his four-volume book on the subject. Accordingly, the title of the first volume of his major work (1873) expressed his conviction: "Human Society as an Actual Organism" (Die menschliche Gesellschaft als realer Organismus).

The level of metaphor, rather than identity, is often a feature of discussions of the body politic. This metaphor has successively illustrated the changes in physiology and medicine, being Galenic until the seventeenth century, then Harveyan, and so on. Its legacies to us are such concepts and expressions as "head" of state, "nerves" or "nerve center" of government, "ills" of society, and their "cures."[14] All such metaphoric expressions include analogies between functions of the animal and the human bodies, including aspects of medicine and public health, producing such social analogues of medical or health science as "normal" and "pathological." Such analogies, we may note, do not always create a unique pair of biosocial homologues.[15]

Jean-Jacques Rousseau provides an example of the use of biomedical analogies in the analysis of society. His conclusion borders on identity, declaring unambiguously that the body politic is "a moral being which has a will." The "body politic," he wrote, "can be considered as an organized, living body and similar to that of man":

> The sovereign power represents the head; the laws and customs are the brain, the center of the nervous system and seat of the understanding, the will and the senses, of which the judges and magistrates are the organs; commerce, industry, and agriculture are the mouth and stomach which prepare the common subsistence; public finances are the blood that a wise *economy*, performing the functions of the heart, sends back to distribute nourishment and life throughout the body.[16]

Rousseau combines concepts that are organismic with ideas of the body as a machine, the latter a direct inheritance from Cartesian philosophy and physiology, noting that "the citizens are the body and members which make the machine move, live, and work." He concluded that the citizens, "as body members," cannot "be injured in any way without a painful sensation being transmitted right to the brain, if the animal is in a state of good health" (in Sherover 1974).

Often, especially in organismic analogies of the state or of society, homologies tend to be introduced that are so extravagant that any reasonable critic would have to declare a mismatch. An example is found in a discussion of the body politic that is similar to Rousseau's – Thomas Carlyle's in *Sartor Resartus* (1836). Here Carlyle introduces a close analogy between social entities and parts of the human body. That is, he does not merely present the general functions of various organs (such as the epidermis) as social analogues, but gives a detailed homology, in which "government is, so to speak, the outward SKIN of the Body Politic, holding the whole together and protecting it." He supposes that the "Craft-Guilds, and Associations for Industry" are the "muscular and osseous Tissues (lying under such SKIN), where-by Society stands and works." He even finds that "Religion [is] the inmost Pericardial and Nervous Tissue." The mismatch of homologies needs no further comment.

Two authors of very different sorts, one from the nineteenth century and one from the twentieth, provide additional case histories that illustrate the easy susceptibility of social thought to mismatched homology. The first, Herbert Spencer, was a self-educated sociologist and philosopher; the second, Walter Bradford Cannon, was an eminent scientist who dabbled in sociology. There are many examples of mismatched homology in Herbert Spencer's writings on sociology. One, which even his sympathetic biographer admits is a case of "dubious biology . . . added to pedestrian sociology," is Spencer's analogy between "the coalescence of the Anglo-Saxon kingdoms into England" and the formation of crustaceans (Peel 1971, 178). Here he was introducing his own odd notion that crustaceans, like insects, are "composite animals," in which the segments are independent life units joined together. Perhaps the limit is reached when he refers to the two great national schools of France as "a double gland" intended "to secrete engineering faculty for public use."

The example of Walter Cannon is more interesting than that of Spencer because Cannon was one of the foremost scientific investigators of the twentieth century. His first essay in biological sociology (1932) was titled "Relations of Biological and Social Homeostasis," an exploration of whether analogues of the "stabilizing processes" in animal organisms can be found in "other forms of organization – industrial, domestic or social." Cannon's major field of scientific investigation was the study of self-regulating processes in the human (and animal) body, stressing the role of the "milieu intérieur." He very sensibly undertook the study of social systems in order to find out whether in "a state or nation" there is an "equivalent" for the "fluid matrix of animal organisms." Unfortunately, he did not confine his study to analogies, that is, to the search for social and physiological equivalents "in a functional sense," but developed very specific homologues. Thus, in society he found the equivalent of the fluid matrix for maintaining homeostasis in the living body to be "the system of distribution in all its aspects – canals, rivers, roads and railroads, with boats, trucks and trains, serving, like the blood and lymph, as common carriers [on which] the products of farm and factory, of mine and forest, are borne to and fro." Cannon unwittingly fell into the trap of mismatched homology by making his analogies far too substantive. He simply could not restrain himself from introducing homologies when he was comparing the cells in an organism with the members of a social group, or the lymph and blood with the system of canals, rivers, roads, and railroads.

We may agree with Robert Merton that Cannon made the mistake of introducing "substantive analogies and homologies between biological organisms and social systems." Merton went so far as to describe Cannon's result an "unexcelled . . . example of the fruitless extremes to which even a distinguished mind is driven." This comment is all the more significant in that it occurs in Merton's essay on "Manifest and Latent Functions" (1968, 101n, 102–3), in which he finds "Cannon's logic of procedure in physiology" to be a model for the sociological investigator, recommending that his readers study Cannon's *Wisdom of the Body*, while warning them about "the unhappy epilogue on social homeostasis."

Analogy, homology, and metaphor in attempts to produce a Newtonian social science

The four levels of discourse may be clearly discerned with respect to the use of Newtonian physics in social theory. Later we shall see some examples (Craig, Carey, Walras) of Newtonian homologies, attempts to produce in the social realm a series of concepts and laws having the same form as Newton's law of universal gravity. But others (e.g., Berkeley and Fourier) held only that the system of society at large or of economics is an analogue of the Newtonian system. That is, Fourier believed, society is "ruled" by a simple fundamental law or principle in the same sense in which the Newtonian physical universe is "governed" by the fundamental law of gravity (Fourier 1971b).[17]

Some social scientists, however, merely believed that on the level of metaphor, social science or economics should be like Newtonian physics. This is, apparently, the intent of Hamilton's *cri de coeur* of 1886: "Although far more advanced, relatively, in particular ideas than sidereal philosophy before the time of Newton, it [social philosophy] scarcely less needs the PRINCIPIA MATHEMATICA PHILOSOPHIAE SOCIALIS, or rather the PRINCIPIA PRIMA" (in Bernard and Bernard 1943, 711). In explanation, Hamilton set forth, "in brief, the Newtonian idea of astronomy" by way of "one of its simplest illustrations," which was essentially that there is "no truly philosophical distinction to be taken between MAN and Nature" (Hamilton, quoted in Bernard and Bernard 1943, 711, 712). This leads him to declare that the "Newtonian idea of Sociology is precisely analogous." The ascription of "Newtonian" to sociology, in other words, meant no more to Hamilton than the assertion of "the universality of the causes, or laws, which determine the social condition of mankind, and the consequent identity of the causes which determine the social destiny of an individual and a nation." Here, then is a perfect example of general metaphor.

At this point, let me take note that some historians of economics have used metaphor in a somewhat different and broader sense, to include the use of analogues and homologues plus a general system of values, ideals, and methodological principles. In this broader sense, such neoclassical economists as Jevons and Walras are considered to have gone a step beyond merely introducing into economics the mathematical tools and actual equations of post-Newtonian rational mechanics. They are seen to have attempted to show that economics could be like rational mechanics and accordingly entitled to share in the high esteem accorded this exalted branch of the exact sciences.

Did anyone ever attempt to found a system of social science or economics on the level of identity with Newtonian rational mechanics or the Newtonian system of the world? In my research, I have never found such an example. The reason is that the Newtonian system of the world, the application of Newtonian rational mechanics, does not lend itself to a mechanical model or a visualization in the human mind that can easily be transferred to an image of society at large or to economics. Indeed, although there has been much discussion of the so-called Newtonian world machine, the Newtonian system of the world is not truly a machine in the sense that the major force that holds the system together acts at a distance rather than by physical contract or mechanical linkage as is the case for all mechanical models or working engines. It is impossible to visualize the Newtonian system in the way that the Cartesian cosmology, in its many variant forms, permits one to picture a sea of some kind of matter swirling around and carrying planets and other bodies in orbit. One cannot even make a mechanical model of the Newtonian system. In the Newtonian system, furthermore, there is no equilibrium, no balancing of contrary forces as in the case of a lever. Rather, the Newtonian explanation of the curved or orbital motion of planets and comets is based on the notion that each planet or comet has two independent components of motion. One is along the tangent, a component of linear inertial (nonaccelerated) motion; the other is directed toward the sun, a component of continually accelerated motion of falling inward toward the sun as a result of an unbalanced "central" or centripetal force. These two components, wholly independent because they are perpendicular, carry the planet forward while it falls inward, just as in the case of the falling of a projectile, so that the planet keeps in orbit (see Cohen 1980, in press a). Because of this limitation in the Newtonian system, the only case of identity between it and a social system would be an identity of equations and their derivations and applications.[18] As we shall see, some economists – Jevons, Walras, Fisher, and Pareto, among them – alleged that their equations were identical (or very nearly identical) with those of rational mechanics, but only Walras (Mirowski and Cook, 1990) seems to have made such a claim for specifically Newtonian equations. Even if the equations were identical, however, the result would be a case of homology rather than identity.

The Newtonian laws of Carey and of Walras

Two examples of laws introduced in the social sciences will serve to illustrate the relations between homology and analogy.[19] Both were proposed in the middle of the nineteenth century, one by the French economist Léon Walras, the other by the American economist and sociologist Henry C. Carey; both were intended to be counterparts of the Newtonian law of universal gravity. Walras's and Carey's laws can be considered analogues of Newton's to the degree that both were intended to serve the same function that Newton's law serves in rational mechanics and celestial dynamics.

Carey's law was a part of a general principle of social gravitation. He wrote, "Man tends of necessity to gravitate towards his fellow-man." More specifically, he declared that "the greater the number [of humans] collected in a given space [e.g., in populous cities] the greater is the attractive force there exerted" (Carey 1858–60, 1:42–3). As in Newton's law, Carey's expresses a property of an "attractive force." Carey has his force be as the "number of men" in two places (e.g., cities), which is formally equivalent to Newton's force being directly proportional to two masses. Thus far, there is an apparent homology between the two. The homology fails, however, with respect to the third factor, distance. In Carey's law the force is inversely proportional to the distance, whereas in Newton's law the force is inversely proportional to the square of the distance. The two laws do not, therefore, have the same form; there is not a perfect fit.

Carey's law therefore exemplifies an analogy that suffers from mismatched homology. But now consider the actual concepts in the two laws. Force and distance appear to be conceptual homologues, but the number of humans is a poor homologue for Newtonian mass. Mass is the characteristic concept of Newtonian or classical physics and as such was invented by Newton in his *Principia* (1687, 1713, 1726, Def. 1). Newtonian mass is an invariant property of any body or sample of matter; it does not change when the body is heated or chilled, bent or twisted, stretched or compressed, or transplanted to another location – whether another spot on earth or some place out in space or even on the moon or another planet. In this feature it differs from such a local (i.e., noninvariant) property as weight, which varies with latitude on earth and also with transplantation to the moon or another planet. Newton's concept of mass, as developed in the *Principia,* has two separate aspects: One (inertial mass in post-Einstein terminology) is a measure of a body's resistance to being accelerated or being made to undergo a change in "state," while the other (gravitational mass) is a measure of a body's response to a given gravitational field (i.e., the weight). Newton showed by experiment that the two are equal (bk. 3, prop. 6).

Once Newton's concept of mass is set forth, it becomes apparent that Carey's social equivalent of mass fails as a homologue of Newton's mass.[20] Carey's concept, however, does have the same role or mathematical function in his law that Newton's concept does in his law of universal gravity. In short, the two concepts are used analogously even though they are not homologous.

Let me now turn to Walras's law. Early in his career (1860), Walras wrote a short work entitled "The Application of Mathematics to Political Economy." Here he essayed a Newtonian law of economics, that "the price of things is in inverse ratio to the quantity offered and in direct ratio to the quantity demanded" (Jaffé 1973). This law appears to be an analogue of the Newtonian law of gravity in the sense that it would have the same important role in market theory that the Newtonian law has for the theory of planetary motion. But even if the two laws are analogous in the sense of being functionally equivalent, they are plainly not homologies. The homology fails for two reasons. First, Walras's law depends on a simple inverse ratio (the price is inversely proportional to the quantity offered), whereas Newton's law invokes the ratio of the inverse square (the force is inversely proportional to the square of the distance). Second, Walras's law states a direct ratio of a single quantity or parameter (quantity demanded), whereas Newton's law uses the direct ratio of two quantities (the two masses). Additionally, Walras's law posits a price that is proportional to a "quantity" divided by another "quantity" of the same kind or dimensionality, that is, a pure numerical ratio. Clearly, whatever other faults this law may have, it doubly exemplifies mismatched homology.

These two examples, in addition to illustrating some aspects of analogy and homology, indicate some of the varieties of ways in which the natural sciences have influenced the social sciences. They were attempts to create a Newtonian social science by introducing concepts or laws as the counterparts of those used by Newton in his rational mechanics.

Transfer and transformation: the problem of incorrect science and imperfect replication

One of the problems in using the natural sciences (and mathematics) in the advance of the social sciences is the use of incorrect science. A conspicuous example is provided once again by Carey. In his endeavor to build a science of society on physical principles, centering on Newtonian celestial mechanics, he not only was guilty of mismatched homology, but also fell into the trap of incorrect science. Carey mistakenly believed that in Newton's law of universal gravity, the force between two gravitating masses is inversely proportional to the distance between them, rather than inversely proportional to the square of the distance.[21] Of course, it can be argued that Carey's social science would not have been much improved had he known and used the correct rather than an incorrect law of gravity. But the fact is that he insisted (and more than once) that the social law and the natural law must be identical, and accordingly, he was – by his own standards – guilty of error.[22]

Carey committed another scientific error. Observing that "man tends of necessity to gravitate towards his fellow-man," Carey asked why "all the members of the human family do not tend to come together on a single spot of earth." His answer was that in human society there is the same "simple and universal law," that is, the law of gravity, that keeps the members of the solar system from collapsing into the sun. The planets, some of which have satellites, he noted, have "each . . . its local center of attraction, by means of which its parts are held together." Let that "attractive power be annihilated," and the rings of Saturn, the moons of Jupiter, and our moon "would crumble to pieces and fall inwards upon the body they now attend. So too with the planets themselves" (1858–60, 3:7). Carey apparently believed that the gravity of each planet prevented it from being drawn into the sun, an enormous error. He obviously did not understand that, according to Newtonian principles, if the attractive power of gravity were to be "annihilated," there would then be no force of attraction to cause satellites "to fall inwards upon the body they now attend"; they would, then, move out along the tangent to their respective orbits. And, "so too with the planets" with respect to the sun. Totally oblivious of the errors of his supposedly Newtonian principles, Carey applied his analysis to explain how men gravitate toward cities; if "we were to obliterate these centres of attraction," he wrote, there would arise "a centralized government." He then expatiated on the evils of centralization in U.S. government and the importance of states' rights, using his incorrect analogies.

Carey was not the only writer on the state or society to make a fundamental error in basic Newtonian physics. A similar instance of incorrect Newtonian science appears in Montesquieu's celebrated *Spirit of the Laws* (1748). In discussing the "principle of monarchy," Montesquieu wrote, "It is with this kind of government as with the system of the universe." That is, "there is a power that constantly repels all bodies from the center, and a power of gravitation that attracts them to it" (bk. 3, art. 7). The concept of the "power of gravitation" that "attracts" all bodies to a center is, of course, Newtonian. But Newton's explanation of the "system of the universe" expressly denied any such balance of centripetal and centrifugal forces.[23] Accordingly, Montesquieu was as ignorant of Newton's physics as Carey and was also guilty of invoking incorrect science. It can, of course, be argued that Carey made a simple blunder, an error of ignorance of the exact form of the physical law he was using, whereas Montesquieu just didn't understand the Newtonian principle he was attempting to apply.

Carey and Montesquieu simply had their physics wrong. The case of Adam Smith is quite different because what he took from Newton's physics was perfectly correct *up to a point;* it was merely incomplete. Here I refer to Smith's concept of the "natural price" as the price toward which all others gravitate. In *The Wealth of Nations* (1776, bk. 1, ch. 7), the text delcares that the "natural price" is "the central price, to which the prices of all commodities are continually gravitating." Often cited as an instance of Smith's alleged Newtonianism, this use of gravity is an illustration of imperfect replication. Smith's notion of "all continually gravitating" toward something "central" is clearly an analogue of Newtonian "gravitation," acting on "all" bodies. His analogy at once conjures the Newtonian image of the solar system with "all" bodies (planets, satellites, comets, etc.) gravitating toward the "central" sun. But Smith did not take account of one of the features of Newtonian gravitation, its property of acting mutually between all pairs of gravitating bodies, so that there is always an equal and opposite force. In this case, a complete homology with Newtonian physics would require that the natural price must also gravitate toward all other prices. What this would do to Smith's economic theory I leave to the imagination of specialists. We may, however, conclude that Smith had been using very sound judgment when introducing into his economics only an imperfect replication of a physical concept. Unlike Carey and Montesquieu, Smith was well educated in Newtonian science and wrote eloquently and authoritatively about physical principles in his long essay on the history of astronomy.

Adam Smith's imperfect replication of a physical concept certainly does not constitute grounds for rejecting Smithian economics. Rather, this example should serve as a reminder that economics, despite many possible analogies with physics, is not physics. Here we see an instance of the distinction between analogy and identity mentioned earlier.

The example of Adam Smith is particularly interesting because it brings us to a significant feature of many interactions between the natural sciences and the social sciences, a feature that also appears in the creative interactions between different branches of the natural sciences and even within a single subject such as astronomy. I have called this aspect of innovation "creative transformation," an intellectual leap forward that often occurs when a concept, a method, a principle, or even a theory is transferred from one domain to another (whether within the natural sciences or outside, as to the social sciences). From this point of view, the creative act is seen to be more than merely a direct transfer of an idea to a new domain, more than the exact replication of an idea in a new subject area. Rather, a basic intellectual component of the creative act is the transformation of the original idea.

An example of such a transformation may be seen in the use by Charles Darwin of a fundamental concept of Charles Lyell's. Noting the succession of species in the fossil record, Lyell concluded that there must have been a contest for survival among different species. Darwin took over Lyell's concept in an imperfect version, transforming it into a wholly new and different concept, that there had been (and still is) a contest for survival among different individuals of the same species. In this way Darwin produced one of his most original innovations, what is called "population thinking."

Another example is Newton's transformation of Kepler's concept of "inertia." Kepler held that because of the "inactivity" ("inertia") of matter, a body cannot move of and by itself. Accordingly, whenever (and wherever) a moving force ceases to act, the body on which the force was acting must come to rest. Newton kept Kepler's name but altered the concept, or adopted it only in part or in an imperfect replication. Newton transformed Kepler's idea of inertia into a property of matter by which bodies "persevere" in whatever state they happen to be in, whether of resting or moving uniformly straight forward.

A conspicuous example of such a creative transformation occurred at the very beginning of the scientific revolution, in Kepler's transformation of Copernicus's system of the world. Kepler did not produce an imperfect replication through ignorance. Rather, he transformed the system through violent alterations of some of Copernicus's basic postulates. For example, Copernicus insisted on "circularity" and uniformity in the construction of planetary orbital motions; a primary argument raised by Copernicus against the system of Ptolemy was that the latter did not fulfill these conditions. Yet, by introducing his laws of planetary motion, Kepler presented the Copernican system imperfectly, since he abandoned both circularity and uniformity. From our post-Newtonian perspective, we laud Kepler for having produced a system of the world that went beyond Copernicus and that enabled Newton to find the inverse-square law and the principle of universal gravity. But Kepler's contemporaries and immediate successors did not esteem his imperfect replication or his perversion of Copernican doctrine. Galileo, for example, a friend and correspondent of Kepler's for many years, so disdained Kepler's alterations of the Copernican system that he didn't even mention them in his own presentation of Copernican astronomy. Galileo and others considered that Kepler made an imperfect or unfaithful replication of Copernicus's concepts, but we today honor Kepler for having taken from Copernicus only those parts of his system that were of real use for the advance of science.

Whatever we have to say about Kepler and Copernicus is influenced by our knowledge that Kepler's laws led to Newton's celestial dynamics. We, in fact, have so fully adopted Kepler's modified replication of the Copernican system that we usually call the Keplerian system "Copernican."[24] The literature of the history of science dating from the post-Newtonian era never faults Kepler for his having selected and used only parts of Copernicus's astronomy. Similarly, I have never encountered an economic historian or scholar writing on Smith who faulted him for his creative use of "attraction" in his discussion of the "natural price," for his having selected only part of Newton's law in the construction and presentation of his system of economics. I believe that Smith's imperfect replication of the concept of the Newtonian force of gravity has been adequately justified by the worth of his system of economics to a degree that may render it irrelevant whether he was consciously making a creative transformation or was simply not fully master of Newtonian physics.

Such imperfect interpretations and replications abound in the application of the natural sciences to the social sciences. Since the transfer is based on analogy rather than strict identity, there is no essential reason why the use of a set of concepts or principles need imply that they must have the same form or degree of completeness in the social science as in the generating natural science. Great care must be exercised, therefore, in considering such examples, lest the historical analyst take on the schoolmasterish role of "moral policeman," grading social scientists on the scope and accuracy of their scientific knowledge, rather than recognizing that every use that a social scientist makes of the natural sciences – whether on the level of analogue, homologue, or metaphor – must involve some kind of transformation and, consequently, some degree of distortion, since there can never be a complete one-to-one identity in every detail between two disparate domains of knowledge.

In a brilliant analysis of this problem, Claude Ménard (1988) has gone so far as to argue that if a "conceptual transfer" arising from an analogy is "to be fertile," the analogy must "leave room for the decentralization of the original idea," so as "to preserve an appreciation of the radical differences between the original concept and the object of comparison." As an example, he considers the way in which the "equation of maximum energy of classical mechanics inspired Walras to formulate his theory of maximum satisfaction, but only at the cost of considerable distortion."[25] Part of the distortion observed by Ménard (and by Mirowski and other critics) arises from the "absence of laws of conservation in economics." It is currently a matter of debate whether the omission of the conservation principle distorts the use of the energy analogy to so great a degree as to constitute an irreparable fault in the foundations of neoclassical economics.[26] Indeed, this subject of debate occasioned the conference that gave rise to the present volume. It should be noted that both Vilfredo Pareto and Irving Fisher were so convinced of the parallelism of their systems of economics and rational mechanics that they both drew up tables in which concepts and principles of economics were paired; Fisher even went to the extreme of indicating which concepts were vectors and which were scalars.[27]

It has been alleged (Mirowski 1989) that the founders of neoclassical economics did not fully understand the energy physics and rational mechanics on which they based their system.[28] It is not for a noneconomist to decide whether such a distortion (or, perhaps, distortion by omission of essentials) in the transfer of concepts, laws, principles, and theories is merely a productively useful, imperfect replication or constitutes a simple error of "fact." Carey's social law is not the result of a distortion or a nonorthodox interpretation of Newtonian science, nor of an incomplete version of gravitational physics, but rather a simple error in physics; he just didn't know the correct gravitational law. Similarly, Montesquieu did not distort Newtonian physics, nor did he omit a significant feature (as was the case for neoclassical economists and conservation); rather, he misunderstood or did not know the Newtonian explanation of curved orbital motion.

Whatever our evaluation may be concerning the completeness or exactness of the knowledge of the science being emulated, we should, I believe, keep in mind the many examples of fruitful advances in social thought or science that have arisen from interactions in which the original concept or principle that is transferred may not be fully understood, or perhaps may not be fully grasped in all its aspects. Indeed, it is generally known among social scientists that misinterpretations may often lead to very fruitful results, even when the source is some other social science. A celebrated example from political science is the doctrine of the separation of powers, a central feature in the form of government adopted in the U.S. Constitution. A direct source for this principle, as A. Lawrence Lowell (1937) has documented, is a misreading of the ideas of Montesquieu.

The problem of useless or inappropriate science: direct emulation of Newtonian science

Attempts to make transfers from the natural sciences to the social sciences, notably in applications of Newton's physics, have often produced an inappropriate analogy (or its equivalent, a useless analogy). Some analogies do not provide a gauge of the validity of a social theory, system, or concept or do not introduce some new insight that advances the social science. The analogy – being of no use to the social science – must be deemed inappropriate. Numerous comparisons of the state or society with the Newtonian system of the world enable us to examine this problem.

The notion that gravitational cosmology or the Newtonian system of the world could provide an appropriate analogy for society or the ordering of the state goes back to the days of Newton himself. His disciple Jean-Théophile Desaguliers, author of one of the standard Newtonian textbooks, embodied his hopes in a poem,[29] "The Newtonian System of the World, the Best Model of Government" (1728). In my historical research, I have never encountered a political theorist, a practical politician or political leader, or a natural or social scientist who has ever made use of this curious presentation. It is clearly an example of useless or inappropriate analogy.

A second early example occurs in a work by a contemporary of Newton's, the Scots mathematician John Craig. The latter's *Theologiae christianae principia mathematica* (1699) is obviously a direct emulation of Newton's *Philosophiae naturalis principia mathematica*. Craig was in full command of Newtonian mathematical physics and once suggested to Newton a minor modification of the *Principia* (Cohen 1974). Craig produced a Newtonian law in a social context, a rule for determining the degree of credence to be assigned to the testimony of successive witnesses. He came up with an ingenious Newtonian answer: The reliability of such testimony varies inversely as the square of the time from that testimony to the present, just as the Newtonian gravitational force decreases as the square of the distance. This law is plainly another example of useless analogy.[30]

My third social Newtonian is the philosopher George Berkeley, who, like Craig, was an astute student and critic of Newtonian mathematics and physics. Berkeley sought to apply the science of the *Principia* in a scheme of social organization based on a law of moral attraction in analogy with the Newtonian law of universal gravity. Writing in 1713, the year of the second edition of the *Principia*, Berkeley began his essay by stating the principles of Newtonian celestial dynamics correctly.[31] He concluded that there must be "a like principle of attraction" in the "Spirits and Minds of men," one that draws them together into "communities, clubs, families, friendships, all the various species of society" (Berkeley 1901, 4:186–90; 1935, 7:225–8). Furthermore, just as in physical bodies of equal mass "the attraction is strongest between those which are placed nearest to each other," so with respect to "the minds of men," ceteris paribus, the "attraction is strongest . . . between those which are most nearly related."[32] Although Berkeley correctly stated the Newtonian principles, he did not really make a serious contribution to social science. His analogy is no more than a historical curiosity, a prime example of useless or inappropriate analogy.

Desaguliers, Craig, and Berkeley all tried to use correct principles of Newtonian physical science in the context of a human or social science. Their ultimate failure, and the subsequent failure of every such attempt to produce a strictly Newtonian social science,[33] must lead to the conclusion that Newtonian rational mechanics as such, like the Newtonian system of the world, is an inappropriate analogy for the social sciences.[34]

We have seen that one reason why Newton's dynamics and gravitational system of the world did not provide a useful model for the social sciences was the impossibility of constructing, or even envisioning, a Newtonian machine. The opposite point of view has been expressed by Overton H. Taylor, who alleges that

> Newtonian or classical theoretical physics, with its conception of the physical universe as a mechanical system, and its theory of the "natural laws" of the motions of bodies and the "working" of that system, profoundly influenced the basic concepts and assumptions commonly involved in eighteenth-century theorizings, not only in the "natural" sciences but also in psychology and economic, political, and all social sciences.

Taylor goes on to suppose that "human, economic and political societies came to be generally conceived or thought of as (either literally or by analogy) 'mechanisms' or 'mechanical' systems, operating or functioning through internal processes conforming to or exemplifying discoverable 'natural laws,' i.e., either those of physics (mechanics) or others like them" (1960, 11). Needless to say, Taylor provides no examples of such Newtonian machines, nor does he justify his allegations – shared by many historians – that the concept of such machines is Newtonian. Students of seventeenth- and eighteenth-century science are aware that one of the grounds for severe criticism of Newton's mechanics and his system of the world was precisely that it departed from the strict canons of the "mechanical philosophy," that the Newtonian cosmos was not mechanical.

Economics and inappropriate science: the problem of three bodies

An instructive example from economics enables us to be a little more precise about the limits of inappropriate science. The Belgian statistician Adolphe Quetelet once proposed an analogy of human society and a many-bodied planetary system. One would be composed of material bodies interacting mutually in accordance with the law of universal gravity; the other would consist of mutually interacting human beings (Hankins 1968). This analogy seems at first glance to be very apt, indicating a possible science of social behavior constructed in analogy with the physics of gravitational perturbations. It is a fact, however, that in celestial mechanics only a system of two mutually interacting bodies can have a complete or analytic solution.[35] The problem of a three-body system cannot be solved rigorously, and so astronomers have resorted to the use of geometric or analytic approximations (except for certain special but very significant cases). Even a somewhat restricted example, the motion of the moon about the earth with the perturbing effect of the sun, studied at length by Newton in the *Principia* (bk. 1, sect. 6, prop. 66 and its twenty-two corollaries) and brought to a high level of development by G. W. Hill,[36] leads only to a series of approximations.[37] Eventually, the work of Henri Poincaré and his successor G. D. Birkhoff (1927) led to a new kind of mathematics that enabled some major qualitative properties of such systems to be explored.

A population of many human individuals provides the social analogue of a gravitational many-body problem, of which the difficulties exceed the bounds of ordinary imagination. When Newton first recognized in December 1684 that each planet must pull on the sun with a force equal and opposite to the force of the sun on the planet, he at once became aware of the consequence, that every one of the planets must also continuously and varyingly attract and be attracted by all the other planets. He was appalled by his own conclusion. In his manuscript he wrote, "Unless I am much mistaken, it would exceed the force of human wit to consider so many causes of motion at the same time" (quoted in Hall and Hall 1962, 256, 281).[38] Post-Newtonian scientists have indeed expended considerable energy on devising means of determining perturbations by better and better means of approximation, a necessary condition for taking account of planetary perturbations in computing orbits for ephemerides.

The three-body problem and the associated theory of perturbations in gravitational systems raised an issue of central importance to social scientists, notably economists, in the nineteenth century. In *The Principles of Science* Jevons explained how the "social and moral sciences" were "subjects of enormous perplexity." The equations for supply and demand for "two or three commodities among two or three trading bodies" are so "complicated," he found, that "scientific methods" could not possibly make any rapid progress in developing this subject. If such difficulties arise in a "comparatively formal science" such as economics, he wrote, "what shall we say of moral science?" Jevons asked rhetorically:

> If we are to apply scientific method to morals, we must have a calculus of moral effects, a kind of physical astronomy investigating the mutual perturbations of individuals. But as astronomers have not yet fully solved the problem of three gravitating bodies, when shall we have a solution of the problem of three moral bodies? (1958, 759–60)

While Jevons did not discuss this problem in his *Theory of Political Economy*, it was introduced in a review of that book by Alfred Marshall in April 1872. "Just as the motion of every body in the solar system affects and is affected by the motion of every other," he wrote, "so it is with the elements of the problem of political economy" (quoted in Pigou 1925, 94–5). These expressions by Jevons and Marshall indicate that, so far as economics is concerned, Quetelet's analogy – while not introducing any scientific error and containing no serious example of mismatched homology – was unproductive and inappropriate for the further development of any social science.

The sentence from Marshall's review was, in turn, quoted by Francis Ysidro Edgeworth (1982, 3:8–9) in his review of the second edition of Marshall's *Principles of Economics* (1891). The three-body problem was central for Edgeworth, as it was for any economist whose goal was to establish his subject on the model of what was then considered the most paradigmatic of all the exact sciences, rational mechanics in general and celestial mechanics in particular. In his first tract on mathematical economics, Edgeworth referred to the sentiments of Jevons and Marshall concerning "the celebrated problem of Many Bodies" attracting one another "according to any function of the distance." Specifically, Edgeworth asked what "can be expected from Mathematics in social science, when she is unable to solve the problem of Three Bodies in her own department." His reply, incidentally, indicates that his command of advanced mathematical dynamics was far above that of Jevons, although not necessarily that of Marshall (Edgeworth 1881, 10–11).[39]

Edgeworth's reply goes beyond simple considerations of Newtonian celestial mechanics to introduce principles of Lagrange and Hamilton that almost make readers believe they are looking at a work by Paul Samuelson in our own time. Pointing out that one cannot solve the many-body problem "numerically and explicitly," Edgeworth nevertheless was aware that the principle of Lagrange could be used to gain results that would satisfy "the soul of the philosopher with the grandest of generalisations," namely, that the time integral of energy always tends toward a maximum (1881, 10–11). His conclusion led to important consequences for economics. The time integral of energy ("the principal object of the physical investigation") became, for Edgeworth, "analogous to that accumulation of pleasure which is constituted by bringing together in prospect the pleasure existing at each instant of time, the end of rational action, whether self-interested or benevolent." In other words, "The central conception of Dynamics and (in virtue of pervading analogies it may be said) in general of Mathematical Physics is *other-sidedly identical* with the central conception of Ethics." Accordingly, after some further argument,[40] he concluded that " 'Mécanique Sociale' may one day take her place along with 'Mécanique Céleste,' throned each upon the double-sided height of one maximum principle, the supreme pinnacle of moral as of physical science."

Consideration of the three-body problem (Edgeworth 1881, 11–12) is of special interest in the present context because it shows how an apparently intractable problem may inspire the creation of new mathematics, which,[41] in turn, results in new directions for the social sciences. But at this point we must depart from "Newton's rational mechanics" or the "rational mechanics of the *Principia*" and introduce post- or non-Newtonian principles such as virtual velocities or virtual displacements, energy and its conservation, and new principles such as those of Lagrange, Laplace, and especially Hamilton.

A particularly important line of modern mathematics grew out of studies of the intractability of the three-body problem and of those properties of dynamical systems in general that do not permit analytic solution.[42] Pioneered by the great French mathematician Henri Poincaré (1892–9) and carried to new heights by the American mathematician G. D. Birkhoff (1927), this new approach to the study of the differential equations of dynamical systems[43] became a major force in generating the present discipline of topology. In our present context, we may take note that Birkhoff predicted some practical applications of his work to such fields as social theory, the study of personality, the investigations of population growth, and biological systems. In particular, he believed that such use might be made of the parts of his research dealing with "the stability of recurrent and non-recurrent systems about the position of equilibrium and in the neighborhood of periodic motions in the case of variational systems" (Birkhoff and Lewis 1935; reviewed in Cohen 1937). Roy Weintraub (1991) has shown how the "Poincaré-Birkhoff tradition in dynamics" influenced "the stability analysis of [Paul] Samuelson, and thus a generation of mathematical economists trained from his 1947 book."[44]

Let me return for a moment to Quetelet. He never worked through his proposed analogy in any detail. Perhaps he intended nothing more than that a general theory of society might be modeled on Laplace's *Système du monde*, which he had studied during his years of apprenticeship in Paris. But even in this case, the analogy would have to be judged unfruitful since no such theory of society has ever been constructed. Today we know some reasons why this is so, most notably because in Laplace's day energy considerations had not achieved the important role in mechanics that was to come later in the century and because, in particular, there was as yet no conservation law (Elkana 1974; Cohen 1981a). Consequently, considerations of minimum and maximum had not yet achieved the significance for mechanical systems that was to come later in the century. Rational mechanics as reformulated by Hamilton in the mid-nineteenth century changed the character of that classical branch of physics in a way that provided almost at once a suitable analogue for some of the primary founders of marginalist or neoclassical economics (Mirowski 1989).

Newtonian social science as metaphor

Thus far I have been considering how certain social scientists sought direct social analogues or homologues of such concepts of Newtonian science as gravitation, of such laws or principles as a force inversely proportional to the square of the distance, of the law of universal gravity itself, of the Newtonian system of the world, and of the theory of gravitational perturbations. They failed to find an appropriate Newtonian paradigm. They never succeeded in producing a satisfactory Newtonian model for a social science on the levels of identity, analogy, or homology. This bleak conclusion does not, however, imply that a Newtonian paradigm has never been part of the social sciences. Rather, we must seek that missing paradigm in a different kind of metaphor.

I shall examine this useful paradigm in three historical examples of Newtonian influence on the social sciences. First, there is the Newtonian goal of creating a science of society or of human action founded on an "experimental" (i.e., experiential or empirical) base. Newton himself sanctioned this methodology in declarations that he had produced his science from experiment and observation by a Baconian process of induction. Such assertions abound in his *Opticks* (1704, 1717–18), a work that differs from the *Principia* in developing its subject by direct appeal to experiment, rather than by the use of mathematical techniques.[45] In the "Queries," at the end of the *Opticks* (enlarged in successive editions: English 1704, Latin 1706, English 1717–18), Newton even set forth a research program for experimental science. Since this work concluded with a discussion of morals, it could be considered a model for producing a "moral" science on an empirical Newtonian foundation.[46]

A primary figure in the search for an empirical "moral Newtonianism," a new science of behavior, was David Hume. He presented his *Treatise of Human Nature* (first published in 1738) as "an attempt to introduce the Experimental Method of Reasoning into Moral Subjects." His goal was to produce a system of moral philosophy that would be the equivalent of what Newton had done in natural philosophy (see Force 1990, ch. 10). He believed he had discovered in the psychological principle of "association" a "kind of attraction, which in the mental world will be found to have as extraordinary effects as in the natural, and to show itself in as many and as various forms." In short, he believed that psychological phenomena exhibit mutual attraction.[47] If, as Hume believed, human behavior and social action are regulated by social laws, there is implied the possibility of a social science, one in which, as Hume wrote, "consequences almost as general and certain may sometimes be deduced . . . as any which the mathematical sciences afford us."[48]

A somewhat different form of the Newtonian paradigm appears in a more general metaphor, which assumed that a social science will be Newtonian even if it is based on concepts, principles, and laws that are not in any sense homologues of Newton's concepts, principles, and laws. In this metaphor, it is only required that the principles organize the sciences of "man" in a similar (analogous) fashion to the way Newton's law of gravitation became an organizing principle for his celestial physics. This variety of Newtonian sociology appeared in the opening years of the nineteenth century in the system of Charles Fourier, who believed he had found such a law and had used it to create a Newtonian sociology. Fourier claimed that he was the first person to have discovered the scientific laws of human nature and that these could now be applied to change or redirect individual human behavior and the social interactions of groups.[49] Announcing his discovery of a "calculus of Harmony" in 1803, he deplored the fact that past scientists had found only "the laws of physical motion," whereas they should have discovered (as he had done) "the laws of social motion." Newton and other physicists had found laws only for the "useless" motions of material bodies, but he had discovered the laws of the motions that mattered because their application would improve the conditions of humanity (Fourier 1971b).

The Newtonian style: Malthus's theory of population

The last variety of the Newtonian metaphor that I will explore is perhaps the most significant. It embodies adapting the Newtonian paradigm to social science by appropriating his method in general, using what I have called the Newtonian style.[50] This style does not refer to the set of mathematical techniques used by Newton – the techniques of geometry and trigonometry, algebra, proportions, infinite series, or fluxions (i.e., the calculus) – but rather to the stages of contrapuntal interactions between imagined or ideal systems and those observed in physical nature.[51]

The *Principia* begins with an idealized world, a simple mental construct, a "system" of a single mathematical particle and a centrally directed force in a mathematical space. Under these idealized conditions, Newton freely develops the mathematical consequences of the laws of motion that are the axioms of the *Principia*. At a later stage, after contrasting this ideal world with the world of physics, he will add further conditions to his intellectual construct – for example, by introducing a second body that will interact with the first one and then exploring further mathematical consequences. Later, he will once again compare the mathematical realm to the physical world and revise the construct – for example, by introducing a third interacting body.[52] In this way he can approach by stages nearer and nearer to the conditions of the world of experiment and observation, introducing bodies of different shapes and composition and finally bodies moving in various types of resistant mediums rather than in free space.[53]

The *Principia* thus displays both the physics of an ideal world and the problems that arise because ideal conditions differ from the world of experience. For example, Newton shows that Kepler's first two laws of planetary motion are true only for the mathematical or ideal condition of a single point mass moving about a mathematical center of force; he then develops the actual ways in which the pure form of Kepler's laws must be modified to fit the world of observation.[54] Similarly, his own first law of motion is "true" only in such an ideal mathematical world, where there are no other interacting bodies and no resisting mediums. The *Principia* can be accurately described as a work in which Newton explores, one by one, the ways in which ideal laws must be modified in the external world of experiment and observation.

An analogous procedure was adopted in Thomas Malthus's *Essay on Population*.[55] As everyone knows, Malthus stated a basic principle that human life increases naturally in a geometric (i.e., exponential) ratio. Malthus's primary statement of his principle reads, "Population, when unchecked, increases in a geometric ratio" (1959, ch. 1: 2). A later version says that "all animals, according to the known laws by which they are produced, must have the capacity of increasing in a geometrical progression." This law is plainly not the result of a Baconian induction from a mass of observations. In fact, the law is true only of an unchecked population; a good part of Malthus's *Essay* is in fact devoted to evidence that populations do *not* so increase and to explanations of why this is so.

Malthus does not say that populations do increase in a geometric or exponential ratio; he says explicitly that this *would* be the case of a population *if* it were not checked. The similarity of this statement and Newton's first axiom or law of motion will be immediately apparent. Newton did not write that all bodies move uniformly straight forward or stay at rest. Rather, he said that a body will maintain one or the other of those two "states" – "nisi quatenus illud a viribus impressis cogitur statum suum mutare" (except to the extent that it is forced by impressed forces to change its state). Malthus is following the style of the *Principia* in seeking the reasons why the laws in the world of nature differ from those in the world of pure abstractions.

In a similar manner, Malthus's *Essay* can be described as an investigation of the ways in which the world of nature exhibits "checks" on an otherwise natural or exponential ideal population growth. The major subject is why real populations do not increase geometrically as they would in an ideal or imagined world. That this comparison of Malthus and Newton is not farfetched can be seen in the fact that, in the *Essay*, Malthus cited Newton in terms of the highest respect even though Newton never wrote a word about populations or their increase. Additionally, it is a fact that Malthus had excelled in mathematics and mathematical physics while an undergraduate at Cambridge, where he had actually studied the *Principia* as well as commentaries on the Newtonian natural philosophy.[56]

In Malthus's thinking about population, the analogue of the Newtonian physical paradigm actually led him to a gloomy conclusion related to a second law. If a population were to increase naturally, there would have to be a concomitant increase in the available food supply. But Malthus's second law was that the food supply can increase only arithmetically and so cannot ever be sufficient to nourish a naturally increasing population, which increases geometrically. Therefore, there must be some active force that limits natural population growth. Just as Newton in the *Principia* sought the reasons why the ideal laws of Kepler do not hold in the physical universe, so Malthus sought the reasons that kept the population from increasing geometrically. He concluded that there must be a set of checks on the natural geometric population growth.[57]

The only population checks that Malthus could at first envisage were a species of "Vice and Misery," that is, disease and famine. Later on, Malthus decided that the reproductive or multiplicative property of human populations need not be assigned to some inalterable natural force but could be under the control of personal power or human will. This point of view gave room for an escape from the previous gloomy conclusions by considering the potentialities of the checking force of moral restraint.[58] He had abandoned a strict Newtonian position by introducing, however weakly, the possibility of social amelioration by the force of human will.

Newton's physics did not ever produce any useful analogies or homologies for the social sciences. Yet as is shown by the example of Malthus and others, the Newtonian natural philosophy did have its effects on the social sciences, but on the level of style and metaphor. The case of the missing paradigm has been solved. Newton's science has been of use to the social sciences – not as a source of direct analogues or homologues, but in that domain of metaphor that I have called the Newtonian style.

Notes

Portions of this chapter – especially those relating to the relations among metaphor, analogy, homology, and identity – are developed in a different manner and in greater detail in I. B. Cohen (1993, ch. 1).

I gratefully acknowledge the support given to my research, on which this contribution is based, by the Richard A. Lounsbery Foundation, and take special note of the continued kindness and concern of the director, Mr. Alan McHenry.

1. In Cohen (1993), I deal with other social sciences.
2. These are, traditionally, anthropology, economics, history, political science, psychology, and sociology; see, e.g., George Homans (1967, 3). For the classification of behavioral sciences, see Bernard Berelson, "Behavioral Sciences," in the *International Encyclopedia of the Social Sciences.* See especially Spiro (1971).
3. I personally dislike the term "Newtonianism" in the same way and to the same degree that Voltaire rejected "Newtonian." He wrote that in France natural philosophers called themselves "Cartesians," just as historically there had been "Aristotelians," but he never heard of a mathematician calling himself a "Euclidean," and in England he never encountered anyone who called himself a "Newtonian." "It would seem," he wrote, "that it was only error that gave a name to a sect."
4. For a discussion of this episode and also the desire for a Newton of chemistry by Wilhelm Ostwald and Otto Warburg, see Cohen (1980).
5. I shun the anachronistic use of the term "celestial mechanics" (invented by Laplace a century after Newton) in relation to Newton's dynamics of celestial systems.
6. The two varieties of Newtonian natural philosophy – the mathematical rational mechanics and celestial dynamics of the *Principia* and the experi-

mental natural philosophy of the *Opticks* – engendered two rival scientific traditions of the eighteenth century. The *Opticks*, although exact (in the sense of containing measurements and quantitative laws), does not develop the proofs of propositions by the use of mathematical techniques as is done in the *Principia*. That is, the proofs in the *Opticks* do not make use of algebraic equations or their equivalents in ratios and proportions; there are no fluxions, infinite series, trigonometric identities, etc., as in the *Principia*. Rather, each of the propositions is followed by a "Proof by Experiments." On the difference between these two traditions, see Cohen (1956).

7. The best general survey of these developments is Dugas (1955).

8. These four categories are developed further in Cohen (1993, in press a). The latter work, "Analogy, Homology and Metaphor in the Interaction of the Natural Sciences and the Social Sciences, with Special Reference to Economics," is based on a symposium at Duke University in April 1991 on the theses developed by Mirowski (1989).

9. These examples of royal rhetoric may be contrasted with a somewhat different statement made by James I when he likened the expanding metropolis of London to the spleen, "whose increase wastes the body" (McIlwain 1918, 343; Hale 1971, 111, n19); for here he was basing his rhetoric on a physician's acquaintance with the function of the spleen. That is, he was invoking an analogy of the operations of a city and the physiological functions of a specific organ. In this context, we must remember that at that time the king was a sort of physician who performed a number of medical roles: His "royal touch," e.g., could by physical contact allegedly induce a cure for scrofula (Bloch 1973, esp. 11–91).

10. Aristotle defined analogy as a special subset of metaphor that depends on a ratio of the form: As A is to B, so C is to D; by analogy we attribute A to D, rather than B, and attribute C to B. We may note that this manipulation of the ratio fulfills the definition of metaphor since it attributes qualities (A and C) to things (D and B) to which they do not apply. That is, A : B :: C : D does not logically imply the result that A : D :: C : B. An example is: As evening is to day, so old age is to life. Analogy yields the result that evening is the old age of day and that old age is the evening of life.

11. The etymological roots (*homos*, or "similar," and *logos*, or "proportion") indicate that homology and homologous and homologue may legitimately have a general meaning of similarity.

12. In evolutionary biology, homologous has the strict signification of a correspondence in the type of structure of parts or organs of different organisms resulting from their descent from some common remote ancestor.

13. For a more complete discussion of analogy and homology, with examples drawn from anatomy and from the social sciences, see Cohen (in press a).

14. The economist and social thinker William Graham Sumner was writing in this tradition when he attacked the "amateur social doctors" who, he said, were like "the amateur physician," since they "always begin with the ques-

tion of remedies," without "any knowledge of the anatomy and physiology of society."

15. For example, Paul von Lilienfeld and his contemporary A. E. F. Schäffle both believed in an analogy between society and a living organism, but whereas – from a structural and functional point of view – Lilienfeld affirmed that the human individual is the social counterpart of the biological cell, Schäffle concluded that the family unit must have this role (Cohen in press a, ch. 1).

16. An alternative translation, made by G. D. H. Cole, is published in Sherover (1974).

17. Fourier's social Newtonianism will be discussed later; see note 49.

18. For a good account of the failure of Newtonian physics to produce a social science, see Mayr (1986).

19. This section is almost identical to section 7 of Cohen (in press a) and may be skipped by those who have read that article.

20. Carey's concept does have a quality of invariance. If a given population were to be transplanted from one place to another, or the temperature were to change, or the members of the population were to huddle closer together, the number of individuals would remain the same. But over time, even relatively short periods, the size of any given human populations (or even the number of male members of a given population) will change because of deaths (and births). Other properties of Newtonian mass are clearly not matched in human populations.

21. In Carey's table of contents (1958–60, 1:xiv, §5), he refers to "the laws of being" as "the same in matter, man, and communities," so as to conclude, "In the solar world, attraction and motion [are] in the ratio of the mass and the proximity."

22. Although this error stands out like a sore thumb to anyone who is even slightly familiar with elementary physics, it has not been noted by Carey's critics. Thus, Sorokin (1928, 11) and Stark (1962, 156–60) discuss Carey's law at length, quoting or paraphrasing his version of Newton without any sense that it is incorrect.

23. Montesquieu also says that honor, providing the equivalent power of the gravitating force, sets the parts in motion. But Newtonian universal gravity does not set the parts of the solar system in motion; it only changes or constantly redirects their original motion and so prevents them from moving out along the tangent. In short, Montesquieu has misunderstood the Newtonian concept of the attractive force of gravity and has grafted it onto the older cosmology that Newton's *Principia* directly refuted. Montesquieu's introduction of the primary Newtonian concept, universal gravity, may therefore be taken as an instance of scientistic metaphor, an example of incorrect science, and serves to illustrate the determinant power of the scientific climate of opinion.

24. For further details, see Kuhn (1957), Koyré (1973), Cohen (1980), and Owen Gingerich's article on Kepler in the *Dictionary of Scientific Biography*.

25. "In fact," Ménard writes, Walras "recognized the formal nature of the analogy, for rareté is defined by subjective experiences. In the attempt to render economics a 'physico-mathematical' science, subjective experience is reinterpreted as an ordering of utilities, the calculation of compatabilities amongst choices, and their aggregation."

    However, Mirowski and Cook (1990) have taken a different position, namely, that "Walras did not understand the physics of his time very well, and therefore was not capable of prosecuting a valid analogical comparison (192).

26. Mirowski (1989, 242–54) has documented the way in which Joseph Bertrand and Hermann Laurent faulted Walras for his mathematical physics, as Laurent and Vito Volterra later faulted Pareto.

27. Fisher's table is reproduced in Mirowski (1989), together with a critique; Pareto's table is reproduced in Cohen (in press a, §6). Both tables may also be found in Cohen (1993, ch. 1).

28. For a counter to Mirowski's assertions, see, e.g., Hal Varian (1991).

29. Henry Guerlac once described it as perhaps one of the worst in the English language.

30. For two centuries and more, Craig's book with its Newton-like laws has usually been presented as an example of the kind of aberration to which Newtonian science may lead. His whole book can, in fact, be considered an extended example of inappropriate analogy. Yet a recent study by Stephen Stigler (1986b) has shown that Craig made a serious contribution to applied probability, "that his formula for the probability of testimony was tantamount to a logistic model for the posterior odds."

31. There is a "secret, uniform and never-ceasing principle," he wrote, that draws the planets "towards each other and towards the sun." This "principle" prevents the earth "as well as the other planets" from "flying off in a tangent line."

32. Berkeley drew from his analogy a number of conclusions about individuals and society, ranging from the love of parents for their children to a concern of one nation for the affairs of another and of each generation for future ones. The social law of moral attraction gives us our "sense of humanity," he wrote, and our recognition that "the good of the whole is inseparable from the good of the parts."

33. Some writers have tried to trace an influence of Newtonian rational mechanics (or even the Newtonian system of the world) in the U.S. Constitution. On this subject, see Cohen (in press b).

34. Of course, the subject of rational mechanics in general – i.e., post-Newtonian rational mechanics (including the extensions made by such mathematicians as Lagrange, Laplace, Hamilton, and others, plus considerations of energy, etc. – have influenced economists. There are numerous examples of the fruitful use of the analogy of rational mechanics in general – or of post-Newtonian and, actually, non-Newtonian mechanics –

by economists. On this topic, see further Mirowski (1989) and especially Weintraub (1991).

35. The reason why a two-body problem is "rigorously solvable" is that "the two integrals of the different equations of motion are sufficient to yield the two variables r and theta as functions of the time." But as soon as the number of bodies (or "mass-points") becomes greater than two, the "problem of describing their motion becomes insolvable" because "the differential equations of motion for n mass-points, when $n > 2$, have no other integrals than those of the two-body problem; namely, the energy integral, the integrals of area, and the integrals stating the uniform motion of the center of mass of the system" (Finlay-Freundlich 1958, 27).

36. For a brief but incisive account of the history of the general and restricted problems of three bodies, and of Hill's contributions in particular, see Moulton (1962), esp. the historical sketches following chs. 8 and 9.

37. "The struggle with the three-body problem is the characteristic feature in the whole development of celestial mechanics," according to E. Finlay-Freundlich. The "aim is either to derive general theorems which may be obtained without the knowledge of a general solution of the problem, or to render the problem solvable by a further simplification – *problème restreint* – or, lastly, to obtain a numerical approximation of the solution" (1958, 1–2).

38. Newton's advance to this extraordinary conclusion occurred during December 1684 or January 1685. Newton's text may be found in both the Latin original and an English version in Hall and Hall (1962, 256, 281). For the significance of Newton's recognition of interplanetary perturbations, see Cohen (1981b).

39. Although Marshall forbore to use higher mathematics in his writings on economics, he had received a solid grounding in this area at Cambridge.

40. He went on: "This general solution, it may be thought, at most is applicable to the utilitarian problem of which the object is the greatest possible sum total of universal happiness. But it deserves consideration that an object of Economics also, the arrangement to which contracting agents actuated only by self-interest tend is capable of being regarded upon the psychophysical hypotheses here entertained as the realization of the maximum sum-total of happiness, the relative maximum, or that which is consistent with certain conditions" (1881, 11).

41. The technical aspects of the three-body problem are given in two great standard works (Tisserand 1889–96 and Whittaker 1927). More recent treatments of theoretical and practical aspects of celestial mechanics at large and the three-body problem in particular are given in Moulton (1962) and in Brouwer and Clemence (1961); see also Finlay-Freundlich (1958).

Of great importance, especially for the historical notes in the supplement, is Wintner (1941). For a general background, especially valuable for the early periods, see Marcolongo (1919).

42. Not only was there a study of various infinite series that would enable astronomers (and, later, astronauts) to gain practical or useful solutions to particular systems of three (and even more than three) bodies, but there developed a study of abstract systems in which questions such as recurrence and stability became central.

43. In relation to the development of this area, special attention must be given to Poincaré's "last geometric theorem," announced in 1912, but without a general proof. The finding of a solution to a problem of this importance, one that had baffled the foremost mathematician of the age, was a dramatic event – all the more so in that the discoverer was a young, twenty-seven-year-old American, G. D. Birkhoff (1927). A proof and an extension of his results for general dynamic systems was treated in Birkhoff (1966).

44. Roy Weintraub also notes that the formalization used by Samuelson "to present and organize his analysis" was that of dynamic systems, "taken largely from the work of G. D. Birkhoff and others, notably the mathematical biologist A. J. Lotka." Samuelson was thus able to clarify "the distinction between statics and dynamics" and to produce a "comprehensive theory that obliterated the distinction between equilibrium as a behavioral outcome and equilibrium as a mechanical rest point" (Weintraub 1991, p. 103 and ch. 3).

45. Throughout the *Opticks*, Newton (1704) presents the subject, proposition by proposition, with a "Proof by Experiments."

46. The role of the *Opticks* in generating a tradition of Newtonian science that was experimental and nonmathematical is displayed, with many examples, in Cohen (1956).

47. The literature on Hume is vast. Among recent literature, special attention may be called to the important works by Duncan Forbes (1970, 1976, 1977), of which the most important in the present context is (1977).

48. Hume's ideas were translated and transformed by the French psychologist-philosopher Helvétius, who openly declared his aim to "treat morals like any other science, and to make an experimental morality like an experimental physics." He put forth the doctrine that morals relate to the "interest of the public, that is to say, of the greatest number," and it followed that justice is the performing of "actions useful to the greatest number." The importance of Helvétius can be seen in Jeremy Bentham's evaluation: "What Bacon was to the physical world, Helvétius was to the moral. The moral world has therefore had its Bacon; but its Newton is yet to come." There was no doubt in Bentham's mind concerning who that Newton would be.

49. Henri de Saint-Simon, a major precursor of Auguste Comte (who served for a while as his secretary), also developed a Newtonian kind of sociology (see Manuel 1962). The basic difference between Fourier's gravitational sociology and Saint-Simon's is that the latter attempted to apply Newton's law to the social realms, while Fourier claimed to have been a second

Newton, having discovered an equivalent of the gravitational law, one that applied to human nature and social behavior. Fourier likened his discovery to Newton's, even alleging that, like Newton, he had been led to it by an apple. He claimed that his own "calculus of attraction" was part of his discovery of "the laws of motion missed by Newton."

50. This concept of a Newtonian "style" is developed in Cohen (1980); abbreviated and more general presentations may be found in two other works (Cohen 1981b, 1990).

51. The appeal of this style, displayed in the development of the subject of rational mechanics in the *Principia,* was that it did not depend on making specific experiments as did the procedure of the *Opticks.* Nor, as we shall see in the case of Malthus, did it necessarily require the use of any of the mathematical techniques developed by Newton.

52. In this work, in section 11 of book 1 of the *Principia,* Newton establishes the science of celestial mechanics (see esp. prop. 66 of book 1 and its corollaries).

53. An advantage of this "style" was that it enabled Newton to consider mathematical principles of natural philosophy freed from physical constraints and yet to produce a system that could, in the end, be applied – as in book 3 of the *Principia* – to the system of the world. Furthermore, because he was basing the development of the subject on a mathematical construct he was not inhibited by such philosophical prejudices as the abhorrence of any force acting at a distance.

54. Props. 1–3 of book 1 of the *Principia* prove that the area law is a necessary and sufficient condition for a centrally directed force acting continually on a body with an initial component of inertial (linear) motion that is not directed toward that center. Prop. 11 proves that in the case of an ellipse, the force in question must be as the inverse square of the distance from the center of force.

55. Thomas Robert Malthus's *An Essay on the Principle of Population as It Affects the Future Improvement of Society* was published anonymously in 1798 in a version often known as the "first essay." It is readily available in two reprints, one of which (1970, edited by Antony Flew) also contains Malthus's *A Summary View of the Principle of Population* (1830), which was originally published without the author's name on the title page. The other reprint (Malthus 1959) has no editorial apparatus but does include a foreword by Kenneth E. Boulding.

The text of the second edition (1803) was so completely revised and expanded that it is generally considered "almost a new book," sometimes referred to as the "second essay." The text of this edition (reprinted from the seventh edition, 1872, but without the appendixes) is also available (1914).

See Malthus (1976) and, for recent editions, Cohen (in press b).

56. It has been argued by Anthony Flew (1985, ch. 4, §1) that Malthus's Newtonian interpretation of his own fundamental population law led him

into a significant intellectual trap of importance for social theory. We may see this feature on Malthus's thought as a property of social science akin to Newtonian natural science. The latter is posited on the concept of mass as a primary and necessary property of matter, said by Newton to be another name for inertia, a universal property. In the physics of Newton's *Principia*, mass can never be altered, no matter where a body is placed or to what physical strains it may be subjected; as a result of the properties of mass, a body's condition or state of motion or rest is unalterable except by the interposition of some external accelerating force. Malthus seems to have considered the tendency of population to increase geometrically to be "natural" in the sense of similarly being a fixed and unalterable property of life.

57. This inescapable conclusion has been described as a shattering of "all utopian dreams of universal egalitarian abundance."

58. This new factor was introduced into the preface to the *Second Essay on Population* as a "restraint from marriage," which is not replaced by "irregular gratifications." The alteration of the number of checks from two to three was intended by Malthus, as he said, "to soften some of the harshest conclusions of the First essay."

References

Berkeley, George. 1901. "Moral Attraction." In Alexander Campbell Fraser, ed., *The Works of George Berkeley*, vol. 4, pp. 186–90. Oxford: Clarendon Press, 1901. (This essay is also reprinted in *The Works of George Berkeley, Bishop of Cloyne*, ed. A. A. Luce, vol. 7, pp. 225–8. London: Thomas Nelson, 1935.)

Bernard, L. L., and Bernard, Jessie. 1943. *Origins of American Sociology: The Social Science Movement in the United States*. New York: Crowell.

Birkhoff, George David. 1913. "Proof of Poincaré's Geometric Theorem," *Transactions of the American Mathematical Society*, 14:14–22.

Birkhoff, George David. 1927. *Dynamical Systems*. New York: American Mathematical Society (Colloquium Publications, vol. 9). (A revised edition, with introduction, bibliography, and notes by Jürgen Moser, was issued by the American Mathematical Society [Providence, RI] in 1966.)

Birkhoff, George David, and Lewis, D. C., Jr. 1935. "Stability in Causal Systems," *Philosophy of Science*, 2:304–33.

Bloch, Marc. 1973. *The Royal Touch: Sacred Monarchy and Scrofula in England and France*, trans. J. E. Anderson. London: Routledge & Kegan Paul; Montreal: McGill–Queen's University Press.

Brewster, David. 1843. *Letters on Natural Magic*. New York: Harper & Brothers.

Brouwer, Dirk, and Clemence, Gerald M. 1961. *Methods of Celestial Mechanics*. New York: Academic Press.

Cannon, Walter. 1932. "Relations of Biological and Social Homeostasis." In *The Wisdom of the Body*, pp. 305–24. New York: Norton.

Cannon, Walter. 1941. "The Body Physiologic and the Body Politic." Presidential Address to the American Association for the Advancement of Science. *Science*, 93:1–10.

Carey, H. C. 1858–60. *Principles of Social Science*, 3 vols. Philadelphia: Lippincott.

Carlyle, Thomas. 1896. *Sartor Resartus*. Boston: Ginn.

Cohen, I. B. 1937. *The Billiard Ball Problem and the Recurrence Property of Dynamical Systems*. Honors thesis, Harvard University.

Cohen, I. B. 1956. *Franklin and Newton*. Philadelphia: American Philosophical Society (reprint, Cambridge, MA: Harvard University Press, 1966).

Cohen, I. B. 1974. "Isaac Newton, the Calculus of Variations, and the Design of Ships." In Robert S. Cohen, J. J. Stachel, and M. M. Wartofsky, eds., *For Dirk Struik: Scientific, Historical, and Political Essays in Honor of Dirk J. Struik*, pp. 169–87. Dordrecht: Reidel.

Cohen, I. B. 1980. *The Newtonian Revolution: With Illustrations of the Transformation of Scientific Ideas*. Cambridge University Press.

Cohen, I. B., ed. 1981a. *The Conservation of Energy and the Principle of Least Action*. New York: Arno.

Cohen, I. B. 1981b. "Newton's Discovery of Gravity," *Scientific American*, 244:166–79.

Cohen, I. B. 1982. "The *Principia*, Universal Gravitation, and the Newtonian Style." In Zev Bechler, ed., *Contemporary Newtonian Research*, pp. 21–108. Dordrecht: Reidel.

Cohen, I. B. 1990. "Newton's Method and Newton's Style." In Frank Durham and Robert D. Purrington, eds., *Some Truer Method: Reflections on the Heritage of Newton*, pp. 15–57. New York: Columbia University Press.

Cohen, I. B., ed. 1993. *The Natural Sciences and the Social Sciences: Some Critical and Historical Perspectives*. Dordrecht: Kluwer.

Cohen, I. B. In press a. "Analogy, Homology and Metaphor in the Interaction of the Natural Sciences and the Social Sciences, with Special Reference to Economics." In Neil de Marchi, ed., *Non-natural Social Science: History of Political Economy*. Durham: Duke University Press.

Cohen, I. B. In press b. *Science and the Founding Fathers: Jefferson, Franklin, Adams, Madison* (New York: Norton).

de Marchi, Neil, ed. In press. *Non-natural Social Science: History of Political Economy*. Durham: Duke University Press.

Dugas, René. 1955. *A History of Mechanics*, trans. J. R. Maddox. Neuchâtel: Editions du Griffon; New York: Central Book.

Edgeworth, F. Y. 1881. *Mathematical Psychics: An Essay on The Application of Mathematics to the Moral Sciences*. London: Kegan Paul.

Edgeworth, F. Y. 1982. *Papers Relating to Political Economy*, 3 vols. New York: Burt Franklin (reprint of original edition of 1925).

Elkana, Yehuda. 1974. *The Discovery of the Conservation of Energy*. London: Hutchinson.

Finlay-Freundlich, E. 1958. *Celestial Mechanics*. London: Pergamon.

Flew, Antony. 1985. *Thinking About Social Thinking: The Philosophy of the Social Sciences*. Oxford: Basil Blackwell.

Forbes, Duncan. 1970. Introduction to the reprinted edition of David Hume, *History of Great Britain: The Reigns of James I and Charles I*. Harmondsworth: Penguin.

Forbes, Duncan. 1976. "Sceptical Whiggism, Commerce and Liberty." In A. S. Skinner and T. Wilson, eds., *Essays on Adam Smith*, pp. 179–201. Oxford University Press.

Forbes, Duncan. 1977. "Hume's Science of Politics." In G. P. Morice, ed., *David Hume, Bicentenary Papers*, pp. 2–12. Edinburgh: Edinburgh University Press.

Force, James E. 1990. "Hume's Interest in Newton and Science." In James E. Force and Richard H. Popkin, *Essays on the Context, Nature, and Influence of Isaac Newton's Theology*, ch. 10. Dordrecht: Kluwer.

Fourier, Charles. 1971a. *Design of Utopia: Selected Writings of Charles Fourier*, ed. Frank Manuel, trans. Julia Franklin. With an introduction by Charles Gide and foreword by Frank E. Manuel. New York: Shocken.

Fourier, Charles. 1971b. *Harmonian Man: Selected Writings of Charles Fourier*, ed. Mark Poster, trans. Susan Hanson. Garden City, NY: Doubleday.

Hale, David George. 1971. *The Body Politic: A Political Metaphor in Renaissance English Literature*. The Hague: Mouton.

Hall, A. Rupert, and Hall, Marie Boas, eds. 1962. *Unpublished Scientific Papers of Isaac Newton*. Cambridge University Press.

Hamilton, Robert S. 1886. *Present Status of the Philosophy of Society*. New York: Westcott.

Hankins, Frank H. 1968. *Adolphe Quetelet as Statistician*. New York: AMS Press.

Hetherington, Norriss. 1983. "Isaac Newton's Influence on Adam Smith's Natural Laws in Economics." *Journal of the History of Ideas*, 44:497–505.

Homans, George C. 1967. *The Nature of Social Science*. New York: Harcourt, Brace, & World.

Jaffé, William. 1973. "Léon Walras's Role in the 'Marginal Revolution' of the Late 1870s." In R. D. Collison Black, A. W. Coates, and Craufurd D. W. Goodwin, eds., *The Marginal Revolution in Economics: Interpretation and Evaluation*, pp. 113–38. Durham, NC: Duke University Press.

Jevons, W. Stanley. 1958. *The Principles of Science: A Treatise on Logic and Scientific Method*. New York: Dover (reprint of second and final edition of 1887).

Koyré, Alexandre. 1973. *The Astronomical Revolution – Copernicus, Borelli, Kepler*, trans. R. E. W. Maddison. Ithaca, NY: Cornell University Press.

Koyré, Alexandre, and Cohen, I. B. 1972. *Isaac Newton's Philosophiae Naturalis Principia Mathematica: The Third Edition (1726) with Variant Readings*. Cambridge, MA: Harvard University Press.

Kuhn, Thomas S. 1957. *The Copernican Revolution*. Cambridge, MA: Harvard University Press.

Lilienfeld, Paul von. 1873. *Gedanken über die Sozialwissenschaft der Zukunft*. Erster Theil: "Die menschliche Gesellschaft als realer Organismus." Mitau: E. Behre's Verlag.

Lowell, A. Lawrence. 1937. "An Example from the Evidence of History." In

Harvard Tercentenary Conference of Arts and Sciences, *Factors Determining Human Behavior*, pp. 119–32. Cambridge, MA: Harvard University Press.

[Malthus, Thomas Robert]. 1798. *An Essay on the Principle of Population as It Affects the Future Improvement of Society.* London: Printed for J. Johnson.

Malthus, Thomas Robert. 1830. *A Summary View of the Principle of Population.* London: John Murray.

Malthus, Thomas Robert. 1914. *An Essay on the Principle of Population.* With an introduction by T. H. Hollingsworth. London: Dent.

Malthus, Thomas Robert. 1959. *Population: The First Essay.* With a foreword by Kenneth E. Boulding. Ann Arbor: University of Michigan Press.

Malthus, Thomas Robert. 1970. *An Essay on the Principle of Population and A Summary View of the Principle of Population,* ed. Antony Flew. Harmondsworth: Penguin.

Malthus, Thomas Robert. 1976. *An Essay on the Principle of Population – Text, Sources and Background, Criticism,* ed. Philip Appleman. New York: Norton.

Manuel, Frank E. 1962. *The Prophets of Paris.* Cambridge, MA: Harvard University Press.

Marcolongo, Roberto. 1919. *Il problema dei tre corpi da Newton (1687) ai nostri giorni.* Milan: Ulrico Hoepli.

Marshall, Alfred. 1891. *Principles of Economics,* 2d ed. London: Macmillan.

Mayr, Otto. 1986. *Authority, Liberty and Automatic Machinery in Early Modern Europe.* Baltimore: Johns Hopkins University Press.

Ménard, Claude. 1988. "The Machine and the Heart: An Essay on Analogies in Economic Reasoning," *Social Context,* 5:81–95.

Merton, Robert K. 1968. *Social Theory and Social Structure.* New York: Free Press.

Mirowski, Philip. 1989. *More Heat Than Light: Economics as Social Physics, Physics as Nature's Economics.* Cambridge University Press.

Mirowski, Philip, and Cook, Pamela. 1990. "Walras' 'Economics and Mechanics': Translation, Commentary, Context." In Warren J. Samuels, ed., *Economics as Discourse,* pp. 189–215. Boston: Kluwer.

Montesquieu, Charles. 1966. *Spirit of the Laws.* New York: Hafner.

Moulton, Forest Ray. 1962. *An Introduction to Celestial Mechanics,* 2d ed. New York: Macmillan.

Newton, Isaac. 1704. *Opticks . . .* London: Printed for Sam. Smith and Benj. Walford.

Newton, Isaac. 1979. *Opticks, or a Treatise of the Reflections, Refractions, Inflections & Colours of Light.* Based on the fourth edition, London, 1730. With a foreword by Albert Einstein, introduction by Edmund Whittaker, preface by I. Bernard Cohen, and analytical table of contents by Duane H. D. Roller. New York: Dover.

Peel, J. D. Y. 1971. *Herbert Spencer: The Evolution of a Sociologist.* New York: Basic.

Pigou, A. C., ed. 1925. *Memorials of Alfred Marshall.* London: Macmillan.

Poincaré, Henri. 1892–9. *Méthodes nouvelles de la mécanique céleste.* 3 vols. Paris:

Gautier-Villars. (An English translation edited by Daniel Goroff, with an important historical introduction, has been published [New York, 1993] in three volumes by the American Institute of Physics of New York.)

Poincaré, Henri. 1912. "Sur une théorème de géometrie," *Rendiconti del Circolo Matematico di Palermo*, 33:1–34.

Sherover, Charles M., ed. 1974. *Annotated Edition: The Social Contract or Principles of Political Right by Jean Jacques Rousseau*. New York: New American Library.

Smith, Adam. 1776. *An Inquiry into the Nature and Causes of the Wealth of Nations*. London: W. Strahan & T. Cadell.

Smith, Adam. 1904. *An Inquiry into the Nature and Causes of the Wealth of Nations*, ed. Edwin Cannan. London: Methuen (reprint, Chicago: University of Chicago Press, 1976).

Smith, Adam. 1976. *An Inquiry into the Nature and Causes of the Wealth of Nations*. Oxford: Oxford University Press.

Sorokin, Pitirim A. 1928. *Contemporary Sociological Theories*. New York: Harper & Brothers.

Spencer, Herbert. 1897. *The Principles of Sociology*, 3d ed. New York: Appleton.

Spiro, Herbert J. 1971. "Critique of Behavioralism in Political Science." In Klaus von Peyme, ed., *Theory and Politics, Festschrift zum 70.Geburtstag für Carl Joachim Friedrich*, pp. 314–27. The Hague: Martinus Nijhoff.

Stark, Werner. 1962. *The Fundamental Forms of Social Thought*. London: Routledge & Kegan Paul.

Stigler, Stephen M. 1986a. *The History of Statistics: The Measurement of Uncertainty Before 1900*. Cambridge, MA: Harvard University Press.

Stigler, Stephen. 1986b. "John Craig and the Probability of History: From the Death of Christ to the Birth of Laplace," *Journal of the American Statistical Association*, 81:879–87.

Taylor, Overton. 1960. *Classical Liberalism*. Cambridge, MA: Harvard University Press.

Tisserand, E. 1889–96. *Traité de mécanique celéste*, 4 vols. Paris: Gautier-Villars.

Tyndall, John. 1861. *The Glaciers of the Alps*. Boston: Ticknor & Fields.

Varian, Hal. 1991. Review of Philip Mirowski, *More Heat Than Light*, in *Journal of Economic Literature* 29:595–6.

Weintraub, E. Roy. 1991. *Stabilizing Dynamics: Constructing Economic Knowledge*. Cambridge University Press.

Whittaker, E. T. 1927. *A Treatise on the Analytical Dynamics of Particles and Rigid Bodies, with an Introduction to the Problem of Three Bodies*. Cambridge University Press.

Wintner, Aurel. 1941. *The Analytical Foundations of Celestial Mechanics*. Princeton, NJ: Princeton University Press.

CHAPTER 4

From virtual velocities to economic action: the very slow arrivals of linear programming and locational equilibrium

IVOR GRATTAN-GUINNESS

Introduction

Scenario

In the early nineteenth century, the principle of virtual work and other assumptions in analytical mechanics led to forays into equilibrium and optimization in economic contexts. Forays toward linear programming appeared in embryo forms at various times between the late eighteenth and the mid-nineteenth centuries, with a very clear formulation put forward by J. B. J. Fourier in the 1820s; but then they fell largely into desuetude. From 1900 to 1940, various studies concerning linear inequalities and/or convexity were carried out in many different branches of pure and applied mathematics; but they also did not launch linear programming, where progress remained slow until an extraordinarily rapid establishment after the Second World War. Similarly, some traces for nonlinear programming were laid, largely in connection with mechanics, but they were not seized when that topic advanced in the 1950s.

In another area, in 1829 two young French scientists, G. Lamé and B. Clapeyron, thought up all the basic ideas and applications of locational equilibrium; but their work made no impact, not even on the concerns of their own distinguished later careers. The topic saw only fitful and partial advances for the next century before establishment was effected.

Presentation

At the factual level this chapter is concerned with these three cases of mathematical economics, which saw their birth in France during this

91

period and continued there and in other countries afterward. Each of them grew out of aspects of mechanics, which will be specified in the following section, along with an outline of the context of French science at that time.

But beneath these facts lie many *missed opportunities* – nonfacts, indeed, in that the stimuli initiated by the French were *not* developed either by them or their successors, so that the theories had to be largely re-created in our time. Thus, none of these protodisciplines developed into a full-fledged topic for over a century after their basic conceptions. Possible reasons for these delays are considered in the concluding section, followed by some general remarks about the scope and limits of analogies.

Throughout the chapter the word "economics" refers not only to parts of the subject matter covered by economic theory today, but also to topics now seen as belonging to operational research and economic geography. For most of the period discussed, none of these disciplines existed as such, so it is inadmissible to impose the corresponding disciplinary boundaries. When I do confine my remarks to the discipline of economics, I will refer to it in this way.

The background in mechanics

The French community of mathematicians

Along with the growth of industry and commerce, the need for more refined and developed means of transport, and the military ambitions of Napoléon, a vast growth took place in engineering and technology in France after the French Revolution, especially during the First Empire (1804–15) and the Restoration (1815–30). The consequences for science and mathematics were quite considerable; they both gained a status unmatched in any other country of the time, and they involved engineering to a unique degree. The whole scenario is far too vast even for summary here; a detailed account of many features is given in Grattan-Guinness (1990a). It will suffice here to cite two points.

First, the single main concern of research mathematics lay in the development and application of the calculus. This topic and its related subjects (series and functions, and the theory of equations) were greatly extended, to a considerable degree by problems posed by finding solutions to differential equations. The main area of application of the calculus was mechanics, which also vastly extended across all its areas (mathematical astronomy, planetary mechanics, engineering mechanics, corporeal mechanics [including foundational questions], and some molecular mechanics). In addition, mechanics broadened into mathematical physics with the initial mathematicizations of parts of heat theory, physical optics, electricity, and magnetism (including their connection in electromagnetism).

Second, the community of professional mathematicians divided by research interests into two almost equal groups of main figures (about twenty members each across the period 1800–40). The emphasis on engineering led to the emergence, among the growing profession of scientists, of the first group composed of figures called the *ingénieurs savants*, who not only passed their careers within some (civil or military) organization, but also oriented their research work around such needs (Grattan-Guinness 1993). The most well known members of this group include L. Carnot, G. G. Coriolis, C. Dupin, P. S. Girard, J. N. P. Hachette, G. Monge, C. L. M. H. Navier, J. V. Poncelet, G. de Prony, and L. Puissant. The second group concentrated more on theoretical and general applications of mathematics and on its "pure" side; by and large, they included the more eminent mathematicians as such. Their ranks included A. M. Ampère, A. L. Cauchy, J. B. J. Fourier, A. J. Fresnel, J. L. Lagrange, P. S. Laplace, A. M. Legendre, L. Poinsot, and S. D. Poisson.

The principle of virtual velocities

Members of both groups worked in the calculus and mechanics, although differences in their motivations is evident (Grattan-Guinness 1989). Within mechanics itself, three main traditions were in place by 1800 (Grattan-Guinness 1990b). One of them took Newton's three laws of rest and motion as its base; the second, which Lagrange promoted as a version of variational mechanics, was based on the principles of d'Alembert, of least action and of virtual velocities; and a third was based on the conservation of energy (or "*force(s) vive(s)*," to use the preferred term of the time) and their exchange with work. There was considerable competition between the three traditions concerning both legitimate foundations and levels of generality (and in particular concerning cases of disequilibrium, such as impact, as well as situations of equilibrium).

This third of these traditions is known to historians of economics, in that its development by *ingénieurs savants* Carnot, Navier, Coriolis, and Poncelet (Grattan-Guinness 1984; 1990a, ch. 16) constituted an essential background for the energy physics of the mid-nineteenth century (Mirowski 1989, ch. 2), which was such an important stimulus for many sciences (including economics). My concern here, however, lies chiefly within Lagrange's ambit; for in his *Mécanique analytique* (1788) he offered a reduction of dynamics to statics via d'Alembert's principles and of the phenomena of mechanics to equilibrium by an emphasis on "the principle of virtual velocities" (as he called it; the use of "work" as a technical term is due to Coriolis). For him it stated that if any system of bodies or point-masses $\{m_r\}$ in equilibrium were slightly disturbed by a system of forces $\{F_r\}$, to be displaced by velocities (or distances in unit time) $\{ds_r\}$, then

$$\Sigma_r F_r \, ds_r = 0. \tag{1}$$

Although Lagrange gave this principle a major place in his mechanics, he offered no proof of it. Thus, considerable interest was taken around 1800 in proving it; participants included Lagrange himself, Laplace, Fourier, de Prony, Ampère, and Poinsot, and some of these men and certain other authors worked on the matter for several decades afterward (see Lindt 1904). It is from this context that two of the three cases discussed in this chapter were to spring.

Linear programming and its false starts

Fourier's insights

Fourier's proof (1798) of (1) was based on various uses of the principle of the lever. Of greater import here, however, is his passing observation that (1) could be stated in terms of inequality rather than as an equation. Over the years he came to extend this insight into a general "analysis of inequalities," as he called it. In the 1820s he published three accounts or examples of his theory (Grattan-Guinness 1994, art. 3). He had a complete basic understanding of linear programming: the formation of the convex set with linear edges; the specification of the feasible region by inequalities (although he wrote "<" rather than "≤"); and the search through it for optimal value(s) of the objective function, or else just the specification of the feasible region. Moreover, he even presented a method for the elimination of variables to find the solutions (or to detect the lack of them) and a strategy for finding the minimax value(s) of the function. On the latter aspect, he would have been aware of such conditions applied to the minimax theory of errors by R. J. Boscovich, Laplace, and de Prony between 1760 and 1800.

This jargon is ours, but the ideas it denotes are Fourier's. Moreover, he had an excellent range of applications in kind: equilibrium problems in mechanics, election returns, and statistical situations such as errors of observations. In addition, he had become a major figure in French science. Yet linear programming did not establish itself from this excellent start; of his followers, only Navier and A. A. Cournot continued the attack, and by the early 1830s it was largely dead. One reason may well have been the lack of effective and general methods of solution. In particular, we know that linear algebra is an essential means of manipulation; but its very tardy arrival on the general mathematical scene in the early years of this century left linear programming behind as one of its casualties.

Yet here is a beautiful example of missed opportunities; for in 1829, just while Fourier was encouraging colleagues to take up his new topic, Cauchy and J. C. F. Sturm independently outlined basic essentials of the spectral theory of matrices, in the (different) context of superposed simple-state solutions to systems of ordinary differential equations (Hawkins 1975). However, neither they nor anyone else recognized the importance of their perceptions!

For the rest of the nineteenth century, we see only very occasional renewals of activity toward linear programming. A striking example is G. Boole in the 1850s concerning bounds on the values of a compound probability as a function of its component probabilities, which he formulated as an exercise in manipulating inequalities. Despite his considerable knowledge of the history of mathematics, he showed no awareness of previous work of this kind; and his attempts made virtually no impact on later probabilists (Hailperin 1991).

Near misses in the twentieth century

The situation did not improve much during this century, although the mathematical contexts were richer (Grattan-Guinness 1994, art. 4). Not only did matrix algebra, especially matrices, come into late flower, but a North American interest in linear inequalities developed in the 1920s. Elsewhere in mathematics, H. Minkowski's concern for the "geometry of numbers" in the early years of the century gave prominence to convex regions; his conception was applied from 1910 to various problems in mathematical analysis (including, in a nice touch, Fourier series) via the notion of function spaces. Occasionally, minimax theorems were studied – for example, by C. de la Vallée Poussin in 1911. Even some signs of linear programming were evident, in the Hungarian mathematician J. Farkas around 1900, his compatriot A. Haar in the 1920s, and above all the Jewish mathematician T. Motzkin in the late 1930s, with an extensive and beautiful study of linear inequalities that contained versions of the simplex and transportation theorems (Motzkin 1936). Finally, the theory of games was studied by J. von Neumann in papers of 1928 and 1936.

However, these developments played a *very* small role in the establishment of linear programming as a branch of mathematics (Grattan-Guinness 1994, art. 5). In the United States, a major initiative grew out of war work by G. B. Dantzig and others in connection with questions concerning military organization; the similarity with the theory of games was noticed by Dantzig and von Neumann in 1947 (Dantzig 1982), and then the field developed with amazing speed. Within the discipline of economics itself, Koopmans was perhaps the principal figure; by the 1960s linear programming had lost some status there, although it grew to become a staple item in business studies. In addition and slightly earlier, work by L. V. Kantorovich, V. V. Novozhiloff, and others had developed the subject in the Soviet Union independently (and again without much knowledge of the prehistory), in the context of industrial economic planning; however, in contrast to the U.S. euphoria, progress after the war was hindered by Marxist objections to the element of choice which the theory allowed.

Three classes of missed opportunity are worth stressing. I take them, in rough chronological order of arrival. First, while linear programming developed in close relationship with mathematical economics, that field played very little role in the prehistory. For example, from the 1830s onward Cournot made major contributions to mathematical economics, but he made *no use* of the linear programming that he had done under Fourier's influence only a few years earlier, even though, for example, his demand and supply curves were usually concave or convex. Again, in the mid-1930s, A. Wald was producing linear models of production that mathematically looked very much like our topic in close proximity to von Neumann's work, publishing even in *the same journal* (Ingrao and Israel 1990, ch. 7); yet connections were still not made, even though, by then, economists were aware of the need to impose inequalities to avoid solutions involving negative prices (Weintraub 1985).

Second, the importance of the Second World War emphasizes by contrast the total nondevelopment of the theory during or after the First World War, although many of the same logistical problems were present and just about enough pertinent mathematics was available for at least some progress to have been possible.

Third, in their study of "the theory of games and economic behaviour," von Neumann and Morgenstern (1944) were virtually doing linear programming, with excellent diagrams of convex regions and objective functions, and von Neumann himself had produced his minimax theorem. However, he did not think out his theory in terms of linear programming: For him the mathematical horizon opened up quite elsewhere, toward fixed-point properties. His orientation is not at all surprising: At that time topology was growing in importance as a branch of mathematics with great rapidity. In addition, his enthusiasm for formalizing mathematical theories, evident in his 1928 paper, had been dampened by Gödel's incompletability theorem of 1931; so he switched his interests somewhat, more toward automation theory and algorithms in general and thereby weakened the link between game theory and equilibrium/optimization. Furthermore, his colleague von Morgenstern had been developing his own antipathy to mechanical modeling of economic equilibria, especially as practiced by the neoclassical tradition.[1]

Nonlinear programming and its nonbackground

The basic theorem

Soon after the establishment of linear programming, its nonlinear variant began to develop, based on the following theorem proved in Kuhn and Tucker (1950). They studied the optimization of a convex function $f(\mathbf{x})$ of a point $\mathbf{x}$ ($= \{x_i\}$) in an n-dimensional region that was specified by m concave differential functions $\{g_s(\mathbf{x})\}$. By using variational arguments, they found conditions under which optimization of f would occur at a point z in the region and m multipliers $\{k_j\}$ could be found such that

$$\sum_{i=1}^{n} \left\{ (x_i - z_i) \, [\partial\{f(\mathbf{x}) + \sum_{s=1}^{m} k_s g_s(\mathbf{x})\} \, / \, \partial x_i |\mathbf{x} = \mathbf{z}] \right\} \geq 0. \qquad (2)$$

What is the prehistory to this result?

Forays in the foundations of mechanics

In fact, theorems of this form had a long genesis and use, primarily in connection with the foundations of mechanics (Grattan-Guinness 1994, art. 7). Fourier had been aware that his theory was not restricted to linear constraints, and Cournot and especially the Russian mathematician M. A. Ostrogradsky, who had spent some years in Paris, discussed the use of inequalities in variational mechanics in two papers of the 1830s.

A different initiative was taken by C. F. Gauss in 1829, when he asserted that the motion of a system of mass-points moving under the action of impulses and under restrictions of some kind occurred with the smallest value of "constraint" (*Zwang*). This word took a special meaning here: It referred to the sum of the product of each mass and the square of the distance D between the point to which it would have moved during an infinitesimal time interval, if able to do so free of the restrictions, and the point where it actually arrived. The form of the constraint expression was the same as that used in least-squares regression, which he had studied in the 1800s.

Gauss's proposal used inequalities to express the least value held to pertain to the motion. In addition, it related to two other principles of mechanics: d'Alembert's, which was also concerned with D in equilibriate situations of the system; and virtual work in its usual equational form, which could be read as stating the first-order condition of complete differentials for minimizing the constraint function. The relationships between these various principles, and also with that of least squares and Fourier's advocacy of inequalities, were matters of study from time to time, particularly by German mathematicians; quite a concentration of work occurred around 1900. Illustrious names such as C. J. Jacobi, A. F. Möbius, C. Neumann, R. O. S. Lipschitz, H. Hertz, L. Boltzmann, and P. Stäckel can be mentioned, and they were joined by the American J. W. Gibbs and also by Farkas.

The bearing of all these considerations upon nonlinear programming is that, apart from no stipulation of convexity or concavity on the functions, forms of expression very close to (2) were frequently involved, with the multipliers serving as factors associated with the constraint functions. Yet by 1950, none of this prehistory seems to have featured in the discovery of (2) or in its immediate uses and applications (Kuhn 1976). A specific class of statements in mechanics – more than analogy, therefore – was passed over.

Locational equilibrium: sudden rise, sudden fall

The standard history

If the preceding two cases exemplify false starts and nonstarts, then this final one is a complete sleeper: a clear and comprehensive presentation of a theory that had no impact whatsoever on its rediscovery later. As with linear programming, the history is sketchy, with disconnections and repeats (Franksen and Grattan-Guinness 1989, pt. 1), although economic theory in general was very much concerned with situations of equilibrium of various kinds (Ingrao and Israel 1990). It runs briefly as follows.

Some of the classical economists, such as Adam Smith and D. Ricardo, allowed for spatial factors in determining equilibrium or optimizations, although not to a major extent. More detailed considerations of spatial aspects came only occasionally, and from less distinguished sources such as J. H. von Thünen's *Der isolierte Staat* of 1826 on the location of demand for agricultural products and W. Launhardt's *Mathematische Begründung der Volkswirtschaftslehre* of 1885 on the exchange and transportation of goods. Launhardt found that he had been partly anticipated by Cournot's work in mathematical economics, which was apparently very little known forty years after its publication.

A more significant advance was made by Alfred Weber, in his *Über die Standort der Industrien* of 1909. When considering the location of a single production facility supplied by three sites, he was inspired by E. Mach's history of mechanics to make a mechanical model by suspending over a horizontal circle three weights, in the directions of the sites and of magnitudes proportional to their perceived economic importance, and locating the desired facility by joining together the strings and letting the system find equilibrium under gravity.

This model, and extensions of it to several sites, is the backbone of locational equilibrium. But it did not gain wide treatment until the 1950s, especially in Germany (following its main known origins), and to some extent in the United States (with Kuhn once again playing a role). Progress was then rapid and spread into economic geography also (Smith 1981). But its prehistory is eclipsed by the fact that all the basic components of the theory, and several extensions and refinements, had been conceived *with complete clarity* a century earlier, in 1829, by Lamé and Clapeyron.

The careers of Lamé and Clapeyron

Our heroes belonged to the group mentioned in the subsection on the French community of mathematicians, though at the time in question they were junior members and – much more seriously – were out of Paris. They were students at the École Polytechnique two years apart in the mid-1810s; then they studied at the École des Mines in Paris and became good friends. One binding factor was their left-wing political stance, which gained them displeasure from the Catholic Bourbon regime that ruled during the Restoration. Now, links had been established between French and Russian engineers during the Imperial period, and when the Czar requested that they be continued, Lamé and Clapeyron were sent in 1820 to become members of the Corps des Voies et Communications in St. Petersburg, the main institution in Russia for civil engineers. They spent ten years there (Bradley 1981) and produced a wide range of joint research: our concern is with their paper "Memoir on the Application of Statics to the Solution of Problems Relative to the Theory of Least Distances," which was published in the journal of the Corps in which they worked (Lamé and Clapeyron 1829).

After their return to France in 1831 (by which time the Bourbons had fallen in the revolution of July 1830), the two men continued to collaborate on matters relating to engineering and society; for example, with two other colleagues they published a book in 1832 outlining a system of national transport, with especial concern for railways. But after their career tended to drift apart, Lamé filling many main teaching posts in Paris (and not working in mathematics oriented around engineering), while Clapeyron worked largely with engineering concerns (including the first substantial mathematical study of Sadi Carnot's ideas on thermodynamics).

The content and inspiration of their paper

During the Restoration some of the *ingénieurs savants* became involved with aspects of efficiency of artifacts and constructs: for example, in Paris, Girard on the best choice for lock systems on a canal, and Navier (before Lamé and Clapeyron) on the advantages of the new method of railways over road travel. Mathematically, these problems were usually treated via the usual first- and second-order conditions for optimizing some function; but in formulating locational equilibrium, Lamé and Clapeyron achieved an extraordinary extension of these ideas (Franksen and Grattan-Guinness 1989, pt. 2).

The 1829 paper contains an analysis of locating a single facility for a set of given sites – the example often now called the depot or warehouse problem. The solution was found mechanically, by suspending appropriately sized weights over pulleys located at the sites and joining the strings at a small ring before releasing the system to find equilibrium. Among other situations, they considered nonlinear constraints, where a site could be moveable (such as a boat working along a stretch of a river); here they proposed that the string pass over a second pulley following the path concerned. Using a military example, they also allowed for two facilities to be determined from the same sites, possibly with different constraints applying to each. Finally, in the problem of the distribution of stones for the efficient maintenance of roads, they even perceived that there was available to the researcher a degree of arbitrariness (and thus decision) in the prior distribution of the sites themselves; this is the grid factor, as their successors called it in the early 1970s when it finally came to be recognized. Points made in their discussion, such as a multiplicity of optimizing solutions or none at all, show that they must have constructed the model and tested it out.

The link with mechanics was clearly indicated in the opening part of the 1829 paper, where they referred to the principle of virtual velocities as the source of the equilibriate conditions. As mentioned in the subsection on virtual velocities, the proofs of the principle were offered around 1800. In particular, Lagrange (1798) himself gave one in which he placed a system of mass-points by pulley blocks joined together by a thread and supporting a weight at one end. He repeated it in 1811, as detailed in the first volume of the second edition of his *Mécanique analytique*. The quality of the solution is not at issue here; the point is that Lamé and Clapeyron surely were aware of it. In the same year, Poisson gave a proof of the principle in the first edition of his textbook on mechanics for use by students at the École Polytechnique (1811, 240–51); it was based on a different argument due to Laplace, but it also used strings connecting masses. Lamé and Clapeyron certainly knew of this presentation, for I own the copy of the textbook that Clapeyron bought while a student at the École Polytechnique. It is probable that they took either Lagrange or Poisson (or both) as their stimulus for their theory.

The "reception" of the paper

Although by 1829 they had been away for ten years, Lamé and Clapeyron had kept in touch with their *confrères*. For example, in 1828 they sent a long paper to the Paris Académie on elasticity theory, and this and several other papers were published in Paris (and also in the *Journal für die reine und angewandte Mathematik*, recently launched in Berlin by the engineer A. L. Crelle). Some of these articles were reprints of their St. Petersburg article, which was published in 1829.

However, despite the growing interest in questions of optimization already mentioned, that paper gained no *éclat*. The only published reaction seems to have been a short review in 1829 by Sturm, then a young visiting mathematician to Paris from Geneva (and, we recall from the section on Fourier's insights, just inventing the rudiments of matrix theory). The review appeared in the mathematics series (of which he was then the editor) of the general science review journal, the *Bulletin général des sciences et de l'industrie*. Around six hundred words in length, it was quite competent, but it did not perceive the significance of the authors' achievement.

Even Lamé and Clapeyron themselves seem to have forgotten their work: The only later reference that I know of is a paragraph, largely consisting of quotations from Sturm's review, in a self-notice of his work that Lamé wrote in 1839 in an unsuccessful bid for a vacancy at the Académie. Their paper came to light only when my astonished eyes fell upon it when conducting a literature search of the *Journal des voies et communications*.

Concluding comments

In praise of indeterminism: the importance of nonevents

Historians are accustomed to describing, and sometimes explaining in some way, what happened in the past (or, at least, those parts of it that they choose to study in the first place). Two historiographical points have arisen here, however: the nonevents, and the types of events that are passed over. When admitted, nonevents can be examined, and the three cases described here contain many excellent examples. The latter point deserves further mention, for our context is the history of mathematics, which is marginal to the practice of the history of science and virtually out of sight for historians in general – in great contrast to its importance in events that are supposed to be their concern (Grattan-Guinness 1990c).

The principal question is: Why did such oversights and delays occur? (The brand-X corollary is: What nonevents are spoiling the scientific progress today?) When the context looks good – nice problems, at least partial answers available, promising prospects for development – why nevertheless were opportunities missed, especially on the scale and for the extraordinary lengths of time involved here? Imagine if the traces evident and published in the 1820s and 1830s had been seized, then three important branches of mathematical economics (and some related topics) could have been pursued actively a century earlier than was actually the case, and the general history of the subject would have been different.

Some social "blocking" factors can be stressed, although they provoke further (interesting) questions. First, in all three cases, many of the main figures were not major mathematicians, at least at the time involved, or else the work in question was not a major concern in their career (Gauss, Fourier): Remember that von Neumann was explicitly *not* a linear programmer in his work on games and that Lamé and

Clapeyron were at an early stage of their careers. In other words, these problems did not capture the attention of leading mathematicians of the times. Second, national differences are evident: linear programming developed mainly in the United States, but much of the mathematical background was central European; again, Lamé and Clapeyron were forced to be in Russia at the crucial time.

But even after granting a place to individual oversights and social (non-)contacts, some of the delays seem to be hard to understand. In particular, recall the following: the silence over Fourier's beautifully clear statement of linear programming, even though he was a major authority in *other* work (in Fourier analysis, the theory of equations, and heat theory) and though economic optimization in general was a topic recognized to be of growing importance; Cournot's short memory span when he began to develop aspects of mathematical economics; the almost total amnesia of Lamé and Clapeyron during three more decades of active professional and academic work after their return to Paris; von Neumann's long orientation toward fixed points rather than convexity and optimization; the extremely modest place of mathematical economics in the prehistories of topics in which it became central when the flowerings eventually took place.

From mechanics to economics

We are concerned with the (non-)transfer from the supposedly hard science of mechanics (to be precise, statics) to the softer terrain of economics via algebra and mathematical analysis. (The full story is complicated still more by the gradual and slow import of probability theory and statistics in mechanics and economics: I have not treated this aspect here, as it does not bear significantly upon these cases.) At first blush it seems clear that equilibrium in a mechanical system is "like" a situation of economic balance (Ingrao and Israel 1990), that detecting optimal values in a dynamic situation may resemble a strategy to achieve an economic best return, or that costs and returns may equal out in something like a conservation law of mechanics or physics (Mirowski 1989); but how much content carries over in practice?

In the case of linear programming, the principle of virtual velocities led to a formulation in terms of inequalities; and while that aspect can be developed further, in both the linear and the nonlinear theories (Franksen 1969), it lost much of its relevance in the later exegeses. Linear programming comprises a particular union of linear algebra, convexity, inequalities, and optimization – branches of mathematics that were not necessarily in touch with each other. Thus, the back-

ground is variegated, and a missing element could be crucial in pre-
venting opportunities for further progress from being spotted. The
same situation obtains for (non-)linear programming, with the addition to the recipe of some differential calculus and other aspects of
equilibrium mechanics: In this case, the absence of the requirement of
convexity or concavity on the functions f and $\{g_s\}$ in formulas in mechanics resembling (2) is critical. With these considerations in mind,
part of the historical explanation of the oversights noted in the previous subsection may be that the analogies are much clearer to us after
the fact than they were to the historical figures of the day, when the
connections were much easier to miss.

The case of locational equilibrium is somewhat different in that the
link with the principle of virtual velocities is much stronger; while
Lagrange's "proof" was only an intuitive presentation rather than a
pukka line of argument, it would have been enough to give to Lamé
and Clapeyron their basic insight. However, the link with mechanics
may also have prevented them from seeing the full potential of the
analogy on which they had seized and so cast their marvelous achievement out of their minds and away from contemporaries' attention.

Finally, the lack of mathematical methods, especially those furnished by linear algebra, was undoubtedly a serious handicap for
linear programming (recall the irony over Cauchy and Sturm in
1829), and possibly for locational equilibrium also. (Matrix theory did
not "arrive" in the discipline of economics until the 1930s, being imported by émigré physicists such as T. J. Koopmans and H. Hotelling.)
Further, let us not take for granted the lack of techniques: Had any of
our three cases gained more acclaim and interest than in fact occurred, then the missing techniques might have developed more
rapidly – so that, for example, the importance of Cauchy and Sturm
would have been more rapidly recognized.[2]

Roles for analogies

But more general questions can be posed. Analogies are central to our
three cases. We are concerned with more than one (branch of a)
science being considered together, and the possible influence (in principle, positive or negative) of one science upon another. This question
is, in my view, of great significance to the philosophy of mathematics,
including its creative aspects when both problem and theory formation are at hand; for it involves the notion of *how* one theory gains
meaning within another one – whether explicit *application* of one
theory to another one is involved or whether analogy alone is at hand.

The prime philosophical issue is the extent to which "structure-similarity" between theories in different contexts may obtain (Grattan-Guinness 1992).

In particular, the varieties of mechanics stressed in the subsection on virtual velocities raises the question of which analogy one would wish to pursue in the first place; for the interest in situations of disequilibrium, such as shock and impact in the engineers' tradition of energy mechanics initiated by Carnot, specifically *rejected* the Lagrangian assumption that the work expression in (1) could always be an exact differential dP and so admit a potential P upon integration. Thus, analogies drawing on energy mechanics contain an element of contradiction with those in which equilibrium plays a central role in the economic theory.

Complications such as these raise historical questions concerning the measure of understanding of the mechanics or physics held by the pioneers of mathematical economics from which their analogies were being drawn. It seems that in many cases competence was limited (Mirowski 1989, esp. chs. 5–7); yet the incompetent transfer of theories from one science to another one does *not* forbid fruitful results from being obtained. In the context of energy physics, for example, the case of S. Freud (mis)reading H. von Helmholtz is very instructive (see Elkana 1983).

Some deep questions are raised by these incidents. An (un)familiarity with the literature, national differences, and parochialism are not all that is involved here; the strength and weakness of analogies also play roles. Despite the deep attachment of economists to analogies from mechanics and physics, two possibilities here did not make the mark. Connections and their absence are our main historiographical topics, the understanding of context our chief aim. Moreover, only two examples have been discussed here in detail. In closing, here is another:

> The cultural lag of economic thought in the application of mathematical methods is strikingly illustrated by the fact that linear graphs are making their entrance into transportation theory just about a century after they were first studied in relation to electrical networks, although organised transportation systems are much older than the study of electricity.[3]

Notes

For comments I am indebted to O. I. Franksen and P. Mirowski, as well as my discussant E. R. Weintraub.

1. Von Neumann did link equilibria with systems of inequalities at the Berlin seminar in 1928 but did not publish it. For this information and other points made in the text at this point I am indebted to Roy Weintraub; the full version appears in *Towards a History of Game Theory* (Weintraub 1992). Regarding Gödel, von Neumann heard of the theorem from Gödel's own first public announcement at a *Weinerkreis* meeting in September 1930 and soon found the corollary concerning consistency for himself (Dawson 1984), so the impact of these results must have been considerable.
2. A similar point can be made about functional equations. They have been well used in mathematical economics, but only in recent years; however, they have a long if modest history back to the eighteenth century, with mechanics as one of the motivations (see the bibliography in Aczel 1966).
3. Koopmans and Reiter (1951, 258). The absence of economic theory from the history of graph theory is corroborated by Biggs et al. (1976).

References

Aczel, J. 1966. *Lectures on Functional Equations and Their Applications* (New York: Academic Press).

Biggs, N. L., Lloyd, K., and Wilson, R. J. 1976. *Graph Theory, 1736–1936* (Oxford University Press).

Bradley, M. 1981. "Franco-Russian Engineering Links: The Careers of Lamé and Clapeyron, 1820–1830," *Annals of Science*, 38:291–312.

Dantzig, G. B. 1982. "Reminiscences About the Origins of Linear Programming," *Operations Research Letters*, 1:43–8. (A slightly revised version appears in *Mathematical Programming: The State of the Art*, ed. A. Bachem, M. Grotschel, and B. Corte [Berlin: Springer, 1983], 78–86.)

Dawson, J. W., Jr., (trans. and ed.) 1984. "Discussion on the Foundation of Mathematics," *History and Philosophy of Logic*, 5:111–29.

Elkana, Y. 1983. "The Borrowing of the Concept of Energy in Freudian Psychoanalysis," in M. Ranchetti, ed., *Psicoanalisi e storia della scienza*, 55–80 (Florence: Olschki).

Fourier, J. B. J. 1798. "Mémoire sur la statique . . . ," *Journal de l'École Polytechnique*, 2 (cah. 5):20–60. Also in *Oeuvres*, 1:475–521.

Franksen, O. I. 1969. "Mathematical Programming in Economics by Physical Analogies," *Simulation* 12 (June): 297–314; 13 (July): 25–42; 13 (August): 63–87.

Franksen, O. I., and Grattan-Guinness, I. 1989. "The Earliest Contribution to Location Theory? Spatio-Economic Equilibrium with Lamé and Clapeyron, 1829," *Mathematics and Computers in Simulation*, 31:195–220.

Grattan-Guinness, I. 1984. "Work for the Workers: Advances in Engineering Mechanics and Instruction in France, 1800–1830," *Annals of Science*, 41:1–33.

Grattan-Guinness, I. 1989. "Modes and Manners of Applied Mathematics:

The Case of Mechanics," in D. Rowe and J. McCleary, eds., *History of Modern Mathematics*, 2:109–26 (New York: Academic Press).

Grattan-Guinness, I. 1990a. *Convolutions in French Mathematics, 1800–1840: From the Calculus and Mechanics to Mathematical Analysis and Mathematical Physics*, 3 vols. (Basel: Birkhäuser; and Berlin: Deutscher Verlag der Wissenschaften).

Grattan-Guinness, I. 1990b. "The Varieties of Mechanics by 1800," *Historia mathematica*, 17:313–38.

Grattan-Guinness, I. 1990c. "Does History of Science Treat of the History of Science? The Case of Mathematics," *History of Science*, 28:147–73.

Grattan-Guinness, I. 1992. "Structure-Similarity as a Cornerstone of the Philosophy of Mathematics," in J. Echeverria, T. Mormann, and A. Ibarra, eds., *The Space of Mathematics*, 91–111 (Berlin: De Gruyter).

Grattan-Guinness, I. 1993. "The *Ingénieur Savant*, 1800–1830: A Neglected Figure in the History of French Mathematics and Science," *Science in Context*.

Grattan-Guinness, I. 1994. " 'A New Type of Question': On the Prehistory of Linear and Non-linear Programming, 1770–1940," in E. Knobloch and D. Rowe, eds., *The History of Modern Mathematics*, vol. 3 (San Diego: Academic Press).

Hailperin, T. 1991. "Probability Logic in the Twentieth Century," *History and Philosophy of Logic*, 12:71–110.

Hawkins, T. W. 1975. "Cauchy and the Spectral Theory of Matrices," *Historia mathematica*, 2:1–29.

Ingrao, B., and Israel, G. 1990. *The Invisible Hand: Economic Equilibrium in the History of Science* (Cambridge, MA: MIT Press).

Koopmans, T. C., and Reiter, S. 1951. "A Model of Transportation," in H. W. Kuhn, ed., *Activity Analysis of Production and Allocation*, 222–59 (New York: Wiley).

Kuhn, H. W. 1976. "Nonlinear Programming: A Historical View," in R. W. Cottle and C. E. Lemke, eds., *Nonlinear Programming*, 1–26 (Providence, RI: American Mathematical Society).

Kuhn, H. W., and Tucker, A. W. 1950. "Nonlinear Programming," in J. Neyman, ed., *Proceedings of the Second Berkeley Symposium on Mathematical Statistics and Probability*, 481–92 (Berkeley and Los Angeles: University of California Press).

Lagrange, J. L. 1798. "Sur les principes des vitesses virtuelles," *Journal de l'École Polytechnique*, 2 (cah. 5):115–18. Also in *Oeuvres*, 7:315–21.

Lamé, G., and Clapeyron, B. P. E. 1829. "Mémoire sur l'application de la statique à la solution des problèmes relatifs à la théorie des moindres distances," *Journal des voies et communications*, no. 10:26–49. An English translation and commentary are in Franksen and Grattan-Guinness (1989).

Lindt, R. 1904. "Das Prinzip der virtuellen Geschwindigkeiten: seine Beweise und die Unmöglichkeit seiner Umkehrung bei Verwendung des Begriffes 'Gleichgewicht eines Massensystems,' " *Abhandlungen zur Geschichte der Mathematik*, 18:145–95.

Mirowski, P. 1989. *More Heat Than Light: Economics as Social Physics, Physics as Nature's Economics* (Cambridge University Press).

Motzkin, T. 1936. *Beiträge zur Theorie der linearen Ungleichungen* (Jerusalem: Azriel). (English translation: Rand Corporation report T-22 [1952]; also in T. Motzkin, *Selected Papers*, vol. 2 [Basel: Birkhäuser, 1983], 1–80.)

Poisson, S. D. 1811. *Traité de mécanique*, 1st ed., 2 vols. (Paris: Courcier).

Smith, D. M. 1981. *Industrial Location: An Economic Geographic Analysis*, 2d ed. (New York: Wiley).

von Neumann, J., and Morgenstern, O. 1944. *The Theory of Games and Economic Behaviour*, 1st ed. (Princeton, NJ: Princeton University Press; 2d ed., 1947; 3d ed., 1953).

Weintraub, E. R. 1985. *General Equilibrium Analysis: Studies in Appraisal* (Cambridge University Press).

Weintraub, E. R., ed. 1992. *Towards a History of Game Theory* (Durham, NC: Duke University Press).

CHAPTER 5

Qualitative dynamics in economics and fluid mechanics: a comparison of recent applications

RANDALL BAUSOR

Time permeates our existence, saturating our very being. Nevertheless, few things are as difficult to comprehend and as hard to model mathematically. Although the invention of the calculus thrust dynamics dramatically forward, only the simplest cases proved solvable. In many important cases, directly solving systems of differential equations is intractable. Alternative techniques are required.

Modern methods investigate the qualitative properties of entire families or flows of trajectories rather than solving for a single trajectory determined by particular parameters and initial conditions. Fundamental to this alternative approach is the identification of initial conditions and parameter values at which structural qualities change, thereby revealing much about the underlying processes governing motion.

These qualitative techniques, which involve the topological properties of the flow, have been applied to several scientific disciplines. Their reception, however, has been uneven. They have had successes in the study of the motion of fluids, for example, but have met less enthusiasm, if not open hostility, among economists.

This chapter documents and explains the differing reception of the mathematics of qualitative dynamics in economics as opposed to hydrodynamics. The first section outlines the mathematics involved, especially the notion of structural instability and its role in generating complex motion. The second describes application of these techniques to two problems in fluid mechanics. The third examines attempts to employ similar methods in economics, arguing that they have not brought great success there. Finally, the fourth section suggests that the contrast between acceptance of the same mathematics in these two fields arises first from their different empirical and evidentiary foundations and second from the distinct cultural and metaphorical background of each. The comparison reveals as much about

109

the underlying intellectual attitudes of each as about the phenomena they engage.

Qualitative dynamical analysis

Problems in solving for individual trajectories of nonlinear motion motivated alternative approaches. Rather than considering solutions individually, modern methods investigate whole families of paths and ascertain the qualitative properties of these collective flows rather than the quantitative properties of individual elements in the flow.

Consider the equation

$$d\mathbf{x}/dt = f(\mathbf{x}),\tag{1}$$

where $\mathbf{x}$ is a real vector and t is a real variable. Here the initial-value problem is to find a function $F(\mathbf{x}_0, t) = \mathbf{x}(t)$ such that the value of the function $F(\cdot)$ is the point occupied by the trajectory anchored at x_0 and t_0 at time t. Alternatively, qualitative dynamics focuses attention on the properties of entire families of trajectories generated by (1). Following Guckenheimer and Holmes (1983), we say that the vector field f defined on domain $U \subseteq R^n$ generates a flow (another function) $\phi_t: U \to R^n$, where $\phi_t(x) = \phi(\mathbf{x}, t)$ is a smooth function defined for all $\mathbf{x} \in U$ and t in an open interval of the real line. That is, ϕ contains all the solutions of $d\mathbf{x}/dt = f(x_0)$ for all $x_0 \in U$. Thus, $\phi_t(U)$ is the set of points to which elements of U at t_0 have flowed at time $t \in I$. $\phi(t)$ reflects the changes in U as it flows from t_0 to t. Rather than discerning the peculiar properties of each element in the flow, qualitative dynamics investigates the global properties of the flow in its domain of definition, especially concentrating on structural changes in those global properties.

Although one seeks global properties of the flow, this may be exceedingly complex, so we begin by examining its local properties. To do this requires comparing neighboring trajectories and assessing changes in the flow resulting from changes of the parameters governing $f(\mathbf{x})$. That is, we examine the qualitative consequences of perturbations of the flow. Topological equivalence and structural stability make this possible.

Continuing to follow Guckenheimer and Holmes (1983, esp. 38–42), the structural stability of a map depends on the topological equivalence of all small perturbation of it. Formally,

> If $F \in C^r(r^n)$, $r, k \in Z^+$, $k \le r$, and $\varepsilon > 0$, then G is a C^k perturbation of size ε if there is a compact set $K \in R^n$ such that $F = G$ on the set $R^n - K$ and for all $(i_1, \ldots, i_n)$ with $i_1 + \cdots + i_n = i \le k$ we have $|\,(\partial i/\partial x^{i1}, \ldots, \partial x^{in})(F - G)| < \varepsilon$. (38)

Since F and G may be either vector fields or maps, we can use this sense of closeness to define structural stability once we identify topological equivalence:

> Two C^r maps, F, G, are said to be C^k *equivalent* or C^k *conjugate* ($k \leq r$) if there exists a C^k homeomorphism h such that $H^0 F = G^0 h$. C^0 equivalence is called *topological equivalence*. . . . Two C^r vector fields, f, g, are said to be C^k *equivalent* ($k \leq r$) if there exists a C^k diffeomorphism h which takes orbits $\phi_t g(\mathbf{x})$ of f to orbits $\phi_t g(\mathbf{x})$ of g, preserving senses but not necessarily parametrization by time. If h does preserve parametrization by time, then it is called a conjugacy. (38)

The power of these equivalence concepts lies in the fact that they carry orbits to qualitatively equivalent orbits. That is, the homeomorphism h (diffeomorphism in the case of vector fields) carries stationary points of F to stationary points of G, and closed orbits of F to closed orbits of G. Precisely this orbit equivalence lays the groundwork for qualitative dynamics, for it supports comparison of the qualitative structures of different maps or vector fields. In particular,

> A map $F \subset C^r(R^n)$ (resp. a C^r vector field f) is *structurally stable* if there is an $\varepsilon > 0$ such that all C^1, ε perturbations of F (resp. of f) are topologically equivalent to F (resp. f). (39)

Thus, a map or flow is structurally stable if its basic qualities are invariant with respect to small changes in the parameters governing it. Its essential characteristics – does it contract onto an attracting fixed point, oscillate along a closed path, or aperiodically worm its way through time, for example – are not altered by tiny perturbations of it. The quantitative particulars of its motion respond, but its essential character is fixed. In particular, topological equivalence preserves sinks, saddles, and sources. Further, it is at points of structural instability or bifurcations of the flow that qualitative change occurs. These locations of metamorphosis of the flow thus attract considerable attention.

To investigate these points of structural instability, we explicitly introduce a vector of parameters μ, so that the bifurcation set – the parameter values at which the flow is structurally unstable – can be identified. Thus, rather than equation (1), we write

$$d\mathbf{x}/dt = f_\mu(\mathbf{x}). \qquad (2)$$

Varying the parameters μ typically changes the quantitative nature of the corresponding flow, but so long as the system is structurally stable no transformation of its qualitative behavior occurs. At parameter values that are structurally unstable, however, the system is said to bifurcate in that qualitatively new behaviors arise and interesting things occur. For example, the period-doubling route to chaos progresses through a sequence of bifurcations introducing orbits of doubled periodicity until aperiodic orbits finally emerge. Returning to (2), an equilibrium occurs when

$$f_\mu(\mathbf{x}) = 0.$$

According to the implicit function theorem, so long as the determinant of the Jacobian matrix of $f_\mu(\mathbf{x})$ is nonvanishing (it has no zero eigenvalue), the equilibria can be defined as smooth functions of μ. Such a function is called a "branch" of equilibria. At parameter values where the Jacobian determinant equals zero, however, such branches may intersect, thereby forming a bifurcation of the flow. The following example, along with much of the material of this section, is taken from Guckenheimer and Holmes (1983, 118–19).

Let $f_\mu(\mathbf{x}) = \mu x - x^3$, so that the Jacobian is $\mu - 3x^2$. Clearly $x = 0$ is an equilibrium for all values of μ and is uniquely so for $\mu \le 0$. Stability in this region can be easily verified. If $\mu > 0$, however, additional equilibria appear whenever $\mu = x^2$. It is interesting that at values of μ greater than the bifurcation point $(0,0)$, equilibrium $x = 0$ has lost its stability, which was acquired by the two new branches of equilibria given by $x = \mu^{1/2}$. There has been, that is, an exchange of stability from the original branch to the new branches of equilibria at the point of bifurcation. Furthermore, an unstable branch has emerged. Qualitatively, at $\mu = 0$ the flow has been transformed from one in which a single stable equilibrium exists to one in which three exist, of which two are stable and one (which had formerly been stable) is now unstable. Although such bifurcations of equilibria are important to understanding the global properties of dynamical systems, they are by no means the only bifurcations. More generally, for example, there may be bifurcations of periodic orbits.

To establish what transpires at points of bifurcation, one examines the neighborhoods surrounding the bifurcation. In linear systems one pursues the eigenvalue problem. Eigenspaces are invariant under the flow, and those corresponding to eigenvalues with negative real parts contract onto the fixed point while those corresponding to eigenvalues with positive real parts expand away from it. Consequently, these eigenspaces are, respectively, stable and unstable invariant sets of the flow. The subspace corresponding to eigenvalues with zero real parts is the center eigenspace, neither stable nor unstable, and may harbor more complicated motion (or none at all).

Equilibria of nonlinear systems also have stable, center, and unstable invariant sets of the flow. Unlike the linear case, however, these invariant sets are not subspaces, but generally curving manifolds. According to the stable manifold theorem, hyperbolic fixed points of the flow – those for which the linearization contains no zero or purely imaginary eigenvalues – have stable and unstable manifolds of the same dimension and tangent to, within some neighborhood, the corresponding eigenspaces of the linearized flow. By taking the union of local stable manifolds as time flows backward (unstable manifolds as time flows forward), one defines global stable (and unstable) manifolds. These manifolds stretch out from an equilibrium and may curve violently, becoming intricately intertwined with one another. Indeed, the stable and unstable manifolds of the same or distinct fixed points may intersect, thus providing a basis for complicated motion in the flow. A fixed point for which the intersection of its stable and unstable manifolds is nonvoid is known as homoclinic.

If there are zero or purely imaginary eigenvalues, however, things are even more complicated, for then one must additionally consider the center manifold, which is analogous to the center eigenspace of linear motion. Here, motion neither contracts nor expands. Moreover, uniqueness and smoothness of the center manifold are generally problematic. Nevertheless, study of the center, stable, and unstable manifolds can provide rich insights into the behavior of dynamical systems and reveals information about the topological equivalence class to which the flow belongs. Recall, too, that fixed points are not the only phenomena for which invariant manifolds can be constructed and analyzed. Other limit sets, including closed orbits, can be subjected to analogous methods. One of the most significant applications of these techniques has been to the analysis of so-called chaos. Chaotic deterministic motion resembles the randomness of stochastically shocked systems. It is not governed, however, by probabilistic chance, but by the intensely complex motion endogenous to the flow itself.

Two properties characterize chaos. First, motion tends to be irregular in the sense that it does not congeal onto fixed points or closed periodic orbits. It is not repetitive and, thus, apparently random. Such behavior is highly structured, however, by the stable, unstable, and center manifolds attached to limit sets. This structure is revealed not only by the equivalence class of a flow, but also by the progression of structural instabilities leading toward chaos. In the case of homoclinic fixed points, for example, stable and unstable manifolds intersect and may become intimately twisted about one another and the center manifold.

This infinitely fine texturing of the flow relates to the second characteristic of chaos – extreme sensitivity to initial conditions. There may be regions in which the stable manifold lies arbitrarily close to the center or unstable manifolds. Moreover, these regions may have fractal structure so that their borders may be so finely grained that arbitrarily small deviations in initial conditions yield qualitatively different trajectories. Not only can motion be complex, but the relationships between the invariant manifolds of that motion can also be complex.

Qualitative dynamical analysis deepens insight into complex deterministic motion by providing the tools to perceive the structure of the flow rather than simply seeing a single path. Indeed, from the viewpoint of the flow's complex structure, solving for any particular trajectory (as in classical approaches) seems to yield relatively little information. Examining the qualitative structure of the flow, in contrast, can yield understanding into the morphogenesis of complexity. In particular, it reveals that chaos is *always* accompanied by lapses from stability. A globally attracting equilibrium contradicts either of the two essential properties of chaos. Instability somewhere in the system is essential.

We now pursue description of the application of qualitative dynamical analysis to the study of fluid mechanics and competitive economics. Contrasting its reception in these two fields reveals the workings of each and informs insight into how pure mathematics penetrates scientific discourse.

Application of qualitative dynamics to the study of the motion of fluids

Newton's law of motion and the laws of thermodynamics anchor the theory of fluid mechanics. Since the motion of a stream or ocean current can be fantastically complicated, investigators concentrate on experimentally simplified and analytically abstracted special cases. We examine two of these: Rayleigh–Bénard convection and Taylor–Couette flow.

The first example, Rayleigh–Bénard convection, involves the motion of a fluid contained between two flat, parallel, and rigid plates. The lower plate is maintained at a uniformly higher temperature than the upper, and the horizontal extent of the plates (ideally infinite, but in experimental practice necessarily finite) is much greater than the vertical distance between the plates. Although this relatively simple and stylized case may appear of little relevance to natural phenomena, it informs a wide variety of applications ranging from motion of the atmosphere to motion within the earth's mantle.[1]

As the fluid is warmed from below, density increases upward. The lower, warmer fluid is more buoyant and is stabilized, if at all, by the fluid's viscosity. If the temperature gradient between the plates grows sufficiently great, the lower layers rise and the denser upper layers tend to sink in plumes. The onset and structure of this motion has been subjected to considerable scientific effort. Moreover, Prigogine (1980) identifies the rolling cells of motion characteristic of Rayleigh–Bénard convection under some parameter values as a comparatively simple example of a spontaneous large-scale far-from-equilibrium dissipative structure (Prigogine 1980, 88–90).

The velocity field of the fluid obeys the Navier–Stokes equation

$$\partial \mathbf{v}/\partial t + \mathbf{v} \cdot \nabla \mathbf{v} = -\nabla P/p_0 + \mathbf{g} + \upsilon \nabla^2 \mathbf{v}, \tag{3}$$

where P is pressure, p is density, υ is the kinematic viscosity, and $\mathbf{g}$ is the gravitational acceleration. A diffusion equation

$$\partial T/\partial t + (\upsilon \cdot \nabla)T = \lambda \partial^2 T, \tag{4}$$

where T is temperature and λ, the thermal diffusivity, governs the temperature field of the fluid. Obviously, if the temperature gradient is zero, no motion occurs. Similarly, if the gradient of T is sufficiently small the relative buoyancy of the warmer lower regions is insufficiently great to overcome the fluid's viscosity, and again the velocity field remains at an equilibrium of no motion.

Study of this problem establishes the stability properties of this motionless equilibrium and then locates the "Bénard instability" at which convection commences by determining the parameter values at which the eigenvalues of the linearized flow have positive real parts. This is usually phrased in terms of the dimensionless number R, called the Rayleigh number, where

$$R = \{\alpha(\Delta T)gd^3\}/\lambda \upsilon, \tag{5}$$

α is the thermal expansion coefficient, and d is the distance between the two plates. At the onset of steady convection and the emergence of Rayleigh–Bénard convection cells, there is an exchange of stability from the purely conductive state to that of steady rolling cells. The convective state is also subject to a variety of instabilities (see Bhatachariee, 1987, ch. 2, for details). Much of the qualitative analysis of convection motion in this system has been in terms of an additionally simplified model.

The Lorenz model relies on a Galerckin projection of the hydrodynamic equations to achieve a system of three coupled ordinary differential equations.[2] Lorenz's equations (following Sparrow 1982) can be written

$$dx/dt = \sigma(y - x),$$
$$dy/dt = rx - y - xz,$$
$$dz/dt = xy - bz, \tag{6}$$

where the variables x, y, z are proxies, respectively, for the rate of convective turning, the horizontal variation in temperature, and the vertical variation in temperature. The parameters σ and r are proportional, respectively, to the Prandtl and Rayleigh numbers, and b reflects the physical porportions of the region investigated. $r = 1$ denotes the point at which convection commences and locates the vicinity within which the Lorenz model most closely approximates the fluid's true motion according to the Navier–Stokes and diffusion equations.

This system has been studied extensively. To ascertain its qualitative properties, let r vary while σ and b are constant values of 10 and $\frac{8}{3}$ respectively.[3] As is now well known, the origin is always a stationary point, being stable if $r < 1$. At $r = 1$, however, a pitchfork bifurcation occurs in which the origin loses its stability (becoming a saddle point when $r > 1$). Simultaneously, two new fixed points appear and are sinks until a Hopf bifurcation appears at $r = \sigma(\sigma + b + 3)/(\sigma - b - 1)$. Thereafter, all the fixed points are saddles, but nonetheless an attracting set exists. Here the motion becomes complex, for the system contains a branched strange attractor, and motion settles into persistent aperiodicity.

The qualitative analysis of these regions corresponds to phases of the Rayleigh–Bénard convection. When r is small so that the origin is a sink, the corresponding physical behavior is the purely conductive phase. When r lies between 1 and the Hopf bifurcation (at approximately 24.74) the two stable fixed points correspond to the Rayleigh–Bénard convection in coherently structured rolling cells. Above the bifurcation, however, the behavior changes qualitatively, loses its periodic rolling, and becomes turbulent. Quantitatively, the system's behavior varies within each of these three regions – for example the two stable fixed points between the pitchfork and the Hopf bifurcations vary with the particular value of the parameter r, but qualitatively the system is equivalent in having one unstable and two stable fixed points.

Thus, we see how the qualitative analysis of this system informs a deeper understanding of the physical problem by identifying and analyzing as bifurcations of the mathematical flow the phase transitions in the motion of the fluid. Metaphorically, it emphasizes the distinction between types of motion and deemphasizes the exact positioning of that motion. Moreover, it provides an analytical basis for conceptualizing the progression through qualitatively different states from laminar conduction to turbulence. This remains metaphorical, however, for the interesting dynamical properties of the Lorenz equations emerge only in regions of parameter values far removed from those at which its approximation to the underlying equations of motion ($r = 1$) are known to be valid.

A second example of the qualitative approach to hydrodynamics also arises from the well-established Navier–Stokes equation. This is the so-called Taylor–Couette flow of a liquid confined between two concentric rotating cylinders.[4] Here, the flow, in which particles generally rotate, also progresses through distinct phases. At low Reynolds numbers (indicating low relative rotational velocity) the flow is smoothly circular. As the relative speed between the inner and outer cylinders increases, stacked layers or "cells" of motion develop in which, in addition to the main rotation around the axis, a circular component of motion within the cell and orthogonal to the main direction of flow appears. Consequently, instead of flowing around the axis in circles, each particle now spirals around, but within its own cell. Further increases in the Reynolds number produces more complicated flow as the motion within each cell becomes chaotic, even though the stacked cellular structure remains intact.

Similarly, analysis of the engineering of the mixing of fluids also invokes concepts from qualitative dynamics. Ottino (1989) experiments with the mixing of paints confined between an outer cylinder and an offset rotating inner cylinder. In this case, the concern is to disrupt the laminar flow through stretching and folding to achieve a thorough mixing of the fluid. Efficient mixing is likened to the Smale horseshoe, and the stretching and folding that interweaves layers in a closed two-dimensional flow resembles the intricate intertwining of manifolds characteristic of the sensitive dependence on initial conditions of chaotic motion.

Qualitative modeling of these phases and the transitions between them provides a theoretical and conceptual skeleton on which to drape scientific knowledge. Although exact correspondence between experimental evidence and analysis of "toy" models is impossible, the link appears to be reasonably strong. Rayleigh–Bénard convection cells and Taylor cells of stacked rotation can both be observed in the laboratory. Thus, the scientific program of modeling phase transitions in fluid flow can proceed, if only for the highly stylized and highly simplified flows, within laboratory apparatus and truncated models.

Moreover, there has been a persistent link between theorizing and experimental observation in the qualitative analysis of fluid mechanics. Despite an occasional penchant for computer simulation, the whole exercise has never wholly escaped the evidence of real fluids really moving. In the cases of Rayleigh–Bénard convection and Taylor–Couette flow, there have been well-recognized phenomena to explain qualitatively. Theory and phenomenon have not stretched unaccountably far apart.

The analysis of economic dynamics and the economics of competitive chaos

Economists, like hydrodynamicists, face apparently noisy and erratic phenomena. Prices always change, for example, and the pattern of that change is rarely discerned with ease. The most widely accepted modeling approach presumes that such phenomena are governed by random variables. Consequently, economic systems are perceived as vulnerable to exogenous shocks. Their apparently unpredictable behavior arises in response to random inputs to an otherwise inherently well-behaved system.

A few economists have been promoting an alternative modeling technique with far different metaphorical significance for our understanding of economic processes. They advocate the use of complex deterministic dynamics, including qualitative dynamics, to argue that the economy might be inherently erratic, that its trajectory might be acutely sensitive to initial conditions, and that its apparently random motion might be generated by endogenous competitive processes. Since these efforts impute the source of complex variability onto the internal workings of market systems, they diametrically oppose the "rational expectations" school.

Applications of qualitative arguments to nonlinear economic processes first appeared about twelve years ago. Benhabib and Nishimura (1979) examined a Hopf bifurcation in the emergence of closed periodic cycles in models of economic growth. Shortly thereafter, Day (1982, 1983) and Benhabib and Day (1981, 1982) published models capable of deterministic chaos showing that competitive processes might be sources of chaotic motion and describing how an economy might progress from a simply and predictably behaved system through sequences of qualitative transitions to complex aperiodic flow. Grandmont placed this literature on a more solid analytical basis (1985, 1987) arguing that chaotic competitive dynamics could justify interventionist macroeconomic policies to nudge the system onto an alternative trajectory or to manipulate parameters to alter the flow.

Much of this literature seeks to demonstrate the possibility of deterministic chaos in overlapping generations models of competitive processes, referring to Li and Yorke (1975) to argue the generality of chaotic motion. Since much of it refers to "toy" examples such as the logistic (Day 1982, Baumol and Quandt 1985) or the Lorenz equations (Benhabib and Day 1981), however, they serve more to illustrate hypothetical possibilities than to compel scientific acceptance. Deep *economic* motivation for the particular equations of motion have not been readily forthcoming.

Moreover, although the qualitative aspects of nonlinear economic dynamics have certainly been discussed, especially in Benhabib and Nishimura (1979), Grandmont (1985 and 1989), and Day and Walter (1989), they have been employed primarily to depict the stepping stones to chaos rather than to establish the significance of phase transitions in their own right. This is particularly clear in Day (1982) and Grandmont (1985). An interesting, albeit speculative, exception is Day and Walter (1989), who stretch the time span from a few dozen years to a few dozen millennia. Extended, detailed, and profound investigation of the qualitative structure of economic dynamics per se, however, has been generally neglected by the profession. Economists have employed qualitative methods more to run toward chaos than to investigate phase transitions for their own sake.

Perhaps this is because no particular equations of motion are either analytically or empirically compelling.[5] Without confidence that particular differential equations adequately model the true motion of competitive processes, no great scientific compulsion to trust much to its particular bifurcation structure emerges. The logistic and the Lorenz equations may be mathematically intriguing, but that alone is insufficient for them to become vital to economics. Analytical indeterminacy breeds empirical inquiry.

Consequently, considerable effort has been recently dedicated to the empirical investigation of nonlinear economic dynamics. Virtually all of this work attempts to distinguish deterministic chaos from random stochasticity in historical time series. Next to none of it explicitly searches for phase transitions or bifurcations of the economic flow.

The principal empirical technique for studying nonlinear economic dynamics follows the work of Grassberger and Procaccia (1983) and Wolf et al. (1985). Introduced to economists largely through the efforts of Brock (1987), Brock and Dechert (1988), and Barnett and Chen (1988), these techniques attempt to ascertain whether a historical sequence of numbers is consistent with motion on a strange attractor. One estimates the dimension of the sequence and the spectrum of its Lyapounov exponents.[6] A variety of other studies have now applied these ideas to economic data. These include Brock and Sayers (1988), Barnett and Choi (1989), and Scheinkman and Le Baron (1989). Although there has been some evidence of nonlinearity, especially in Barnett and Chen (1988) and in Scheinkman and Le Baron (1989), Brock and Sayers (1988) were unable to reject the hypothesis that macroeconomic aggregates are stochastically random rather than chaotic. Overall, this evidence has not clearly spoken in favor of nonlinear deterministic dynamics as a source of the observed erratic behavior. Consequently, most economists have not been dislodged from the view that exogenous random shocks account for the erratic motion detected in empirical data.

Significantly, these techniques cannot isolate bifurcations, since they presume all the data arise from the same side of a structural instability. Since they test for motion on a strange attractor, they necessarily cannot adjudicate whether or not the dynamic system has undergone a bifurcation during the time span covered by the data, thereby perhaps creating or destroying such a hypothetical attractor. Empirical methods *presuming* one qualitative type of motion cannot be used to identify transitions between qualitatively distinct phases. In particular, they presume that the data follow one trajectory along a given manifold generated by an unknown process whose parameters are fixed. Thus, the primary evidentiary devices economists use presuppose a constancy itself inconsistent with the fundamental insights achievable from the qualitative analysis of dynamics. The parameter rigidity required for these empirical tests cannot cope with bifurcations of the flow.[7] Moreover, these methods cannot identify the underlying equations of motion, which is necessary for the scientific pursuit of qualitative economic dynamics.

Not surprisingly, therefore, most economists tend toward caution and skepticism in using the mathematics of so-called chaos and in the employment of qualitative dynamics. Except as a parable telling of the possibility of sliding toward endogenous stochasticity, qualitative dynamics now finds only a negligible application in competitive economics. To many economists, it appears as yet another ephemeral fad. See, for example, Boldrin (1988) and Baumol and Benhabib (1989). And in recent years, Brock's enthusiasm has markedly waned (1989). Certainly there has been no great shift from the dominant view that competitive processes are inherently stable, and that observed irregularities in economic outcomes result from exogenous random shocks. Nonlinear determinisitic dynamics, in general, and qualitative dynamics, in particular, remain peripheral to most economic research.

The concluding section contrasts the success with which qualitative dynamical methods penetrated fluid mechanics with the indifference with which economists reacted to them. Different empirical methods and differences in the scientific authority with which particular models (particularly equations of motion) could be endorsed, rather than necessarily inherent phenomenological differences, explain why qualitative dynamical analysis has thrived in application to hydrodynamics, relative to economics.

The scientific applicability of qualitative dynamics in fluid mechanics and in competitive economics

Complex dynamical analysis is well named. Little about it could be termed simple, and frequently the quantitative analysis of it and of trajectories through complex flows is insurmountably difficult. Progress in its qualitative analysis may, however, prove fruitful. To achieve this, however, local behavior of the flow must be investigated at points of bifurcation. This requires examination of the stable, unstable, and center manifolds at degenerate points in the flow, and this cannot be fulfilled without reference to the equations of motion.

This allows us to identify our first major distinction between qualitative dynamics as applied in fluid mechanics as opposed to economics. In the former the velocity field of a fluid flow can be authoritatively expressed by the Navier–Stokes equations. With its roots in Newtonian mechanics and with considerable tradition and experience behind it, appeal to this equation is scientifically legitimate. Reliance upon "toy" systems dependent upon it, such as the Lorenz equations, may be questioned, but the underlying equations are not generally regarded as dubious, irrelevant, and/or ad hoc.

Nothing even remotely analogous graces economic dynamics. No analytical or empirical foundation supports any particular equations of macrodynamic motion. None speaks with generally accepted authority, and all appear to be dubious and ephemeral. Microfounded systems face similar problems. Any equations of motion compatible with the Walrasian *tâtonnement* might be acceptable, but none, and none of their bifurcating families, can be endorsed uniquely. Consequently, the core analytical material with which to apply qualitative methods, and which is satisfied by the Navier–Stokes equations in hydrodynamics, has never been developed by economists. Thus, for most economists, any attempt to apply qualitative arguments and to derive insights about equivalence classes of dynamical systems appears ad hoc and never attains a scientific bona fide. Neither empirical evidence nor analytical reasoning renders any unique family of functions scientifically compelling.

A second separatrix between fluid mechanics and economics stems from the attitudes of their practitioners toward stability. Anybody who has ever mixed paint or stirred milk into coffee has encountered instability in a fluid flow. Anyone who has ever heated a thin layer of oil in a skillet, or competently cooked oatmeal has encountered structural instabilities of Rayleigh–Bénard convection. For students of fluid mechanics, structural instabilities of dynamical systems are widespread and unavoidable.

By inclination and training, however, economists abhor instability. Reared on the presumption of local stability of markets bolstered by the global-stability Lyapounov arguments of Arrow et al. (1959), for them it is an unwelcome oddity. To most economists competitive processes that rule the economy are inherently dynamically stable.[8] Mathematically interesting dynamics and certainly "chaos," in contrast, *require* instability somewhere. However, the exchange of stability between fixed points or closed orbits typifies bifurcations, and this means deviations from stability are present. Bifurcations of the flow, with their alteration of a dynamical system's equivalence class, are the central topics of qualitative dynamics, and the exchange of stability at a bifurcation necessarily entails instability of some sort.

Few economists are keen on any of this. For them, instability of competitive processes manifests only a palsied malfunctioning of the invisible hand. Their most cherished attitudes toward markets and their most central presumptions about how the economy should be governed are all profoundly challenged by analyses conditioned on systemic instability. As an exception to prevailing views, Grandmont (1985) is admirably explicit about how sensitivity to initial conditions mandates actively interventionist macroeconomic policies. To deliberately nudge the economy onto a nearby and preferred path explicitly rejects laissez-faire platitudes.

Thus, many professional economists are inherently skeptical about qualitative dynamics. The validity of the most important normative propositions of economics is threatened if the economy fails to occupy an equivalence class containing a unique globally attracting equilibrium. To introduce structural instability is to speak from a culturally alien milieu and to challenge deeply held beliefs.

A third and final factor explaining why qualitative dynamics has thrived more vigorously in hydrodynamics than in competitive economics lies in the empirical methods of each. Whereas fluid mechanics can rely on laboratory experiments to simplify and control phenomena, the economist has no laboratory and no experimental apparatus with which to generate evidence. Access to laboratory experimentation provides many advantages. In particular, it allows observing behavior under varying parameter values. This has been particularly true of the qualitative approach to the motion of fluids. Experiments such as those of Libchaber (1987) and Threlfall (1975), in which Rayleigh–Bénard convection is induced at a variety of Rayleigh numbers, are an indispensable component of a scientific research program's incorporation of qualitative dynamics into its analytical repertoire. There can be no substitute for observing the onset of convection and its later transitions to chaos and turbulence. Economics has produced nothing analogous in attempting to detect the critical transition points along the route to chaos.

Empirically, economists cannot begin with controlled phenomena but must go straight to the wild, as it were. It is as if the student of fluid mechanics had to begin with Niagara.[9] Lacking laboratories, economists must do without experimental control. Thus, they cannot empirically calibrate a route-to-chaos story based in qualitative dynamics. For them, such a story remains entirely prescientific and wholly metaphorical so long as no empirical technique for identifying phase transitions exists. Instead, economists possess a growing heap of studies attempting to demonstrate whether or not chaos is present in their data. Grassberger–Procaccia tests have generally been inconclusive, and there has been no consensus that evidence demands abandoning stochastic models subject to exogenous shocks.

This empirical route could never have amassed evidence regarding bifurcations of a flow. Grassberger–Procaccia tests have meaning only *on* a strange attractor and so cannot identify the bifurcations of the dynamical system leading to the existence of chaos. Passing such tests argues that the system has been within one equivalence class. Thus, economists are empirically empty-handed in founding a definite theory in qualitative dynamical analysis.

Given the conceptually alien reliance upon instability implicit in qualitative dynamics, the absence of any clear empirical need to adopt its methods has left it largely neglected by economists. Initially skeptical and uncomfortable with its metaphorical implications and empirically unmotivated to explore it, this terrain has been generally avoided.

Contrasting applications of qualitative dynamics in hydrodynamics and mainstream economics reveals much about each. Previous acceptance of unstable phenomena rendered hydrodynamics more accepting of qualitative dynamics than were their colleagues in economics, who had long fed on arguments for globally stable equilibria. Whereas the former were conditioned in favor of these tools by long experience with unstable flows, the latter were congenitally discomforted by the threat to the invisible hand's capacity to reliably govern the economy. Thus, the cultural backgrounds of both fields predisposed each to its own ultimate intellectual outcome. Empirical evidence gathered (or neglected to be harvested) over the last two decades and the means of its acquisition reinforced these natural inclinations. Armed with its Navier–Stokes equation and with laboratory procedures, fluid mechanics successfully obtained evidence regarding phase transitions that accords acceptably with theoretically derived results. Economists have not. They have no generally scientifically accepted equations of motion from which to derive theoretical propositions about phase transitions, and they have neither empirical evidence about nor empirical means to get such evidence about phase transitions at bifurcating points of a flow. Thus, whereas the hydrodynamicist's observations have elevated the confidence with which qualitative dynamics engages their research, economists' observations reinforce neglect and doubt.

In science as in much of the rest of human affairs, what we already believe influences what we will observe and what we will believe. What now seems to be true governs what we will come to accept as true. Our current state of knowledge, including our methods of acquiring and processing observations, guides what we will see and what we will believe.

Notes

1. Much of this characterization of Rayleigh–Bénard convection follows Bhattacharjee (1987).
2. The Lorenz model was introduced in Lorenz (1963) and has been subjected to immense scientific and mathematical scrutiny. Sparrow (1982) is an excellent presentation of its properties.
3. These particular values are most commonly encountered and have been used by Lorenz (1963), Sparrow (1982), and Guckenheimer and Holmes (1983).
4. See Mullins (1991) for an intuitive discussion.
5. In addition to Debreu (1970), Dierker (1987) and Mas Colell (1985) offer excellent discussions of regular economics.
6. These are nonlinear analogues of eigenvalues, so that if any are positive, instability of some sort is present. If they lie on both sides of the origin, then "chaos" may be present. It is interesting to consider that the Grassberger–Procaccia tests on which economists have seized are to detect motion on strange attractors. Recall that strange attractors occur only in dissipative

systems and thus are not necessary either for aperiodicity or for sensitive dependence on initial conditions, which may also arise in conservative dynamical systems. Moreover, since solution of an optimal control problem requires the existence of a Hamiltonian, its flow must be conservative and therefore cannot reside within a strange attractor, even if it is "chaotic." Thus, for an economic time series to pass the Brock test for "chaos" is prima facie evidence that it is not the outcome of a rational process in the sense that it solves a problem of nonlinear optimal control.

7. The apparent problems of empirically accounting for regime changes, e.g., around World War II in Sheinkman and Le Baron (1989), may be related to changing parameters of the flow and conceivable change in equivalence class of the dynamic system. No existing econometric technique could examine such a possibility.

8. Here also is the fount of their temptation to analytically expel all sources of erratic and stochastic motion to exogenous random shocks.

9. Experimental economics is a new field in which controlled experiments are conducted on groups in highly stylized venues of social interaction. This novel empirical approach may some day provide a richer and more precise foundation for economic dynamics.

References

Arrow, K. J., Block, H. D., and Hurwicz, L. 1959. "On the Stability of the Competitive Equilibrium II," *Econometrics* 27: 82–109.

Barnett, W., and Chen, P. 1988. "The Aggregation-Theoretic Monetary Aggregates are Chaotic and Have Strange Attractors." In *Dynamic Econometric Modeling,* Proceedings of the Third International Symposium in Economic Theory and Econometrics, ed. W. Barnett, E. Berndt, and H. White. Cambridge University Press.

Barnett, William, A., and Choi, Seungmook S. 1989. "A Comparison Between the Conventional Econometric Approach to Structural Inference and the Nonparametric Chaotic Attractor Approach." In *Economic Complexity: Chaos, Sunspots, Bubbles, and Nonlinearity,* ed. William A. Barnett, John Geweke, and Karl Shell. Cambridge University Press.

Baumol, William J., and Benhabib, Jess. 1989. "Chaos: Significance, Mechanism, and Economic Applications." *Journal of Economic Perspectives* 3, 1(Winter):77–105.

Baumol, William J., and Quandt, R. E. 1985. "Chaos Models and the Implications for Forecasting." *Eastern Economic Journal* 11 (January–March):3–15.

Benhabib, Jess, and Day, Richard H. 1981. "Rational Choice and Erratic Behavior." *Review of Economic Studies* 48:459–71.

Benhabib, Jess, and Day, Richard H. 1982. "A Characterization of Erratic Dynamics in the Overlapping Generations Model." *Journal of Economic Dynamics and Control* 4:37–55.

Benhabib, Jess, and Nishimura, K. 1979. "The Hopf Bifurcation and the

Existence and Stability of Closed Orbits in Multisector Models of Optimal Economic Growth." *Journals of Economic Theory* 21:421–44.

Bhattacharjee, J. K. 1987. *Convection and Chaos in Fluids.* Singapore: World Scientific.

Boldrin, Michele. 1988. "Persistent Oscillations and Chaos in Dynamic Economic Models: Notes for a Survey." In *The Economy as an Evolving Complex System,* Proceedings of the Evolutionary Paths of the Global Economy Workshop. ed. Philip W. Anderson, Kenneth J. Arrow, and David Pines, pp. 49–75. New York: Addison-Wesley.

Brock, William A. 1987. "Distinguishing Random and Deterministic Systems: Abridged Version." In *Nonlinear Economic Dynamics,* ed. J. M. Grandmont, pp. 168–95. New York: Academic Press. (Originally published in *Journal of Economic Theory* 40 (1986): 168–95.)

Brock, William A. 1989. *Differential Equations, Stability, and Chaos in Dynamic Economics.* New York: North Holland.

Brock, William A., and Dechert, W. D. 1988. "Theorems on Distinguishing Deterministic from Random Systems." In *Dynamic Econometric Modeling,* Proceedings of the Third International Symposium in Economic Theory and Econometrics, ed. W. Barnett, E. Berndt, and H. White, pp. 247–65. Cambridge University Press.

Brock, William A., and Sayers, C. 1988. "Is the Business Cycle Characterized by Deterministic Chaos." *Journal of Monetary Economics* 22:71–90.

Day, Richard H. 1982. "Irregular Growth Cycles." *American Economic Review* 72:406–14.

Day, Richard H. 1983. "The Emergence of Chaos from Classical Economic Growth." *Quarterly Journal of Economics* 98:201–12.

Day, Richard H., and Walter, Jean-Luc. 1989. "Economic Growth in the Very Long Run: On the Multiple Phase Interaction of Population, Technology, and Social Infrastructure." In *Economic Complexity: Chaos, Sunspots, Bubbles, and Nonlinearity,* ed. William A. Barnett, John Geweke, and Karl Shell, pp. 283–9. Cambridge University Press.

Debreu, Gerard. 1970. "Economies with a Finite Set of Equilibria." *Econometrica* 38:387–92.

Dierker, Egbert. 1987. "Regular Economies." *The New Palgrave: A Dictionary of Economics,* vol. 4, ed. John Eatwell, Murray Milgate, and Peter Newman, pp. 123–6. London: Macmillan.

Grandmont, Jean-Michel. 1985. "On Endogenous Competitive Business Cycles." *Econometrica* 53:995–1096.

Grandmont, Jean-Michel. 1987. "Stabilizing Competitive Business Cycles." In *Nonlinear Economic Dynamics,* ed. Jean-Michel Grandmont. New York: Academic Press.

Grandmont, Jean-Michel. 1989. "Local Bifurcations and Stationary Sunspots." In *Economic Complexity: Chaos, Sunspots, Bubbles, and Nonlinearity,* ed. William A. Barnett, John Geweke, and Karl Shell, pp. 995–1096. Cambridge University Press.

Grassberger, Peter, and Procaccia, Itamar. 1983. "Measuring the Strangeness of Strange Attractors." *Physica* 9D:199–208.

Guckenheimer, John, and Holmes, Philip. 1983. *Nonlinear Oscillations, Dynamical Systems, and Bifurcations of Vector Fields*, 2d ed. New York: Springer.

Li, T. Y., and Yorke, J. A. 1975. "Period Three Implies Chaos." *American Mathematical Monthly* 82:895–992.

Libchaber, A. 1987. "From Chaos to Turbulence in Benard Convection." In *Dynamical Chaos*, Proceedings of a Royal Society discussion meeting, M. V. Berry, I. C. Percival, and N. O. Weiss, pp. 63–9. London: Royal Society.

Lorenz, E. N. 1963. "Deterministic Non-Periodic Flow." *Journal of Atmospheric Science* 20:130–41.

Mas Colell, Andreu. 1965. *The Theory of General Economic Equilibrium: A Differentiable Approach*. Cambridge University Press.

Mullins, Tom. 1991. "Chaos in Physical Systems." In *Fractals and Chaos*, ed. A. J. Crilly, R. A. Earnshaw, and M. Jones, pp. 237–45. New York: Springer.

Ottino, Julio. 1989. "The Mixing of Fluids." *Scientific American* 260, 1(January): 56–67.

Prigogine, Ilya. 1980. *From Being to Becoming: Time and Complexity in the Physical Sciences*. San Francisco: Freeman.

Scheinkman, Jose A., and Le Baron, Blake. 1989. "Nonlinear Dynamics and GNP Data." In *Economic Complexity: Chaos, Sunspots, Bubbles, and Nonlinearity*, ed. William A. Barnett, John Geweke, and Karl Shell, pp. 213–27. Cambridge University Press.

Sparrow, Colin. 1982. *The Lorenz Equations: Bifurcations, Chaos, and Strange Attractors*. New York: Springer.

Threlfall, D. C. 1975. *Journal of Fluid Mechanics* 67:17.

Wolf, A., Swift, J. B., Swinney, H. C., and Vastano, J. A. 1985. "Determining Lyapounov Exponents from a Time Series." *Physica* 160:258–317.

CHAPTER 6

Rigor and practicality: rival ideals of quantification in nineteenth-century economics

THEODORE M. PORTER

Neoclassical economics, now dominant in the English-language world, emerged out of the so-called marginal revolution beginning in the 1870s. In retrospect, and in the eyes of some of the leading protagonists as well, it seems clear that the crucial change here was nothing so limited as a new theory of value. It was the serious introduction of mathematical reasoning to economics. It is only a slight exaggeration to say that mathematical methods constituted economics as an academic discipline.[1] This conquest of economics by mathematics has become the most lively and exciting area of research in the current history of economics. On the whole, historians of this episode have come to agree with the actors themselves, that the model of the natural sciences contributed crucially to the reformulation of economics. To say this is by no means necessarily to praise neoclassical economics. While economists generally consider their ties to physics a matter to celebrate, historians often have not. Thus, many are inclined to blame inappropriate copying of physics for the willingness of neoclassicals to tolerate bizarrely unrealistic assumptions and to place everything historical, cultural, institutional, and even psychological outside the framework of economic analysis. One of the least sympathetic portraits, by Philip Mirowski (1989), indicts neoclassical economics precisely for its unimaginative copying of energy physics. If true, it is easy to understand why economic assumptions and models might seem to caricature the motives and behavior of real, flesh-and-blood human actors.

I take it as well established now that the model of natural science played a key generative role in the creation of mathematical economics. Indeed, it is not too strong to speak of deliberate imitation, at least for some of the pioneer neoclassicals. But we cannot explain the shape assumed by neoclassical economics so simply. Successful imitation is anything but straightforward. The most indiscriminate copying will not suffice to create a perfect correspondence. What begins as imitation, if it succeeds, must inevitably take on a life of its own. I have argued this point elsewhere in regard to the Belgian astronomer and statistician Adolphe Quetelet. His fanatical commitment to the model of celestial mechanics did not suffice to create a successful "social physics," but rather introduced subtle changes in the way the mathematics he sought to apply was interpreted, changes that subsequently were imported back into the natural sciences (Porter 1985). Mathematical economics, too, has become an important resource for the biological sciences, and even occasionally for the physical ones.

I am concerned here with a different obstacle to unimaginative imitation: that the natural disciplines present nothing like a single model of scientific theory or method. This is not simply a matter of the very different resonances of physics and biology, which since Alfred Marshall at least have been familiar, perhaps to the point of stereotype, among economists. Biology, after all, was a loser in the battle for the soul of economics.[2] Here I will ignore biology and consider economics in the context of its relations to the so-called exact sciences, meaning mathematics, physics, and closely related areas of engineering. There is already within the notion of "exact" science a major ambiguity, crucial for much of the modern history of economics, between what we may call quantification and mathematization. Mathematization implies theoretical formulation in the language of mathematics, emphasizing derivations involving the manipulation of terms to reach new results. Quantification, as used here, refers first of all to purely or partly empirical operations, such as measurement, counting, and statistical analysis. High neoclassical economics assigns a distinctly subordinate place to these forms of quantification and reveres deductive mathematics. Physics and engineering are, to say the least, far more ambivalent about the priority of theoretical mathematics. Of course, economists and physicists alike prefer not to dwell on the distinction, aspiring instead to a fruitful union of mathematical theory and empirical or experimental data. The experimental tradition in physics, though, has been consistently strong, whereas the collection and analysis of empirical information have in the last century become increasingly peripheral to academic economics. To the extent that economists have aimed to pattern their discipline after physics, their principal model has been theoretical physics, not experimentation. This choice was a highly consequential one. There were, I will show, other alternatives, which if anything were closer to the physics model.

Certainly an infatuation with physics never required the hypertrophy of mathematical theory. Until late in the nineteenth century, theoretical physics was not even an acceptable specialty of physics (Jungnickel and McCormmach 1986). Of course, physicists regarded theory as important, but almost never in isolation from experiment, and their customary rhetoric emphasized experimental fact, not mathematical rigor. This is not to say that quantification was of secondary importance, though. A culture of experimental and observational quantification became dominant in physics during the first half of the nineteenth century, so that by 1850 reports without measurements could scarcely be taken seriously.[3] Even then, the purely theoretical paper remained exceptional and was likely to be viewed as vaguely subversive.[4] Meanwhile, vast efforts were devoted to the collection of quantitative data, ranging from stellar coordinates to thermal and electrical conductivities to tide levels. Although in some cases the quantification of measurements was necessary to make them commensurable with mathematical theory, in others there was not even a gesture at theoretical modeling or prediction. It does not at all follow from this that physicists were unwilling ever to let theory run ahead of measurement. Nor can we infer that they were uniformly or even typically scornful of economic abstractions. But they were unlikely to be struck dumb by the appearance of deductive rigor in economic science. If they were not well disposed to classical political economy for other reasons, it was easy to find justification within their own disciplinary traditions to join lay critics and denounce it as baseless theorizing.

None of these scientist-critics aimed to deny the legitimacy of theory, not even in political economy. Nor did they commonly denounce a premature use of mathematics. They objected, rather, to "loose" theorizing. The precision and rigor of quantitative methods were held up as a cure for this looseness. The cure might be a matter simply of deflating excessive pretensions. This was the aim of William Whewell, who despised Ricardian economics and who tried to recast economic reasoning in mathematical form in order to show that its more objectionable conclusions could not stand up to exact investigation. More commonly, physical scientists interested in economics looked to reconstruct it on an empirical basis, to displace abstract theory or at least supplement it with a healthy infusion of measurement and statistics. They were, to follow the distinction already proposed, committed first of all to quantification, and only secondarily to mathematization.

Such a scheme for economics was by no means predestined to failure. The strength of the quantifying impulse in economics in the nineteenth century is attested to by the burgeoning field of statistics. As I will discuss later, an alternative political economy based on an alliance of statistics, physical measurement, and thermodynamics was pursued on more than one occasion by physicists and engineers as well as economists. Marginal economics in the form that was introduced in the 1870s, in contrast, was very much a program of mathematization, one that did not condemn quantification, but was willing to defer it indefinitely. Though patterned in important ways after physical statics, this was not the economics of choice for physicists, and it permitted theory a degree of autonomy from measurement that went well beyond what is normally condoned even in twentieth-century physics.

Mathematical discipline for theorists

Pure theory was never so dominant in classical political economy as the standard image purveyed by commentators and historians would suggest. Even within the apostolic succession of Adam Smith, Thomas Robert Malthus, David Ricardo, and John Stuart Mill, we find a huge amount of empirical and sometimes historical material mixed up with theoretical deductions in the main works of all but Ricardo. The same holds for Marx. Perhaps a few French authors, such as Say and Bastiat, can be categorized with Ricardo. Against them one should place a whole host of economic authors concerned with the statistics of production and trade, monetary history, the condition of the poor, the general advance of prosperity, and public health. Still, the basic theoretical doctrines of political economy had wide currency, appearing sometimes as catechisms. They were easily mobilized for public debate, where they provided ready answers to hot issues of public policy. They upheld an ethic of individualism: Free exchange increased everyone's utility; trade unions could not help the working classes; poor laws aggravated the problem of pauperism; agricultural tariffs enhanced the ability of parasitic landlords to suck up the surplus production of the industrious classes. These policy doctrines were not universally admired. Neither was the idealization of an atomistic world of self-interested economic actors. But no theoretical tradition of comparable elegance, simplicity, or rigor was developed by the opponents of classical political economy. Instead, critics learned to attack its abstraction, its indifference to empirical fact, and its blindness to history, institutions, and legal structures.

It took some time for this opposition to form its own intellectual traditions. When it did, in the 1860s and 1870s, it was under the banner of historicism. Historicism was strong in England, France, and the United States, but almost everyone recognized that its intellectual center was Germany. The historical school became a hotbed of German antimodernism. It was organicist, holistic, antiliberal, and more than a little antiscientific. At least it opposed strenuously the idea that natural science could be a model for historical and humanistic studies. Similar, though generally more moderate, views were characteristic also of historical economics in the United Kingdom and the United States (Kadish 1982; Koot 1987). One naturally infers from this that the classical economists stood for the ideal of science, though perhaps in an exaggerated form. Thus, we would expect to see mathematical and quantitative reasoning deployed by the allies of classical political economy and opposed by its critics.

This is wrong. The central propositions of classical political economy were not expressed mathematically, much less used to predict quantities that could be measured statistically. Jean-Baptiste Say explained why. He insisted, naturally, that political economy must be based on fact. The alternative was the lamentable *esprit de système* that had made it possible to believe gravity was caused by *tourbillons* of invisible matter rather than simple, mathematical forces. But as with every other science, not just any fact would do. A heavy object may be suspended in air by the jet of a fountain, without defying the law of gravity. In the same way, interest rates may for a time diverge from risk, though the law of their equality prevails just the same. The problem is perturbing causes, which conceal the simple laws governing phenomena in economics and mechanics alike. Economics cannot be based on mere statistics, any more than physics can rest on casual observations of carts and fountains. The facts that support economic reasoning must be like the experiments of physics, well grounded and carefully isolated. A mass of indiscriminate observations, all mixed together, is worthless. Perturbing causes cannot prevent economics from attaining general principles, but they make economic prediction impossible. To test economic theory against statistics is invalid and otiose. And if exact predictions cannot be made, there is little reason to try to make economics mathematical.[5]

Statistics provided an ideal of social and economic knowledge that was often placed in radical opposition to the deductions of Ricardo, Say, and Marx. The German historical school was at least as dedicated to statistics as to economic history, and it, in alliance with official agencies, provided the main support for public statistics in late-nineteenth-century Germany. German social reformers pointedly contrasted empirical, factual statistics with the baseless deductions and blind dogmas of Manchester liberals and revolutionary socialists. In Victorian England, statistical writing was deployed in support of the political ambitions and liberal presuppositions of the economists, though even there statistics were most often assembled to endorse paternalistic or state-directed reform, not laissez-faire.[6] And in England too, statistical factuality was sometimes held up as an alternative to the theoretical excesses of the economists.

The great British advocate of statistics in opposition to political economy was Richard Jones. Significantly, Jones was largely responsible for the organization of Section F, Statistics, of the British Association for the Advancement of Science (Goldman 1983; see also Henderson, Chapter 18, this volume). Section F, in turn, formed the kernel of the Statistical Society of London, ancestor of the modern Royal Statistical Society. Jones did not succeed in turning London statistics into a bastion of opposition to Ricardian economics. Certainly, though, he had allies. The one who concerns us here is William Whewell, Jones's lifelong friend and literary executor, and himself an early member of the Statistical Society's governing council. Whewell was not an active social statistician. Nor did he perform original work in historical economics. Instead, he contributed to Jones's cause by writing a mathematical exposition of Ricardian economics. This may seem an improbable alliance: Why should the great enemy of deduction in economics have been supportive of its mathematization? Whewell claimed that mathematics, with its high standard of rigor, could bring out the doubtful assumptions and errors of reasoning in Ricardo's argument. Mathematics would impose discipline on theoretical political economy and block its indiscriminate application.

Economics was by no means Whewell's major intellectual concern. He was a polymath – a leading scientific organizer; master of Trinity College, Cambridge, and thinker and writer on educational subjects; an astronomer, physicist, geologist, and mineralogist. He devoted much of his scientific effort to "tidology," the science of tidal movement, involving the collection of enormous amounts of quantitative data, which he hoped could be brought into accord with mathematical predictions. He is best known now as the author of the three-volume *History of the Inductive Sciences* followed by the two-volume *Philosophy of the Inductive Sciences* and a last one, *On the Philosophy of Discovery*.

Whewell's philosophical outlook is the obvious place to begin seeking an understanding of his critical approach to political economy (Hollander 1983). We find, to begin, that political economy is not a topic of Whewell's history or philosophy. This was, after all, history teaching by example, and its author found nothing in political economy that could fit it to be a model for other scientific investigations. On the contrary, he thought political economists had much to learn from the example of the more successful disciplines, meaning the natural sciences. So Whewell criticized Ricardian economics not because he thought the model of natural science inappropriate for political economy, but because political economists had departed too far from the historical pattern of successful scientific investigation.

That pattern involved, first of all, induction. Whewell professed admiration for Francis Bacon, and we find him arguing over and over that science should proceed by induction to successively broader generalizations. The temptation must be resisted to leap from a few casually observed facts to vast, all-embracing principles and proceed thereafter by the easy path of deduction. This last is, of course, what he thought Ricardo had done. His mathematical Ricardianism was intended mainly as a destructive project, to join political economy to mathematics and thereby to "make nonsense of it."[7]

For the more positive task of reconstructing political economy, he had a close ally. This was Jones, a friend since their undergraduate days together at Cambridge. Whewell wrote often to Jones, encouraging his research and complaining about his opponents, from the late 1820s until Jones's death in 1855. He wrote in 1828, for example, that if the political economists "will not understand common sense because their heads are full of extravagant theory, they will be trampled down and passed over; and it will be the height of indolence and bad management if you allow other heels to take the *pas* of yours in this most meritorious procession" (Todhunter 1876, 2: 94). As Whewell's remark implies, Jones was somewhat remiss in finishing his work and publishing; although his comparative study of rent came out in 1831, the projected succeeding volumes never appeared, and his next major publication was in 1858, three years after he died. This was due to Whewell, a prolific author, who had become his literary executor. Whewell (1859) praised Jones's reliance on induction and cited with approval his doctrine that Ricardo's theory of rent could apply at most to "farmers' rents," which were to be found almost nowhere outside Britain and the Netherlands. Mere deduction applies to nothing at all unless it takes customs and legal arrangements into account.

Whewell's commitment to induction was anything but pure, and it is probably a mistake to make this the crucial factor in his opposition to Ricardo. To be sure, he emphasized its importance throughout his life, especially whenever he had occasion to discuss political economy. That science, he argued in 1860, violates "the precepts that we must classify our facts before we generalize, and seek for narrower generalizations and inductions before we aim at the widest" (Whewell 1860, 298). As a member of the council of the London Statistical Society, though, he quickly became disillusioned with its radical commitment to facts, to the exclusion of all expressions of opinion. "I am afraid you will think me heterodox," he wrote the Belgian statistician Quetelet in 1835, but investigation depends on working theories if it is to get beyond unconnected facts. "Theories are not very dangerous, even when they are false (except when they are applied *to practice*)" (Whewell 1835). He insisted, against Mill, that induction can never be mechanical, that it is meaningless to talk abstractly of causes A, B, C, and effects a, b, c. Induction should be based on facts, but there is an irreducible element of intuition involved in any discovery of causes or laws, and Whewell believed that hypotheses are invaluable for guiding investigation even if the end result might be to discard them for some other explanation. Jones, for one, came to believe that Whewell's philosophical writings departed too far from a proper inductivism (see de Marchi and Sturges 1973).

We should not think of Whewell's views on method as abstract and monolithic. Political economy he regarded as something distinctive, deserving of his sharpest barbs. Clearly it was not immaterial that Ricardo had reached conclusions the reverend master of Trinity College found thoroughly unappealing. He complained repeatedly of the premature application of political economy to practice. In particular, he opposed Ricardo's notion of class conflict, that the landed classes were tending to absorb an ever increasing fraction of production in the form of rent, at the expense of the productive members of society.[8] Still, his remarks on method were no mere disguise for naked political antipathies. His great objection to Ricardo the theorist was not simply the rigidity of his deductions, but also their looseness. Ricardo's methods seemed to him weak. Verbal reasoning is too slippery. It does not require that the premises be made clear and permits auxiliary hypotheses to slip in unnoticed. It provides no clear checks against errors of reasoning. Verbal methods, in short, are too weak to guarantee correct reasoning and too imprecise for their results to be tested against those uncompromising judges, experiment and observation. Mathematical economics could overcome these defects. The result, of course, might often be to show that we are not yet able to succeed at deductive reasoning, that our premises are not sufficiently in accord with the world. But this, too, is valuable to know. Exact results, even if faulty, are to be preferred to imprecise, sweeping conclusions, to "the statements which we perpetually receive from the economists, of that which must necessarily be but yet is not, and to general 'truths,' to which each particular case is an exception" (Whewell 1831, 61).

Whewell's professed goal in his mathematical writings on Ricardian political economy was to eliminate this looseness. He did not expect important practical results from the enterprise: "Mathematical calculations," he conceded, cannot "supply the place of moral reasoning." One can no more reduce the business of the world to mathematics than mechanics can be used to understand the working of machines when we ignore friction, resistance, and the imperfection of materials. But Ricardo and others had based their reasoning on so few principles that mathematical solutions were readily available and, indeed, "might have been done in a few pages." In this way, the reasonings would have been made "almost infallible," and the mathematical results "could be compared with practice so as to show whether the problem was approximately solved or not" (Whewell 1829).

Given all this, it is hard to be surprised at Whewell's conclusions. Ricardo had allowed dubious tacit assumptions to creep into his argument. Once exposed and made explicit, Ricardo's qualitative assumptions could be judged against historical and empirical work of men such as Jones. Whewell did not himself work out theory to the point of quantitative predictions that could be compared with statistics, but he seemed not to anticipate its total vindication. He claimed also to find mistakes in Ricardo's abstract verbal reasoning. Ricardo erred, for example, in his inference of the effect on rent or profits of growing English prosperity, and of the sector upon which taxes of various descriptions would ultimately fall. Not that Whewell believed the mathematician could reach decisive, exact conclusions on these points. His purposes were more critical than constructive: to show "of what kind and how many are the data on which the exact solution of such problems may depend" (Whewell 1829, 1831). Mathematics should not supplant empirical investigation but could clear the ground for it by revealing the weakness of verbal deductions.

Specific grievances also lay behind several other economic efforts by men trained in natural science and economics in the late nineteenth century. The most common whipping boy in the 1860s and 1870s was the wages fund doctrine. This was an old doctrine of imprecise meaning – from one standpoint, it amounts to little more than a balancing of accounts. But it also provided an opportunity, or pitfall, for those infected by the Ricardian vice. All other things being equal, this fund is a limit on wages, and though in reality the other things are never equal, and though even if they were, wages might not have reached that limit, this doctrine did provide language of some use to those who were unfavorably disposed to trade unions. Collective bargaining, it was sometimes argued, is useless, since it cannot expand the fund available for wages. Or if one group of workers, through effective organization, gets more, it must come from the pockets of their less greedy fellows.

Fleeming Jenkin, who achieved some note in the history of mathematical economics for his papers on the graphical representation of the laws of supply and demand, was moved to this effort by a desire to clear up the wages fund doctrine. Jenkin wrote his papers in 1868 and 1870, while a professor of engineering at the University of Edinburgh, and he may be counted with James Clerk Maxwell, William Thomson (Lord Kelvin), and P. G. Tait among the notable Scottish mathematical physicists of the nineteenth century. He was a classmate of Tait and junior of Maxwell at the Edinburgh Academy, and he became very close to Thomson, when the two joined in planning and laying submarine telegraph cables. He also had known physical labor, having worked his way up from an apprenticeship as an engineer, and as Robert Louis Stevenson put it, he knew the working classes too well to regard them "in a lump" (1887, 1:xlix). He was not, however, an opponent of political economy, and in particular he spoke repeatedly in favor of free trade. No devout enemy of the economists could end a paper as Jenkin did: "Whatever school of religion or philosophy we belong to, we cannot deny that each man, acting rationally for his own advantage, will conduce to the good of all" (Jenkin 1870, 2:105).[9]

The verbal argument from the wages fund principle against the possibility of workers benefiting by trade unions has a certain plausibility, he allowed. Certainly there will be a tendency for whatever reduces profits to reduce also the fund available for wages. But there is a fallacy here: "The motion of a body is not determined by one force only" (Jenkin 1868, 2:9). The problem with the wages fund argument is that it does not tell us how this fund is determined; it is in fact affected by a myriad of circumstances, all of which can affect the rate of wages. How is the fund determined precisely? We don't know, said Jenkin: "No economist has hitherto stated the law of demand and supply so as to allow this calculation to be made" (2:15). Here was an obvious desideratum. To work out the interaction of causes required, if not an abstract mathematical formulation, at least generalizable quantitative techniques. So Jenkin, like Whewell, took to mathematics out of frustration with verbal reasoning that was, perhaps inherently, too vague to permit understanding in detail. Unlike Whewell, Jenkin thought his mathematics adequate to make a real contribution to an understanding of the problem, not mainly an agent of debunking. But it is significant that his conclusion was to pronounce the solution indeterminate, at least without a considerable improvement in the empirical data.

The task was to find the equilibrium between supply and demand. These are, of course, functions of price – or, in the particular problem here addressed, of the wage rate. But the shape of these curves is not given timelessly by nature. They depend, as Jenkin put it, on states of mind – of the capitalist and of the workers. "The laws of prices are as immutable as the laws of mechanics, but to assume that the rate of wages is not under man's control would be as absurd as to suppose that men cannot improve the construction of machinery" (Jenkin 1870, 93). Hence, so-called "laws" of demand and supply "afford little help, or no help, in determining what the price of any object will be in the long run" (Jenkin 1870, 87). Unorganized laborers are at a great disadvantage; those who do not bargain collectively are like goods to be unloaded in a bankruptcy sale. Hence, organization into trade unions most certainly can improve the worker's lot. How much? In a subsequent paper on the incidence of taxes, Jenkin suggested empirical measurement of supply and demand schedules to resolve the effects of taxation experimentally, and the same methods would apply to wage studies (Jenkin 1871–2). But given the mental component that he emphasized so heavily in the determination of wage rates, prediction here might well be beyond the capability of the political economist's art.

Quantitative programs for political economy

Whewell's anti-Ricardian campaign is suggestive of the ways in which mathematical reasoning could be turned against deductive political economy. It did not offer a positive program of quantification. Neither Whewell nor Jenkin wrote mathematical theory in a form that would yield predictions of statistical results. And despite Whewell's warm embrace of induction, he made almost no effort to gather the economic facts he so piously defended. Jones of course did. His ideal economics was to be thoroughly statistical and untheoretical. Whewell wondered if this might be going a bit too far, though he clearly preferred it to the opposite extreme. So did Charles Babbage, Whewell's contemporary, best known even in his own day for his "calculating engine." Babbage was a founding member of the Statistical Society of London and the author of a very successful book on the machinery question. No more than Whewell or Jones did he admire classical political economy: The "closet philosopher," he wrote, is too little acquainted "with the admirable arrangements of the factory" (Babbage 1833, 156). On these matters, Babbage practiced while Whewell preached. The effects of machinery were arguably the greatest economic issue of the time, a major concern of much early-nineteenth-century empirical work on political economy (Berg 1980). Babbage allied himself unambiguously with those who would measure and count, not with theorists. This included many "practical men," such as members of parliament, who allowed that Ricardo might be right in theory but insisted that such abstractions could never be adequate for a legislator facing a complex world (de Marchi 1974). It was also the prevalent view among natural philosophers who wrote on political economy.

One may be tempted to regard this empirical attitude as characteristically British, especially in the time of Whewell and Babbage. In a way it was, but the greatest success of statistical economics came in imperial Germany. There, the mathematical approach to political economy was in sharp opposition to the individualism of the classicals. There also, the historicist revolt was so strong as almost to extinguish deductive economics. In just one German-language university did it thrive – in the Vienna of Carl Menger and his students. Menger is often grouped with Jevons and Walras because of his marginal utility theory, but unlike them he made no use of mathematics. His economics was not only nonmathematical, but also largely nonquantitative. It is curious but revealing that in the great *Methodenstreit* between followers of Menger and Gustav Schmoller, we find mathematics mainly on the side of *Historismus*, not with the deductivists. Of course, the mathematics involved consisted not mainly of deductive models, but rather statistics. Still, there were a few prominent figures who went beyond presenting numbers and sought to develop higher methods to analyze them. G. F. Knapp and Wilhelm Lexis, in particular, saw themselves as champions of mathematical precision *and* faithfulness to the complexities of experience, as against the indefinite generalizations of the verbal deductivists in Vienna, Paris, and Manchester.

The historical school economists, even more than Whewell, were opposed to the classicals and neoclassicals on moral grounds. They objected particularly to the individualism of traditional political economy, to its assumption that principles regulating the behavior of individuals could be posited independently of the larger community to which these individuals belonged. This was, they thought, to place humanity in the realm of nature and of mechanical law. Humans belong to the domain of history and of progress – to free communities that gradually change, along with the individuals who make them up. In place of selfish utilitarianism, the historicists called for social responsibility, to be expressed partly through free associations such as worker cooperatives and partly through the activity of the state.

But here, as almost always, intellectual convictions cannot be reduced to mere ideology, even if ideology is often an important component of economic views and approaches. That Knapp and Lexis were not prisoners of anti-Enlightenment, antiliberal dogmas is strongly evidenced by their devoted pursuit of mathematical social science. Knapp, in his much later autobiography, reports equal disgust dating back to his student years in the early 1860s with unimaginative statistical compilations and deductive political economy. The former seemed to him vacuous. The latter he called a useless *Gymnastik*, a mere student exercise without scientific value and inapplicable to real problems. To be sure, he conceded, political economists have often written intelligently about practical matters. But they do so in their examples, and for this purpose the dogmatics are put aside (Knapp 1927). As a doctoral student at Göttingen, Knapp was put to work on the wages fund doctrine. He concluded that it was fallacious. There are, he argued, too many variables for a rigorous solution to the problem of distribution, even in Thünen's "isolated state." Thünen, he held, was forced to treat some quantities as independent variables that in fact were dependent ones. Hence, the "general, absolute validity, that Thünen ascribes to [his equation] . . . , is lacking, and it most certainly does not hold in the real world" (Knapp 1865, 12). Knapp would eventually make his mark as an economic historian in studies of peasants and agriculture, but his first serious social studies were statistical. He worked for a time as director of a government statistical office, in Leipzig. He also wrote mathematical works on demography – the one demonstrably practical area of exact social science, since those methods were used to calculate life insurance and annuity premiums.

Wilhelm Lexis criticized Menger for his failure to incorporate mathematics into economics, but he also was skeptical of the mathematical marginalist theory of Walras. These abstract propositions are valuable, he conceded, but they show no more than tendencies. They do not give a "reliable predetermination of actual events, and cannot by themselves decide the measures to be taken in pursuit of goals in economics" (Lexis 1881, 427). His response to the gap between economic theory and practical concerns was to emphasize the study of disturbing forces, which can be identified and estimated only through empirical research. In particular, he pursued something rather like what we know in the twentieth century as mathematical statistics. Neither Lexis nor Knapp was the patient, disinterested observer of society that their critique of the theoretical excesses of classical economics might seem to demand. Lexis aimed throughout to demonstrate that humanity was not subject to natural laws, independent of time and place. Using statistical methods he aimed to demonstrate, with the conclusiveness of mathematics, that moral and social behavior vary greatly over time and place and that societies cannot be reduced to a sum of autonomous individuals (Porter 1987; Wise 1987). And beyond social metaphysics, his statistical research also supported the gentle interventionism of the "academic socialists" in the Verein für Sozialpolitik. Effective state activity, he believed, presupposed adequate expertise. The test of this expertise was empirical adequacy, and mathematical reasonings had to be held to this standard if they were to be usefully applied to practical questions. Of course, he and Knapp did not reach a perfect accord between theoretical understanding and quantitative measures either. Their statistical methods, though, were calculated to manage the economy, while classical deductions showed mainly why political authorities should leave it alone.

The economics of engineers and physicists

Engineers are often required by their profession to practice economics. Physicists, at least in their familiar capacity as researchers, generally are not. But the line between physics and engineering has not always been very sharp. The gap was kept narrow through most of the nineteenth century as a result of the great importance in physics and engineering first of steam engines, and then of electricity. Especially in the early part of the century, relations between thermodynamic and economic ideas were extremely close. Each made use of ideas from the other. By no means was economics simply parasitic on physics; economic and physical ideas grew up together, sharing a common context. An economic point of view formed the root of thermodynamics. But this was not mainly a matter of physicists depending on the work of Ricardo or Say. The economic mentality at issue here was associated more closely with accounting than with high theory. And this economic conception itself already integrated a labor theory of value with a set of analogies involving engines (Wise 1989–90).

This fruitful confrontation of physics with engineering and economics first took place in France. It was closely associated with the culture of the École Polytechnique, created during the French revolution to enlist science in the service of the French state, especially in view of its pressing military needs. It was the great French scientific and engineering school, the first institution to make science and mathematics central to the education of engineers. Its raison d'être was to produce knowledge that was at once mathematically elegant and useful. After 1815, the French found themselves decades behind the British in the technology of the steam engine, and engines became an important topic of scientific as well as engineering inquiry (Fox 1986). These engineers were not content to approach steam engines as a problem of craft skill and merely technical ingenuity. They were scientists, and they sought an adequate scientific vocabulary for talking about the effectiveness of engines. An adequate vocabulary, naturally, presupposed the possibility of measurement. In this context was introduced the crucial physical notion of work.

For physicists and engineers like J. V. Poncelet, Charles Dupin, and Louis Navier, work referred to something more physical and more readily quantified than labor. It came to be defined as a product of weight and the height to which it was raised, the action of a force through a distance. But this was not merely a physical unit. It was also a measure of labor power, of work in the colloquial and economic sense. With it one could compare machines with humans or animals. One could talk about efficiency and productivity. The transmutation of heat and electricity into work became conceivable, indeed measurable. This was an important ingredient in the formulation of the doctrine of energy conservation (Grattan-Guinness 1984, 1990; Mirowski 1989).[10]

With the transfer of French physics to Britain, the rich concept of work was introduced as well. There, as Norton Wise has shown, work, meaning energy, became the basis for an alternative economics. The economics of energy was ideally suited to measurement, for it permitted the productivity of labor to be assessed against an absolute, physical standard. The champions of energy economics were not generally hostile to free trade, laissez-faire, or the other leading doctrines of classical political economy. Neither, though, were they content with an economic science that was mainly theoretical. Here was a form of economic reasoning and, more crucially, a system of economic practice that would permit scientists to judge the productivity of machines and labor, as well as to improve them. In this economics, statistics of factories, workers, and production meant something. Quantification could aid administration, could guide the improving activities of engineers and reformers (Wise 1989–90).

In Britain, the most important early champion of the new French physics of work was Whewell, author of an 1841 textbook entitled *Mechanics of Engineering*. Whewell wanted to raise engineering above mere craftsmanship, to introduce physical theory in alliance with physical measurement. His book made the foot-pound the common unit of laboring force. This had many advantages. Crucial among them was that it could readily be expressed in quantitative terms, to compare the labor of machines, animals, and humans. The advantage of machines could thus be expressed in familiar terms. James Thompson, brother of the famous physicist William and himself a distinguished engineer, gave a typical calculation in 1852. His pump, he found, could lift water at the rate of 22,700 foot-pounds per minute. A man can lift only 1,700 foot-pounds per minute, and that only for eight hours in a day, so that the pump was doing the work of forty men. Physical work, as Wise remarks, was here literally labor value (Wise 1989–90).

Even more crucially, this formulation permitted a clear distinction between useful work and waste, and indeed gave a quantitative expression of efficiency. This was invaluable to the industrial engineer and also to the reformer and philanthropist. Calculation could be used to determine an optimal mix of machine labor with human labor. James Thomson calculated to decide whether it was energetically advantageous to boil urine as fertilizer, thereby producing an increase in food for human workers, or to employ the coal fire directly for productive work (Wise 1989–90). At about the same time, William Thomson showed how energetic and monetary calculations could be combined to reach an optimum in telegraphy. Once he had learned how to measure the retardation of signals in a wire, it became "an economical problem, easily solved . . . to determine the dimensions of wire and covering which, with stated prices of copper, gutta-percha, and iron, will give a stated rapidity of action with the smallest initial expense" (quoted in Wise and Smith 1987, 326). And with this we begin to discover the benefits of energetic calculations for friends of the poor and working classes, especially those hailing from the Gradgrind school. R. D. Thomson, of the Glasgow Philosophical Society, looked forward to the day "when the light of science will enable the guardians of the poor to manage our poverty-stricken fellow men by precise and definite rules" (quoted in Wise 1989–90, 224). To this end, the Glaswegians were pleased to make use of a tabular presentation of the nutritive value of various food items: beans, peas, wheat, rye, oats, cabbage, and turnips. R. D. Thomson presented the nutritive values of various types of bread, in comparison with costs, to aid in minimizing the cost of supplying energy to human labor power. This was, as Wise remarks, rather like measuring the energy content of coal or the efficiency of machines. Lewis Gordon, another Glaswegian and the first professor of engineering in a British university, appreciated that measuring physical labor power and weighing bread yielded comparable numbers. Together they enabled the engineer to design and run factories with a maximum of efficiency.

The economics of energy here implied no rejection of the more customary medium of economic quantification, money. Its crucial feature was the search for standard, comparable units. This was a form of economics patterned after physics that aimed far less at theoretical elegance than at practical management and efficiency. The contrast with the mathematical economics of the marginalists could scarcely be more vivid. And the economics of quantified energy, unlike that of mathematized utility, won the interest and even enthusiasm of contemporary physicists.

One can find a similar approach, even more coherently developed, in France. "Engineers do economics while others talk about it," argued one twentieth-century French polytechnician (F. Caquot, quoted in Divisia 1951, x). The École Polytechnique and the École des Ponts et Chaussées had long recognized that the business of the engineer required a familiarity with economic ideas. There were, however, enduring doubts about whether the writings of those who called themselves political economists were capable of supplying what the engineers needed. Classical economics was, some argued, too impractical, too qualitative, too dogmatic. The engineers cultivated their own economic tradition, which borrowed sometimes more, but often less, heavily from Say, Rossi, Garnier, and other classical French economists.

One important Polytechnique engineer, whose work overlapped in important ways with Fleeming Jenkin's, was Émile Cheysson. Cheysson was a member of the French civil engineering corps, the Ponts et Chaussées. He was also a pioneer of graphical statistics and an influential social reformer in the tradition of Frédéric Le Play, whose monographic study of selected family budgets Cheysson saw as complementary to statistical method.[11] Cheysson called statistics indispensable for the management of men, for social engineering. He wanted to use them to divert economics from its abstractions, emphasizing instead the "study of the conditions that produce the well-being, the peace and the life of the greatest number" (quoted in Elwitt 1986, 67).

Predictably, Cheysson took physics as his model for political economy. Economics, of course, suffered by the comparison. It lacked, he said, a common unit: The value of money is too changeable, and utility is impossible to measure; unlike many predecessors, he did not pursue energy as an alternative.[12] Hence, he argued, economics can make no pretense to the rank of an exact science. "Despite ingenious attempts," he proclaimed in 1882, "the rigorous procedures of algebra have been proven sterile in application to this order of phenomena, for the equations are incapable of embracing all the facts" (Cheysson 1911b, 2:48). But Cheysson did develop ideas that tended to the mathematization of decision making. His outstanding contribution on these lines was his article on the geometry of statistics, first published in an engineering journal in 1887. It aimed to extend the skills of the engineer to business decisions about products, supplies, markets, and prices. Unlike the political economy of Walras and Jevons, with which he was well acquainted, it was not a mere abstraction, "speculative analysis," but a quantitative tool developed for practical reasons to solve practical problems in public and private affairs. It would permit decisions to be made without groping toward an optimal price or tax rate through trial and error, but instead by solving such problems directly.

Cheysson advocated graphical methods for finding optima of this sort, though he conceded that analytical methods could attain the same results. Analysis, he remarked, required mathematical sophistication and lacked the intuitive appeal of that *langue universelle,* graphical statistics. Also, the graphical method is quite simple. Suppose we want to determine how much to charge for railway travel on some line or network. We must plot two curves, one of demand and one of costs, each as a function of charge per kilometer. From them we can calculate a curve of net revenue, which the company aims to maximize. The highest point on this curve is the solution. Sometimes extrapolation will be required, but only when the company has always charged rates on one side of this optimum. In that case, the potential benefits even of an approximate solution are very great. He gave as an example the Austrian Nordbahn, whose rates had always been far too high to maximize the profitability of the company. Such errors seemed especially egregious given that the public interest demands rates below this point of maximum profits. Cheysson's methods were not limited to transport problems. They could also be used to establish optimal wage rates for workers, and thus provide powerful tools of social betterment. And they could guide investment decisions or the setting of tax and tariff rates (Cheysson 1911a, 1: 185–218).[13]

Cheysson, though a loyal engineer, had a multifarious career, most of it outside the Corps des Ponts et Chaussées. Still, his economic interests were in many ways typical of French state engineers. Nowhere was practical economic quantification more skillfully developed in the nineteenth century. The Corps des Ponts et Chaussées was an administrative agency, not just a team of engineers. As François Etner observes, it was charged with budgeting and choosing among projects, "all in the name of the public interest and in accordance with rules that should be written, public, and non-discriminatory" (1987, 115).[14] In the interest of rationalization, these engineers endeavored to make physical parameters such as mechanical efficiency, friction, and wear commensurable with costs of construction, maintenance, and operation. Choice of materials in a road or the decision about steepness of grades and sharpness of curves on a railroad were economic problems, as was recognized in any number of papers by state engineers on the construction of routes.[15] An outstanding example is the solution to the problem of road maintenance given by Jules Dupuit, the only one of these engineers to gain a lasting international reputation among economists. It was unmistakably an economic solution, in which physical measurements were in the end translated into monetary terms (Dupuit 1842).

Dupuit's reputation survives among economists because he used the principle now known as "diminishing marginal utility." He did not invent it as the basis of a program of mathematical deductions, but rather to attain a satisfactory measure of the public benefits of a railroad or canal. It is significant that Walras, the French-language pioneer of marginal utility theory, disdained to include the engineer Dupuit among his precursors, and in a way Walras was right. For purposes of calculation, though, Dupuit wielded his principle very effectively. It was designed as an improvement on some formulas proposed by Navier, who introduced this form of cost–benefit quantification in an attempt to show that the benefits of a canal would normally far exceed the revenue it brought in. The best measure of benefits, Navier proposed, is not tolls charged, but costs saved – the product of volume of goods moved on a canal by savings per ton-mile over transportation on the roads. Dupuit declared this formula far too generous. Much of the traffic on the canals depends on their low charges and would not move at all if water transport were not available. These shipments do not yield benefits equal to the full difference between road and canal shipping costs, but only the difference between actual costs on the canals and the increase in value resulting from the transportation. As the cost of transport goes down, the volume will go up. Hence, the total benefit due to the canal cannot be the product of volume with cost differential, but must instead be represented as the area under a curve that plots the number of units that would be transported on a rail line or canal as a function of the toll charged (Dupuit 1844, 342; see also Ekelund and Hébert 1978; Smith 1990). Dupuit assumed, with eminent reasonableness, that, as tolls go up, usage will go down. This corresponds with the doctrine of diminishing marginal utility.

Dupuit did not suppose that these curves could be plotted directly from statistics. If, however, rates had varied over time, one could surmise something about the shape of the demand curve. At least his quantities were observable in principle, quite unlike the personal utility of the next generation of economists. And Dupuit's general strategy for calculating the benefit of public works became standard for guiding policy on their construction and pricing. His methods were taught, for example, in the authoritative textbooks on the economics of public works published toward the end of the century by Clément-Léon Colson, also of the Corps des Ponts. Colson was not a man of speculative bent. He complained of those economic authors who are content to reason deductively and mathematically, and thus "have often deviated completely from real facts in their most ingenious theories" (Colson 1907, 39). Engineers, he stressed, are practical men. Their economics should stay close to the facts, to statistics, so that it will be useful in administration. This, indeed, was Corps dogma. François Divisia, in a later celebration of the economics of French engineers, did not conceal his scorn for pure economics:

> How far we are from its resonant controversies that go round and round through the decades or the centuries, from its clever and subtle dissections, the games of mandarins, from its previsions that are just the opposite of reality one time in two, from its experiments that really aren't and that lack even the value of a lesson in facts. Economics! Is it, after all, anything more than a job well done, what all our engineers can do? (1951, 101)

Walras confronts the polytechnicians

The differences in view separating mathematical economists from engineers and physicists are compellingly illustrated by the career of Léon Walras, generally viewed by modern mathematical economists as the most important neoclassical pioneer. Two recent books show to what extent Walras took his mathematics from standard works of physics, particularly from potential theory in statics (Mirowski 1989; Ingrao and Israel 1990). One might have expected a cordial welcome for mathematical economics from those trained in modern physics. Walras certainly hoped for one. Recent studies of Walras and A. A. Cournot, noting their almost complete isolation from the French legal and literary school of political economy, have tried to connect them instead to the mathematical and engineering traditions of the École Polytechnique (Ménard 1978; Dumez 1985). The relations between mathematical economics and French engineering were important ones. They were, however, exceedingly stormy. Their history highlights the differences between economic mathematization and quantification.

Cournot's 1838 book can reasonably be called the first serious work of mathematical economics. It was, in its time, a complete failure, despite the considerable reputation of its author. He was not actually a polytechnician, but a graduate of the École Normale Supérieure. Among his classmates was Walras's father Auguste. The École Normale was a school of science and scholarship that educated teachers and researchers. This may be contrasted with the École Polytechnique, whose mission was, of course, to train engineers. There is considerable ambiguity here, since the curriculum at the Polytechnique was strongly oriented around mathematics. Especially in its first decades, up to the 1820s or 1830s, it was the central institution of French science and mathematics. Pure mathematics helped to maintain its standing as an elite institution in a conservative society. Yet, as Jean Dhombres (1987) has argued, the practical ethos of engineering and management was already strong there in the 1820s, and it became even more dominant as the century advanced.

Cournot, no engineer, aimed to sharpen up economic theory by rewriting it in terms of general mathematical functions. He took care, though, to frame his theory in terms of observable economic quantities – money and prices. He set out by showing how to use the method of least squares to chart the changing value of precious metals, based on an explicit analogy with astronomy. In this way he hoped to establish a fixed unit, to facilitate reliable measurement, and to permit comparisons across time. Thus, one cannot call Cournot indifferent to the investigation of economic quantities, and it is significant that the model of natural science entered his reasoning most explicitly where he was most concerned with measurement. But his books on economics and probability were written mainly from the standpoint of a mathematician, and scarcely more than Whewell did he have a workable vision of a quantitative economics (Cournot 1838, 1843). As Claude Ménard points out, Cournot's strategy of economic mathematization depended on excluding history, with its irrationality and perpetual disequilibrium. Cournot was willing to pay the price of mathematical rationality by excluding the whole domain of *économie sociale,* all the complications that would be as mud to the pellucid waters of pure economic reasoning. The "logical reconstruction" effected by Cournot's mathematical approach was made possible by his willingness to assume pure rationality and not to limit himself to what could be ascertained empirically or applied to policy. Real economic decisions, he conceded, involve so many complex factors that practical sagacity outweighs scientific apprehension (Ménard 1978).

Walras was a great admirer of Cournot. He claimed in his correspondence to have gone beyond Cournot mainly in the purity and rigor of his methods. "You," he wrote, "follow a route that takes immediate advantage of the law of large numbers and leads to numerical applications, while my work remains free from that law on the terrain of rigorous axioms and of pure theory."[16] To be sure, he did not always discuss his work this way. In his letters to Jules Ferry, the French minister of education, he was much more eager to claim practical relevance for his theoretical insights, or even to hold that some pressing problem such as railroad rates could not be solved until economic theory was better developed.[17] And Walras, unlike Cournot, did write on practical issues. He even became active twice in campaigns for economic reform: first, at the beginning of his career, in favor of free trade, and then, near its end, as an advocate of land socialization. But the interpretation of his own work he sketched for Cournot is at least defensible. Cournot framed his theory mainly in terms of macroscopic variables such as the quantity of money. Walras's originality as a theorist owes principally to his deductions from an abstract model of free exchange, leading to an even more abstract theory of general equilibrium. His microeconomic approach, like most, could be used as a language to describe the behavior of a profit-maximizing firm, but this was not why Walras developed it.

Walras was no polytechnician. His mathematics was not good enough to succeed in the competition for entry. He did study as an external student at the École des Mines, which, like the École des Ponts, accepted as ordinary students only the most elite graduates of Polytechnique. He was not entirely indifferent to applications of social mathematics. He served briefly as actuary for a Swiss insurance company. He sent not only letters to Ferry about railroad rates, but also, in 1875, a long memoir. He hoped that pure economics would guide practice in these areas. In 1873 he wrote his colleague at Lausanne, the engineer Antoine Paul Piccard, that "by introducing into pure political economy the precision of definitions and the rigor of deductions that prevails in pure mechanics, . . . most rules of applied political economy" could be demonstrated mathematically.[18] This was, however, by no means direct and simple. Pure political economy, he held, should be constructed on the model of astronomy – "the type to which, sooner or later, the theory of social wealth must converge." It will study "natural facts" of human behavior, which are more basic than social conventions and which "impose themselves on the human will." Such laws can be expressed in abstract mathematics and provide the proper foundation of political economy. Adam Smith and J. B. Say had never gone beyond what he called "applied" political economy. He anticipated that in the future this would be grounded on his more fundamental theory. But we still have not reached the practical rules of economic policy. They were to be given by a third subdiscipline, "social economy," which would connect with the deepest level of theory only through the mediation of the second.[19]

And even this was an expression of youthful enthusiasm, written in 1862 before Walras had any specific vision of mathematical economics. By 1876, when he published his Eléments d'économie pure, he had already become more pessimistic. Later he virtually stopped claiming policy applications. Asked for official advice about tariffs in 1881, for example, he answered that he did not command the detailed knowledge of the conditions of Swiss industry to justify a recommendation and that he lacked the interest to devote the needed time to it. "I am a man of pure theory," he explained. He still hoped that others would take the trouble to define a more rational practice on the foundation of his theory, but he saw no reason to be very hopeful.[20]

This remoteness of Walras's theory from practice was recognized also by engineers and seems to account for their lack of interest in his work. Only in retrospect, out of bitterness, did Walras reciprocate their disdain. At first he courted them assiduously, for he had no other supporters. He tried to gain entry to the Institute of Actuaries, a group of Polytechnique graduates dedicated to the quantitative study of economic problems who took insurance mathematics as their model. Walras's general equilibrium theory was too abstract to interest them. Although they were quite able to understand it as pure mathematics, they could never see the point (Dumez 1985).

The history of Walras's relations with them is instructive. In 1873, he presented a paper at a meeting of the Académie des Sciences Morales et Politiques in Paris in hopes of making his work known to the leading French economists. Disappointed, though not completely surprised, by their incomprehension, he was correspondingly pleased to hear afterward from Hippolyte Charlon of the newly formed Circle of Actuaries. Charlon offered its journal as an outlet for the economist's work. Walras, in reply, declared himself pleasantly surprised to discover that he was not so isolated in France as he had thought.[21] He soon sent Charlon a memoir, the crucial chapter of the Eléments d'économie pure, for separate publication in the hope of drawing attention to his forthcoming book. After a long delay, caused by internal disagreement among the actuaries, Charlon explained that the *Journal des actuaires français* had decided not to publish his memoir. Although Charlon had found it "very remarkable and abounding in sound ideas," it was also "off the practical and positive course along which we have directed our Journal. There is a crowd of sciences that, more than political economy, employ or could employ mathematical methods. This is no reason for them to be the object of our publication." There seems, he speculated, to be an unfortunate "incompatibility of humor between economists and actuaries."[22]

This incompatibility resurfaced in the correspondence between Walras and Hermann Laurent in 1898. The Circle of Actuaries had fallen into abeyance in 1880; Laurent was the moving force in its revival, in 1890, as the Institute of Actuaries. Like Charlon he had studied at Polytechnique. He was also a distinguished physicist and mathematician, and he took the model of the physical sciences very seriously. In his correspondence with Walras, he wondered whether economic comparisons over time might be facilitated by using a measure of energy, rather than currency or utility, as the standard economic unit. That is, he wanted economics to be based on measurement, and this could not be accomplished with a fluctuating unit like money. His aim was to make economics more practical, which, he explained, required that it be made mathematical.[23]

He was no enemy of Walras. He published in 1902 a short book on political economy "according to the principles of the Lausanne school" of Walras and his successor, Vilifredo Pareto (Laurent 1902). But, while applauding their mathematical turn, he wanted to associate it with something more practical than the abstract laws of exchange. He argued that a proper course in economics should involve four main parts: statistics, "economic facts," theory of financial operations, and theory of insurance. This did not entirely exclude the more abstruse theories of economists, for he included Walrasian pure theory within his category of economic facts. Mathematics could at least elevate economics to a proper science, he held, but only if it was closely linked with the study of empirical reality. This for him implied careful attention to statistics: Economics without statistics would be like physics without experiment. "I consider statistics not merely as an auxiliary to political economy," he wrote, "but as its fundamental base. It is its experimental part. Political economy can never become a true science, genuinely useful, until the day when its reasonings can conduct its premises to well-made observations, and when its conclusions can be verified by other appropriate observations."

Laurent can by no means be said to have achieved this. He did take the goal seriously enough to include a substantial discussion of statistics in his treatise on political economy and then in 1908 to publish another little book on statistics (Laurent 1908). It was not devoted to the collection of useful administrative numbers, but to probabilistic techniques for analyzing data and estimating precision that Laurent regarded as the foundation of statistics. He wanted to see economics and statistics become more like the science of the actuary. Actuaries had succeeded in making probability mathematics indispensable for insurance companies. He looked forward to a day when political economy could boast of a like practical value.

In his exchange of letters with Walras, he explained that an effective economics must be dynamic. To compare measurements across time, one needed a stable unit. His candidate for this was energy. He was deeply skeptical of Walras's ineffable "utility." Walras responded with as much patience as he could manage that energy was a valid economic measure only if it were equivalent to utility at the margin – which he doubted. He then admitted that dynamic formulas had no place in his theory. "In my desire to establish patiently the basis of a new science, I have so far more or less confined myself to the study of the phenomena of economic statics."[24] Laurent was not at all satisfied with this evasion, and subsequent correspondence did nothing to resolve their disagreement. And Laurent was his closest contact in the Institute of Actuaries. The stubborn indifference of the others to his work fed his paranoia. They had deliberately excluded him from their company. The Institute of Actuaries, he told its secretary, was controlled by the same malign influence that had ruined political economy in France. To others, he offered the opinion that there was no "profound knowledge" or intellectual vitality to be found there.[25]

The failure of Walras to win influence in the Circle of Actuaries, or to develop practical economic tools of his own, sheds much light on the relation of marginalist economics to practical calculation. This was largely an autonomous tradition, cultivated by administrators with problems to solve rather than by academic theorists. The highly abstract models from which Walras built a theory of general equilibrium contributed nothing to the decision processes of engineering administrators. The philosopher Renouvier, also a polytechnician, complained to Walras that the gap "between the science and the art of the engineer-economist (if you will permit me this expression)" is much greater than "that between the science and art of the engineer-mathematician."[26]

It was not only among the engineers in France that Walras's theory failed. He won few adherents, and almost no followers. This failure is naturally somewhat disconcerting to neoclassical economists, who view Walras's work as the discovery of an important scientific truth. Accordingly, there have been various attempts to explain his nonreception, with results that are on the whole convincing. Mathematical economics triumphed in Britain and the United States as part of the professionalization of the field, and its success is difficult to explain in other terms (Coats 1967; Stigler 1982).[27] The weak interest it stimulated in France is due in large part to the lack of opportunity for professionalizing economics in the French university system. Political economy was part of the training for civil servants and engineers. It won a place in the universities in the 1880s, but in the law faculty rather than among the sciences. It was, in short, taught mainly for administrative purposes. This was ruinous for Walras. Mathematical political economy was the sort of thing that only an academic economist could love.

Economics, physics, and mathematics

The pioneers of neoclassical economics depended heavily on mathematical physics for the theoretical structure they imposed on their discipline. The rediscovery of these interdisciplinary links is one of the most welcome developments in the recent historiography of economics (Kingsland 1985; Ingrao and Israel 1990). Drawing inspiration from statics and energy physics, economists built up a set of mathematical models as impressive and as demanding as are to be found in any natural science. Yet the story I have told here suggests a generally unenthusiastic reaction to deductive or mathematical economics on the part of physicists. William Whewell applied mathematical reasoning to Ricardo precisely in order to reveal his question-begging assumptions and to display his errors. Physicists and engineers in both Britain and France developed their own economic frameworks, which were thoroughly quantitative and yet quite alien to the mathematics of the early neoclassicals. One should not exaggerate the point. Certainly there were physicists, such as Vito Volterra, who applauded the research of the neoclassicals. But these were rare. More typical is Simon Newcomb, the U.S. astronomer and influential spokesman for "scientific method." Newcomb was an admirer of political economy and highly favorable to the project of making it more scientific. He was a teacher of Irving Fisher. He wrote an introductory treatise on political economy, which is full of mechanical analogies to economic processes. Yet, although the works of Walras and Jevons had been out for a decade, he did not even employ the calculus, the indispensable mathematical basis for marginal economics. He insisted that a fruitful economics must be closely linked with statistics. And he criticized Jevons, arguing that it was useless to make subjective feelings the foundation for economics. One must instead focus on actions, human behavior, which alone can be properly quantified (Newcomb 1885; Moyer 1992).

Walras was perpetually frustrated by this attitude. His desperate search for allies included appeals to such giants of theoretical physics as Poincaré. In Poincaré's philosophy he found inspiration, or rather justification. "One of the masters of modern science," he rhapsodized, "has concluded that masses are nothing but coefficients which are conveniently introduced into the calculations." Is it not the same, he continued, with the crucial economic concepts of utility and scarcity (rareté)? (in Mirowski and Cook 1990, 213). With this inspiration, Walras approached Poincaré for his approval. And he received in reply an ambivalent letter, favorable enough that Walras thereafter quoted from it on every possible occasion. But Poincaré was devoutly committed to applied mathematics and did not fail to notice that utility is a nonmeasurable magnitude. While it may legitimately be introduced as an arbitrary function in the premises, he allowed, it must disappear from the conclusions or these will be devoid of sense and interest. He also wondered about the premises of Walras's mathematics: It might be reasonable, as a first approximation, to regard men as completely self-interested, but the assumption of perfect foreknowledge "perhaps requires a certain reserve."[28] The mathematician Joseph Bertrand was less charitable. He found an essential contingency in the idealized economic marketplace, so that the price of a commodity would depend on the order of transactions and would not be determined by supply and demand curves. More generally, he concluded that the economic world was too slippery for mathematics and that practical knowledge in this domain is superior to mathematical abstractions (Bertrand 1883).[29]

Why were physicists so unreceptive to mathematical economics? It is, I think, wrong to suggest, as Mirowski has, that the marginalists were bumblers and that the physicists detected logical flaws to which the economists remained oblivious. The nub of the matter is that the physicists and engineers discussed here were unable to see the point of a purely theoretical economics. With very few exceptions, physicists and engineers took measurement to be more central than mathematical deductions to their discipline. They applied this standard even more stringently to economics than to physics because economics was not for most of them a pure research interest, but rather an aid to administrative decisions. Mathematical economics was detached from practice throughout the nineteenth century. So it was naturally more appealing to those who were indifferent to, or even opposed, centralized economic administration than to those who were looking to rationalize economic decisions. Whewell, who used mathematical reasoning mainly to undermine the policy prescriptions of Ricardian economics, appears exemplary from this standpoint. Toward the end of the century, Herbert S. Foxwell identified as one of the great merits of the new marginalist theory of Jevons and Marshall to have "made it henceforth practically impossible for the educated economist to mistake the limits of theory and practice or to repeat the confusions which brought the study into discredit and almost arrested its growth" (Foxwell 1886–7, 88). He even considered that mathematical and historical economics were allies in opposing the misapplication of theory. Mathematical economics, it seems, had the great virtue of demonstrable irrelevance, which was morally preferable to spurious relevance.

Few economic quantifiers, though, were content with demonstrated irrelevance. We should certainly not suppose that only engineers and physicists had the methodological or quantitative sophistication to apply economic numbers and calculations usefully to practice. By far the majority of practicing economists in the nineteenth century, and well into the twentieth century, were specialists in banking, commerce, or transport, not abstract theory.[30] And they too most often worked independently of abstract mathematical theory.[31]

This failure to make much use of theoretical economics in relation to practical and political questions applies even to the mathematical economists themselves. This is no surprise in relation to Walras, who found pure theory taxing enough and lost interest in the scientific study of practical economic issues. It is perhaps more surprising that we find almost nothing of the new marginalist economics in the policy writings of William Stanley Jevons and Alfred Marshall, each of whom nurtured a lifelong interest in economic affairs. The work of Jevons is especially revealing. He was an active and exceptionally sophisticated statistician. He was willing to make the effort of gathering up statistical information to learn about the causes of poverty or the conditions of trade. He even employed the mathematical theory of probability to infer fluctuations in prices, to demonstrate the exhaustion of coal reserves, and to detect an unwonted relationship between sunspot cycles and commercial crises (see Morgan 1989). Jevons was, in short, an avid quantifier. Yet one never encounters a word about marginal utility theory in his statistical writings. It may well be that in the long run he hoped to see statistics used in order to measure utility functions (Howey 1960).[32] But he never worked any of this out, never integrated his various economic interests. His own polymathy made him all the more conscious of a need for specialization. "The present chaotic state of Economics arises from the confusing together of several branches of knowledge. Subdivision is the remedy. We must distinguish the empirical element from the abstract theory, from the applied theory, and from the more detailed art of finance and administration. Thus will arise various sciences" (Jevons 1957).[33] From this standpoint, his much-advertised claim that economics should be mathematical because it is intrinsically quantitative rings hollow.

Marshall's economic thought is too complicated, too contradictory, to be divided into neat compartments. As is well known, he came to economics from Cambridge mathematics. By the time he published his *Principles of Economics* (1890), his mathematical enthusiasm was sufficiently diminished that he consigned all mathematics to a set of appendixes. Any mathematical result that cannot be expressed in natural language should be burned, he urged. And he preached that economics should follow biology rather than physics as its model.[34] This last point was honored mainly in the breach. And in place of mathematics he made extensive use of graphical representations. Those were idealized, never summaries of actual data.

The ambiguities of Marshall's economic style and pronouncements reflected a deep ambivalence of aims. He was a thoroughgoing professionalizer, earnestly committed to the creation of an effective economic discipline. At this he was remarkably successful. But he also wanted to educate potential businessmen in economics, to promote a chivalrous ethic that would reduce disparities of wealth without requiring heavy-handed bureaucratic intervention. He was not looking to train economic experts, but gentlemen, like those who led the Civil Service. He tried to make prominent political leaders feel welcome in the British Economic Association, provided they deferred to the academics on scientific issues. For their purposes, the cultivation of judgment was more important than the inculcation of quantitative skills. Probably his aims were incompatible (see Winch 1990). We need not worry much about the contradictions they generated. Neither professionalization nor the education of gentlemen called for much reliance on measurement or quantification, and as A. W. Coats remarks, Marshall feared the possible victory of empirical over "scientific and analytical" economics.[35] Occasional intrusions from the sphere of public discussion, such as debates about the gold standard, led Marshall to work for a time with statistics. Like Jevons and Francis Ysidro Edgeworth before him, he conducted this discussion without drawing on the mathematics of marginal economics (see Marshall 1926; Porter 1986).[36]

This remoteness from measurement and quantification was associated with a remoteness of neoclassical economic theory from practice, which, as I have argued, is one explanation for the indifference, even hostility, of many engineers and physicists to the new economics. To physicists in the era of Kelvin and Helmholtz, a theory was only meaningful if its terms were susceptible to measurement. Such views were especially common among those who were close to engineering and who wanted to see physics put to use. But it was also a moral ideal, an ideal of discipline, restraint, and humility. Just how severely it should be applied was contested in late-nineteenth-century physics. Kelvin, for example, criticized Maxwell for introducing terms into his theory that could not be measured. He argued, famously, that "when you can measure what you are speaking about and express it in numbers you know something about it; but when you cannot measure it in numbers, your knowledge is of a meagre and unsatisfactory kind" (quoted in Wise and Smith 1987, 327–8). Social scientists have often failed to realize that this was intended as an attack on the "nihilism" of theory. Indeed, Norton Wise and Crosbie Smith (1987) have urged that the willingness of Maxwell's school to relax this practical imperative, to allow a greater autonomy for mathematical theory, reflected the increasing professionalization of physics at the end of the nineteenth century in Britain. This suggests a parallel with the development of neoclassical economics. But the mathematical economists took their hypertrophy of theory much further than the Maxwellians. Maxwell and his followers tried always to come back to experimental predictions, matters of potential measurement, at the terminus of any theoretical excursion. Physicists were widely agreed that the proof of theory was in measurement.[37]

While neoclassical economists may have derived much of their mathematical theory using analogies with physics, they were very far from accepting the prevailing standards of physics as a practice. That practice was and is strongly associated with experimental quantification, and by no means first of all with mathematical theory. It would be invidious and seriously misleading to suggest that dissenters from the neoclassical approach have more nearly succeeded in following the pattern of physics. Clearly, though, it was the early econometricians who took most seriously the problem of measurement.

A fine example is Wesley Mitchell, head of the National Bureau of Economic Research and an active contributor to economic policy under

Herbert Hoover. Mitchell, somewhat audaciously, referred to neoclassical theory as "qualitative" and called for a major infusion of quantification into economics. By this he meant statistical measurement:

> Economists who practice quantitative analysis are likely to be chary of deserting the firm ground of measurable phenomena for excursions into the subjective. . . . If my forecast is valid, our whole apparatus of reasoning on the basis of utilities and disutilities, or motives, or choices, in the individual economy, will drop out of sight in the work of the quantitative analysts, going the way of the static state. (1925, 4)[38]

He complained that the "qualitative" theory of Jevons and Marshall "plays so small a role in our work as specialists in public finance and banking, in accountancy and transportation, in business cycles, marketing, and labor problems" (5). It poses the wrong issues and asks questions that cannot be addressed with quantitative methods. Hence, economic theory must "reformulate its problems" (6) and "change not merely its complexion, but also its content" (3).

Mitchell did not fail to allude to the physical sciences as a model for economic research. Scientific knowledge comes from the laboratory, he declared. Social statistics provide the laboratory of the economist. In physics, "we rely, and with success, upon quantitative analysis to point the way; and we advance because we are constantly improving and applying such analysis" (1919, quoted in Alchon 1985). It is obvious to us, as it was to Mitchell, that official statistical collections are not the same as laboratory results. They lack the crucial element of experimental control, which permits natural scientists to proceed not mainly by trying to describe a world that exists independently of their activity, but rather by creating a controlled microworld of artificial technologies in which their theories are valid.[39] Still, as Mary Morgan (1989) points out, econometrics succeeded in appealing to physicists, especially in the heady days of the early 1930s when the Econometric Society was founded. Nancy Cartwright (1989) has argued that inference from data by econometricians is in important ways strikingly similar to that by quantum physicists.

The ethos of neoclassical economic theory, in contrast, seems alien to that of physics, even if much of its mathematics did come from statics and thermodynamics. To be sure, physical theory too has in this century become increasingly autonomous from experiment and measurement. But to find a form of theory so detached from practice and data as is characteristic of neoclassical economics, we must look to mathematics rather than physics. Margaret Schabas (1989) points to the mathematical logic of Augustus DeMorgan and George Boole as the background to Jevons's mathematization of economics (see also Black 1973). Logic, though not yet integral to the mathematics discipline, was rapidly becoming so, as mathematics moved increasingly from realism to formalism. The incomprehension that Walras met so often reflected similar tendencies. He complained that too many readers expected mathematical economics to mean numbers and formulas, when he was using instead the theory of functions. As John Maynard Keynes remarked in 1921: "The old assumptions, that all quantity is numerical and that all quantitative characteristics are additive, can no longer be sustained. Mathematical reasoning now appears as an aid in its symbolic rather than its numerical character." And then he added, "I . . . have not the same lively hope as Condorcet, or even Edgeworth, éclairer les sciences morales et politiques par le flambeau de l'Algèbre."[40] This tendency to identify mathematics with formalism rather than formulas became all the more dominant in the 1930s and 1940s, when general equilibrium theory was established as the most prestigious research field in the economic discipline. The migration of mathematicians into economics was crucial for the establishment of this new research style (Ingrao and Israel 1990).

As Herbert Mehrtens argues, modernism in mathematics meant precisely a retreat from the world of space and time, flesh and blood. The paradise of mathematicians, identified already by Gauss in 1802, was a place in which *Geist* was no longer confined by space, nor chained to a ponderous, suffering body. David Hilbert, the Göttingen mathematician who gave modernism its authoritative formulation, was characteristically indifferent to the debate over Euclidean and non-Euclidean geometries. Geometry is not the mathematics of space; it is self-subsistent. It proceeds by positing axioms and deriving theorems, and if the results lead to no contradictions, the system is by definition mathematically true. Mathematics does not describe a world, but posits one. It is a language of symbols that refers to nothing outside itself. "The new language of mathematics does not need to be made certain in relation to an exterior reality, because it makes itself certain through its own work" (Mehrtens 1990, 68).[41]

Mehrtens explains the modernist turn in mathematics partly in terms of its professionalization, which permitted far more isolation from the problems of the sciences than had been possible previously. This disciplinary autonomy, he adds, is part of what makes mathematics exemplary for modernism generally. In economics, the mathematical turn served important defensive purposes as well. The mathematization of economics was key to its professionalization. It provided disciplinary identity and a standard of competence that discredited outsiders (Stigler 1982; see also Maloney 1985). It lifted economic discourse decisively out of the domain of public discussion, eliminating the threat that the pronouncements of economists would seem to be no more than a slightly obscure version of common sense. To the mere citizen, the obscurity of economic theory would henceforth be complete.

Wesley Mitchell was perplexed at this dedication of economists to marginal theory. Other economists, he noted, had defended economic mathematics as essential shared knowledge, which could hold the discipline together in the face of rampant specialization. But why, he asked, should economists tolerate a core of knowledge that is so useless in regard to every part of the periphery? Neoclassical theory can hardly succeed even at this when it plays so little role in any variety of economic practice (Mitchell 1925). Mitchell, though, failed to anticipate that neoclassical theory might *become* the dominant specialty, and thus, like Hilbert's mathematics, no longer depend for its perpetuation on any ability to describe the world. Further, its very dearth of content was for some purposes an advantage. One is reminded of the role of abstract art in fin-de-siècle Vienna, which the authorities approved for monumental buildings precisely because it lacked content and historical meanings. Any art with real content was unacceptably polarizing in a fractured, multinational state (Schorske 1980; Silverman 1989). Mathematical neoclassicism, while presupposing a broadly liberal individualist basis for economic order,[42] was almost neutral with respect to the narrower but more numerous issues of policy that must lead to endemic conflict in a genuinely political economy. The adoption of mathematical foundations served not only to translate emotion-charged issues into a technical language, but even more to create a basis for agreement that could be viewed as deeper than mere applications. A few splinter groups, most notably the Marxists, have refused to accept this narrowing and evasion. But from the standpoint of the dominant school, such dissenters are negligible. The abstract formalism of neoclassical mathematics has served admirably in preserving the unity of the economics discipline.

Conclusion

Mathematics is never neutral, never simply a technically superior way of accomplishing what practitioners of the social and natural disciplines are already doing. Its triumph in economics was associated with a vast change in the practices of that field. Alternative uses of mathematics and quantification have had sharply variant implications. Quantification and statistics were associated primarily with the management of economic affairs, often though not always in the public domain. Political economy was long a storehouse of arguments for not attempting to disrupt the spontaneous workings of the market. Some of the earliest mathematizers of economics, notably Whewell and Jenkin, aimed to neutralize this ideological message by showing that its arguments against public action rested on doubtful assumptions or even errors of reasoning. Mathematics has tended to render theory more nearly neutral, or at least to put more space between the economic discipline and the hubbub of political and commercial affairs.

Neoclassical theory has remained aloof not only from controverted issues, but also from the problems of practical management. For similar reasons, the pioneering mathematical economists established very little contact between neoclassical theory and statistics or measurement. Quantification and mathematization, in short, have been very much isolated from one another. Though the political conflicts between theory and practical quantification have been alleviated, differences involving aims and methods have persisted. The mathematization of theory has done nothing to harmonize it with statistical numbers. Whewell hoped that a demonstration of the irrelevance of theory would drive it from the field, leaving room for empirical and statistical study. Instead, the relative neutrality of mathematical theory has made it all the more satisfactory as a basis of professional economic discourse.

In this respect, as Donald McCloskey (1991) argues, modernist economics shares a good deal with modernist mathematics.[43] Its practitioners opened a wide rift between mathematical theory and measurement long before physicists or mathematicians could boast of anything comparable. Nineteenth-century physicists and engineers who had occasion to engage themselves with economic questions and to assess the merits of mathematical economic theory rarely saw eye to eye with the economists. Their economics tended strongly to the quantifying, managerial form. Many reacted to neoclassical theory with incomprehension. Sometimes, as in Laurent's exchange with Walras, they simply misunderstood it. When they misunderstood, though, it was in part because they had been brought up to think even less of theory without measurement than of measurement without theory.

The scientific ideal is often taken, not least by economists, as monolithic. It helps greatly to support this illusion when the broad domain of quantitative reasoning, extending from counting and measuring to mathematical deduction, is understood as a single, unified body of conceptions and techniques. The history of modern economics shows, as strikingly as any field, that this is a misconception. Imitating natural science is anything but an unproblematic endeavor.

Notes

The research for this chapter was generously supported by the Earhart Foundation, the Thomas Jefferson Memorial Foundation, and the John Simon Guggenheim Memorial Foundation. I thank Bruce Caldwell, Lorraine Daston, Neil de Marchi, and Philip Mirowski for helpful comments.

1. It is an exaggeration mainly because new historical and institutional approaches provided for several decades a strong alternative to the mathematics of the neoclassicals, in both Britain and the United States. Finally in the mid-twentieth century, these were relegated to the fringes of the discipline. See Ross (1991) and Coats (1988).

2. Gordon (1973) argues that even Marshall was unable to provide a persuasive model of a biological style of economics, though Camille Limoges and Claude Ménard, Chapter 13, this volume, show how his mechanical picture was framed by biological analogies. I have discussed in broad terms the diverse ways in which social thought has been patterned after the natural sciences in Porter (1990).

3. A phenomenon not limited to physics. A wide literature now touches on these issues from various standpoints; see Cannon (1978), Porter (1986), Smith and Wise (1989), Hacking (1990), Gooday (1990), Olesko (1991), and Wise (1994). For the eighteenth century, see Frängsmyr et al. (1990).

4. Perhaps the most extreme case of this is the reaction to Thomas Young's wave theory of light, admittedly by a liberal critic rather than a specialist in physical science: "It is difficult to argue with an author whose mind is filled with a medium of so fickle and vibratory a nature. . . . A mere theory . . . is the unmanly and unfruitful pleasure of a boyish and prurient imagination, or the gratification of a corrupted and depraved appetite" (Brougham 1803, 452).

5. See Say (1803); also Ménard (1980). Say provided an important model of systematic political economy for Ricardo and James Mill; see Halévy (1955). Henderson (1985, 407) mentions the use of a language of "disturbing causes" by classical political economists in England to fend off the statisticians.

6. The statisticians generally favored particular reforms, not systematic state intervention. See Coleman (1982) and Cullen (1975).

7. Whewell to Jones, July 23, 1831, in Todhunter (1876, 2:353). Whewell's negative intentions are also clear from two letters of 1829 to Jones, quoted in Henderson (1990, 16).

8. He investigated this conclusion mathematically, then assessed it against the empirical evidence supplied by Jones, particularly in Whewell (1862), lecture 5.

9. On Jenkin, see Wise (1994).

10. Comparative measurements of human and machine labor power go back to the beginning of the eighteenth century, especially in France; see Lindqvist (1990).

11. On Le Play's differences from the statisticians, see Hacking (1990, ch. 16).

12. There was a continuous though relatively inconspicuous tradition of energeticist economics dating from about the 1870s. For the most part it was deliberately subversive of mainstream economics. See Juan Martinez-Alier (1987).

13. This was originally published in 1887 in *Le génie civil*. For a modern discussion of this article, see Hébert (1974) and especially Desrosières (1986). By this time, graphic methods came naturally to engineers, at least in France; see Lalanne (1846).

14. See also Porter (1991).

15. For example, Coriolis (1835) and Reynaud (1842). Reynaud, however, concluded that the formulas connecting grades with costs of operation were too imperfect to be relied upon and that informal techniques of quantification were best.

16. Walras to Cournot, March 20, 1874, letter 253 in Jaffé (1965); hereafter WC.

17. Walras to Ferry, March 11, 1878, letter 403 in WC. See also letter 444 to Ferry. One must recall that Walras was looking to Ferry to find him an appointment in a French university.

18. Walras to Piccard, October 25, 1873, letter 239 in WC.

19. Walras to Jules du Mesnil-Marigny, December 23, 1862, letter 81 in WC.

20. Walras to Hirsch, January 18, 1881, letter 487 in WC.

21. Letters from Hippolyte Charlon, September 22, 1873, and to Charlon, October 15, 1873, numbers 234 and 236 in WC. On the Circle of Actuaries, see Zylberberg (1990).

22. Hippolyte Charlon to Walras, January 30, 1876, letter 347 in WC.

23. WC, vol. 3. Such dissatisfaction was not unique to Laurent. See, e.g., Geddes (1883–4, 950–63).

24. Laurent to Walras, November 29, 1898, and reply December 3, 1898, letters 1374 and 1377 in WC.

25. See three letters from Walras to Léon Marie from the end of 1899, numbers 1430, 1433, and 1434, and letter 1409 to Georges Renard, probably sent July 1899, in WC.

26. Renouvier to Walras, 18 May 1874, letter 274 in WC.

27. See, however, Schabas (1991), who argues against the identification of mathematical with professional economics.

28. Poincaré to Walras, 1901, letter 1496 in WC.

29. The best study of the reaction of mathematicians to Walras and to mathematical economics is Ingrao and Israel (1990). Central to their account is the skepticism of mathematicians and physicists because of doubts about economic mathematics unsupported by measurement.

30. See the important new work by Alborn (1991) and Klein (in press).

31. Hutchison (1969) remarks that, increasingly after 1870, economists' policy recommendations had at most a tenuous base in systematic theory. This is not to say that they were purely empirical. Certainly economists valued, for example, the keen awareness of unintended consequences taught by Adam Smith.
32. For a fuller discussion of the relations between utility and demand in Jevons's work, see Bostaph and Shieh (1987).
33. Maloney (1985) calls Jevons a "polymathic specialist."
34. Numerous remarks by Marshall on the dangers of excessive mathematization, the need for economic biology, and the like can be found in Pigou (1925). See also Marshall (1920).
35. Coats (1967, 713), quoting from a letter by Marshall to J. N. Keynes.
36. Hutchison (1953, 91) remarks that when dealing with policy questions, Marshall relied not on mathematical solutions to maximization problems, but on detailed factual study.
37. There is now a wide literature on measurement in nineteenth-century physics. Here I am relying mainly on Smith and Wise (1989). See also Hunt (1987).
38. I thank Mary Morgan for calling my attention to this article. Neoclassical theory may still be less important for economic applications than is, e.g., mathematical statistics. Tribe (1991).
39. See Hacking (1983); also Latour (1987), who points out that results of the laboratory do not remain confined to a microworld, but instead spread out along networks and remake the larger world. I have discussed the problem of networks and standardization in relation to statistics and the applied social sciences (Porter 1992a; see also 1992b).
40. (To illuminate the moral and political sciences with the lamp of algebra.) From the *Treatise on Probability,* quoted in Skidelsky (1983, 223).
41. My discussion draws on my review of Mehrtens (1990) in Porter (1992c).
42. The political consequences of these presuppositions of economic analysis are emphasized by Martin (1978).
43. The similarity of economics to mathematics has also been argued by Rosenberg (1992, ch. 8).

References

Alborn, Timothy. 1991. *The Other Economists: Science and Commercial Culture in Victorian England.* Ph.D. dissertation, Harvard University.

Alchon, Guy. 1985. *The Invisible Hand of Planning: Capitalism, Social Science, and the State in the 1920s.* Princeton, NJ: Princeton University Press.

Babbage, Charles. 1833. *On the Economy of Machinery and Manufactures,* 3d ed. London: Charles Knight.

Berg, Maxine. 1980. *The Machinery Question and the Making of Political Economy, 1815–1848.* Cambridge University Press.

Bertrand, Joseph. 1883. "Théorie des richesses," *Journal des savants* (September):499–508.

Black, R. D. Collison, 1973. "W. S. Jevons and the Foundation of Modern Economics," in R. D. Collison Black, A. W. Coats, and Craufurd D. W. Goodwin, eds., *The Marginal Revolution in Economics*, 98–112. Durham, NC: Duke University Press.

Bostaph, Samuel, and Yeung-Nan Shieh, 1987. "Jevons's Demand Curve," *History of Political Economy* 19:107–26.

Brougham, Henry. 1803. "Bakerian Lecture on Light and Colors," *Edinburgh Review*, 1:450–6.

Cannon, Susan Faye. 1978. "Humboldtian Science," in *Science and Culture: The Early Victorian Period*, 73–110. New York: Science History Publications.

Cartwright, Nancy. 1989. *Nature's Capacities and Their Measurement*. Oxford University Press.

Cheysson, Emile. 1911a. "La statistique géometrique," in *Oeuvres choisies*, 1:185–218. Paris: Rousseau. Originally published in 1887 in *Le génie civil*.

Cheysson, Emile. 1911b. "Le cadre, l'objet et la méthode de l'économie politique," in *Oeuvres choisies*, 2:37–66. Paris: Rousseau.

Coats, A. W. 1967. "Sociological Aspects of British Economic Thought (ca. 1880–1930)," *Journal of Political Economy*, 75:706–29.

Coats, A. W. 1988. "The Educational Revolution and the Professionalization of American Economics," in William J. Barber, ed., *Breaking the Academic Mould*, 340–75. Middletown, CN: Wesleyan University Press.

Coleman, William. 1982. *Death Is a Social Disease: Public Health and Political Economy in Early Industrial France*. Madison: University of Wisconsin Press.

Colson, Clément-Léon. 1907. *Cours d'économie politique, professé à l'École Nationale des Ponts et Chaussées*, 2d. ed., vol. 1, *Théorie générale des phénomènes économiques*. Paris: Gauthier-Villars & Felix Alcan.

Coriolis, G. 1835. "Premiers résultats de quelques experiences comparative de differentes natures de grés employés au pavage . . . ," *Annales des Ponts et Chaussées: Mémoires*, 7:236–40.

Cournot, A. A. 1838. *Recherches sur les principes mathématiques de la théorie des richesses*. Paris.

Cournot, A. A. 1843. *Exposition de la théorie des chances et des probabilités*. Paris.

Cullen, Michael. 1975. *The Statistical Movement in Early Victorian Britain: The Foundations of Empirical Social Research*. Hassocks: Harvester.

de Marchi, N. B. 1974. "The Success of Mill's *Principles*," *History of Political Economy*, 6:119–57.

de Marchi, N. B., and R. P. Sturges. 1973. "Malthus and Ricardo's Inductivist Critics: Four Letters to William Whewell," *Economica*, 40 (November):379–93.

Desrosières, Alain. 1986. "L'ingénieur d'état et le père de famille: Emile Cheysson et la statistique," *Annales des mines: Série gérer et comprendre*, (March):66–80.

Dhombres, Jean. 1987. "L'École Polytechnique et ses historiens," Introduction to A. Fourcy, *Histoire de l'École Polytechnique*. Reprinted Paris: Belin.

Divisia, F. 1951. *Exposés d'économique: L'apport des ingénieurs français aux sciences économiques.* Paris: Dunod.

Dumez, Hervé. 1985. *L'économiste, la science, et le pouvoir: Le cas Walras.* Paris: Presses Universitaires de France.

Dupuit, Jules. 1842. "Sur les frais d'entretien des routes," *Annales des Ponts et Chaussées: Mémoires,* 3:1–90.

Dupuit, Jules. 1844. "De la mésure de l'utilité des travaux publics," *Annales des Ponts et Chaussées, Mémoires,* 8:332–75. Translated in 1952 in *International Economic Papers* 2:83–110.

Ekelund, Robert B., and Robert F. Hébert. 1978. "French Engineers, Welfare Economics, and Public Finance in the Nineteenth Century," *History of Political Economy,* 10:636–68.

Elwitt, Sanford. 1986. *The Third Republic Defended: Bourgeois Reform in France, 1880–1914.* Baton Rouge: Louisiana State University Press.

Etner, François. 1987. *Histoire du calcul économique en France.* Paris: Economica.

Fox, Robert. 1986. Introduction to Sadi Carnot, *Reflections on the Motive Power of Fire,* 1–57. Manchester: Manchester University Press.

Foxwell, H. S. 1886–7. "The Economic Movement in England," *Quarterly Journal of Economics,* 1:84–103.

Frängsmyr, Tore, John Heilbron, and Robin Rider, eds., 1990. *The Quantifying Spirit in the Eighteenth Century.* Berkeley: University of California Press.

Geddes, Patrick. 1883–4. "An Analysis of the Principles of Economics," *Proceedings of the Royal Soceity of Edinburgh,* 12:943–80.

Goldman, Lawrence. 1983. "The Origins of British 'Social Science': Political Economy, Natural Science, and Statistics," *Historical Journal,* 26:587–616.

Gooday, Graeme. 1990. "Precision Measurement and the Genesis of Physics Teaching Laboratories in Victorian Britain," *British Journal for the History of Science,* 23:25–51.

Gordon, H. Scott. 1973. "Alfred Marshall and the Development of Economics as a Science," in Ronald N. Giere and Richard S. Westfall, eds., *Foundations of Scientific Method: The Nineteenth Century,* 234–58. Bloomington: Indiana University Press.

Grattan-Guinness, Ivor. 1984. "Work for the Workers: Advances in Engineering Mechanics and Instruction in France, 1800–1930," *Annals of Science,* 41:1–33.

Grattan-Guinness, Ivor. 1990. *Convolutions in French Mathematics,* 3 vols. Basel: Birkhäuser.

Hacking, Ian. 1983. *Representing and Intervening.* Cambridge University Press.

Hacking, Ian. 1990. *The Taming of Chance.* Cambridge University Press.

Halévy, Elie. 1955. *The Growth of Philosophic Radicalism,* Mary Morris, trans. Boston: Beacon.

Hébert, Robert F. 1974. "The Theory of Input Selection and Supply Areas in 1887: Emile Cheysson," *History of Political Economy,* 6:109–13.

Henderson, James P. 1985. "The Whewell Group of Mathematical Economists," *Manchester School,* 53:404–31.

Henderson, James P. 1990. "Induction, Deduction and the Role of Mathematics: The Whewell Group vs. the Ricardian Economists," *Research in the History of Economic Thought and Methodology*, 7:1–36.

Hollander, Samuel. 1983. "William Whewell and John Stuart Mill on the Methodology of Political Economy," *Studies in the History and Philosophy of Science*, 14:127–68.

Howey, R.S. 1960. *The Rise of the Marginal Utility School, 1870–1889.* Lawrence: University of Kansas Press.

Hunt, Bruce J. 1987. " 'How My Model Was Right': G. F. FitzGerald and the Reform of Maxwell's Theory," in Robert Kargon and Peter Achinstein, eds., *Kelvin's Baltimore Lectures and Modern Theoretical Physics*, 299–321. Cambridge, MA: MIT Press.

Hutchison, Terence W. 1953. *A Review of Economic Doctrines, 1870–1929.* Oxford University Press.

Hutchison, Terence W. 1969. "Economists and Economic Policy in Britain After 1870," *History of Political Economy*, 1:231–55.

Ingrao, Bruna, and Giorgio Israel. 1990. *The Invisible Hand: Economic Equilibrium in the History of Science*, trans. Ian McGilvray. Cambridge, MA: MIT Press.

Jaffé, William, ed. 1965. *Correspondence of Léon Walras and Related Papers*, 3 vols. Amsterdam: North Holland.

Jenkin, Fleeming. 1868. "Trade Unions: How Far Legitimate?" in Jenkin (1887, 2:1–75).

Jenkin, Fleeming. 1870. "The Graphic Representation of the Laws of Supply and Demand, and Their Applications to Labour," in Jenkin (1887, 2:76–106).

Jenkin, Fleeming. 1871–2. "On the Principles Which Regulate the Incidence of Taxes," in Jenkin (1887, 2:107–21).

Jenkin, Fleeming. 1887. *Papers, Literary, Scientific &c.*, 2 vols., ed. Sidney Calvin and J. A. Ewing. London: Longman, Green.

Jevons, William Stanley. 1957. *Theory of Political Economy*, 5th ed. London: Macmillan.

Jungnickel, Christa, and Russell McCormmach. 1986. *Intellectual Mastery of Nature: Theoretical Physics From Ohm to Einstein*, 2 vols. Chicago: University of Chicago Press.

Kadish, Alon. 1982. *The Oxford Economists in the Late Nineteenth Century.* Oxford University Press.

Kingsland, Sharon. 1985. *Modeling Nature: Episodes in the History of Population Ecology.* Chicago: University of Chicago Press.

Klein, Judy L. In press. *Time and the Science of Means: The Statistical Analysis of Changing Phenomena, 1830–1940.* Cambridge University Press.

Knapp, Georg Friedrich. 1865. *Zur Prüfung der Untersuchungen Thünens über Lohn und Zinsfuss im isolierten Staate.* Braunschweig: F. Vieweg.

Knapp, Georg Friedrich. 1927. *Aus der Jugend eines deutschen Gelehrten.* Stuttgart: Deutsche Verlag.

Koot, Gerard M. 1987. *English Historical Economics, 1870–1926: The Rise of Economic History and Neo-Mercantilism.* Cambridge University Press.

Lalanne, Léon. 1846. "Sur les tables graphiques et sur la géometrie anamorphique appliquée à diverses questions qui se rattachent à l'art de l'ingénieur," *Annales des Ponts et Chaussées, Mémoires,* [2]:11.

Latour, Bruno. 1987. *Science in Action.* Cambridge, MA: Harvard University Press.

Laurent, Hermann. 1902. *Petit traité d'économie politique, rédigé conformément aux préceptes de l'école de Lausanne.* Paris: Charles Schmid.

Laurent, Hermann. 1908. *Statistique mathématique.* Paris: Octave Doin.

Lexis, Wilhelm. 1881. "Zur mathematisch-ökonomischen Literatur," *Jahrbücher für Nationalökonomie und Statistik,* N.F. 3:427–34.

Lindqvist, Svante. 1990. "Labs in the Woods: The Quantification of Technology During the Late Enlightenment," in Tore Frängsmyr, John Heilbron, and Robin Rider, eds., *The Quantifying Spirit in the Eighteenth Century,* 291–314. Berkeley: University of California Press.

Maloney, John. 1985. *Marshall, Orthodoxy, and the Professionalisation of Economics.* Cambridge University Press.

Marshall, Alfred. 1920/1938. *Principles of Economics,* 8th ed. London: Macmillan.

Marshall, Alfred. 1926. *Official Papers.* London: Macmillan.

Martin, Brian. 1978. "The Selective Usefulness of Game Theory," *Social Studies of Science,* 8:85–110.

Martinez-Alier, Juan. 1987. *Ecological Economics.* New York: Basil Blackwell.

McCloskey, Donald. 1991. "Economics Science: A Search Through the Hyperspace of Assumptions," *Methodus,* 3:6–16.

Mehrtens, Herbert. 1990. *Moderne – Sprache – Mathematik: Eine Geschichte des Streits um die Grundlagen der Disziplin und des Subjects formaler Systeme.* Frankfurt: Suhrkamp Verlag.

Ménard, Claude. 1978. *La formation d'une rationalité économique: A. A. Cournot,* Paris: Flammarion.

Ménard, Claude. 1980. "Three Forms of Resistance to Statistics: Say, Cournot, Walras," *History of Political Economy,* 12:524–41.

Mirowski, Philip. 1989. *More Heat Than Light: Economics as Social Physics, Physics as Nature's Economics.* Cambridge University Press.

Mirowski, Philip, and Pamela Cook. 1990. " 'Economics and Mechanics': Translation, Commentary, Context," in Warren Samuels, ed., *Economics as Discourse: An Analysis of the Language of Economists,* 206–13. Boston: Kluwer.

Mitchell, Wesley. 1919. "Statistics and Government," *Journal of the American Statistical Association,* 16:223–36.

Mitchell, Wesley. 1925. "Quantitative Analysis in Economic Theory," *American Economic Review,* 15:1–12.

Morgan, Mary. 1989. *The History of Econometric Ideas.* Cambridge University Press.

Moyer, Albert E. 1992. *A Scientist's Voice in American Culture: Simon Newcomb and the Rhetoric of Scientific Method.* Berkeley: University of California Press.

Newcomb, Simon. 1885. *Principles of Political Economy.* New York.

Olesko, Kathryn M. 1991. *Physics as a Calling: Discipline and Practice in the Königsberg Seminar for Physics.* Ithaca, NY: Cornell University Press.

Pigou, A. C., ed. 1925. *Memorials of Alfred Marshall.* London: Macmillan.

Porter, Theodore M. 1985. "The Mathematics of Society: Error and Variation in Quetelet's Statistics," *British Journal for the History of Science,* 18:51–69.

Porter, Theodore M. 1986. *The Rise of Statistical Thinking.* Princeton, NJ: Princeton University Press.

Porter, Theodore M. 1987. "Lawless Society: Social Science and the Reinterpretation of Statistics in Germany, 1850–1880," in Lorenz Krüger, Lorraine Daston, and Michael Heidelberger, eds., *The Probabilistic Revolution,* vol. 1: *Ideas in History,* 351–75. Cambridge, MA: MIT Press.

Porter, Theodore M. 1990. "Natural Science and Social Theory," in R. C. Olby et al., eds., *Companion to the History of Modern Science,* 1024–43. London: Routledge.

Porter, Theodore M. 1991. "Objectivity and Authority: How French Engineers Reduced Public Utility to Numbers," *Poetics Today,* 12:245–65.

Porter, Theodore M. 1992a. "Objectivity as Standardization: The Rhetoric of Impersonality in Measurement, Statistics, and Cost-Benefit Analysis," in Allan Megill, ed. "Rethinking Objectivity," *Annals of Scholarship,* 9:19–59.

Porter, Theodore M. 1992b. "Quantification and the Accounting Ideal in Science," *Social Studies of Science,* 22:633–652.

Porter, Theodore M. 1992c. "Review of Herbert Mehrtens, *Moderne – Sprache – Mathematik.*" *American Historical Review,* 97:157–158.

Reynaud, Léonce. 1842. "Tracé des routes et des chemins de fer," *Annales des Ponts et Chaussées: Mémoires,* 2(2):76–113.

Rosenberg, Alexander. 1992. *Economics: Mathematical Politics or Science of Diminishing Returns?* Chicago: University of Chicago Press.

Ross, Dorothy. 1991. *The Origins of American Social Science.* Cambridge University Press.

Say, Jean-Baptiste. 1803. *Traité d'économie politique.* 2 vols. Paris: Discours préliminaire.

Schabas, Margaret. 1989. *A World Ruled by Number: William Stanley Jevons and the Rise of Mathematical Economics.* Princeton, NJ: Princeton University Press.

Schabas, Margaret. 1991. "Mathematics and the Economics Profession in Late Victorian England," in Joanne Brown and David van Keuren, eds., *The Estate of Social Knowledge,* 67–83. Baltimore: Johns Hopkins University Press.

Schorske, Carl. 1980. *Fin-de-Siècle Vienna: Politics and Culture.* New York: Knopf.

Silverman, Debora L. 1989. *Art Nouveau in Fin-de-Siècle Paris: Politics, Psychology, and Style.* Berkeley: University of California Press.

Skidelsky, Robert. 1983. *John Maynard Keynes: Hopes Betrayed, 1883–1920.* New York: Viking Penguin.

Smith, Cecil O. 1990. "The Longest Run: Public Engineers and Planning in France," *American Historical Review,* 95:657–692.

Smith, Crosbie, and M. Norton Wise. 1989. *Energy and Empire: A Biographical Study of Lord Kelvin.* Cambridge University Press.

Stevenson, Robert Louis. 1887. "Memoir of Fleeming Jenkin," in Jenkin (1887, vol. 1).

Stigler, George. 1982. "The Adoption of the Marginal Utility Theory," in *The Economist as Preacher and Other Essays,* 72–85. Chicago: University of Chicago Press.

Todhunter, Isaac, ed., 1876. *William Whewell, D. D.: An Account of His Writings,* London: Macmillan.

Tribe, Keith. 1991. "The Economic Metric," *Economy and Society,* 20:411–22.

Whewell, William. 1829. "Mathematical Exposition of Some Doctrines of Political Economy." Reprinted 1971 as Whewell, *Mathematical Exposition of Some Doctrines of Political Economy.* New York: Kelley.

Whewell, William. 1831. Review of Richard Jones, *An Essay on the Distribution of Wealth and on the Sources of Taxation,* British Critic, 10:41–61.

Whewell, William. 1835. In cahier 2644, Quetelet Papers, letter to Adolphe Quetelet. Brussels.

Whewell, William. 1859. "Prefatory Notice," in Whewell, ed., *Literary Remains Consisting of Lectures and Tracts on Political Economy of the Late Richard Jones.* London: Murray.

Whewell, William. 1860. *On the Philosophy of Discovery.* Reprinted 1871, New York: Burt Franklin.

Whewell, William. 1862. *Six Lectures on Political Economy.* Cambridge University Press.

Winch, Donald. 1990. "Economic Knowledge and Government in Britain: Some Historical and Comparative Reflections," in Mary O. Furner and Barry Supple, eds., *The State and Economic Knowledge: The American and British Experiences,* 40–70. Cambridge University Press.

Wise, M. Norton. 1987. "How Do Sums Count: On the Cultural Origins of Statistical Causality," in Lorenz Krüger, Lorraine Daston, and Michael Heidelberger, eds., *The Probabilistic Revolution,* vol. 1: *Ideas in History,* 395–425. Cambridge, MA: MIT Press.

Wise, M. Norton. 1989–90. "Work and Waste: Political Economy and Natural Philosophy in Nineteenth-Century Britain," *History of Science,* 27:263–317, 391–449; 28:221–61.

Wise, M. Norton. ed. 1994. *The Values of Precision.* Princeton, NJ: Princeton University Press.

Wise, M. Norton, and Crosbie Smith. 1987. "The Practical Imperative: Kelvin Challenges the Maxwellians," in Robert Kargon and Peter Achinstein, eds., *Kelvin's Baltimore Lectures and Modern Theoretical Physics,* 324–48. Cambridge, MA: MIT Press.

Zylberberg, André. 1990. *L'économie mathématique en France, 1870–1914.* Paris: Economica.

PART III

Uneasy boundaries between man and machine

Economic man, economic machine: images of circulation in the Victorian money market

TIMOTHY L. ALBORN

Introduction

The centrality of the healthy body to nineteenth-century social discourse has recently received much scrutiny from people working in a whole range of disciplines (see Coleman 1982; Gallagher 1986; Haley 1978; Mirowski 1989). A common focus has been the rise of public health movements in England, France, and the United States, the leaders of which conceptualized society as a corporate body in danger of contamination from its unhealthy individual members. Catherine Gallagher, for instance, takes the case of the English reformer Henry Mayhew, who suspected urban nomads of physically and morally polluting the vulnerable producing classes; she isolates a passage from Mayhew's *London Labour and the London Poor,* where he identifies "the pickpockets – the beggars – the prostitutes – the street-sellers . . . – the sailors and such like," who "prey upon the earnings of the more industrious portions of the community." Besides accusing this class of numerous forms of moral depravity, Mayhew medically diagnosed them as suffering "a greater determination of blood to the surface of the body, and consequently a less quantity sent to the brain, the muscles being thus nourished at the expense of the mind" (quoted in Gallagher 1986, 90). Such suspicions established the circulatory system – physical as well as economic – to be at once vital and menacing to the well-being of Victorian society. By circulating the products of capitalism, Mayhew's nomads performed an essential role in the marketplace: So no matter how much he feared their ascendence, he could not wholly reject them without rejecting the marketplace itself.

Gallagher uses Mayhew's fears as a means of setting body language in the context of the industrial transformation of English society:

173

from the pastoral setting of the eighteenth century, when the circuit between production and consumption could still be imagined (and was, by Malthus) as taking place within the same household, to the mid-nineteenth century, when functions of production and exchange were carried out by different members of society. This change in social structure redefined the problem of the body in Victorian social criticism, from the Malthusian threat of individually healthy bodies threatening to swamp the nation with overpopulation, to the nearly reverse threat of a healthy corporate body being contaminated by its members. Gallagher appeals to Mayhew, she writes, to help her "understand the revisions leading to that peculiar Victorian discourse in which loathing 'mere life' and obsessively examining it are parts of one impulse" (1986, 104). At the same time, Mayhew's contradictory image of circulation appears as the self-indictment of a social critic whose attachment to capitalism prevents him from reaching a satisfactory solution to the problem of corporate contamination. The same strategy is at work in William Coleman's study of the nineteenth-century French hygienist Louis Villermé, which reiterates that a body-centered social criticism wedded to capitalist ideology was a dead-end proposition (1982, xviii–xix, 277–306).

The cultural power and political dilemmas inherent in nineteenth-century circulatory language were not restricted to their appearance in debates over public health. The Victorian money market is another obvious place to look for problematic images of circulation. Coins and bank notes circulated during much of the early nineteenth century in more or less healthy doses, and contemporary observers seldom missed an opportunity to compare the motion with the life-giving circulation going on in the human body. Since most work in monetary history has tended to be informed by present-day concerns about economic thought and policy, however, the cultural meanings of circulation in this context have largely been overlooked.[1] This is a mistake, both from the perspective of the cultural historian and of the economist. The cultural historian can learn much by extending valuable observations about language's social role into previously underexplored regions. The economist can learn much, in turn, about how ideas and practice interact by observing the important role of language in conditioning the direction of a debate.

Upon investigation, circulation in the Victorian money market turns out to be rife with the same contradictions that make it at once so interesting and problematic for historians of public health. Bank notes, every bit as much as Mayhew's urban nomads, were viewed to be simultaneously necessary and threatening to the British economy.

By economizing coin, bank notes facilitated a hitherto unimaginable volume of fiscal and commercial undertakings: from creating and funding England's national debt to assisting domestic trade. But by replacing the tangible commodities of gold and silver with the more flimsy promise of a financier's good word, bank notes also suggested dangerous levels of risk. Adam Smith captured this tension, although he could not have anticipated its full importance, in Book 2 of the *Wealth of Nations* when he had recourse to the "violent metaphor" of a "waggon-way through the air" to describe the "judicious operations of banking."[2] Smith's suggestion was that bank notes were economically beneficial since they freed exchange from the constraints of metallic currency but were also potentially dangerous, since they suspended commerce "upon the Daedalian wings of paper money" rather than allowing it to "travel about upon the solid ground of gold and silver" (1776/1979). His metaphor was violent because he feared the threat paper money posed to the slower-paced "natural" economic order, but his commitment to growth pushed him at the same time to call a well-organized banking system judicious. Nineteenth-century economists introduced less violent (and less curious) metaphors to describe note circulation, but they could not undo its problematic relation to the natural language of laissez-faire.

The case of the money market hence offers a new point of confirmation in a gathering supply of evidence about the problematic location of circulation in Victorian culture. In addition, studying circulatory language in the Victorian money market has the potential of answering two vital historical questions left mainly unresolved by writers like Gallagher and Coleman. The first question concerns the social power of the analogy itself: Given the contradictions, how did circulatory images not only survive in Victorian discourse, but flourish? The second question concerns the changing social context that the analogy occupied: What happened to the role of circulatory language after the transition to the modern British economy was complete? Most studies of circulation in public health have succeeded only in pinning the cultural problem of contradictory language to the economic context of industrialization, without waiting around to see what transpired once the economy had reached maturity. In the realms of public health and social welfare, for instance, the mature economy produced a new set of concerns relating more to stagnation and the "underclass" than to Mayhew's circulatory obsessions. Similar transitions are apparent in the money market, and it is useful to ask how these changes were registered in the contemporary language community.

In this chapter I offer some general (and necessarily schematic) suggestions to sort out the issues raised by these two questions, followed by a more specific case study involving circulatory images in the Victorian money market. The first question can best be addressed by observing the *imprecision* of circulation when used as a Victorian analogy. Although eighteenth-century circulatory analogies mainly linked events to the "natural" function of circulating blood, by the nineteenth century the analogy might refer to mechanical functions as well. Steam circulated through an engine in the same manner as blood through a human body, and the result was that when a third object metaphorically "circulated," the precise connotation was open to interpretation. I propose that this dual potential of circulatory language appeared in a specific social and political context: namely, the ambiguous overlapping in Victorian society between centralized economic administration (signifiable by the "machine" interpretation of circulation) and laissez-faire naturalism (signifiable by the "body" interpretation). Advocates of either version of economic agency could refer to circulation as a defense of their own position, a critique of their opponents' stance, or both at once, as called for by the occasion. Circulation's imprecision as an analogy, in other words, rendered it especially well suited to the transitional nature of the early Victorian economy.

Circulation's imprecision was not, however, as suitable to the late-nineteenth-century British economy, when capitalists had come closer to agreeing where to draw the line between central administration and laissez-faire. Certain "mechanical" features of the economy, such as railway monopolies and an intricate credit structure, had by this time proven their utility beyond much debate. In the process, specific limits to the "natural" laws of laissez-faire became firmly established through the authority of Mill's *Principles* and a series of legislative acts. Circulatory images remained available as component parts of economic discourse, to the very large extent that people and things continued to circulate: Late-nineteenth-century tradesmen still transported goods from producer to consumer, and bank notes still made the circuit from cashier to wage earner and back. But economists, by and large, now looked elsewhere for their images. They were increasingly content to accept existing economic conditions as their starting point, rather than using their discourse to negotiate the proper mixture of intervention and individualism, and they reached for a new set of natural images to describe the more restricted problems that now sparked their interest.[3] Debate in the mature economy had shifted to a new point, where talk of circulation was no longer capable of carrying the argument forward.

In this case study of the Victorian money market, I will attach these general reflections about language to specific actors and interests.

The only way to analyze the cultural significance of language, in the money market elsewhere, is to locate and evaluate the people who employed it. In this case, two groups of people were mainly active in appealing to different images of circulation: private and joint-stock bankers. In the 1830s the latter group presented their institutions as strong and efficient machines, which were more suitable than individual private bankers for circulating currency in the new conditions of industrial England. Rather than convincing the public that they were saviors, however, joint-stock banks came to occupy the same paradoxical location in social discourse as Mayhew's street seller. Banks with large capitals did signify physical strength in circulating currency through the Victorian money market, but their very strength also signified danger. Larger banks held the potential of more disastrous bank runs, and the unprecedented scale of such enterprises threatened to diminish individual moral responsibility over the economy. They paralleled the social critic's suspicion that muscularity and rapid circulation were being exerted at the expense of moral and mental supervision. The fate of the joint-stock bank took a turn for the better only when circulating currency became subsumed by more centralized banking techniques on a macroeconomic scale, relying on *non*circulating checks and other bookkeeping expedients. With this transition, new physical analogies (in this case between the money market and the nervous system) gradually replaced popular fears about circulation as commercial bankers discovered a less problematic language to accompany their increasingly influential role as overseers of the English economy. In the final section of this chapter, I examine the transformed language of the late Victorian money market, by focusing on the efforts of Walter Bagehot to teach his fellow bankers how to move beyond the controversial image of circulation.

Language that circulated: body, machine, and nature

Circulatory language flourished in Victorian England because it provided a common reference point for two divergent contemporary themes: the self-sufficiency of a "natural economy" to regulate commerce, and humanity's mechanical dominion over nature. The first appeal to circulation, to a self-regulating economy, dated back to the eighteenth-century context of Adam Smith. Here the circulating image was blood, and Smith's moral was to let the economy (or human body) function free from outside interference. The second, more recent, appeal referred to any number of human-controlled circulatory mechanisms, of which the steam engine was the most common.

Here the moral was to utilize human ingenuity to supplement the "natural" workings of the economy. Although these two variant appeals to circulation would ultimately come into conflict in different ways, they were not necessarily antagonistic. As long as the parties who exercised dominion over nature were individual enterpreneurs, their activities did not inherently contradict Smith's model of an "invisible hand" that guided the actions of autonomous economic agents. Individuals could manipulate nature via mechanical circulatory agents without impeding their own (or others') free circulation in the economy, or at least so Smith argued. It was only with the advent of large-scale machinery, requiring new forms of cooperation among economic agents, that the mechanical uses of circulatory language came into conflict with its body-centered uses. In this new context, supplementing nature also implied supplementing the natural metaphor of economic individualism with "mechanical" powers like central administration and joint-stock financing.

Adam Smith's economic image of circulation, referring to the body-centered analogy of a self-regulating economy, appeared in the eighteenth century amid a number of other similarly "natural" circulatory languages. Different appeals to circulatory images informed several competing economic discourses including physiocracy, mercantilism, Smith's logic of free trade, and Malthusian agrarianism. What distinguished such appeals from each other was the specific type of circuit implied by the common analogy, which in turn corresponded with different respective proposals for state intervention. For the physiocrats, the only circuit worth discussing was that connecting agricultural production and capital expenditure. In their system circulation was literally as well as figuratively a natural phenomenon, since they sought the origin of the circulatory process in the natural augmentation of wealth from the productive powers of the soil. Industrial expenditure was unnaturally "sterile" for the physiocrats precisely because it existed outside this circuit. Mercantilists, in contrast, ignored the origins of economic circulation and focused on the process by which goods traversed trade circuits between countries. Pressed by the political incentive to outcompete national rivals, they presented as only figuratively "natural" whatever circulation of goods was needed for augmenting domestic trade, without tracing their country's prosperity back to the *primum mobile* of universal economic production (Tribe 1978; see also Appleby 1978).

The physiocratic and mercantilist appeals to circulation accompanied specific proposals for the role of the state in regulating the production and flow of goods. Physiocrats argued for state support of

efficient agricultural techniques in order to assist national food production and discouraged industrial undertakings as subtracting from
the state's net gain. Mercantilists favored protection of domestic ex-
ports in order to ensure a productive circuit of incoming monetary
wealth. Between these two schools of thought, Adam Smith inter-
vened with his famous arguments in favor of the division of labor and
universal free trade. He used circulatory language in this context
mainly to disabuse his opponents of their alleged errors. The physiocrats were mistaken, he argued, because they had neglected the role
of labor in adding value to goods. Apart from this correction, he
allowed the circulatory language of Quesnay's *Tableau* to stand more
or less intact: inasmuch as he located the origin of circulating wealth
in the produce of land, to be enhanced but never created ex nihilo by
the division of labor. Smith performed more radical surgery on the
circulatory language of the mercantilists, on whose colonial policies he
blamed "many dangerous disorders." He compared the protected
eighteenth-century trade route between England and the United
States to a "great blood-vessel, which has been artificially swelled beyond its natural dimensions, and through which an unnatural proportion of the industry and commerce of the country has been forced to
circulate"; and he feared the imminent stoppage of the vessel that was
soon to accompany the American Revolution (Smith 1776/1979).[4]

   Although Smith never expressly commited himself to circulation as
an organizing metaphor in the fashion of the physiocrats and mercantilists, his criticisms of those two schools implied an alternative model
of the economy as a healthy body with blood flowing freely and
equally through all its veins. This implicit image was rhetorically successful, in that it allowed Smith to depict his foes as meddling quacks
whose "artificial" intervention went against God and nature. When he
turned from his critical use of circulatory language to a more constructive model of economic activity, however, his commitment to a freely
circulating market became problematic. The chief difficulty here was
Smith's insistence that the division of labor was the main mechanism
by which circulating goods gained in value. At the same time, he
needed to embed that mechanism in his more general story about a
freely circulating commodity market in order to defend laissez-faire
as the surest path to growth. He attempted to do exactly that by
presenting the division of labor as "not originally the effect of any
human wisdom" (Smith 1776/1979, 25). But this presentation was
undercut by his own observations that capitalists had an unhealthy
tendency to form monopolies and to stultify the human cogs who
worked their machinery. As a result, he found it necessary to conclude

The Wealth of Nations by returning to the statesman as ultimately responsible for making sure the economy did in fact freely circulate, in the dual sense of individual competition and a socially mobile labor force (Tribe 1978, 106–9).

Smith's second thoughts about the self-sufficiency of a freely circulating economy received devastating confirmation in the writings of Malthus and his successors. Malthus's introduction of the population principle added new and problematic meaning to the circulatory metaphor. Now, a healthy circulation of goods, in Smith's sense of the term, might actually be harmful to the system as a whole, if this circulation induced consumers to reproduce beyond their means. As Malthus originally proposed this quandary, he took its moral to mean that it was necessary to narrow the circuit between production and consumption as tightly as possible, in order to keep people aware of the looming limit of overpopulation (Gallagher 1986). Later in life, he came closer to facing the facts of economic growth. By the fifth edition of the *Essay on the Principle of Population* (1817), he revised consumption to include desire for luxury goods as well as the purely biological desire for nourishment, and as early as 1806 he was willing to include "a taste for the conveniences and comforts of life" as a primary condition for postponing the positive checks of pestilence and war (see Gilbert 1980). These changes reextended the acceptable circuit of goods back toward Smith's vision of commercial society, but they also reintroduced Smith's problem of embedding industrial production in a body-centered metaphor. Malthus, and successors like Thomas Chalmers, appealed to the new concept of moral restraint to keep business activity within the "natural" circuit imposed by the population principle. But as Boyd Hilton has observed in his study of Christian political economy, the introduction of restraint as a mediator in a natural circulatory system necessarily invoked an arbitrary distinction between "healthy" and "unhealthy" commercial activities: "Risk being inseparable from profit, the line between fair trade and foul is impossible to draw" (1988, 121–2). The Malthusians essentially found themselves back in Smith's quandary, of proposing a "natural" economic system that required an external statesman to dictate what constituted sufficiently natural behavior.

As Malthus and Chalmers were busy drawing lines between restraint and excess, the "machinery question" of the 1820s and 1830s was in the process of first displacing the body in circulatory language, then ultimately offering a way to combine machinery and body in the problematic but temporarily effective manner that would come to define Victorian social reform. Writers like Charles Babbage and Andrew Ure, as well as complicitous economists like J. R. McCulloch, obsessively appealed to the machine as a way out of the Malthusian problem of a healthy body leading to an unhealthy society. Their defense of machinery rested on three related arguments. First, machines would massively extend the productive capacity of the English people, allowing them to keep ahead of the population race indefinitely. Second, if workers were busy making new machines they would have less time to make babies. And finally, at the most basic level, machines literally replaced bodies in the production of wealth (see Berg 1980). People like Babbage celebrated machines in the context of an overdetermined Puritan fantasy about mechanical labor. While factories provided humanity with a consumer's paradise of new products, according to this story, they also reduced the sinful penchant for overconsumption by subordinating human desire to rigid principles of engineering. Railways, for instance, which were routinely praised for opening up vast new markets in remote regions of England, were simultaneously lauded for "introducing their rigid mechanism into the habits of the people" by means of time tables (Anon. 1851).

But such writers soon discovered that machines, once they had entered the marketplace, created as many problems as they had solved, not the least of which being the dilemma of what to do with all the labor that had been displaced. Although machinery advocates argued that technological unemployment was only a temporary drawback to economic growth, social critics persistently reminded them of the increase in crime, disease, and poverty that had followed in the wake of industrialization. Such critics, representing camps as diverse as Tory paternalists and Luddites, presented machinery as "unnatural" and argued that the attempt to square Smith's laissez-faire naturalism with the new machinery had been a failure: Bodies and machines, they implied, simply did not mix. Proponents of growth retaliated by installing a strong administrative machinery of central government boards, outside the realm of the natural economy, to seep up the dregs of industry. As many writers have noticed, this strategy worked very well for mending specific problems as they arose without ever addressing the underlying causes of social crisis. At the heart of what Gallagher (1986, 97) has called this "endlessly generative" nature of early Victorian social reform was the unavoidable fact that the dregs who remained after the machinery had done its work – the physical bodies whose central location in the economy rendered them especially vulnerable to displacement – were not nearly as disposable as the machinery advocates had surmised.[5]

The machinery advocates' "solution" to the industrial displacement of labor was, of course, merely a dressed-up version of the Smithian–Malthusian recourse to a hypothetical statesman whose job it was to determine arbitrarily the natural limits of economic activity. But what their solution was dressed up as was significant: a politically potent alliance between liberal Tories and utilitarian social reformers that ensured active government intervention instead of closet moralism.[6] The Victorian reformers' statesman was not at all hypothetical, as the succession of poor laws and factory acts in the 1830s testifies. Furthermore, Victorian social reform, and complementary developments in classical economic theory, went much further than Smith and Malthus in carefully mapping out a boundary between the "natural" realm of free circulation and the "mechanical" realm of state-controlled circulation. Such boundary construction is evident in the efforts of various Ricardian heirs, including Mill, Merivale, and Senior, to distinguish between the "science" of political economy and the "art" of legislation (see, e.g., Merivale 1837).

During this still-transitional stage of economic growth, however, merely alleging that boundaries between the natural and the mechanical existed was not enough. The classical economists' allegations helped form a powerful ideology, but they did not always reflect (or transform) practice (see Dentith 1983). As a result, Marx had little trouble rejecting their economic science as "vulgar," and actual owners of machinery implicitly rejected their legislative art by cheating on the factory acts. Marx's tragicomic description in *Capital* of Leonard Horner unsuccessfully striving to enforce the ten-hour workday represents, among other things, the practical difficulty that continued to exist through the mid-nineteenth century in balancing the forces of free competition and central planning (Marx 1867/1987). And it was owing to this difficulty that circulatory language remained a popular form of discourse for theorists and practitioners alike. As long as the theory's language was itself imprecise, theorists could make precise-sounding demarcations between theory and practice that were not necessarily undercut by practical "falsifications" of their science.[7] More obviously, practitioners and popularizers reveled in the pliability of circulatory language, which facilitated the evasion or opposition of strictures that had been politically imposed by their own class. A factory boss could strenuously defend his machinery as the most efficient way of circulating goods through the economy, then turn around and appeal to the natural laws of laissez-faire if a legislative body informed him that the human cost of such machinery was too great to be permitted full freedom of movement.

The divergent relationship between ideology and practice in the

Victorian economy, which circulatory language helped facilitate, was capable of surviving only in a very specific social and political environment. Economists could remain imprecise about empirical content, and capitalists could comfortably disregard the ideological assertions of political economy, only as long as prosperous business conditions and a more or less quiescent labor force allowed them to do so. A combination of commercial stagnation and working-class enfranchisement in the 1870s and 1880s prodded economists and capitalists to clarify, to themselves and to their public, exactly where they drew the line between natural laws and mechanical dominion over nature and society. In the 1890s a new debate emerged among economists over the scope and method of their field, only this time supplemented by the rise of professional institutions to enforce disciplinary rigor. At the same time, social legislation acquired more bite than it had achieved earlier in the century, as capitalists slowly began to recognize the unproductive side effects of strikes and unhealthy workers (see Maloney 1985; Winch 1969). In this context circulatory language receded into the background. Although it did not disappear, it stopped serving as a focus for negotiating economic boundaries; these boundaries had finally been negotiated, and the task of economic discourse had accordingly changed. The discussion that follows recounts a single instance of such a movement away from circulatory language, as it transpired in the Victorian money market.

The machine in the market: the dilemma of joint-stock banking

The British money market underwent its own version of the "machinery question" in the 1830s and 1840s, with parallel consequences in the domain of circulatory language. In this case the antagonists were joint-stock bankers, who promised to bring to the economy new levels of efficiency and rates of growth, and private bankers, who feared their competitors would first drive them out of the market, then drive the market beyond the brink of stability. In both language and institutional arrangements, the antagonists repeated the polarization of machine and body that marked the contemporary introduction of mechanical improvements in industry. Joint-stock bank managers and directors advertised their institutions as mechanical marvels, capable of replacing the residue of recently failed private banks with the streamlined security of a large array of shareholders and a standardized system of accounting. They claimed that the circulation of bank notes, long a fitful and untrustworthy affair when left in the hands of individual financiers, would now exhibit the speed and regularity of a steam engine. Private bankers did their best to counter this attack by claiming to be better at personally supervising the nation's note circulation and by preying on shareholders' suspicions of untried financial "experiments." As in the broader machinery question, the banking debate reached a partial resolution when practical flaws in the joint-stock bankers' mechanical promises raised the issue of state intervention. The Bank Charter Act of 1844 signified the appearance of a new form of machinery, this time set in motion by Parliament, to enforce an arbitrarily determined set of "natural" limits to the potentially destabilizing effects of joint-stock banking machinery.

The banking debate was as much about the ability of different sides to utilize available cultural and social resources as it was about economic performance. It was through their utilization of culture that private bankers managed to score a victory in the debate, by expertly combining personal connections and rhetorical elegance in convincing legislators to pass the Bank Charter Act. As long as the debate was restricted to competing images of circulation, this victory hindered the joint-stock bankers' ability to reform financial administration along more centralized lines. The establishment of an act that appealed to machinery *outside* the money market drove advocates of joint-stock bankers to defend their trade using the individualistic language of Adam Smith. In both language and practice, their retreat away from a "mechanical" circulatory analogy impeded the administrative "mechanization" of banking. This section describes the rise and fall of joint-stock banks in the limited sense of their ability to manipulate circulatory language and practice to their benefit. The final section then proceeds to examine how joint-stock bankers discovered a way out of their dilemma, by looking for noncirculatory financial techniques.

Joint-stock banks were first allowed in England after a severe commercial crisis in 1825. Before that time English banks had been limited to six partners or less, creating two types of bankers: rich London families who served aristocrats, and provincial traders whose capital often proved inadequate during times of monetary pressure. To create a niche for themselves in this already-crowded market, the new commercial bankers used tactics that were wholly consistent with the political and economic agenda of contemporary machinery advocates. Against the London family bankers, they used the then-current language of electoral reform in an effort to break their monopoly of patronage and government protection. Against the traders they used the antiphysical rhetoric of the machinery advocates to distinguish their systematic administration from the shopkeeper mentality that pervaded banking in the provinces. Such a bodily threat was articulated by one of their leading spokesmen, James W. Gilbart, who predicted dire consequences if England continued to entrust its banking to shopkeepers: "Calculate, if you can, . . . how many female hearts have burst with anguish at seeing the wretchedness of their husbands and children . . . the system of [private] banking has produced more wretchedness in this country than any war, famine, or pestilence with which the land was ever scourged" (1859, 397–8).

Joint-stock bankers contrasted their own glistening machinery with the allegedly pestilent physical debilitation caused by failed private banks. In his *Practical Treatise on Banking*, first published in 1827, Gilbart presented himself as an experienced engineer who had acquired "a perfect acquaintance with all the details of this complicated machinery" (119). The centerpiece of the joint-stock bank system was the head office, where the general manager, aided by "experienced and unbiased inspectors" supervised a uniform hierarchy in which "each branch must have a good system of book-keeping, and the system must be uniform in every branch" (1834/1837, 136). His bank managers and clerks, he stressed, were professionals who did not mix with merchants and manufactures since "any attempt to unite two or more distinct trades must be regarded as a retrograde movement towards barbarism" (1859, 48). Such rhetoric paralleled public health reformers' arguments in favor of the division of labor, specialization, and periodical inspection; and with it came the same suspicion of contamination from physical circulation – in this case, circulation of bank notes. At his bank, the London and Westminster, Gilbart kept a watchful eye over provincial issuing banks that deposited notes with him and repeatedly stressed the facility of central administration as an antidote to potentially dangerous local relations of production and distribution. "To form a system of country joint-stock banks," he concluded, "without a central joint-stock bank in London, would be to form . . . a solar system without a sun" (1827, 400).

On the face of it, the joint-stock bankers' sales pitch had much going for it. Their target customers were the traders and manufacturers who themselves were experimenting with more standardized methods of bookkeeping and factory management and who were socially barred from seeking accommodation from preindustrial London bankers. But what the managers in the head office did not anticipate was that local social and economic links between "shopkeeper" banks and their customers were often strong enough to keep the best loans out of joint-stock hands. Leading local merchants who banked on the side, for instance, often threatened to stop trading with townsmen who took their banking elsewhere. Additionally, some of the more progressive private bankers in London proved happy to accommodate the more obviously solvent railway concerns. If joint-stock bankers wished to compete, their only recourse often was to lend on more risky securities – which, in turn, threatened to swamp the money market with an excess of accommodation paper and bank notes. To make matters worse, even if they could have limited the loan market to a class of undoubtedly solvent customers, the share market remained open to a whole underclass of speculators who had no qualms about cloaking their fly-by-night financial projects in the commercial bankers' rhetoric of strength and stability (Alborn 1991).

Such market realities soon sullied the pristine mechanical image of joint-stock banks. The same corporate structure that had promised improvement was now conceived to be contaminated and prone to transmit its diseased state to the social body. Critics in the popular press lashed out at corporate banks, whose directors valued self-interest over careful regulation of the nation's delicate circulation, and blamed economic instability on the uncontrolled temptation to purchase shares in banks and other joint-stock sponges of surplus capital. Their language was tinged with a common fear of parallel problems in the human body, as when the economist Robert Torrens compared joint-stock bank directors to "a surgeon, who had wounded an artery, instead of having opened a vein" (1837, 43) or when a Glasgow newspaper columnist reasoned from economic cause to physiological effect in the midst of a railway mania in 1843: "The temperature of the blood is regulated by the stock exchange barometer. It is warmed by the excitement of gain, or chilled by the mortification of loss . . . Now and then we see a smoke-dried shopkeeper efflorescing into a rosy west-ender, and incontinently all minds are unsettled."[8]

While corporate banks suffered the pains of this rhetorical backlash, private bankers and Bank of England directors seized the opportunity to regain ground in the competitive money market. Taking advantage of the unstable status of profit-making administrative machinery, they redepicted joint-stock banks as ill conceived and dangerous machines that shared little in common with the heroic engines of industry, and sold this new image to politicians. The bankers Samuel Jones Loyd and G. W. Norman enacted this strategy at the end of the 1830s with a campaign to centralize note issue in the Bank of England and attach the circulation of notes to the supply of bullion, in order to prevent bank directors from exerting discretionary powers.[9] Although the London bankers' immediate joint-stock competitors in the

City did not possess the power to issue notes, their campaign still affected banks like the London and Westminster, which served as an agent for many issuing country banks and which naturally suffered from any general distrust of the principle of joint-stock banking. Since no London private bankers issued their own notes, a central bank would not affect their fortunes one way or the other. In short, bankers like Loyd and Norman advocated centralized administration in the one area of banking from which they were immune, as a vaccine against the spread of joint-stock machinery in all aspects of banking.

Private bankers and Bank of England directors were well-connected socially and intellectually for pursuing their currency reform schemes. Their large personal wealth paid for the privilege of roaming freely in circles that were not, as yet, strictly limited to professional social scientists. As treasurer of the Royal Society, the banker J. W. Lubbock flattered Babbage with the promise of patronage while suggesting the dangers of joint-stock banking; and Norman and Loyd, at the Political Economy Club, could suggest to the economists Nassau Senior and Robert Torrens that a central bank of issue was a proper exception to the laws of free trade, classifiable (as Senior would have it) under the "art of legislation." In addition, economists had already been half-convinced by the sterling precedent of David Ricardo, whose earlier advocacy of a national bank of issue was revived in the 1830s by his brother Samson. With such powerful allies, Loyd managed to convince Sir Robert Peel to pass the 1844 Bank Charter Act, which called for a separate issuing department of the Bank of England, restricted the privilege of issuing notes to those banks already in possession of it, and limited all notes printed in England to a fixed amount regulated by the supply of bullion in the issuing bank (Fetter 1964, 171–2, 194–7).

The Bank Charter Act and the "currency principle" on which it was founded clothed an arbitrarily selected limit to commercial activity in an allegedly "natural" appeal to the gold standard. In doing so it repeated a strategy often used in appealing to state machinery to limit the expansion of a mechanized economy. The fact that the gold standard was arbitrary and only "natural" by analogy was demonstrated to everyone's satisfaction after the discoveries of new gold between 1848 and 1851, which showed that the constant supply of gold before that time had been more a coincidence than a natural dictate.[10] Furthermore, the Bank Charter Act also failed to deliver on its promise to produce more caution in the behavior of businessmen. As in the case of the factory acts and kindred examples of state machinery countering abuses of market machines, capitalists easily invented ways to circumvent the allegedly "natural" limitations that the Bank Charter Act imposed on their activities. Even before 1844, new forms of currency had been developed, including checks and bills of exchange, that were entirely outside the purview of the new legislation. As a result, the act failed to prevent commercial crises in 1847, 1857, and 1866, all of which resulted from a combination of wayward bills of exchange and imprudent dealings with foreign markets.

Despite its shaky scientific foundation and practical failings, however, the Bank Charter Act did succeed in what was arguably Loyd's main motive for its enactment: It wrested the language of centralized machinery from his corporatist rivals and forced them to defend their trade in the body-centered language of economic individualism. Joint-stock bankers were forced into that position at least as long as they continued to express the benefits of finance in circulatory language, the "mechanical" version of which had been thoroughly discredited in the course of the currency debate.[11] It was, in fact, in the years surrounding the 1844 act that advocates of joint-stock banking reversed their earlier emphasis on central machinery in favor of a radical defense of autonomy for individual banks across England. This was the argument of the "free banking" school, whose leading spokesman was the erstwhile banking "machinery" advocate, J. W. Gilbart. He and his allies asserted that bankers regulated their circulation in accord with local fluctuations in supply and demand and should therefore not be required to attach their issues to the supply of gold in the Bank of England.[12] While the free bankers necessarily continued to defend the mechanism inherent in joint-stock administration, their defense in the 1840s shifted to Adam Smith's unfortunate attempt to embed mechanistic language in a more general account of a freely circulating "natural" economy. As this chapter's final section shows, that strategy turned out to be even less suited to the position of joint-stock banking at midcentury than it had been for Adam Smith seventy years before.

At one level, the joint-stock bankers' turnabout in images of circulation represented a simple retreat into the only available rhetorical space left vacant by Loyd. Rich examples can be found of such bankers reacting against the same machinery they had once brandished in their advertisements merely because that machinery was now advocated by their competitors. Gavin Bell, author of *The Philosophy of Joint-Stock Banking*, scoffed in 1844 that trade would go on as before under the new law, "while the philosophers at the centre were amusing themselves in examining, and adjusting all the nice points of their beautiful new machine" (75). And Gilbart warned, in 1851, that in the next monetary pressure, England would be "like 'a cat in an air-pump,'" whose survival depended on "the views and theories of the philosophic statesmen who may at the time be performing the experiment" (76). Loyd's rhetoric also had deeper effects on London finance. With a newfound suspicion of machinery among London's large joint-stock banks came increasingly conservative lending policies. In contrast to the 1830s, when Gilbart had supported fellow joint-stock companies with loans as well as words, after the Bank Charter Act he went out of his way to identify railways and "companies of all sorts" as "securities on which commercial banks do not like to make advances" (1851, 347). Increasingly, the fiscal strategies of London joint-stock banks became harder to distinguish from that of their private competitors. It might be said, indeed, that the consummation of Loyd's efforts to control the circulation of bank notes came twenty years after the 1844 act, when his bank merged with Gilbart's London and Westminster, and Loyd could affirm that "the old concern still exists, though brought into new association and conducted by new parties."[13]

Beyond body versus machine: deposit banking and commercial crises

Loyd's victory, because it was both economically and rhetorically limited to restricting the circulation of notes, was bound to be short-lived. His ability to force the original cast of joint-stock bankers into a rhetorical corner and his success in affecting their commercial practices ultimately stood for little more than a retirement medal for an old-fashioned financier. The same incompleteness that saddled the Bank Charter Act's exclusive focus on circulation was bound, sooner or later, to take its toll on the currency school's more general effort to restrict the modern machinery of the joint-stock banking profession. If the original leaders of that profession were slow to realize this point and continued for a time to fight rearguard battles against Loyd using the outmoded language of circulation, this fact only postponed the inevitable. Even as the currency school and the free bankers argued in the 1840s, in fact, another contingent was paving the way for a new language and a new monetary policy. This contingent, called the "banking school" by monetary historians, was led by Thomas Tooke, who co-wrote the massive *History of Prices* with the statistician William Newmarch, and James Wilson at the *Economist*. They argued that since the majority of bank transactions, by the 1840s, were accomplished by discounting mercantile bills or writing checks on deposits, controlling note issue alone would have little effect on the stability of the money market. Tooke and Newmarch reasoned from this premise to support a central bank that could exercise discretionary power through regulating the interest rate – a conclusion that pleased neither bankers, who felt threatened enough by the Bank of England already, nor libertarian legislators, who worried that a discretionary bank would be overly monopolistic (see Fetter 1964, ch. 6). But the banking school had time on its side, as well as the undeniable fact that circulating notes were fading out as England's primary mode of currency. They also had the eventual support of Walter Bagehot, Wilson's son-in-law and successor at the *Economist,* whose evolutionary perspective produced a more persuasive analysis of the money market than any of those in the 1840s.

In 1873 Bagehot published *Lombard Street* in an effort to sweep away the *"debris"* (1968–86, 9:89) of the earlier controversies and to equip English businessmen with the necessary tools to get by in "a most vigorous and adult world which then [had been] small and weak" (9:49). In this stronger, more mature money market, Bagehot consigned circulation to the realm of recent history. His historical approach left him room for a revised set of economic palliatives and physiological metaphors, while keeping the threatening but vital image of circulation near enough at hand to serve both as a warning against impropriety and a paean to past progress. In the economic sphere, the checking account had indisputably replaced note circulation as the primary locus of exchange, and corporate banking was in England to stay. In the sphere of body language, at least as far as Bagehot was concerned, the nervous system had replaced the circulation of blood as the central metaphor to describe the money market: Commercial panics were "species of neuralgia," not cases of overflowing blood (9: 73). Bagehot incorporated both of these transitions into his evolutionary vision of society, which had already found articulation in *Physics and Politics* and which itself had received much impetus from Bagehot's own experiences on Lombard Street during the monetary pressure of the mid-1860s.

Amid a spate of mid-Victorian efforts to relate natural science and social progress, *Physics and Politics* was unique in spurning any mention of the circulatory system. For his purposes, Bagehot found a more useful physical analogy in the nervous system, with its "connective tissue" and instant electronic messages from the brain to all parts of the body. With the help of the popularizing physiologists Thomas Huxley and Henry Maudsley, he could translate nervous action into cultural transmission and embark on such favored topics as the development of national character and political wisdom. In a nutshell, *Physics and Politics* describes an evolutionary process beginning with prehistoric savages, whose active biological impulses spur them onward to forming small groups. From these groups nations are formed among those individuals who excel at imitating leaders, creating the "cake of custom" that is vital to national character. Finally, the "age of discussion" develops tolerance among individuals in those nations (like England) lucky enough to make it to the final stage of civilization (Bagehot 1872/1948).

Bagehot mentioned the money market only twice in *Physics and Politics*, but both times shed crucial light on the sources of his evolutionary thinking and on his extension of that logic in later economic writings. Each case arose as an example of a different form of atavism still evident in Bagehot's England. The first appeared in a discussion of the imitative impulse, which, as the main ingredient in the cake of custom, had the potential of keeping nations in a state of "modern savagery" if continued too long. Bagehot turned to the money market to show that "the grave part of mankind are quite as liable to these imitated beliefs as the frivolous part," citing the herd mentality on Lombard Street that constantly exaggerated the high and low ends of the business cycle (1872/1948, 99). The second atavism in the money market went even further back, to the "disposition to excessive action," which had been "victorious in barbarous ages" but now threatened to disrupt civilization. Commercial manias, he claimed, were caused "in some degree . . . by the wish to get rich; but in a considerable degree, too, by the mere love of activity" (195).

Both forms of atavism occupied center stage in a series of diagnostic articles Bagehot wrote for the *Economist* during a rise and fall of the stock market between 1864 and 1866, less than a year before he began work on *Physics and Politics*. The money market in 1864, he announced, had become "a vast borrowing machinery . . . in which a vast number of persons give a surprising trust to one another," marking a "very late and not a very easy step in civilization" (1968–86, 9:422). Checks had all but replaced circulating notes, which in comparison had been "a most coarse form of credit" (9: 436). But to Bagehot's nose, the denizen of Lombard Street still smelled of the modern savage, stuck in his "cake of custom," whose life he would later describe as "twisted into a thousand curious habits" (1872/1948, 124). In the neighborhood of the Bank of England, he wrote, "A man of business feels that there is something strange, that he has got out of his usual element, that he is in the realm of unnatural complexity, not in the realm of natural simplicity" (1968–86, 9:440).[14] During a panic, these unusual leftovers from a bygone era threatened to gain the upper hand. People stopped writing checks, started hoarding notes, and

ultimately demanded gold from the bank – descending the evolutionary scale toward increasingly tactile forms of currency.

Yet if evolutionary language informed Bagehot's dour diagnosis of
the economy, it also served paradoxical duty as an apologetic for English economic progress. Even while repeating his warnings about the
money market's extreme "delicacy" in *Lombard Street,* he placed atavistic tendencies into a progressive Darwinian framework: "The rough
and vulgar structure of English commerce is the secret of its life," he
claimed, "for it contains the 'propensity to variation,' which, in the
social as in the animal kingdom, is the principle of progress" (1968–
86, 9:49).[15] This was no simple statement that the fittest survived, as
would be proclaimed by American social Darwinists in a later generation; rather, Bagehot appealed to evolution in an attempt to confine
the "rough and vulgar" traits of the English money market in the past,
where they could be safely celebrated. He constantly harked back to
the "natural state of banking" that relied on circulating notes and self-
interest, but just as firmly denied that such a state was suitable for the
present (9:53).

At least in part, Bagehot's historicization of circulation marked an
effort to put the problematic image of note circulation behind him,
without wholly embracing the alternative mechanical model of banking. Such a motive is evident in his effort to guard against the atavistic
appearance of what he called "the natural heat of imaginative faculty"
on Lombard Street – a palliative that, not surprisingly, recalled his
celebration of the "age of discussion" in *Physics and Politics.* Rather
than resting secure in mechanical rules, whether administered by the
state or by private enterprise, Bagehot proposed to inject bankers with
a healthy dose of discussion: as he put it, "such wider culture as would
give those men other keen intellectual interests" (1968–86, 10:46–8).
Because notes had diminished in importance since the 1840s, regulating the circulation was no longer a feasible solution to monetary pressure. But in his attempt to calm bankers' nerves, to soothe the savage
beasts on Lombard Street, Bagehot sincerely hoped for a way out of
future commercial crises. This solution, like that of the banking
school, translated into a call for discretionary centralized banking, but
with the added safety feature that bankers' discretion would be
molded by higher education and guarded by public opinion.

While Bagehot's palliative may strike the modern reader as something of a panacea, it suited the emerging English banking profession's own aspirations for status as well as their attempts to distance
themselves from the "rough and vulgar" world of supply and demand. Leading bankers, such as *Bankers' Magazine* editor Robert

Harry Inglis Palgrave, refined Bagehot's evolutionary narrative in articles contrasting England's delicate deposit system with the circulation of notes in industrializing countries.[16] His lesson was that bankers should feel good about the progress their forebears had accomplished through the dangerous process of note issue, while guarding against ever returning to that earlier, more competitive stage of banking. In the depressed money market of late Victorian England, this lesson made increasing sense to bankers and politicians alike. Bankers were fast discovering that the best way to stay afloat was by conspiring to establish artificially high interest rates, by playing the margins in centralized clearing facilities, and last but not least, by cooperating with the Bank of England. Politicians, whose loyalty to free trade was already being severely tested at the close of the nineteenth century, were starting to reconsider discretionary central banking as a possible means of ensuring economic stability. Once bankers had chosen to unite in a single profession rather than slinging insults across intramural rifts, the once-crucial distinction between body and machine waned in significance. Palgrave, for instance, found little difficulty collapsing that distinction into a single warning against the overriding depression-era fear of monetary collapse: "What is to be done," he asked in 1886, "if the mainspring which sets all our machinery in motion were snapped, if the heart whose pulsations vivify the whole of our business body politic were stopped?" (146). This question, intended as rhetorical, represented a rhetorical victory for bankers who were no longer constrained by competition and political opinion to make a choice between economic machine and man.

Notes

1. For a bibliography of typical sources, see Bordo (1986).
2. "Waggon-way" was the common eighteenth-century term for a railway.
3. On the transition from economists' use of discourse as a negotiating tool to their use of discourse within a consensual set of boundaries, see Winch (1972). The connection between this transition and the choice of natural images is implicitly treated in many of the other contributions to this book, as well as in Mirowski (1989).
4. On the physiocrats, see Smith (1776/1979, 674–6).
5. See Berg (1980, ch. 13) on the contradictory nature of bourgeois social reform strategies in early Victorian England.
6. Peter Mandler (1990) has most recently detailed this alliance for the case of poor law reform.
7. For the time being I leave this statement as more a suggestion than an assertion, to be supported in more detail in my later discussion of the

currency school. On the general matter of theoretical precision and practical falsification, see de Marchi (1970).

8. Excerpt from the *Glasgow Citizen,* reprinted in *Economist* 1 (1843): 601.
9. Loyd was a partner in the banking house of Jones Loyd & Co. of Manchester and London; Norman was a Bank of England director who sided with Loyd in order to secure a monopoly for Bank of England note issue and to rebuff criticisms that the bank's discretionary policy was untrustworthy. All Bank of England directors shared Norman's view on a single issuing bank, although some (notably Horsley Palmer) held out for continuing the bank's discretionary powers. See Collins (1972) and Fetter (1964, ch. 6).
10. On the effect of the gold discoveries on bullionist thought, see Goodwin (1970).
11. One strident opponent of the Bank Charter Act, for instance, uncritically accepted Loyd's restrictive definition of currency as forms of exchange "actually passing from hand to hand" (Bell 1841, 54).
12. The clearest presentation of Gilbart and the free banking school can be found in White (1984, chs. 3 and 4). White correctly distinguishes the free bankers, who argued against any central banking control, from the "banking school" (featuring Thomas Tooke and discussed later), which shared the free bankers' antipathy to the Bank Charter Act but advocated discretionary central banking. Significantly, a majority of leading joint-stock bankers at least initially preferred Gilbart's alternative to the currency school over Tooke's.
13. S. J. Loyd Overstone to Lewis Loyd, March 30, 1864, in Gregory (1936, 1:281). A similar sign of the times was the admission of the major London joint-stock banks to the clearing house in 1856, after more than twenty years of exclusion.
14. The contrast between the "unnatural" system of central banking in England and a "natural" (really preternatural) state, conceived by Bagehot as a multiissue system, became one of the central themes in *Lombard Street.*
15. Bagehot's reference to the money market as "delicate" is another signification of the "age of discussion," which he referred to in Bagehot (1872/1948, 184) as "a plant of singular delicacy."
16. See, e.g., Palgrave (1873, 1876, 1877). On significant differences between Bagehot and Palgrave, see Alborn (1991, ch. 6).

References

Alborn, Timothy L. 1991. "The Other Economists: Science and Commercial Culture in Victorian England." Ph.D. dissertation, Harvard University.
Anon. 1851. "Railways: Progress and Effects," *Economist* 9: 953.
Appleby, Joyce. 1978. *Economic Thought and Ideology in Seventeenth-Century England.* Princeton, NJ: Princeton University Press.
Bagehot, Walter. 1948. *Physics and Politics* (1872). New York: Knopf.

Bagehot, Walter. 1968–86. *Collected Works of Walter Bagehot*, ed. Norman St. John-Stevas. London: The Economist.

Bell, Gavin. 1841. *The Currency Question*. London.

[Bell, Gavin.] 1844. "Free Trade in Banking," *Bankers' Magazine* 1: 68–75.

Berg, Maxine. 1980. *The Machinery Question and the Making of Political Economy*. Cambridge University Press.

Bordo, Michael David. 1986. "Explorations in Monetary History: A Survey of the Literature," *Explorations in Economic History* 2: 339–415.

Coleman, William. 1982. *Death Is a Social Disease: Public Health and Political Economy in Early Industrial France*. Madison: University of Wisconsin Press.

Collins, Michael. 1972. "The Langton Papers: Banking and Bank of England Policy in the 1830s," *Economica* 39: 47–59.

de Marchi, N. B. 1970. "The Empirical Content and Longevity of Ricardian Economics," *Economica* 37: 257–76.

Dentith, Simon. 1983. "Political Economy, Fiction and the Language of Practical Ideology in Nineteenth-Century England," *Social History* 8: 183–200.

Fetter, Frank W. 1964. *Development of British Monetary Orthodoxy, 1797–1875*. Cambridge, MA: Harvard University Press.

Gallagher, Catherine. 1986. "The Body Versus the Social Body in the Works of Thomas Malthus and Henry Mayhew," *Representations* 14: 83–106.

Gilbart, James W. 1827. *A Practical Treatise on Banking*. London.

Gilbart, James W. 1837. *History and Principles of Banking* (1834). London.

Gilbart, James W. 1859. *The Logic of Banking: A Familiar Exposition of the Principles of Reasoning, and Their Application to the Art and Science of Banking*. London.

Gilbert, Geoffrey. 1980. "Economic Growth and the Poor in Malthus's *Essay on Population*," *History of Political Economy* 12: 84–96.

Goodwin, Crauford D. W. 1970. "British Economists and Australian Gold," *Journal of Economic History* 30: 405–26.

Gregory, T. E. 1936. *Westminster Bank through a Century*, 2 vols. London: Westminster Bank Ltd.

Haley, Bruce. 1978. *The Healthy Body and Victorian Culture*. Cambridge, MA: Harvard University Press.

Hilton, Boyd. 1988. *The Age of Atonement: The Influence of Evangelicalism on Social and Economic Thought, 1795–1865*. Oxford: Clarendon Press.

Maloney, John. 1985. *Marshall, Orthodoxy and the Professionalisation of Economics*. Cambridge University Press.

Mandler, Peter. 1990. "Tories and Paupers: Christian Political Economy and the Making of the New Poor Law," *Historical Journal* 33: 81–104.

Marx, Karl. 1987. *Capital*, 3 vols. (1867). New York: International Publishers.

Merivale, Herman. 1837. "Definitions and systems of political economy," *Edinburgh Review* 66: 73–102.

Mirowski, Philip. 1989. *More Heat Than Light: Economics as Social Physics, Physics as Nature's Economics*. Cambridge University Press.

Palgrave, R. H. Inglis. 1873. "Notes on Banking in Great Britain and Ireland,

Sweden, Denmark, and Hamburg," *Journal of the London Statistical Society* 36: 27–152.

Palgrave, R. H. Inglis. 1876. "Banking in Sweden," *Bankers' Magazine* 36: 905–10.

Palgrave, R. H. Inglis. 1877. "On the Influence of a Note Circulation in the Conduct of Banking Business," *Transactions of the Manchester Statistical Society* 14: 71–152.

Palgrave, R. H. Inglis. 1886. "The Country Banker," *Quarterly Review* 162: 133–55.

Smith, Adam. 1979. *An Inquiry into the Nature and Causes of the Wealth of Nations* (1776). Oxford: Clarendon Press.

Torrens, Robert. 1837. *A Letter to the Right Honourable Viscount Melbourne.* London.

Tribe, Keith. 1978. *Land, Labour and Economic Discourse.* London: Routledge & Kegan Paul.

White, Lawrence. 1984. *Free Banking in Britain: Theory, Experience, and Debate, 1800–1845.* Cambridge University Press.

Winch, Donald. 1969. *Economics and Policy: A Historical Study.* London: Hodder & Stoughton.

Winch, Donald. 1972. "Marginalism and the Boundaries of Economic Science," *History of Political Economy* 4: 325–43.

CHAPTER 8

The moment of Richard Jennings: the production of Jevons's marginalist economic agent

MICHAEL V. WHITE

The effect of applying Physiology and Psychology to Political-economy will evidently remove this branch of learning from the condition of a political to the condition of a physical and a meta-physical science.

Richard Jennings (1856, 110n)

Introduction

Some years ago, George Katona argued that, while mainstream economic analysis generally "continues to disregard psychological studies, it is not devoid of psychological assumptions. Most commonly it proceeds on the premise that human beings behave mechanically," so that they are effectively depicted as "automatons." Hence, orthodox economics should be "described as 'economics with mechanistic psychology,' rather than as 'economics without psychology' " (1975, 5, 6). This chapter attempts to provide a historical perspective on that mechanistic approach by explaining how it first appeared in postclassical (or marginalist) supply and demand theory. Specifically, the chapter is concerned with the depiction of economic behavior in W. S. Jevons's *Theory of Political Economy* (1871; hereafter *TPE*). This was the first postclassical English text that depicted the theoretical object of "scientific" political economy as a type of constrained optimization, discussed all prices in terms of "the laws of supply and demand" and explained all economic actions in terms of marginal utility, using the calculus and geometry. One reason for focusing on *TPE* is that its detailed treatment of the behavioral theory distinguished it from the work of the other postclassical pioneer, L. Walras (Jaffe 1983, ch. 17). The representation of behavior set out in *TPE* has remained fundamentally unchanged in orthodox theory, despite subsequent attempts to discard the notion of utility and to sever any connection with psychology (Wong 1978).

The principal argument of this chapter is that it is readily understandable why the orthodox theory is so mechanistic, once its basis is identified. That basis can be found in Richard Jennings's *Natural Elements of Political Economy* (1855), which drew upon the discourse of physiological psychology to present "natural laws" of economic behavior in functional terms. This was possible because most economic actions were explained as reflexes. Jevons was able to utilize this discourse in part because Jennings argued that the theory made behavior analogous to a gravitational force. The explanation could then be incorporated within the framework of the "correlation of forces," which provided a unified explanation for the motion of all material phenomena in terms of the interconvertibility of force. Jevons was familiar with this because of his previous training and work in physics. He was then able to develop a theory of exchange based on the metaphor of a "balance" of forces. Jennings's approach, however, created a substantial problem because the existence of reflex actions raised the problem of "free will." Since Jevons simply claimed in *TPE* that all economic activity was the result of free will, we conclude that his explanation of economic action was incoherent.

The chapter has five sections. The first explains how Jennings provided the theory of economic behavior for Jevons and why this inaugurated a new approach to the explanation of consumption behavior. The second considers the mechanical metaphors used by Jennings, explaining how Jevons was able both to use and to modify them. The third discusses the appearance of physiological psychology by the early 1850s and how it was used as a resource by Jennings to formulate his behavioral theory. The fourth section then explains how physiological psychology raised the problem of free will and how Jevons responded to this in *TPE*. Finally, since it has been argued that Jennings's work played a negligible role in the production of *TPE*, the fifth section shows how the problems raised by physiological psychology explain a number of comments Jevons made when he was first formulating the marginalist theory.

The natural laws of economic action

Jevons argued in *TPE* that it was "the inevitable tendency of human nature" to "satisfy our wants to the utmost with the least effort – to procure the greatest amount of what is desirable at the expense of the least that is undesirable – in other words, to maximize comfort and pleasure" (1871, 44, 69). Similar statements as to general behavioral motives can be found in the work of previous political economists such as Nassau Senior, J. S. Mill, and J. E. Cairnes. It is important, however, to distinguish such general motives from the more specific "principles or axioms" of behavior (Jevons 1871, 24), which were the *differentia specifica* of the marginalist economic agent. The axioms were deemed to be universal laws as Jevons explained in 1876: "The laws of political economy treat of the relations between human wants and the available natural objects and human labour by which they may be satisfied. These laws are so simple in their foundation that they would apply, more or less completely, to all human beings of whom we have any knowledge." Given that the behavioral laws "may be considered universally true as regards human nature" (Jevons 1905, 196, 197), the utility theory could represent the actions of economic agents without reference to any social conditions of their existence. The marginalist principles of the science of political economy could thus be explained without reference to a particular type of society.[1]

There were two natural laws of behavior. The first was for consumption, where the final degree of utility *"varies with the quantity of commodity, and ultimately decreases as that quantity increases"* (Jevons 1871, 62 OE; cf. 53–8).[2] The second law was for labor, defined as *"any painful exertion of body or mind undergone with the view to future good"* (1871, 164 OE). Its "law of variation" was that "as labour is prolonged the effort becomes rapidly more and more painful" (1871, 166, 168). With the combination of the behavioral motive and specific laws, it was possible to set out the theory of "the mechanics of human interest" (1871, 24) or, as in the second edition, *"the mechanics of utility and self-interest"* (Jevons 1970, 90 OE). One example of this mechanics was the equilibrium point, where, at the margin, "the pleasure gained" from consuming a commodity was "exactly equal to the labour endured" in either directly producing or working to indirectly obtain the commodity through wages (1871, 169). Jevons's analysis of this is shown in Figure 8.1. The diagram represents the work decision for a "free labourer" producing "enough to support himself." Units of marginal utility and disutility are represented along the ordinate. The marginal utility of the output produced is indicated along *pq*, with the marginal utility and disutility of work represented by *abcd*. The labor cease point is then at *m*. The marginal productivity of labor is assumed constant so that units of labor correspond monotonically to the marginal product and *Ox* indicates units of labor. With the marginal return to labor reflecting its productivity, Jevons described *Ox* as representing the "amount of produce or the day's wages" (1871, 166, 169–72).[3]

This analysis was one of the "most important points of the theory" (Jevons 1871, 38), in part because the theory of behavior (or "action")

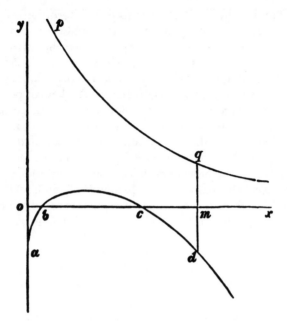

Figure 8.1. Jevons's work decision diagram. From Jevons (1871, 168).

played a crucial role in the initial production of Jevons's marginalist analysis in early 1860. His diary entries and some letters from that time indicate a remarkably rapid shift in his theoretical approach. In early February, Jevons recorded that he was working on an aggregate distribution theory in a mathematical form, with "value to [be] established on the basis of labour." Two weeks later, however, he wrote that he had "blundered" on the topic and now "supposed" that he had arrived at "a true comprehension of *Value*" (Black 1973–81, 7:120 OE). Letters written in June and November indicate that Jevons was sketching a new theoretical approach and that he was particularly concerned with the importance of his new explanation of utility (Black 1973–81, 2:410–11, 422).

A reconstruction of the reasons for Jevons's dissatisfaction with the labor theory of value suggests that, in his initial distribution "model," he was unable to explain ground rent with both capital and labor as inputs. However, once he had the marginal utility theory of behavior, he reformulated the rent analysis with labor as the only variable input. The different analytical orientation thus depended on the new theory of action. This was made more clear in Jevons's first public presentation

of the theory (Jevons 1863, 1866b) than it was in *TPE* (White 1991a).[4]
An attempt to explain how this theory was produced is hampered by
contradictory statements from Jevons as to his sources. In the first
edition of *TPE*, he claimed that he had "sketched out" the theory "almost irrespective of previous opinions" (1871, vii). In the second edition, however, he wrote that "I have carefully pointed out, both in the
first edition and in this, certain passages of Bentham, Senior, Jennings
and other authors, from whom my system was, more or less consciously,
developed" (Jevons 1970, 63). Although it is customary to present
Jevons as drawing on Bentham for the behavioral theory in *TPE*, it
should be noted that Jevons did not attribute a marginal utility theory
to the "dry old Jeremy." Only three analysts were presented as anticipating his approach in that regard – Nassau Senior, Thomas Banfield, and
Richard Jennings. As far as Senior is concerned, Jevons's account involved a distortion of Senior's analysis, which is more akin to a lexicographic consumption theory (White 1992a). This suggests that Jevons
read Senior in that misleading fashion after he had formulated the
marginal utility theory. Much the same point can be made about
Banfield's analysis, which, as Jevons acknowledged, was inconsistent
with the theory of action in *TPE* (Jevons 1871, 49–51, 64).[5] It is possible, however, to find a presentation of the marginalist behavioral
theory in Jennings's *Natural Elements* (hereafter *NE*).

Jennings argued that political economy was a "science of human
actions," founded on universal "laws of [human] nature" (1855, 41,
20), identified from the relation between body and mind: "As the
human body is universally found to be framed after the same type . . .
so the human mind, whatever idiosyncrasies it may exhibit in particular instances, is universally found to offer to the philosophical observer the same general class of natural phenomena" (195). Two universal laws were of fundamental importance in this regard. The first
law concerned consumption:

> With respect to all Commodities, our feelings show that the degrees of
> satisfaction do not proceed *pari passu* with the quantities consumed, –
> they do not advance equally with each instalment of the Commodity
> offered to the senses, and then suddenly stop, – but diminish gradu-
> ally, until they ultimately disappear, and further instalments can pro-
> duce no further satisfaction. In this progressive scale the increments
> of sensation resulting from equal increments of the Commodity are
> obviously less and less at each step. (98–9)

As Jevons noted in *TPE*, when he included a longer quotation from
NE from which this quote is taken (1871, 65–8; cf. Jennings 1855, 96–
9), Jennings was the "writer" who had "most clearly appreciated the

nature and importance of the law of [diminishing marginal] utility" (Jevons 1871, 64–5).

Jennings's second law of human behavior, which also dealt with functional "increments of sensation," concerned labor. At first, any effort expended would produce "indifferent" or even "pleasurable" sensations, but eventually, "pain" would be felt (1855, 116). The nub of the law of labor variation, which Jevons cited in full (1871, 166–8), was:

> Between these . . . points . . . of incipient effort and of painful suffering, it is quite evident that the degree of toilsome sensations endured does not vary directly as the quantity of work performed, but increases much more rapidly, like the resistance offered by an opposing medium to the velocity of a moving body.
>
> When this observation comes to be applied to the toilsome sensations endured by the working classes, it will be found convenient to fix . . . the average amount of toilsome sensation attending the average amount of labour, and to measure from this point the degrees of variation. If, for the sake of illustration, this average amount be assumed to be of ten hours' duration, it would follow that, if at any period the amount were to be supposed to be reduced to five hours, the sensations of labour would be found, at least by the majority of mankind, to be almost merged in the pleasures of occupation and exercise, whilst the amount of work performed would only be diminished by one half; if, on the contrary, the amount were to be supposed to be increased to twenty hours, the quantity of work produced would only be doubled, whilst the amount of toilsome suffering would become unsupportable. (Jennings 1855, 119–20)

With the combination of the two behavioral laws, "the mystery of action is solved" (1855, 142) and Jennings emphasized that the explanation for any wage rate would have to be couched in terms of the interaction between the "positive value" attached to the "pecuniary reward" for work (which would follow the consumption sensation law) and the "Negative Value" accompanying the "toilsome feelings" of work (187). Figure 8.1 shows how Jevons could have translated *NE*'s account into an analysis and diagram of work effort and the labor "cease-point" for a representative laborer, since Jennings had argued that action would cease when a person became indifferent between sensations (85). Jevons then reworked his rent analysis in that light (White 1991a).

It should be noted here how Jennings's analysis signaled a new approach to consumption theory in political economy. Prior to the publication of *NE*, the dominant explanation had been presented in lexicographic terms, which allowed that there were two aspects to consumption. The first was that commodities were arranged in a hierarchy from necessities to luxuries, while the second was that the degree of want felt for a particular commodity would decline with successive units of it. In this account, the hierarchy was the most important component of the explanation, and explicit allowance was made for interdependence in consumption.[6] While Jennings's analysis allowed for a hierarchy, he effectively transformed the categories of the lexicographic framework.

To explain consumption, Jennings used a distinction between "common" and "special" sensations, the effects of which were made to correspond with the consumption of necessary ("primary") and luxury ("secondary") commodities (1855, 81–102). Nerves of common sensation conveyed sensations of resistance, temperature, gratification of appetite, and stimulation. Special sensations were conveyed specifically by one of the five organs of the senses and included appreciation of color, beauty of form, and melody.

It was important to distinguish between "relative" and "absolute" effects so as to explain "the changes in the degree and duration of sensations" that followed changes in the quantities of commodities consumed. As far as the relative aspect was concerned, Jennings acknowledged that secondary commodities could not be appreciated without the primary wants first being met. Relative sensations thus depended on the consumption of other commodities. This explained the hierarchy of consumption, which was taken as effectively given and subject to change only over long periods of time (Jennings 1855, 93, 94–6, 104). The second, "absolute" aspect was concerned only with changes in sensations produced by successive units of a commodity. It was here that Jennings argued that "the increase of sensation resulting from equal increments of the Commodity are obviously less and less at each step" (99), an argument that Jevons cited subsequently as a statement of diminishing marginal utility (discussed earlier). Jennings then claimed that it was possible to posit a "law" for the "general variation of sensations" by noting that "for equal changes in the quantity of Commodities, the change in the amount of satisfaction derived from Primary Commodities is greater than the change in the amount of satisfaction derived from Secondary Commodities" (102). The analytical significance of the commodity hierarchy was thus reduced to differences in the "quantity of sensations" and hence to an illustration of the "law of the variation of sensations" (99). It was Jennings's simultaneous inversion and transformation of the lexicographic approach that Jevons was to exploit by depicting utility as a single-valued function. Although Jevons acknowledged that there was a hierarchy of consumption, this became a subordinate aspect of the marginalist analysis since luxury and necessary commodities could in principle be represented by utility diagrams with different slopes and were thus illustrations of the one law. The final step in Jevons's analysis was to treat all commodities in the analysis as capable of being exchanged at the margin, thus dissolving the significance of the hierarchy in the lexicographic account.

For Jennings, it was possible to explain "value" in political economy as a "complex *mental* conception" that consisted of ascribing an attribute to objects based on memory and the anticipation of service provided by an object. Exchangeable value was thus the value of objects that could be exchanged (1855, 178, 72 OE). Value had two aspects, static and dynamic. The static examined relative exchange value (i.e., relations of quantity in a particular space) and thus dealt with "phenomena of co-existence," measured by commodity prices. The dynamic, by contrast, examined the rate of change of exchange values through time and thus dealt with "phenomena of succession," or the manufacture of exchangeable objects. The link between the two aspects of value was that changes in consumption and price led to changes in value, which induced changes in production (28, 30, 72–3, 135, 204). While *TPE* was restricted to a static account of exchange, Jennings provided a further suggestion, which Jevons pursued in his quest to produce a "scientific" political economy.

At the outset of *NE*, Jennings explained that one "object" of his treatise was to attack an epistemological argument made by J. S. Mill and J. E. Cairnes. This was that political economy dealt with laws that were tendencies, so that their effects were never clear precisely in the *"concrete"* because of *"disturbing causes."* For Jennings, however, the argument was unsatisfactory because it could not establish the validity of theoretical propositions, which, instead, had to be formulated "to represent observed *facts.*" Nevertheless, "we are still far distant from that knowledge of *numerical* laws which is the characteristic of the higher branches of Science. . . . This is the field which now claims the attention, and will hereafter produce the laurels of the scientific political-economist" (1855, 3–6, 26 OE).

Like Jennings, Jevons acknowledged that such numerical laws were difficult to produce and that the subject was not capable of "exact measurement." However, in the early 1860s, he began an attempt to calculate statistical and mathematical price "laws" for particular commodities that would explain consumption in terms of marginal utility. This project was frustrated by computation problems, but one result can be seen in *TPE* with the formulation of a price law for the King-D'Avenant price–quantity table (White 1989). Jevons's formulation drew upon William Whewell's treatment of the same topic in some early papers to the Cambridge Philosophical Society (1829). In this regard, *NE* must have been something of a bibliographical gold mine for Jevons. Quite aside from the references to the exchange school of political economists (Senior, Whateley, and Bastiat), Jennings quoted a passage from Whewell's early work in the Philosophical Society's *Transactions* on *NE*'s title page.[7] In consulting *Transactions*, Jevons could also have found Tozer's mathematical work on political economy, which was mentioned in the first edition of *TPE* (Jevons 1871, 16–7).

Mechanics, force, and energy

Jevons's attraction to Jennings's argument was not simply because it provided a theoretical solution to his initial problem with a value and distribution theory. It was also because Jennings couched his explanation in terms of mechanical metaphors that Jevons could recognize because of his training and work in chemistry, meteorology, and therefore mechanics.

In the unfinished *Principles of Economics*, Jevons noted that previous economists, such as J. S. Mill, had argued that "labour creates nothing, but merely draws from the crust of the globe the materials which are to be utilised." This was in keeping with the older "law . . . in physics . . . that man can neither create nor annihilate matter" (Jevons 1905, 68). Jennings also relied on this device, arguing that "matter receives improvement" in production, was "transferred" in commodity exchange, and "absorbed, or resolved into other elements" in consumption. It was, then, the "universal relation of mind to matter" that explained a "large proportion" of sensations, emotions, and actions in political economy. In particular, the analytical "field" of the discourse was that "betwixt mind and external matter which is offered by the organisation of the human body" (Jennings 1855, 10, 18, 27). To explain the actions of the body, Jennings treated matter as a vehicle for "force," so that the "Natural laws [of behavior] which are permanent and invariable" were akin to those of "mechanical force" and "may now be . . . compared to the moving force of gravitation." Since "human action produces, or resists mechanical force, makes durable impressions on matter, or causes motion," the natural laws of behavior had the same veracity or "stability of other natural laws . . . [such as] the gravitation or coherence of matter" (Jennings 1855, 17, 136, 141, 148, 159).

This analysis was given a more detailed treatment in *TPE*, where Jevons made marginal utility analogous to a gravitational force. The dominant metaphor in the analysis was that of a "balance" of forces. The mind of the economic agent, for example, was represented as balancing the forces of pleasure and pain, so that exchange was depicted as a balance using the analogy of a lever in equilibrium (Jevons 1970, 144–7). Consistent with this, the work decision for a laborer was explained as a balance between pleasure and pain (Jevons 1871, 163, 169, 174, 180), and Figure 8.1 was effectively made analogous to a gravitational force field. While the representation of the consumption utility curve in the figure as a gravitational force is readily identifiable (White 1991b), the representation of labor in the same way may appear puzzling. However, this point can be clarified by examining how Jevons followed a suggestion by Jennings in an attempt to "verify" the marginalist project.

In the extract from Jennings's discussion of work effort that Jevons cited in *TPE*, it was argued that the "degree of toilsome sensation" increased rapidly with the work performed, "like the resistance offered by an opposing medium to the velocity of a moving body" (Jennings 1855, 119; Jevons 1871, 166). If this was grist to Jevons's mechanistic mill, a few pages before Jennings had offered the following suggestion to "test" the proposition:

> Let any muscular effort be made, as, for example, let the arm be extended in a horizontal direction, and be held there, counteracting the force of gravitation: the first sensations may be the indifferent, or perhaps agreeable sensations of activity and of power, arising from the exercise of the muscular sense; but the sensations which succeed assume a different complexion, and progressively merge into sensations of resistance, of a necessity for effort, of a consciousness of a force equal or superior to our own, and ultimately of a painful reluctance to persist: such are the class of sensations which may be distinguished as the sensations of Physical Labour. (Jennings 1855, 116–7)

In early 1870, Jevons reported three experiments that were designed to "throw some light upon the chemical and physiological conditions of muscular force" to begin "defining the mathematical relations upon which the science of economy is founded" (1870, 158). Two of the experiments were unsatisfactory because they did not result in a mathematical law that could be explained by "mechanical principles." The third, however, was more satisfactory. It involved holding weights in the hand with an outstretched arm and recording the time for which the weights could be supported. In this case, work (the "useful effect") was calculated as the product of weight and time. First reported in *Nature*, the experiment was then described in *TPE* as illustrating the "laws forming the physical basis of Political Economy" (Jevons 1871, 195). Perhaps not surprisingly, a diagram of Jevons's results looks like the labor disutility curve in *TPE* (Haughton 1871, 290). As already noted, in the early 1860s, Jevons had attempted to calculate mathematical price laws for a number of commodities, which would provide statistical verification of the utility theory in consumption. It seems reasonable to suggest that Jevons's "work" experiment was suggested also by Jennings and dated from about the same time, with the aim of verifying the labor component of the utility theory.

The assumption of constant labor productivity, which Jevons used in the labor cease point diagram, also seems to have been derived from Jennings. (In the long quotation from Jennings [1855, 119–20] that Jevons cited in *TPE*, it was argued that a doubling or halving of the work day would change output in the same proportion.) This debt was obscured, however, by Jevons's claim that the assumption also applied to cases of "machine labour" (1871, 172). While Jennings possibly drew upon the analysis of "labouring force" in Whewell's mechanics (Wise 1989, 417–24), Jevons's reference to machine labor was apparently taken from Babbage's *Economy of Machinery* and assumed a different set of means and relations of production to that of the "free labourer" case in *TPE*. In a similar manner, the debt to Jennings for the work experiment was obscured in *TPE* because Jennings received no mention. Instead, Jevons linked his experiments with the discussion of efficient work loads (the "economy of labour") by Babbage. Drawing on the work of Coulomb, Babbage discussed work in terms of the expenditure of force in moving matter (1835, 18–20, 30–7).[8]

Jevons regarded Babbage's *Economy* as an "exquisite work" that "anticipates the modern doctrines of the relations of the natural forces" (Jevons 1866a, 143n). This reference was consistent with his use, until the mid-1860s, of Grove's notion of the correlation of forces as a conservation principle in his work. Whatever else Jevons may have read in the ten years since 1860, he was reminded of that topic by John Tyndall's reconciliation of the conservation of force and of energy frameworks. As Tyndall noted, a moving force had "a definite mechanical measure in the amount of work it can perform," while including the analysis of muscular force in an energy framework (1865, 136–8, 143). It was Tyndall's article that converted Jevons, by early 1866, to the energy metaphor subsequently used in *TPE* (White 1991b, 65–9).

By the time that Jevons came to write *TPE*, he considered that gravitational forces could be explained by the energy conservation principle. Hence, he wrote that each laborer began the day with a given amount of "spontaneous energy" that "begins to be rapidly exhausted" with work.[9] With the pain of the intensity of labor indicated by the "amount of muscular force undergone in a certain time," it was necessary that "a workman . . . recover all fatigue and recommence with an undiminished store of energy" (Jevons 1871, 166, 169, 197). Jevons thus appears to have been attempting to represent the labor disutility analysis as isomorphic with a process in which potential energy was replaced with kinetic energy at work, much as he thought that the consumption element of Figure 8.1 could be represented as an energy field (White 1991b). However, no attempt was made to demonstrate that in a coherent manner. In part this was because, as Jevons acknowledged, he could find no physiological explanation to match the energy metaphor and his experimental results (1870, 159).

When Jevons described the relationship between the amount and the intensity of work, he claimed that "long experience has led men, by a sort of unconscious reasoning, to select that rate of work which is the most advantageous" (1871, 191–2). This Panglossian statement, with its reference to "unconscious reasoning," was remarkably similar to one previously made by Thomas Laycock (Danzinger 1982, 126). Laycock's work was instrumental in the formulation of the discourse of physiological psychology. That discourse enabled Richard Jennings to first outline the mechanics of behavior, which Jevons subsequently explained with the energy conservation principle.

Physiological psychology

In the early 1840s, the dominant English theory of wants, perception, and behavior that political economists could draw upon was associationist "psychology." This discourse, which now appears as more an epistemology than a psychology,[10] considered that complex mental events, such as knowledge and experience, could be accounted for by a combination of sensations and perceptions felt by the body and registered in the mind. The formation of mental phenomena was dependent on the similarity and/or repeated juxtaposition of sensations and perceptions over space and time. These could then be "internalised" – for example, by memory, through an association of ideas so that behavior subsequent to the initial stimulation could be explained by the mind's operation (Young 1973, 111).

In the early nineteenth century, Thomas Brown, whose work was cited by Jennings more than thirty years later, attempted to produce a theory of mind, reconciling associationism with the role of touch and muscle senses in revealing the external world in the mind. Still, the conceptual focus remained one of a "mental physiology," which was not carried out with any direct analysis of the nervous system. James Mill then used Brown's analysis in his theory of knowledge, albeit emphasizing muscle sense to the exclusion of touch (Smith, 1973, 92; Young 1970, 97). One crucial effect of the epistemological dominance in such discussion was that while it was acknowledged that the mind had powers that organized units of knowledge, the characterization of behavior tended to be conducted in terms of responses to external stimuli, thus emphasizing a "passive sensationalism" (Young 1970, 114).

It would be misleading to characterise the eighteenth-century conceptualization of the mind–body relationship in terms of a simple Cartesian dualism, since by midcentury two essential components of that dualism (the indivisibility of the mind and the notion of free will) had been challenged from within associationism (Young 1973, 111). By the early nineteenth century, however, a more decisive challenge to the previous century's conceptualization of a mind–body hierarchy was made in Britain and on the Continent. Analysts such as Flourens, Muller, Bell, and Hall argued for a division between types of reflex actions centered in the spinal cord, dealing with the lower, "automatic" regions of the body, and those actions ordered by the "soul," delineating the controlling regions of the brain (Jacyna 1981, 111; Smith 1981, 46). The notion of the reflex was subsequently made more precise and applied to the "higher" regions of the nervous system, which could then be conceptualized in terms of sensorimotor connections and reflex mechanisms (Smith 1981, 46; Danzinger 1982). By the 1840s and 1850s, an important point in such analyses was that the essential unit of the nervous system was the ganglion – a nerve nucleus served by afferent and efferent nerves. A series of those units were understood to be "largely autonomous centres of reception and innervation" (Jacyna 1981, 112). The significance of the ganglia for analysis of the cerebrospinal column was that the notion of reflection could be used to explain a number of cerebral functions. Although the continuity between various parts of the nervous system in terms of reflexes and sensorimotor connections was not "fully" established until the 1870s, it was possible by midcentury to explain human actions in such a way that the role of "the mind" was, to a significant extent, "epiphenomenal" (Smith 1981, 46, 164).

During the 1850s, the conceptual basis and thrust of associationist psychology was shifted abruptly with the incorporation, in theories of behavior, of the physiological analyses of sense organs and sensory processes that had been produced between the 1820s and the 1840s.

The significance of the physiological work of the 1820s and 1830s is apparent from the formulation of the Bell–Magendie "law" of spinal nerve roots, which enabled a "structural localisation of sensory and motor functions" – that is, the identification of nerves of sensation as contrasted with those stimulating muscles that moved parts of the body. The sensorimotor division of nervous function could be appropriated by psychology, precisely because the division was "a nervous (structural or mechanical) analogue for the psychological events of sensation and reaction" (Smith 1973, 82, 83).

By stressing the importance of relations between movement, the nervous system, and "in-born" patterns of coordination, it was also possible to provide an explanation for the body's spontaneous movements that were prior to and independent of previous external stimuli and consequently mental "associations." The organism became active, not simply reactive, in its own right because movement could precede sensation (Hearnshaw 1964, 12). To some extent, the nub of the explanation became the analysis of such spontaneous movements that were independent of and even opposed to those required by the "will." These were then linked to the experience of pleasure and pain, so that the organism could adapt its behavior to the ends or purposes of avoiding pain and attracting pleasure. Motor impulses could then become purposive movements by the association of ideas with them, even though there need be no voluntary activity on the part of the brain in bringing them about. It was necessary to incorporate "willed" activity, which was both conscious and voluntary, in such an analysis. However, with the emphasis on "activity as a primary psychological fact" and with the analytical means to delineate motion and purposive action, "association psychology had changed radically from an epistemological science to a psychological science of feeling, knowing and doing" (Young 1970, 120).

The work of Alexander Bain, particularly in his *The Senses of the Intellect* (1855) and *The Emotions and the Will* (1859), has been considered to be "the meeting-point of experimental sensory-motor physiology and the association psychology" (Young 1970, 101), producing the new discourse of physiological psychology. While Jevons was to indicate the relevance of Bain's work in *TPE*, W. B. Carpenter (1813–85), a colleague of Bain's, provided the point of entry for political economists to first appropriate the new discourse of behavioral action via Jennings's *NE*. Carpenter was professor of physiology and of forensic medicine at University College Hospital, London. As the author of the influential *Principles of Human Physiology*, first published in 1842, he "may be said to have played the same role from the physiological side that Bain played from the psychological side in uniting the two disciplines"; for it was Carpenter, "drawing heavily from Bain before the publication of Bain's major work" (Young 1970, 212n) who "combined" physiology and psychology by adding chapters on the latter to the fourth (1853) and fifth (1855) editions of his *Principles*.[11]

For Carpenter, organisms encountered matter, with its effects of resistance and "ponderosity," through sensations conveyed by the tactile senses of touch and muscular exertion, as well as the mental sense of effort. The connection between *"feelings of Pain and Pleasure"* and sensations was explained as "the necessary associations of those feelings, by an original law of our nature, with the sensations in question." For human beings, the "springs of human actions" were to be found in "instinct," which produced automatic (reflex) actions, and "intelligence," which produced volitional or voluntary actions. Pleasure and pain were not the only feelings humans could have, but they were important since they were associated with reflex actions (Carpenter 1888, 10, 16, 85, 100, 171, 173 OE).

Jennings's discussion of the "natural laws" of human action that were relevant in political economy for the explanation of consumption, work, and wealth accumulation depended on Carpenter's delineation of reflex actions, which occurred without the "attention" of the will, some even taking place if the mind was unconscious (Jennings, 1855, 136). Such actions could be based in various parts of the nervous system, from the nerves of the limbs to the cerebral cortex, although it was necessary to distinguish between the body's "Automatic Mechanism which constitutes the fundamental and essential part of the nervous system" and the cerebrum (Carpenter 1888, 100). The automatic apparatus was composed of the sensory ganglia and the thalamus. Figure 8.2 reproduces Carpenter's diagram of the general plan of the automatic apparatus in relation to the cerebral cortex. Jennings (1855, 136–41) closely and explicitly followed this account when detailing the natural laws of political economy.

Although Jennings referred in a number of places to economic actions that were governed by the will (1855, 10, 22, 125, 135), he noted that these occurred "much less frequently than is commonly supposed" (132). Instead, a good deal of activity was regulated behavior, consisting of actions that were "simply automatic or instinctive," performed "without the attention, or the intention, or even the excitement of consciousness in the mind of the agent." These reflex actions, which Carpenter had discussed, were "now universally recognised by psychologists" as resulting from the "involuntary education of the senses" through experience. The "two great branches of the subject,"

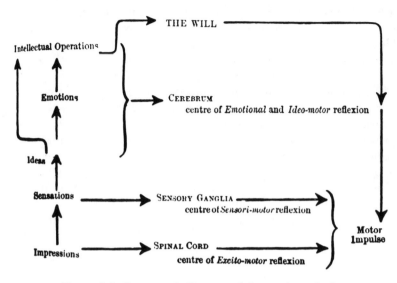

Figure 8.2. Carpenter's diagram of the cerebrospinal apparatus.

consumption and production (the latter really an analysis of work types and "effort"), could be explained in that manner. They were distinguished by their relation to different trunks of nerve fibers in the body. Consumption dealt with the effects of matter external to the body, producing "impressions" on the afferent fiber trunks, which led to the sensorium, resulting in mental "sensations." Production, by contrast, involved the body acting on external matter. This produced impressions on the efferent trunks leading from the sensorium, which, in turn, acted on muscles producing mechanical force. Such movements, which "originate" in the spinal column and not in the brain, constituted the "natural laws" of political economy that could be observed statistically by the method of averages (Jennings 1855, 46–9, 81–2, 136–8, 143). As Jennings summarized the argument:

> The laws . . . of human action are, in the same sense in which other laws of Nature are so, fixed and invariable, – the conditions under which they operate are undoubtedly subject to the interposition of the human will, but their results are, in the absence of such interposition, certain, and therefore subject to provision where sufficient knowledge has been attained to determine the existing conditions of phenomena, and to trace their consequences. Of all the direct connections of cause and effect, this, perhaps, appears the most paradoxical – that our own organs should ever without our con-

sciousness minister, like fairy hands, to our Desires, and even to our Ideas and our Sensations. (140–1)

To a significant extent, then, behavior could be depicted as a set of actions that were simultaneously purposive, automatic, and either conscious or unconscious. It was the notion of the reflex that allowed this "reconciliation of purposiveness with automatism" (Smith, 1973, 85) to designate an individual "organism" in terms of neurophysiological organization. At the same time, it was possible to allow for the effects of the environment on the organism in a functional manner. In the case of human beings, this enabled a distinction between "individual" and socialized behaviors and depended on the notion of learned reflexes that incorporated environmental effects. The corollary was that, just as people could learn reflex actions by the replication of uncontrolled events, it would be possible to direct them into new action paths by changing their environment. For Jennings, most economic activities consisted of reflex actions, and the mass of the population did not exercise free will to any significant extent.

Carpenter's analysis could have enabled Jennings to formulate his argument in terms of degrees of sensation using the manner in which the *Principles of Human Physiology* depicted feelings of pleasure and pain and stressed that they could be understood as "natural laws" of behavior with empirical or statistical correlates:

> The vividness of Sensations usually depends on the degree of *change* which they produce in the [nervous] system, [rather] than on the *absolute amount* of the impressing force; and this is the case with regard alike to special sensations. Thus, our sensations of Heat and Cold are entirely governed by the previous condition of the parts affected. (Carpenter 1888, 153–4 OE)

He also referred to "that diminution of the force of Sensations which is the ordinary consequence of their *habitual* recurrence" (155 OE). It had to be recognized, however, that the statistical laws, "in their primary sense, are simply expressions of *phenomenal uniformities*" or "comprehensive expressions of aggregates of particular facts . . . giving no rationale of them whatever" (629, 693 OE). This notion of statistical laws was common at the time, and Jevons was to use it in *TPE* (White 1989).

In concluding this section, two points show how, in using physiological psychology as a resource, *NE* marked a break with the work of previous analysts in British political economy. First, Jennings showed that it was possible to distinguish between "natural laws" of behavior and the social manifestations of those laws. In the previous work of supply and demand economists, this distinction was not made clearly.

To Thomas Banfield, for example, "man is . . . above all a free agent" with wants and aspirations. Yet he still made some muted allowance for the effects on people's behavior of "the circumstances in which they are placed" (Banfield 1848, 5, 11). *NE* showed, however, that it was possible to first banish the "social" with the designation of a new theoretical object. Instead of an undifferentiated "man," there was the human body conceptualized as a neurophysiological system/organism. Social behavior could then be accounted for by the organism's environment and could be observed with statistics.

Second, the new theoretical object of the body enabled a different conceptualization of behavior to explain the "system of action." Whereas Banfield posited a fixed order of want fulfillment, which, as Jevons noted, was incompatible with marginalism, *NE* showed that it was possible to posit a theory of action with a calculating neurophysiological organism. Combining the principles of consumption and production, Jennings could portray economic action in a way that was fundamentally the same as the subsequent marginalist supply and demand theory. In direct contrast with Banfield, the acquisition of commodities by an agent depended on

> whether the sensations of pleasure that are derived from the possession of objects which constitute property, and which are greater than, and prevail over, the sensations of toil that accompany the efforts by which alone they are commonly produced, or the consequent conception of value set upon these objects, or the will to labour for the purpose of producing, and to exercise self-denial for the purpose of calculating them. (Jennings 1855, 195–6)

Given the behavioral motivation of pleasure "attraction" and pain "revulsion" (45), the agent learned to calculate and thus to act through replication.

The citadel of the will – the Bain of Jevons's theory

The discourse of physiological psychology by the early 1850s was the result of a series of analytical responses to problems that emerged "within the framework of contemporary social systems" (Smith 1973, 79). The social conditions of existence of the discourse included, at various times: the challenge posed by the "anti-establishment" and "popularist" movement of phrenology; the study of hypnosis and of diseases, especially "nervous disorder and mental illness," both of which were components of the reorganization of hospitals and mental asylums in the nineteenth century; and, the acquisition of an institutional area of independence for psychology and physiology from medical studies (79, 81, 86). Because of its implications for child rearing, the treatment of alcoholism, and the legal defense of insanity (Daston 1978, 192; Smith 1981), the discourse necessarily had significant political implications for the discussion of those issues.

The political impact of physiological psychology was actually much wider than the preceding paragraph suggests. Once human behavior could be explained, to varying degrees, as predetermined by the body's neurophysiological organization, it could be argued that human behavior approximated a "materialist automatism" within the epistemological premises of scientific naturalism, which "reached something of a high point in Britain in the 1860s and 1870s" (Smith 1981, 9). According to this approach, the rhetoric of which was "saturated with concepts and terminology from mechanics" (Porter 1986, 196), scientific knowledge produced regulated or determined explanations of worldly phenomena that were thus "reduced to the parameters of matter and motion" in a deterministic or mechanistic fashion (Daston 1978, 194). In that respect, psychology could be viewed as simply one aspect of "a unified Science of Physics," as W. K. Clifford noted in 1874 (Daston 1978, 201).[12] This link was made by Carpenter (1857), when he claimed that mental events should be analyzed in terms of the correlation of forces framework: "[There is] a 'correlation' between nerve-force and mental agency, which is not less complete than that which has been shown to exist between nerve-force and electricity" (392–3). Bain followed suit, arguing that it was possible to explain the correlation of mind and body (i.e., psychophysiological parallelism) by "extending" the "doctrine" of the "Correlation . . . [or] Equivalence . . . [or] Indestructability of Force" to the "mind" (1867, 373).

By making the notion of voluntary behavior problematic, the concept of reflex action called the evaluation of "value, purpose and ethical conduct" into doubt, precisely because such evaluation depended on behavior being voluntarily undertaken so that a person was responsible for his or her actions. With the increasing circumscription of voluntary behavior, the analytical area of moral philosophy was correspondingly circumscribed so that the discussion of values and purpose, under the general heading of ethics, was apparently capable of analysis only in terms of what Henry Sidgwick referred to in 1874 as "the mysterious citadel of the 'Will' " (Daston 1978, 194, 201).

The debate over scientific naturalism can, in part, be seen as an instrument of "professionalization" by a number of prominent scientists, promoting a "model" of knowledge production directed against "the religious beliefs of the clergy and other scientists [who] could and did directly influence evaluation of work, patronage of research, and appointments in scientific institutions, the universities, and the public schools" (Turner 1978, 366). Beyond this particular context of conflict between "science and religion," the physiological psychology of Bain and his confrères raised a further political danger for conservatives such as the Unitarian James Martineau (discussed in the next section). If that discourse obliterated the disjuncture between psychical and physical nature, between mind (the "spiritual") and matter (the "material"), then the claims of the Christian church(es), based on the authority of the Scriptures, to lay down ethical prescriptions were under attack. This was held to threaten both the social position of the clergy and the stability of the social order; for just as the predominance of God/the Spirit over behavior entailed a system of hierarchy and subordination, the ecclesiastical organization was an inherent component of the ordering of the social structure. Without an "external power" that could prescribe an ethical ordering for the world, the regulation of both individual behavior and the existing set of social relations were threatened by the forces of "liberal radicalism" (Jacyna 1981, 110, 118, 120, 122–3).[13] That problem exercised W. B. Carpenter in his attempts to reconcile Christianity with physiological psychology (Smith 1977). Carpenter's solution to the dilemma between automatism and free will was to argue that while the will could only select and not cause actions (with volitional activity thus restricted within the choices available), it was capable of acting as a vehicle for "attention." Appropriate educational instruments would carry out the "riveting" of attention onto acceptable "ideas" so that the body's automatic apparatus would then determine behavior.

Jennings relied on Carpenter's *Human Physiology* to delineate laws of behavior but does not seem to have been particularly concerned by the ethical/political implications of that analysis in the terms just described. This may have been for three reasons: first, because of the political assumptions he made (for instance, the working classes were to be acted upon); second, because the political furor over physiological psychology became critical only after the late 1850s; and third, because he did not deem it politically necessary to demonstrate that market exchanges manifesting voluntary behavior produced an economically optimal outcome. For Jevons in the early 1860s, neither the second nor the third of those reasons could be taken for granted (see White 1989, 1992b).

While Jennings followed Carpenter, it was Alexander Bain's *Emotions and the Will* (1859) to which Jevons referred in *TPE* (1871, 19,

31, 39, 40).[14] Bain's work "profoundly changed" association psychology, integrating it with sensorimotor physiology and formulating an explanation of action, encompassing both perception and behavior, by making the sense of activity fundamental to the human being (Smith 1973, 95). The crux of his work was the link between sensation and motor phenomena (i.e., the nerves exciting muscular activity) (Young 1970, 119). Nevertheless, Bain argued that his theory was not "materialistic" – neural events did not cause mental events since both sets of events occurred in a direct correspondence. Aspects of consciousness correlated with motor nerve processes, so that there was a parallelism between the passive and active modes of consciousness and the sensory and motor delineation of neural processes (Young 1970, 73, 75; Daston 1978, 197, n123).[15] The private world of "the conscious" remained impenetrable, but because of psychophysical parallelism, behavior could be studied as "the observable correlates of mental events" (Daston 1978, 201; 1982).

Bain also argued that the exercise of the will depended on the body's physiological organization. According to his account, since the nervous system was capable of "spontaneous" (i.e., nonreflex) actions, it would experience muscular sensation. Such sensory experience amounted to the "experiential aspect" of the will, so that knowledge of the latter was dependent on the experience of volition (Boring 1957, 240). The problem, however, with this account of the existence of free will was that spontaneous actions were inseparable from, indeed determined by, the body's physiological structure. Free will was thus dependent on the specific physical/material context in which actions occurred, so that it could be held to be illusory. Bain was thus only evading the problem when he also defended the traditional role of introspection being used in conjunction with the psychophysiologists' experimental work (Smith 1973, 117, n35). In that respect, he followed J. S. Mill, who, while he greeted Bain's work enthusiastically, considered that the "ultimate facts of knowledge" corresponded to what were, in the final instance, "unanalysable states of consciousness" and that the development of knowledge was still fundamentally dependent on traditional introspective methods (Smith 1973, 120, n130; 1981, 59–60). Bain's ambiguity on the role of the will and hence voluntary activity was replicated in *TPE*.

Arguing that individual feelings of pleasure and pain underlay all actions, Jevons followed Bain in arguing that "every mind is . . . inscrutable to every other mind, and no common denominator of feeling is possible." This meant it was impossible to compare directly the "amount of feeling in one mind with that in another" so that "we cannot weigh, or gauge, or test the feelings of the mind; there is no unit of labour, or suffering, or enjoyment" (Jevons 1871, 21, 9). Nevertheless, such feelings prompted economic activity, so that "it is from the quantitative effects of the feelings that we must estimate their comparative amounts" (13–14). It was the will's role to act as the "final judge" on the "equality or inequality of feelings," which correspond to the events in the world "outside" the individual, so that its "oscillations are minutely registered in all the price lists of the markets." Drawing also on Quetelet's *l'homme moyen,* Jevons then claimed that the "general form of the laws of Economy is the same in the case of individuals and nations" and that statistics could be used to "verify" the utility theory (14, 21).

It is important to note that, in his *Principles of Science,* Jevons indicated that he was aware of the ethical issues raised by physiological psychology when, in discussing the arguments raised by scientific naturalism, he referred to the analysis of "mental phenomena." If such phenomena were "capable of treatment by the balance and the micrometer, can we any longer hold that mind is distinct from matter?" If not, "our boasted free will becomes a delusion." With "the uniform action of material causes" then explaining all events, it would be possible to "preclude the hypothesis of a benevolent Creator" (Jevons 1877, 736).[16] While Jevons rejected that conclusion (see later), the shifting terminology he used in *TPE* to describe the nature of "individual" and aggregate decision making provides further evidence that he was aware of the arguments about ethics that the physiological psychologists' work had raised. The designation of a mechanics of action suggests clearly the problem of automatism and scientific naturalism as it was understood by his contemporaries. Yet in discussing the inevitable tendency of human nature to choose the "greater apparent good," Jevons, explicitly referring to Bain's work, initially argued that the resultant choices were manifestations of "voluntary activity," that is, "a manifest of the will" (Jevons 1871, 19, 31). Subsequently, however, the manifestation became that of the "will or inclination" (46), where the latter category is ambiguous since it could refer to either willed or reflex activity. The ambiguity was then thrown into sharp relief via an introductory comment to a long quotation from Jennings's *Natural Elements* in which Jevons noted that the text "treats of the physiological groundwork of Economy, showing its dependence on physiological laws" (1871, 65). (The reference to the "groundwork" was taken directly from Jennings 1855, 18.)

Jevons seems to have been aware since 1860 of the ethical/political furor that accompanied the postulation of such reflex physiological laws (see later). Yet until the quotation from Jennings, there was no mention in *TPE* of the "dependency" of the action theory on them. *TPE* could thus maintain a theory of the mechanics of law-governed action, which was simultaneously voluntary, only by confusion. At first, activity was manifestation of the "will," then "inclination," until it was finally acknowledged that it was dependent to some unspecified extent on the existence of reflexes. It might be argued that Jevons was drawing on the ambiguities over willed behavior in Bain's account, but it is noteworthy that *TPE* made no attempt to acknowledge, let along confront, the problem of voluntary versus involuntary actions that Bain's exposition entailed. Indeed, in the "Introduction" to *TPE*'s second edition, the conceptual fudging was ironically made clear with this statement: "The science of economics . . . is in some degree peculiar, owing to the fact, pointed out by J. S. Mill and Cairnes, that its ultimate laws are known immediately to us by intuition, or at any rate, they are furnished to us ready-made by other mental or physical sciences" (Jevons 1970, 88).

The fudging occurred because Jevons failed to mention that Cairnes explicitly rejected basing economic analysis on psychophysiological laws as outlined by Jennings, and Jevons was well aware of Cairnes's objections. Jevons also failed to explain how an analysis based on "intuition" was reconcilable with one based on "laws" from other physical sciences since this was precisely what the opponents of physiological psychology argued was not possible (see later). Jevons further confused matters when he cited Bain's *Emotions and the Will:* "No amount of complication is ever able to disguise the general fact, that our voluntary activity is moved by only two great classes of stimulants; either a pleasure or a pain, present or remote, must lurk in every situation that drives us into action" (Bain 1859, 460; quoted in Jevons 1871, 31). The confusion resulted from citing Bain only on "voluntary action" and ignoring the problem of involuntary activity, which, as already noted, Jevons subsequently acknowledged was the "groundwork" of the action theory. Without a satisfactory resolution of the problem, however, Jevons's account of the "mechanics of human interest" as voluntary activity was incoherent.

Jevons in 1860: ruminating on free will

The remarkable similarities between the behavioral theories in *NE* and in *TPE*, when coupled with the speed with which Jevons switched to a marginalist theory in 1860, suggest that it is unlikely that Jevons "discovered" Jennings's text after he went to Manchester in 1863

(Howey 1960, 12–13).[17] This section considers some further evidence which suggests that, in 1860, Jevons was familiar with and troubled by the issues raised by physiological psychology.

Since Jennings's text was not widely known and rarely referred to, how could Jevons have located it? In July 1860, he wrote to his brother that he had "studied the subject [of political economy] independently and originally . . . and read some dozens of the best works in it" (Black 1973–81, 2:416). One possible candidate for his reading list would have been J. E. Cairnes's *Character and Logical Method of Political Economy* (1857), because, with its publication, Cairnes "had come to notice" in the late 1850s (Checkland 1951, 161n; see also Gooch 1920, 57). If Jevons had read *Character* with its general deference to J. S. Mill's approach to political economy, he could hardly have failed to notice the hostile treatment that Cairnes gave to Jennings's *NE* and to H. D. Macleod's *Theory and Practice of Banking*. Cairnes not only criticized Jennings and Macleod in long notes through the text, but also considered them important enough to discuss again in two appendices (Cairnes 1857, 176–83). As Jevons noted in *TPE*, Cairnes was the only exception to economists having failed to pay "the slightest attention" to *NE* (Jevons 1871, 65).

That Jevons was considering the issues raised by Jennings at the time that he announced his break with a labor theory of value is indicated by a number of his diary entries in early 1860. In early February, he recorded that he was working on his mathematical theory of political economy, and on February 19 he announced that he had previously "blundered" by using a labor theory of value. Two days before this, he recorded that he was "reading up the *Nervous System*."[18] This was possibly a reference to Marshall Hall's *Memoirs of the Nervous System* (1837), a discussion of reflex "sensori-motor" acts, which had influenced the early work of W. B. Carpenter (Jacyna 1981, 111).[19]

It is noteworthy that at the time Jevons began to outline his marginal utility approach, he was particularly concerned with the free will question. The context and form of his comments provide further indirect support for the argument that Jennings's text was of crucial importance in Jevons's early work. In two letters written in June and November of 1860, where Jevons outlined concepts that were to form the basis of his "true theory of Economy," the discussion of the theory was immediately followed or preceded by a reference to metaphysics. This was not in itself remarkable, since, at that time, Jevons was enrolled in a course entitled "Philosophy of Mind and Logic" at University College, London (Black 1972, 123). However, the terms of his comments are interesting. In the June letter, for instance, immediately following the claims for the theory ("so thorough-going and consistent, that I cannot now read other books on the subject without indignation"), Jevons wrote: "I am extremely interested in Metaphysics. . . . The ultimate question of philosophy that between idealism and materialism is necessarily an insoluble one, but one also on which we cannot avoid speculating with interest. Nor can I say that I yet feel bottom, I am somewhat . . . out of my depth" (Black 1973–81, 2:411). If Jevons had relied on Jennings's *NE* and, therefore, the work of the physiological psychologists in depicting behavior in a mathematical functional manner, it would not be surprising if he was ruminating on the specific metaphysical problem of "idealism and materialism"; for by early 1860, a storm had broken over physiological psychology couched in precisely those terms.

The harbinger of the storm was James Martineau's review, in the April 1860 *National Review*, of Bain's *Senses and the Intellect* (1855) and *Emotions and the Will* (1859). In posing the question "What Is 'Psychology'?" Martineau launched a trenchant attack on the possibility of a physiological psychology. Bain's account of the nervous system was "lucid, exact and compendious," but as far as psychology was concerned, it was "altogether foreign and intrusive," for it introduced "the language and methods" of the natural sciences into mental and moral philosophy, a procedure that should be rejected. To connect a "physiological exposition" with a subsequent analysis of "intellectual" processes was to "tincture" psychology "with a language of materialistic description, at once unphilosophical and repulsive." Psychology was concerned with "self-consciousness" (introspection), to which the very language and methods of physiological description were foreign. It was as if an artist were "to paint his Madonna with the skin off. It is recommended neither by scientific precision, nor by illustrative good taste" (Martineau 1891, 538, 542, 543, 545). For Martineau, since psychology required a reflecting subject, a knowing and willing self-conscious mind, it was primarily subjective and thus not a "natural" science (see Cardno 1955, 124–5).[20]

In *TPE*, Jevons rejected this argument of a complete divorce between the language and methods of the natural and moral sciences when he defended his approach to economic theory (Jevons 1871, 3). Nevertheless, his fudging over the voluntary nature of economic activity might suggest that he was worried by the type of criticism that Martineau had voiced. In June 1860, having announced his commitment to the mathematical behavioral approach, he acknowledged in the same letter that he was "out of his depth" in metaphysics, in terms that are consistent with the criticisms leveled at Bain's work in Martineau's review, published two months before.

Then, in the November 1860 letter containing further references to the marginalist economic theory and metaphysics, Jevons announced he was more interested in "moral philosophy" and was attending "Mr. Martineau's mental philosophy class at Manchester New College, which is close at hand in University Hall" (Black 1973–81, 2:421–2). Jevons's brother thought that this was peculiar:

> It seems to me rather odd of you attending Martineau's metaphysical lectures. . . . The truth about Metaphysics is not to be put in a book or treatise. I am inclined to think that the tendency of the present age is to deprecate the importance of Metaphysical studies and stick to exact science and practical knowledge. (Black 1973–81, 2:424)

Yet viewed in this sequence of events, Jevons's attendance at Martineau's lectures was not at all "odd." Martineau was one of the two full-time professors at the New College, which was founded originally as "the principal institution of higher education in arts and theology for Unitarians" (Black 1973–81, 2:421n). Moved to London in 1853, the college was "established to supply the theological element omitted from University College's curriculum" (Woodfield 1986, 7). The younger brother of Harriet Martineau, James was an influential intellectual force in the northern Unitarian power bloc of intellectuals and businessmen, having previously been professor of moral and mental philosophy as well as political economy when the New College was at Manchester. Martineau was, in other words, part of the "social background in which Jevons had been reared and his return to University College had brought him back into it" (Black 1972, 125).[21] While Jevons clearly disagreed with Martineau's attack on physiological psychology as such, he might well have been troubled by a fellow Unitarian's attack on that discourse as materialistic and to that extent "unethical."

Jevons's attendance at Martineau's lectures can thus be explained by Jevons attempting to reconcile the behavioral basis for his new economic theory, drawn from Jennings's *NE* and the work of the English physiological psychologists,[22] with the terms of Martineau's attack.[23] As it turned out, that was not particularly difficult. In general, Jevons was unimpressed by Martineau's arguments, announcing near the end of the lecture series that he remained convinced of "the objective certainty of our knowledge." He was not "sorry" he had attended the lecture, "if only to know what out and out metaphysics is." Nevertheless, he told his brother that he had found the lectures "a great labour," complaining that Martineau "pursues a steady course through the clouds." Moreover, he was highly critical of the lecturer's knowledge of physiological psychology: "When he does become comprehensible he generally goes palpably wrong; thus a few days since he astonished me by asserting that the tactual & muscular feelings are all one – that you cannot feel unless your *muscles* are in play."[24]

Insofar as Martineau's initial criticism had created something of a dilemma for Jevons, his experience was a specific example of the difficulties facing many scientists during that period in dealing with the conflict between "science" and "religion." By 1870, however, that debate had been absorbed in the discussion of the relation(s) between "mind" and "matter" (Block 1986, 380). As already indicated, Jevons referred to that issue in his *Principles of Science*, where he argued that science could not disprove the existence of the Creator. This was because of the incompleteness of scientific knowledge in the face of the "infinite . . . extent and complexity" of the universe. While science could posit the existence of various natural laws, knowledge of their causes was incomplete, and the Creator's role was thus possible in both the "original conformation of the material universe" and in "sudden and unexpected changes" where the possibility of "sudden catastrophes" could not be precluded (Jevons 1877, 739–41, 742, 746). Jevons's position thus seems to have been that it was possible to reconcile the claims of science and religion but that analysis of them should be kept quite separate analytically. Such compartmentalization of "belief" and "knowledge" was a common solution adopted in the disputes of the period.[25]

Conclusions

When J. E. Cairnes assessed Jennings's *Natural Elements* in 1857, he argued that a political economy based on such "laws of mind" was unnecessary (the basis for human behavior was known already), too complicated (it required a detailed knowledge of both psychology and physiology), and misleading (a satisfactory political economy could not be based on universal "mental principles"). Cairnes concluded that if political economy was "to be treated in this way, it is evident that it will soon become a wholly different study from that which the world has hitherto known" (1857, 181). The conceptualization of the domain of political economy was indeed to change dramatically when Jevons appropriated Jennings's analysis in the next decade. By depicting human behavior in mechanistic functional terms, however, Jevons both inherited and created for political economy a series of analytical problems. In particular, *TPE* became part of "a silly season," between roughly 1850 and the early 1870s, when "there was a zany intellectual ferment in discussion of determinism and free will" (Hacking 1983, 455).[26] Jevons's theory of the economic agent bears all the hallmarks of that "ferment," although his solution was to arbitrarily label the laws of action as voluntary in *TPE*. In this respect, Jevons provided a striking illustration of Ian Hacking's suggestion that "conceptual incoherence which creates philosophical perplexity is an historical incoherence between prior conditions that made a concept possible, and the concept made possible those prior conditions" (1981, 17). It should be noted, however, that Jevons's experience was not unique, for consideration of similar problems flowing from the scientific naturalism associated with physiological psychology can also be found in the early work of that other English marginalist, Alfred Marshall (Raffaelli 1990a, 1990b).

Notes

1. While this chapter is concerned with Jevons's natural laws of behavior, it should be noted that he did not claim that the laws became manifest in precisely the same ways in all situations, since they "may receive widely different applications in the concrete" (1905, 198). Drawing on Quetelet's notion of *l'homme moyen*, Jevons claimed that the theory could be verified by using statistics of average prices and quantities transacted in markets. This assumed a normal distribution of behavior, so that the theory could also explain the behavior of different races and classes. For this reason, the analysis was not concerned with individuals per se (White 1992b). Jevons's use of the "error law" was virtually a matter of faith (1877, 383–4).
2. In this chapter, OE denotes original emphasis.
3. Jevons's formal treatment of the argument was as follows. With x representing a unit of output, l representing a unit of labor effort, and u representing the utility of a commodity, then dx/dt is the marginal rate of production, dl/dt the degree of painfulness of labor, and du/dx the final degree of utility from the output, "whether [the laborer] consumes it himself, or exchanges it." Labor's "reward" was thus equal to $dx/dt \cdot du/dx$, and laborers would work up to the point or "moment" where the marginal pain of work was equal to the marginal pleasure of the reward. The equilibrium condition $dl/dt = dx/dt \cdot du/dx$ would then represent "the length of time which will be naturally selected as the best term of labour." With a constant rate of production, the equilibrium condition would become $du/dx = dl/dx$ (1871, 171–3).
4. The two early versions of the theory were both written in 1862. The longer version, however, was first published in 1866.
5. For a brief comparison of the approaches of Banfield and Jennings, see the section entitled "Physiological Psychology."
6. See White (1992a) and the references cited therein.

7. "The most profitable and philosophical speculations of Political Economy are however of a different kind: they are those which are employed not in reasoning *from* principles, but *to* them" (Whewell 1831, 43 OE). A member of the landed gentry, Jennings (1814–91) attended Trinity College, Cambridge, when Whewell was master. Subsequently, Jennings entered the law and, by 1859, was high sheriff of Carmarthenshire (Stark 1943, 165n; Howey 1960, 227).

8. The way that Jevons referred to Coulomb's work in the first edition of *TPE* (Jevons 1871, 193–4) might suggest that he was directly familiar with the concept of work as developed in late-eighteenth-century French mechanics (see Grattan-Guinness 1984). However, Jevons's discussion of Coulomb basically consisted of unacknowledged quotations from Babbage (1835, 30–1). In the second edition of *TPE*, a long (acknowledged) quotation from Babbage on fatigue and work was added to the text (Jevons 1970, 214). For a discussion of Babbage in this context, see Wise (1989, 410–17).

9. In the second edition, "spontaneous energy" was changed to "overflowing energy" (Jevons 1970, 190).

10. As Smith (1973, 76) has noted, while theories of the mind can be called "psychological," the term is somewhat anachronistic in this context.

11. For details of Carpenter, see Hearnshaw (1964, 19–23) and Young (1970, 210–15).

12. For discussion of scientific naturalism, see Turner (1974a, ch. 2).

13. See also Turner (1974b). Heyck (1982, ch. 4) provides a useful overview of the science versus religion debates.

14. It should be noted, however, that Jevons had certainly read the fifth edition (1855) of Carpenter's *Human Physiology* by 1862 (Jevons 1862, 86n). For details of Bain's biography and his work, see Hearnshaw (1964, 1–4) and Young (1970, ch. 3).

15. For a summary of the argument, see Bain (1867).

16. Jevons also noted that there "are scientific men who assert that the interposition of Providence is impossible, and prayer an absurdity, because the laws of Nature are inductively proved to be invariable" (1877, 736). This was a reference to the "Prayer Gauge Debate" of 1872–3 (Turner 1974b).

17. For the reasons already discussed, I disagree with Howey's (1960, 12) conclusion that Jevons's "early statements" on economic theory "do not show . . . any similarity of form or expression that would hint that he had studied Jennings carefully."

18. Jevons Archive, John Rylands University Library of Manchester, Item JA6/4/5.

19. Alternatively, Jevons might have been referring to Charles Bell's *The Nervous System of the Human Body* (3d edition, 1836) (Jacyna 1982, 235n).

20. Jacyna (1981, 120, 123) argues that, in the 1860s, Martineau saw physiological psychology as synonymous with the views of the "radical" wing of the Liberal Party – a grouping identified with J. S. Mill, Fawcett, Leslie Stephen, and W. K. Clifford – and that Martineau was a "leading exponent" of a conservative response to that radicalism.

21. Martineau's attack was first published as "Cerebral Physiology: Bain," in the *National Review*, 10 (1860): 500–21. In the same year, that journal published a review of *Poems and Essays* by Jevons's cousin, W. Caldwell Roscoe (1823–59). The text had been edited posthumously by R. H. Hutton, another relative, who had been principal of Manchester New College in 1852 (Woodfield 1986, 7). In July 1861, Jevons's review article entitled "Light and Sunlight," which had been commissioned by Hutton, was published in the *National Review* (Jevons 1861).

22. One other possible (non-English) influence on Jevons's formulation of the behavioral theory is suggested by Ekelund and Hebert (1975, 250). After noting that *TPE*'s utility theory was "at least based . . . partially on physiological theory," they argue that "in this connection Jevons specifically noted the Weber–Fechner studies of stimulus and response." However, no citation is provided to support the argument. I have found one reference by Jevons to "Fechner's law, Wundt's curve of pleasure and pain," but this was in a review of Edgeworth's *Mathematical Psychics*, where Jevons was citing Edgeworth's sources (Jevons 1881, 581). As far as Jevons's early work is concerned, it should be noted that Fechner's *Elemente der Psychophysik* was published only in 1860 (Boring 1957, ch. 14). Stigler (1965, 113–15) sketches the subsequent discussion of the Weber–Fechner law by economists, while Howey (1960, 95–103) concentrates on Edgeworth, noting that the German work was known in England as "psychophysics" by the late 1870s. Howey suggests that the Weber – Fechner law can be considered analogous to marginal utility theory because both argue that "the responses of the individual decrease in some way as the amount of stimulus increases." However, Howey argues, the two analyses were also quite different because psychophysics was concerned with "*sensations* associated with weight, distance, tones and the like," which could not be summed, unlike marginal utility. Moreover, psychophysics was concerned with measurement in laboratory experiments, an approach that was "shunned" initially by the marginal utility theorists, who appealed instead to "common experience" (Howey 1960, 98–9 OE). Clearly, however, this was not the case for Jevons (as described earlier). The basis for the similarities can be explained by psychophysics being the German variant of physiological psychology. Like its English counterpart, it began in the 1830s with work on reflex actions.

23. Jevons seems to have maintained amicable relations with both Bain and Martineau since they provided testimonials for him, which he used in his application for the chair at Owens College in 1866 (Black 1973–81, 3:107, 111). Bain was an examiner at University College London when Jevons was a student there in the early 1860s.

24. Letters to T. E. Jevons, April 4 and 28, 1861, OE, in the Seton–Jevons Collection, Seton Hall University. In his discussion of the possible theoretical continuities between Bentham, Martineau, and Jevons, Professor Black cites the following passage from Martineau's *Types of Ethical Theory:*

"I carried into [my moral and metaphysical speculations] . . . a store of exclusively scientific conceptions, rendered familiar in the elementary study of mathematics, mechanics and chemistry" (Martineau 1886, viii). Black (1972, 124 n3) considers this to mean "Martineau would certainly have appealed to Jevons." However, Martineau went on to point out that while this was his initial approach, he had rejected it by the late 1840s. To explain "human phenomena" in terms of "the maxims of mechanical causality" was to take the approach of a "tight-swathed logical prig" (Martineau 1886, ix, x).

25. For a summary of the various approaches taken by scientists on the question, see Brock and MacLeod (1976, 59). An earlier statement of Jevons's position can be found in an 1864 letter to Sir John Herschel (Black 1973–81, 3:60), after Herschel had rejected a request to sign the "Theological Declaration of Scientific Men." For the declaration and Herschel's reaction, see (60n); Brock and MacLeod (1976, esp. 47).

26. See also Hacking (1981). Unfortunately, Hacking does not discuss the work of the English physiological psychologists.

References

Babbage, C. 1835. *On the Economy of Machinery and Manufactures.* 4th ed. London: Knight.

Bain, A. 1859. *The Emotions and the Will.* London: Parker.

Bain, A. 1867. "On the Correlation of Force in Its Bearing on Mind," *Macmillan's Magazine,* 16:372–83.

Banfield, T. C. 1848. *The Organization of Industry, Explained in a Course of Lectures Delivered in the University of Cambridge in Easter Term, 1844,* 2d ed. London: Longman, Brown, Green, & Longmans.

Black, R. D. C. 1972. "Jevons, Bentham and De Morgan," *Economica,* 39(154): 119–34.

Black, R. D. C. 1973–81. *Papers and Correspondence of William Stanley Jevons,* vols. 2–7. London: Macmillan.

Block, E. 1986. "T. H. Huxley's Rhetoric and the Popularization of Victorian Scientific Ideas: 1854–1874," *Victorian Studies,* 29(3):363–86.

Boring, G. 1957. *A History of Experimental Psychology.* New York: Appleton-Century-Crofts.

Brock, W. H., and MacLeod, R. H. 1976. "The Scientists' Declaration: Reflections on Science and Belief in the Wake of *Essays and Reviews,* 1864–5," *British Journal for the History of Science,* 9(1):39–66.

Cairnes, J. E. 1857. *The Character and Logical Method of Political Economy.* London: Longman, Brown, Green, Longman, & Roberts.

Cardno, J. A. 1955. "Bain and Physiological Psychology," *Australian Journal of Psychology,* 7(2):108–20.

Carpenter, W. B. 1855. *Principles of Human Physiology,* 5th ed. London: Churchill.

Carpenter, W. B. 1857. "The Phasis of Force," *National Review*, 4(8):359–94.
Carpenter, W. B. 1888. *Principles of Mental Physiology*, 6th ed. London: Kegan Paul Trench.
Checkland, S. G. 1951. "Economic Opinion in England as Jevons Found It," *Manchester School*, 19:143–69.
Danzinger, K. 1982. "Mid-Nineteenth British Psycho-Physiology: A Neglected Chapter in the History of Psychology," in Woodward and Ash (1982, 119–46).
Daston, L. J. 1978. "British Responses to Psycho-Physiology, 1860–1900," *Isis*, 69(247):192–208.
Daston, L. J. 1982. "The Theory of Will Versus the Science of Mind," in Woodward and Ash (1982, 88–115).
Ekelund, R. B., and Herbert, R. F. 1975. *A History of Economic Theory and Method*. New York: McGraw-Hill.
Gooch, G. P. 1920. *Life of Lord Courtney*. London: Macmillan.
Grattan-Guinness, I. 1984. "Work for the Workers: Advances in Engineering Mechanics and Instruction in France, 1800–1830," *Annals of Science*, 4(1):1–33.
Hacking, I. 1981. "How Should We Do the History of Statistics?" *I and C* (8):15–26.
Hacking, I. 1983. "Nineteenth Century Cracks in the Concept of Determinism," *Journal of the History of Ideas*, 44(3):455–75.
Haughton, S. 1870. "On the Natural Laws of Muscular Exertion," *Nature*, 2:324–5.
Haughton, S. 1871. "On the Natural Laws of Muscular Exertion II," *Nature*, 3:289–93.
Hearnshaw, L. S. 1964. *A Short History of British Psychology, 1840–1940*. London: Methuen.
Heyck, T. W. 1982. *The Transformation of Intellectual Life in Victorian England*. London: Croom Helm.
Howey, R. S. 1960. *The Rise of the Marginal Utility School*. Lawrence: University of Kansas Press.
Jacyna, L. S. 1981. "The Physiology of Mind, The Unity of Nature, and the Moral Order in Victorian Thought," *British Journal for the History of Science*, 14(2):109–32.
Jacyna, L. S. 1982. "Somatic Theories of Mind and the Interests of Medicine in Britain, 1850–1879," *Medical History*, 26(3):233–58.
Jaffe, W. 1983. *William Jaffe's Essays on Walras*. New York: Cambridge University Press.
Jennings, R. 1855. *Natural Elements of Political Economy*. London: Longman, Brown, Green, & Longmans.
Jennings, R. 1856. *Social Delusions Concerning Wealth and Want*. London: Longman, Brown, Green, & Longmans.
Jevons, W. S. 1861. "Light and Sunlight," *National Review*, 13(25):1–26.
Jevons, W. S. 1862. "Spectrum Analysis," *London Review*, 18:80–100.

Jevons, W. S. 1863. "Notice of a General Mathematical Theory of Political Economy" (1862), in *Report of the Thirty-Second Meeting of the British Association for the Advancement of Science*, 158–9. London: Murray.

Jevons, W. S. 1866a. *The Coal Question: An Inquiry Concerning the Progress of the Nation, and the Probable Exhaustion of Our Coal Mines*, 2d ed. London: Macmillan.

Jevons, W. S. 1866b. "Brief Account of a General Mathematical Theory of Political Economy," *Journal of the Statistical Society*, 19:282–7.

Jevons, W. S. 1870. "On the Natural Laws of Muscular Exertion," *Nature* 2:158–60.

Jevons W. S. 1871. *The Theory of Political Economy*. London: Macmillan.

Jevons, W. S. 1877. *The Principles of Science: A Treatise on Logic and Scientific Method*. 2d ed. London: Macmillan.

Jevons, W. S. 1881. Untitled review of F. Y. Edgeworth, *Mathematical Psychics*, *Mind*, 6:581–3.

Jevons, W. S. 1905. *The Principles of Economics: A Fragment of a Treatise on the Industrial Mechanism of Society, and Other Papers*, ed. H. Higgs. London: Macmillan.

Jevons, W. S. 1970. *The Theory of Political Economy*, ed. R. D. C. Black. Harmondsworth: Pelican.

Katona, G. 1975. *Psychological Economics*. New York: Elsevier.

Macpherson, C. B. 1973. *Democratic Theory: Essays in Retrieval*. Oxford University Press.

Martineau, J. 1886. *Types of Ethical Theory* (1885), 2d edition, vol. 1. Oxford: Clarendon Press.

Martineau, J. 1891. "Bain's Psychology" (1860), in *Essays, Reviews and Addresses*, vol. 2. London: Longmans, Green,

Porter, T. M. 1986. *The Rise of Statistical Thinking, 1820–1900*. Princeton, NJ: Princeton University Press.

Raffaelli, T. 1990a. "The Analysis of the Human Mind in the Early Marshallian Manuscripts," in G. Becattini et al., eds., *Alfred Marshall's "Principles of Economics," 1890–1990: International Centenary Conference*, 1–20. Florence: Facolta di Economic e Commercio, Universita di Firenze.

Raffaelli, T. 1990b. "Marshall's Analysis of the Human Mind," in *The Early Philosophical Writings of Alfred Marshall*. Marshallian Studies no. 6. Florence: Dipartimento di Scienze Economiche, Universita Degli Studi di Firenze.

Rizvi, S. A. T. 1991. "Specialisation and the Existence Problem in General Equilibrium Theory," *Contribution to Political Economy*, 10:1–20.

Shapin, S., and Barnes, B. 1976. "Head and Hand: Rhetorical Resources in British Pedagogical Writing, 1770–1850," *Oxford Review of Education*, 2(3): 231–54.

Smith, R. 1973. "The Background of Physiological Psychology in Natural Philosophy," *History of Science*, 11(2):75–123.

Smith, R. 1977. "The Human Significance of Biology: Carpenter, Darwin and the *vera causa*," in U. C. Knoepflmacher and G. B. Tennyson, eds., *Nature and the Victorian Imagination,* 216–30. Berkeley and Los Angeles: University of California Press.

Smith, R. 1981. *Trial by Medicine: Insanity and Responsibility in Victorian Trials.* Edinburgh: Edinburgh University Press.

Stark, W. 1943. *The Ideal Foundations of Economic Thought.* London: Kegan Paul, Trench, & Trubner.

Stigler, G. J. 1965. *Essays in the History of Economics.* Chicago: University of Chicago Press.

Turner, F. M. 1974a. *Between Science and Religion: The Reaction to Scientific Naturalism in Late Victorian England.* New Haven, CT: Yale University Press.

Turner, F. M. 1974b. "Rainfall, Plagues, and the Prince of Wales: A Chapter in the Conflict of Religion and Science," *Journal of British Studies,* 13(2):46–65.

Turner, F. M. 1978. "The Victorian Conflict Between Science and Religion: A Professional Dimension," *Isis,* 69(248):356–76.

Tyndall, J. 1865. "The Constitution of the Universe," *Fortnightly Review,* 3(14):129–43.

Walsh, V., and Gram, H. 1980. *Classical and Neoclassical Theories of General Equilibrium.* Cambridge University Press.

Whewell, W. 1829. "Mathematical Exposition of Some Doctrines of Political Economy." Reprinted in Whewell. (1971). *Mathematical Exposition of Some Doctrines of Political Economy (1829, 1831, and 1850).* New York: Kelley.

White, M. V. 1989. "Why Are There No Supply and Demand Curves in Jevons?" *History of Political Economy,* 21(3):425–56.

White, M. V. 1991a. "Jevons's 'Blunder' Concerning Value and Distribution: An Explanation," *Cambridge Journal of Economics,* 15(2):149–60.

White, M. V. 1991b. "Where Did Jevons' Energy Come From?," *History of Economics Review,* (15):60–72.

White, M. V. 1992a. "Diamonds Are Forever (?) Nassau Senior and Utility Theory," *Manchester School,* 60(1):64–78.

White, M. V. 1992b. "Bridging the Natural and the Social: Science and Character in Jevons' Political Economy." Working paper, Monash University, Economics Department.

Wise, M. N. 1989. "Work and Waste: Political Economy and Natural Philosophy in Nineteenth Century Britain (II)," *History of Science,* 27(78):391–449.

Wong, S. 1978. *The Foundations of Paul Samuelson's Revealed Preference Theory.* London: Routledge & Kegan Paul.

Woodfield, M. 1986. *R. H. Hutton, Critic and Theologian: The Writings of R. H. Hutton on Newman, Arnold, Tennyson, Wordsworth and George Eliot.* Oxford University Press.

Woodward, W. R., and Ash, M. G., eds. 1982. *The Problematic Science: Psychology in Nineteenth-Century Thought.* New York: Praeger.

Young, R. M. 1970. *Mind, Brain and Adaption in the Nineteenth Century.* Oxford University Press.

Young, R. M. 1973. "Association of Ideas," in P. P. Weiner, ed., *Dictionary of the History of Ideas,* 1:111–18. New York: Scribner.

CHAPTER 9

Economics and evolution:
Alfred James Lotka and the economy
of nature

SHARON E. KINGSLAND

There is a natural affinity between evolutionary ecology and economics, because ecology is concerned with the ways in which limited resources are allocated among different uses and users. Yet the interaction between these two disciplines has been a recent development of
the past twenty-five years, in part because ecologists have only slowly,
and with much resistance, accepted the validity of mathematical modeling in their science. In the 1970s ecologists, aided by optimization
modeling drawn from engineering, began seriously to use economic
models and modes of thought, in some cases transferring concepts
directly from economics into biology, in other cases rediscovering economic principles in the context of their biological studies.[1]

At the same time, economists began to investigate ecological models
and to examine how they might be generalized and applied to economic processes (Goodwin 1987). The ecological models that drew
their attention were mathematical analyses of predator–prey interactions, which had been investigated independently by Italian physicist
Vito Volterra and U.S. mathematician Alfred James Lotka in the
1920s and 1930s. These models, along with parallel studies of population growth and competition, formed the backbone of theoretical
population ecology, which in conjunction with population genetics was
emerging in the 1960s as one of the most active and controversial
areas of ecology. Population biology investigated the relations between
ecological and genetic strategies and evolutionary processes, in particular to discover under what conditions fitness might be maximized.
These developments in evolutionary biology have, in turn, been applied to economic theories of the firm, although the validity of the
biological analogy has been contested, as discussed by Neil Niman,
chapter 14, this volume.

Although there is a long history of cross-fertilization between biol-

231

ogy and economics, the interchange between the two disciplines has only recently been pursued with any seriousness as far as mathematical modeling is concerned. Those who have explored this mathematical field recently are largely unaware that A. J. Lotka was the first person to attempt, as early as 1914, a direct transfer of mathematical methods from economics into ecology. In the light of Lotka's early interest in bioeconomic analogies, it is all the more interesting that later economists would draw upon other parts of Lotka's work – his analysis of two-species interactions and his demographic analyses of stable populations – without apparently being aware of how deeply his thinking about biology was influenced by the economics literature. This essay is about Lotka's efforts to develop a mathematically rigorous "economy of nature," an idea that in turn harkened back to the earlier bioeconomic analogies of Herbert Spencer and Henri Milne-Edwards, as well as to the mathematical economics of William Stanley Jevons.

A. J. Lotka (1880–1949) made his main reputation in demography, where he is now recognized for his work in stable population theory (Coale 1987; Vance 1959). His most important demographic analyses were done after he joined the Metropolitan Life Insurance Company as a statistician in 1925. But in the two decades preceding this move, he nurtured a different ambition: to create an entirely new field of science called "physical biology," which would analyze biological systems in thermodynamic terms. He developed this program in his best known book, *Elements of Physical Biology* (1925), which was the culmination of two decades of work. To develop the basis for his new science, Lotka drew on a wide literature in the natural and social sciences. This included the mathematical work in economics that was having an impact on U.S. economists at the turn of the century.

The breadth of Lotka's interests and the original way in which he synthesized these fields under the umbrella of physical biology made his book, paradoxically, both unique and typical at the same time. It was unique in not belonging squarely within any established discipline. In fact, his efforts to create a new discipline failed, and his book was too eclectic to become part of the canon of any field. This is not to suggest that he lacked readers: Lotka's ideas were picked up sporadically in many fields, especially by people who were receptive to interdisciplinary thinking. He made people think about things differently, he inspired them, and this stimulating effect created something like a cult following. Sometimes such "cult figures" can have significant roles in the history of science because they are able to translate ideas and methods across disciplines. Lotka's importance lay in his effectiveness as a translator.

His position as a cult figure raises problems for assessing his impact on a given discipline. Lotka was read by economists – Paul Samuelson, for one – and his impact on such people could be explored further. But it is not as a historian of the discipline of economics that I approach him. Instead, I wish to explore what Lotka's program meant and what vision of U.S. life it set out. Unusual though Lotka may have been as an interdisciplinary thinker, the project that he envisioned reflected concerns about the future of U.S. society that were typical of his age. Also typical was his search for solutions that relied heavily on the promise of mathematics and on the scientization of the world picture, solutions favoring the leadership of the scientific expert in an age that celebrated expertise. I shall use Lotka therefore as an expression of the U.S. *Zeitgeist* of the 1910s and 1920s and then examine how the context of this vision changed from the time his book first appeared in 1925 to the 1950s, when it was reprinted posthumously under the title *Elements of Mathematical Biology*. In order to discuss Lotka's impact in a way that does not lose sight of his own visions and goals, I shall discuss his influence on Herbert A. Simon, who as an economist must be considered a maverick, but whose interdisciplinary approach most closely resembled what Lotka himself was trying to do.

Lotka's plan for physical biology was modeled directly on physical chemistry, itself a new discipline emerging at the end of the nineteenth century. In 1901 Lotka graduated from the University of Birmingham, where he studied physics under John Henry Poynting, who was in the Maxwellian school, and in 1901–2 he traveled to Leipzig to study under Friedrich Wilhelm Ostwald, the founder of the energetics school of physical chemistry. These two men stimulated Lotka's interest in physical biology as a discipline analogous to physical chemistry. He began to delineate the scope of the discipline after he moved to the United States in 1902.

Physical chemistry emphasized thermodynamic principles and mathematical analysis, so Lotka imagined that physical biology must treat the organic world as a giant energy transformer. One could then apply the same mathematical analysis to the study of these transformations as had been developed in physical chemistry. Lotka wanted to reformulate biology as a branch of physics, where biological relationships would be related back to physical principles, specifically to the laws of thermodynamics. The kinds of biological problems he focused on in this context were largely ecological, involving the cycling of material and energy through the organic world. His writings included analysis of such problems as nutrient cycling, population growth, predator–prey interactions, and the meaning of biological fitness. For later ecologists, the attraction of his work lay in its anticipation of ecosystem analysis, as well as his mathematical analysis of population growth and two-species interactions (Kingsland 1985, chs. 2 and 5). In this chapter I discuss a part of Lotka's work that has not received much notice from ecologists, namely, his application of economic ideas to the problem of ascertaining how fitness was maintained.

To trace the origins of this synthetic project, we must look beyond Poynting and Ostwald to Herbert Spencer. Lotka was impressed by Spencer's efforts to derive a general law of evolution that could unify all historical processes. Spencer's statement of the law boiled down to the assertion that all processes entailed a progressive unfolding or evolution from simple homogeneous states to complex heterogeneous states. But Lotka realized that Spencer needed to be updated: He reasoned that as these evolutionary processes involved exchanges of matter and transformations of energy, then the laws of thermodynamics were basic to understanding organic evolution.

When Lotka spoke of evolution, he meant it in the broad sense used by Spencer, signifying a progressive unfolding and increase in complexity, analogous to the evolution of the embryonic organism, but involving the entire organic and inorganic world. He was not especially interested in the more limited biological meaning of one species diverging into two or more new species. Lotka believed it would be profitable to analyze the evolution of the entire world system as a whole. He compared the world to a giant engine or, using an image familiar in thermodynamics, to a giant mill wheel: This analogy was the starting point for Sadi Carnot's analysis of the ideal heat engine, which was later reformulated into the second law of thermodynamics. Lotka had been particularly impressed with the way his teacher J. H. Poynting had explained the heuristic significance of Carnot's ideal engine.

The first problem was to understand how thinking of the world as a giant energy transformer changed one's perspective on the laws governing biological processes. Could the law of natural selection be restated to answer the larger question: To what end did natural selection lead with respect to the energy flow of the organic system taken as a whole? The laws of thermodynamics, coupled with Spencer's formula for a general progressive law of evolution, gave Lotka a hint of how to proceed. He believed that thermodynamic principles led to the conclusion that natural selection should increase the total mass of the organic system, as well as the energy flow through the system. Here we have a thermodynamic explanation for the directionality of evolution. The idea of evolutionary progress was linked to the idea of capturing energy in the organic system and using it more efficiently.

The second problem was to relate the operations of the giant world engine to the activities of the individual organisms. What did this evolutionary principle mean for the individual and its ability to adjust and to remain competitive, or fit? Physicists had suggested a link between fitness and use of energy: Ludwig Boltzmann had pointed out in 1886 that organisms were engaged in a struggle for energy. Wilhelm Ostwald believed that organisms that could transform energy most efficiently would be more perfect and that this perspective would be important in evaluating the progress of human civilization. It was Spencer, however, whose blend of physics, biology, and economics proved most suggestive.

Spencer had recognized that evolutionary progress, reduced to individual terms, was an economic problem, a question of balancing various costs and benefits. There was, he believed, a balance in each individual between the costs of maintenance and the costs of reproduction. The individual had a finite quantity of energy to expend on these activities. This need to balance cost of maintenance with the cost of reproduction constrained how natural selection could act. Spencer believed that natural selection could not, all else being equal, produce an increase both in fertility and in individual maintenance at the same time, except by increasing efficiency. As he put it, the vital capital invested in an organic change had to bring a more than equivalent return. An evolutionary change, if it increased adaptation, must produce a more efficient performance of an action. Increased efficiency was achieved by a division of labor: There would then be a surplus of vital capital, which could be distributed into maintenance and reproductive activities (Spencer 1896, 2: pt. 6, secs. 363, 364, 373–7).

These ideas echoed the analysis of the economy of the organism developed in the 1850s by the French physiologist Henri Milne-Edwards, with whose work Spencer was well acquainted (Russett 1989, 131–40). Milne-Edwards had stressed the idea of the division of labor as a biological law. His views of the organic economy were clearly influenced by early-nineteenth-century French political economy, not surprisingly, given that he taught at the École Centrale des Arts et Manufactures starting in 1831.[2] One likely source of the analogy was Jean-Baptiste Say, who had reworked Adam Smith's *Wealth of Nations* to stress the importance of the division of labor as a means of improving the level of civilization (Say 1845, 77–84). Milne-Edwards introduced his "law of the division of labor" into zoology as early as 1827 but explored the economic model more clearly in his text of 1851, *Introduction à la zoologie générale*, where the division of physiological labor became a perfecting principle of organic life. Thus, the simple polyp was described as "a poorly directed workshop where each worker is in charge of the entire series of operations necessary for the construction of an object, and where consequently the number of hands all engaged in the same labors influences the quantity but not the quality of the product" (36). Higher in the animal kingdom, functions became diversified through the specialization of tissues, and the animal as a result was qualitatively superior.

Darwin, as we know, was influenced by Milne-Edwards's concept of the division of labor as a perfecting principle and in the *Origin of Species* applied the idea to the ecological world, arguing that natural selection would promote a division of labor within the organic world, that is, it would tend to produce greater diversity of species (Ospovat 1981, chs. 8 and 9). And if natural selection promoted greater diversity, then it could also be seen as a mechanism of progress, for a result of this increased diversity was the creation of the higher forms of life. Darwin did not push the analogy between organic evolution and economic principles very far, but Spencer was bolder in drawing these connections.

The central problem was to determine how individuals ought to allocate their energies in different activities. Following the Benthamite utilitarian tradition, Spencer connected an individual's activities first to feelings of pleasure and pain, and ultimately to the idea of biological fitness. Species would survive and be fit if pleasurable feelings were closely correlated with activities that supported life (1896, 124–5). His analysis, like so much of his armchair reasoning, had been full of broad generalizations supported by a few hypothetical examples. Lotka, who believed that a more rigorous analysis was needed, looked for a mathematical theory of economic activity that would provide a better heuristic device for exploring the connection between biological and economic quantities. He found his answer in William Stanley Jevons's *Theory of Political Economy* and in the early economic works of Vilfredo Pareto.

These were both natural choices for someone trained in physical science, for the metaphors and formalisms of thermodynamics were embedded in neoclassical theory. Jevons had developed his mathematical approach reasoning by analogy with the physical sciences, especially mechanics. *The Theory of Political Economy* was meant to formulate a science of economic mechanics universal in scope. Viewing economics as analogous to the physical sciences dealing with statics and equilibrium, Jevons tried to develop a program of scientific economics from Bentham's "hedonistic principle," creating out of the combination a "calculus of pleasure and pain" (1879, vii).[3] As Margaret Schabas has argued, Jevons used mathematics not so much with the intention of increasing the degree of certainty of his science, but as a way of adding clarity and precision to the formulations and also as a heuristic tool of a method of discovery (1990, ch. 5). To Lotka, the analogy between economic mechanics and his idea of physical biology, with its roots in energetics, must have appeared obvious. And for Lotka also, mathematical reasoning was to be used as a method of discovery, as opposed to a method of demonstration. Pareto had pursued the analogy between economics and rational mechanics even more aggressively than Jevons had (Mirowski 1989).[4] To him, Lotka turned for his concept of marginal ophelimity, Pareto's (1971) definition of utility.

But it was Jevons's work that provided the direct model for how to state Spencer's bioeconomic analogies in more precise form. Reasoning that the fitness of a species depended on the way the individual distributed its labor among various activities, Lotka assumed there would be some particular distribution that would produce an optimum benefit (and therefore greatest adaptation). Such a distribution could be attained only if the individual were capable of valuing things at their "true" or "objective" value. The problem was to discover how to determine the objective value in biological terms, in other words, how to relate value to biological fitness. Lotka's original forays into this question, published in 1914 and 1915, closely paralleled the parts of Jevons's discussion dealing with the concept of value and the theory of labor, especially his discussion of how labor might be divided to produce the greatest amount of utility with the least amount of pain.

In the biological counterpart, individuals would distribute their labor to make the rate of increase per individual a maximum. In this way, Lotka arrived at a definition of the value of a commodity in relation to the rate of increase, which at the same time was a measure of fitness (1914, 416). He expressed this relation mathematically as:

$$V_j = \frac{\partial r}{\partial m_j},$$ (1)

where V_j is the objective value of a given commodity, r the rate of increase per head (which, assuming exponential growth for the population, is equal to the birthrate minus the deathrate), and m_j the mass of the given commodity consumed per unit time per head. This equation related the value of a commodity (in this case, a food) to its effect, when consumed, on the rate of increase of the indidividual consumer, all other variables being held constant.

The rate of increase per head, known as the Malthusian parameter r, was designated the index of fitness. Then one could dissect the rate of increase into the various demographic and behavioral components that affected it: These were the individual mechanisms underlying fitness. In the biological example such parameters as population growth and age structure also had to be considered; Lotka's interest in demography added a third mathematical dimension to the analysis, complementing the methods that he derived from physical chemistry and economics. An appropriate question might be, for example, How efficient is a given behavior in relation to fitness? Or how do errors in the valuation process come to influence this efficiency? These questions remained abstract and qualitative, for Lotka did not have specific numerical examples of these relationships. Energy was certainly of value to the organisms, and the value of a food in energy terms might be gauged by its contribution to fertility, but this was a far cry from determining that value numerically. There was no known equivalent in the animal community to the standard of measurement represented by market prices in the human community.

In Lotka's more mature treatment in the *Elements*, these problems remained unsolved. He could only conclude that the formulas were useful because they revealed the relations between economic and biological quantities, even if they could not be applied to numerical examples. Moreover he firmly rejected the suggestion that there was any simpleminded relation between physical and economic quantities. Just because energy was of value to the organism, this did not warrant the assertion that economic value was a form of energy (1956, 355). He also played down in his later work the connections between his ideas and those of Spencer and Jevons, adopting an alternative proto-game theory approach based on an analogy with chess as a model of the "battlefield of life" (330–57). Game theory as a field of research developed in the 1940s following the publication of John von Neumann and Oskar Morgenstern's *The Theory of Games and Economic Behavior*, in 1944. Von Neumann's work had started in the 1920s but was not well known; Lotka's ideas seem to have arisen independently and had no relation to game theory as it later developed. It is, however, an interesting example of a way of thinking about biological relations in terms of strategic choices, as though one were playing a game. Comparing the relations of the organism to the environment to that of chessmen on a chessboard, he imagined that each organism carried around with it certain "zones" of influence and mobility, according to its sensory and motor capabilities. The dimensions of the zones determined how the individual could interact with the environment, just as the rules of chess determined how the chessmen could move across the board.

The interesting questions arose by considering how these relations could be changed. First, one could change the character of the zones (the sensory and motor apparatus), which was like changing the rules of the game by allowing the chessmen to move differently. Second, one could change the relation between organisms and environment, while leaving the zones intact, which was like changing the strategy of the players. Lotka then asked what effect these changes would have on the rate of increase. Returning to economic analysis, he arrived at the principle that, given free choice, the behavior of the individual would favor the growth of the species. However, he realized that an animal did not consciously maximize its rate of increase; rather, it maximized some other quantity analogous to "pleasure." Therefore, a well-adapted species was one whose behavior was adjusted to maximize something analogous to pleasure, which would automatically also maximize the rate of increase. This brought him back to Spencer's "hedonistic principle," and he was unable to apply the game analogy in any specific fashion.

Lotka apparently had an almost obsessive enthusiasm for mathematical modeling, but obsessiveness aside, there was a larger agenda to his book, a search for a way to engineer progress by rationalizing and controlling behavior. His main concern was the relationship of humans to technology. Lotka was not just offering a new way of analyzing biological problems, but also making an argument concerning the individual's predicament at a time of overwhelming technological growth. His interpretation of natural selection as a mechanism for increasing energy flow and efficiency, which was quite unlike the usual biological way of thinking about evolution, was meant to demonstrate the unity of man and nature, to show that human activity was intimately tied in with the operation of the vast world engine.

The starting point was his image of technological aids as the sensory and motor organs of the social organism, the body politic. The point of view was holistic. "Man and machines," he declared, "today form one working unit, one industrial system. The body politic has its organs of sight and hearing, its motive energies, its moving members, in close copy of the primitive body of man, of which it is a magnificent and intensified version."[5] Both Spencer and Ostwald had expressed similar ideas. Spencer had developed the analogy between the organism and the body politic in considerable detail: He had likened the nerve fibers of a vertebrate to telegraph wires. Ostwald compared the evolution of machinery to organic evolution and stressed the importance of studying civilization from the point of view of technical science.

As with these authors, Lotka's notion of the body politic was intended to show that the evolution of the social organism through technological expansion was part of a natural process that contributed to the individual's unity with nature. The solution to the stresses of a modern industrial age was to bring the individual into harmony with nature's schemes. A new kind of individual and a new definition of individualism were called for; here Lotka parted with Spencer. Working with nature did not imply a society governed by selfish attitudes or the hedonistic visions of a brave new world, but a society of altruistic individuals who had risen above selfishness to become, in Lotka's words, collaborators with nature. His viewpoint was progressive and forward-looking, his vision of human evolution a gradual movement toward a harmonious, cooperative, and efficient society of the future.

These ideas were mirrored in many different forms in the literature of the time, during which the theme of industrial expansion and society's response to it echoed in popular magazines and professional journals alike. The expansion of U.S. industry at the turn of the century stimulated many pronouncements on people's duty to suppress their unruly individualism and to contribute to the growth of the modern, industrial society. This was the theme of Horatio Alger's popular novels. With wit, daring, and luck, his heroes might overcome their impoverished beginnings, but these heroes were no rebels: They ended up by quietly settling into the proper place in society. Whether technology was seen to be a beneficial or malevolent force, the question of the day was: How would people respond and adjust to the changes of the new age?

References to progress measured by the efficient use of energy permeated this literature. In 1901, for instance, Brooks Adams argued that nature favored organisms that were most efficient in their use of energy. The future society, according to Adams, would have rulers skilled at administering "masses vaster than anything now existing in the world," and laws and institutions would "take the shape best adapted to the needs of the mighty engines which such men shall control" (165). As H. G. Wells observed in 1906, the country seemed to be at a turning point in its great surge of growth, a change from the "first phase of a mob-like rush of individualistic undertakings into a planned and ordered progress" (70–1).

But industrialization was also producing a society fragmented and polarized along class and racial lines. Some felt that the stresses of modern society could be blamed on the technological changes that science had wrought. Lotka wanted to dispel this idea that technology had an alienating effect by grounding the vision of a planned and ordered progress in the basic laws of nature. Far from being alienating, technology was a means by which people could achieve unity with nature through the combined actions of the body politic, on the condition that they kept up with the progress of technology and suppressed any selfish tendencies that interfered with the social organism. More science, not less, was the guarantee of progress. Lotka was advocating a kind of secular millenarianism, a vision of a new society transfigured and guided to greatness by an elite intelligentsia who understood how to fulfill the "great World Purpose" (1956, 428). Dorothy Ross (1991) has surveyed the vast literature in the social sciences that addresses the theme of the response to industrialism, showing how social science attempted to lift the United States outside of history by constructing a means of engineering the future.[6] In some respects Lotka's book represents a microcosm of U.S. postwar society, a single text in which one finds a condensed expression both of the anxieties of the age and of the millenarian vision that was the professional middle-class response to this anxiety.

Progressing through such examples as these on the economy of nature, Lotka's book offered a wide-ranging set of reflections on behavior and how it might be rationalized through the application of mathematical techniques drawn from various sources, including physical chemistry and demography. Although the book was largely mathematical, Lotka moved quickly from one example to another, avoiding plunging the reader into the esoteric details that normally characterized treatises in mathematical subjects. His discussion of the mathematics of systems of differential equations, for instance, was laid out clearly and briefly in a few pages. The book could be read with profit by interdisciplinary thinkers looking for innovative ways of applying mathematical methods to social as well as biological problems. For such people, Lotka helped to translate mathematical methods and physical concepts into terms they could understand and apply in their own fields.

One such reader was Henry Schultz, who as an avid neoclassical economist was intrigued by the analogies between energy physics and economics. Lotka's book was one of his favorites, and he had his students at the University of Chicago read it. Among those students was Herbert A. Simon, who read Lotka in 1936 and, like his teacher, made it one of his favorite books. The value of Lotka's work lay not only in its mathematical framework and transfer of ideas across disciplines, but in its sophisticated approach to the use of analogies. Lotka realized that an incidental similarity based on loose analogy was not sufficient to justify the application of physical laws and techniques to other disciplines. He was always concerned that the use of analogy should be based on an actual identity between the systems being considered.

Simon (1959) reviewing the second edition of Lotka's book, *Elements of Mathematical Biology*, published in 1956, explained what had made this eclectic work stimulating to people of his generation and why, as late as 1959, he would continue to refer his students to the book. Most important was Lotka's clarity in expounding certain ideas that were current at the time, especially those having to do with equilibrium systems. Lotka's book provided an exceptionally clear discussion of the mathematics of systems of differential equations in the context of a general discussion of statics and dynamics and examination of various types of equilibria. Simon noted that Paul Samuelson's (1942) analysis of the relations of statics and dynamics in the 1940s was indebted to Lotka's discussion of the problem. Weintraub (1991, ch. 3) has explored the possible connection between Lotka and Samuelson in more detail, suggesting that because of the widespread academic interest in Pareto's sociology at Harvard University in the 1930s, Lotka's book and its analysis of equilibrium systems would have found a receptive audience (see also Russett 1966).[7] Later in 1967 and 1971 Samuelson returned to Lotka's work, this time to apply the predator–prey models developed by Lotka and Volterra to economic theory (see Samuelson 1972, 473–86, 487–90).

Lotka's discussion of the displacement of equilibrium was a forerunner of cybernetics; as Simon noted, there was much in Lotka's book that seemed to anticipate later developments in mathematical theory, as well as in ecology and social science. Simon considered Lotka to represent an "imaginative forerunner" who "creates plans of exploration that he can only partly execute, but who exerts great influence on the work of his successors" more by asking interesting questions than by solving them (Simon 1959, 493). For Simon, the value of the book was not only in the examples discussed, but in the way Lotka used mathematics as a heuristic tool. In most social science texts, mathematics meant statistical analysis. Like Lotka, Simon was interested in using mathematical modeling as a method of discovery, not simply as a method of demonstration. Lotka's book was one of the few places one could turn, outside economics, for examples of how to use modeling in a creative way in the social sciences. Simon also credited F. W. Richardson's *Generalized Foreign Politics* (1939) and Nicholas Rashevsky's *Mathematical Theory of Human Relations* (1947) as important influences. In Simon's collection of essays, *Models of Man, Social and Rational,* all three are acknowledged as influences on his mathematical approach to human behavior and human rationality (1957, xi). These essays were the basis for the course Simon taught on mathematical social science.

The essays in *Models of Man* were intended to develop a theory of human action that encompassed both the rational and the nonrational aspects of human behavior. They built on Simon's work, begun in 1935, in the field of decision making and administrative organization. The purpose of this kind of analysis was to gain control over human behavior: "The behavior of a rational person can be controlled . . . if the value and factual premises upon which he bases his decisions are specified for him" (1991, 193). In approaching the problem of controlling behavior, Simon developed an interdisciplinary approach that cut across economics, political science, social psychology, sociology, learning theory, logic, and statistics. What unified the essays was their interest in creating a "science of man that will accommodate comfortably his dual nature as a social and as a rational animal" (1957, vii; see also Miller 1990).

Simon's program of mathematizing the human sciences, in contrast to Lotka's efforts to found a new discipline in physical biology, was highly successful. Changes in the institutional context of U.S. science were at least partly responsible for Simon's and Lotka's different levels of achievement; in particular we should note the greater role that the military was to play in mathematical science after the war and how this influence was felt in the social sciences. To explain his own development, Simon recalled the postwar influence of the Cowles Commission for Research in Economics, which ran weekly seminars at the University of Chicago on mathematical economics and econometrics that drew economists from around the world. The commission had close connections with the RAND Corporation, the think tank for research and development that was funded largely by the air force and was devoted mainly to studies relating air force strategy and national security. RAND was also at the center of developments in cybernetics and computing, attracting academics from around the country, who, in addition to working on military problems, explored applications of the theory of decision making and game theory. Simon, while serving as a consultant at RAND starting in 1952, worked out part of the analysis of the decision-making process that went into the essays collected in *Models of Man* (esp. 164–7).

Lotka had been only indirectly aiming at a "science of man," while ostensibly trying, albeit unsuccessfully, to create a new branch of biology as a subset of physics. Nevertheless, his book was clearly motivated in part by anxieties about the direction of U.S. society and the role that science and technology should have in shaping the future. This concern, expressed through the metaphorical discussion of the body politic, motivated the unusual interdisciplinary project that Lotka undertook but could not complete before his death in 1949. Completion of the project would rest in the hands of a later generation. Although scientists like Simon began their work in the 1930s, and therefore to some extent shared Lotka's cultural experiences, it was the postwar context, with the creation of the "military-academic complex," that promoted interest in applied mathematics and its use in all aspects of human life. Thus, just as Lotka could use advances in mathematics, which themselves were products of industrial development, to improve on Spencer in the early twentieth century, so Simon, using mathematical advances that were called forth by new military and technological needs, could bring some of Lotka's ideas to fruition.

Notes

1. The range of economic thinking in ecology was reviewed by Rapport and Turner (1977). A more important impetus for the use of optimization models in ecology has been engineering, especially operations research. On optimization modeling, see Oster and Wilson (1978).
2. Milne-Edwards's use of this analogy has been examined in Limoges (in press).
3. Lotka used the 1911 edition, which has the same text.
4. Chapter 5 of Mirowski (1989) discusses the physical analogies underlying neoclassical economic theory.
5. A. J. Lotka, manuscript of a projected book, in the A. J. Lotka Papers, Princeton University Archives. Lotka incorporated the ideas for this book into the concluding chapters of *Elements of Physical Biology;* see esp. chs. 33 and 34.
6. Ross's thesis is that the development of social science helped to preserve the nationalist ideology of U.S. exceptionalism that was threatened by industrialization and the loss of religious authority in the early twentieth century.
7. Russett discusses the Pareto circle at Harvard; she refers to Lotka's book in passing without, however, indicating whether the book was well known among this group. Statistician Edwin B. Wilson, a member of the Pareto group, did review Lotka's book when it first appeared, but his comments were ambiguous, concluding with the remarks that it was beyond the abil-

ity of the reviewer to describe the book's merits or assess its faults. See Wilson (1927).

References

Adams, Brooks. 1901. "The New Industrial Revolution," *Atlantic Monthly*, 87:165.

Coale, A. J. 1987. "Stable Population Theory," in J. Eatwell and M. Milgate, eds., *The New Palgrave*, 4: 466–9. New York: Stockton Press.

Goodwin, R. M. 1987. "Predator–Prey Models," in J. Eatwell and M. Milgate, eds., *The New Palgrave*, 3: 936–7. New York: Stockton Press.

Jevons, W. S. 1879. *The Theory of Political Economy*, 2d ed. London.

Kingsland, Sharon E. 1985. *Modeling Nature: Episodes in the History of Population Ecology*. Chicago: University of Chicago Press.

Limoges, Camille. In press. "Milne-Edwards, Darwin, Durkheim and Division of Labour," in I. B. Cohen, ed., *The Relations between the Natural Sciences and the Social Sciences*. Princeton, NJ: Princeton University Press.

Lotka, Alfred J. 1914. "An Objective Standard of Value Derived from the Principle of Evolution," *Journal of the Washington Academy of Science*, 4:409–18, 499–500.

Lotka, Alfred J. 1915. "Efficiency as a Factor in Organic Evolution," *Journal of the Washington Academy of Science*, 5: 360–8, 397–403.

Lotka, Alfred J. 1956. *Elements of Mathematical Biology*. New York: Dover. Originally published as *Elements of Physical Biology* (1925).

Miller, Carolyn R. 1990. "The Rhetoric of Decision Science, or Herbert A. Simon Says," in H. Simons, ed., *The Rhetorical Turn: Invention and Persuasion in the Conduct of Inquiry*, 162–84. Chicago: University of Chicago Press.

Milne-Edwards. 1953. *Introduction à la zoologie générale; ou considérations sur les tendances de la nature dans la constitution du règne animal*, 2d ed. Paris: Masson.

Mirowski, Philip. 1989. *More Heat Than Light: Economics as Social Physics, Physics as Nature's Economics*. Cambridge University Press.

Ospovat, Dov. 1981. *The Development of Darwin's Theory: Natural History, Natural Theology, and Natural Selection, 1838–1859*. Cambridge University Press.

Pareto, V. 1971. *Manuel of Political Economy*, trans. A. S. Schwier. New York: Kelley.

Rapport, David J., and James E. Turner. 1977. "Economic Models in Ecology," *Science*, 195: 367–73.

Ross, Dorothy. 1991. *The Origins of American Social Science*. Cambridge University Press.

Russett, Cynthia E. 1966. *The Concept of Equilibrium in American Social Thought*. New Haven, CT: Yale University Press.

Samuelson, Paul. 1942. "The Stability of Equilibrium: Linear and Non-Linear Systems," *Econometrica*, 10: 1–25.

Samuelson, Paul. 1972. *The Collected Scientific Papers of Paul A. Samuelson*. Cambridge, MA: MIT Press.

Say, Jean-Baptiste. 1845. *Cours complet d'économie politique pratique*, 6th ed. Brussels, 1845.

Schabas, Margaret. 1990. *A World Ruled by Number: William Stanley Jevons and the Rise of Mathematical Economics.* Princeton, NJ: Princeton University Press.

Simon, Herbert A. 1957. *Models of Man, Social and Rational: Mathematical Essays on Rational Human Behavior in a Social Setting.* New York: Wiley.

Simon, Herbert A. 1959. Review of Lotka, *Elements of Mathematical Biology*, *Econometrica*, 27: 493–5.

Simon, Herbert A. 1991. *Models of My Life.* New York: Basic.

Spencer, Herbert. 1896. *The Principles of Biology*, 2 vols. New York: Appleton.

Vance, R. B. 1959. "The Development and Status of American Demography," in P. M. Hauser and O. D. Duncan, eds., *The Study of Population: An Inventory and Appraisal*, 286–313. Chicago: University of Chicago Press.

Weintraub, E. Roy. 1991. *Stabilizing Dynamics: Constructing Economic Knowledge.* Cambridge University Press.

Wells, H. G. 1906. *The Future in America: A Search after Realities.* London: Chapman & Hall.

Wilson, E. B. 1927. *Science*, 66: 281–2.

PART IV

Organic metaphors and their stimuli

Fire, motion, and productivity: the proto-energetics of nature and economy in François Quesnay

PAUL P. CHRISTENSEN

Chez nous, pour nous, tout est physique, et le moral en dérive.
Quesnay in a marginal note to a text of
Mirabeau (Weulersse 1910, 122)

Introduction

The history of economic thought since the mid-seventeenth century has been characterized by a succession of models that attempt to ground economic ideas in the methodologies, conceptual structures, and mathematics of the natural sciences. While mechanics and the idea of a self-adjusting economic machine have provided the most well known examples in classical and neoclassical theory, it is less known that physiology played a crucially important role in shaping the early development of the classical model. From Hobbes to Quesnay, the dominant set of metaphors shaping the conceptual structure of the economic theory of production and exchange were drawn from physiology and the comparison of the economy to the living body (and the larger economy of nature).[1]

For early economists whose starting point was production, physiology provided an obvious set of analogies. Nature, like the economy, was produced by the self-activity of living organisms. It depended on the extraction and transformation of nutritive and other materials from the earth, which were circulated and consumed. And it reflected design and organization in its parts and its totality. Conceptually, early economists drew on many related domains: mechanics, matter theory, theories of activity and motion, chemistry, and physiology.

I will argue that Quesnay's economic theory of production and circulation (the *Tableau économique*) and his unique theory of agricultural productivity (and manufacturing sterility) reflect not only his

249

physiological model of the circulation of blood (as Foley [1973] argues), but also his physical, chemical, physiological, and "ecological" theory of the production and circulation of materials in nature. These processes in turn fundamentally depend on the circulation of a dynamic, active, and life-giving ether. As Mirowski (1989) has convincingly shown, neoclassical theory was structured by the conceptual and mathematical framework of nineteenth-century analytical mechanics and field theory (which postulates motion and productive potential at every point of input space). Preclassical and classical theories had their own theories of motion and activity underpinning production and exchange. In Quesnay's case, this was a theory of an active and subtle matter (shaped by Leibnizian, Epicurean, and chemical influences) combined with a theory of immanent design.

Despite the fact that Quesnay spent the greatest part of his working life as a surgeon and physician and wrote a number of works on medicine and a major treatise on physiology, his natural philosophy and physiology and their connection to his economics have not received systematic study. Sutter's (1958) survey of Quesnay's physiological and medical ideas gives only a cursory and unsympathetic account of Quesnay's physiology.[2] The portrait that has been drawn is that of a "derivative Cartesian" (Foley, 1976), closer in spirit to early-eighteenth-century mechanism than to the concerns of Enlightenment philosophy and biology.[3]

At the same time, historians of economic theory have sought to disassociate his economic theory from any fundamental connection with his natural philosophy or metaphysics. Schumpeter (1954) argues that "neither the theological nor the naturalist element was really the point from which (the physiocrats) started. They merely expressed the results of economic analysis in this theological or naturalist form *after* they had established them" (49–50; emphasis in original). Meek (1962) approvingly quotes Schumpeter and adds that while it would be wrong "to dismiss the divine and ideal elements in [the Physiocratic formulations," it would be equally wrong to claim "that their ideas about 'natural law' somehow lay *at the basis* of their economic analysis" or that the latter was "derived from their philosophy" (373).[4]

Schumpeter, Meek, and others assert that there is no significant influence running from Quesnay's natural philosophy and metaphysics to his economics. But they provide no investigation of his scientific ideas – his matter theory, his ideas about motion in nature and organisms, his use of conservation principles, his treatment of biological generation, or his ideas of productivity in the "economy of nature." Quesnay's natural philosophy, in particular his theory of the causes of activity in matter and in physiology, provides a completely neglected connection with his economics. I will show that Quesnay's theory of matter and activity is the key to understanding his productivity doctrines and the material circulation of the *Tableau économique*.

First, the chapter reviews the mechanistic theories that dominated physiology in the early eighteenth century. Second, it sets out Quesnay's arguments about bleeding as background for his treatment of the structure of the circulation of materials and money in the economy. Third, it introduces the main themes of the two editions of his major physiological work. It attempts, fourth, to consider some of the main thinkers and ideas that influenced the major statement of his physical theory in the second of the two editions. Fifth, it takes up the specific theories and arguments that characterize his natural philosophy and physiology generally and those that he will obviously employ in his economics. The last two sections show how his ether theory of motion and change and regenerative processes in nature offer an explanation of his singular theory of productivity and the structure and exchanges of the *Tableau*.

Mechanistic physiology

Quesnay has been regarded, along with Vaucauson and Le Cat, as one of the leading adherents in France of the mechanistic physiology, which had been developed by the followers of Galileo, Descartes, and Newton – chiefly, Baglivi, Borelli, Bellini, Pitcairne, Cheney, and Boerhaave.[5] According to the mechanist view of the seventeenth and early eighteenth centuries, everything in nature could be reduced to operations of matter and motion (as matter was reduced to extension). All nature from the particles of homogeneous matter to chemical compounds, living bodies, and the motion of the planets operated according to the same mechanical principles. Life reduced to movement and living organisms to machines. Mechanics governed the complex and subtle operations of living things just as they did the visible mechanisms of a clock.

In English physiology, Harvey's revolutionary discovery of the circulation had inaugurated a very fruitful alliance between the Aristotelian biological ideas championed by Harvey and the more mechanistic orientation of many of his followers. Chemical, vitalistic, and mechanical theories were all considerably advanced in the third quarter of the seventeenth century. But this diversity was soon overwhelmed by the great success of Newton's dynamics and the impetus Newton gave to the voluntarist view of God's omnipresent activity in nature. Just as chemistry in the hands of Boyle was increasingly oriented to physical or mechanistic explanations, physiology in the age of Newton became a study of fluid hydraulics and forces (whose source lay outside the body and remained unexplained). The body was a hydraulic machine of circulating fluids. Sickness and health were viewed as a question of the balance of forces in the humors (fluids) of the body.

The treatment of motion and activity in the mechanical philosophy was, to a considerable extent, shaped by religious beliefs and the need to avoid a confrontation with religion. In contrast to the tendency of the Aristotelian and Epicurean traditions toward materialist explanations of inherent activity, the mechanical philosophies of Descartes, Boyle, and Newton were characterized by a "supernaturalistic ontology of action" (Hutchinson 1983, 325; Pyle 1987). Matter was entirely passive. God had created matter with properties of extension, inertia, and mobility. Motion came from outside; it was not a property or quality of matter. God had provided for motion by creating a certain quantity at creation or through his continuous action in the universe. Matter on its own (or in organized form) could neither move nor think.

Whereas traditional biology had explained the activity, organization, and direction of life by a hierarchy of vegetative, sensitive, and intelligent faculties or souls, Descartes reduced the involuntary physiological processes of the body to mechanical processes and eliminated the vegetative and animal souls from physiology. Sensitivity and thought were confined to humans and attributed to an immaterial rational soul (Staum 1980, ch. 1; Roger, 1986). The soul (analogous to motion) was an immaterial principle or explanation of human activity.

Mechanical explanations were likewise applied to nutrition and generation, the main faculties of the vegetative soul. Classical and Renaissance naturalists had treated nutrition as the source of the body's innate heat. Food and a vital component from the air were linked to an invisible or slow "combustion" responsible for the body's motion (Mendelsohn 1964; Hall 1969).[6] Mechanists, by contrast, confined the role of food to the materials used for the growth and replacement of tissue. The body's heat was explained by the friction caused by the hydraulic and mechanical operations of the body that wore away the material tissue of the body at a great rate, especially in the smaller vessels. These parts were "continuously ground away and impaired and must consequently require continual reparation by new particles" (Boerhaave 1742 1:85). The lungs were a bellows to cool this heat.

The question of motion was simply avoided. Inert matter could not move itself, and neither could one explain how an immaterial spirit moved matter. Boerhaave, as a good Newtonian, writes that "we are wholly ignorant of the origin and communication of motion in bodies" (1742, 1:71). He compares the body to a clock. It requires only one original cause to put it in motion and once in motion will continue to perform its several actions during the space of time for which the wheels and works are adapted (1:310–11).

Generation was likewise radically reinterpreted. Aristotle, Galen, Harvey, and even Descartes had supposed that organisms were formed by epigenesis, that is, by the successive organization of parts from nutritive substances. But how could passive matter organize itself? Any attempt to explain the organization of matter into the rich variety and complex structures of plants and animals by the self-activity of living bodies raised the Epicurean heresy. The mechanists (Swammerdam, Malebranche, and others) adapted the doctrine of preformation (all organisms develop by simple enlargement from the germ) to a theory of "emboitment": All organisms were created by God at the beginning of the world and carried as tiny germs (each generation smaller than the last) in the loins of the first parents (Roger 1963, 1986). Preformation through encasement thus preserved a creationist ontology and a mechanical explanation of growth (Roe 1981).

By the mid-eighteenth century, the inadequacies of the mechanistic program were increasingly evident and under challenge. The mechanistic theory of matter in which corpuscles of some homogeneous substance were united in various sizes, shapes, and motions to form the visible elements of the world had failed to provide any predictive account of the operations of chemistry or the "stubborn" irreducibility of the chemical elements (Schofield 1970; Thackeray 1970, ch. 6).[7] Passivity of matter was, moreover, particularly at odds with the manifest activity of matter evident in chemical, electrical, and biological phenomena – for example, in the sensitivity of living tissue. Nor could preformation and the theory of preexistent germs offer a satisfactory theory of biparental heredity, of hybrids, of monsters, or of the regeneration of the severed parts of crabs and other animals. The regeneration of Tremblay's polyp, discovered in 1740, was particularly perplexing to mechanists. Severed into numerous pieces, each part was regenerated as a complete organism. Did a separate soul reside in each part, each with the power of generation? All this evidence of the ceaseless activity of nature provided support for a resurrection of a biologically oriented materialism (Roger 1963, 457–68).

But it takes a theory to beat a theory. In the 1830s and early 1840s, new theoretical frameworks emerged in France that variously combined elements from Locke's epistemology, the methodology and matter theory of Newton's *Optics*, Liebniz's theories of immanent design and the inherent activity of matter, the matter theory of the Epicureans and Spinoza, and the chemical and vitalistic approach to physiology and medicine of Stahl and the German tradition. A key element in the new ideas was a belief in the inherent (immanent) activity of nature centered either on the inherent activity of matter or on a vitalistic account of organisms. Neomechanists, materialists, and vitalists together challenged the hegemony of traditional mechanism in chemistry, biology, physiology, and medicine (Roger 1903; Moravia 1978).

As we will see, Quesnay did not remain indifferent to these new theoretical currents. A chronological examination of his major physiological works provides evidence of the continuing development of his thought: his early iatro-mechanism, the increasing importance of chemistry and its philosophy in his work, his materialist explanation of the inherent activity of nature, his adoption and development of the new theory of epigenesis, and his vision of the intrinsic powers present in biological structures. We will then see how he applies these ideas of production, generation, and motion to economics.

Bleeding and equilibrium in the circulatory system

Quesnay was a surgeon practicing in a small town outside Paris when he challenged the bleeding theories of Jean-Baptiste Silva, a court physician and member of the faculty of the University of Paris. Silva (1727) had applied the mechanistic theory of Bellini to sustain an argument for bleeding the lower limbs in cases of fevers, smallpox, and other maladies of the head and superior regions.[8] Quesnay cuts through Silva's highly speculative arguments with the relentless application of a model based on the simplest principles of hydrostatics.

According to Silva, bleeding a vein (the *evacuation*) "attracts a much greater quantity of blood" into the vein, the neighboring veins, and the artery that supplies these veins than is taken by the evacuation. This quickened and enlarged flow of blood in the region of the bleeding is called the *derivation*. The result was a correspondingly large reduction in the quantity and velocity of blood flow in regions served by opposing or distant arterial branches (the *revulsion*) (1727, 2–3).[9]

Silva uses these "theoretical principles" to give the decision whether to bleed from the arms, the foot, or the throat. Bleedings are derivative or revulsive to the extent that they direct blood toward or away from a particular part of the body. Bleeding an arm is revulsive with regard to the inferior (lower) parts of the body, which receive their blood by the trunk of the descending artery. Bleeding the foot is revulsive in regard to the parts served by the superior (upper) arteries. Thus, one would bleed the feet (and not the arms) to cure an inflamation or fever in the head (Silva 1727, 4; Delauney 1906, 218–19).

Quesnay writes that he found Silva's doctrines very different from his own. To satisfy himself, he "had recourse to a project which I made for fixing my ideas and directing my practice" (Quesnay 1730, iii). This was to apply the principles of the "laws of hydrostatics" to a very simple model of the circulation and to construct "a hydraulic machine" to "convince myself . . . in all manner of facts that I had drawn out and demonstrated from universally received principles" (iii). He later describes this apparatus as "a tube of tin divided into two equal branches" (Quesnay 1750, 159).[10]

Quesnay begins wtih a very simple example (1730, 2–6).[11] Assume a flow of eight seaux per minute through the large branch, which divides equally into four seaux in the two smaller branches. An opening is made in one of the latter, and two seaux per minute is removed (the evacuation).[12] Because of the lower resistance (due to the opening), the current will flow faster in this branch. The lower resistance will also direct the flow away from the branch that has not been cut until an equilibrium is reestablished in the amount of liquid flowing through each pipe (beyond the opening in the case of the first), that is, three seaux will flow through the terminous of each branch in which the resistance is equal. The derivation is the five seaux flowing in the first branch before the opening (two seaux evacuated by bleeding and the three seaux that flows through the length of the branch). Quesnay defines the revulsion as the smaller flow of three seaux in the uncut branch. His "First Fundamental Proposition" (Prop. 3) is that the derivation is greater than the revulsion only by the amount of the evacuation, that is, $D(5) - R(3) = E(2)$ (1730, 2–6).

Silva had argued that the mass of blood projected toward the cut (the derivation) and the reduction in the distant and opposing parts (the revulsion) are each larger than the amount taken by the evacuation. Quesnay disagrees and says that "the resistance will only diminish as much as one takes of the blood" (1730, 28). The "first and principal effect" of the bleeding for Quesnay is the augmentation of quickness in the flow (the derivation). Since the blood flows more quickly in the vessels where there is a derivation than in those where there is a revulsion, it is the derivation (and size of the evacuation) that matters most and not the revulsion (80).

Because of the evacuation, the flow of the blood and other humors in the immediate area is accelerated, disturbed, and agitated. The engorged and blocked canals are cleared. The glands and other flows are less compressed, filtrations are facilitated, and the humors that circulate in the canals are moved more liberally. In addition, the proportion of the chyle in the blood is increased. The "great effect" of the bleeding is the augmentation of the freshness (*crudité*) of the blood and not Silva's principle of "revulsion" (Quesnay 1730, 103–6, 120).

Quesnay constantly appeals to theory. The body is treated as a simple hydraulic structure that operates according to the basic principles developed from initial definitions and propositions. In a much expanded 1750 version of his bleeding theory, he adopts a more discursive mode of argument. He twice asserts that the body is *not* to be compared to a simple hydraulic machine (11, 17).[13] He now argues that the elasticity of the organic vessels and changes in the air pressure within the vein and on the body must be taken into account. Bleeding releases air as well as blood from the veins. The compression of the external air shrinks the vessel in proportion to the fluid taken and the vessel cannot be depleted. The "pretended" depletion cannot take place and is contrary to the laws of nature (1750, 17). Quesnay recognizes the much greater complexity presented by bodies composed of elastic vessels. His new arguments reflect the work of Stephen Hales on the elasticity of air and the vessels of the body.[14]

Before leaving Quesnay's bleeding theory, it is worth remarking on Foley's suggestion of the influence of Quesnay's circulatory model on his treatment of expenditure flows in the *Tableau économique*. "Just as . . . the circulation of blood in the body falls into two large subdivisions," one flow feeding the head and arms and the other radiating out to supply the lower trunk and legs, the same "two fold division is found in Quesnay's economic analysis." Economic expenditures "emerge from a common source in the collective coffers of the landlords and immediately subdivide into two flows" following the circulation scheme and that of the "tubes of tin" (Foley 1976, 124, 126).

The correspondence is more extended. In addition to the flow to the head and arms (the landlords), the arterial trunk divides into two systems (farmers and artisans), one going to each side of the body. This treatment of the arterial circulation has been a primary feature of medical texts since Galen. Each channel, Quesnay emphasizes, repeatedly divides and subdivides, carrying blood "to irrigate all the parts" (Quesnay 1730, iii). In a subsequent discussion of the friction in the smallest vessels, Quesnay calculates that the mesenteric artery divides into 37,418 branches (1736, 242). Having made such calculations of the repeated divisions of the blood flow, he was well prepared to recast the aggregate flow of economic expenditure to the parts of the social body in similar terms. The *Tableau économique* divides not only expenditures but farmers and artisans into progressively smaller groups, each depending on progressively reduced streams of money and commodity exchanges. The body provides the map of the structure and operation of the socioeconomic system.

The Animal Economy: the two editions

Quesnay's refutation of Silva brought him to the attention of the powerful La Peyronie, head of the Royal Academy of surgeons, who introduced him to the future Duke of Villeroy.[15] He joined the household of the Duke, who provided him with the needed leisure for physiological and medical studies and sponsored him as a member of the Academy of Science in Lyon. In 1736, he published his *Essai phisique sur l'oeconomie animale*,[16] a much simplified version of Boerhaavian chemistry and physiology.[17]

The title indicates a concern with the physical principles or fundamental laws governing physiology.[18] The central focus of the work, however, is not mechanics, but chemistry – the elements that form the "mixtes" or compounds that in their turn form the structures and fluids of the body. Chemistry was not only central to the study of physiology and to medicine;[19] its prominence in Quesnay's *Essai* signals a degree of epistemological and conceptual distance from mechanistic reductionism. Quesnay, we will see, allies himself with those chemists who saw the need to establish an autonomous discipline whose principles of combination were not satisfactorily explained by physics (see Moravia 1978, 51; Guedon 1979).

The *Essai* is prefaced by a long methodological "Discourse," which stresses the dependence of theory on experience and indicates the strong influence of Locke.[20] He proposes two rules: "never supposing beyond that which experience instructs us" and "never asserting by a simple chain of consequences, the truths we uncover by experience." Medicine is very complex, and those who abandon themselves entirely to reason will fall into error (Quesnay 1736, xxii, xxxii).

The 1736 *Essai* is divided into three umbrella chapters. The first treats the chemistry of the six elements (fire, air, water, earth, oil, and salt), the second the basic humors made from the aliment that nourish and regulate the body, and the third the solid parts and temperaments (the latter regarded as a disposition of the solid parts). The first topic taken up is a discussion of the nature of matter. While physicists maintain in theory that matter is always divisible, in experience division has always stopped at a "certain genre of molecules" that resist all attempts at further division (1736, 2–3). These are the elements or principles on which physiology is grounded. Of the six elements, fire and air are active; the rest, like matter itself, are entirely passive.

Fire is a very subtle matter or fluid that is responsible for producing all the effects manifest in nature. Oil and salt are qualifiedly included with the basic elements. Quesnay's justification indicates something important about how he thinks nature works. He asks if oil and salt should be excluded, since little remains when they are put to the test of destruction by fire, that is, of distillation. The evidence that they are elements comes from experiments in agronomy: "Smoking the earth" can renew its fertility because "the salts and sulfurs of mixes which are released return to the womb of the earth where they in turn contribute anew to the reproduction of the mixes" (1736, 6). This hint of the "ecological" circulation of materials is more explicitly spelled out in the second edition.

In a long note, Quesnay disavows any theoretical speculation on "first principles," such as the existence of a vacuum, an ether without motion, an ether that is the principle of all activity, or the nature of fire. All such "first knowledge," he says, is not useful or necessary to the art of healing, which is concerned only with immediate causes and effects. Medical doctrine is independent of the hypotheses of the physicists on the nature of the elements and first causes and "all their different fashions of moving subtle matter and of animating the universe" (1736, 2–3).[21]

In the three-volume edition of 1747, which is essentially an entirely new work, Quesnay ends his silence on metaphysics.[22] He effusively praises the "celebrated Boerhaave, who has reordered all the teaching of physiology. But this "great master" presents his lectures on physiology as an "atomique usage of parts," which is insufficient "for judging the method he has followed (and) the light he has drawn from physics for explaining the mechanisms of the body." To understand his doctrine, "it is necessary to be instructed in the principles and proofs on which they have been established" (1747, 1:3–4). Boerhaave, Quesnay writes, goes knowledgeably into the action of the stomach on the aliments but "has passed lightly over the first physical causes which give motion to the parts" (7). It is thus necessary to undertake a discussion of the intelligence and direction by which physiology operates, its first principles, and the first causes of its motion.

The 1747 *Essai* is thus marked by the attention it gives to first principles: the nature of matter and form, the nature and sources of motion, the productions of chemistry, and the functions of the vegetative, sensitive, animal, and rational souls in the living body. Volume 1 provides a detailed treatment of the elements, including a two-hundred-page chapter on fire and the active ether, which provides the motion that animates the living world and effects all the changes that take place in nature.[23] Volume 2 is devoted to the chemistry of acids, bases, and salts and the "mixtes" and molecules that make up the fluid and solid parts of the body. Volume 3 includes a section on the humors, a coverage of the vegetative, animal, sensitive, and intellectual faculties (souls), and sections on the circulation and temperaments. The *Essai* is more a philosophical treatise on the nature of activity in animate and inanimate nature. Its chief focus is an extensive consideration of the vegetable, animal, and reasonable faculties in animals and humans.[24]

Conceptual influences

What has drawn Quesnay out of his silence on the nature of matter and motion? Quesnay will now explicitly develop the dependence of the operations of chemistry and physiology on a conception of an inherently active matter – an extremely active and subtle ether whose source is the light of the sun and whose circulation between the animal, vegetable, and mineral kingdoms is used to explain all the motions and changes in nature, including the "productions" of chemistry and the vital processes of generation, nutrition, sensitivity, muscular movement, and so on. This activity-bearing ether is, in turn, joined to the regulative powers and capacities of the structures and organs of the body. These faculties or capacities are a vital machine. Like a machine, they require a source of motion, and they direct and regulate the forces and powers supplied to them by the ether.

Quesnay's physiology is an eclectic mix of neomechanistic and vitalistic themes. To attempt to locate these themes in relation to the philosophic currents with which they are intertwined, we look briefly at some of the writers and positions that appear to have influenced his natural philosophy.

First, there is his acceptance of Locke's "sensationalism" and the physiological and corpuscular matter theory with which it was connected (the Epicurean atomism championed by Gassendi and taken over into the physiology of Willis, Mayow, and others). Locke's system of "physical influence" of the body on the soul was given an extremely wide hearing in France in the 1730s and 1740s (see Yolton 1991). This included his suggestion, heretical to many, that God might have endowed matter with the capacities of thought.[25] Quesnay rejects the innate ideas of Descartes. Like his mentor, La Peyronie, he posits a theory of reciprocal influence, indeed, a unity of body and soul.[26] Reasoning about the relationship of the body and soul had proceeded in ignorance of the light of anatomy and physiology (Quesnay 1747, 3:163–7). Sensation, discrimination, and thought are clearly regarded as faculties of the body.

Second, his work reflects the penetration of Newtonian theories in France. Quesnay was a disciple of Boerhaave, who was considerably influenced by Newtonian mechanics and methodology. Quesnay knows and uses the important contributions of Stephen Hales in the physico-chemistry of elastic and fixed airs and physiological fluids. He is considerably influenced by the neomechanistic philosophy of Maupertuis, who with Clairaut was an early scientific advocate of Newton's physics and cosmology in France.[27] And he knows the "Newtonian" program of Buffon, which extended from agronomy and forestry to natural history.[28] An essential legacy of Newton for French science and biology was his emphasis on forces and active principles, which, with a shift in metaphysics, played a central role in the revival of theories of active matter in the eighteenth century.[29] By adding force to matter and motion, Newtonian physics adds a fundamental category to biological explanation (Roe 1981, 18).[30]

Third, Quesnay embodies the increasingly important role that chemistry plays in the shaping of French natural philosophy in the eighteenth century. Chemistry became an autonomous discipline fundamental to an understanding of the processes of nature. This reflected the growing influence of Stahl, whose critical contributions to the analysis and composition of compounds was widely known by leading French chemists.[31] Stahl's chemical theories were disseminated by Rouelle's lectures at the Jardin du Roi, which were attended by a generation of scientists and intellectuals (Eklund 1971; Guedon 1979). While Quesnay's specific chemical commitments remain to be determined, it is clear that he takes the side of the anti-Newtonians, who refuse to reduce chemical attractions to a general inverse-square law and occult principles. Rather, chemistry operates by the principle of affinities mapped out by Geoffroy and developed by Rouelle and others (Quesnay 1747, 1:83, 363).

A central topic of chemistry was the theory of fire. In contrast to the dynamic theory of heat as an internal motion of particles, most eighteenth-century chemists adopted a substantial theory of fire – a subtle material whose activity explained heat, light, fluidity, combustion, and so on. Boerhaave's *Elementa chemiae* (1731) played a central role in the development of a substance approach to fire and offered a mechanistic account of fire as a universal instrument in chemical processes. His Newtonian caution about causes limited a speculative linking of matter theory, chemistry, and life processes.

Stahlian chemistry, in contrast, offered a more unified explanation of the activity of nature centered on phlogiston – the material principle of fire or flammability (Eklund 1971). As a primary consituent of certain minerals and present in different degrees in plants and animals (e.g., in the oils), phlogiston was the common material principle that connected by its circulation the vegetable, animal, and mineral kingdoms. From decaying plants and animals, phlogiston was incorporated in minerals in the earth, taken up by plants, passed on to animals in their food, and returned to the air and the earth. Between 1718 and 1723, Stahl had developed

> a remarkable picture of self-moving and self-supporting nature . . . conceived as a dynamic interrelated unitary chemical system of minerals and metals, plants and animals including the atmosphere. It was maintained, apparently, without a direct intervention of a divine agency by the circulation of combining and resolving (the elemental) and inflammable principles of matter. (Teich 1982, 19)

Hoffmann, a student and colleague of Stahl, combines a corpuscular theory of matter with Leibniz's dynamic theory of motive force to provide a mechanistic treatment of physiological functions. The processes of the body are based on the operation of a highly subtle and active ether which serves as the material principle of animation (Duchesneau 1991).[32] Quesnay's treatment of the ether has a broad similarity with that of Hoffmann, although he develops it in a more materialist direction. Quesnay's ether similarly extends the Boerhaavian theory in a materialist direction and connects it to a vision of the interdependence of "ecological" and physiological processes. All activity in nature, animate and inanimate, depends on the circulation of this invisible and active material element.

Fourth, the late 1730s and 1740s were witness to a revival of animistic and previtalistic ideas in medical theory. Stahl's antimechanistic medical theory (1707), with its emphasis on organization, final purposes, and an immaterial animate principle differentiating life from nonlife, was to play a significant role in this resurgence (Hall 1969; Staum 1980). Living things had self-locomotion and sensitivity. In France, the University of Montpellier became a center of early vitalist teaching and its export.[33] Vitalists and neomechanists agreed that "pure" mechanism could not explain vital processes such as generation, sensitivity, control of the pulse, and other involuntary motions. There was a need for an intelligence and directing force within organisms.[34] Vitalists attributed this to a unique principle of life. Nonorthodox mechanists used the same language. Quesnay, for his part, restores the nutritive, animal, and reasonable souls to physiology and argues for a vital principle (which he finds in the activity of the material ether operating conjointly with the determinative powers and capacities of the body).

Fifth, there is the influence of Leibniz's metaphysics and theory of the inherent activity of matter. In place of God's continual intervention in the world (Newton's voluntarism), Leibniz had posited an omniscient God who had created a world with sufficient powers to govern itself.[35] Maupertuis, who knew Leibniz's theory of *vis viva* from Bernoulli (1727), had made a critique of its conservation in response to the perceptive questions of Madame du Châtelet in the late 1730s. One fruit of this reexamination was his formulation of the principle of least action (see Dufrénoy 1963). He adopts the metaphysical principle that the basic principle of the design and operation of the universe is economy of action and expense (Maupertuis 1748, 8, 21). He also adopts Leibnizian ideas in regard to the activity of matter and extends the fundamental qualities of matter from extension, impenetrability, durability, mobility, and the like to self-motion, sensitivity, and perception. His application of these ideas to a theory of biological generation (see the next item) and in a theory of the transformation of species (Glass 1959) was to have immense importance for French biology.[36]

An important influence in the spread of Leibnizian ideas was Du Châtelet's *Institutions de physique* (1740), which sought to synthesize Newton's theory of motion with the mechanistic and metaphysical foundation of Leibniz, and her 1744 dissertation on fire (which Quesnay cites). Both works develop a Leibnizian conception in which matter is characterized by the power to act. Buffon, who was close to Maupertuis and the Cirey circle (Du Châtelet, Voltaire, and König) in this period, was another important source of Leibnizian ideas.[37]

Sixth, there is the decisive influence of Maupertuis's (1744) development of an epigenetic theory of biological generation along mechanistic lines. What is particularly significant is the way he applies his new metaphysics and matter theory to generation. He rejects the arguments of orthodox mechanism that generation is based on a unique creation (the preexistence of germs). He marshals the argument of the prodigious production of seeds of trees and the sperm of male animals to demonstrate that the idea of the encasement of preexistent germs is impossible at the level of matter theory and physiological organization.[38] Ancestors simply could not house the germs of this profusion. Generation is accomplished by natural processes working in time. God is shown by the regularity and operation of the physical laws he has designed. Maupertuis suggests a neomechanistic cause:

Generation works by attractive forces (crediting Geoffroy's ideas of selective affinity or relations between different kinds of particles) and suggests an "instinct" that causes the particles of matter to unite (indicating again the influence of Leibniz).[39]

A seventh influence on Quesnay was La Mettrie. Protégé of Maupertuis, friend of Quesnay, and former student of Boerhaave, La Mettrie had spent a decade translating Boerhaave's chemical and medical works into French.[40] His *Histoire naturelle de l'âme* (1745), published clandestinely, develops a materialist approach to physiology. He argues the unity of the soul and the body from the outset. He is critical of Descartes for excluding "metaphysical forms" and hence active properties of matter. He draws on Leibniz for a concept of self-active matter that includes a conception of motive force and sensitivity. He reintroduces the distinctions made by the ancients between the vegetative, sensitive, and rational souls and relates the faculties that plants and animals have of nutrition, generation, self-motion, sensitivity, and thought to the activity of matter.[41]

That Quesnay has a considerable affinity with the ideas of La Mettrie is indicated by La Mettrie's praise of Quesnay's *Traité du feu* for its "ample commentary on the doctrine of the ancients" on the role of heat and cold in the production of forms that this author "demonstrates by all the researches and experiments of modern physics."[42] It is apparent from La Mettrie that both writers were considerably influenced by the Epicureanism of Guilliame Lamy (and the Oxford physiology of Willis and others that Lamy had taken up). He credits Quesnay for "subtly reviving" the ether in the generation of all forms and indicates that Lamy had developed the role of the ether in the same way but without having to limit his argument (presumably from the fear of the censors). Quesnay's close relation with La Mettrie is further indicated by extensive borrowing (Quesnay's first chapter reads as a summary of the first eight chapters of La Mettrie's book) and by the praise that this writer subsequently bestows on him for extending the "physical" foundation of the Boerhaavian program.[43]

Production and generation in nature

In contrast to the Cartesian elimination of Aristotelian forms and the vegetative and animal souls from physiology, Quesnay restores the ancient concepts to a central place in the chemistry and physiology of the second edition of his *Essai phisique svr l'oeconomie animale*. He begins with a discussion of matter and the forms to which it is susceptible. All the productions of nature, from the elements and compounds with which chemistry is concerned to the processes of physiology, are concerned with changes in forms. These transformations require a motive force – an active material principle. This is provided by the principle or element of fire, "the universal agent which operates all the changes which take place in bodies" (1747, 1:37).

The principle of fire that Quesnay uses to explain the various productions of chemistry, including the complex "mixtes" of salts, acids, oils, and so on that form the body, is explained in turn by the ether of ancient physics. This ether, universal and atomistic, is the only active element of matter. Extremely subtle and active, it penetrates the pores of grosser bodies and is responsible for establishing the structure of these bodies as well as being the causal force of the changes that take place in chemical processes. As the material agent that puts the internal particles of a body in motion, it is the explanation of heat (1:62). Similarly, it "is the action of the sun on the ether which communicates the light to us and which produces the heat which the sun occasions" (1:114) on which all the operations of nature depend. This active substance is thus the material principle that explains the generation, nutrition, and motive activity of living things. It is the vegetative soul and the source of the fire that vivifies animals. It is what the ancients called the soul of the world (1:177–83).

Consideration of physiology proper begins in volume 3, chapter 12, with a section on the "solid parts" of the body, followed by chapters on the vital principle and the vegetative and animal souls. Of particular interest to us is the way in which he immediately links the activity of the solid parts (tissues and organs) with the ether or motion substance that both forms the substance of the body and provides its animating principle. The discussion of the solid parts begins with a consideration of the basic unit of physiological organization – the tissues that are used to construct the various vessels and parts. These are the smallest vessels that serve the nutrition and generation of the body's various parts. Curiously, these are not the blood vessels but the smallest vessels of the nerves that supply the "suc nouricier" of homogeneous nutrient material from which all the parts of the body are constructed. It is only in these smallest and most delicate of vessels (which form the cavities of the solid parts) that the humors move sufficiently slowly so as to construct, nourish, and repair the parts.[44]

Chapter 13, entitled "Vital Principle," is concerned with "the premier material agent which gives life, movement, and sensitivity to the parts of the body. This first principle, as "physiciens" have nearly always maintained, consists in the "very subtle and active" fluids of the nerves. Movement is explained by the presence of blood throughout the muscles. "Muscles . . . have in truth a force which is communicated to them by the blood which flows continually in their fibers and which puts them in contraction" by a processes of entrapping the blood in the fibers. This interception depends again on the "premier force" that arrests the blood and directs the force of its movement. The nerves determine and excite the movement (1747, 3:108–10). The source of the movement is the active power of the ether, which is apparently obtained from the mixed air in the atmosphere by the respiration (this is not clearly explained).[45]

Production in living things is considered under the heading of the "vegetative soul" (3:ch. 15). Those such as Descartes who reject the vegetative soul in order to give an account "by pure mechanism" of all the faculties and operations in plants, beasts, and humans have forgotten the motive power and the direction that is precisely the vegetative soul by which the ancient philosophers used to give an account of these faculties (3:120). He gives the example of the digestive faculty of the stomach. What marks the precise moment when it will move? It is apparent that there is a degree of sensitivity or activity in the organs and its tissues. Impressions received by the organ excite its movement and direct its action.[46]

These actions have been compared to the much grosser operations of machines – for example, to a watch. Everyone knows the intelligence and skill that has gone into the metallurgy, the design, and the construction of a watch. Many seem to ignore the much greater intelligence and design that has entered into the hidden structures and operations of the body (3:120–1).

The productive powers of the body are again underlined when Quesnay takes up the idea of some philosophers who think that the intellectual soul forms the body that it animates. But by what power can that soul alone, deprived of organs, move on matter? The life of the body – its organic movements, digestion, the action of the heart, the circulation of the blood, and other operations – are independent of consciousness and the feeble knowledge of the reasonable soul. As the ancient philosophers understood, some other principle is needed "for constructing our parts and directing the movements of life and all the operations of the Animal Oeconomy." This principle is the vegetative soul, which is "infinitely more intelligent, more knowledgeable, more powerful than our reasonable soul" (3:126–7).[47]

Since Quesnay has already established that the vegetable soul is the same as the ether, the materialist basis of his argument should be reasonably clear. But this is an argument about which he necessarily must be cautious. He states the counterargument. Many ancient philosophers have confounded this "formative intelligence" with matter. They have known the universal intelligence only by its sensible productions, which appear to reside in matter. This constrains the knowledge they have been able to obtain on the relations between intelligence and matter. Can such feeble conjectures be sufficient for regarding thought as an attribute or property of matter (3:128)?

While this argument appears to support the orthodox view that thought is not a dependence of matter, he presents the evidence of experiments by La Peyronie that thought depends on the organs of sense and the faculties of the body (3:130). What can be brought against the evidence of these "experiences"? Apparently, only the limits of what we can know of these matters. Study of animal economy, he admits, has induced the belief that intelligence is dependent on matter.[48] Such arguments and facts would "lead to consequences very false" (132). But taken as a whole, the thrust of his argument is the dependence of thought on the body and matter. The arguments he presents in rebuttal as his own position are the tactical arguments of a skeptic.[49]

It is not only the study of physiology that has induced the belief that intelligence is dependent on matter. Physical knowledge "even more seducing" has supported this conjecture:

> One recognizes that there is a first agent in matter by which everything is executed in nature, which moves everything, which is the cause of all generation and all destruction; it is a fire, a matter aetherial or subtle, extremely active, which has the property of all the movement which animates the universe; it is an immense sea which contains all the sensible bodies which it intimately pentrates and which it works all the changes which happen there. (3:133)[50]

In an apparent reference to Leibniz and his followers, Quesnay writes that some philosophers have believed that the small parts of this fluid are intelligent beings moving with design who form and direct everything in the universe, who think effectively and continually, and who know everything independently of any union with organized bodies (3:133–4). But he rejects this imaginative view. Why don't these small particles sense by themselves when the functions of the organs are suspended? If the souls of men are formulated from this same material, who don't they all have this universal intelligence? Why does each human have particular and limited ideas? Physics, he says, "dissipates all the resemblances which favor this absurd opinion" (136–8).

But what are Quesnay's views on the extent of sensitivity in matter? He has clearly stated that ether is the vegetative soul and the first principle that animates bodies. Does he accept the neo-Leibnizian view of Maupertuis and others that *particular* kinds of matter have latent capabilities of sensitivity, perception, and the like that in sufficient aggregation and organization, can produce thought and intelligence in living beings?[51]

In rejecting the Leibnizian monad, he cites his *Traité du feu* for the proof that ethereal matter does not direct itself or its movement but is throughout determined by the grosser bodies (3:138). This is the material cause that works all the changes known to us in chemical "mixtes" (the ether or principle of fire). "It is a material agent which carries movement" and puts everything in action. He cautions, however, that this material agent should not be confused with the universal intelligence "which forms the laws, ordains and directs all the movements." This matter "does no more" by its movement in the body than the air moved by the wind or the water of a river does in moving a mill or some other machine. The ether can be regarded only as a "universal instrument" that moves in the "mixtes" according to the "author of nature which is this supreme being we know by the Soul Vegetative" (139).

This return to the animating powers of an ether identified with the soul of the world appears to place Quesnay's own position well within the orbit of materialist tradition. This conclusion is strengthened if we recall the role of ether in the form of the "nourishing fluid" in the generation and nutrition of the solid parts. It is perhaps significant that Quesnay omits a discussion of nutrition (the first faculty of the vegetable soul) at this point in the chapter and turns instead to generation (the second faculty of the vegetable soul). His theory of nutrition would have only strengthened the materialist thrust of the argument. His "public" position is thus a combination of the "solidist" emphasis he takes from Boerhaave and an underlying materialism of the subtle and active ether or general fire.

We have already noted La Mettrie's (1745) praise of Quesnay for reviving the ancient doctrine of the ether and its "premier role" in the formation of bodies. The links between La Mettrie and Quesnay and the physician, G. Lamy, are important in a number of respects. Lamy's theory draws on the combustion physiology of Mayow and the work of Willis on the sensitive soul in animals, which in turn reflect the inspiration of Gassendi's atomism. (Stahl will similarly draw on these writers for his theory of fire or phlogiston.) And Lamy provides a model for subsuming the operations of the sensitive and rational soul to the vegetative soul and the latter's connection to the general operations of the ether.

A long quote from Lamy indicates his view of the ether and how he assimilates it to an explanation of sensitivity:

The visible fire has a great deal of this spirit, air some, and water much less, the earth very little. Between the mixes, the minerals have less, the plants more, and the animals very much. This fire, or this spirit is their soul, which is augmented within bodies by the means of the aliment and which is separated within the chyle and becomes in the end capable of sentiment, thanks to a certain blending of humors, and to the particular structure of the organs which forms the animated body. (Quoted in La Mettrie 1745, 47)[52]

The quote goes on to indicate that the expression of this sentiment in the organs of various plants, animals, and humans depends not only on its concentration in particular humors, but also in the differences in organization between these bodies. Sensitivity and activity are inherent in the ether, but their expression and direction in the humors and organs of the body are a function of the physical and chemical organization of the body.

The second half of the chapter, entitled "Vegetative Faculty," offers a detailed consideration of generation. Quesnay begins by stating that the "radical or primitive forms of bodies reside more in the solids than in the liquids":

The determinative powers or faculties of material direction depend principally on the organization of these solid parts. And this organization, . . . ordained and fixed by the Universal Intelligence, is executed by mechanistic movements; i.e. by movements constantly subject to general laws, simple, invariable, and uniform. (Quesnay 1747, 3:140)[53]

He compares the mechanisms in the body to the operation of a loom ("machines directrices") used in the fabrication of quality cloths and tapestries whose forms are "strongly composed and the product of purely mechanical movements." These machines, designed by an artisan but operating automatically, present a gross idea of the more subtle construction of the body (3:141).

The textile analogy continues. All generation in bodies starts with some small portion of body already organized. This is the *plastic form* or loom by which the other organized parts of the same body will be successively formed.[54] This "first principle of organization" is found in the seminal fluids ("semences") produced by the parents from the same organization that has furnished these fluids (3:141).[55] The organization of the body reproduces itself through time.

The source of activity comes from the ether. This is compared to the worker who gives movement "to these machines which reproduce themselves." The textile analogy extends to the spinning of fibers. The smallest vessels carry nutrients to the site where the new fabrication is taking place. These form the filaments of tissue that provide "the first warp of our parts." The tissues are formed little by little. The analogy of directed looms also suggests a programming analogy. New vessels are established in an order "according to the directions necessary for composing new organic parts" (1747, 3:143).[56]

Quesnay rejects the theory of the preformation and preexistence of germs – the idea that all the germs were created at the beginning of the world and carried within the loins of the first parents. This opinion, which is founded on the infinite divisibility of matter, "revolts the imagination" (3:143). Such divisibility is entirely inconsistent with physical and chemical knowledge. All the processes of nature depend on the elements, which have a given size. To show the impossibility of the encasement view, Quesnay mobilizes the evidence of the volume of plant matter and seed that can be produced from a large tree by growth, by propagation from roots and shoots, and from seed. The parts of bodies cannot be formed at the same time but must follow an elaboration and development in time on the basis of parts previously developed (146–7).

Quesnay's concern is to establish a theory of the underlying causes common to all generation. He uses the extensive observations and facts obtained in the study of plant generation to find similarities in animal generation, where observation has been more difficult. On the basis of the plant model, he argues for the male fertilization of the egg in animals (which Maupertuis had rejected on the authority of Harvey). Each domain of nature provides models or analogies relevant to others (1747, 3:155, 158).

All generation in nature works by the cooperation of "a small number of determinate causes," which are sufficient for executing the "most grand operations of nature."[57] Quesnay again reminds the reader that all this takes place by the principles established in his *Traité du feu* (3:158). He is emphasizing the determinate causes that were invented and established by the author of nature, and the reader will remember how his long essay (and chapter) links these causes to the operation of the ether.

The coupling of the "determinative powers" of organic structures to the active powers of the ether (and suggestion of the formation of these structures by the action of the ether in nutrition and generation) points toward a materialist approach of a quite different order than the analogy of the machine and its motive power (each attributable to divine design and activity). Whether Quesnay fully embraced the radical possibilities inherent in the materialist alternative or would ally himself firmly to the vision of an eternal natural order replicating its organization through time is open to question. What is not in question is how intimately involved he is in the central debates of his time.[58] We now turn to how Quesnay's conception of the dissipative but regenerative operations of nature shapes his economic theory of production.

Generation in economics: the physical productivity doctrine

In 1749 Quesnay became the personal physician of Madame de Pompadour and was installed at court as "ordinary surgeon" to the king. He was now able to turn from physiology to a long-standing interest in agriculture and the economy. Marmontel reports that he was "lodged in very cramped quarters in the entresol above Mme de Pompadour" and that he "occupied himself from morning to night with nothing but rural economy":

> Below us they were deliberating concerning war and peace, the choice of generals, the dismissal of ministers, while we, in the entresol, argued about agriculture, calculated the net product, or sometimes dined gaily with Diderot, D'Alembert, Duclos, Helvétius, Turgot, Buffon; and Mme de Pompadour, not being able to induce this troop of philosophers to come down to her *salon*, came up herself to see them at table and chat with them. (Marmontel 1804, 28, 33–4)

The points of contact between Buffon and Quesnay on the question of agriculture and economy are intriguing. Buffon's patron at the Jardin du Roi was Mme. de Pompadour. In addition to his efforts to propagate Newtonian science (which included his translation of Stephen Hale's *Vegetable Statics*), Buffon had translated Jethro Tull's *The New Horse-Ploughing Husbandry* (Hanks 1966, 132).[59] He also knew Petty's *Essays on Political Arithmetick*, which he cites in several works dating from the 1730s.[60] Quesnay's application of the methods of political arithmetic are evident in the statistical data on French agriculture in his article "Grains" (1757) in the *Encyclopédie*. The "Maxims," which accompany the *Tableau économique*, repeatedly emphasize the superiority of horse cultivation over the "petite culture" of oxen and men.

We can also expect that Quesnay was conversant with the extension of epigenetic theories of generation in the late 1740s and early 1750s by Buffon, Needham, and Maupertuis. These theories continue to maintain a connection with theories of active matter. Maupertuis (1751) suggests that "some principle of intelligence – something resembling what we call desire, aversion, memory – might exist in the smallest particle of matter." Buffon (1749) develops a theory of "organic molecules" or living matter distinct from inert matter (and the mechanism of an "interior mould").[61] Needham (1748) argues that "it seems plain that there is a vegetative force in every microscopical point of matter."

Thus, when Quesnay employs the language of generation in his economic writings to characterize and defend his theory of the exclusive productivity of agriculture and the sterility of manufacturing and commerce, his language resonates with the meanings it takes from his own physiological writings and from the biological work of his contemporaries. This meaning is not confined to physiology but involves the larger economy of nature: the circulation and regeneration of vital materials within the womb of nature. Nature reproduces itself. This regeneration involves an ongoing reconstitution of the material qualities and motive forces that are requisite to the life of plants and animals. Materials circulate back to nature and are recomposed in appropriate compounds and reinvested with the delicate and subtle ether that has been dissipated in the physical and chemical operations of life and activity.

What are the implications of this doctrine for economics? Meek (1962) has called Quesnay's doctrine of the exclusive productivity of agriculture the "really essential and distinctive element of the physiocratic model" (378). It has been interpreted by modern economists as indicating that only agriculture is capable of yielding a surplus of output over inputs (in both *physical* and *value* terms), in contrast to manufacturing, which is "inherently incapable of yielding any disposable surplus over cost in terms of value" (1962, 379–1).[62]

But this characterization docs not grasp the ontological difference that Quesnay posits between agricultural and manufacturing processes and products. He calls agriculture a "generation" of riches or wealth, while manufacturing merely transforms items of wealth already in existence and thus is only an adding together of value. What, however, is the meaning of generation as a coming into existence? Since Quesnay certainly accepts the principle of the conservation of matter, there cannot be any question of something being created from nothing.

In the exposition of his doctrine in "Grains" (1757), Quesnay writes that agriculture produces the subsistence and costs of the cultivating class plus the real wealth (surplus) that flows as revenue to the landlords. Industrial work, however, does not increase wealth. It "destroys in the form of subsistence as much" as it produces. "The principle of wealth lies in the source of men's subsistence" (in Meek 1962, 73).

Plants and animals require certain types of materials for subsistence. Production and consumption destroy certain qualities and organization in the materials that they use and that must be restored before economic production can go on. This includes, in particular, their component of the element of fire (ether).

Certainly manufacturing can create new forms that delight the eye or serve important needs. The foundation of Quesnay's natural philosophy would be put in question if this were not the case. What manufacturing does not do in Quesnay's theory is provide new subsistence and prime materials. Manufacturing, in Quesnay's view of the circuit of production, takes its raw materials and its subsistence (which include its motion) from the land. It consumes and transforms subsistence and prime materials already in existence.

His "Sur les travaux des artisans" (Dialogue on the work of artisans) (1766) adds the language of creation to that of generation in characterizing agricultural production and again calls manufacturing only an "*adding together* of items of wealth which are combined with one another." It is necessary, Quesnay says, to distinguish the combination of raw materials and "consumption of things" already in existence from the "*generation* or creation of wealth which constitutes a renewal and *real* increase of renascent wealth" (original emphasis). The "production of wealth" should not be confused with "the forms given to their goods by artisans, builders, handicraftsmen, manufacturers, etc" (in Meek 1962, 207–8). Manufacturing is clearly involved in changing the forms of materials, but it does not thereby produce or generate subsistence and prime materials.

Quesnay's line of defense here is not on the question of which sectors are productive in the sense of generating a surplus, but on the issue of the "physical existence" of specific material products. The products the artisan needs to buy "are in existence before the artisan buys them. . . . Trade (and artisan production) . . . by no means generates them" (in Meek 1962, 215). Agriculture, however, is a new production or generation because it brings these items into physical existence, that is, it brings materials with specific qualities and potencies into being.

Quesnay goes on to distinguish between the "circle or process of circulation of money," which shifts from one hand to another, and the more fundamental circulation of the "distribution of the products which are annually regenerated through the work of the productive class." Money "is not consumed" in contrast to the products annually regenerated by the productive class and sold to the sterile class (the artisans). These items are eventually all consumed. "This distribution terminates directly and completely in consumption" and begins all over again with reproduction (in Meek 1962, 224–5).

Manufacturing activity is, of course, a process of making new forms. But in Quesnay's conception of natural production, agriculture, which takes place in the larger context of the ecological circulation of materials, involves a transformation of elements and chemical compounds, in particular, a restoration of the organic form of the chemical "mixtes," and in addition, a reinvesting of protoenergetic potential in these physical and chemical substances. Manufacturing, which takes its materials and subsistence from the land, is only a consumer of these materials and "energetic" substance. What Quesnay misses, of course, is the economic construction, outside the system of ecological renewal, of new circuits of nonrenewable, non-agricultural materials and fuels from the vast storehouses of nature and the coupling of these with the evolution of new designs and organizations.

Production and circulation in the *Tableau*

The physical conception of material production and circulation developed by Quesnay can be used to offer a new reading of the *Tableau économique* (1758). Since its publication, the *Tableau* has raised perplexing questions of explanation. Modern readers have seen the progressively diminishing expenditures of the zigzag as an early version of a Keynesian expenditure analysis, where the initial revenue (say, 600 livres) spent by the landlords, half on food and half on the products of industry, repeatedly divide into smaller and smaller purchases in a descending geometric progression: $600 \rightarrow 300 \rightarrow 150 \rightarrow 75 \rightarrow 37.5 \rightarrow 18.75 \ldots$ (see Figure 10.1).[63]

But such an interpretation gives primary weight to the flow of expenditure (and effectively asserts that demand creates the flow of products). By failing to fully trace the flow of physical output, which takes place by the monetary exchanges, historians of theory have not provided a complete picture of the circulation. They have not shown what happens to the "net product" depicted in the center column of the table, and they have not explained the complete circuit of money in the *Tableau*. Herlitz (1961) claims, for example, that the original *Tableau* "is incomplete because it does not touch the problem of the conversion of the net product into money . . . or say anything about the payment of revenue" (17). Eltis (1984) similarly writes that "it is not clear . . . what happens to the economy's stock of money," which the landlords hold at the beginning of the year (23).

The key to explaining the circulation of the net product and the circulation of money is a step-by-step analysis of the physical flows of

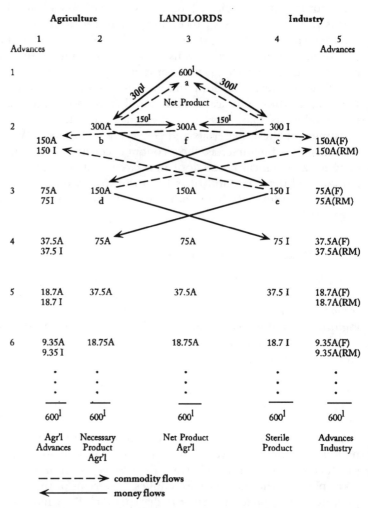

Figure 10.1. *Tableau économique* of François Quesnay.

the *Tableau.* Any exchange is simultaneously an exchange of goods (previously produced) for money.

The analysis begins at the end of the production processes of the previous year. The landlords begin the process of exchange by spending the 600-livre rent they have received in the previous period from the farming class. Quesnay assumes that they divide their expenditure equally between the agricultural and industrial sector, 300^l going to one side of the diagram to buy the products of the urban sector (expenditure ac) and 300^l going to the other side to buy the products of the farmers (expend ab). This gives the landlords 300^l of industrial goods (300I) and 300^l of agricultural goods (300A), which they will consume in the following year.

Quesnay assumes that the farmers and artisans spend their income in the same way: half on expenditures of the other class and half on expenditures within the class (1759, ii–iii). The farmers in row 2 have produced 600^l of agricultural product: 300A in column 2, which will cover their expenses and subsistence, and 300A of surplus or net product in column 3. After selling 300A to the landlords, they spend 150^l of their receipts on industrial goods (expenditure be) and the remaining 150^l on agricultural goods (expenditure bf). This reconstitutes the necessary inputs (advances) they need for next year's activity: the 150I and 150A in column 1 they will use to produce 600^l of agricultural output in the following period.

The artisans of row 2 produce 300^l of output (300I), which is sold to the landlords (ac). They use their receipts to purchase 150A from the farmers in the primary circulation (cd) and the 150A that remains in the net product column (cf).[64] This gives them the 300A (subsistence and raw materials) they will need for the following year. This exchange completes the physical circulation of the net product of row 2. The farming class in row 1 now holds 300^l (from the sale of the net product), and each sector is in possession of the advances it needs for the following year.

The farmers and artisans in each successive row produce themselves in the same way. The division of each production class and expenditure flows in the *Tableau* into progressively smaller and smaller units can be seen to map to the circulatory system of the body. Each successive flow is matched to an appropriately scaled "vessel" or site of production and exchange. This provides more support for Foley's (1973) claim for a physiological inspiration of the zigzag structure.

At the end of this infinite division and subdivision of expenditures, all the product has been circulated to the appropriate position for next year's production and consumption. Each class has the inputs it needs for the next year. The farmers have 600^l of agricultural goods and industrial goods, which they will turn into $1,200^l$ worth of total product in the next season (a new net product of 600^l). The industrial sector has, on its side, the 600^l of subsistence and raw materials that it will transform into 600^l of artisan products. Artisans thus transform materials and convert values. Their net product is zero.

By selling the 600^l net product of the agricultural sector in the center column (3), half to themselves and half to the artisans, the farmers have the 600^l of money they need to pay their rent. The assertion that the original *Tableau* does not account for the circulation of money or the payment of rent in money is incorrect. The *Tableau* involves "two" ciirculations, one of money and a more fundamental circulation and distribution of physical products. Just as eighteenth-century chemists saw the chemical tables of Geoffroy as a reprise or summary of the material circulation of nature (Guedon 1979), so Quesnay's *Tableau économique* provides the structural relations of the circulation of materials in the economy.

Conclusion

Of the numerous examples of the use of theories of nature to construct economic theories, few are as systematic as François Quesnay's application of the ideas of physiology to economics. In no other case is the theory applied so completely the author's own. For Quesnay, the theory of natural generation provides the materials and motive forces for the construction of the economy.

We have reviewed Quesnay's iatro-mechanical model of the circulation of the blood. As Foley (1973) argued, the structure of the *Tableau économique* reflects the bifurcating structure of the blood's circulation. But we can also see an image of the body itself in the *Tableau*. Each node of exchange represents a physical site of production and consumption through which the subsistence, raw materials, and products are cycled. The "tissue" structures and exchange circuits are appropriately matched in a descending scale.

We have used Quesnay's suggestion of two circulations, one of money and one of the distribution of materials, to reexamine the *Tableau économique*. By matching each monetary expenditure with a commodity exchange, we have traced the physical distribution of output and shown how the net produce (center column) is exchanged. Since the exchange of the net product leaves money in the hands of farmers (all other exchanges are money for goods), this provides the funds to be paid as rent to landlords. Two long-standing problems in the interpretation of the *Tableau* are solved.

An investigation of Quesnay's theory of matter and natural production has been used to develop a reinterpretation of the Physiocratic theory of productivity. Standing behind Quesnay's theory of the exclusive productivity of agriculture is a model of the production and circulation of materials in the economy of nature. The key element keeping this system of material circulation and generation in motion is a highly subtle and active ether – the matter of fire – which is used to account for all the motions, chemical changes, and body processes (nutrition, fermentation, muscle motion, etc.). The ongoing processes of nature involve, on one side, the production and reconstitution of forms and forces and, on the other, destruction and dissipation. Economic production and consumption depend, in this view, on a one-way flow of subsistence and raw materials from nature through the economy and, hence, on a reconstitution and regeneration of these vital forms and motive potencies. Thus, the physiology and ecology of natural production and its dynamic or "energetic" substance provide Quesnay with a model of the structure, the material flows, and the motion substance of economic production. A substance approach to value directly follows (see Mirowski 1989, 159).

Notes

I would like to thank James Bono, Ivor Grattan-Guinness, Jean-Claude Guedon, Shirley Roe, Phillip Sloan, Thomas von Foerster, and Sue Weinberg for generously sharing their knowledge of the eighteenth century with me. I am especially indebted to Sloan for suggesting a closer examination of the connection between Quesnay, Buffon, and Enlightenment biology and to Guedon for his insights about eighteenth-century chemistry and neomechanistic explanatory strategies. None is responsible for the uses to which I have put their informed help.

1. I have discussed Hobbes's use of Harvey's physiology in Christensen (1989).
2. Quesnay, Sutter (1958) says, "did not have, properly speaking, a biological conception" and he was indifferent to "the great problems" that convulsed his contemporaries (210). This makes it rather difficult to understand the considerable attraction that Diderot and other Enlightenment thinkers had to Quesnay's physiological ideas.
3. Kubota (1958) treats Quesnay's epistemology and psychology in relation to Malebranche and Locke. Foley (1973) limits his investigation to Quesnay's model of the circulation of the blood. Both writers neglect Quesnay's physiology.
4. In a similar vein, Vaggi (1987) argues that Quesnay's economic theories are formulated and defended on value, not physical terrain (ch. 4). An exception to this position is Oncken (1888), who saw Quesnay's physiological studies as the foundation of his "philosophic-economic studies." Quesnay, he adds, tended to found metaphysics on physiology (in Rosenfield 1979, 739–40).
5. On the development of mechanical physiology, see Frank (1980), Schofield (1970), and Brown (1981, 1987).

6. In traditional physiology, food maintained the innate heat or fire that was the source of motion in the body. Several of Harvey's followers (Ent, Digby, Charleton, Mayow, and others) advanced a "nitre" theory in which an active element in the air combined with a "fuel" in the food to produce combustion in the body (Guerlac 1953; Frank 1980, 258–74). For the mechanists, food was exclusively building material.

7. Schofield (1970) notes "the failure of mechanism to come to grips with a major part of chemical phenomena – the persistent identity of certain substances and the regularity of varying combinations" (209–10).

8. Silva's views are described by Haller (1757), Delaunay (1906), and Foley (1973, 1976).

9. Haller supports Silva against Senac but mentions Quesnay's opposition only in passing. For Haller (1757), the critical question is "whether bleeding accelerates also the motion of the arterial blood as laid down in the Bellinian doctrine" (94). Foley (1976) mistakenly argues that Silva's "key" claim was "that the revulsion was greater than the derivation" (123). Rather, Silva argues that the revulsion and the derivation were greater than the quantity evacuated by the bleeding.

10. He subsequently repeated the same experiments in a more complex apparatus, which he refers to as "tubes more composed" (Quesnay, 1750, 159).

11. This example is presented twice in both the 1730 and 1750 "editions." In the later book he also presents the figures he obtained from his physical model (1750, 159–63, 168–73).

12. I have changed Quesnay's example from six seaux to eight to more clearly distinguish the evacuation and revulsion.

13. But starting on p. 154, Quesnay reprints the entire 1730 text with only minor changes in wording.

14. Buffon translated Hales's *Vegetable Statics* (1727) into French in 1735. Sauvages translated the *Haemastatics* (1733) in 1744.

15. Quesnay was closely associated with La Peyronie as "secrétaire perpétuel" of the academy from 1740. "Due to La Peyronie, Paris had become the surgical center of the world in the eighteenth century" (Garrison 1929).

16. He also published a companion volume on medical treatment, *L'art de guérir par la saignée* (1736).

17. Boerhaave had published his chemistry lectures in two volumes and physiology in five volumes. Quesnay's dependence on Boerhaave was noted by the physician Burette, who accused him of plagiarism (Hecht 1958, 228) and by Haller and La Mettrie. In his parody of French physicians, La Mettrie says of *The Animal Economy* that "it is Boerhaave put into pieces; the right lessons to be worn by the French" (La Mettrie 1746, in Schell 1904, 206).

18. The term "animal economy" was ubiquitous in iatro-mechanics. This usage may reflects Malebranche's and Leibniz's conception that God's design of Nature employed an economy of means to ends (see Elster 1975, p. 189). This conception is poorly achieved in the first edition of the *Essai* but plays a greater role in the second (1747) edition.

19. In the 1747 edition of the *Essai*, Quesnay says that chemistry is to physiology what mechanics is to general physics (1747, 1:3).
20. La Peyronie was a disciple of Locke's "sensationalism" (see Yolton 1991). Voltaire's famous letter (1734, no. 13) had popularized Locke in France. According to Fox-Genovese (1976), Quesnay had copies of Voltaire's books and knew them well.
21. Quesnay's silence is consistent with Boerhaave's injunction that a good scientist avoids first causes (1742, 1:71).
22. Effectively, theories of matter and motion.
23. Quesnay explains fire and light by the activity of a subtle ether whose motion is the cause of all the operations in nature including the circulation of materials between the soil and atmosphere, plants, and animals. These ideas go far beyond Boerhaave to embrace Gassendi and Leibniz. They appear to be especially influenced by Stahl, whose emphasis on the conservation of matter in a self-moving and self-supporting nature was a principle contribution to Enlightenment thought (Teich 1982). On Stahl's influence on French chemistry and theory of fire see Eklund (1971). Stahlian chemistry was given a considerable development by Rouelle, who gave private lectures in pharmacy and chemistry in Paris from 1738 and, from 1742, as "demonstrator" at the Jardin du Roi. Rouelle emphasized chemical affinity and the autonomy of chemistry from domination by Newtonian physics (see Guedon 1979). Diderot, Turgot, and Lavoisier among many others were pupils of Rouelle (Rappaport 1960, 1961).
24. Quesnay's sustained interest in psychology is indicated by a lost article, "Fonctions de lâme," which was withdrawn from the Diderot's *Encyclopédie* after its suppression. It has never been published. For the considerable role that the sensitive soul played in opposition to iatro-mechanics, see Moravia (1978).
25. Voltaire's famous letter (1734, no. 13) "highlighted the suggestion of thinking matter and located Locke in the context of such deistic and materialist writers as Collins, Toland, and Spinoza" (Yolton 1991, 38).
26. Quesnay will draw on La Peyronie's studies of the effect of brain damage on the body's ability to move the soul. La Peyronie made extensive studies and operations on patients with brain injuries and attempted to discover the place in the brain where the soul interacted with the body (Yolton 1991, 102–5). Three of the four *Mémoires* that Quesnay wrote for the Academy of Surgeons were on brain operations (Rosenfield 1979, 275).
27. In 1732, Maupertuis showed how Newton's idea of the flattening of the earth at the poles could be tested by "means of astronomy and geography." This was confirmed by the measurements of three French expeditions, one being his famous voyage to Lapland (cruelly caricatured by Voltaire, who championed Newtonian metaphysics against the growing influence of Leibniz).
28. Voltaire declares that he is a member of the Newtonian Party in France of

which Buffon is the head. On Buffon's essential role in introducing English science, see Hanks (1966).

29. In the "Queries" of his *Optics,* Newton presents a conception of nature working in a perpetual circulation by the operation of active or "vivifying principles" that could not be subsumed under the laws of mechanics. His appeal to chemistry and etherial principles as keys to unraveling the secrets of nature was to have a major impact on eighteenth-century thinkers who rejected his voluntaristic conception of activity sustained by divine agency (Heimann and McGuire 1971; Heimann 1973). A distinction between the quasi-positivistic methodology of the *Principia* and the inductive and even materialist approach of the *Optics* is made by Guerlac (1965) and Cohen (1956).

30. For the influence of British ideas in French biology, see Roger (1963, 418–35).

31. Boerhaave had been considerably influenced by Stahl's chemistry but had been unwilling to undertake a systematic reformulation of the subject (Donovan and Prentis 1980, 21).

32. Hoffman's *Medicina rationalis* (1718–41) was translated into French by Bruhier (1739–43).

33. La Peyronie, Quesnay's mentor, had influential connections with Montpellier. Louis de La Caze, a Montpellier-trained physician to the king, was in Paris in the 1730s and provided a conduit for ideas and aspiring students, including Venel and Bordeu (who was La Cazes's nephew). See Roger (1970–1). Venel wrote important chemistry articles for the *Encyclopédie.* Bordeu, a vitalist and materialist, was the physician in Diderot's *d'Alembert's Dream.*

34. Sauvages (1740) argues that Cartesian physicians had usurped the role of the soul as the cause of vital motions. Because the body is a hydraulic machine, it needs an immaterial supply of motion to replace what is lost through friction. The machine of the body cannot work without an immaterial principle. Following Newton, he located these "motive potencies" in the forces God impressed on matter (French 1990, 106–7; Martin 1990, 131–2).

35. Having rejected the voluntaristic metaphysics of Descartes but committed to his physical naturalism, many French thinkers were reluctant to accept Newton's weak and equivocal metaphysics.

36. Maupertuis (1748) also attacks the Newtonian argument from design. God's power is evident in the world not in the myriad detail of the universe, but in the operation of the principle of economy. On Maupertuis's central place in the emergence of natural-law arguments, see Tonnelli (1959). For Quesnay's view of an immanent natural order, see (Quesnay 1958, 2:729–42). Tonnelli (1987) argues the considerable convergence in the epistemological approaches of Maupertuis and Quesnay. The idea of a God who employed the principle of an economy of means to ends in creating the world was a feature of the thought of Leibniz and Male-

branche (see Elster 1975). The belief in a natural harmony, order, and principle of economy will reverberate between political economy and physics.

37. Phillip Sloan (1979) has shown the significant influence of Leibniz and Wolff on Buffon's biological ideas, including the primacy he gives to historical explanation and the distinction between "abstract" ideal orders and the "real and physical" order. The ontological primacy Buffon gives to nature traces to Leibniz. Buffon praised Du Châtelet's synthesis of Wolffian metaphysics and Newton's mechanics (Lyon and Sloan, 1981).

38. Quesnay's treatment of generation will considerably extend these arguments, especially in the budding and sprouting of plants (1747, 3:143–9).

39. Maupertuis (1744, chs. 17–18). See Roger (1963, 477–9; Hoffheimer (1982), and Roe (1981). In 1751, Maupertuis advocates the presence of a principle of intelligence in the particles of matter, i.e., of "desire, aversion, memory."

40. The *Institutions de médicine* (Paris, 1743–1750) included Haller's "lengthy and valuable notes" (Vartanian 1974, 605).

41. La Mettrie (1745, chs. 1–8). See Roger (1963, 487–90), Thomson (1981, 33–40; 1988).

42. It is possible that Quesnay prepared this work for the competition of the Academy of Sciences on the subject of fire in 1738. The competition was won by Euler and two Cartesians. Mme. Du Châtelet and Voltaire were runners up. Quesnay cites Du Châtelet and Voltaire in his chapter on fire (1747, 1:55, 57).

43. La Mettrie (1748) calls Quesnay "this grand experimenter," one of the "rare geniuses" of his time, and "the eagle of surgery . . . who, to the shame of the (medical) faculty a professional surgeon, found himself in a position to dig deeper into, to pursue in depth and to embellish Boerhaave's doctrine, to which he has substantially added; since it is certain that in the last edition of his *Animal Economy*, he took as his point of departure the physics which our celebrated author kept to in the *Institutions*" (quoted in Rosenfield 1979, 266).

44. Quesnay sets the argument out in the context of the growth of the foetus, which is initially deprived of the blood. By implication, if I am interpreting him correctly, the process of nutrition (tissue formation) is independent of the blood.

45. The air, which has 1/800th the weight of water, has eight hundred times as much ether (Quesnay 1747, 3:111).

46. Haller refers to tissue irritability in his presentation of Boerhaave's medical treatise in 1739. The concept had an important development by Glissen (1672) whose work was known to the Montpellier faculty.

47. A similar separation of the soul and animal life from vegetative process (the influence of Leibniz and Christian Wolff) is made by Caspar F. Wolff in 1759 (Roe 1981, 109). Wolff disavows Stahl's attribution of vital activities to an immaterial soul. La Mettrie (1745), following Lamy and the

Oxford physiologist Thomas Willis, privileges the sensitive soul (Thomson 1988).

48. These included the studies that indicate how sensation and thought depend on the functioning of the organs of the body and are deranged when these are disturbed (3:130).

49. Tonelli (1987) places Quesnay "in the tradition of the grand skeptics" (77). Quesnay, rather, uses the moderate skepticism of Locke and Hume to avoid too close an identification with dangerous ideas. He had strong social and political incentives to escape censorship.

50. This is Quesnay's own view in the chapter on fire.

51. I am indebted to Jean-Claude Guedon for this characterization of the methodological strategy of the neomechanists.

52. La Mettrie does not identify the quote. It appears to be taken from Lamy (cf. Spink 1960, 117–18), but Lamy is cited within the body of the quote. Roger (1963) regards Quesnay as a traditional mechanist and fails to note any connection to this theory. He observes of La Mettrie that "we quit here the dynamism of Aristotle to return to Epicurus and the Gassendian conception of the igneous soul" (1963, 489).

53. The language of "determinative powers" indicates something of Quesnay's philosophical position. Malebranche called the idea of natural powers "the most dangerous error in the philosophy of the ancients (cited in Pyle 1987, 226).

54. Quesnay's *plastic forms* or automatic loom may be compared to Buffon's (1749) "internal mould," to Needham's (1748) model of filaments in the generation of microorganisms, and to Bonnet (1762), who regarded the germ as a preformed net of fibers (see Bowler, 1973; Lyon and Sloan 1981; and Roe 1985; Roger 1989).

55. Clearly, Quesnay is aware of the contributions of Maupertuis (1744, 1745), who advances the theory of two "semences" in the context of a restoration of Harvey's theory of epigenesis (see Hoffheimer, 1982). Quesnay mobilizes considerable evidence from botany and compares the fertilization of the female seed by pollen to the fertilization of eggs in animals by the semen (1747, 3:147–52).

56. La Mettrie (1745), in his concluding discussion of the vegetable soul, says that modern philosophers have not drawn out the properties of matter – "the principle of its movement and the principle of its determination – which are two things absolutely individual and inseparable" (48–9).

57. These arguments that intelligence and design are embodied in the laws of nature, that nature produces its effects by an economy of causes, and that one finds God in the principles of motion (3:158, 185) clearly recall the ideas of Maupertuis that it is in the laws of motion (and economy) that one searches for the evidence, intelligence, and design of God.

58. Diderot had a considerable interest in Quesnay's physiology (see Strenski 1967). He also saw chemical theory, its epistemology, and its insight into nature's operations as a model for philosophy. His attendance at Rouelle's

lectures for three years in the early 1750s indicates how much importance he gave to this science (Guedon 1979). He was also attracted for a time to the Physiocratic idea of a natural law linking the order of society to immutable laws governing the operations of nature (Strenski 1967; Perkins 1979). On Diderot's shift from deism and purposeful order to a philosophy of "energetic materialism," see Dixon (1988).

59. Buffon turned his work over to the naturalist Duhamel du Monceau, who published his own translation in 1750. Buffon, who owned several iron-making establishments in Burgundy, also published a work on silva-culture, which reflected his concern with maintaining supplies of charcoal for iron making.

60. He cites Petty in his essay on "the probabilities of life," which was not published until 1777 (Roger 1977, 95).

61. Buffon treats nutrition as production by a kind of flame or fire by which animals "assimilate and convert into their own substance every matter which may serve them for food" (1749, vol. 1, in Lyon and Sloan 1981, 179–81).

62. It may be noted that this was not the primary meaning attached to it by Dugald Stewart and Thomas Malthus, two writers considerably influenced by Physiocratic ideas.

63. See Herlitz (1961). Robert Eagly (1974) says Quesnay constructs a model of expenditure–income interactions in which the original expenditures of the landlords "set in motion an infinite (and converging) series of exchanges" (19–20).

64. Contrary to Quesnay's statement, this is not an "intrasectoral" purchase. It is, however, consistent with the "sterility" assumption that applies to artisan production. To produce 300^l of output, requires 300^l of input (150RM and 150F).

References

Boerhaave, H. 1741. *A New Method of Chemistry*, 2 vols., trans. P. Shaw. London: T. Longman (orig. 1735).

Boerhaave, H. 1742. *Academical Lectures on the Theory of Physic, being a transl. of his "Institutes,"* 6 vols. London: W. Innys, 1742–6 (orig. 1724).

Bonnet, C. 1762. *Considérations sur les corps organisés*, vol. 1. Amsterdam: M. M. Rey.

Bowler, P. J. 1973. "Bonnet and Buffon: Theories of Generation and the Problem of Species," *Journal of the History of Biology*, 6(2), pp. 259–81.

Brown, T. 1981. *The Mechanical Philosophy and the "Animal Economy."* New York: Arno.

Brown, T. 1987. "Medicine in the Shadow of the *Principia*," *Journal of the History of Ideas*, 48 (Oct.–Dec.), pp. 624–48.

Buffon, G. L. L. 1749. *Histoire naturelle, générale et particulière*, vol. 2: *Histoire des animaux*. Paris: L'Imprimerie Royale.

Christensen, P. 1989. "Hobbes and the Physiological Origins of Economic Science," *History of Political Economy*, 21:4, pp. 689–709.

Cohen, I. B. 1956. *Franklin and Newton*. Philadelphia: American Philosophical Society.

Cunningham, A., and French, R., eds. 1990. *The Medical Enlightenment of the Eighteenth Century*. Cambridge University Press.

Delaunay, Paul. 1906. *Le monde médical parisien au dix-huitième siècle*. Paris.

Dixon, E. L. 1988. *Diderot, Philosopher of Energy*. Oxford University Press.

Donovan, A., and J. Prentiss. 1980. "James Hutton's Medical Dissertation," *Transactions of the American Philosophical Society*, 7 (6), pp. 2–47.

Duchesneau, F. 1991. "La physiologie mécaniste de Hoffmann," *Dix-huitième Siècle*, 23, pp. 9–22.

Dufrénoy, M. L. 1963. "Maupertuis et le progrès scientifique," in *Studies on Voltaire and the Eighteenth Century*, vol. 25. Oxford: Voltaire Foundation, pp. 519–87.

Duhumel du Monceau, H. L. 1750. *Traité de la culture des terres, suivant les principes de M. Tull*, vol. 1. Paris.

Eagly, R. 1974. *The Structure of Classical Economic Theory*. New York: Oxford University Press.

Eklund, J. 1971. *Chemical Analysis and the Phlogiston Theory, 1738–1772*. Ph.D. Diss., Yale University.

Elster, J. 1975. *Leibniz et la formation de l'esprit capitaliste*. Paris: Aubier Montaigne.

Eltis, W. 1984. *The Classical Theory of Economic Growth*. New York: St. Martin's.

Foley, V. 1973. "An Origin of The *Tableau Economique*," *History of Political Economy*, 5 (Spring), pp. 121–50.

Foley, V. 1976. *The Social Physics of Adam Smith*. West Lafayette, IN.: Purdue University Press.

Fox-Genovese, E. 1976. *The Origins of Physiocracy*. Ithaca, NY: Cornell University Press.

Frank R. G. (1980). *Harvey and the Oxford Physiologists*. Berkeley and Los Angeles: University of California Press.

French, R. 1990. "Sickness and the Soul: Stahl, Hoffmann, and Sauvages on Pathology," in Cunningham and French, eds. (1990), pp. 88–110.

Garrison, F. 1929. *History of Medicine*, 4th ed. Philadelphia: Saunders.

Glass, B. 1959. "Maupertuis, Pioneer of Genetics and Evolution," in B. Glass, O. Temkin, and W. L. Straus, eds., *Forerunners of Darwin: 1745–1859*, pp. 51–83. Baltimore: Johns Hopkins University Press.

Glissen, Francis. 1672. *Tractatus de Natura Substantiae Energetica*. London: Flesher.

Guedon, J.-C. 1979. "Chimie et matérialisme: La stratégie anti-Newtonienne de Diderot," *Dix-huitième Siècle*, 2, pp. 185–200.

Guerlac, H. 1953. "John Mayow and the Aerial Nitre," *Actes du Septième Congrès d'Histoire des Sciences* (Jerusalem), pp. 332–49, reprinted in Guerlac (1977), pp. 245–59.

Guerlac, H. 1965. "Where the Statue Stood: Divergent Loyalties to Newton in the Eighteenth Century," in Earl R. Wasserman, ed., *Aspects of the Eighteenth Century*. Baltimore: Johns Hopkins University Press. Reprinted in Guerlac (1977), pp. 131–145.

Guerlac, H. 1977. *Essays and Papers in the History of Modern Science*, pp. 245–59. Baltimore: Johns Hopkins University Press.

Hall, T. S. 1969. *Ideas of Life and Matter: Studies in the History of General Physiology: 600 B.C.–1900 A.D.*, 2 vols. Chicago: University of Chicago Press.

Haller, A., von. 1757. *A Dissertation on the Motion of the Blood and on the Effects of Bleeding*. London: Whiston & White.

Haller, A., von. 1803. *First Lines of Physiology*. Troy, NY: O. Penniman; orig. 1747.

Hanks, L. 1966. *Buffon avant "l'Histoire Naturelle."* Paris: Presses Universitaires de France.

Hecht, J. 1958. "La vie de François Quesnay," in Quesnay (1958), vol. 1, pp. 211–91.

Heimann, P. M. 1973. "Nature Is a Perpetual Worker": Newton's Aether and Eighteenth Century Natural Philosophy," *Ambix*, 20, (Mar.), pp. 1–25.

Heimann, P. M. 1978. "Voluntarism and Immanence: Conceptions of Nature in Eighteenth-Century Thought," *Journal of the History of Ideas*, 39 (2), pp. 271–83.

Heimann, P. M., and J. E. McGuire. 1971. "Newtonian Forces and Lockean Powers: Concepts of Matter in Eighteenth Century Thought," *Historical Studies in the Physical Sciences*, 3, pp. 233–306.

Herlitz, L. 1961. "The *Tableau Economique* and the Doctrine of Sterility," *Scandinavian Economic History Review*, 9 (1), pp. 3–55.

Hoffheimer, M. H. 1982. "Maupertuis and the Eighteenth-Century Critique of Preexistence," *Journal of the History of Biology*, 15 (1), pp. 119–44.

Hutchinson, K. 1983. "Supernaturalism and the Mechanical Philosophy," *History of Science*, 21, pp. 297–333.

Kubota, A. 1958. "Quesnay: Disciple de Malebranche," in Quesnay (1958), vol. 1. pp. 169–96.

Kuczynski, M., and R. Meek, eds. 1972. *Quesnay's Tableau Economique*. New York: Kelley.

La Mettrie, J. O. 1745. *Histoire naturelle de l'âme*, translated into English by M. Charp (The Hague: J. Neaulme).

La Mettrie, J. O. 1746. *La politique de la médicine de Machiavel*. Paris.

La Mettrie, J. O. 1748–50. *L'ouvrage de Pénélope ou Machiavel en médecine par Alatheius Demetrius*, 3 vols. Berlin.

Lyon, J., and P. R. Sloan. 1981. *From Natural History to the History of Nature*. Notre Dame, IN: University of Notre Dame Press.

Marmontel, J.-F. 1804. *Mémoires*. Paris: Peelman.

Martin, J. 1990. "Sauvages's Nosology: Medical Enlightenment in Montpellier," in Cunningham and French, eds. (1990), pp. 111–37.

Maupertuis, P. 1735. "Sur les loix de l'attraction" (1732), in Maupertuis (1974), vol. 1, pp. 160–71.

Maupertuis, P. 1744. *Dissertation physique à l'occasion du nègre blanc* (Leyde), modified version: *Vénus physique* (The Hague: 1745), in Maupertuis (1974), vol. 2, pp. 1–35.

Maupertuis, P. 1748. "Accord des différentes loix de la nature" (1744), in Maupertuis (1974), vol. 4, pp. 1–23.

Maupertuis, P. 1751. *Système de la nature: Essai sur la formation des corps organisés*, in Maupertuis (1974), vol. 2, pp. 139–84.

Maupertuis, P. 1974. *Oeuvres* (1756), 4 vols. Hildesheim: George Olms.

Meek, R. 1962. *The Economics of Physiocracy – Essays and Translations*. London: Allen & Unwin.

Mendelsohn, E. 1964. *Heat and Life: The Development of the Theory of Animal Heat*. Cambridge, MA: Harvard University Press.

Mirowski, P. 1989. *More Heat Than Light: Economics as Social Physics, Physics as Nature's Economics*. Cambridge University Press.

Moravaia, S. 1978. "From *Homme Machine* to Homme Sensible: Changing Eighteenth Century Models of Man's Image," *Journal of the History of Ideas*, 39(1), pp. 45–59.

Needham, J. T. 1748. "A Summary of Some Late Observations upon the Generation, Composition, and Decomposition of Animal and Vegetable Substances," *Philosophical Transactions* (London: Royal Society of London), 45, pp. 615–66. (An expanded French version, *Nouvelles observations . . .*, appeared in 1750.)

Oncken, A. 1888. *Oeuvres économiques et philosophiques de François Quesnay*. Paris: Jules Peelman.

Perkins, J. 1979. "The Physiocrats and the Encyclopedists," *Studies in Eighteenth Century Culture*, vol. 8 (Madison: University of Wisconsin Press), pp. 323–36.

Pyle, A. J. 1987. "Animal Generation and the Mechanical Philosophy: Some Light on the Role of Biology in the Scientific Revolution," *History and Philosophy of the Life Sciences*, 9, pp. 225–54.

Quesnay, F. 1730. *Observations sur les effets de la saignée . . . fondées sur les lois de l'hydrostatique*. Paris: C. Osmont.

Quesnay, F. 1736. *Essai phisique sur l'oeconomie animale*. Paris: G. Cavelier.

Quesnay, F. 1747. *Essai physique sur l'oeconomie animale*, 3 vols., 2d ed. Paris: G. Cavelier.

Quesnay, F. 1750. *Traité des effets de l'usage de la saignée*. Paris: d'Houry.

Quesnay, F. 1759. *Tableau économique*, 3d ed., in Kuczynski and Meek, eds. (1972).

Quesnay, F. 1766. "Sur les travaux des artisans," in Quesnay (1958), vol. 2, pp. 885–912.

Quesnay, F. 1958. *François Quesnay et la physiocratie*, 2 vols. Paris: Institut National de l'Economie et Démographie.

Quesnay, F. 1965. *Oeuvres économiques et philosophiques de F. Quesnay*, ed. A. Oncken. Paris: Jules Peelman, 1888; reprinted Darmstadt: Scientia Verlag Aalen.

Rappaport, R. 1960. "G.-F. Rouelle: An Eighteenth-Century Chemist and Teacher," *Chymia*, 6, pp. 68–101.

Rappaport, R. 1961. "Rouelle and Stahl – The Phlogistic Revolution in France," *Chymia*, 7, pp. 73–102.

Roe, S. 1981. *Matter, Life, and Generation: Eighteenth-Century Embryology and the Haller–Wolff Debate*. Cambridge University Press.

Roe, S. 1985. "Voltaire Versus Needham: Atheism, Materialism, and the Generation of Life," *Journal of the History of Ideas*, 46 (1), pp. 65–88.

Roger, J. 1963. *Les sciences de la vie dans la pensée française du XVIIIe siècle: La génération des animaux de Descartes à l'encyclopédie*. Paris: Armond Colin.

Roger, J. 1970–1. "Méthodes et modèles dans la préhistoire du vitalisme français," *Actes du XIIe Congrès International d'Histoire des Sciences, 1968*, pp. 101–8. Paris: A. Blanchard.

Roger, J. 1977. "Introduction and Annotation," in G. L. C. Buffon, *Un autre Buffon*, pp. 93–6. Paris: Hermann.

Roger, J. 1979. "Chimie et biologie: Des 'molécules organiques' de Buffon à la 'physico-chimic' de Lamarck," in *History and Philosophy of the Life Sciences*, pp. 43–64. Naples.

Roger, J. 1986. "The Mechanistic Conception of Life," in D. Lindberg and R. Numbers, eds., *God and Nature: Historical Essays in the Encounter Between Christianity and Science*, pp. 277–95. Berkeley and Los Angeles: University of California Press.

Rosenfield, L. C. 1979. "La Mettrie and Quesnay, physician-*philosophes* of the Enlightenment," in A. Bingham and V. Topazio, eds., *Enlightenment Studies in Honour of Lester G. Crocker*. Oxford: Voltaire Foundation.

Sauvages, F. B., de. 1740. *On the Cause of Vital Motions (Dissertatio medica de motuum vitalium causa)*. Montpellier.

Schell, G. 1904. "Quesnay, avant d'être économiste," *Revue d'Économie Politique*, 18, pp. 177–212.

Schofield, R. E. 1970. *Mechanism and Materialism: British Natural Philosophy in an Age of Reason*. Princeton, NJ: Princeton University Press.

Schumpeter, J. A. 1954. *Economic Doctrine and Method*, trans. R. Aris. New York: Oxford University Press.

Silva, J. B. 1727. *Traité de l'usage des différentes sortes de saignées, principalement de celle du pied*. Paris.

Sloan, P. R. 1979. "Buffon, German Biology, and the Historical Interpretation of Biological Species," *British Journal for the History of Science*, 12, pp. 109–153.

Spink, J. S. 1960. *French Free-Thought from Gassendi to Voltaire*. London: Athalone Press.

Staum, M. S. 1980. *Cabanis: Enlightenment and Medical Philosophy in the French Revolution*. Princeton, NJ: Princeton University Press.

Strenski, E. 1967. "Diderot for and against the Physiocrats," *Studies on Voltaire and the Eighteenth Century*, 57, pp. 1435–55.

Sutter, J. 1958. "Quesnay et la Médecine," in Quesnay (1958), vol. 1, pp. 197–210.

Teich, M. 1982. "Circulation, Transformation, Conservation of Matter and the Balancing of the Biological World in the Eighteenth Century," *Ambix*, 29 (1), pp. 17–27.

Thackray, A. 1970. *Atoms and Powers: An Essay on Newtonian Matter-Theory and the Development of Chemistry*. Cambridge, MA: Harvard University Press.

Thomson, A. 1981. *Materialism and Society in the Mid-Eighteenth Century: La Mettrie's discours préliminaire*. Geneva: Librairie Droz.

Thomson, A. 1988. "L' Homme-machine, mythe ou métaphore?" *Dix-huitième Siècle*, 20, pp. 367–76.

Tonelli, G. 1959. "La nécessité des lois de la nature au XVIII siècle et chez Kant en 1762," *Revue d'Histoire des sciences et de leurs applications*, 12 (3), pp. 225–40.

Tonelli, G. 1987. *La pensée philosphique de Maupertuis: Son milieu et ses sources*. Hildesheim: Georg Olms.

Vaggi, G. 1987. *The Economics of François Quesnay*. Durham, NC: Duke University Press.

Vartanian, A. 1974. "La Mettrie," *Dictionary of Scientific Biography*.

Voltaire, F.-M. A. 1734. *Lettres écrites de Londres sur les Anglais*. Basel.

Weulersse, G. 1910. *Le mouvement physiocritique en France de 1756 à 1770*. Paris: Felix Alcan.

Yolton, J. W. 1991. *Locke and French Materialism*. New York: Oxford University Press.

CHAPTER 11

Organism as a metaphor in German economic thought

MICHAEL HUTTER

Introduction

Why go back to those turbid Teutonic tomes written by the likes of Adam Müller, Friedrich List, Albert Schäffle, or Othmar Spann? The attraction has very contemporary explanations. The recent controversy about the relevance of physics to the development of economic theory has kindled a more general discussion on the role of metaphors. It is unclear whether metaphors are just a coincidental device, clearly distinct from the theory's internal structure, or whether they constrain and direct the theory for which they have been appropriated.

To shed some light on this question, it may be helpful to examine the role of biological processes as a source of inspiration for economists. They were, at times, even more popular than physical metaphors. Yet today, biological analogies to economic processes are widely considered a failure. Apparently, then, some metaphors are more successful than others. What caused the failure of biological images? Is it a feature within the biological paradigm, or is it a problem of transferring the basic structure of biological systems to the structure of economies?

This chapter surveys a subset of the biological approaches to economic theory, namely, those based on a comparison between biological "organisms" and economies as parts of social "organisms." Organic approaches were particularly popular in German thought, and this chapter will restrict itself to German texts. Until the 1930s, organic comparisons were widely considered a viable alternative to mechanistic interpretations of social and economic action. Since then, "organism" has been discredited as a social metaphor not only because of its apparent scientific sterility, but also (and this is the graver cause) because of its suspected contribution to national socialist ideology. Going back to the turbid tomes, then, was not like approaching the wisdom of the ancients with a feeling of veneration. It was more like sifting through a rubbish heap, touching texts that had been declared not only useless but, worse, dangerous.

There is a further reason for picking up the old debate. Recent work in social theory has begun to model economies as well as organizations and institutions as self-referential, autonomous communication systems. The autonomy of such systems has been likened to the operational closure of biological bodies and single cells. The new social theories, however, are structured in a way that is clearly distinct from the older, organic theories. Exploring the difference may be a way of finding out under what conditions biological metaphors are appropriate for social and, more narrowly, for economic processes.

The use of the organic metaphor in German economic thought was woven into the more general intellectual discourse. In many cases, "organism" was used as a primitive notion, a term known and accepted by both writer and reader. Changes in the economic meaning of the metaphor took place along with changes in the intellectual context. The second section of this chapter outlines briefly the general history of the organism metaphor. In the third section, the history of the metaphor in German economic thought is reconstructed. The fourth section relates the findings to contemporary social systems theory.

Organism as a social metaphor: the context

"Organon" meant "tool" in ancient Greek parlance. Aristotle was the first to use it as a medical term, signifying a part of the body (1) that is structured, (2) that performs a function, and (3) whose existence depends on the existence of the entire body. Throughout the Middle Ages, the term was used in Latin and Greek texts in meanings similar or identical with "part of the body." The transfer from Latin to the modern languages, however, was slow and halting (Ballauff and Scheerer 1971, 1320). "Organismus" – as a term for an entity consisting of organs – was first used by G. E Stahl (*Theoria medica vera*, 1708) instead of the then-current "corpus organicum" (Scheerer 1971, 1331). The term is a neologism, and Stahl introduced it explicitly in opposition to "mechanism," thus indicating an early challenge to the Cartesian paradigm. Half a century earlier, Descartes had, in one bold stroke, replaced the multiplicity of scholastic elements, substances, forms, qualities, and quantities with two distinctions: The distinction between *res cogitans* and *res extensa* differentiates the unobservable world of thinking from the observable world of physical appearance; the distinction between *body* and *motion* is sufficient to explain all the phenomena in the physical world (Ballauff and Scheerer 1971, 1330; Specht 1966, 102–3). Living bodies are no exception to the paradigm. What used to be explained by a moving "soul" could now, at least to an astounding degree, be explained by the push and pull of physical forces.

The new theory did not yet know the limits of its applicability.[1] Stahl responded to the indiscriminate application of the mechanistic approach as it spread through Europe. But the limits of applicability remained vague throughout the eighteenth century. In consequence, those who used living bodies as economic metaphors, like Quesnay and Turgot, mingled their references to artificial contraptions, like clocks, and those to natural processes, like metabolism, because the distinction was simply not yet established.[2]

It was Kant who clearly defined "organism" through three criteria in his *Kritik der Urteilskraft:*

1. The idea of the whole determines form and connection of the parts.
2. The parts determine themselves mutually.
3. The organic whole reproduces itself in its totality.[3]

Note that the definition is very general and applicable to a wide variety of phenomena, natural as well as social. Indeed, it was by no means obvious in 1785 which of the emerging sciences would be able to use the newly coined term to the greatest advantage. Until the 1830s, organisms were the object of observation in natural science, in language philosophy, and in social philosophy.[4] In all three fields, highly complex "bodies" with obvious, yet unintelligible structures invited the attempt of being interpreted as organisms.

The new science of *biology* had the most striking success in exploring such organisms. First, the old notion of organs was positioned more precisely between fibre and tissue on one side and the total organism on the other side. "Every organ," states J. C. Reil in 1795, "is independent and self-sufficient, it works for itself and through itself through the energy of its own forces" (quoted in Ballauff and Scheerer 1971, 1320).[5] The conditions under which organs respond with specific reactions began to be observed carefully. The discovery of cells – already predicted in 1759 by K. E. Wolf (Scheerer 1971, 1331) but not accomplished until the 1830s – opened the door to a seemingly complete physiological explanation. The change of organisms over time was, after a long and winding discussion,[6] determined as a process of variation, selection, and stabilization. Only after the breakthrough of evolutionism was the scientific connection between animal organism and human organism accepted (Mayr 1984, 281). The most recent step in the explanation of organic reproduction concerns the discovery of sequentially arranged amino acids serving as a code for the continuity of a genotype.[7]

The history of the metaphor in *language philosophy* is difficult to trace because that science had had no independent existence until then. In fact, it was literary expression, beginning for the German language with Herder and Goethe, that led to the awareness that we live within languages, that languages grow and die, that all experience is expressed in the same mode as fiction, like a novel or a romance – whence comes the name for the literary movement. Romantic philosophy and philology led, on the empirical plane, to intensive research into existing vocabularies, their changes, and their mutual relationships. On a methodological level, the harvest was much richer than the common prejudice about romantic yearning for a fictional past suggests. Still, the problem of observing the universe of discourse within one's own discourse proved intractable in logical terms. By the 1850s, descriptive historical methods prevailed, and organism was reduced to a vague generality. In the 1880s, particularly through Dilthey's proposal of a distinct methodology for the humanities, the issue of *Verstehen*, or Understanding, gained new interest,[8] and that interest has been maintained throughout the work of authors like Georg Simmel, Ludwig Wittgenstein, Martin Heidegger, Hans-Georg Gadamer, and Gotthard Günther.

The history of the metaphor in *social science* was influenced by concurrent developments in general philosophy and by the successes of its biological application. The metaphor of the "social body" goes back to antiquity. The notion of a hierarchically structured "corpus" dominated the Middle Ages, Hobbes's *Leviathan* being just one example. As the notion of the individual emerged and grew during the sixteenth and seventeenth centuries (Luhmann 1986), the question of society's "elements" arose. Contractual, individualistic theories of social change gained credibility and acceptance. A countermovement was built on Kant's new general definition of organism. Fichte, for instance, observed in 1796 that the citizen sustains the state in the same way in which, "in an organic body, every part sustains the whole and is, in turn, sustained by it" (Scheerer 1971, 1340). Authors of the Romantic movement, like Baader and Schelling, assume the state as the natural form of social organization.

French and English authors took a more general view in describing the forces that hold together and change societies. Comte, the first to propose a sociological system,[9] explicitly referred to the organic nature of the entity whose composition he wanted to explore. He limited his observations, however, to those aspects of social action that produce the "spontaneous order of a society" by an equilibrating process and to those that change it through an evolutionary process; "adapting, as he tells us, the terminology of the zoologist H. de Blainville, he called the former Statics and the latter Dynamics" (Schumpeter 1954, 417). Herbert Spencer's emphasis on the differentiation of functions within societies, on society's self-regulation, and on its continuous evolution has been very productive for sociological research in the twentieth century (Parsons 1961). However, his belief in the simultaneous self-determination of the individual led him to a notion of individual evolution that has gained doubtful fame as social Darwinism (Mayr 1984, 307). It seems that the popularity of Spencer's work helped to spread the credibility of organic metaphors for social description. But since the elements of his theoretical analysis were rigidly individualistic, that credibility was not supported by an adequate research program. Organic sociology did continue outside of Germany, as in the work of René Worms (1926) but faltered, as well, in the 1930s.[10]

German sociology was strongly influenced by the interpretation that Hegel had given to Kant's ideas. Hegel outlined a new alternative to the old question of society's "purpose": Society does not strive for religious fulfillment; it is also not adequately described in terms of biological survival; rather, its purpose is the progress of a specific quality called *Geist*. *Geist* suggests the "will" or "mind" of conscious individuals, but it also suggests the collective nature of "spirit" as in team spirit. The most adequate translation, reflecting some of this ambiguity, seems to be "thought." Thought constitutes the specific quality of social organisms. Thought (or *Geist*) may take various institutional forms as it progresses through history, like state law or religion. Hegel's own preference for the status quo is of little relevance. His philosophy of history marks the beginning of German Idealism as a vigorous current of philosophical thought (Barth 1915). From then on, virtually all interpretations of society as an organism started from the explicit distinction between a biological organism and a thought organism (*Geistiger Organismus*). It is this orientation that sustained the application of the metaphor well into the twentieth century, long after the naive biological analogies had been discarded. Many of the major contributions to German philosophy and sociology had their roots in idealist tradition. There were, however, other attempts to interpret society, particularly the state, in explicitly biological terms.[11] Hegelian *Geist* disappeared as a guiding term in the 1930s.[12] It was destroyed first by ideological misinterpretation, then by the physical eradication of German academic culture. After World War II, idealist and organic references are found only rarely in the philosophical or sociological debate.[13] There were, however, successful advances in biology that led to more generally applicable results about the characteristic features of organisms. In particular, von Bertalanffy (1950, 1968) proposed a "general system theory" that interpreted organisms and social entities as open systems. We will return to these developments in the closing section.

Organism as an economic metaphor: the texts

Setting the criteria for exploration

Now on to the turbid tomes. From the preceding section it should be clear why there is no need to assume an organic school of economics in German thought to explain the continuing use of the metaphor. In the intellectual air from 1790 to 1940, cross-currents of conversation ran from biology to sociology and philology and vice versa. Moreover, organic metaphors were in widespread colloquial use. What are, then, the criteria for identifying those contributions to economic theory that not only used "organic" as a superficial synonym for "continuous" or "connected," but actually drew implications for their explanation of economic action and economic development? I have used four criteria:

1. Organic economic analysis is sociological in approach. The economy, therefore, is discussed as an integral part of society.
2. The observable form of the total social organism is discussed. Various candidates like state, nation, community, and *Volk* are conceivable, but one of them must be chosen.
3. The relationship between individual will and the purpose of the social organism is discussed.
4. Comparisons with specific anatomical and physiological characteristics of biological organisms are explored; new discoveries in biology are tested for their applicability to social phenomena.

These four criteria have been applied to the German economic literature since 1790. The result can be interpreted as the erratic, yet ongoing development of an organic paradigm well into the twentieth century. I have chosen to concentrate the exposition on the texts of ten authors, published between 1806 and 1939. A few remarks and quotes are assembled to give a flavor of the argument in texts that do not share our contemporary theoretical bias. As a trade-off, all other work had to be relegated to notes.[14] The choices were made with a view to highlighting changes in the organic paradigm, not with respect to the overall scientific value of a contribution. Before dealing with each text in particular, a brief outline of the sequence may be helpful.

Müller's *Elemente der Staatskunst* (1809) and List's *Nationale System der politischen Ökonomie* (1841) represent an early, theoretically simple organic approach. Roscher's *System der Volkswirtschaft* (1854) and Knies's *Politische Ökonomie vom Standpunkt der geschichtlichen Methode* (1853) are central works in the German historical tradition that demonstrate the strong dependence on organic thought. Von Lilienfeld's *Gedanken über die Sozialwissenschaft der Zukunft* (1873–81) and Schäffle's *Bau und Leben des socialen Körpers* mark the high point and the failure of a research program relying strongly on biological analogy. Menger's *Untersuchungen über die Methode der Sozialwissenschaften* (1883) contributes to the new individualistic, contractarian paradigm, but a large part of the text deals with an exact definition of the organic approach. Spann's *Fundament der Volkswirtschaftslehre* (1918) revives the Romantic movement; many of the biological connotations have been dropped, and the notion of a nation's purpose is prominent. Sombart's *Drei Nationalökonomien* (1930) distinguishes the relative explanatory power of social paradigms. The economic organism is transferred into a system of hierarchically composed meaning. Finally, Eucken's *Grundlagen der Nationalökonomie* (1939) contains a morphological theory of economic order that demonstrates how his thought, which became decisive in shaping Germany's postwar economy, had been shaped, in turn, by a paradigm that was, in essence, still organic.

Elemente der Staatskunst ([1809] 1922) and *Das Nationale System der politischen Ökonomie* (1941)

Adam Müller's *Elemente* (Elements of State Art) contains thirty-six lectures, given to educated, mostly aristocratic lay circles while the author lived in Dresden, trying to make a living as a free-lance writer.[15] Being of common descent, Müller sided with the conservative political powers. His modest career reached a high point when he was appointed Austrian consul in Leipzig in 1816. The *Elemente* is colored by opposition to Smithian laissez-faire policies, but it is driven by a more ambitious desire to make sense of economic action within the context of national organic unity. The nation is patterned after

Fichte's "state": The encompassing community is the whole that determines the parts and is reproduced by them. The basic force is the "living force of the personal interrelation between all members of the community" (Spann 1928, 93). In order to exemplify the content of the *Elemente*, lecture 18, "On the Individual (Use-) Value, and on the Social (Exchange-) Value of Things," shall serve to illustrate the style and the theory of the text.

Müller opens with the argument that everything has a private character through use, and a civil (*bürgerlich*) or social (*gesellig*) character through exchange. Therefore, everything is private property and, at the same time, national property:

> If a thing is called useful, then it is claimed that it has value in relation to civil society, that is, as should be sufficiently clear, that it receives a really personal character through the state, by which it serves the state just as we corporeal persons do. A useful thing is owned the way a person is owned: It is protected like a person, in spite of the rotten Roman Law, which cannot grasp this relationship and gives to the owner the right over life and death, while the police and the finance laws of the same state contradict this absolute right and have to cancel it in innumerable cases. (Müller [1809] 1922, 151–2)

The exchange value of things is expressed as money:

> Money is an idea; or, if that word should be still offensive [twenty years after Kant] money is a property inherent in all individuals of civil society, through which they can connect themselves more or less with the other individuals, or disassociate connected individuals. (153)

As that "property of being money" is developed in fabrication and industry, national wealth increases:

> The more every individual thing or person in the state connects itself with all others, the more it makes itself into money: The more concentrated and alive becomes the state, the more dexterous it moves, the greater are its emanations of force, the more it can produce. (155)

It follows that "products" can be understood only in their social context. National product is not the "sad, dead sum of all single private productions" within the span of a year; it must include "the time and the force of centuries" into its calculations (157). An example is the dependency of state credit on the change of factors in its environment:

> This sum changes invisibly every second; no algorithm masters it; its rise and fall follows deeper laws. The real, not substitutable inner and outer national forces give the sum . . . being or not being; it is based on the most uncertain and the most certain that a man may give or pay, on his word, on a *national word*, and this national word is

based, in turn, on that on which every single thing really depends, as economic theory should show, on the *national force*. (158)

The lecture shows several typical features. A theory of productivity is developed that emphasizes, besides land, labor, and physical capital, a fourth factor: thought capital,[16] including items that today are labeled human capital or social capital. Mainly the fourth factor drives the productive life force of the social organism, called, indiscriminately, state or society. Money, as well as property, is considered an "idea," which makes it possible to articulate social value. Money can be expressed through metal pieces, but it is more adequately interpreted as a word, that is, a promise of future national production.

It remains beyond question that Müller simply postulated the purpose of his social organism, first by identifying it with the political aims of state bureaucracy and landed gentry, later by identifying it with a religious authority. Yet the approach yielded a perspective with surprising connections to contemporary thought. It may be true that Müller introduced "a number of wholly inoperative metaphysical conceptions," as Schumpeter has charged (1954, 421). But it is doubtful whether the world of philosophic vision is as distinct from the world of economic analysis as Schumpeter believed.

Friedrich List wrote his *Nationale System* (National System of Political Economy) about thirty years after Müller's *Elemente* in 1838. The original version is French, since List had responded to the annual prize question of the Académie des Sciences Morales et Politiques in Paris. The question was: "If a nation wants to establish liberty of commerce or to change its tariff laws, which are the facts it ought to take into consideration in order to reconcile in the most equitable manner the interests of national producers and those of the mass of consumers?"

List had led an unsteady and perilous life for the cause of industrialization and liberal, yet national, trade. He had lost his chair in political economy, been jailed, emigrated to the United States, returned as U.S. consul to Leipzig, and worked as an activist and pamphleteer for the new railroad companies and other causes of industrial progress. List ran across the fateful prize question in 1837, after a management position at the Dresden–Leipzig railroad had been refused to him. The manuscript was, in his own words, written within a few weeks because of other pressing demands on his time (Salin and Sommer 1927, 32–3). The jury did not choose a winner of the contest. List was downcast, but still could be brought to edit a German edition in 1841. He killed himself a few years later in a state of failure and depression.

In spite of the differences in time and political conviction, the theoretical elements of the two texts are remarkably similar. List shares Müller's fundamental belief in the reality of a social organism called nation. List attributes a more independent role to the individual than does Müller, and he envisions the final attainment of a global republic in the future, but the social forms of his time are national entities. Like Müller, he attributes the growth of nations to productive forces. The *Nationale System* emphasizes the relevance of the legal order, of education, infrastructure, and institutions. It points out the interdependence of the various productive forces within a nation. Apparently, the postulate "the whole which is more than the sum of its parts" serves as an organic explanation for the productivity of the nation.[17] List also advocated a differentiated position in tariff policy, eliminating tariffs within the nation (a major impediment to intra-German trade), and maintaining them in relation to other, more advanced nations. Here, of course, lies a considerable difference between the two authors: Müller orients his organic nation toward the past, romanticized as a medieval corporate community; List orients his nation toward the future, idealized as a technically developed nation. In support, he sketches a rudimentary step theory, leading from hunting societies all the way to the perfect economic state (*Der vollendete Wirtschaftsstaat*) – a goal reached, in his opinion, only by England and (almost) France. But despite these opposite interpretations of the arrow of time, both Müller and List operate from the same holistic position, based on the same "life forces." Müller, who sides with the conservatives, emphasizes the control and guidance by the state. List, who sides with the progressives, emphasizes the protection of infant-industry investment and the importance of long-range policy planning.

The *Nationale System* continued to be a source of inspiration for economic policy rather than economic theory. List, more than any other author of his age, was able to describe the particular historical development and contemporary state of the major national economies around the globe, descriptions that take up a good part of his text. Hildebrand even claimed that List had forced German economists to historical study (quoted in Spann 1928, 119). But the claim seems exaggerated since historical study was gaining in popularity in all the literary and social sciences during the 1840s.

Das System der Volkswirtschaft (1854) and Die Politische Ökonomie vom Standpunkt der geschichtlichen Methode (1853)

Wilhelm Roscher's *System der Volkswirtschaft* (System of the Folk-Economy) and Karl Knies's *Politische Ökonomie* (Political Economy

from the Perspective of the Historical Method) are the classical texts
of the older historical school and have been described and analyzed
many times.[18] Here, they will be considered only with respect to their
dependence on the organic paradigm.

That dependence is, in fact, considerable. Let us take, as a prime
example, the term *Volkswirtschaft*. It was a standard term of the time,
and it has remained so until today. The reality of a *Volk*, perceived as a
community of thought, institutionalized in an organized state, seemed
so self-evident that it was considered beyond the scrutiny of scientific
inquiry. At this point, it seems worthwhile to remark on the difficulty
in translating the term *Volk*. Both of the possible English equivalents,
"people" and "folk," carry a strong individualist connotation. *Volk*,
however, refers exclusively to the social phenomenon; there is no
individualist interpretation. *Volk* is, at least since Hegel, considered an
entity of thought, a culture. But it was easy, as we shall see, to reduce
the term to a biological, that is, race-defined interpretation.

For both Roscher and Knies, the metaphysical unity of *Volkscharakter*
and *Volkswirtschaft* is beyond question.[19] New is the approach taken to
analyze the performance of that collective organism: In both cases,
individuals are endowed with various "drives." For Roscher, individuals have a selfish drive that guides their actions in private economic
life and a community-oriented drive (*Gemeinsinn*) that guides them in
public life. For Knies, the human soul is not to be fragmented, but
still, self-love is complemented by a sense of justice, community, and
the like. The postulated opposite drives, however, lead to a dilemma:
Which one of the drives is decisive for a theory of production and a
theory of value? Both assume that the selfish drive determines short-
term productivity and exchange value, while the long-term development of a society and its economy is determined by the "life force"
that drives that "organism of a higher order" (Knies). Here, the two
authors part company. Roscher assumes a background from which
everything emanates, "which may be called life force or species or
god's thought" (quoted in Weber 1973, 19), but he pursues an empirical research program with the modest intention of "pushing back"
that background. In order to do so, historical facts are collected as if
they were natural phenomena – the species "*Volk*" is likened to the
species "elephant" (Weber 1973, 11). Furthermore, the theoretical
tenets of the classical theorists are applied to policy problems to an
extent that has led Roscher's text to be judged simply as "historical
sauce over a classical dish" (quoted in Winkel 1977, 93). Knies, in
contrast, refuses any mechanistic regularity for the description of historical processes. To him, the *Völker* are, in turn, individual parts of

the larger organic unity of humanity. In the totality of human development, every *Volk* develops with a stable internal homogeneity, performing its individual historical role and function. Political economy (or
Volkswirtschaftslehre), as a science, must concern itself with the laws of
emergence. These laws, however, depend on the ability of individuals
to act irrationally, yet in accordance with the life force of the social
organism.

Note that Roscher and Knies already grant a more differentiated
role to the individual than Müller and List did. Knies's insistence on
the irrational individual was eventually transposed into a version compatible with the mechanistic paradigm by proposing the existence of
"creative individual minds." Authors ranging from Spann to Schumpeter transferred the life force from collective thought (*Volksgeist*) to
the minds of individual leaders (*geistige Führer*).

Gedanken über die Sozialwissenschaft der Zukunft (1873–81) and *Bau und Leben des socialen Körpers* (1875–8)

Paul von Lilienfeld's *Gedanken* (Thoughts on the Social Science of the
Future) began to appear in 1873. Albert Schäffle's *Bau und Leben*
(Anatomy and Life of the Social Body) had its first edition between
1875 and 1878, and sharply revised editions appeared in 1881 and
1896. We are now faced with a new generation of the organic paradigm. The successes of the natural sciences were well known by the
1870s, and they were a constant challenge to social science. Some
social scientists, particularly economists, emulated explanatory patterns from the physical sciences. The concept of energy was borrowed
from observation of the physical universe and was found highly useful
in explaining phenomena like relative prices (Mirowski 1989). Other
social scientists emulated biological patterns. They interpreted the
concept of energy as a life force, but they constantly struggled with a
more adequate formulation of the internal, reproducing force of social "systems," as they began to be called by von Lilienfeld and
Schäffle.

As with all organic approaches, the new version was sociological in
nature. But sociological in the 1870s did not mean the vague communities and superficial states of Müller and List; nor was sociology
content with the collection of empirical details on human history. The
work of Comte and his followers had given much finer structure and
detail to the various sections of society. Could not the complexities of
an industrializing society be compared to the anatomical structures
and their morphology (as Haeckel had developed), to the flow of

organic forms in evolution (as Darwin had discovered), and to the new knowledge about social psychology (as Wundt had found)? The prospects must have seemed inviting to uncover the hidden similarities between the two types of systems, particularly if one believed that the Hegelian notion of thought evolution answered the question about the social organism's life force.

Both von Lilienfeld and Schäffle must be considered primarily as sociologists. They deal with the economy in the due course of their lengthy survey of the social body.[20] Von Lilienfeld's attention to the economy is slight. Schäffle, instead, had had early economic training and slowly expanded the scope of his research to the entire society. But the economy plays, in his system, an irreplaceable role for the anatomy and the physiology of the social body.

Although *Bau and Leben* found a certain amount of critical acclaim, it should be noted that both von Lilienfeld and Schäffle were on the periphery of established science. Von Lilienfeld, as a German-Russian, wrote his texts in virtual isolation; Schäffle, like List, began his career as a professor of *Nationalökonomie*, but after a stint as minister of commerce in Vienna and the publication of his antihistoricist work, he never held another chair and lived and worked as a free-lance scientist and social reformer.

The structural features of von Lilienfeld's *Gedanken* will be outlined briefly. He characterizes "organism" through five criteria: unity, suitability (*Zweckmäßigkeit*), ability of nonrepetitive movement, specialization of organs, and capital formation (*Capitalisierung*). The notion of capital formation is von Lilienfeld's primary claim to our attention. He transfers it from social observation to natural observation, just as division of labor had been transferred by others. Thus, he believes to have found a property common to all organisms. First, he defines everything produced by man that is not used for immediate (*unmittelbar*) consumption as capital. He then argues:

> Every organism concentrates and accumulates its forces not only in his single parts. Endowed with organic unity, he must by necessity concentrate itself in itself . . . this tendency of forces to a common center, the ability to live and to develop its specific forms and boundaries represents a capital which is generated in every single organism and is transferred to following generations as life germ [the metaphor "germ" has been separated now from the older "life force"], as ability for a specific development . . . from this perspective, the whole organic nature represents in its totality incessantly growing capital, due to continuous accumulation, transformation and concentration of nature's forces. (von Lilienfeld 1873–81, 66–7)

Given his five criteria, von Lilienfeld proceeds to apply various natural laws of biology to the social organism. The first law is the discovery of cells as elementary particles of living bodies. Lilienfeld declares the nerve cells of human individuals – which are also, as he observes, the instruments of man's knowledge of the world – to be the cells of the social body. These cells are structured through individual nerve systems, but also through the intercellular substance (*soziale Intercellularsubstanz*) of capital: buildings, railroads, books, money, law, ideas, and so on (see Barth 1915, 343). The social body, therefore, becomes visible through its capital structure.

Von Lilienfeld's approach makes parts of humans as well as goods into the elements of his social structure – an approach similar to the one chosen by Schäffle. For both, the consequence of that theoretical choice is confusion between a nonmaterial and a material interpretation of unity: The elaboration of the system oscillates between a normative orientation toward a transcendental ethical goal attributed to the social organism[21] and an empirical-realist orientation that picks out biological observations and transfers them rather arbitrarily to social phenomena. The further features of von Lilienfeld's system are noted only summarily: Society is divided into physiological (economic), morphological (legal), and tectonic (political) spheres; social growth takes place according to the sequence of morphological forms suggested by Haeckel – as in natural evolution, forms are related in three dimensions, a temporal sequence (*nacheinander*), a spatial simultaneity of different stages (*nebeneinander*), and an ontogenetic repetition of phylogenetic development (*übereinander*); finally, anomalies of the social system, like pathologies of biological bodies, are considered treatable with therapies.

No doubt, *Gedanken* exaggerates the congruence between natural and social systems to a sometimes grotesque degree, and it provides little explanation for social change. But it unfolds the analogies with great consistency into a complex taxonomy, if not theory, of society.

Albert Schäffle's *Bau und Leben* was a much more successful text, measured by its popularity and the discussion it engendered. It shared, as already mentioned, some of the basic structural defects of von Lilienfeld's system and remained an elaborate, erudite taxonomy, filled and ornated with the biological knowledge of the age, even though it contains a number of remarkable theoretical insights (Borchardt 1961). Some of the main features of the text will be discussed.

Schäffle, from the outset, distinguishes the social body from the biological body:

At the top of the life phenomena in our earthly world of experience stands human society, the social body, composed in peoples (*Völker*) and their private and national institutions. Constructed of the substances and moved by the forces of anorganic and organic nature, it is yet a living body of a different (*eigener*) kind. The human or civil society, a much higher form than the societies of animal peoples, is a purely psychically [*geistig* is now translated as a psychologist's notion of the mind] caused indivisible life community of organic individuals, performed through symbols (*Ideenzeichen*) and technical actions (*Kunsthandlungen*). . . . The consciously performed, shall we say "ideal" coherence between connected organic individuals through symbolizing and technical actions – this is what constitutes the totally peculiar signature of the social body. (Schäffle 1881, 1:1)[22]

Schäffle's *geistiger Organismus* is held together by means that are less material than von Lilienfeld's capital: He mentions voice, language, writing, and the technologies for communication, transport, production, and traffic that lead to a community of imagining, feeling, wanting, and acting (Schäffle 1881, 1:7). The various connections are distinguished into six varieties: unity through language, through common values, through order (law and morals), through power and coercion, through production, and through spatial continuity (accumulation). Only one of these connections is economic in nature. Schäffle likens it to the metabolism of natural organisms; economic institutions are likened to various forms of body tissue.

Schäffle's discussion of the economy touches all of the then-current topics of economic theory. First, there is a theory of value. Economic value is of central importance, it "reigns the production, circulation and consumption of goods. It is the compass of all economic motion" (quoted in Fabian-Sagal 1909, 67). Value is determined by human utility and by cost – "the double face of goods in the social metabolism" (82). Apart from the wording, the argument sounds rather Marshallian.[23] Second, there is a peculiar definition of goods. "If the economy is really society's metabolism, . . . all substances which enter it at a cost for a purpose of social maintenance must be considered economic goods" (Schäffle 1881, 2:206–7). In consequence, material objects and physical labor are goods as well as the so-called idea goods, those for "representing, communicating, conserving and continuing ideas." As society increases in complexity, the demand for idea goods increases exponentially. While material goods increase in cost because of their physical scarcity, idea goods can be produced cheaply and used repeatedly. Thus, their utility is "inexhaustibly continuing and regenerating, it is truly 'aere perennius' " (Schäffle 1881, 1:34).

It must be noted again that Schäffle, like von Lilienfeld, defines both individuals and goods as elements of the social organism, with shifting emphasis as to their relevance. To his contemporary economists, that seemed a daring step away from the production-oriented classical paradigm. But to contemporary idealist philosophers, it seemed a rather incoherent attachment to material connotations within a study of psychic, mental, or thought connections (see Barth 1915, 361–2). Schäffle also suggests a theory of the firm that follows liberal Smithian lines, even if the images differ:

> We can . . . compare an enterprise to an independent body floating through the social universe; its path is determined by the attractive force of highest gain and the repulsive force of threatening losses . . . capitalism then is a composition of millions of individual labor and wealth entities into one national and international production organism under the guidance (*Oberleitung*) of enterprising capitalists who compete for the highest profit. (Quoted in Fabian-Sagal 1909, 164)[24]

Beyond this perception of capitalism, Schäffle envisions a future development of society toward a harmonious state, which he calls "socialism." He describes the features of his socialist utopia in great detail – with public production and the public calculation of labor and capital values through a "social clearinghouse" (Schäffle 1881, 3:335). But all of his details are derived from considerations external to the theory. The theory is unable to forecast anything because the driving force of the system can never be identified. When pressed to an explanation in the elaborate 500-page section on the "laws of social development," a Spencerian world of the survival-of-the fittest individuals and collectivities is suggested, although with numerous details about the various stages and mechanisms of development. The present stage of that development is, to him, a state of individual liberty, regulated by contractual forms. The future state of harmonious socialism can be reached only if it is possible to maintain the private interests of labor and capital; otherwise "a necessary consequence is widespread laziness, disorder, and unemployment from below, pure arbitrariness and whim from above and anarchy on the whole" (Schäffle 1881, 3:345).

Bau und Leben was a sufficiently complex and rich text to leave its traces in the work of many contemporaries. Besides, Schäffle was a popular contender in the policy debates of his day and thus more influential than some of his academic colleagues. Schmoller integrated many of Schäffle's concepts and ideas (Hutter 1992);[25] even Menger mentions the text favorably (1969, 170). One might argue, however, that Schäffle's contributions to economic theory are quite independent of his organic paradigm. That is inevitably true, since otherwise they would not have been preserved in a theory based on the individualist paradigm.

Untersuchungen über die Methode der Sozialwissenschaften (1883)

Carl Menger's *Untersuchungen* (Investigations on the Method of the Social Sciences)[26] is, of course, not part of the organic tradition. Quite to the contrary, it defends the "atomistic" paradigm against the dominating historical and organic paradigms. Thus, one of the three parts of the book is dedicated to the "organic understanding of social phenomena." In distinguishing his own method from the organic tradition, Menger arrives at a clear restatement of the social metaphor, and he is able to clarify to what extent the notion of a common will is expendable in explaining the emergence of institutions. Two similarities between natural and social organisms are conceded: a certain analogy between the function of organs and the function of social constructs, and an analogy between the emergence of apparently highly suitable organs and the unreflected origin of useful institutions. To the degree in which such analogies hold, a social research program comparable to natural anatomy and physiology seems appropriate.

Menger proceeds to show the limits of such an approach in those cases where the analogy does not hold or where (pragmatic) reasons have led to the conscious choice of new conventions. There remains a large number of institutions that cannot be attributed to conscious action. How can they be explained without assuming a force called "common will"?

Menger's answer, his celebrated theory of the emergence of institutions, is well known. Pure self-interest leads individuals to choose alternatives that are, as he calls it, the "resultant" of all individual interests (1969, 180). In a daring act of theoretical imperialism, he calls such institutions "organic." Menger arrives at his solution by sticking closely to his atomistic assumption. There are no links of communication or thought, no symbolic or technical actions needed to explain social institutions. It is noteworthy that Menger chooses money as the empirical example to be discussed in at least stylized detail. In the case of money, the institution can be represented by a material commodity. No signs, symbols, or other forms of communication seem necessary for the explanation. Such an argument, however, seems much less plausible in the case of language, state, or law.[27]

Menger's plea was to accept the exact atomistic method alongside the dominant methods. In time, he believed, more and more phenomena of the social world would become the object of his theory. The progress of the atomistic method, however, was much quicker. Within the time span of the next generation, the organic approach lost most of its scientific credibility. The paradigm lingered on in public usage and through the teachings of old-fashioned academics, but the wave of the future at the turn of the century was atomistic.[28]

Fundament der Volkswirtschaftslehre (1918)

After World War I, the mechanistic paradigm prevailed in economic thought. Value, production, and capital theory were subject to a new dimension of formal rigor. Now, every economic text that attempted to build on the central notion of organic unity had to legitimize that position. Othmar Spann's *Fundament der Volkswirtschaftslehre* (Foundation of the Science of the Folk-Economy) combines an updated version of Hegelian idealism with a revival of romantic ideas and a moderate use of conventional classical theory. The biological connotations of organism play practically no role in the text. But it continues the economic metaphor on a more abstract, more specifically social level.

Society is, for Spann, a living world of thought, regenerating itself through its own internal force. The economy has a peculiar position within society because it has no independent purpose. It is a system of means that serves the fulfillment of the social purpose.[29] Therefore, the economy must be studied as an assemblage of functions (*Leistungen*) for the social purpose. Only then can one understand the economy's contribution to human spirituality (*menschliche Geistigkeit*). If one limits the investigation to quantities of goods, exchange ratios, and costs, one will only produce an objective and dead image of the economy. Spann's central concept is *Gegenseitigkeit*, to be translated as "reciprocity" or "interdependence." All the functions within an economy are interwoven; their performance depends on each other and cannot be analyzed separately. Thus, the "universalist" approach starts from the assumptions opposite to the "individualist" approach. Spann accepts the applicability of optimizing behavior for single economic actors; he even uses the principle of equality at the margin for allocative choices. Much of his terminology in these sections follows Menger, his predecessor in Vienna. But the activity of isolated units does not constitute organic unity. Spann identifies three reasons for a unification of the total economy:

1. Capital of higher order. That category includes virtually everything of a public nature that would influence economic activity: public goods provided by the state and the communities,
   contract law, and all other kinds of commercial law, building
   regulations, monetary order, and so on. Spann compares capital of higher order to the trunk of a tree, whereas normal
   capital is the branch, and the actual performance is the fruit
   (1929, 109).

2. Competition in the trading economy (*Verkehrswirtschaft*).[30]
   Competition integrates the individual desires into the composition of the economic structure, as it is given through
   capital of a higher order: "The selfish wish to have a villa at
   the sea only leads to 'economy' if the actions which it initi-
   ates fit themselves into a composed structure of means (*Glie-
   derbau von Mitteln*) . . . through the objective requirements of
   the composed structure, the motivating reason must be
   reshaped into a reason for incorporation (*Eingliederungs-
   grund*)" (Spann 1929, 152). Through competition, the mor-
   phologically correct proportion of activities within the economic structure is achieved and constantly adjusted.

3. Aim orientation (*Zielverbundenheit*) of the economy. Aim orientation can be generated through the similarity of tastes and
   opinions in a region or a nation. Spann calls it *völkische
   Wirtschaft* and sees it organized either as a moderately capitalist or a corporate economy. Aim orientation can also be generated through collectivist centralized organization, but he considers that possibility to be utopian.

Spann goes into great detail to characterize the various stages of
maturity that an economy passes on its way to community maturity
(*Gemeinschaftsreife*). These details are of lesser interest in our context. It
should be emphasized, however, that Spann does not pursue the approach to give *Geist* a more objective, science-based meaning through
social psychology as Schäffle had tried to do. He returns to Romantic
notions of an external, higher purpose. But in reintroducing them a
century later, they become dangerous: By now, it has indeed become
possible to force a purpose upon a society consciously. Sombart is probably right when he argues that Spann's theory is not even Hegelian, but
basically scholastic: It aims not for progress toward an unknown future,
but for the stability of a corporate world whose hierarchy of values is
already known (Sombart 1930, 36–8). The complex mixture of traditionalist, reactionary elements and modern ingredients made Spann's

version of organic theory highly popular for the two decades between the wars.[31]

Die Drei Nationalökonomien (1930) and Die Grundlagen der Nationalökonomie (1939)

Werner Sombart's *Drei Nationalökonomien* (Three National Economies) and Walter Eucken's *Grundlagen der Nationalökonomie* (Foundations of the National Economy) do not use organism as an economic metaphor. If they mention the term, then it is in a condescending manner. Yet the influence of the organic paradigm can be shown rather easily in the two texts.

In Sombart's work, the economic organism has been replaced by the "economic system." An economic system is "a certain organisation of economic life within which a certain economic ideology (*Wirtschaftsgesinnung*) dominates and a certain technique is applied" (Sombart 1916, 22). In his first great research program, Sombart attempted to unfold in a "genetic-systematic" manner the emergence of the system of capitalism. In doing so, he wanted to fuse three perspectives or methods, the theoretical-abstract perspective, the realist-empirical perspective (the terms are taken from Menger), and the political perspective, which "orients all phenomena towards one ideal" (Sombart 1916, 22). The ideology or spirit characteristic for capitalism is defined as "a frame of mind (*Seelenstimmung*), woven out of entrepreneur spirit and citizen spirit into a unified whole" (329).[32]

This approach is deepened and clarified in *Die Drei Nationalökonomien*. Sombart first describes a judgmental (*richtende*) theory with scholastic underpinnings – the Romantics and Spann fall into this category – and an ordering (*ordnende*) theory, which adapts the methods of the natural sciences. But he drives toward a third variety, namely, understanding (*verstehende*) theory. That theory is part of a larger sociology; it is a social and cultural science. Its fundamental objects are economic systems. The basic heuristic principles are the opposition of statics and dynamics (or development), the opposition of organism and mechanism (or folk economy and exchange economy), and the notion of value. At this point, the argument takes a new twist: Sombart introduces the hermeneutic problem of understanding in explicitly Heideggerian terms (Sombart 1930, 192). The observer is seen to be within his subject matter; he observes from the inside. The community, then, is a community of understanding. There can be no understanding without reference to a community (200). Sombart goes on to categorize three kinds of understanding. The understanding of meaning (*Sinnverstehen*) relates to the basic ideas and categories of an economic system; the understanding of objective economy (*Sachverstehen*) relates to differing styles of production or distribution; the understanding of motivation (*Seelverstehen*) relates to the drives and purposes of single individuals. On the basis of these forms of understanding, economics can be reconstructed as one of the humanities (*Geisteswissenschaften*): "If we are a science like the exact natural sciences, then our research has only value in as much as it leads to practical use . . . in this case the theory of national economy would have no meaning. It can only maintain its meaning if we consider it as a *Geisteswissenschaft* which carries its value in itself" (342).

In Eucken's text, the metaphor of "organism" is replaced by "economic order" (*Wirtschaftsordnung*). Eucken states a failure of classical theoretical science to explain the variability of economic life. He also rejects the historical approach and Spann's universalist theory. He sets himself the task of solving the "great antinomy" between theoretical and historical approaches.[33]

Older attempts to explain economic development like the historicist's "steps" or the "styles" (Spiethoff, Müller-Armack) and "systems" (Sombart) of contemporary authors are rejected because they assume some externally given sequence of development, whereas Eucken wants to be able to understand every stage of development "in its own existence" (Eucken 1944, 57, quoting Ranke). For this purpose, he suggests the notion of economic order: "The economic process takes place always and everywhere within a historically given economic order" (Eucken 1944, 61–2). Various parts of the economy have particular orders, "but all these particular orders fit into each other and are simply members (*Glieder*) of the total order" (63). Such orders can grow, or they can be introduced as constitutions. The scientist's difficulty consists in recognizing the entire structure of a concrete economic order in its complexity.

Economic orders can be broken down into their structural components with the aid of a matrix of market forms. The forms range from perfect competition to full monopoly, on both the supply and the demand sides. This "morphological apparatus" (Eucken 1944, 149) can now be applied to determine the characteristics of a particular historical economic order. Eucken suggests a basic distinction between centrally administered economies and trade economies, but still every order remains an individuality that "results from the selection of the realized pure forms whose number is limited and easy to survey (*übersehbar*)" (203). A derivation of dynamic theory must also recognize the distinction between process and order. Finally, the interdependence of all economic action demands a reintegration of business administration into economics and a circumspect execution of economic policy measures. "Every single policy measure influences the total order and the total process, and this total context, which should be the measure of economic policy decisions, can only be recognized by national economic science through the application of morphology and theory" (288).

Communication systems: a new chapter of the organism story?

A short introduction to contemporary systems theory

In economic thought, the organic paradigm has been considered a failure. It submerged when the mechanist paradigm proved more successful in explaining production, prices, and, to a tiny degree, growth. Only vestiges of it remain in the institutionalist tradition and in individualized versions of the Viennese tradition, like Hayek's "spontaneous order." But worse than being a failure, the paradigm played a considerable role in the emergence of an ideology in whose spirit tens of millions of people were killed and continents were devastated. If that metaphor were to be touched again, then it would have to be with a set of tools clearly identifying those features that have caused its previous failure and its disastrous misapplication.

There have been advances in philosophy, logic, biology, and sociology that possibly fulfill the requirements for continuing the organic approach: Systems theory and its continuation in cybernetics have yielded the concept of self-regulating open systems; language theory and formal logic have yielded new insights into the process of communication and understanding; biological research has advanced to a point where the self-reproduction of an organism's basic units can be precisely described. Out of these developments has emerged a theory of self-reproducing social systems that is able to treat societies and parts of societies, like economies, as organisms in the metaphoric sense in which Kant had defined them.[34] The new theory is explicit on all three of the Kantian criteria: interrelation of parts and elements, reproduction of the organism, and maintenance of the organism's "idea" or, more profanely, its border.

Interrelation of parts and elements. The issue of determining the social body's elements is never discussed explicitly in the organicist literature. It seemed perfectly obvious that natural individuals are the elements of the social entity. Yet we can trace difficulties with this assumption in all the texts. Roscher and Knies try hard to distinguish between "Gemeinsinn" and "Eigensinn." Lilienfeld suggests nerve cells as social elements; Schäffle adds material goods. For Sombart and Eucken, individuals are the dominating forces, and the unity of Sombart's system and Eucken's order are even harder to justify. There are attempts, then, to question the designation of humans as social elements. But the attempts are weak; the validity of the traditional assumption seems too obvious.

It is the apparent obviousness that obscures the fact that such a designation still is an act of choice on the part of the observer. The observer chooses the metaphor, and the observer must choose the equivalents between the two realms of meaning that are being compared. It is a choice with severe consequences. Once it has been made, any larger social entity must be thought of as a composite of separate individuals, held together by vague notions of a pragmatic nature: groups, teams, firms, communities. It is quite reasonable in this situation to stick to the individualist assumption and make the most of it, as Menger did in his penetrating analysis. Adding a "common will" or "communal sense"[35] simply turns the theory into a tautology.

In modern social systems theory, another choice is made. The elements of any social entity or "body" are assumed to be *communication events*. That choice seems indeed much more artificial than the traditional one, and it needs a little explanation: "Communication" refers to the most fundamental property of social processes. Meaning or information is transferred from one location of the system to another location. The transfer is not a physical transfer, because there is no matter involved. The transfer refers, rather, to the reappearance of the same feature in a later message. "Information," wrote Gregory Bateson (1972, 381), "is a difference which makes a difference in some later event." Since the term "information" has been preempted by Shannon and Weaver's (1949) technical interpretation, the term "communication" is suggested. Communication, then, notes the remarkable phenomenon that address A sends a message containing many differences; A observes that B reacts to the message by repeating some of the differences; A then continues the conversation by repeating some of the differences in B's message. Neither of the two will ever know how his counterpart has processed or "understood" the message. Nevertheless, the two addresses are able to continue their dialogue under the supposition that they understand each other. A communication event occurs whenever an action repeats the differences contained in a previous action.[36] Clearly, such events are tiny, and they are highly volatile. Yet they are linked into endless chains of conversation and dialogue, using language, writing, music, and, last but not least, money as their medium.[37] Society can now be perceived as the total stream of communication, as it takes place in highly conditioned environments of skilled humans[38] and specialized machines.[39] We can – to return to our subject – define the economy as the totality of all messages that are performed using the communication medium of money. Thus, we gain a perspective of the economy that focuses on the communicative process rather than on material activities. Such a perspective is less novel than it may seem: There is a strong current in contemporary microeconomics that considers *transactions* to be the basic units of economic investigation.[40] The new social theory suggests that the communication aspect of a transaction, that is, the payment of money, is more relevant in defining an economy than is the material aspect, that is, the exchange of goods.

Reproduction of the organism. The older organic theories never come to a convincing explanation of social continuity and growth. If humans are chosen as elements, then it seems consistent to leave social reproduction up to them as well. But how? Surely, social reproduction must not be biological in nature. Whenever it is, the transfer of the metaphor has been left out, and we are left with a biological, race-oriented theory that dresses up as a social theory.[41] Hegelian philosophy offers a solution: The social entity continues itself through "dialectical" movement. One idea leads antithetically to the next one. Thus, the social continuity is transferred to a continuity of thoughts in individual minds. Unfortunately, such continuity is observable only in explicit messages. It seems quite possible to develop such a perspective into a communication perspective. But Hegelian idealism is firmly based on the primacy of identity. To start with difference as a basic notion implies no less than a reconstruction of the entire edifice. There were also other attempts to position social reproduction. Schäffle, for instance, assigns the role to education. Again, the proposal sounds compatible to a communication perspective. But as always with Schäffle, the thought remains isolated; it is not developed into meaningful propositions.

The new social theory has a different option for expressing social reproduction: Communication events are linked by "copying" differences out of previous events. In fact, they would not exist if there were no previous events to refer to and if there was not an expectation of future events that will, in turn, refer to them. The process of copying can be observed quite well in chains of payment: A money sign, for instance, a coin, is passed from one person to another. Person A offers that particular sign for economic value; person B accepts it. Next, person B offers the coin to a third person, who, in turn, accepts it. The coin has now been used in two subsequent transactions. The coin in B's hand has rendered service twice: first, as a medium for the response to A; second, as a medium for the offer to C.[42] The message has *duplicated* itself by appearing in two events.

Thus, we are able to define a process of reproduction in purely social terms.[43] Is the process akin to the duplication of genetic matter in biological phenotypes? Its semantic genesis would suggest that it is. After all, "code" is a social metaphor for a natural process. But more than that, we can observe that the duplication of messages contains mistakes and misrepresentations that have the same effects as variations and mutations of genetic matter. Social reproduction can then be thought of as an evolutionary process, without having to refer to external innovation as a driving force of change.[44]

Border maintenance. The identity or "idea" of the social organism was of a higher, religious nature for Müller and for Lilienfeld. It was technically defined for List and vaguely transcendental for Schäffle and Spann. In every case, the outlines of society were somehow known to the observer, as if such perception were as easy as the visual perception of animals and plants.

The new social theory treats the distinction between a social system and its environment as a serious and methodically complex problem. Social systems appear and disappear, they seem to be dormant for decades, and they can grow rapidly under favorable environmental circumstances. In what sense can we say, then, that the system has a notion of itself, of its own borders, of its own identity? It has been suggested that social systems reproduce themselves through their own elements – they are operationally closed. Just like plays, which have no other goal or purpose than the continuity of the play, the systems continue themselves. All the information about the borders of the play are contained in the moves – there cannot be, by definition, any outside information.[45] As a consequence, the system can only react to internal changes. Even the environment is observable only inasmuch as it has been translated into internal communication. We can easily verify that proposition with respect to the "money game"of the economy or the "truth game" of science. Metaphors are, in effect, an attempt to plant new differences into the ongoing conversation play of a discipline. If the metaphor is picked up and continued, then new aspects of the world can be talked about.

The sense of identity that social systems develop varies greatly from the team spirit of a rowing crew to the vague feeling of togetherness in a language community. But still, there seems to be an interest of the system to continue its own existence. That self-interest belongs to the same logical category as the self-interest of biological organisms. Yet it is clearly distinct from the material survival common to natural beings. It is, primarily, an interest in the continuity of the communication events that constitute the play.[46]

Conclusion

The new social theory could only be sketched in the previous section. But even that attempt creates some distance to the older texts, and it allows us to clarify or even explain some aspects of the organicist tradition.

We have seen that the organic approach failed because of the assumption that natural individuals must be the elements of society. A methodologically correct use of the metaphor requires that biological details have their social equivalents. Unless an organic model starts from purely social elements (like communication events), it cannot transfer the metaphor adequately when it comes to reproduction and self-interest.

The sequence of texts presented in the preceding section is, in itself, an example for the development of a communication play. The texts were all messages in a larger conversation.[47] There was, as many contributions to this volume show, a much broader stream of scientific development in which organic and social metaphors crisscrossed frequently and fruitfully.[48] There was, as is to be expected, a particularly intensive interchange within the German-speaking literature. There was also a vivid exchange of ideas with the other European language areas. That larger stream of development demonstrates how difficult it is to change established communication patterns and to give new meaning to old concepts. The concept of "state," for instance, changed dramatically between 1806 and 1939, yet Müller and Eucken were each mired in their respective perceptions. The development also demonstrates how authors' intentions are often ignored by the conversation. Texts relate to previous texts, irrespective of the value judgments of the authors. An example is Marshall's emphasis on organization and the lack of notice that the texts interpreting and reformulating Marshall have taken.[49] Such divergence, however, is not arbitrary. The ability to pick up an argument and to reproduce it depends on the ease with which a convincing story can be told. As long as there were no adequate formulations for a theory of organization (and they are still lacking), all attempts remained descriptions without internal consistency, and in consequence, they were left out when the bare bones of Marshallian theory became part of the economists' "oral tradition."

But this, of course, is not the end of the story. In fact, it may be a beginning. As the basic structure of a logic adequate for articulating social processes slowly emerges, we may soon be able to transfer more of the richness of biological knowledge to the observation of societies. Organism, as a metaphor for social systems, may have its most productive phase yet to come.

Notes

The investigation reported here was aided by a student research group. My thanks go to Martin Berger, Ansgar Münsterjohann, Volkmar Rohr, and Rainer Venghaus for their valuable help. Some points were sharpened and corrected thanks to detailed comments by Warren Samuels.

1. "At the price of an obstinate metaphysical problem a cleaning of the world of substance from the admixtures of spirit is made plausible" (Jonas 1973, 83). Here, as in all the following texts, the translations are mine.
2. For an inquiry into the use of mechanistic and organic metaphors by Quesnay, see Rieter (1983, 1990) and Christensen, Chapter 10, this volume.
3. Quoted after Barth (1915, 101–3). Kant is also among the first authors to point out that the new term "organization" is used to advantage ("sehr schicklich") in describing administrative reforms of the state bureaucracy (Scheerer 1971, 1352). But he also, like Herder, speaks of animal bodies or of entire nature as being "organized."
4. The distinction into these three general fields follows Foucault (1966).
5. Note that, at the time, the use of the term "force" was not yet limited to mechanistic force. Reil establishes an alternative source for such a force that is more precise than a tautological reference to "vital" forces.
6. But note that the interior of cells, the so-called protoplasm, was considered to be the basic "life substance" until the 1930s. See Mayr (1984, 525).
7. It is remarkable that "genes" were initially suggested by Johansen in 1907 as "a kind of measurement unit," i.e., as a fictional device. See Mayr (1984, 590).
8. Dilthey, in turn, traces his theoretical roots to Schleiermacher, Scherer, and Schelling. See Rothacker (1930).
9. At about that time, the meaning of the term "system" changed from indicating a thought system to indicating an observable system.
10. The French strand of development did not distinguish organic and mechanistic organization quite as sharply as the German authors did. For a penetrating analysis see Schlanger (1971). Another attempt, now rarely remembered, is Whitehead's attempt at a vitalist-organic philosophy. He

argued that the continuity of existence consists of a sequence of atomic events that forms a nexus because of the constructive inclusion of the past in every new present. See Jonas (1973, 149–50).

11. See, e.g., Oppenheimer (1900) and Hertwig (1922). A survey of that period in German sociology is compiled in Kruse (1990).
12. For a survey of neoidealism in the Anglo-Saxon world, see Phillips (1970).
13. For an exception, see Jonas (1973).
14. This holds, with particular regret, also for the work of Karl Marx.
15. At the same time, Müller edited the literary magazine *Phoebus*, together with H. von Kleist.
16. Müller associates the four factors with the "elements" of femininity, masculinity, youth, and age. It is these scholastic inclinations that have contributed to ruining his reputation.
17. Authors with similar approaches could be mentioned. For instance, F. Schmitenners's *National-Ökonomie oder Wirtschaftslehre* (1839) also postulated that the organic combination of forces within the state lead to an increase in national product. See Priddat (1991).
18. See Schumpeter (1954) and Winkel (1977).
19. On Roscher and Knies, see Weber (1973, 11–16 and 142–5, respectively).
20. The *Gedanken* fill five volumes; the first edition of *Bau und Leben* spanned four volumes.
21. Schäffle shares the traditional idealist position – with an Aristotelian twist, according to Priddat (1990). Von Lilienfeld, however, has excluded spiritual activities from his definition. He attributes them to a separate, hierarchically superior organism that is of a religious nature. See Barth (1915, 344).
22. See Foucault (1966) on the historical meaning of "signature."
23. Fabian-Sagal (1909) sees similarities with Cassel; Borchardt (1961), with Walras. But the connections seem a bit strained.
24. An important incentive in this context are innovator rents. See Fabian-Saga (1909, 152).
25. Schmoller, in spite of his prominence and power, had little influence on theory development. He integrated the concepts of other authors liberally into his work, and Schäffle is no exception. Schmoller's contribution to economic policy or reform is another matter.
26. A recent translation renames it *Problems of Economics and Sociology*.
27. Menger attached an appendix that deals with the origin of law – one of the central fields for applying the organic paradigm. Here, he argues that people realize the necessity of constraints for fancy and for arbitrariness. Therefore, they form "convictions" about such constraints. Still, he maintains that there is "wisdom which is not understood" (*unverstandene Weisheit*) in institutions like the common law – a fact that should hinder unreflected intervention and reform (Menger 1969, 283).
28. The notion of organism, however, does not disappear from Menger's writings. There is a strong emphasis in his late unpublished work on

perception and the "chemism" of feelings as explanatory factors of economic behavior. Organism, in its psychological interpretation, thus continues to influence economic results.

29. Note the analogous interest in the relationship between means and ends in the Robbins tradition. The difference lies, of course, in the assumption about who or what generates the ends.

30. There exists an old distinction in German economic thought between *Verkehrswirtschaft*, which encompasses the profit-oriented activities of private actors, *Gemeinwirtschaft*, which includes communal activities of an economic nature, and *Widmungswirtschaft*, which entails philanthropic giving.

31. It was not only Spann's version of organic theory that prospered at the time. An example of a text that relates to Schäffle and explicitly opposes Spann is Weddigen's *Organismusgedanke in der Wirtschaftstheorie* (1939). The author declares the classical law of first increasing, then decreasing returns as the central theorem of economic theory and argues: "The precondition for the validity of this claim – unrecognized until now – consists in a sufficient, independent (*selbsttätig*) ability of the economic formation (*Gebilde*) [a term used very frequently in the literature of the time] to adapt, reorganize and rearrange the factors of production. They have to substitute each other in a certain kind of self-regulation to make the best of the new situation created through the one-dimensional change of input . . . from here follows the organic essence (*Wesenheit*) of economic theory, arranged systematically around the purely theoretical law of productivity" (6).

32. More intricate connections between Sombart and the Romantics are compiled in Betz (1991).

33. It should be noted that Eucken's father, Rudolf Eucken, was one of the protagonists of neoidealism. See Eucken (1915).

34. The major contributions are by Luhmann (1984b, 1988). See also Baecker (1988) and Hutter (1990).

35. A comparison with the notion of "common sense" as it was used in English philosophy seems instructive. Apparently, the German (Kantian) interpretation implies a visible community, whereas the English (Humean) interpretation implies a community of thought.

36. Such actions that specialize in formulating differences through sound or signs are called messages. It may seem that the perception of messages depends on an observer, while the existence of human beings is given. But that would be a mistake: There is a long and continuing debate about what constitutes a human. A short while ago, Pygmies were excluded; today, the status of embryos is contested.

37. The proximity to theories that start from discourse is quite clear. Most of the available texts are less clear, however, on the primacy of discourse over its participants. See Klamer, Chapter 2, this volume, and the introduction of communication issues in Moore, Chapter 20, this volume.

38. Individuals do not disappear in communication systems theory, as it is often claimed. Rather, they are split into two kinds of appearances: First,

they appear in social systems inasmuch as they contribute to the ongoing communication – transmitting their thoughts in "symbolic actions," to use Schäffle's term. But only the communication acts are observed. Second, they appear as separate consciousness, which are, in themselves, auto-poietic self-reproducing systems. But the reproduction of consciousness takes place outside of communication, and the communication takes place outside of consciousness. The neglect of that basic distinction has led the idealist movement into mistaking consciousness for communication. The distinction is logically necessary because systems are distinguished from their environment through the environment's higher degree of complexity; for communication events, consciousness, and life forms constitute their environment, and they are inaccessibly complex. Communication can only respond to events that have been brought down to its level and form of complexity. The inaccessibility of consciousness for purposes of communication becomes painfully clear as one searches for access to one's mind in order to write a conference paper.

39. "Society consists of communication, it consists only of communication, it consists of all communications. It reproduces communication through communication. Whatever happens as communication is thus operation and, at the same time, reproduction of society. Neither in the environment nor with the environment of society can there be communication. In consequence, the communication system society is a closed system. It is, however, only possible in an environment, thanks to psychic conscious-ness, thanks to organic life, thanks to physical materialization, thanks to the evolution of suns and atoms. Society registers this situation by estab-lishing itself as an open system. It communicates about something – about topics which concern its environment or itself or the actually occurring communication. Thus, society is a closed and an open system at the same time, and communication is the form of the elementary operation which performs and reproduces this combination" (Luhmann 1984a, 311).

40. Limoges and Ménard, Chapter 13, this volume, relate to that position.

41. This critique holds for Spencer as well as for Spann.

42. The coin does not constitute the message. It serves as a medium that makes it possible to articulate a particular payment message.

43. Murphy, Chapter 19, this volume, claims that mechanism and organism cannot be distinguished sharply because both try to "explain structure as if it were deliberately designed for its function." The notion of self-reproduction, as it is developed here, sets organic structure quite clearly apart from mechanic structure.

44. The Schumpeterian approach, to which I allude here, is one of the varia-tions of the Vienna tradition. Following the explorations of Menger, Schum-peter places the vital force into the creativity of individuals. Such a move seems compatible with the neoclassical tradition, but it presumes abilities that go way beyond the utility field notions of Edgeworth and Hicks.

45. This is the reason why the organicist authors refer to higher authority. They, too, can only perceive those systems in which they are participating.

They recognize the plays because they recognize certain events as moves in a particular play. The term "play" is used here in the sense of improvised, possibly artistic action. Games with given rules and given aims leave little room for genuine play.

46. It must be noted that the self-referential nature of the processes observed makes the existence of a play a prerequisite to identifying a specific communication event. There is no objective outside definition. The exposition of the theory, as it is attempted here, suffers from the constraint of linearity while trying to model a circular process.

47. Care was taken to present the material (or, rather, the messages) as texts, rather than as something produced by an author.

48. See, particularly, White, Chapter 8, on Richard Jennings and Alborn, Chapter 7, on the Victorian money debate. Of course, Mirowski's (1989) account of the development of the energy metaphor is another contribution showing the scope of the interaction.

49. Compare Limoges and Ménard, Chapter 13, and Schabas, Chapter 12, this volume.

References

Baecker, Dirk. 1988. *Information und Risiko in der Marktwirtschaft.* Frankfurt: Suhrkamp.

Baecker, Dirk. 1992. "The Writing of Accounting," *Stanford Literature Review* 1(7):123–32.

Ballauff, T., and E. Scheerer. 1971. "Organ," in J. Ritter, ed., *Historisches Wörterbuch der Philosophie,* 1317–26. Darmstadt: Wissenschaftliche Verlagsgesellschaft.

Barth, Paul. 1915. *Die Philosophie der Geschichte als Soziologie.* Leipzig: Reisland.

Bateson, Gregory. 1972. "A Reexamination of Bateson's Rule," in *Steps to an Ecology of Mind,* 379–99. New York: Ballantine.

Betz, Horst, 1991. "Werner Sombart and German Romanticism," in *Proceedings of the Conference "Werner Sombart, Social Scientist,"* manuscript, Heilbronn.

Biddick, Kathleen. 1992. "Comment on David Moore," unpublished manuscript.

Borchardt, Knut. 1961. "Albert Schäffle als Wirtschaftstheoretiker," *Zeitschrift für die gesamte Staatswissenschaft* 117:610–34.

Esposito, Elena. 1992. *L'Operazione dell' Osservazione: Construttivismo e teoria dei sistemi sociali.* Milan: Angeli.

Eucken, Rudolf. 1915. *Die Träger des deutschen Idealismus.* Berlin: Ullstein.

Eucken, Walter. 1944. *Die Grundlagen der Nationalökonomie.* Jena: Fischer. (Original edition 1939.)

Fabian-Sagal, Eugenie. 1909. *Albert Schäffle und seine theoretisch-nationalökonomischen Lehren.* Dissertation, University of Zürich.

Foucault, Michel. 1966. *Les mots et les choses.* Paris: Gallimard.

Hertwig, Oscar. 1922. *Der Staat als Organismus.* Jena: Fischer.

Hutter, Michael. 1990. "The Self-Organisation of the Economy," in K. Dopfer and K. F. Raidle, eds., *The Evolution of Economic Systems,* 100–10. London: Macmillan.

Hutter, Michael. 1992. "Historicist Biologism and Contemporary Evolutionism: Where Is the Difference?" Discussion paper, Witten/Herdecke University.

Hutter, Michael. 1994. "Communication in Economic Evolution: The Case of Money," in R. England, ed., *Evolutionary Concepts in Contemporary Economics.* Ann Arbor: University of Michigan Press.

Iht, Arnold. 1927. *Die menschliche Gesellschaft als sozialer Organismus. Die Grundlinien der Gesellschaftslehre A. Schäffles.* Zürich: Speider & Wurzel.

Jonas, Hans. 1973. *Organismus und Freiheit.* Göttingen: Vandenhoek & Rupprecht.

Klamer, Arjo. 1992. "The Loss of the Economic Subject," unpublished manuscript.

Knies, Karl. 1853. *Politische Ökonomie vom Standpunkte der geschichtlichen.* Braunschweig: Schwetschke.

Kruse, Volker. 1990. "Von der Historischen Nationalökonomie zur historischen Soziologie: Ein Paradigmenwechsel in den deutschen Sozialwissenschaften um 1900," *Zeitschrift für Soziologie* 19(3):149–65.

List, Friedrich. 1841. *Das nationale System der politischen Ökonomie.* Stuttgart: Cotta.

Luhmann, Niklas. 1984a. "Die Wirtschaft der Gesellschaft als autopoetisches System," *Zeitschrift für Soziologie* 13:308–27.

Luhmann, Niklas. 1984b. *Soziale Systeme.* Frankfurt: Suhrkamp.

Luhmann, Niklas. 1986. "The Individuality of the Individual: Historical Meanings and Contemporary Problems," in T. Heller, M. Sosna, and D. Wellbery, eds., *Reconstructing Individualism: Autonomy, Individuality, and the Self in Western Thought,* 313–25. Stanford, Calif.: Stanford University Press.

Luhmann, Niklas. 1988. *Die Wirtschaft der Gesellschaft.* Frankfurt: Suhrkamp.

Luhmann, Niklas. 1990. *Die Wissenschaft der Gesellschaft.* Frankfurt: Suhrkamp.

Mayr, Ernst. 1984. *Die Entwicklung der biologischen Gedankenwelt.* Berlin: Springer. (Original English edition 1982, "The Growth of Biological Thought," Cambridge, MA: Belknap Press.)

Menger, Carl. 1969. *Untersuchungen über die Methode der Sozialwissenschaften, und der politischen Oekonomie insbesondere.* Tübingen: Mohr. (Original edition 1883.)

Mirowski, Philip. 1989. *More Heat Than Light: Economics as Social Physics, Physics as Nature's Economics.* Cambridge University Press.

Müller, Adam. 1922. *Elemente der Staatskunst.* Leipzig: Kröner. (Original edition 1809.)

Oppenheimer, Franz. 1900 "Nationalökonomie, Soziologie, Anthropologie," *Zeitschrift für Sozialwissenschaft* 3:485–93, 621–32.

Oppenheimer, Franz. 1926. *System der Soziologie.* Jena: Fischer.

Parsons, Talcott. 1961. *Introduction to Herbert Spencer's "Study of Sociology."* Ann Arbor: University of Michigan Press.

Phillips, D.C. 1970. "Organicism in the late 19th and early 20th centuries," *Journal of the History of Ideas* 31:413–32.

Priddat, Birger. 1991. *Der Ethische Ton der Allokation. Zum Verhältnis von Ökonomie und Ethik in der deutschen Nationalökonomie des 19. Jahrhunderts.* Baden-Baden: Nomos.

Rieter, Heinz. 1983. "Zur Rezeption der physiokratischen Kreislaufanalogie in der Wirtschaftswissenschaft," in H. Scherf, ed., *Studien zur Entwicklung der ökonomischen Theorie III*, 55–100. Berlin: Duncker & Humblot.

Rieter, Heinz. 1990. "Quesnays Tableau Economique als Uhren-Analogie," in H. Scherf, ed., *Studien zur Entwicklung der ökonomischen Theorie IX*, 57–94. Berlin: Duncker & Humblot.

Roscher, Wilhelm. 1854. *Das System der Volkswirtschaft.* Stuttgart: Cotta.

Rothacker, Erich. 1930. *Einleitung in die Geisteswissenschaften.* Tübingen: Mohr.

Salin, E., and A. Sommer. 1927. *Einleitung zu Friedrich Lists "Das natürliche System der politischen Ökonomie,"* 3–37. Berlin: Hobbing.

Schäffle, Albert. 1881. *Bau und Leben des Socialen Körpers.* Tübingen: Laupp.

Scheerer, E., 1971. "Organismus," in J. Ritter, ed., *Historisches Wörterbuch der Philosophie*, 1330–58. Darmstadt: Wissenschaftliche Verlagsgesellschaft.

Schumpeter, Joseph. 1954. *History of Economic Analysis.* London: Allen & Unwin.

Shannon, Claude, and W. Weaver. 1949. *The Mathematical Theory of Communication.* Urbana: University of Illinois Press.

Sombart, Werner. 1916. *Der moderne Kapitalismus.* München: Duncker & Humblot.

Sombart, Werner, 1930. *Die drei Nationalökonomien.* Berlin: Duncker & Humblot.

Spann, Othmar. 1928. *Die Haupttheorien der Volkswirtschaftslehre.* Leipzig; Quelle & Meyer.

Spann, Othmar. 1929. *Fundament der Volkswirtschaftslehre*, 4th ed. Jena: Fischer. (Original edition 1918.)

Specht, Rainer. 1966. *René Descartes.* Reinbek: Rowohlt.

von Bertalanffy, Ludwig. 1950. "An Outline of General System Theory," *British Journal of Philosophy of Science* 1:139–64.

von Bertalanffy, Ludwig. 1968. *General System Theory.* New York: Braziller.

von Lilienfeld, Paul. 1873–81. *Gedanken zur Sozialwissenschaft der Zukunft.* Hamburg.

Weber, Max. 1973. "Roscher und Knies und die logischen Probleme der historischen Nationalökonomie," in J. Winckelmann, ed., *Gesammelte Aufsätze zur Wissenschaftslehre.* Tübingen: Mohr.

Weddigen, Walter. 1939. "Der Organismusgedanke in der Wirtschaftstheorie," *Zeitschrift für die Gesamte Staatswissenschaft* 95 (1):1–22.

Winkel, Harald. 1977. *Die deutsche Nationalökonomie im 19. Jahrhundert.* Darmstadt: Wissenschaftliche Buchgesellschaft.

Worms, René. 1926. *Die Soziologie. Wesen, Inhalt und Beziehung zu anderen Wissenschaften.* Karlsruhe: Braun.

CHAPTER 12

The greyhound and the mastiff: Darwinian themes in Mill and Marshall

MARGARET SCHABAS

When economists think of joining their subject with biology, it is Alfred Marshall who springs to mind for his celebrated remark that "the Mecca of the economist is economic biology rather than economic dynamics" (Pigou 1925, 318). His endorsement of the same motto as Darwin regarding nature's inability to take leaps has also been taken to suggest that Marshall was profoundly influenced by Darwin (see Niman 1991). It is certainly very tempting, and quite easy, to tell the following story. Darwin's *Origin of Species* (1859) propelled biology into a respectable scientific field such that economists could then turn to it to emulate, in place of physics. More specifically, Darwin's insights greatly reinforced long-standing appeals by economists to competition, equilibrating mechanisms, and historical explanation. Most of all, his thoroughgoing materialism transformed our conception of human psychology and morality. Both were products of our evolutionary history and thus at bottom just refined instincts. Economists could discard, once and for all, appeals to a human nature designed by the deity.

I will challenge this view. More specifically, I will show that there is little evidence that Darwinian biology shaped the content or even the broader context of early neoclassical economics, particularly as represented by Marshall. In doing this, I do not wish to suggest that economic theory and the theory of evolution have nothing in common. On the contrary, biological and economic reasoning have been closely intertwined since the Enlightenment. But there is probably as much Linnaeus in Adam Smith as Darwin in Marshall.[1] Even John Stuart Mill's conception of the economic order is arguably more at one with the broader tenets of Darwinian biology than is Marshall's. By making these claims, I am weaving quite a large piece of historical cloth and ask in advance that the reader forgive the many holes that might be formed here and there. I believe that the threads intertwine well enough, but one might not want to wear the finished cloth to dinner with the Queen. Speaking of which, I will confine my study to Victorian England, in part because of limitations of space and time and in part because that is the period I know best.

Thanks to the perceptive work of Robert M. Young, historians have also come to see Darwin and his contemporaries within a much broader context than as simply a solution to the problems of extinction and the geographical distribution of life forms. As Young has put it, the central debate of the nineteenth century was "man's place in nature," a debate that was thrashed out in numerous disciplines, including theology, political economy, anthropology, and psychology, as well as biology. More important, the disciplinary boundaries at the time were highly permeable. As Young has put it, "In the nineteenth-century debate there was an intimate mixture of psychological, social-philosophical, biological and theological issues" (1985, 78). Certainly, the wall between the natural and moral sciences was far less firm than holds today.

One striking fact to keep in mind is that prominent British economists alive in the decades after 1859 responded favorably to Darwin. John Stuart Mill remarked in a letter of 1860 that Darwin's book "far surpasses my expectation" (Mill 1972, 695), and William Stanley Jevons compared Darwin (and Spencer) to Newton in terms of "revolutionising . . . all our views of the origin of bodily, mental, moral, and social phenomena" (Jevons 1877, 762). Marshall first read Darwin, with much enthusiasm, during his "apprenticeship years" as a member of the Grote Club (Whitaker 1977, 194) and in the opening sections of his *Principles of Economics,* Marshall explicitly acknowledges the importance of Darwin's theme of historical contingency (Marshall 1920, 42). In Chapter 13, this volume, Claude Ménard and Camille Limoges have argued that Darwin's (and Ernst Haeckel's) insights on the division of labor permeate Marshall's insights in book 4 of the *Principles.*[2]

Darwin was a palatable tonic for economists if only because his analysis of the economy of nature read like classical political economy applied to the natural realm. But did Darwin in fact use economic ideas in his research? The most reliable piece of evidence to advance this thesis is Darwin's debt to Malthus. Scott Gordon (1989) has persuasively argued not only that Darwin misunderstood Malthus, but that there is very little evidence to support the claim that Darwin was familiar with the literature on classical political economy. In short, Darwin was remarkably indifferent to political economy, particularly for a well-educated Briton of his day. He was a naturalist first and foremost, and much preferred the company of his beetles and earthworms than that of political economists.

I support Gordon's position, but still believe that the similarities between Darwin's model of nature and classical economics are too strong to be merely coincidental. I have argued elsewhere that Charles Lyell may have been the agent who imported some concepts from classical economics into biology.[3] As Martin Rudwick (1979) and Salim Rashid (1981) have demonstrated, Lyell cultivated an interest in political economy during the 1820s, both by reading the main texts on the subject and by attending John Ramsey McCulloch's lectures. He was also a close friend of Nassau Senior's. There are distinct traces of Smith and Ricardo in his lengthy discussion of the economy of nature in volume 2 of *The Principles of Geology* (1832). Darwin received a copy of Lyell's second volume while on the *Beagle,* and there can be no doubt that it had a profound impact on his own conceptual genesis, arguably as much or more than his visit to the Galapagos Islands. Unwittingly, Darwin may have appropriated many ideas from classical economic theory via Lyell. But this appeal, like the purported influence of Malthus, best hangs on the fact that Victorian economists drank Darwin with such relish.

Precisely because Darwin's struggle for existence in the economy of nature resonated with extant economic doctrine, economists may have been disinclined to take the trouble to understand the intricacies of his theory. That seems to be the case with both Mill and Marshall. Darwin's theory of descent with modification is, by any standards, a very sophisticated piece of reasoning. Arguably, it takes years to absorb the details of the theory (e.g., the concept of fitness) and appreciate its explanatory richness. Few, if any, at the time absorbed Darwin's populationist notions of a species. And some, such as Jevons, found Darwin's reluctance to impute progress to the evolutionary scheme quite troubling (Jevons 1890, 273–4). Spencer's sanguine gloss on the biological process was much more appealing to Victorian economists, who were the first to insist that they pursued their subject as the road to a higher good.

On the few occasions when Marshall draws analogies to things biological, most of his images, such as the cycles of birth and death, might as well have come from Aristotle.[4] Oddly enough, Marshall's essay, "Mechanical and Biological Analogies in Economics" (1898), contains not one reference to evolutionary biology. And apart from the analysis in book 4 on the division of labor, no use is made of Darwinian mechanisms in his *Principles,* other than one fleeting reference to the principle of the survival of the fittest, a phrase that originated with Spencer, not Darwin. The careful exegesis of Marshall's biological fragments by A. L. Levine (1983) suggests only a cursory appreciation for Darwinian processes. The discussion of a social organism and appeals to statics and dynamics most likely came from Auguste Comte, whom Marshall much admired.[5] Certainly, the numerous claims by Marshall that appeals to biological analogies ought to be made only after economics has reached a certain level of maturity, via appeals to physical analogies, has a distinct Comtean ring to it.

Marshall makes much ado about human wants and activities in the opening chapters of his *Principles*. As John Dennis Chasse (1984) has argued, these passages are emblematic of the broader philosophical framework of Marshall's work. Like Marx, Marshall was struggling to come to terms with our species-being. The debt, however, is to Hegel and Spencer far more than to Darwin. Much the same, I might add, is true for Jevons. He usually lumped Spencer and Darwin together when referring to evolutionary biology, but in his discussion of human nature it is Spencer who receives a full endorsement.[6]

Perhaps we have been looking in the wrong place. It is the broader implications of Darwin, rather than the specific mechanism of natural selection, that might have molded neoclassical economics. The intricate web that forms our cultural history lends considerable plausibility to this claim. But the problem lies in detecting the specific strands. One possible candidate may be that at least in the eyes of his contemporaries, Darwin had reduced man to an animal. There is a degree of truth in this, though it needs to be qualified. In one respect, Aristotle had linked man with the animals and plants with his doctrine of the three souls. And when Linneaus devised the grouping of mammals, he had no difficulty in placing man in that group and assigning a taxonomic name, albeit with a singular entry, of *Homo sapiens*. Young (1985, 24) sees Malthus as instrumental in breaking down these distinctions, insofar as he treated man as an animal, and thus we already have, before Darwin, a secularized conception of human nature. But only with Darwin is the argument made that man is related by descent with every other living form, and thus that even human intelligence and morality are simply refined instincts.[7]

Are there signs that this very profound and novel perspective made its way into economics? I think not, at least in the early neoclassical era of Marshall. Comparisons between human and animal behavior reach back to at least the eighteenth century. Think of Bernard Mandeville's *Fable of the Bees* or the writings of David Hume. It was never (or rarely) imagined, however, that human nature might resemble animal nature because of a common ancestor. Comparisons were normally drawn in order to emphasize the uniqueness of human reason and the universality of other propensities. In the opening sections of his *Wealth of Nations*, Adam Smith notes that the faculties of reason and speech are to be found only in humans, hence our ability to engage in economic exchange. I hesitate to claim that the converse of this is not to be found in the neoclassical literature. Indeed, Jevons once quipped that "I should not despair of tracing the action of the postulates of political economy among some of the more intelligent classes of animals" (1905, 197). But we can gather from a letter to his wife that this was intended more as a joke (Jevons 1977, 4:182). No one seems to have developed the idea at the time. Only quite recently have economists, in tandem with ecologists, begun to break down that age-old assumption about the unique behavior of homo economicus (see Hirschleifer 1977).

More modestly, Darwin's theory implied that one seek the roots of human nature in human physiology. This message may have been what propelled Jevons and Edgeworth to adopt a reductionist view of psychology, although I know of no concrete evidence to confirm this connection. Jevons worked much more along the lines of Benthamist introspection, and Edgeworth drew inspiration from the German school of experimental psychology (see Creedy 1986, 28–9). In fact, an evolutionary psychology does not necessarily entail reductionism of mind to matter. According to Young, the case of David Hartley and Erasmus Darwin demonstrates that "associationist psychology, suitably extrapolated, becomes evolution" (1985, 71). In short, evolutionary biology underdetermines the theory of psychology one might endorse. A commitment to viewing human traits as refined instincts still permits one to stake out many different positions along the material–mental continuum.

Robert Richards's excellent study of the subject gives the impression that Darwin was forced to resort to a considerable amount of hand waving in this as in other areas of his work. His conviction that our social and sympathetic capacities were instinctive rather than learned was supported by observations of other animals. What enabled us to become moral creatures was our ability to deliberate. If another species were to develop a similar ability to reason, coupled with social instincts, it too would acquire a moral sense (Richards 1987, 210). In this emphasis on deliberation, it would seem that Darwin was at one with Bentham. But as Richards has persuasively argued, Darwin's theory "overturned utilitarianism" (218). The differences much outweighed the similarities, as Darwin himself fully realized. The good was not to be sought in the consequences of actions, nor grounded in a self-interested view of human action, but found in what nature deemed viable for the community as a whole. Nor was pleasure the mainspring of human action for Darwin. Individual pleasure may have no cash value in the evolutionary scheme of things (217–42).

The Marshall Papers at Cambridge contain an interesting, hitherto neglected manuscript in Marshall's writing (undated, but according to Rita McWilliams and archivist Frances Willmoth, a youthful work), entitled "The Law of Parcimony." Since Marshall never published this essay, and since it is most likely an early piece, perhaps we cannot weigh it too heavily. Nevertheless, its twenty-five pages contain more musings on Darwin than any subsequent letter or extant manuscript by Marshall; in fact, he explicitly declares toward the start that he is "at present concerned only with the scientific aspect of Darwin's book," which, judging from other remarks, we can take to be the *Origin of Species*.

The "law" itself was coined by Sir William Hamilton in 1837 (with the more common spelling of parsimony) to dictate that no more causes or forces should be assumed than are necessary to account for the facts. For reasons that are obscure, Marshall explores the law in the context of Darwinian biology and the psychology of Étienne-Bonnot de Condillac and Alexander Bain, among others. The thrust of his jejune discussion is to place severe limitations on the reliability of both areas of inquiry. Marshall notes, for example, Darwin's "naive simplicity" and his tendency to "exceed the authority which experience can give" his fundamental principles. Darwin can only conjecture as to what might have been the common ancestor of two living species, and when it comes to complex organisms, like the human eye, he runs into severe difficulties (as Darwin rightly noted).

For our purposes here, the most interesting portion of this document is Marshall's frequent comparisons and contrasts between biology and psychology, particularly on the subject of methodology. He recognizes the importance of analogical reasoning, coupled with Occam's razor. There is, in his view, "a remarkable analogy and a still more remarkable difference between the fundamental methods of his [Darwin's] investigation and those of psychology." Whereas in Darwin's case, the phenomena are homogeneous, when it comes to psychology, Marshall submits, the phenomena are irreducibly heterogeneous. Psychological inquiry thus runs up against major obstacles. "Between the idea of a sensation and an idea of similarity between sensations there is no relation." And when it comes to connecting the ideas formed by the different perceptual faculties, like taste and smell, analogical reasoning breaks down altogether.[8]

Comte had already voiced, in considerable detail, the difficulties of connecting social physics to physiology, though he maintained that the "homogeneity" of the phenomena offered a glimmer of hope (Lenzer 1975, 95). Social inquiry must start with the individual, but social physics proper has its own set of phenomena, those that pertain to the social organism. Post facto, it is difficult to map Darwinian evolution and associationist psychology onto the Comtean ladder, though they would presumably fall somewhere in the nexus of social physics and physiology (with the proviso that they met positivist standards in the first place). Perhaps it was this task that prompted Marshall's train of thought, although Comte is not explicitly cited. Spencer is mentioned a couple of times, and he too dwelled on the problem of the homogeneity of phenomena for a given domain of inquiry. In any event, Marshall seems to have shut the door quite firmly on linking any further those two disparate branches of knowledge. If Darwin was to have left his mark on Marshall's economics, it was not via psychology. The negative tenor of the essay, together with Darwin's expressed opposition to utilitarianism, seems to put the burden of proof on those who would wish to urge a strong influence of Darwin on Marshall's conception of mental processes and moral principles.

Let me turn now to Mill and compare him to Darwin, with whom he was virtually contemporaneous. By elucidating the different direction in which Mill was moving, I hope thereby to suggest that Darwin's impact was that much the less on Mill's successors. I do not wish to imply that intellectual history always proceeds in a linear fashion, that once one philosopher parts company with a tradition, all those who follow him or her do so as well. But in this case, Mill strikes me as an important transitional writer between the classical and neoclassical economists and, particularly on the question of man's place in nature, the approach he took was instrumental in rendering neoclassical economic ideas all the more distinct from those of the earlier period.

Even for contemporaries, Mill (b. 1806) and Darwin (b. 1809) had much in common. Both, for example, were secularists in a time when theological premises were more commonplace. Both were empiricists by temperament and eschewed the more idealist metaphysicians that could be found across the Channel. And both emphasized the view that historical contingencies alter human nature. Arguably, Mill saw human nature as more malleable than did Darwin, since he did not pay much attention to the constraints of physiology. Indeed, Mill did much to set man apart from nature. John Robson has argued that Mill was "not happy about man's animal nature, and would willingly see most of its urgings suppressed" (1976, 148). In his posthumously published essay "On Nature" (written in 1852–3, before the publication of Darwin's *Origin*), Mill argues that "the ways of Nature are to be conquered, not obeyed" (1874/1969, 10:381). This is true with respect to both physical nature – hence human technology – and human nature itself: "The duty of man is the same in respect to his own nature as in respect to the nature of all other things, namely not to follow but to amend it" (10:397). Like Hume, Mill repudiates any appeals to nature for canons of the just or the good. Humans are in fact able to do better, to surpass the daily cruelty one finds in the natural realm: "All praise of Civilization, of Art, of Contrivance, is so much dispraise of Nature; an admission of imperfection, which it is man's business, and merit, to be always endeavouring to correct or mitigate" (10:381).

The contrast with Darwin is quite striking.[9] Darwin tended to belittle man by contrast with the powers of nature. As he put it: "Natural Selection . . . is as immeasurably superior to man's feeble efforts, as the works of Nature are to those of Art" (1859, 115). But Mill believed just the opposite. As he put it, "Civilization in every one of its aspects is a struggle against the animal instincts. . . . It has artificialized large portions of mankind to such an extent, that of many of their most natural inclinations they have scarcely a vestige or a remembrance left" (1848/1965, 2:365). Only by combating our "animal instincts" can we begin to alleviate poverty. Only industry will thwart the tendency toward diminishing returns and enable society to achieve a higher standard of living.

To a large extent, Mill has here broken free of the natural fetters that are so prevalent in the Malthusian view of the world. Human institutions – the correct ones at least – can surmount the problems of population growth or diminishing returns in agriculture. Not that man should dominate nature in its entirety. Mill's vision of the stationary state speaks to a healthy balance between human society and the natural world. He makes an appeal for what we would today call biodiversity and conservation of the wilderness, if only to permit the enjoyment of complete solitude when one communes with nature. The point to grasp is that Mill and Darwin were already diverging on the question of man's place in nature. Just as Darwin was bringing man into nature, Mill was taking him out, and there is no indication that subsequent economists have reversed the trend.[10]

With the early neoclassicists, the economic order has been placed squarely within the realm of the artificial. Human deliberation, the striving for pleasure, is the source of all economic phenomena; even capital is recast subjectively – as that which will yield utility in the future – rather than in terms of a specific set of wage goods. Wealth is no longer a product of nature, as the Physiocrats had once maintained.

Nor were Smith's and Malthus's appeals to natural constraints relevant. Utility is infinitely expansible and can take any form one so desires. The economy is entirely man-made, in the full sense of the term.

One major consequence of Darwin's theory that commentators have noted is that it lent enormous force to a belief in the uniformity of nature. As Darwin himself noted, "When we look at the plants and bushes clothing an entangled bank, we are tempted to attribute their proportional numbers and kinds to what we call chance. But how false a view is this!" (1859, 125). Every speck of life on that bank is there because of the laws that govern the organic realm.

Mill, however, had already advanced this doctrine of the uniformity of nature in his *System of Logic*, some fifteen years before Darwin published the *Origin of Species*. Taking stock of the long list of extant laws in the natural sciences, Mill contended that there could be no other explanation of this fortunate state of affairs than the fact that nature was indeed uniform. Jevons advanced much the same argument, pointing to the established body of laws in physics. It does not appear to have been the case, then, that Darwin's findings were critical in elevating convictions among economists on this matter, although they were certainly welcome reinforcement.

Peter Bowler has argued that Darwin's specific version of evolution was never predominant in the Victorian period. Since the so-called Darwinian synthesis of the 1930s and 1940s, we have come to pay homage to Darwin above all (though we have also had to ignore his Lamarckian leanings and his allegiance to continuous variation), but during the mid-nineteenth century there were many other "transformationist" notions circulating among naturalists. Lamarck's ideas were taken seriously, as were the ideas of Geoffroy Saint-Hilaire and Richard Owen (see Kohn 1985, 260). And there were others who adhered either to the transformationism of Naturphilosophie or to outright creationism. Bowler has put it as follows:

> If Darwin's radical insights catalyzed the transition to evolutionism but were ignored by most "post-Darwinian" thinkers, are we justified in treating the emergence of the selection theory as the key event in the theory's history? . . . I suspect that the world is not yet ready for a survey of evolutionism in which Darwin does not play a pivotal role. Nevertheless, in my view, our current fascination with Darwin's discovery of natural selection is at least in part an artifact of modern biology's commitment to the synthesis of selectionism and genetics. (1983, 24)

Even if this is an overstatement, it most surely holds for Darwin's views on human nature. Arguably, not one naturalist at the time agreed with his specific views on human psychology and morality (Richards 1987, 234). Nor were they willing to accept his repudiation of purpose in nature. The task I have set myself here seems to have been a search for a red herring. Darwin could not have influenced Mill or Marshall because he was not influential – period. I do not wish to go that far, however. Bowler's position, in my view, is the product of a malaise with the oversaturated Darwin industry. Of course, Darwin was a central figure in Victorian England, as Mill, Jevons, and Marshall fully recognized. My claim is only that it is difficult to identify specific Darwinian elements in economic thought at the time.

Scott Gordon (1973) once noted that while Marshall voiced the prospect of leading economic theory toward the true Mecca of biology, no one has managed to carry out the task. More recently, A. W. Coats (1990) has echoed that sentiment. But, in fact, the Mecca was reached long before Marshall, in the mid-eighteenth century, and was then shrouded in clouds. Marshall's appeal may be better understood as one of his romantic sighs to a time now lost, in part, I conjecture, because of his Hegelian conviction that the fundamental laws of the economic realm are historical.

Indeed, were it not for those remarks made by Marshall, we would probably not have bothered to look for Darwin's influence in the first place. If the current trend in the history of biology is closer to the truth, we can safely abandon this quest, since Darwin was not supremely important after all, at least not until the 1930s and 1940s. And by then, neoclassical economics had matured, both as a body of knowledge and as a professional unit, such that its external membranes were virtually impervious to viruses from such distant fields as evolutionary biology.

Why the greyhound and the mastiff? One theme I wish to highlight is that comparisons between man and animals took place long before Darwin. Those who know Adam Smith will quickly recognize the reference: "By nature a philosopher is not in genius and disposition half so different from a street porter, as a mastiff is from a greyhound" (Smith 1776, 120). Custom and education are what tend to single out one man for the life of philosophy, another for street portering. Smith thereby leaned much more to nurture than to nature in explaining specific human attributes.

When it comes to explaining economic phenomena, however, Smith emphasized the attributes that distinguish human beings from other animals. It is because we all share the natural propensity to truck, barter, and exchange, as well as the lifelong desire to better our condition, that the human economy has law and order. Virtually every major economist since then has endorsed, either wittingly or unwittingly, this line of reasoning. Today, we may be more finely pigeonholed in terms of our predilection for risk, but we are all still basically alike when it comes to the means by which we actualize our desires, beliefs, and intentions in the commercial realm. In short, economists for the past few centuries have emphasized the uniqueness and uniformity of human nature, and any support they may seek from Darwin, Lamarck, or E. O. Wilson is basically beside the point.

Notes

This chapter was first presented at the annual meetings of the American Economics Association (Washington, DC, 1990). I thank Scott Gordon, Mary Morgan, Lynn Nyhart, Robert Richards, and A. W. Coats for comments and criticisms.

1. Linnaeus's treatises on the economy and polity of nature (1750s) are replete with economic concepts. Adam Smith, in turn, was a great admirer of Linnaeus and had several of his works in his personal library. There are only a few explicit references to Linnaeus in Smith's essay "Of the External Senses," but I have suggested that there may have been more points of intersection. See Schabas (1990a).

2. I am not entirely convinced by their argument. In the Marshall Papers at Cambridge University (Box 6, Item 13), there is an undated, presumably early, draft on the division of labor, but it contains no references to biology. Nor is there a need for such a source, since the disanalogies are strong. First, Darwin's division of labor came about without organization (invisible hand), a feature that was in Smith, perhaps, but not in Marshall. Second, there is no clear-cut analogue to the Darwinian mechanism of natural selection in Marshall. Marshall could point to the diversity of firms, but what filled the place of the laws of heredity, let alone the principle of superfecundity? Third, as Ménard and Limoges acknowledge, Marshall's concept of the representative firm was purportedly a reversion back to essentialist thinking, despite Darwin's own brilliant grasp of populationist processes.

3. See Schabas (1990a). Let me add, however, that my argument is by no means airtight. I simply lend weight to the view that if economics was explicitly imported into biology, then Lyell was the more likely merchant.

4. In his manuscript "The Law of Parcimony" (to be discussed later), Marshall harks back to Aristotle's maxim that nature does nothing in vain. If one were to go in search of organizing principles in which the biological and the economic intersect, this seems to be a worthy candidate.

5. He praises Comte for his genius and for showing "how complex social phenomena are," though he did not endorse Comte's view that economics had no right to a separate existence. See Pigou (1925, 163) and Marshall (1920, 636).

6. On Marshall's appreciation of Hegel and Spencer, see Pigou (1925, 11), Whitaker (1977, 193), and Groenewegen (1990). Benjamin Jowett, one of the few who held sway over Marshall, expressed a distinct pleasure in seeing an element of Hegelianism in Marshall's *Principles*. See an unpublished letter of September 18, 1890, from Benjamin Jowett to Alfred Marshall, in the Marshall Papers at Cambridge University. Jevons attributed the recent "revolution" in moral philosophy to Herbert Spencer (Jevons 1890, 289). How different was Spencer from Darwin? According to Robert Richards, quite a lot. Spencer was a thoroughgoing Lamarckian, and while Darwin also accepted the principle of the inheritance of acquired characteristics, Spencer was far more reluctant to assimilate the principle of natural selection. In other words, he was never a Darwinian, even granting Darwin's Lamarckian leanings. See Richards (1987, 291–4).

7. See John R. Durant, "The Ascent of Nature in Darwin's *Descent of Man*" (in Kohn 1985, 283–306), for a discussion of Darwin's enthusiasm to promote man's animal origins.

8. John Maynard Keynes recollects Marshall's belated wish to have devoted himself to psychology. It may have been this youthful insight into the complexity of the subject that initially steered Marshall in other directions. See Pigou (1925, 37).

9. Alan Ryan (1974) has lent weight to the view that Mill was somewhat uneasy about Darwin's theory.

10. Marshall, e.g., speaks of man's "command over nature." (1920, 207).

References

Black, R. D. Collison. 1990. "Jevons, Marshall and the Utilitarian Tradition," *Scottish Journal of Political Economy* 37:5–17.

Bowler, Peter J. 1989. *Evolution: the History of an Idea.* Berkeley and Los Angeles: University of California Press.

Burrow, J. W. 1966. *Evolution and Society: A Study in Victorian Social Theory.* Cambridge University Press.

Chasse, John Dennis. 1984. "Marshall, the Human Agent and Economic Growth: Wants and Activities Revisited," *History of Political Economy* 3 (16): 381–404.

Coats, A. W. 1990. "Marshall and Ethics," in Rita McWilliams Tullberg, ed., *Alfred Marshall in Retrospect.* Aldershot: Edward Elgar.

Creedy, John. 1986. *Edgeworth and the Development of Neoclassical Economics.* Oxford: Basil Blackwell.

Darwin, Charles. 1859. *The Origin of Species by Means of Natural Selection.* London: John Murray (Penguin reprint edition, 1968).

Gordon, H. Scott. 1973. "Alfred Marshall and the Development of Economics as a Science," in R. N. Giere and R. S. Westfall, eds., *Foundations of Scientific Method: The Nineteenth Century.* Bloomington: Indiana University Press.

Gordon, H. Scott. 1989. "Darwin and Political Economy: The Connection Reconsidered," *Journal of the History of Biology* 22:437–59.

Groenewegen, Peter. 1990. "Marshall and Hegel," *Économie Appliquée* 43:63–84.

Hirschleifer, Jack. 1977. "Economics from a Biological Viewpoint," *Journal of Law and Economics* 20:1–52.

Jevons, William Stanley. 1876. "The Future of Political Economy." Reprinted in *The Principles of Economics and other Papers*. 1905. Henry Higgs, ed. London: Macmillan.

Jevons, William Stanley. 1877. *The Principles of Science*, 2d ed. London: Macmillan.

Jevons, William Stanley. 1890. "Utilitarianism," in *Pure Logic and Other Minor Works*. Robert Adamson and Harriet A. Jevons, eds. London: Macmillan.

Jevons, William Stanley. 1977. *Papers and Correspondence of William Stanley Jevons*, vol. 4. R. D. C. Black, ed. London: Macmillan.

Kohn, David, ed. 1985. *The Darwinian Heritage*. Princeton, NJ: Princeton University Press.

Lenzer, Gertrud, ed. 1975. *Auguste Comte and Positivism: The Essential Writings*. Chicago: University of Chicago Press.

Levine, A. L. 1983. "Marshall's *Principles* and the 'Biological Viewpoint': A Reconsideration," *Manchester School* 51:276–293.

Lyell, Charles. 1830–3. *Principles of Geology*, 2 vols. London: John Murray.

Maloney, John. 1985. *Marshall, Orthodoxy, and the Professionalisation of Economics*. Cambridge University Press.

Marshall, Alfred. 1898. "Mechanical and Biological Analogies in Economics," reprinted in Pigou (1925).

Marshall, Alfred. 1920. *Principles of Economics*, 8th ed. London: Macmillan.

Marshall, Alfred. N.d. "The Law of Parcimony," unpublished manuscript in The Alfred Marshall Papers, Box 11 (11). The Marshall Library, Cambridge University.

McWilliams, Rita. 1969. "The Papers of Alfred Marshall Deposited in the Marshall Library," *History of Economic Thought Newsletter* 3:9–19.

Mill, John Stuart. 1848. *Principles of Political Economy*. Reprinted in J. M. Robson, ed. 1965. *The Collected Works of John Stuart Mill*, vol. 2. Toronto: University of Toronto Press.

Mill, John Stuart. 1874. "On Nature," in *Three Essays on Religion*. Reprinted in J. M. Robson, ed. 1969. *The Collected Works of John Stuart Mill*, vol. 10. Toronto: University of Toronto Press.

Mill, John Stuart. 1972. *The Later Letters of John Stuart Mill: 1849–1873. The Collected Works of John Stuart Mill*, vol. 15 Francis E. Mineka and Dwight N. Lindley, eds. J. M. Robson, gen. ed. Toronto: University of Toronto Press.

Mischel, Theodore. 1965. " 'Emotion' and 'Motivation' in the Development of English Psychology: D. Hartley, James Mill, A. Bain," *Journal of the History of the Behavioral Sciences* 1:123–44.

Moss, Laurence. 1982. "Biological Theory and Technological Entrepreneurship in Marshall's Writings," *Eastern Economic Journal* 18:3–13.

Niman, Neil B. 1991. "Biological Analogies in Marshall's Work," *Journal of the History of Economic Thought* 13:19–36.

Pigou, Alfred C., ed. 1925. *The Memorials of Alfred Marshall.* London: Macmillan.

Rashid, Salim. 1981. "Political Economy and Geology in the Early Nineteenth Century: Similarities and Contrasts," *History of Political Economy* 13:726–44.

Richards, Robert J. 1987. *Darwin and the Emergence of Evolutionary Theories of Mind and Behavior.* Chicago: University of Chicago Press.

Robson, John M. 1976. "Rational Animals and Others," in Robson and Michael Laine, eds., *James and John Stuart Mill: Papers of the Centenary Conference.* Toronto: University of Toronto Press.

Rudwick, Martin J. S. 1979. "Transposed Concepts from the Human Species in the Early Work of Charles Lyell," in L. S. Jordanova and Roy S. Porter, eds., *Images of the Earth: Essays in the History of the Environmental Sciences.* Chalfont St. Giles: British Society for the History of Science.

Ryan, Alan. 1974. *J. S. Mill.* London: Routledge & Kegan Paul.

Schabas, Margaret. 1990a. "Ricardo Naturalized: Lyell and Darwin on the Economy of Nature," in Donald E. Moggridge, ed., *Perspectives on the History of Economic Thought.* London: Edward Elgar.

Schabas, Margaret. 1990b. *A World Ruled by Number: William Stanley Jevons and the Rise of Mathematical Economics.* Princeton, NJ: Princeton University Press.

Schweber, S. S. 1977. "Darwin and the Political Economists: Divergence of Character," *Journal of the History of Biology* 10:195–289.

Schweber, S. S. 1985. "The Wider British Context in Darwin's Theorizing," in Kohn (1985).

Smith, Adam. 1776 (1986). *The Wealth of Nations.* Andrew Skinner, ed. Middlesex: Penguin.

Smith, Adam. 1982. "Of the External Senses," in *Essays on Philosophical Subjects.* W. P. D. Wightman, ed. Indianapolis, IN: Liberty Classics.

Smyth, R. L., ed. 1962. *Essays in Economic Method.* London: Gerald Duckworth.

Thomas, Brinley. 1991. "Alfred Marshall on Economic Biology," *Review of Political Economy* 3:1–14.

Whitaker, John. 1975. *The Early Economic Writings of Alfred Marshall, 1867–1890,* 2 vols. London: Macmillan.

Whitaker, John. 1977. "Some Neglected Aspects of Alfred Marshall's Economic and Social Thought," *History of Political Economy* 9:191–7.

Whitaker, John, ed. 1990. *Centenary Essays on Alfred Marshall.* Cambridge University Press.

Worster, Donald. 1985. *Nature's Economy: A History of Ecological Ideas.* Cambridge University Press.

Young, Robert M. 1985. *Darwin's Metaphor.* Cambridge University Press.

CHAPTER 13

Organization and the division of labor: biological metaphors at work in Alfred Marshall's *Principles of Economics*

CAMILLE LIMOGES and CLAUDE MÉNARD

It has been well said that analogies may help one into the saddle, but are encumbrances on a long journey.

Marshall (1898)

Though Alfred Marshall, as early as 1941, had been declared "long dead" by Jacob Viner, it can hardly be denied that some of the major ideas developed in the *Principles of Economics,* the first edition of which appeared one century ago, are still at the core of modern economics.

One could easily pay tribute to the author who relabeled "political economy" as the now-familiar "economics" and who restructured a substantial part of the discipline according to a sequence that continues to organize our microeconomics textbooks: from consumption and production theories to market equilibrium and to the theory of distribution. But Marshall is now best remembered for his analysis of market forces at work from temporary to longrun equilibrium, with the associated cost functions and the correlated problems of the nature of the supply curve and of its intersection with the demand curve. Certainly these concepts have been reshaped and elegantly expressed in mathematical form. As far as the content is concerned, they remain a very substantial part of the hard core of economics.

Hence, Marshall's contribution is mostly identified with Book V of the *Principles.* Nevertheless, there has been renewed interest recently in other aspects of the magnum opus. Several authors (Ménard 1979; Moss 1982; Levine 1983; Mirowski 1984, 1989; Niman 1991; Thomas 1991; Hodgson in press) have reexamined some neglected contributions of Marshall; and most of them, because of the influential debate on the methodology of economics, devoted a great deal of attention to the analogies at work in the *Principles.* Moreover, almost all these

336

analysts concluded that the biological metaphors in that book at best led to a dead end and at worst were a hodgepodge of eclectic and unhelpful ideas picked up mostly from Spencer.

The purpose of this chapter is to dispute this judgment. It is our view (1) that the biological analogies at work in the *Principles* were carefully selected in relation to the notion of the *division of labor;* (2) that reading Adam Smith through the glasses of Darwin and his reinterpretation of Milne-Edwards, Marshall significantly reshaped this notion and firmly embedded it into his concept of *organization;* and (3) that this is crucial for understanding the logic of the *Principles* and the production of such other key concepts as *returns, economies of scale,* and *internal* and *external economies.* It is also our contention that Marshall understood fairly well some fundamental aspects of the biology of his time, well enough to try developing a solution to the economic problems he was confronting. These problems were related to the division of labor and organization, that is, to the representation of the supply side. To avoid unbearable prospects, Marshall's approach led him to introduce the notion of the *representative firm,* a notion that ought to be seen as regressive.

Therefore, a careful examination of the *Principles* reveals a complex process of transference of notions between biology and economics. It helps us as well to understand why such an essential notion as organization, given its association with the doomed idea of the representative firm, had to be neglected by economists for so long.

These views will be developed as follows. The first section surveys the recent literature on the role of analogies in Marshall's *Principles* and discusses their interpretation. The second section presents what we consider a consistent interpretation of book 4 based on the coupling of the concepts of the *division of labor* and of *organization.* The final section clarifies the significance of the biological references at work in Marshall. We conclude by restating the importance of the concept of the division of labor as a go-between linking economics and biology.

On some misinterpretations

Several papers have been published over the past ten years that intend to reassess the use and meaning of biological analogies in Marshall's *Principles.* Almost all of them are concerned with the question: Why is it that Marshall, contrary to what he intended to do, failed to introduce biological ideas at the core of the research program in economics? The emphasis on this problem is related not only to the renewed interest in methodological questions in our discipline, but also to the resurgent idea that a research program inspired by biology could be developed in economics (see, e.g., Hirshleifer 1977; Nelson and Winter 1982). The contributions that we are concerned with here can be distributed on a spectrum of interpretations, of which the two ends would be represented respectively by Mirowski (1984, 1989) and Niman (1991).

Basic views

Mirowski's thesis is twofold: Biological analogies are not important either for understanding the "marginalist revolution" or for interpreting Marshall. As plainly stated in 1984 and reprinted without changes in 1989, neoclassical economics "can be explained by parallel developments in physics in the mid-nineteenth century," for example, as a species of energetics as elaborated by the physicists in the 1840s (1984, 363; 1989, 262). Therefore, all attempts to introduce biological metaphors were condemned and never had any significant effect on the research program in economics (1989, 271; this is also the predominant view in Ménard 1981a).

As for Marshall, despite the fact that Mirowski considerably reduces his contribution by considering him a "popularizer" rather than a discoverer, biological references would not play any central role in the intellectual structure of the *Principles*. Their function would be peripheral: They were introduced to make energetics metaphors palpable to an English audience (1984, 375);[1] and they were used by Marshall as part of a strategy to make economics acceptable to a scientific community strongly influenced by the successes of biology (1989, 265).[2]

A recent paper by Niman (1991) occupies the other end of the spectrum. He feels that biological metaphors are important for understanding Marshall and the subsequent history of economics; and he suggests a careful interpretation of these metaphors. Using largely, and adequately, a paper published by Schweber in 1980, Niman points out in his articles that the commonality between economics and biology lies in the division of labor (1991, 24). He even goes a step further and relates the process of the division of labor to the Marshallian concept of organization through the creation of wealth: "The hability to satisfy wants depends not only on the characteristics of the individuals within a population, but also on the organization of activities designed to satisfy those wants" (1991, 25). But he says very little about this (less than three pages out of sixteen) and does not produce any specific analysis of the representation of the division of labor at work or of the peculiarities of the very notion of organization. In fact, he is essentially interested in biological analogies as an attempt to develop a dynamic approach. Economic growth would be fundamentally predicated upon the conception of firms: The "tree in the forest" image[3] could therefore designate the evolution "from a less coherent to a more coherent form" (28), without any specification by Niman of what this might mean. On a global level, growth could be understood through a very Spencerian interpretation of "compound evolution," a phrase that, however, never occurs in Marshall's work (Niman 1991, 26–7).

Such an interpretation is typical of most recent analyses of the role of analogies in the *Principles,* as illustrated by Levine (1983), Thomas (1991), or Hodgson (in press). "Evolution" is considered to be the key word in Marshall's references to biology: A Lyell–Darwin mixture (Levine 1983; see also Schabas, Chapter 12, this volume), as revisited by Spencer (Thomas 1991; Hodgson in press), would allow Marshall to describe society as an "organism," where the evolutionary principle would reconcile the biological firm and the mechanical market, the tree with the forest (Niman 1991, 31). Moreover, these readings of Marshall as a by-product of Spencer tend to put the emphasis on analogies related to very global problems, like time, irreversibility, secular movement, and the interaction with the environment. Though most authors already mentioned are sympathetic to Marshall, one cannot but have the clear impression that biological analogies at work in the *Principles* would inspire some general views of the evolution of firms and society and, at best, would suggest a possible approach to economy as a biosystem (Levine 1983), while the operational Marshall would all be in Book V, that is, in the mechanics of the markets.

Unsolved problems

This is not to say that all crucial problems related to these biological analogies are ignored. The centrality of the supply side is underlined by several authors (Bharadwaj 1978; Mirowski 1984, 1990), but in relation to the difficulties of the static interpretation of the adjustment between supply and demand developed in Book V, not in relation to the very nature of what an organization is. (There is almost no mention of the fact that organization is considered a factor of production, of a very special type.) Similarly, the fact that Marshall insisted so much on the division of labor and reinterpreted Adam Smith in that regard is mentioned (Niman 1991; Thomas 1991), but not analyzed. Last, but not least, the ambiguity of the notion of the representative firm has been underlined, and Levine (1983) already noticed the crucial role of this image "to hold biological factors constant" and therefore to pursue the study of markets *as if* they were governed by physical laws (see also Niman 1991). But there is no close examination of the links between this problem and the difficulties raised in Book IV, in relation to the notion of organization.

It is the purpose of the next section to explore these neglected aspects. A preliminary question must be asked, though: Why is it that the specific content of Book IV, where most biological metaphors are developed, has not been looked at more carefully?

Our interpretation would suggest that such knowledgeable authors as those already discussed have been trapped by the conjunction of three different problems. First, though most of them are quite critical of what economics has become today, their investigations remain dominated by the current approach in microeconomics, focused on how markets can be characterized. Therefore, very much like most contemporary economists, they give only passing attention to what has long been considered, from Adam Smith to Alfred Marshall, and is still looked at by some of us, as an essential foundation for understanding the structures and the dynamics of changing markets, namely, the division of labor and its consequences on firms as vectors of change. Second, as historians, they have not avoided the pitfalls of anachronism. If their reading of Marshall is first hand, their interpretation of the analogies at work in the *Principles,* and particularly the biological analogies, is almost exclusively based on secondary sources – and moreover, sources broadly concerned with recent developments in evolutionary biology – rather than on close examination of the biology at Marshall's time.[4] Third, there is some ambiguity about what analogies are. All contributors are looking for explicit images, "figures of speech" (Levine 1983). But there is very little notice, if any, of analogies as a purposeful transfer of concepts from one domain to another to help restructure and eventually solve problems that were already raised by the borrowing discipline (Menard 1981a).

It is our view, developed in the next sections, that such a transfer is at stake in Book IV of the *Principles,* where the production of the central concept of *organization* by Marshall is made possible through a reinterpretation of the *division of labor* that owes much to Darwin and Milne-Edwards.

Organization as organism: a threatening analogy

Most commentators have focused their attention on Book V of the *Principles* and its analysis of market mechanisms. But the fundamentals are developed before, in Book III, which introduces a modern theory of the consumer to establish the demand function, and more importantly in Book IV, where the supply side is conceptualized through a theory of production.[5] The notion of organization is elaborated as a central part of this theory. Indeed, it plays a fundamental role, which sheds light on Marshall's interpretation of productive processes and on his philosophy of economics as well.

Some ambiguities

According to the title of Book IV, "organization" should be considered a factor of production, to be added to land, labor, and capital. Chapter 1 is ambiguous, however, since Marshall seesm to regard organization as a characteristic of capital: "Capital consists in a great part of knowledge and organization. . . . Knowledge is our most powerful engine of production; it enables us to subdue Nature and force her to satisfy our wants. Organization aids knowledge; it has many forms" (IV.1.1).[6] But he adds, "The distinction between public and private property in knowledge and organization is of great and growing importance . . . and partly for that reason it seems best sometimes to reckon Organization apart as a distinct agent of production" (IV.1.1).

This very cautious and, one must add, ambiguous introduction of the notion of organization must be understood in relation to Marshall's strategy, designed to convey his message as if in continuity with the classics. But the notion is thereafter considered fully justified as a distinct one – moreover, *the* central one – and is developed at considerable length in six of the thirteen chapters of Book IV. Indeed, it is organizations that articulate all factors of production into a coherent structure of production so that, in Marshall's view, it would not be possible to understand the very functioning of a modern economy in the absence of that notion.

There is another difficulty to tackle, partaking of the very ambiguity of the then-unfamiliar notion of organization. Three different approaches can be identified in the *Principles,* corresponding to divergent contemporary developments in economics. At a very general level, of particular importance in chapter 8, "organization" is considered a sort of vital principle, the action of organizing at work in any social system: Marshall's "social organization" (IV.8.3) is very close to Weber's "social and economic organization" (1947) as well as to Arrow's description of market economies as "one large class of organizations" (1974). Chapter 9 delineates more precisely the notion of organization, already associated with the word "industrial." This should not be understood, however, as our modern industrial organization, which focuses on the analysis of market structures. It is more general and concerns the characteristics of economic activities – whether manufacture, agriculture, or commerce – in such a developed stage that they can be dissociated from other activities – religious, political, military, and so on (IV.8.3). Finally, there is the "business organization" (IV.12.1), which corresponds to the basic unit in which the production of goods and services is implemented and which exemplifies the central problem of all modern economic organisms: that of coordination (IV.9.7).

To summarize, "organization" can designate, depending on context, the structuring principle of a social system, the structural characteristics of economic activities in a developed society, or the basic unit of production. But there is a strong unity, articulating these three levels, one backed by the concept of the division of labor.

Social organization and the laws of nature

The starting point of Marshall's analysis of organizations is a biological analogy. More specifically, it is his belief that there is "a fundamental unity of action between the laws of nature in the physical and in the moral world," a unity that justifies "profound analogies which have been discovered between social and especially industrial organization on the one side and the physical organization of the higher animals on the other" (IV.8.1).

What social organizations and higher animals share is a developmental process based on *two common principles:* "an increasing subdivision of functions between . . . separate parts on the one hand, and on the other a more intimate connection between them" (IV.8.1). In other terms, it is the coupling of *differentiation* and *integration* that characterizes social organizations and explains their development according to the equivalent of the Darwinian law of "divergence and the survival of the fittest." In economics, differentiation means division of labor, and integration means coordination.[7]

This provides the key for interpreting the history of social organizations. "In early times" (IV.8.3), division of functions was rudimentary, as in the caste system, and well suited to the environment. Low differentiation meant rigidity of organization: Functions were determined once and for all; positions of individuals were fixed by traditional rules; social relations were determined *priori;* and methods of production were repetitive. Such a system, once well adapted, had growing difficulties in dealing with an environment of scarce resources. It had to change drastically, as shown in the "modern organization," namely, "the Western world" (IV.8.3). Here we have a social organization in which functions are separated: Economic activities are distinct from ceremonial or military activities, and there is a growing division of labor between "the different ranks of industry" as well as "between different individuals in the same rank." The result can be contrasted with that of the primitive organization: There is plasticity, so that methods of production continuously and rapidly change, while the positions of the individual and the social relations of classes "are now perfectly variable."

Marshall refers here to Spencer (one of very few references to that author), but it is on a point of secondary importance.[8] Indeed, in our view, and on this we oppose most commentators, the key issue in these pages is not this very sketchy comparison between two forms of organizations, but rather what this comparison purports to *illustrate:* the structural impact of a progressing division of labor on social organization. In regard to this issue, the key references are not to Spencer, but to Charles Darwin, Adam Smith, and Ernst Haeckel (see the section "The Representative Firm").[9]

Despite his use of analogy to higher animals to make sense of the division of functions in society, Marshall is conscious that economics is *not* biology and is cautious enough to delineate the two at the very beginning of his analysis. "When we come to human beings" (IV.8.2), the fundamental difference is that an organization is not only responsive to its environment, but can also model its environment through "command over nature" (IV.8.5). In economics the fit organisms are those that "profit by their environment," but also that "benefit their environment" (IV.9.7). Therefore, when extended to social organizations the laws of Nature have to be specified. First, as noticed by Adam Smith, there are "general advantages" to the division of labor, but also "many incidental evils which it involves" (IV.8.4), particularly when it induces identification of general interest with interests of certain individuals. Second, in social organizations, individual behavior must be explained by motivations that are not purely individualistic (Marshall is very critical of the principle of selfishness – see IV.8.2 and also I.1.4), and that largely depend on collective values and social commitment:

> Thus the struggle for existence causes in the long run those races of men to survive in which the individual is most willing to sacrifice himself for the benefit of those around him; and which are consequently the best adapted collectively to make use of their environment. (IV.8.2)

Third, social organization is not exclusively a "natural organization." Because humans are characterized by language and reason, as emphasized by Adam Smith (1776, bk. 1, ch. 2), they have the capacity to modify their own characters, "by thought and work; by the application of the principles of Eugenics . . . and by the appropriate education of the faculties of either sex" or through a more egalitarian distribution of wealth (IV.8.5).

Modern organization and the efficiency constraint

But it is in the Western World, the most complex social organization so far, that the centrality of the division of labor can best be understood. It may be characterized as a stage where activities are separated and clearly identified, so that economic activity (or "industrial organization" in Marshall's words) has a life of its own, within which there are subdivisions ("divison between trades") and where "manufacturing operations" (IV.9.1) are of a particular importance. The modern economic organization can also be identified with the predominance of *efficiency:* Confronting the scarcity of resources, those species will survive competition that can best use available resources, which means minimizing their costs and maximizing their output.

In Marshall's *Principles,* therefore, *the fundamental rule of modern economics,* that of a rational (maximizing) behavior, is *introduced through a biological metaphor,* that of the survival of the fittest, a principle discriminating among individuals – for example, firms, – as well as among species – for example, trade activities.

Now, economic efficiency will ensure the survival of the *fittest,* not necessarily the best (IV.8.1); and it will do so through the division of labor. The Smithian concept is then reshaped to fit this Darwinian view.

There are four major characteristics of the division of labor that will improve efficiency and give a comparative advantage to one social organization over another or to specific parts (industrial sectors, individual firms, etc.) within it. First, and this is traditional Smithian argument, *routinization* will increase productivity, improve the quality of products through standardization, and implement more flexibility among workers (IV.9.2 and IV.9.5). Second, it will do so because routine means *mechanization:* "When the action has thus been reduced to routine it has nearly arrived at the stage at which it can be taken over by machinery" (IV.9.2). This process will induce improvements of machines and an upward shift in the qualification of labor: "Machinery constantly supplants and renders unnecessary . . . purely manual skill" (IV.9.3), therefore enlarging the scope of activity for skilled workers. This is the foundation of a third characteristic, best understood through its underlying comparison with biology. In complex organisms, "perfectly reflex actions . . . performed by the responsibility of the local nerve centres" must be differentiated from "deliberate movements," which "require the attention of the chief central authority." But here the analogy is reversed: Complex living beings are explained by comparison with manufactures, since in a complex organism, "there is probably something like an organized bureaucracy of the local nerve centres" (IV.9.1, n. 1). Such reasoning is very much that of Milne-Edwards, borrowing the notion of the division of labor from Adam Smith to apply it to biology, a move to be renewed by Darwin (see Limoges in press; and the section titled "The Representative Firm"). In manufacturing processes, routines are analogous to "reflex actions," while complex decisions are similar to "deliberate movements." As a result, the more complex an economic organization is, the more room there is for *sophisticated functions* (IV.9.3). Fourth, and of major consequence is that specialization will be chiefly associated with large firms. In the long run, there is a "tendency to increase the scale of manufactures and to make them more complex" (IV.9.3). Thus, in economics, but not in biology for sure, *complex usually means big.*

There are conditions for such large organizations to be successful, and these conditions can be interpreted as parts of the selective process. "Largeness of markets" is necessary (IV.9.3), both in terms of demand for a specific product and in terms of diversification of that demand (to create "niches" as we would say today). Goods under consideration must be such that there are available technologies to implement mass production (IV.9.3). There must be specialized machinery as well as skilled workers, and there must also be an efficient utilization of these scarce resources. To avoid the destruction of such a complex organization, "sufficient work should be found to keep it well employed" (IV.9.7); otherwise, it will regress. Only organizations that can benefit fully from "internal" as well as "external" economies will survive and develop (IV.9.7).[10] True, it is in this context that Marshall introduced this famous distinction, now fully integrated into modern theory. And he does so in a very Darwinian manner, as we will show in the section "The Representative Firm," linking external economies to the localization of firms – for example, to "the advantage of diversification in the inhabitants of the same region" (Darwin 1859, 115).

But if the division of labor acounts for the prosperity of complex organizations, as compared with more elementary forms, and is significantly related to large scale through some selection mechanism, then as we will show there are two major problems that economic theory has to deal with.

From coordination to domination

The increasing complexity associated with the growing division of labor will generate a coordination problem, and the efficiency of specialization can benefit organizations up to the point where risks of monopoly power arise, thus eliminating or reducing competition.

In living beings, complexification and related problems of coordination could be reconciled in the development of the neural system. What might be the equivalent in a developed economic organization? Marshall's answer is: businessmen or, to be more exact, the *entrepreneurial function*. It is surprising that this notion has been so poorly developed in economics, and Marshall's contribution almost ignored. (The usual reference for the nineteenth century is to Jean-Baptiste Say; see Hebert and Link 1982.) Indeed, that notion plays a central role in the *Principles*.

Though the vocabulary fluctuates ("businessmen," "merchants," "entrepreneurs" are used interchangeably), the concept is quite clear. Marshall intends to distinguish without any ambiguity two functions that have "to be broken up" (IV.12.2): the ownership of capital, particularly in its modern shareholding form, and the function of "organizer of production" (IV.12.5). This last function is the one that interests him because it concerns the fundamental coordination problem of a complex organism.[11] Three basic aspects are associated with this function. The entrepreneurs "adventure or undertake . . . risks: they bring together the capital and the labour required for the work; they arrange or engineer its general plan, and superintend its minor details" (IV.12.2). As risk takers, they have to assume the "risks of buying and selling" (IV.12.4), to "forecast the future" about their own and other trades to get a view of the general level of activity (IV.12.4), and to search for new markets (IV.12.5). As *assembleurs*, they must find the best possible machinery and understand its use, and more important, they must be "leaders of men," "choosing," "interesting," and controlling them (IV.12.5; see also VI.7.3). Finally, entrepreneurs have to integrate all these organs and components into a consistent framework, they have to "engineer" them in defining an exact program of production and in monitoring it, and they must control the functioning of the hierarchical system and choose its appropriate incentives (IV.12.10). Keeping all these aspects in mind, Marshall developed a classification of organizational forms that is very similar to the one proposed by Adam Smith (1776, bk. V, ch. 1) – distinguishing individual or family firms, partnership, joint-stock companies, and cooperatives – with the notable difference that he looked at their comparative advantages in the context of an evolutionist interpretation.[12] There are obviously what we now call "organizational costs" associated with these functions, of which Marshall was very conscious (IV.12.3): Finding the appropriate businessmen, assembling the skilled workers, acquiring information on their qualifications and performance so as to monitor them adequately, and controlling them with incomplete information are very costly. But on the whole, according to Marshall, such a complex organization is very similar to that of higher animals: It is superior in terms of adaptability and, therefore, in terms of capacity to survive.

To survive and to expand

While there is no simple relation among living beings between the fittest organism and its size, in the economic world the advantages of the division of labor are closely related to "the advantages of production on a large scale," as is "best shown in manufacture" (IV.11.1), particularly where joint-stock companies are predominant. These advantages are (1) economies of skill, through the capacity to attract "men with exceptional natural abilities" (IV.11.3); (2) economies of machinery, through the use of specialized machines and the capacity to improve existing ones (IV.11.2); (3) economies in buying larger quantities of inputs at lower costs (IV.11.2); (4) advantages as sellers, since there are possibilities to sell more diversified products to a larger number of customers through a systematic policy of advertising (IV.11.2); (5) gains in attracting the best "businessmen" (e.g., managers) and in allowing them, through the division of labor, to "keep [their] mind[s] fresh and clear for thinking out the most difficult and vital problems of [their] business" (IV.11.4); and finally (6) expanded capacities to deal advantageously with bankers and to borrow capital at lower cost (IV.11.5).

These advantages are those that will be attributed, later in the economic literature, to multidivisional forms of organization (Williamson 1975). Put in a dynamic context and interpreted in a Darwinian framework, they could mean the elimination of individuals, namely, less specialized firms with a lower level of the division of labor, but of species as well – for example, of "trade activities." In the long run, it means that large concentrated sectors and large firms with monopoly power could prevail, threatening the very existence of competitive markets.

Division of labor: a hazardous concept

Marshall believed in the necessity of *restricting the advantages of the division of labor* and develops two lines of arguments to do so. First, he points out the advantages of small firms in several sectors of activity. Small organizations can compete against large ones because of lower organizational costs, because of their ability to monitor workers more efficiently ("The master's eye is everywhere," IV.11.4), because they can benefit from external economies (through a better access to "trade-knowledge," IV.11.4), and because they can occupy specialized niches where economies of scale are difficult to obtain (IV.11.6). Obviously these are not very strong arguments – with the possible exception of the last one – when compared with those favoring big organizations. There is a need for something more convincing.

The now-famous notion of a *representative firm* is precisely designed as such an argument. The analogy of "the trees and the forest" (IV.13.1) allows Marshall to introduce the idea of a life cycle within species – for example, within each industry. The possibility for one firm to absorb all its competitors in the sector or to get some monopoly power over them would be analogous to the dominance of an individual's progeny over the whole species: It is limited only by the exhaustion of its vitality.[13] Certainly, large firms do not always die, but their expansion is constrained by the decay of their coordinating capacities and by the rise of younger firms. The representative firm is then described either as "an average firm" or, not equivalently at all in our view, as "a normal" one:

> Our representative firm must be one which has had a fairly long life, and fair success, which is managed with normal ability, and which has normal access to the economies, external and internal, which belong to that aggregate volume of production; account being taken of the class of goods produced, the conditions of marketing them and the economic environment generally. (IV.13.2)

This is hardly a rigorous concept. It was, in the late 1920s, the source of a major controversy on the origins, existence, and consequences of increasing returns (Ménard 1981b). The problem raised was clear enough: If the division of labor generates increasing returns and results in monopoly power, then the model of pure competition among small firms appears inadequate to account for market economy. Though there has been no clear outcome to that debate, economic theory still continues to assume internal limits – the rationale of which is all but clear – to increasing returns.

It has been suggested by Robertson (1931), Levine (1983), and even, though more ambiguously, by Niman (1991) that the notion of a representative firm, later extended to "representative worker" and "representative employer" (VI.1.7), was intended primarily to introduce a dynamic representation of steady growth. On the contrary, in our view, it is a deus ex machina, introduced in extremis by Marshall in the very last chapter of Book IV of the *Principles* to escape some unbearable consequences entailed by the biological analogy structuring the whole book.[14]

As Levine (1983) and Niman (1991) noticed – though, significantly, they did not develop the idea – advancing the image of the representative firm actually was moving a step backward: It eliminated the richness of the concept of the division of labor to reintroduce an indifferentiated world of buyers and sellers operating in a static world regulated by static laws.

Marshall did not engage in that move because of an insufficiency of the analogy per se. On the contrary, it is in exhibiting differences between the usages of the concept of the division of labor in economics and in biology that Marshall realized the threatening potency of the analogy. If in living beings the advantages of differentiation are selected by the environment and concern populations, in economics the division of labor is implemented by individual organizations that can benefit by eliminating their competitors, particularly since they can favorably remodel their environment, at least up to a certain point.

Backing up from the consequences of the analogy, Marshall abandoned the concept of organization. Indeed, in Book V, the notion has disappeared. This is a severe loss for theoretical economics, brought about by a regression to a pre-Darwinian viewpoint: Substituting *representative firm* for *organizations*, Marshall shifted back from population thinking to traditional typological thinking. On this he was to be followed by most contemporary economists.

The representative firm: the outcome of a biological dilemma

It is our contention that Marshall's construction of the notion of representative firm at the end of Book IV did not come, as often asserted, from loose analogies that proved too weak for economic theorizing. Quite the contrary, Marshall's use of biological analogies was anything but loose. It is precisely because of a tight coupling between economics and biology, because the borrowing of biological concepts went beyond metaphorical rhetorics and structured economic thinking, that the notion of the representative firm could appear as the solution to the threatening problem already delineated. Moreover, the very notion of a representative firm could be firmly grounded in traditional biological thinking.

Before presenting the evidence sustaining these points, let us restate a crucial methodological rule: In the history of any science, hindsight may prove at times illuminating, but it is not permissible to account for a theoretical construct by later developments of the sciences. This is why we must ignore what we now know about evolution theory as it unfolded after Marshall's time. Marshall's work has to be understood on its own terms, from the viewpoint of what *he* thought was known, of what he read and commented on. Fortunately for us, he is quite explicit about the literature that went into his thinking.

A tightly woven network

Concerning the division of labor, Marshall was not simply a reader of Adam Smith. He read, as emphasized earlier, Smith through the eyes of Darwin and eventually found support for his interpretation of Darwinian biology in "a brilliant paper by Haeckel, *Arbeitstheilung in Menschen- und Thierleben*" (IV.8.1, n. 1). This provided him with an understanding of the division of labor as embedded in organizations. Darwin had developed this understanding in part from his reworking of the concept of a *division of physiological labor* coming from the French naturalist Henri Milen-Edwards, whose thinking, in turn, was rooted in Adam Smith's notion of a social and technical division of labor. This clarifies how Marshall's theorizing was integrated within an already tightly woven historical network of interrelationships between economics and biology.

At the beginning of chapter 8 (IV.8.1), Marshall clearly states the connection between the division of labor and the struggle for existence, or competition:

> The doctrine that those organisms which are the most highly developed, in the sense in which we have just used the phrase,[15] are those which are most likely to survive in the struggle for existence, is itself in process of development. It is not completely thought out either in its biological or its economic relations. But we may pause to consider the main bearings in economics of the law that the struggle for existence causes those organisms to multiply which are best fitted to derive benefit from their environment.

At the end of this paragraph Marshall, in the early editions of his book, gave as his authorities "the writings of Herbert Spencer on this subject, Bagehot's *Physics and Politics*, and Hearn's *Plutology*." Interestingly, from the sixth edition (1910) on, all these references are deleted and Haeckel's "brilliant paper" becomes the sole authoritative source.

"On Division of Labour in the Life of Nature and of Mankind" is a lecture given by Ernst Haeckel to a general audience in the lecture room of the Berlin Craftsmen Association in December 1868. It was published in Berlin the year after and again, with minor changes, in 1878, this time in a collection of his "popular" contributions to the theory of animal development (Haeckel 1878). Marshall does not indicate which edition he is referring to, but it does not matter here because what was of interest to him remained unchanged from one edition to the other.

In his lecture Haeckel emphasized that the division of labor exists not only in human societies and in some "societies" of insects, but also in animals that though they appear as a whole to form an individual, in fact are colonies or an aggregation of differentiated individuals. His favorite example seems to have been that of the siphonophores.

Siphonophores are an order of specialized hydrozoan invertebrates, the best known of which is no doubt *Physalia*, the Portuguese man-of-war. These organisms live in large colonies composed of modified polypoid and medusoid individuals, generally displaying high polymorphism. The different functions of the colony are fulfilled by the different types of individual components: Locomotion is the function of the swim bladder, whose gas content is regulated so that the colony can float or sink below the surface and which is modified pulsating medusae; feeding is carried on by the polypoid members, each of these polyps having a single tentacle armed with very efficient nematocysts used to paralyze prey, which is then brought to the mouths of the polyps; the products of digestion are shared by all the members of the colony, including the medusoid individuals, through gastrovascular cavities (Haeckel 1869, 17–26; Barnes 1968, 92).

According to Haeckel, the polymorphism shown in animals such as the siphonophores is the result of the struggle for existence. The ancestors of the siphonophores were polyps; later a medusoid form appeared, and both forms were retained in the composition of the new type of organism. Whereas in a society of bees the animals retain their independent morphological existence, in other complex organisms the individuals are physically connected and physiologically interrelated and interdependent. The human body, like that of any higher animal, is nothing but a huge colony of "vielen Millionen von kleinen Stattsbürgern," millions of minute individual citizens, the specialized cells fulfilling diverse functions in the division of labor that keep the body alive (Haeckel 1869, 34).

This was not all Haeckel's idea. In 1851, the German biologist Rudolf Leuckart had already interpreted the morphology of the siphonophore as corresponding to a colony of individuals, modified polyps or medusae, exhibiting division of labor and functioning as a "communist state" (Winsor 1971–2, 315–23). The main novelty of Haeckel's work – and what made it of special interest to Marshall – was his linking of the division of labor with the struggle for existence. This he did very consciously in the wake of Darwin, of whom he was the major German advocate. He had already made the connection explicit three years earlier in his *Generelle Morphologie der Organismen*, to which he refers in his lecture (Haeckel 1868, 37).

Haeckel asserted that it is natural selection, through its "instrument," the struggle for existence (Haeckel 1866, 2:231), that accounts for one of the "fundamental organic laws," the "law of division of Labour or differentiation," which Darwin called "divergence of characters" (1869, 4; 1866, 2:249). This is the very sort of language Marshall himself is using.

The connection with competition

Indeed, Marshall not only took from biology a perspective on the division of labor as embedded in organizations; he also seized upon the centrality of Darwin's connection between the division of labor and the struggle for existence, or competition. This is made clear in the very first pages of chapter 8, Book IV, "Industrial Organization." Indeed, whereas Adam Smith explained the division of labor basically by the human propensity to barter and exchange, and accounted for the limits of its development by the extension of the market, it is Darwin who pointed out, first, that the process of the division of labor in organization is undergone through competition and, second, that the effects of this process are likely to result in monopoly position:

> The advantage of diversification of the inhabitants of the same region is, in fact, the same as that of the physiological division of labour in the organs of the same individual body – a subject so well elucidated by Milne-Edwards. No physiologist doubts that a stomach by being adapted to digest vegetable matter alone, or flesh alone, draws more nutriment from these substances. So in the general economy of any land, the more widely and perfectly the animals and plants are

diversified for different habits of life, so will a greater number of individuals be capable of there supporting themselves A set of animals, with their organization but little diversified, could hardly compete with a more perfectly diversified in structure. (Darwin 1859, 115–16)

He adds later:

As a general rule, the more diversified in structure the descendants from any one species can be rendered, the more places they will be enabled to seize on, and the more their modified progeny will be increased. . . . The modified offspring from the later and more highly improved branches of the lines of descent, will, it is probable, often take the place of, and so destroy, the earlier and less improved branches. (1859, 119)

Again, so that the point could not be missed, he states:

As in each fully stocked country natural selection necessarily acts by the selected forms having some advantage in the struggle for life over other forms, there will be a constant tendency in the improved descendants of any one species to supplant and to exterminate in each stage of descent their predecessors and their original parent. (1859, 121)

It is not our intention to show how these views of Darwin arose from a reworking of Milne-Edwards's ideas. This has been done in some detail elsewhere (Limoges 1970, in press). What matters here is what Marshall read in Darwin, what additional support he found in Haeckel, and what this entailed for his understanding of the outcome of a struggle for existence between organizations undergoing division of labor.

A regressive analogon

The meaning of Darwin's breakthrough is perhaps best made clear by contrasting it with the previous understanding of what the struggle for existence amounted to. Paradoxically, for us living in the post-Darwin era, the competition among organisms was, from the time of Linneaus to that of Darwin, the very mechanism ensuring *a steady-state living world,* a fixed economy of nature. As species were created, they were well adapted to their function in the maintenance of the whole. Each helped, through predation or parasitism, to maintain other species at their equilibrium level, so that proportions remain stable at all time between the population of all species. They would remain indefinitely identical to their predecessors, since any individual carrying a variation and departing from the type of the species would be, by definition so to speak, less well adapted than its competitors in the same species and would be eventually wiped out. The notion that there is some normative essence of a species is what has come to be called the typological species concept (Mayr 1963).

In contrast, Darwin's revolutionary step was to consider any adaptation as a relative affair, no adaptation ever being perfect, so that individual organisms presenting hereditary variations with even incremental advantage in the struggle for existence would eventually prevail and eradicate their competitors through time. There is no such thing as a given type for a species. Any species is nothing but a population of individuals that are all different and all more or less well adapted to conjunctural circumstances. This is the underpinning of the *population concept of the species.*

But what this population concept also entailed is that, in the struggle for existence, the progeny of some individuals will survive, while that of others will necessarily become extinct. What it also entailed, more precisely and more threateningly in Marshall's view, is that the more similar the competing sets of organisms – like firms in the same line of business – the more fierce that competition will be and the more certain it is that those who try to occupy the same "place in the economy of nature" (or niche) will disappear, except the ones best equipped to monopolize the resources. This is how new species emerge according to Darwin, through extinction of their closest competitors, that is, those too similar but not quite as well adapted. This is the principle of "divergence," embodied in what ecologists now call the competitive exclusion principle.

This, it is our central contention, is what proved to be the unbearable consequence of the coupling of the economic and biological processes that Marshall himself stressed: These processes inexorably lead to monopoly as the only possible natural outcome.

Marshall's notion of the representative firm was his response to that challenge; it was not a construct born for some other extraneous purpose. It was moreover a response congruent with biological tradition, though no doubt a regression to pre-Darwinian biology: The representative or typical firm had a clear analogon, the typological species concept, the species as subsuming the individuals under a type that is at the same time a norm. Finally, what seemed to Marshall a permissible biological escape from his dilemma, this falling back on biological typology, under the guise of a representative firm amenable to the physicalist approach, provided the cornerstone for his analysis of equilibrium as developed in Book V.

Conclusion

Because of Marshall's inability to overcome the problems raised by the coupling between economics and biology, the very notion of organization had to be abandoned. This was a turning point in the modern history of economics.

In identifying the centrality of the relation of the concept of organization with that of the division of labor, Marshall opened the possibility for some major progress in the direction suggested by Adam Smith at the very beginning of *The Wealth of Nations*. This breakthrough would have otherwise bccn made possible thanks to the cross-fertilization between economics and biology initiated by Henri-Milne-Edwards and carried further by Darwin. But it would have necessitated a populationist approach to the analysis of the economic agents, coupled with an evolutionist perspective. Trapped by the already available image of market as a mechanistic system where symmetric forces can equilibrate and, most important, unable to reconcile the already standardized view of economic competition with the Darwinian interpretation of the consequences of the division of labor on complex organisms, Marshall shifted back to pre-Darwinian biology, adopting the typological notion of the representative firm. This would eliminate all the unpalatable prospects related to the principle of divergence, or differentiation, but this would also entail the eradication of differentiated economic agents from the central core of theoretical economics.

Marshall's regressive move was to weight heavily on the research agenda of economics. He left us a heritage with which we are still coming to grips.

Notes

The authors would like to thank the participants in the conference "Natural Images in Economics," and especially Professor Philip Mirowski, for their thoughtful and very helpful comments on an earlier version of this chapter.

1. "[He] did render the energetics metaphor palpable for an English audience which would probably have resisted the brash revolution of a Jevons" (Mirowski 1984, 375). Thomas (1991) also develops the idea of "lip service to biological analogy."
2. "Marshall's recourse to biological analogies can be understood as a continuation of that strategy (Ingram's address to the British Association for the Advancement of Sciences in 1878, claiming that political economy resembled biology, so as to resist Galton's drive to oust section F from the

B.A.A.S.), as part of his larger project of building a stable professional identity for economics" (Mirowski 1989, 265). The argument is repeated in Mirowski (1990), though a more detailed examination of why Marshall failed as a theoretician is provided. The title of Mirowski's paper makes explicit his intent: that "Marshall's demand and supply curves made neo-classicism safe for public consumption but unfit for science."

3. For Marshall's use of this image, see note 13.

4. An example illustrates this: the contemporary "population genetics" interpretation of natural selection shared by all of the authors already quoted.

5. The centrality of Book IV in Marshall's analysis can also be supported by looking at some historical evidences. It is well known (see Pigou 1925; Whitaker 1975) that the basic framework of Books III and V (including the mathematical apparatus) was already in place in the early 1880s, probably even earlier. But it took Marshall ten years to "solve" some basic problems confronted in writing Book IV – even more than ten years, according to Marshall's famous letter to A. W. Flux of March 7, 1898: "My confidence in Cournot as an *economist* was shaken when I found that his mathematics re: I.R. increasing returns led inevitably to things which do not exist and have no near relation to reality. One of the chief purposes of my Wanderjahre among factories etc . . . was to discover how Cournot's premises were wrong . . . Cournot's problem (how to reconcile widespread increasing returns with the conviction that monopolization is not the result) occupied me a good deal between 1870 and 1890." Quoted in Pigou (1925, 406–7).

6. Hereafter all quotations are from Marshall's eighth edition of the *Principles* and are referred to by book, chapter, and paragraph according to Marshall's own system.

7. A little earlier, in his final books, Cournot arrived at a similar conclusion, based on a similar analogy with biology. His conclusion was that coordination became such a complex problem that only an *archée*, the equivalent of a central nervous system, could assume the function; and the *archée* could well be the state in Cournot's view. See Cournot (1877) and Ménard (1978, ch. 3).

8. Spencer is mentioned as an authority on the effect of use on the strengthening of organs, an argument mobilized by Marshall against the idea, entertained by some disciples of Smith, of a permanent natural organization. Marshall, however, also emphasizes that modern genetics has cast doubt on the hereditary transmission of such effects.

9. It should be pointed out that all commentators put the emphasis on Spencer, while none pays attention to other references – like the one to Haeckel – or to the disappearance of most references to Spencer in the successive editions of the *Principles* from 1890 to 1920.

10. As is now well known, Marshall defines external economies as those that are "dependent on the general development of the industry," among which the major factor is the concentration of the industry in an area,

e.g., its localization and the related division of labor among types of activity (since they will improve "hereditary skill," i.e., transmission of know-how among workers, facilitate access to "highly specialized machinery" and special skills, and give firms the possibility of benefiting from "the growth of subsidiary trades"). Internal economies are related directly to the advantages of the division of labor within the organization as well as to the organizational efficiency in coordinating these subfunctions (see IV.9.7).

11. Though Marshall uses the term "businessmen" most of the time, we will employ the term "entrepreneur," which is also in Marshall and carries fewer connotations for a modern reader.

12. Though there are many stimulating insights on organizations in Marshall's classification, the analysis of this aspect would go beyond the purpose of the chapter.

13. "But here we may read a lesson from the young trees of the forest as they struggle upwards through the benumbing shade of their older rivals. Many succumb on the way, and a few only survive; those few become stronger with every year, they get a larger share of light and air with every increase of their height, and at last in their turn they tower above their neighbours, and seem as though they would grow on for ever, and for ever become stronger as they grow. But they do not. One tree will last longer in full vigour and attain a greater size than another; but sooner or later age tells on them all. Though the taller ones have better access to light and air than their rivals, they gradually lose vitality; and one after another they give place to others, which, though of less material strength, have on their side the vigour of youth.

"And as with the growth of trees, so was it with the growth of businesses as a general rule before the great recent development of vast joint-stock companies, which often stagnate, but do not readily die" (IV.13.1).

14. Significantly, it was in this chapter that Marshall introduced by far the most changes in the various editions of the *Principles*. See the annotated edition by Guillebaud.

15. In the previous paragraph Marshall refers to the increased subdivision of functions as differentiation, and to integration.

References

Arrow, Kenneth J. 1974. *Limits of Organization*. New York: Norton.

Barnes, Robert D. 1968. *Invertebrate Zoology*, 2d ed. Philadelphia: Saunders.

Bharadwaj, Krishna. 1978. "The Subversion of Classical Analysis: Alfred Marshall's Early Writings on Value," *Cambridge Journal of Economics* 2 (Sept.): 153–74.

Cournot, Antoine A. 1877. *Revue sommaire des doctrines économiques*. Paris: Hachette.

Darwin, Charles. 1859. *On the Origin of Species by Means of Natural Selection*.

London: John Murray. Reprinted with an introduction by Ernst Mayr, Cambridge, MA: Harvard University Press, 1966.

Haeckel, Ernst. 1866. *Generelle Morphologie der Organismen*, 2 vols. Berlin.

Haeckel, Ernst. 1869. *Arbeitstheilung in Menschen- und Thierleben*. Berlin. Off print. Reproduced in Haeckel (1878).

Haeckel, Ernst. 1878. *Gesammelte populare Vertrage aus dem Gebiete der Entwickelungslehre*. Bonn.

Hebert, Robert, and Link, Robert. 1982. *The Entrepreneur*. New York: Praeger.

Hirshleifer, Jack. 1977. "Economics from a Biological Viewpoint," *Journal of Law and Economics* (20): 1–52.

Hodgson, Geoffrey. In press. *Economics and Evolution*. See particularly ch. 7, "The Mecca of Alfred Marshall." Cambridge: Polity.

Levine, A. L. 1983. "Marshall's *Principles* and the "Biological Viewpoint: A Reconsideration," *Manchester School of Economic and Social Studies* 51 (3): 276–93.

Limoges, Camille. 1970. *La sélection naturelle*. Paris: Presses Universitaires de France.

Limoges, Camille. In press. "Milne-Edwards, Darwin, Durkheim and Division of Labour: A Cast Study in Reciprocal Conceptual Exchanges Between the Social and the Natural Sciences." In I. B. Cohen (ed.), *The Natural Sciences and the Social Sciences: Historical Interactions*. Dordrecht: Kluwer.

Marshall, Alfred. 1885. "The Graphic Method of Statistics," *Journal of the Royal Statistical Society*, Jubilee Volume, 251–60. Reprinted in Pigou (1925).

Marshall, Alfred. 1898. "Mechanical and Biological Analogies in Economics," excerpt from "Distribution and Exchange," *Economic Journal*. Reprinted in Pigou (1925).

Marshall, Alfred. 1920. *Principles of Economics*. London: Macmillan. This eighth edition was published in 2 vols. with variorum by C. W. Guillebaud, London: Macmillan, 1961.

Ménard, Claude. 1978. *La formation d'une rationalité économique*. Paris: Flammarion.

Ménard, Claude. 1981a. "La machine et le coeur: Essai sur les analogies dans le raisonnement économique." In A. Lichnerowicz (ed.), *Analogie et connaissance: De la poésie à la science*. Paris: Librairie Maloine. English translation, P. Cook and P. Mirowski. 1989. "The Machine and the Heart: An Essay on Analogies in Economic Reasoning," *Social Concept* 5 (1): 81–95.

Ménard, Claude. 1981b. *Equilibre, asymétrie, conflit: Un siècle de théorie des prix en équilibre partiel*. Paris: Université de Paris I (Panthéon-Sorbonne). Mimeo.

Milne-Edwards, H. 1827. "Organisation." In *Dictionnaire classique d'histoire naturelle*, 12: 332–44. Paris: Rey & Gravier.

Mirowski, Philip. 1984. "Physics and the 'Marginalist Revolution,'" *Cambridge Journal of Economics* 8 (2): 361–79.

Mirowski, Philip. 1989. *More Heat Than Light: Economics as Social Physics, Physics as Nature's Economics*. Cambridge University Press.

Mirowski, Philip. 1990. "Smooth Operator: How Marshall's Demand and Supply Curves Made Neoclassicism Safe for Public Consumption but Unfit for Science," in Rita McWilliams Tullberg, ed., *Alfred Marshall in Retrospect*, 61–89: Aldershot: Edward Edgar.

Moss, Laurence. 1982. "Biological Theory and Technological Entrepreneurship in Marshall's Writings," *Eastern Economic Journal* 8 (1): 3–13.

Nelson, Richard, and Winter, Sidney. 1982. *An Evolutionary Theory of Economic Change*. Cambridge, MA: Harvard University Press.

Niman, Neil B. 1991. "Biological Analogies in Marshall's Work," *Journal of the History of Economic Thought* 13 (1): 19–36.

Pigou, A. C., ed. 1925. *Memorials of Alfred Marshall*. London: Macmillan.

Robbins, Lionel. 1928. "The Representative Firm," *Economic Journal* 38 (2): 387–404.

Robertson, Denis H. 1831. "The Trees of the Forest," *Economic Journal* 40 (1): 80–9.

Schweber, Silvan S. 1980. "Darwin and the Political Economists: Divergence of Character," *Journal of the History of Biology* 13: 189–95.

Smith, Adam. 1776. *The Wealth of Nations*. Reprint (Cannan's edition), Chicago: University of Chicago Press, 1976.

Thomas, Brinley. 1991. "Alfred Marshall on Economic Biology," *Review of Political Economy* 3 (1): 1–14.

Viner, Jacob. 1941. "Marshall's Economics in Relation to the Man and His Times," *American Economic Review* 31 (3): 223–35.

Weber, Max. 1964. *The Theory of Social and Economic Organization* (1947). Translated by A. M. Henderson and Talcott Parsons. New York: Free Press.

Whitaker, John K. 1975. *The Early Writings of Alfred Marshall, 1867–1890*, 2 vols. London: Macmillan.

Williamson, Oliver E. 1975. *Markets and Hierarchies*. New York: Free Press.

Winsor, Mary P. 1971–2. "A Historical Consideration of the Siphonophores," *Proceedings of the Royal Society of Edinburgh*, ser. B, 73: 315–23.

CHAPTER 14

The role of biological analogies in the theory of the firm

NEIL B. NIMAN

While economic analysis has for the most part been satisfied with the theory of the production function serving as the theory of the firm, three notable exceptions (Marshall 1920; Alchian 1950; and Winter 1964, 1971) have attempted to create meaningful theories of the firm utilizing biological analogies. Why such analogies have been used sparingly may be the result of a general trend away from biology in the development of modern economic theory (Schabas, Chapter 12, this volume) or may be more specifically related to the observation (made by Rosenberg, Chapter 15, this volume) that when biology is applied to the theory of the firm, much of what results seems to be more of interest to organizational theorists than to economists. The lack of interest and/or limited appeal of the biological metaphor raises the question of why it may be of value for economics in general, and the theory of the firm more specifically, to appropriate biological analogies. This chapter attempts to answer this question.

The first step toward providing an answer will be to investigate some of the potential reasons why economists might find biological analogies attractive. The appropriation of biology for use in economics is not however without some cost, and therefore the second step will be to identify some of the challenges involved in translating biological concepts for use in the theory of the firm. For example, in what ways is a firm similar to a biological organism? How can rational economic decision making be reconciled with a theory of evolution that relies on random mutation and selection by the environment to explain change? How does competition affect survival?

The conclusion reached is that while the use of biological analogies is not without some difficulty, two possible benefits for economics are provided. First, a biological approach may aid in the description of economic agents and events. If economic activity is not performed exclusively by representative agents, then some system of taxonomy classifying agents and events, along with a description of the processes underlying their behavior, may enhance the ability of economists to explain actual economic events. Second, as evolutionary biology continues to evaluate exactly what constitutes the neo-Darwinian synthesis, economists may gain new insights into what can be done to resolve some of the difficulties contained in their own synthesis.

The use of biological analogies

In accounting for the potential benefits gained from the appropriation of biological metaphors, eight potential reasons immediately come to mind. The first can be attributed to Armen Alchian (1952) in his defense against the attack by Edith Penrose (1952) for misappropriating the biological metaphor. Alchian's response was based on the defense that "the theory I presented stands independently of the biological analogy. . . . In my original article every reference to the biological analogy was merely expository, designed to clarify the ideas in the theory" (601). However, if ease of exposition is the goal, it is not clear that the unfamiliar language of the biological sciences is the best way of presenting complex ideas to the economics profession as a whole.

The second possible explanation for the use of biological analogies can be labeled as the Machiavellian approach predicated on the principle "the ends justify the means." Here biology is looked upon as a framework for promoting ideas and getting them published. A great deal of work in the economics of technological change literature is flirting with the use of biological analogies (see, e.g., Dosi et al. 1988). However, since these authors control only a limited number of professional journals, chances for publication would only be enhanced within a small select group, and thus does not seem to provide a compelling reason for cloaking economic ideas within a biological framework.

The third reason can be identified under the rubric of gamesmanship. The application of biological concepts represents a challenge similar to that encountered by ancient mariners as they explored unchartered territory merely to see if it could be done. Of course, to boldly go where no person has gone before requires that some funding agency will find the project worthwhile. Even though the National Science Foundation (as Mirowski points out in Chapter 17, this volume) seems to have no qualms about sinking large sums of money into economic experiments with rats, there must be other endeavors that have a higher probability of securing funding.

The fourth reason may be one of reverse imperialism. While Jack Hirshleifer (1985) has not been reticent to expose the imperialistic nature of economists, economics may now in turn be falling victim to the imperialism of the sociobiologists. This assumes, however, that the sociobiologists have managed to leap over the barricades and scale the imposing walls surrounding the citadel protecting the inner sanctum of economics. While certainly possible, it is probably easy to dismiss in terms of limited incentives.

The fifth reason may arise from a search for legitimacy. Such a search springs forth from a deep-rooted need to justify economic concepts through formalization or by appealing to the natural sciences. However, given that biological processes are inherently complex, the quantification of certain economic concepts based on biology may not be feasible. Furthermore, as Mirowski (1989) has pointed out, physics has already played an important role in defining the important questions and the techniques required for answering many of the questions of concern to economists. Thus, if economics already has physics, who needs biology?

The sixth reason for incorporating biological concepts may arise from an intellectual deficit in the economics profession. The need to fill the ever-increasing number of professional journals with new advances may be forcing economists who must publish or perish to look outside the profession for new ideas that can be appropriated for use. However, the economics profession has traditionally drawn from the pool of mathematicians and physicists who themselves have only a passing acquaintance with biology. Thus, once again, the potential costs seem to outweigh the benefits.

The seventh reason could result from the creation of a post-Marshallian (with or without the hyphen) economics. Since Marshall himself liberally appealed to biological analogies (Niman, 1991a; Limoges and Ménard, Chapter 13, this volume), the development of a brand of economic theorizing based on the "economics of Marshall" would itself be full of biological references. It may then be possible to emulate the post-Keynesians by creating a cottage industry attempting to explain what Marshall really meant. The difficulty with such a task however is that Marshall was more Spencerian (Niman 1991a) than Darwinian (Schabas, Chapter 12, this volume), and therefore reinterpreting Marshall may provide only a limited forum for incorporating modern evolutionary biology into economics.

The eighth reason can be characterized as the antineoclassical attack. Within this context, economics is accused of being inflexible and far too narrow in its scope of inquiry. However, as long as the primary concern of economics is with establishing and explaining the theory of value, then perhaps Edith Penrose (1952) is correct that "biological analogies contribute little either to the theory of price or to the theory of growth and development of firms and in general tend to confuse the nature of the important issues" (804). In the case of the firm, as long as the theory of price presupposes the existence of products that can be readily exchanged independently of how they are produced, then there is no need for a theory of the firm as something other than a "heuristic device" (Machlup 1967) that follows the decision rule: maximize profits. Therefore, within such a context, the firm is to a large extent superfluous, and thus any theory of the firm (biological or otherwise) does not in this sense contribute anything to the theory of price.

The challenge of using biological analogies

While it is certainly possible to develop a variety of reasons for justifying the use of biological analogies, it is not clear that such justification is necessary. If historians of science such as Schweber (1980) are correct, then much of Darwinism is merely classical political economy applied to the realm of the natural. Under these circumstances, appealing to Darwinism is merely using economics (under the guise of biology) to advance the state of economics. Thus, appealing to biological analogies could be construed as being as natural (or more so) as the appeals that are made to concepts such as Brouwer's fixed-point theorem to prove the existence of a general equilibrium. However, as Schabas (Chapter 12, this volume) has contended, the origins of Darwin's ideas are not so clear and may not be related to classical political economy. Thus, such an argument can be made defensible only when the origins of Darwin's ideas are firmly established.

Another potential approach is to ask the question: What if economics and biology are disciplines that have developed independently but share certain common characteristics? Rather than speculating on what this means, it may be of value as a first step to determine the extent to which similarities exist between disciplines. However, rather than attempting to draw parallels between all of economics and the entire discipline of biology, a more modest goal of comparing smaller subsets seems to be more realistic. Thus, from economics, the theory of the firm, and from biology the subdiscipline of evolutionary biology may be chosen to determine the extent of the similarities or differences between disciplines.

To evaluate the similarities between the theory of the firm and evolutionary biology involves three challenges. The first arises from the need to develop exactly what constitutes the theory of the firm and, from evolutionary biology, whether it is the synthetic theory that is to be used or some variant. Once the corresponding theories have been identified, the second challenge is to translate effectively biological concepts into economic terminology. The third challenge is to determine if a one-to-one correspondence exists between economics and biology (what Cohen, in Chapter 3, this volume identifies as the construction of a homology) and, if it is found that the relationship is not exact, the extent to which it must be modified in order to create a good fit.[1]

Challenge 1: identification

In attempting to create a one-to-one correspondence between evolutionary biology and the theory of the firm, the first step is to identify what exactly constitutes a firm and which theory of evolution is to be utilized. Neither of these is an easy task and both are subject to dispute and some controversy.

One of the unfortunate consequences of the formalization of economic theory in the twentieth century has been the substitution of the theory of the production function for the theory of the firm (Niman 1991b). By making the implicit assumption that firms are in essence "what they produce," they have been classified into industries according to product, and issues pertaining to allocation are discussed exclusively in terms of production possibilities. Joseph Stiglitz (1991) has recently commented: "Many economists argued that there was no need to look carefully into the black box called the firm: firms maximized profits (stock market value); if managers didn't they would be replaced; and firms that didn't maximize wouldn't survive. Accordingly, what went on inside the black box was mere detail. The behavior of the firm could be described completely without knowledge of those details" (15). Thus, while considerable progress is currently underway toward creating a well-defined theory of the firm (Holmstrom and Tirole 1989), an accepted synthesis of current research has yet to be reached.

With respect to evolutionary biology, there does appear to be widespread agreement of the basic tenets underlying the neo-Darwinian synthesis; however, recent developments in fields such as molecular biology and paleontology (Stebbins and Ayala 1981) are applying pressure to promote a broadening of the synthesis. One possible approach being suggested is a hierarchically based approach designed as a supplement (and not a replacement) to the synthetic approach. Eldredge (1985) comments:

> It is often perceived that a hierarchically based evolutionary theory . . . constitutes a strict and total alternative to the synthesis. I – along with Gould, Vrba, Salthe, Damuth, Stanley, and all others who have been moving in the direction of hierarchy theory – have no intention of junking the synthesis (were such action possible). . . . My position here, and the position of all other doubters of the completeness of the synthesis that I know of, is simply that the neo-Darwinian paradigm is indeed necessary – but is not sufficient – to handle the totality of all known evolutionary phenomena. (118–19)

Until the synthetic theory can be modified to incorporate new developments or current research is thoroughly discredited (thereby removing a need to modify existing theory), identifying the concepts from evolutionary biology for translation into economics represents a unique challenge in and of itself.

Challenge 2: translation

To provide a translation from evolutionary biology to economics, the structure of evolutionary theory must first be identified. Evolutionary theories depend on three elements: (1) establishing some basis for change, (2) identifying the source of change, and (3) determining the reason for change. In evolutionary biology, the genetic constitution of the organism identifies the basis for change, mutation and selection provide the source for change, and competition establishes the reason for change. The challenge is then one of finding comparable concepts in the theory of the firm.[2]

The basis for change

Given that the genetic constitution of an organism provides the basis for evolutionary change, the question is whether or not some analogous concept exists within the theory of the firm. If the firm is viewed as a black box where inputs are transformed into outputs according to the rule "maximize profits," then it does not appear to be possible to create the necessary linkage between economics and biology. In a recent survey of the theory of the firm, Holmstrom and Tirole (1989) point out that most of the current work on the firm is based on some type of contracting framework. The firm is viewed as an institutional structure designed to reduce transactions costs. Because information is a primary source of transaction costs and is not widely available, it is difficult to process, and because individuals have different levels of expertise in utilizing information, the costs of managing it are often significantly lower within the context of an organization that encourages specialization in information handling. Within such a context, "the organization must succeed in capturing the returns from informational expertise by alleviating the exchange hazards that inevitably accompany asymmetric information. Consequently, much recent analytical work on organizations has centered on an improved understanding of how one goes about contracting when people know different pieces of information of relevance for the organization as a whole" (Holmstrom and Tirole 1989, 64).

One strategy for reducing transaction costs is the creation of rules. Rules determine the structure of information flows, incentives, and authority – all of which determine if and to what extent profits reach their maximum. Rules are necessary to assist in the monitoring of performance to prevent shirking (Alchian and Demsetz 1972), to help align incentives because of underlying principle–agent problems (Sappington 1991), to structure information flows to facilitate decision making (Marschak and Radner 1972), and to provide supervision (Calvo and Wellisz 1978). How the firm behaves therefore depends on the characteristics of the institution that structures the potential ways in which the firm can act and how successful those actions will be. Thus, the challenge in terms of identifying the basis for change is to find some way to link the rules governing the decision structure (how the firm is organized) and the genetic constitution found in biological organisms.

The source of change

If the structure of rules can serve a function similar to the genetic constitution of an organism, then the next challenge becomes one of determining what motivates change. In the neo-Darwinian synthesis, change is the outcome of an external selection process that chooses from a variety of random mutations. In contrast, the traditional economics approach has been to assume that internal changes originating from conscious, directed decision making lead to the selection of the appropriate external environment. This raises the question of whether the environment selects those firms best suited for survival or whether firms select the appropriate environments that maximize their chances for survival.[3]

The challenge becomes one of how to reconcile conscious direction with a selection process that depends on random changes in diverse populations. Perhaps this point can be best illustrated with an analogy. One view of evolution (Darwinism) is that the environment selects from the gene pool those organisms (economic agents) best able to survive given environmental conditions. Another view (Lamarckism) might suggest that organisms (economic agents) are able to increase their survivability (and that of future generations) by mandating a change in their physical makeup to overcome an adverse environment. (Thus change is not confined to the boundaries of an external selection process.) The first view is consistent with the widely held theory of evolution found in the biological sciences. The second view is perhaps the perspective held by many economists. The differences between these views is found in the degree of autonomy possessed by organisms in their struggle to survive. In other words, to what extent are organisms able to act independently of environmental considerations?

The movement away from the biological perspective contained in the work of Alfred Marshall (1920), to the more mechanical perspectives underlying the microeconomic theory of Hicks (1946) and Samuelson (1947), can perhaps be found in the desire to attribute a greater degree of autonomy to human behavior than a biological approach is willing to provide. With complete autonomy, economic science can focus exclusively on rational economic behavior, independent of social institutions or environmental composition.

Friedman (1953) refers to economic natural selection in building a case in support of the neoclassical position of complete autonomy by employing the "as if" assumption to explain organism and firm behavior. The issue is not whether, given certain environmental constraints, firms are able to actually maximize profits, but rather if it is reasonable to make the assumption that the firms act *as if* they are maximizing some objective function.[4] However, as Sahlins (1976) notes, attempting to explain change in terms of optimizing behavior has profound implications for evolutionary theory because it transforms "selection into the means by which DNA optimizes itself over the course of the generations" (72), rather than being a theory where the environment selects from a heterogeneous pool of organisms – a perspective that is confirmed by Becker's (1976) application of sociobiology to economics.

In evolutionary biology or sociobiology, whatever type of optimizing behavior takes place is designed not to satisfy the demands of the

individual, but rather to ensure the reproductive success of the underlying genetic structure.[5] Thus, while economics and sociobiology may
share the notion that individuals of some sort engage in optimizing
behavior (Becker 1976; Hirshleifer 1977), what such behavior is designed to benefit is significantly different. A broader goal that transcends the happiness or profitability of individual organisms or enterprises exists within the context of sociobiology but is not found in
economics. The elevation of reproductive success to a place of importance implies that profit or utility maximization is important only
insofar as it promotes the transmission of those genes (making success
possible) to future generations. Thus, success is defined in terms of
what happens between generations, rather than the activities that occur within the context of a single generation. The actions undertaken
by organisms are significant only insofar as they provide a window for
observing the success of the underlying genetic structure and the
extent to which they contribute to the survival of such a structure
through procreation.

The concept of reproductive success implies that some genes will be
transmitted to future generations and others will not. The neo-
Darwinian synthesis attempts to explain this process in terms of natural selection. The assumption of some sort of selection process assumes, of course, that variation exists in the population of organisms
(firms) in order for there to be differences that form the basis for
choosing one particular entity over another. However, when the firm
is nothing more than a production function and all firms have equal
access to the same production technology, what forms the basis for the
differences that provide for selection? Perhaps more important, once
all of the "optimal" firms have been selected, what accounts for continued change? If every firm is the optimal firm, then there exists no
basis for future selection and hence no mechanism for initiating
change over time.

Current research in molecular biology provides one possible avenue
for explaining how change occurs. Mutations in molecular biology
take the form of either point (gene) or regulatory (chromosomal)
mutations. Point mutations lead to changes within genes, while regulatory mutations determine which genes have an active role in each
chromosome. Point mutations accumulate at fairly steady rates over
time according to a "molecular clock" at different rates at every position along the DNA molecule (Ayala 1976). Regulatory mutations, by
controlling which genes are dominant (active), alter how genes are
expressed and hence what characteristics will dominate in a particular
organism. Much of the current research in molecular biology (Kimura

1983) indicates that these changes are to a large extent neutral (i.e., result from random drift rather than selection).[6]

Adapting the concepts of point and regulatory mutation to the firm can provide an explanation for how and why firms evolve. If the firm consists of an organizational structure comprised of various assets and a set of rules determining how those assets are to be allocated, then change can result from point mutation (changes in the available assets) and/or regulatory mutations (changes in the rules). While the rules (which are themselves subject to change) may be designed to promote the maximization of some objective function subject to a set of constraints, the existence of point mutations implies that these constraints are also constantly changing. If the assets comprising the constraints facing the firm are placed into the broad categories of human, physical, and technological assets following the same pattern as molecules, then each category of asset will have its own biological clock changing at a different rate (where the rate itself depends in part on how assets are combined).[7]

In assessing the empirical research on molecular evolution, Kimura (1983) offers the following general rule: "Molecular changes that are less likely to be subject to natural selection occur more rapidly in evolution" (308). This rule implies that at the molecular level, neutral evolution by random drift occurs at higher rates than evolution resulting from natural selection.[8] Such a contention would appear to lead to the conclusion that some sort of tendency toward a natural optimum does not exist and that, over time, industries, rather than being characterized by a homogeneous group with each member earning zero economic profits, would be comprised of members who share some but not all of the same characteristics.

The theory of neutral evolution suggests that a significant portion of change is the result of random drift rather than some type of optimizing process. This creates a serious problem for those economists who believe that all economic phenomena can be reduced to the maximization of some objective function subject to a set of constraints. Rather than attempting to explain change on a global level (as attempted by the neutral theory), the economist might contend that only those changes worthy of being selected are of concern. It is not the changes in the constraints or objective function that are important, but rather the relationship between function and constraint. Changes in the rules are significant only if they lead to more efficient uses in the assets, and changes in the assets are of value only if such improvements can be utilized by the rules. Typically then, improvements worth being selected would require both point and regulatory mutations and would include only those regulatory mutations that are best able to take advantage of the changes resulting from point mutations. Thus, only a relatively small number of mutations would fall within the parameters of study, and evolutionary change would be explained in local terms as the environment selects only these "optimal" mutations.

The conception of an optimal mutation, while potentially capable of ascribing some notion of a maximum to the process, can do so only in a very limited sense. While in absolute terms such a mutation might be classified as being optimal, in relative terms it is not clear that such a change would enjoy such a status. While some regulatory changes may make "best use" of point changes, not all point mutations are significant (worthy of being selected by the environment). Hence, what is important is not making the most of all changes, but rather making the most of those changes that the environment determines to be significant. In this sense, optimality becomes a relative rather than an absolute concept within a specific environmental context. Furthermore, it becomes increasingly difficult to determine what exactly constitutes an optimal mutation once it is recognized that mutations leading to a change in the population will ultimately lead to changes in the environment (Lewontin 1983). As the environment evolves, the standard for optimality changes, and what exactly constitutes the relevant environment depends on the time frame chosen. Thus, the idea of an optimal change becomes a historically specific concept whose relevance becomes subject to interpretation.

The reason for change

The conventional representation of the firm as producing a single product and competing within the confines of a single industry characterized by a perfectly competitive market creates another potential stumbling block for the construction of an evolutionary theory of the firm. Evolutionary change results from the selection of those traits best adapted to the peculiarities of the environment. Selection occurs because the environment is not capable of supporting unlimited reproduction within populations. The competitive struggle for the means of survival can result in overpopulation within a species or in the predator–prey relationships between species.

While the idea of a competitive struggle for existing resources is something shared between economics and biology, the nature of competition is substantially different.[9] If the assumption of perfectly competitive markets is used, then firms can sell all of the output they desire at the given market price. Under such an assumption, rivalry stemming from overpopulation cannot occur because, while the market may be limited in terms of the amount of output that can be sold at a given price, each individual firm does not share a similar constraint. Thus, individual firms do not compete for a limited number of potential sales or resources by assumption, thereby precluding the biological conception of struggle within a species.

Removing the assumption of perfect competition for a conception of markets based on imperfect competition does open the door for the construction of a theory of the firm consistent with evolutionary biology, however; merely assuming that individual firms face output constraints does not, however, solve the problem. A "biological" theory of the firm constructed on the principle that firms are not synonymous with the products that are produced requires a conception of rivalry in which competitive advantage is achieved not through the products that are produced, but rather from differences between firms. Firms can gain a competitive advantage not merely by differentiating their product and altering how products are produced, but also by differentiating their cost structures. The structure of costs incurred by an individual firm, while including the costs associated with producing a particular product, also include the costs of constructing, managing, and maintaining the organization. Variation in the genetic constitution (organizational structure) of firms may confer a competitive advantage for a particular firm even though the firm produces the same product offered by competitors. Thus, what is required is a theory of how firms rather than products compete.

Additional difficulties arise when attempting to explain competition as the result of entry and exit, and then attempting to draw the appropriate connections to the idea of the competitive struggle between species in the form of predator–prey relationships in biology. In economics, new firms entering an industry (thereby contributing to the competitive struggle) or ineffective competitors leaving an industry ensure that a stable population of firms (each earning zero economic profits) is reached. Given that firms are defined in terms of the product they produce, such a view of competition leads to a logical inconsistency that makes it difficult to draw the appropriate parallels between economics and biology. If firms are assumed to be synonymous with the products they produce, how can existing firms enter new industries? Entry by existing firms would entail the abandonment of the current product in order to begin producing a different product. Within this framework, exit must be synonymous with death because firms that could not compete in terms of a particular product go out of business rather than repositioning themselves in terms of producing a different product.

The problem exists because when the firm is defined in terms of the product that is produced, entry can occur only by newly created firms, and exit occurs only with the death of a firm. Yet in biology, when existing species prey on each other, the predator does not transform itself once it has consumed its prey. Wolves that prey on deer do not themselves become deer. This does not imply that there exists an insurmountable inconsistency between the notions of competition in economics and biology, but rather that inconsistencies exist in terms of the classification of firms/industries and organisms/species. Within the existing taxonomic system, it is the competition between products rather than competition between firms that dominates economics.

Challenge 3: modification

In attempting to make a direct translation from evolutionary biology to the theory of the firm, it becomes evident that a perfect correspondence does not exist. However, this raises the important question: To what extent does the theory of the firm have to be modified to achieve an acceptable level of consistency? Leaving aside the question of what exactly constitutes an acceptable level, the theory of the firm must be modified in three distinct areas to achieve consistency. Rather than viewing the firm as a black box, some connection must be made between the way the firm internalizes market transactions and the genetic constitution of a biological organism. Once the firm can be conceptualized as something that is analogous to an organism, the problem of reconciling rational economic behavior with a theory of change based on random mutations must be addressed. Finally, differences in terms of the nature of competition must be resolved.

The firm as an organism

One possible avenue for modifying the theory of the firm to create a concept comparable to the genetic constitution of an organism is to adapt the biological concepts presented in Dawkins (1989). The market, substituting for the primeval soup, serves as the location where resources (building blocks) exist. Managers (replicators) seek to unlock the potential gains that can be derived from specialized resources by coordinating how they interact through the creation of rules (genes) that specify how resources are to be combined. Managers are organized into teams (chromosomes) that take on such forms as product divisions or functional groupings. Through cooperation, functional areas or product divisions are linked in order to create an organizational structure that becomes the foundation for the firm (survival machine). Firms then compete for the available profits (nutrients) that are essential for maintaining their existence.

Within the context of such a "biological" firm, the rules that specify how resources are to be allocated and used to support the organizational structure are collectively defined as the genotype of the firm. These rules encompass the policies, procedures, and practices that define the role of the manager, what specific actions are to be undertaken by management, and how these actions are to be performed. Policies serve as the general guidelines that oversee management activities. Procedures formally specify how these activities are to be carried out. Practices consist of those "rules of thumb" and other informal ways of doing things that are used to accomplish the tasks assigned individual managers.

Accounting for conscious directed behavior

Underlying the process of evolutionary change are the forces of mutation and selection. In evolutionary biology, mutations occur randomly, and selection is a process outside the direct control of the organism. In economics, it is commonly assumed that entrepreneurs initiate change, and managers select how changes affect the firm. This raises two important issues. Do changes occur randomly? And are these changes selected by the external environment or internally by management?

If the firm is defined by a set of rules embodied in the organizational structure, then mutations arise from the creation of new rules. New rules in part arise from advances in technology that can improve the quantity and quality of information leading to changes in the way the firm organizes activities. Technological change, while not resulting from random actions by the firms that create the technology, can be viewed as being random from the perspective of the firm that purchases and utilizes the technology. The types of technologies that lead to substantive changes in organizational structure are generally purchased in the marketplace rather than developed internally. Individual firms (to a large extent) do not engineer technology products for use within the context of their own organizations, but rather for sale in the marketplace.

The majority of firms gain access to new technologies through purchases in the marketplace. From the perspective of the firm acquiring new technology, these innovations occur outside their control because they do not have the means to directly specify what technologies are to be produced and made readily available for sale in the marketplace.[10] Thus, while technological change is not itself the result of a random process, from the perspective of the firm that uses the technology, such change can be viewed *as if* it occurs randomly.

Even if the source of change can be attributed to some random process, what happens to conscious directed behavior in the economic model? One possible avenue for preserving a role for directed behavior is to move to the next stage of the evolutionary process. Regardless of how a particular mutation comes into existence, such a change is considered to be significant only if it becomes fixed in the population. Therefore, how a mutation is transmitted to other members of the population is in many ways as significant as the change itself. Evolution depends not only on mutation, but also on some mechanism of inheritance whereby mutations are diffused throughout the population. Conscious directed behavior can be inserted into the evolutionary framework not as the source of change, but as the means for transmitting change.

Rather than viewing conscious behavior as directing substantial changes in the firm (through the creation of mutations), such behavior can be visualized as part of the process that ensures that those mutations best adapted for a particular environment survive. Survival depends on reproductive success, where such success depends on perpetuating the rules comprising the organizational structure (not whether the firm maximizes profits). Reproduction can be viewed as the outcome of some form of "mating" activity in which firms choose potential partners in order to take advantage of new opportunities.

If firms are identified by their organizational structures rather than the products they produce, then the creation of a new firm can be conceptualized as the outcome of two "firms" that join to create a new organizational entity. One firm (entrepreneur) identifies a new opportunity for generating revenues as the result of producing a new product, improving the production of an existing product, or creating a new structure that facilitates production activity. To realize this opportunity, the firm must locate a source of capital. Capital makes it possible to build the new plant, acquire the required technology, or create the new organization that makes it possible to realize the opportunity. In providing capital, the other firm (entrepreneur) is able to acquire some of the gains realized from the opportunity. The result is the merger of two existing firms or the creation of a new firm. Thus, for example, if the opportunity is discovered by an entrepreneur and the source of capital is a bank, the outcome is the creation of a new firm. If, however, one firm chooses to use its capital to acquire an opportunity by purchasing an existing firm, the outcome is a new firm that represents the merger of the two existing firms.

The creation of new firms (as defined by their organizational structures) can be viewed as the outcome of a selection process in which firms (entrepreneurs) select other firms based on the shared needs required to realize a new opportunity. The perceived desirability of a potential partner results from either the availability of capital or the desire to gain access to another firm's technology, products, or market. Just as some organisms choose their mates on the basis of physical or behavioral characteristics, firms select other firms on the basis of the desirability of their organizational structures. Firms are judged as being desirable not necessarily because they are able to maximize profits, but rather because of particular organizational characteristics that other firms find to be "attractive."

The selection of potential partners leading to the creation of new firms provides for directed change without imposing Lamarckism on the evolutionary process. Firms (entrepreneurs) select potential partners rather than desired characteristics for the new generation of firms. Thus, the evolutionary process is not the result of conscious directed behavior leading to the acquisition of characteristics that are then passed on to the next generation of firms; rather, it is subject to direction insofar as the process of "sexual selection" is based on mutual needs and not random behavior.

The nature of competition

Difficulties in terms of assigning a similar role to competition in both biology and economics exist because firms (organisms) are equated with the products that are produced, and industries (species) are subsequently defined in terms of products. Firms often produce a variety of products, compete in a number of industries, and in the case of existing firms, enter new industries by adding on to existing product lines. For the development of a theory of the firm (rather than a theory of markets), these problems suggest a need to create a new taxonomy that explicitly recognizes that firms exist as institutional structures defined not exclusively in terms of the products they produce.

One possible solution would be to classify organisms and firms in terms of a food chain. At the most general level, organisms are classified in terms of the type of food they eat (i.e., whether they are carnivores or herbivores). Animals eat food in order to acquire nutrients necessary for preserving and promoting life. Those animals that are more complex and thus able to digest a wide variety of foods will tend to be larger and, with such an advantage, will prey on smaller animals. The food chain is therefore organized in terms of the size of the organism, where larger (more complex) organisms prey on smaller organisms.

With respect to the firm, food can be thought of as products; and at the most general level, firms can be classified in terms of the broad categories of service-based or manufacturing. Firms (organisms) sell (eat) products (food) in order to acquire profits (nutrients). Firms that sell a greater number of products will possess more complex structures and will tend to be more formidable competitors because of greater experience in terms of managing the complexity of producing a wide range of products, access to a larger number of revenue streams, or a greater access to capital markets. With such an enhanced position, more complex firms will prey on less complex firms.

The benefit of biological analogies

While the modifications that have to be made in economics to establish a close correspondence with evolutionary biology may appear to some as if a round peg is being placed in a square hole, such modifications may for others provide sufficient grounds for returning to the question of what biology has to offer economics. Having handily dismissed eight potential reasons for incorporating biological analogies into the corpus of economics, it now seems appropriate to ask whether any other potential reasons exist. The answer to such a query leads to the addition of two possible reasons for appealing to biology. By providing a possible taxonomy for describing economic agents and events, a biological approach may enhance the ability to explain actual events, thereby offering one possible justification for its use. However, even if biology may not enhance the explanatory power of economics, both evolutionary biology and economics rely on synthetic constructs to present their ideas. While the goals of these syntheses may be different, synthetic theories by their very nature share common materials and methods in terms of their construction. Thus issues surrounding the synthetic theory dominating evolutionary biology may provide insights that will lead to improvements in the synthetic theory that prevails in economics.

Description

In his critique of the use of biological analogies for the development of economic theory, Rosenberg (Chapter 15, this volume) points to the inability of biology to improve the predictive power of economics. If economics is to be judged in terms of its ability to predict, then, according to Rosenberg, biology provides a poor foundation. This poor foundation is in part the result of inherent weaknesses found in evolutionary biology, but is also seen by Rosenberg as resulting from an inability to generalize evolutionary phenomena.

The specific nature of evolutionary phenomena, however, is precisely the reason why some economists have found biological analogies appealing. Alfred Marshall, for example, believed that "the study of theory must go hand in hand with that of facts: and for dealing with most modern problems it is modern facts that are of the greatest use" (1920, 39). Thus, for Marshall, description is as (if not more) important than prediction. To best understand and describe existing circumstances, Marshall contended, "Darwin's development of the laws of struggle and survival gave perhaps a greater impetus to the careful and exact study of particular facts than any other event that has occurred" (1897, 298).

As Alchian (1950) points out, the creation of a theory that is based on actual outcomes rather than hypothesized optimal results does not preclude prediction. It merely establishes the position that prediction is the result of generalized events predicated on factual events. Prediction depends on fictionalized constructs such as the representative firm, but the representative firm must itself be tied to some basis in reality. In this sense, Alchian is using, as he proclaims, "a Marshallian type of analysis combined with the essentials of Darwinian evolutionary natural selection" (1950, 213 n.7).

The issue is not the predictive power of a biological economics, but rather that the generalized constructs forming the basis for prediction are themselves firmly grounded in actual events. It is in the description of these events that biology plays an important role, attempting to prevent economic theory from becoming an intellectual exercise that bears only a passing resemblance to the events that it is trying to explain.

Expansion

By suggesting alternative foundations, a biological approach may also provide the mechanism for influencing the expansion of the core of economic theory. One of the current controversies (summarized in

Ayala 1983) in the theory of evolution is the relationship between micro- and macroevolution. Evolution at the species and higher levels (macroevolution) is thought by a number of paleontologists to be autonomous from microevolution (at the level of the gene or individual organism). The question is whether microevolutionary processes can fully explain the tempo and pattern of change at the macro level, where change may be "punctuated" rather than gradual.[11] This controversy bears a striking resemblance to the ongoing question raised in economics as to whether macroeconomic phenomena can be reduced to microfoundations.

With respect to issues raised by the theory of the firm, the question is whether firms are defined in terms of or independent of their products. If firms and products are not synonymous, then the evolutionary processes governing changes in the firm may not be the same as those processes determining how products evolve. In this sense, product evolution based on punctuated changes can be viewed as being independent from a conception of the firm that follows a path of slow gradual change.

Rather than ignoring distinctions between firms and products, or making the assumption that evolutionary process must be uniform, the hierarchical approach of Eldredge (1985) may provide one possible solution that allows for differences within a single coherent framework. Eldredge explains:

> Genes, organisms, demes, species, and monophyletic taxa form one nested hierarchical system of individuals that is concerned with the development, retention, and modification of information ensconced, at base, in the genome. But there is at the same time a parallel hierarchy of nested ecological individuals – proteins, organisms, populations, communities, and regional biotal systems, that reflects the economic organization and integration of living systems. The processes within each of these two process hierarchies, plus the interactions between the two hierarchies, seems to me to produce the events and patterns that we call evolution. (1985, 7)

By conceiving of two parallel hierarchies – one that focuses on the transmission of information, while the other concentrates on economic organization and integration – Eldredge is able to account for both types of phenomena within a single framework. Evolution is seen as the outcome of changes within each hierarchy and the interactions between the hierarchies. While the notion of evolutionary hierarchies may potentially lead to a rethinking of the neo-Darwinian synthesis, the concept also has potential value in the creation of a broader evolutionary economics.

The view of the firm as a repository, creator, and processor of information, is similar in nature and function to Eldredge's first hierarchy captured by the genome. Within such a context, creating a product becomes the outcome of a series of implicit and explicit contractual relationships. The focus, however, is not on the product itself, but rather on the relationships required to make production possible. Products, in contrast, are the outcome of activities undertaken within the confines of the firm and are subject to the economic forces of the marketplace. The type of economizing that takes place with respect to products revolves around the relationships between firms within the context of the market in a manner that is more compatible with Eldredge's second hierarchy.[12]

Economics stands to gain two benefits with the adoption of a similar hierarchical approach. For the theory of the firm, the firm itself could potentially once and for all be liberated from the traditional view that equates firms with products. Taking such an approach can pave the way for recognizing that institutional innovation (Matthews 1986; Niman 1991b) leading to evolutionary change in the firm can itself promote product and process innovation, thereby promoting evolutionary change in the economy as a whole. But perhaps more important a parallel hierarchies approach would not force the creation of uniform explanations for evolutionary change. In other words, consistency would not be sacrificed if firms and products did not share the same pattern or tempo of change. Furthermore, rather than viewing product evolution or firm evolution as either the same or as distinct entities, a parallel hierarchies approach might stimulate a new research area based on the interaction between firms and products, one that might lead to the development of a broader theory of evolutionary change.

Conclusion

It remains to be seen whether a product-based economics will eventually be replaced by an economics built on foundations provided by a theory of the firm. However, despite the outcome, evolutionary biology can provide useful insights toward the development of a meaningful theory of the firm. Using concepts borrowed from evolutionary biology may be of value by imposing a structure on the thought process that forces distinctions to be drawn that would otherwise go unrecognized because they are not required by a theory of price. The true significance may be not in terms of providing stronger foundations for the current theory of price, but rather in providing the basis for establishing a broader context leading to substantial changes in how the theory of value is formulated. Such a shift may have the result of transforming economics from a discipline in which fictional generalized constructs are created in order to predict, to one in which prediction is an outcome resulting from the creation of generalized constructs built upon a foundation grounded on fact. With such a change, economics may finally find itself in need of a meaningful theory of the firm.

Notes

1. This is, of course, dependent on being able to identify exactly what constitutes a good fit.
2. This difficulty of responding to the challenge can be identified in the following statements by Penrose (1952): "Clearly the one thing a firm does not have in common with biological organisms is a genetic constitution, and yet this is the one factor that determines the life cycle of biological organisms" (808). "The characteristic use of biological analogies in economics is to suggest explanations of events that do not depend upon the conscious willed decisions of human beings" (808). "The explanation of competition in nature is found in the rate of entry. The 'excessive entry' is due to the nature of biological reproduction. But how shall we explain competition in economic affairs where there is no biological reproduction?" (812)
3. For Alchian (1950), "The essential point is that individual motivation and foresight, while sufficient, are not necessary. . . . All that is needed by economists is their own awareness of the survival conditions and criteria of the economic system and a group of participants who submit various combinations and organizations for the system's selection and adoption." Thus, firms are selected by the environment based on how they perform relative to other firms (where success may emerge more as a result of chance than conscious effort).
4. Because many of the recent developments in the theory of the firm begin with the premise that firms are unable to act "as if" they were able to maximize profits, the neoclassical position appears to stand alone, particularly with respect to its appeals to biology in order to justify a position that buttresses the theory of value, but is of little value in the development of a theory of the firm.
5. E.O. Wilson (1975) has commented: "The hypothalamic-limbric complex of a highly social species, such as man, 'knows,' or more precisely it has been programmed to perform as if its responses bring into play an efficient mixture of personal survival, reproduction, and altruism. . . . Love joins hate; aggression, fear; expansiveness, withdrawal; and so on; in blends designed not to promote the happiness and survival of the individual, but to favor the maximum transmission of the controlling genes" (4).

6. In the introduction to his book, Kimura (1983) describes the neutral theory of evolution in the following manner: "The neutral theory asserts that the great majority of evolutionary changes at the molecular level, as revealed by comparative studies of protein and DNA sequences, are caused not by Darwinian selection but by random drift of selectively neutral or nearly neutral mutants. The theory does not deny the role of natural selection in determining the course of adaptive evolution, but it assumes that only a minute fraction of DNA changes in evolution are adaptive in nature, while the great majority of phenotypically silent molecular substitutions exert no significant influence on survival and reproduction and drift randomly through the species" (xi).

7. If these assets are transaction specific, then Williamson's (1985) concept of asset specificity could be incorporated to explain not only why the firm exists, but also why variation exists in the population of firms. Within such a context, point mutations could be used to explain why variations persist over time.

8. This is not to say that the neutral theory based on random drift has supplanted selection as the dominant explanation for evolutionary change. As Stebbins and Ayala (1981) note, "During the last decade no other issue has been more actively debated among evolutionists than the role of random drift" (967). However, even if a larger role can be attributed to random drift, it is not clear that this obviates the synthetic theory. "The 'selectionist' and 'neutrist' views of molecular evolution are competing hypotheses within the framework of the synthetic theory of evolution" (967).

9. The influence of Malthus and concepts such as the division of labor prevalent in classical political economy on the development of Darwin's ideas are discussed in Schweber (1980).

10. It is true that, over time, firms will influence what technologies are developed because only those technologies that can be sold at a profit will be produced and developed. However, if we make the provisional assumption that the market for technology is perfectly competitive, then we can assume that production decisions on the part of technology firms are reached independently of the purchasing decisions by consumers.

11. The notion of punctuated equilibrium is an attempt to explain rapid discontinuous changes in the fossil record. Parallels to the ideas of gradual and punctuated change present in evolutionary biology have been found to exist by Ankar (1986), in the gradual evolutionary theory of Marshall, and the seemingly "punctuated" evolutionary theory of Schumpeter.

12. What is perhaps interesting to note is that with a central focus on the product rather than the firm, the development of an evolutionary economics (Nelson and Winter 1982; Dosi et al. 1988) has taken place primarily on what we have been calling the economic level, while concentration on the gene and the individual organism found in the neo-Darwinian synthesis has promoted the development of an evolutionary biology primarily at the information level.

382   Neil B. Niman

References

Alchian, A. 1950. "Uncertainty, Evolution, and Economic Theory." *Journal of Political Economy* 53: 211–21.

Alchian, A. 1952. "Biological Analogies in the Theory of the Firm: Comment." *American Economic Review* 32:600–603.

Alchian, A., and H. Demsetz. 1972. "Production, Information Costs, and Economic Organization." *American Economic Review* 62:777–95.

Ankar, A. 1986. "Marshallian and Schumpeterian Theories of Economic Evolution: Gradualism Versus Punctualism." *Atlantic Economic Journal* 14:37–49.

Ayala, F., ed. 1976. *Molecular Evolution*. Sinauer: Sunderland.

Ayala, F. 1983. "Microevolution and Macroevolution," in D. Bendall, ed., *Evolution from Molecules to Men*, Cambridge University Press.

Becker, G. 1976. "Altruism, Egoism, and Genetic Fitness." *Journal of Economic Literature* 14:817–26.

Calvo, G., and S. Wellisz. 1978. "Supervision, Loss of Control, and the Optimal Size of the Firm." *Journal of Political Economy* 86:943–52.

Coase, R. 1937. "The Nature of the Firm." *Economica* 4:386–405.

Dawkins, R. 1986. *The Blind Watchmaker*. New York: Norton.

Dawkins, R. 1989. *The Selfish Gene*, new ed. Oxford University Press.

Dosi, G., C. Freeman, R. Nelson, G. Silverberg, and L. Soete, eds. 1988. *Technical Change and Economic Theory*. London: Pinter.

Eldredge, N. 1985. *Unfinished Synthesis*. New York: Oxford University Press.

Eldredge, N., and S. Gould. 1972. "Punctuated Equilibria: An Alternative to Phyletic Gradualism," in T. Schopf, ed., *Models in Paleobiology*, 82–115. San Francisco: Freeman, Cooper.

Friedman, M. 1953. *Essays in Positive Economics*. Chicago: University of Chicago Press.

Hannan, M., and D. Freeman. 1989. *Organizational Ecology*. Cambridge, MA: Harvard University Press.

Hicks, J. 1946. *Value and Capital*, 2d ed. Oxford University Press.

Hirshleifer, J. 1977. "Economics from a Biological Viewpoint." *Journal of Law and Economics* 20:1–52.

Hirshleifer, J. 1985. "The Expanding Domain of Economics." *American Economics Review* 75(6):53–68.

Holmstrom, B., and J. Tirole. 1989. "The Theory of the Firm," in R. Schmalensee and R. D. Willig, eds., *Handbook of Industrial Organization*, 1:61–133. Amsterdam: North-Holland.

Kimura, M. 1983. *The Neutral Theory of Molecular Evolution*. Cambridge University Press.

Lewontin, R. 1983. "Gene, Organism, and Environment," in D. Bendall, ed., *Evolution from Molecules to Men*, 273–86. Cambridge University Press.

Machlup, F. 1967. "Theories of the Firm: Marginalist, Behavioral, Managerial." *American Economic Review* 57:1–33.

Marschak, J., and R. Radner. 1972. *The Economic Theory of Teams.* New Haven, CT: Yale University Press.

Marshall, A. 1897. "The Old Generation of Economists and the New." Reprinted in A. C. Pigou, ed., *Memorials of Alfred Marshall.* New York: Kelley, 1966.

Marshall, A. 1920. *Principles of Economics,* 8th ed. London: Macmillan.

Matthews, R. C. O. 1986. "The Economics of Institutions and the Sources of Growth." *Economic Journal* 96:903–18.

Mirowski, P. 1989. *More Heat Than Light: Economics as Social Physics, Physics as Nature's Economics.* Cambridge University Press.

Nelson, R., and S. Winter 1982. *An Evolutionary Theory of Economic Change.* Cambridge: MA: Harvard University Press.

Niman, N. 1991a. "Biological Analogies in Marshall's Work." *Journal of the History of Economic Thought* 13:19–36.

Niman, N. 1991b. "The Entrepreneurial Function in the Theory of the Firm." *Scottish Journal of Political Economy* 38:162–76.

Penrose, E. 1952. "Biological Analogies in the Theory of the Firm." *American Economic Review* 42:804–919.

Penrose, E. 1959. *The Theory of the Growth of the Firm.* New York: Wiley.

Sahlins, M. 1976. *The Use and Abuse of Biology.* Ann Arbor: University of Michigan Press.

Samuelson, P. 1947. *Foundations of Economic Analysis.* Cambridge, MA: Harvard University Press.

Sappington, D. 1991. "Incentives in Principle–Agent Relationships." *Journal of Economic Perspectives* 5:45–66.

Schweber, S. 1980. "Darwin and the Political Economists: Divergence of Character." *Journal of the History of Biology* 13:199–289.

Shove, G. 1942. "The Place of Marshall's Principles in the Development of Economic Theory." *Economic Journal* 52:294–329.

Simon, H. 1957. *Models of Man.* New York: Wiley.

Simon, H. 1972. "Theories of Bounded Rationality." In C. McGuire and R. Radner, eds., *Decision and Organization,* 161–76. New York: Elsevier.

Stebbins, G., and F. Ayala. 1981. "Is a New Evolutionary Synthesis Necessary?" *Science* 213:967–71.

Stiglitz, J. 1991. "Symposium on Organizations and Economics." *Journal of Economic Perspectives* 5:15–24.

Williamson, O. 1975. *Markets and Hierarchies.* New York: Free Press.

Williamson, O. 1985. *The Economic Institutions of Capitalism.* New York: Free Press.

Wilson, E. O. 1975. *Sociobiology.* Cambridge, MA: Harvard University Press.

Winter, S. 1964. "Economic Natural Selection and the Theory of the Firm." *Yale Economic Essays* 4:225–72.

Winter, S. 1971. "Satisficing, Selection, and the Innovating Remnant." *Quarterly Journal of Economics* 85:237–61.

CHAPTER 15

Does evolutionary theory give comfort or inspiration to economics?

ALEXANDER ROSENBERG

To some economists, evolutionary theory looks like a tempting cure for what ails their subject. To others, it looks like part of a powerful defense of the status quo in economic theory. I think that Darwinian theory is a remarkably inappropriate model, metaphor, inspiration, or theoretical framework for economic theory. The theory of natural selection shares few of its strengths and most of its weaknesses with neoclassical theory, and provides no help in any attempt to frame more powerful alternatives to that theory. In this chapter, I explain why this is so.

I begin with a sketch of the theory of natural selection, some of its strengths and some of its weaknesses. Then I consider how the theory might be supposed to play a role in the improvement of our understanding of economic processes. I conclude with a brief illustration of the problems of instantiating a theory from one domain in another quite different one, employing the most extensive of attempts to develop an evolutionary theory in economics. My pessimistic conclusions reflect a concern shared with economists who have sought comfort or inspiration from biological theory. The concern is to vindicate received theory or to underwrite new theory against a reasonable standard of predictive success. Few of these economists have noticed what the opponents of such a standard for economic theory have seen, that evolutionary theory is itself bereft of strong predictive power (see McCloskey 1985, 15).

Two things to note and set aside at the outset are the historical influence that economic science has had over evolutionary theory from before Darwin to the present day, and the profit that biologists have taken in recent years from developments in economic theory. The influence of Adam Smith and Thomas Malthus on Darwin are well documented. Indeed, they are so well established that more than

384

one opponent of evolutionary theory has attempted to tar it with the brush of laissez-faire capitalism (see Rifkin 1984). (This was, of course, before the fall of the socialist economies of the East.) Darwin himself relates the influence of Malthus on his notion of the survival of the fittest. In recent years, biologists have exploited some significant mathematical results relating to conditions of stability for general equilibria and have adapted insights from game theory to identify evolutionarily stable strategies in animal behavior. Everything I shall say hereafter is perfectly compatible with economic thought having a significant impact on the improvement of biological theory. It is just that the terms of trade are always in the direction from economics to biology and not vice versa. Why is that?

To answer, we need first a brief introduction to the theory of natural selection. This should not be difficult. The theory is breathtaking in its simplicity. It is so easy to understand that Darwin certainly need not have traveled for five years around Latin American to have hit upon it; an hour on the Sussex Downs would have sufficed. Indeed, when Thomas Huxley, one of the theory's most vigorous early exponents, first heard its details, he complained, "How stupid of me not to have thought of it."

Natural selection

Darwin began with some observations. The first is the Malthusian point that organisms reproduce geometrically, and yet the population of most species remains constant over time. From this it follows that there is a struggle for survival, both within species and between members of differing species. Darwin's second observation was that species are characterized by variation among the properties of their members. Darwin inferred that the survivors in this struggle are those variants most fitted to their environments – most able to defend themselves against predators, find shelter against the elements, provide themselves with food, and therefore most able to reproduce in higher numbers. If these traits are hereditary, then they will be represented in higher proportions in each generation until they become unbiquitous throughout the species. This will be especially true for hereditary traits that enhance an organism's ability to procure mates and otherwise ensure the reproduction of fertile offspring. It is crucial to Darwin's theory that variation is large and blind – in any generation there will be differences on which selection can operate, and these differences are not elicited by environmental needs, but are randomly generated. Darwin knew nothing of genetics, and his theory requires only that there be variation and heredity. Modern genetic theory provides for both of these requisites of Darwin's theory. For this reason, genetics is often treated as part of evolutionary theory. Selection, for Darwin, is a misleading metaphor, for his theory deprives nature of any purpose, teleology, design, or intentions of the sort the notion of selection suggests. Nature selects only in the sense that the match or mismatch between the environment and the fortuitously generated variants determine survival and thus reproduction.

So much for the bare bones of the theory. Now some of the details. Darwin knew little about the sources of variation. We know more. Some variation is produced by mutations, but not enough to account for the diversity and the adaptations we actually observe. Most variation, especially among sexually reproducing organisms, is the result of the shuffling of genes through interbreeding across the species. The interaction of different genes with one another and with various features of an environment produces a range of phenotypes that are selected for in accordance with their strictly fortuitous contributions to or withdrawals from survival and reproduction.

However, a single new variant (produced by recombination or mutation), no matter how adaptive, is likely to be swamped in its effects if it appears in a large population. One long-necked giraffe in a million is just not going to make a difference. To begin with, though it can reach food that other animals cannot, it just might be hit by lightning and die before breeding. For another, when the one gene for long necks combines with any of the million or so genes for short necks, the result may just be short necks. For the long-neck genes to make a difference, the number of giraffes with which its bearer breeds must be small, so that copies of the gene in subsequent generations have a chance to combine with one another and produce more long necks. Thus, the structure of the evolving population is important for the occurrence of adaptive evolution: It should be small and make for a certain amount of interbreeding. But if it is too small, a well-adapted population could be wiped out by random forces before it has a chance to expand its numbers.

In addition, for adaptive evolution the environment must remain relatively constant over long periods of time. The environment presents organisms with survival problems. But it takes a generation for the best solutions to these problems to make a difference for the species, for it is only in the relative proportions of the offspring that the best solutions to an adaptational problem have their evolutionary effects. So if an environment changes at rates faster than the generation time of a species, that species will never show any pattern of adaptation. Among animals this is not a serious problem. Most environmental problems – heat, cold, gravity, lack of food in winter, and so on – have been with us for literally geological epochs. And even the generation time of the tortoise – a hundred and fifty years or so – is nothing compared with such epochs. So there has been time and enough stability for a lot of evolution. Nevertheless, critics of Darwinian theory complain that though there has been enough time for the evolution of species, there seems little evidence of transitional forms of the sort we should expect. Indeed, it is an old saw among paleontologists that the fossil record shows mainly that evolution took place elsewhere. Another important thing to note is that in rapidly changing environments, survival puts a premium on generalists who are moderately well adapted to a number of environments over specialists very well adapted to just one sort of environment.

In selecting variants for differential survival, nature works with what variation presents itself and shapes available properties. Thus, it has the appearance of seeking the quick and dirty solution to an adaptive problem, not the optimally adaptive one. Because an organism can make no contribution to evolution unless it survives, nature will work with what is presented to it and will encourage early approximate solutions over late but elegant and exact ones. By the time an elegant solution is available, the lineage may be extinct.

Two other important features of Darwinian evolution are its commitment to gradualism and to individual selection. Neither Darwin nor the majority of contemporary evolutionary biologists believe that evolution has proceeded or can proceed by large changes. Rather, they view evolution as the accretion of large numbers of very small changes over long periods. It is not that great improvements in adaptation over small numbers of generations are impossible. Rather, the evidence such as Darwin understood it – and the genetic mechanism of heredity such as modern geneticists understand it – make such evolutionary jumps highly improbable. Similarly, Darwin shares with modern biologists a conviction that the locus of selection is the individual organism, not larger groups in which individuals participate. If groups of various kinds evolve, then it will be because of the adaptational advantages they accord to individuals who maximize fitness. Groups that disadvantage some of their individual members to increase average fitness, for example, are vulnerable to free riders, who take advantage of benefits groups provide their members while failing to contribute to the provision. These free riders will prosper at the expense of contributors until they have completely displaced them. For groups without enforcement mechanisms, individual selection will always swamp group selection. Moreover, it is hard to see how enforcement mechanisms can emerge in the first place, given individual fitness maximization.

Another feature of evolutionary theory is well worth understanding: its relatively weak powers of prediction. About the only place where there is very strong predictive evidence for natural selection is in laboratory experiments and in what animal and plant breeders call artificial selection. In the lab and on the farm, we can control environmental conditions (reproductive opportunities) stringently enough so that only a narrow class of animals or plants survive and reproduce. The result is relatively rapid changes in the proportions of properties adaptive to our interests as breeders. However, not only have we not produced anything that all will agree constitutes a new species, but, as noted, the fossil record does not help either. Evolutionary biology has no striking retrodiction to its credit, and such predictions as it might make are either very generic or likely to be no more reliable than the initial or boundary conditions to which the theory is applied.

In fact, for much of the century the theory of natural selection has often been stigmatized as completely lacking in evidential bearing, as being an unfalsifiable trivial tautology. The charge is well understood. The theory asserts that the fittest survive and reproduce differentially. But the only applicable uniform quantitative measure of fitness is reproductive rates. Accordingly, the formula becomes those with the highest reproductive rates have the highest reproductive rates. It is therefore no wonder that no evidence can be found that contradicts the theory, nor can we expect to find evidence that strikingly confirms it either. It is no good defending evolutionary theory by rejecting the demand the theory be falsifiable. To do so is just to blame the messenger; for even if strict falsifiability is too stern a test for a scientific theory, it is still a serious weakness of any theory if we cannot identify its causal variables independently of the effects they bring about. And this is indeed the problem for evolutionary theory. A better response to this complaint against the theory is to admit that in general we cannot enumerate what fitness consists in – there are too many determinants of evolutionary fitness to be mentioned in a theory – or whether and how much a property conduces to fitness depends on the environment. And the only thing all determinants of fitness differences have in common is their *effect* on rates of reproduction. So it is natural to measure fitness differences in terms of their common effects. Once we are clear on the difference between fitness and what we use to measure it, the claim that the fittest survive and reproduce in higher numbers is no more vacuous than the claim that increases in heat make thermometers rise.[1]

There are many ways in which organisms can adapt in response to a given environmental constraint. An ice age presents survival problems that can be solved by growing fur, adding layers of fat, changing shape to minimize surface area, migration or hibernation, and so on. And there are many ways in which an environment can change: temperature, humidity, wind, pressure, flora, fauna, CO_2 concentration, and the like. Multiplying the environmental changes times the number of different adaptational responses to each change makes it clear that interesting generalizations about adaptation are not to be found in the expression of the theory itself. In fact, because of this the theory has pretty much taken the form of stochastic models of changes in gene frequencies. By making certain assumptions about the independence of genes (and therefore observable traits of organisms – phenotypes) from one another and adding assumptions about differences in fitness, size of interbreeding population, and the like, the biologist can derive conclusions about the change in gene frequencies over time. The question then becomes whether there are biological phenomena that realize the assumptions of the model well enough so that its consequences can guide our expectations about the phenomena. Instead of seeking general laws about the way in which environmental changes result in adaptations, evolutionary biologists consider which models of changes in gene frequencies most clearly illuminate processes of interest and whether the most illuminating models have interesting features in common. By and large, the number of such predictively powerful models has not been great, and they have had relatively few distinctive features in common. This should be no surprise, for if the models were very successful and had a good deal of structure and a large proportion of assumptions in common, then the most obvious explanation of these facts would be the truth of a simple and powerful theory that unified them all and explained why they worked so well. Such a theory would in fact replace the theory of natural selection whose weakness and lack of predictive content leads biologists to seek models of restricted phenomena instead of general laws.

Economists and evolution

Why should anyone suppose that Darwinian evolutionary theory will provide a useful model for how to proceed in economics? One apparently attractive feature of the theory for economists is the methodological defense it seems to provide neoclassical theory in the face of charges that the theory fails to account for the actual behavior of consumers and producers. Thus, Friedman offers the following argument for the hypothesis that economic agents maximize money returns:

> Let the apparent immediate determinant of business behavior be anything at all, habitual reaction, random chance, or whatnot. Whenever this determinant happens to lead to behavior consistent with rational and informed maximization of returns, the business will prosper, and acquire resources with which to expand; whenever it does not, the business will tend to loose resources and can be kept in existence only by the addition of resources from outside. The process of "natural selection" thus helps to validate the hypothesis or, rather, given natural selection, acceptance of the hypothesis can be based on the judgement that it summarizes appropriately the conditions for survival. (1953, 35)

This argument does reflect a feature of evolutionary theorizing, though admittedly a controversial one. The natural environment sets adaptational problems that animals must solve to survive. The fact that a particular species is not extinct is good evidence that it has solved some of the problems imposed upon it. This fact about adaptational problems and their solutions plays two roles in evolutionary thinking. First, examining the environment, biologists might try to identify the adaptational problems that organisms face. Second, focusing on the organism, biologists sometimes attempt to identify possible problems that known features of the organism might be solutions to. The problem with this approach is the temptation of Panglossianism: imagining a problem to be solved for every feature of an organism we detect. Thus, Dr. Pangloss held that the bridge of the nose was a solution to the adaptational problem of holding up glasses. The problem with inferences from the environment to adaptational problems is that we need to determine all or most of the problems to be solved, for each of them is an important constraint on what will count as solutions to others. Thus, having a dark color will not be a solution to the problem of hiding from nocturnal predators unless the organism can deal with the heat that such color will absorb during the day. However, a color that will effect the optimal compromise between these two constraints may fail a third one, say being detectable by conspecifics during mating season.

Then there is the problem of there being more than one way to skin a cat. Even if we can identify an adaptational problem and most of the constraints against which a solution can be found, it is unlikely that we will be able to narrow the range of equally adaptive solutions down to just the one that animals actually evince. Thus, we are left with the explanatory question of why this way of skinning the adaptational cat emerges and not another one apparently equally as good. There are two answers to this question. One is to say that if we knew all the constraints, we would see that the only possible solution is the actual one. The other is to say that there are more than one equally adequate solutions and that the one finally "chosen" appeared for nonevolutionary causes. The first of these two replies is simply a pious hope that more inquiry will vindicate the theory. The second is in effect to limit evolutionary theory's explanatory power and deny it predictive power.

These problems have in general hobbled "optimality" analysis as an explanatory strategy in evolutionary biology. Many biologists find the temptations of Panglossianism combined with the daunting multiplicity of constraints on solutions to be so great that they despair of providing an evolutionary theory that contributes to our detailed understanding of organisms in their environments.

The same problems bedevil Friedman's conception and limit the force of his conclusion. The idea that rational informed maximization of returns sets a necessary and/or sufficient condition for long-term survival in every possible economic environment, or even in any actual one, is either false or vacuous. Is the hypothesis that returns are maximized over the short run, the long run, the fiscal year, or the quarter? If we make the hypothesis specific enough to test, it is plainly false. Leave it vague and the hypothesis is hard to test. Suppose we equate the maximization of returns hypothesis with the survival of the fittest hypothesis. Then nothing in particular follows about what economic agents do and how large their returns are, any more than it follows what particular organisms do and how many offspring they have. However many the offspring and however much the returns, the results will be maximal, given the circumstances, over the long run. What we want to know is which features of organisms increase their fitness, and which strategies of economic agents increase their returns. And we want this information both to explain particular events in the past and to predict the course of future evolution. For the hypothesis of maximization of returns to play this substantive role, it cannot be supposed to be on a par with the maximization of fitness hypothesis. Rather, we need to treat it as a specific optimal response to a particular environmental problem, rather like we might treat coat color as an optimal response to an environmental problem of finding a color that protects against predators, does not absorb too much heat, is visible to conspecifics, and the like. But when we think of the maximization of returns hypothesis this way, it is clear that maximizing dollar returns is not a condition of survival in general, either in the long or the short run.

As already noted, nature has a preference for quick and dirty solutions to environmental problems. It seems to satisfice, in Simon's phrase. But unlike satisficing, nature's strategy really is a maximizing one. It is just that the constraints are so complicated and so unknown to us that the solutions favored by selection look quick and dirty to us. If we knew the constraints, we would see that they are elegant and just on time. Learning what the constraints are and how the problems are solved is where the action is in vindicating the theory of natural selection, because only this will enable us to tell whether the solution really maximizes fitness, as measured by offspring. Similarly, in economics the action is in learning the constraints and seeing what solutions are chosen. Only this will tell us whether dollar returns are really maximized and whether maximizing dollar returns ensure survival. To stop where Friedman does is to condemn the theory he sets out to vindicate to the vacuity with which Darwinian theory is often charged.

If the theory of natural selection is to vindicate economic theory or illuminate economic processes, it will have to do more than just provide a Panglossian assurance that whatever survives in the long run is fittest. What is needed in any attempt to accomplish this is a better understanding of the theory of natural selection. Such an improved understanding of the theory is evident in Alchian's (1950) approach to modeling economic processes as evolutionary ones.[2]

Alchian's approach is not open to obvious Panglossian objections, nor does it make claims about empirical content that transcend the power of an evolutionary theory to deliver. Still, its problems reveal more deeply the difficulties of taking an evolutionary approach to economic behavior.

To begin with, Alchian's approach reflects the recognition that Darwinian theory's claims about individual responses to the environment are hard to establish, impossible to generalize, and therefore without predictive value for other organisms in other environments. Alchian recognized that the really useful versions of evolutionary theory are those that focus on populations large enough that statistical regularities in responses to environmental changes can be discerned. And he recognized that Darwinian evolution operates through solutions to adaptational problems that are, in appearances at any rate, quick and dirty, approximate and heuristic, and not rationally and informationally maximizing. Like the biological environment, the economic one need not elicit anything like the maximization of returns that conventional theory requires:

> In an economic system the realization of profits is the criterion according to which successful and surviving firms are selected. This decision criterion is applied by an impersonal market system . . . and may be completely independent of the decision processes of individual units, of the variety of inconsistent motives and abilities and even of the individual's awareness of the criterion.
>
> The pertinent requirement – positive profits through relative efficiency – is weaker than "maximized profits," with which unfortunately, it has been confused. Positive profits accrue to those who are better than their actual competitors, not some hypotheticallly perfect competitors. As in a race, the award goes to the relatively fastest, even if all competitors loaf.
>
> . . . success (survival) accompanies relative superiority; . . . it may . . . be the result of fortuitous circumstances. Among all competitors those whose particular conditions happen to be the most appropriate of those offered to the economic system for testing and adoption will be "selected" as survivors. (213–14)

Alchian also recognizes that adaptation is not immediate and is discernible to the observer only in the change in statistical distributions over periods of time, and recognizes that what counts as adaptive will change as the economic environment does. Alchian uses a parable to illustrate the way that the economic environment shifts the distribution of actually employed choice strategies toward the more rational:

> Assume that thousands of travellers set out from Chicago, selecting their roads completely at random and without foresight. Only our "economist" knows that on but one road there are any gas stations. He can state categorically that travellers will continue to travel only on that road: those on other roads will soon run out of gas. Even though each one selected his route at random, we might have called those travellers who were so fortunate as to have picked the right road wise, efficient, farsighted, etc. Of course we would consider them the lucky ones. If gasoline supplies were now moved to a new road, some formerly luckless travellers again would be able to move; and a new pattern of travel would be observed, although none of the players changes his particular path. The really possible paths have changed with the changing environment. All that is needed is a set of varied, risk-taking (adoptable [*sic*]) travellers. The correct direction of travel will be established. As circumstances (economic environment) change, the analyst (economist) can select the type of participants (firms) that will now become successful; he may also be able to diagnose the conditions most conducive to greater probability of survival. (214)

To ensure survival and significant shifts in the direction of adaptation, several other conditions must be satisfied: To begin with, the environment must remain constant long enough so that those strategies more well adapted to it than others will have time to outcompete the less well adapted and to increase their frequency significantly enough to be noticed. Moreover, the initial relative frequency of the most well adapted strategy must be high enough so it will not be stamped out by random forces before it has amassed a sufficient advantage to begin displacing competitors. And of course, it must be the case that there are significant differences among competing strategies. Otherwise, their proportions at the outset of competition will remain constant over time. There will be no significant changes in proportions to report.

What kind of knowledge will such an economic theory provide? Even at his most optimistic, Alchian was properly limited in his expectations. He made no claims that with an evolutionary approach the course of behavior of the individual economic agent could be predicted. Here the parallel with evolution is obvious. Darwin's theory not only has no implications for what will happen to any individual organism; its implications for large numbers of organism are at best probabilistic:

> A chance dominated model does not mean that an economist cannot predict or explain or diagnose. With a knowledge of the economy's requisites for survival and by a comparison of alternative conditions, he can state what types of firms or behavior relative to other possible types will be more viable, even though the firms themselves may not know the conditions or even try to achieve them by readjusting to the changed conditions. It is sufficient if all firms are slightly different so that in the new environmental situation those who have their fixed internal conditions closer to the new, but unknown optimum position now have a greater probability of survival and growth. They will grow relative to other firms and become the prevailing type, since survival conditions may push the observed characteristics of the set of survivors towards the unknowable [to them] optimum by either (1) repeated trials or (2) survival of more of those who happen to be near the optimum – determined ex post. If these new conditions last "very long", the dominant firms will be different ones from those which prevailed or would have prevailed under the other conditions. *Even if* the environmental conditions cannot be forecast, the economist can compare for given alternative potential situations the types of behavior that would have higher probability of viability or adoption. If explanation of past results rather than prediction is the task, the economist can diagnose the particular attributes which were critical in facilitating survival, even though individual participants were not aware of them. (216; emphasis added)

As a set of conditional claims, most of what Alchian says about the explanatory and predictive powers of an evolutionary theory of economic processes is true enough. The trouble is that almost none of the conditions obtain, either in evolutionary biology or in economic behavior, that would make either theory as useful as Alchian or any economist needs it to be. Thus, the attractions of an evolutionary theory for economists must be very limited indeed. Alchian rightly treats the economy as the environment to which individual economic agents are differentially adapted. As with the biological case, we need to know what "the requisites of survival" in the environment are. In the biological case, this is not a trivial matter; and beyond the most obvious adaptational problems, there are precious few generalizations about what any particular ecological environment requires for survival, still less what it rewards in increased reproductive opportunities. We know animals need to eat, breathe, and avoid illnesses and environmental hazards, and the more of their needs they fulfill the better off they are. But we don't know what in any given environment the optimal available diet is or what the environmental hazards are for each of the creatures that are its inhabitants. And outside of ecology and ethology, few biologists are interested in this information in any case, for its systematic value to biology is very limited. Ignorance about these requisites for survival in biology make it difficult to predict even "the types of . . . behavior relative to other possible types that will be more viable." It is easy to predict that all surviving types will have to subsist in an oxygen-rich environment where the gravitational constant is 32 feet/second^2 and the ambient temperature ranges from 45 degrees to minus 20 degrees Celsius. But such a "prediction" leaves us little closer to what we hope to learn from a prediction. The same must be true in evolutionary economics. We have no idea of what the requisites for survival are, and even if we learned them, they would probably not narrowly enough restrict the types that can survive for us to frame any very useful expectations of the future. Of course, this is not an in-principle objection to an evolutionary approach. But consider what sort of information would be required to establish a very full list of concrete, necessary conditions for survival of, say, a firm in any very specific market, and then consider the myriad ways in which economic agents could so act to satisfy those conditions. This information is either impossible to obtain or else, if we had it, an evolutionary approach to economic processes would be superfluous. To see this, go back to Alchian's discussion.

Alchian notes that over time the proportion of firms of various types should change: The proportion of those that are more fit should increase while those less fit should decrease. If environmental conditions last a long time, "the dominant firms will be different from those which prevailed . . . under other conditions." True enough, but what counts as a long time for environmental conditions? In the evolutionary context, "long enough" means at least one generation, and the duration of a generation will vary with the species. In addition the notion of long enough reflects a circularity that haunts evolutionary biology. Evolution occurs if the environment remains constant long enough for the proportion of types to change. Long enough is enough time for the proportions to change. Moreover, when the number of competing individuals is small, there may be change in proportions of types that is not adaptational, but is identified as drift – a sort of sampling error. But what is a small number of individuals versus a large number? Here, the same ambiguity emerges. Large enough means a number in which changes in proportion reflect evolutionary adaptation. The only way in which to break out of this circularity of long enough, large enough, and so on is to focus on individual populations in particular environments over several generations. And the answer we get for any one set of individuals will be of little value when we turn to another set of the same types in different environments or to different types in the same environment.

Can the situation be any better in economics? In fact, won't the situation be far less promising? After all, the environment within which an economic agent must operate does not change with the stately pace of a geological epoch. Economic environments seem to change from day to day. If they do, then there is never enough time for the type most adapted to one environment to increase in its proportions relative to other types. Before the type has had a chance to do so, the environment has changed, and another type becomes most adapted. But perhaps economic environments do not change quite so quickly. Perhaps to suppose that they do change so quickly is to mistake the weather for the climate. Day-to-day fluctuations may be a feature of a more long-standing environment. The most well adapted individual to an environment is not one who responds best to each feature of it, including its variable features, but rather one who adapts best over all on an average weighted by the frequency with which certain conditions in the environment obtain. So the period of time relevant to evolutionary adaptation might be long enough for changes in proportion to show up. For the parallel to evolution to hold up, this period of environmental constancy will have to be longer than some equivalent to the generation time in biological evolution. But is there among economic agents any such an equivalent? Is there a natural division among economic agents into generations? With firms, the generation time might be the period from incorporation to the emergence of other firms employing the same method in the same markets through conscious imitation; with individual agents, the minimal period for evolutionary adaptation will be the time during which it takes an individual to train another to behave in the same way under similar economic circumstances. But these two periods are clearly ones during which the economic environment almost always changes enough to shift the adaptational strategy.

The only way we can use an evolutionary theory to predict the direction of adaptation is by being able to identify the relevant environment that remains constant enough to force adaptational change in proportions of firms. As Alchian tacitly admits, this is something we cannot do: "Even if the environmental conditions cannot be forecast, the economist can compare for given alternative potential situations the types of behavior that would have a higher probability of viability or adoption" (217). This is a retrospective second best. Suppose economically relevant environmental conditions could be forecast. Then, it is pretty clear we would not need an evolutionary theory of economic behavior. Friedman's rationale for neoclassical theory would then come into its own. If we knew environmental conditions, then we could state what optimal adaptation to them would be. And if we could do this, so could at least some of the economic agents themselves. To the extent that they could pass on this information to their successors, Panglossianism would eventually be vindicated in economic evolutionary theory. Economic agents would conform their actions to the strategy calculated to be maximally adaptive, just as Friedman claims. An evolutionary theory of economic behavior is offered either as an alternative to rational maximizing or as an explanation of its adequacy. If rational maximizing is adequate as a theory, evolutionary rationales are superfluous; if it is not adequate, then an evolutionary approach is unlikely to be much better, and for much the same reason: Neither economic theorists nor economic agents can know enough about the economic environment for the former's predictions or the latter's decisions to be regularly vindicated.

Why economics is not Darwinian

One of the features of evolutionary theory that makes it attractive to the economist is the role of equilibrium in claims made about nature. Equilibrium is important for economic theory not least because of the predictive power it accords the economist. An economic system in equilibrium or moving toward one is a system some or all of whose future states are predictable by the economist. Equilibrium has other (welfare-theory-relevant) aspects, but its attractions for economists must in part consist in the role it plays so successfully in physical theory and evolutionary theory. Evolutionary biology defines an equilibrium such that gene ratios do not change from generation to generation, and it stipulates several conditions that must obtain for equilibrium: a large population mating at random, without immigration, emigration, or mutation, and of course, without environmental change. Departures from these conditions will cause changes in gene frequencies within a population. But over the long run, the changes will move in the direction of closer adaptation to the environment – either closer adaptation to an unchanged one or adaptation toward a new one. The parallel to economic equilibrium is so obvious that mathematical biologists have simply taken over the economist's conditions for the existence and stability of equilibria. If a unique, stable market-clearing equilibrium exists, then its individual members are optimally adapted to their environment, no trading will occur, and there will be no change – no evolution – in the economy. But if one or another of the conditions for equilibrium is violated, an efficient economic system will either move back to the original equilibrium or to a new one by means of adjustments in which individuals move along paths of increased adaptation.

In evolutionary biology, equilibrium has an important explanatory role. As far as we can see, populations remain fairly constant over time, and among populations the proportions of varying phenotypes remain constant as well. Moreover, when one or another of the conditions presupposed by equilibrium of gene frequencies is violated, the result is either compensating movement back toward the original distribution of gene frequencies or movement toward a new level of gene frequencies. These facts about the stability of gene frequencies and their trajectories need to be explained, and the equilibrium assumptions of transmission genetics are the best explanations going. In addition they will help us make *generic* predictions that when one or another condition, like the absence of mutation, is violated, a new equilibrium will be sought. Sometimes we can even predict the direction of that new equilibrium. But in real ecological contexts (as opposed to simple textbook models), we can hardly ever predict that actual value of the new equilibrium level of gene frequencies. This is because we do not know all the environmental factors that work with a change in one of these conditions, and among those factors that are known, we have only primitive means of measurement for their dimensions.

Now compare economics. To begin with, we have nothing comparable to the observed stability of gene frequencies that needs to be explained. So the principle explanatory motivation for equilibrium explanations is absent. We cannot even appeal to the stability of prices as a fact explaining equilibrium in economics because we know only too well that neoclassical general equilibrium theory has no explanation for price stability. That is, given an equilibrium distribution and a change in price, there is no proof that the economy will move to a new general equilibrium. (For this reason, general equilibrium theory has recourse to the Walrasian auctioneer and *tâtonnement*.)

There is no doubt that economic equilibrium theory has many attractive theoretical features – mathematical tractability, the two welfare theorems – but it lacks the most important feature that justifies the same kind of thinking in evolutionary biology: independent evidence that there is a stable equilibrium to be explained.

One of the factors giving us some confidence that equilibrium obtains with some frequency in nature is that changes in gene frequencies are not self-reinforcing. If some change also affects gene frequencies, then such change in gene frequencies will rarely precipitate still another round of changes in gene frequencies, and so on, thus cascading into a period of instability. Of course, sometimes evolutionary change is "frequency dependent": If one species of butterfly increases in population size because it looks like another species that birds avoid, then once it has grown larger in number than the bad-tasting butterflies, its similar appearance and the genes that code for appearance will no longer be adaptive and may decline. But presumably the proportions will return to some optimal level and be held there by the twin forces of adaptation and maladaptation.

In the game theorist's lingo, evolutionary adaptational problems are parametric: The adaptiveness of an organism's behavior does not depend on what other organisms do. But we cannot expect this absence of feedback in economic evolution. Among economic agents, the problem is strategic. Economic agents are far more salient features of one another's environment than animals are features of one another's biological environment. Changes in agents' behaviors affect their environments regularly because they call forth changes in the behavior of other agents, and these further changes cause a second round of changes in the original agents' behavior. Game theorists have come to identify this phenomenon under the rubric of the common knowledge problem. Economists traditionally circumvented this problem by two assumptions that have parallels in evolutionary biology as well. It is important to see that the parallels do not provide much ground for the rationalization of economic theorizing in the biologist's practice.

Both evolutionary equilibrium and economic general equilibrium require an infinite number of individuals. In the case of evolution, this is to prevent drift or sampling error from moving gene frequencies independent of environmental changes. In the case of the theory of pure competition, it is to prevent agent choice from becoming strategic. If the firm is always a price taker and can have no effect on the market, then it can treat its choices as parametric. Where the number of interactors is small, the assumption of price taking produces very wrong predictions, and there is indeed no stability and typically no equilibrium.

Is sauce for the biological goose sauce for the economic gander? Can both make the same false assumption with equal impunity? The fact is, though assumptions of infinite population size are false for interbreeding populations, it seems to do little harm in biology. That is, despite the strict falsity of the evolutionary assumption, populations seem to be large enough for theory that makes these false assumptions to explain the evident facts of constancy and/or stability of gene frequencies. In the case of economics, there are no such evident facts, and one apparent reason seems to be the falsity of the assumption of an infinite number of economic agents.

The other assumption evolutionary theory and economic theory traditionally make is that the genes and the agents, respectively, are "omniscient." Genes carry information in two senses. First, they carry instructions for the building and maintenance of proteins and assemblies of genes that meet the environment as phenotypes. Second, they indirectly carry information about which phenotypes are most adapted to the environment in which they find themselves. They do so through the intervention of selective forces that cull maladaptive phenotypes and thus the genes that code for phenotypic building blocks. And as long as the environment remains constant, the gene frequencies will eventually track every environmentally significant, biologically possible adaptation and maladaptation. In this sense the genome is in the long run omniscient about the environment. There are two crucial qualifications here. First there is the assumption of the constancy of the environment, something economic theory has little reason to help itself to. Second, there is the "long run" – another concept evolutionary theory shares with economic theory. Evolutionary biology has world enough and time for theories that explain and predict only in the long run – geological epochs are close enough to infinite not to matter for many purposes. But Keynes pointed out the problem for economics concerning theories that explain only the long run. An evolutionary economic theory committed to equilibrium is condemned at best to explain only the long run.

We know only too well the disequilibrating effects of nonomniscience, that is, how information obstructs the economy's arrival at or maintenance of an equilibrium. Indeed, the effects of differences in information on economic outcomes are so pervasive that we should not expect economic phenomena ever to reflect the kind of equilibrium evolutionary biological phenomena do. Arrow has succinctly summarized the impact of information on equilibrium models:

> If nothing else there are at least two salient characteristics of information which prevent it from being fully identified as one of the commodities represented in our abstract models of general equilibrium: (1) it is, by definition, indivisible in its use; and (2) it is very difficult to appropriate. With regard to the first point, information about a method of production, for example, is the same regardless of the scale of the output. Since the cost of information depends only on the item, not its use, it pays a large scale producer to acquire better information than a small scale producer. Thus, information creates economies of scale throughout the economy, and therefore, according to well-known principles, causes a departure from the competitive economy.
>
> Information is inappropriable because an individual who has some can never lose it by transmitting it. It is frequently noted in connection with the economics of research and development that information acquired by research at great cost may be transmitted much more cheaply. If the information is, therefore, transmitted to one buyer, he can in turn sell it very cheaply, so that the market price is well below the cost of production. But if the transmission costs are high, then it is also true that there is inappropriability, since the seller cannot realize the social value of the information. Both cases occur in practice with different kinds of information.
>
> But then, according to well-known principles of welfare economics, the inappropriability of a commodity means that its production will be far from optimal. It may be below optimal: it may also induce costly protective measures outside the usual property system.
>
> Thus, it has been a classic position that a competitive world will underinvest in research and development, because the information acquired will become general knowledge and cannot be appropriated by the firm financing the research. . . . if secrecy is possible, there may be overinvestment in information gathering, each firm may secretly get the same information, either on nature or on each

other, although it would of course consume less of society's resources if they were collected once and disseminated to all. (1984, 142–3)

If agents were omniscient, these problems would not emerge. Genomes are omniscient so the parallel problems do not emerge in nature, and do not obstruct equilibria. There are no apparent economies of scale operating within species in reproductive fitness. And besides, the information that the environment provides about relative adaptedness is costless and universally available. So there is no problem about appropriability. In the absence of secrecy and the need for strategic knowledge about what other agents know, there is no room in biological evolution for the sort of problems information raises in economics. Once biological systems become social and their interactions become strategic, the role for information becomes crucial. But at this point evolution turns Lamarckian. It is no surprise that when "acquired" characteristics are available for differential transmission, markets for the characteristics will emerge. But at this point Darwinian evolution is no longer operating. In fact, one good argument against the adoption of Darwinian evolutionary theory as a model for economic theory is just the difference made by information. Once it appears in nature, evolution ceases to be exclusively or even mainly Darwinian. Why suppose that once information becomes as important as it is in economic exchange that phenomena should again become Darwinian?

The case of Nelson and Winter

It will be useful to apply some of the omniadiversions already advanced to what is doubtless the most well developed approach to economics inspired by Darwinian considerations (Nelson and Winter 1982). The capstone of two distinguished careers, few books can have had a more disappointing reception in recent economics. I hazard two guesses about why it has fallen stillborn from the presses, both of them natural consequences of what I have argued here. First, the predictive power of Nelson and Winter's evolutionary alternative to neoclassical theory is by their own admission little better than that of the theory of natural selection. And for Nelson and Winter, as for most other economics, predictive improvement is an important criterion of theoretical advance. But predictive power is the least of variation and selection theory's virtues, no matter what discipline it is developed for. No one should have expected more in application elsewhere. Second, Nelson and Winter's theory doesn't really look very different from neoclassical theory: Like other evolutionary theories, it lends itself to equilibria explanations, it reflects the fact that biological evolution fosters constrained maximization, and its interests are in the aggregate of individuals and not in their particular behavior. Except in areas where neoclassical theory is silent, the evolutionary approach is not different enough to make it more than a variation on the theme written in the eighteenth century by Adam Smith.

But once we get past the obvious features of Nelson and Winter's theory, there is a more fundamental problem that deprives it, I fear, of even the prospects of being as good as Darwinian evolutionary theory. If an evolutionary approach to economics is to be something more than a suggestive metaphor, if we are actually to confirm the claim that economic phenomena reflect a process of Darwinian evolution, we must identify in the phenomena the fundamental causal forces that are necessary and sufficient for natural selection. Because it fails to do this Nelson and Winter's theory is at best a metaphorically Darwinian theory that stands or falls on its own, without the support or the drag of Darwin's theory.

Evolutionary biologists and philosophers of biology have identified the following minimal condition for evolution by natural selection: There must be *replicators* and there must be *interactors* (see Dawkins 1976; Hull 1989). A replicator is defined as an entity that passes on its structure intact in successive replications. Thus, a gene is a replicator, but not the only possible replicator. If organisms produce offspring very much like themselves in structure, then organisms are replicators too. The key to deciding whether something is a replicator is what counts as a distinct offspring whose structure can be compared. An interactor is an entity that interacts as a cohesive whole with its environment in such a way that this interaction causes replication to be differential. Organisms are paradigm interactors in evolutionary biology. But they are not the only possible ones: Genes, cells, tissues, and organs interact with their bodily environments in ways that cause more or less copies of the genes to be produced. In fact, some evolutionary biologists have in the past suggested that groups, populations, and even whole species might constitute interactors. This view is no longer widely held (for reasons well understood by game theorists (see Smith 1984). Selection is the process in which differential extinction and proliferation of interactors cause the differential perpetuation of the relevant replicators. Some evolutionary biologists define one other term, the *lineage*, which is the entity that actually evolves, as the proportion of types of interactors in its line of descent changes from generation to generation. It is important to bear in mind that interactors do not evolve; only the lines of descent of which they are composed do.

Nelson and Winter's aim is not simply to wrap economic theory in the mantle of evolution, but to show how economic processes instantiate Darwinian natural selection. Though they do not use the word, they identify the replicator as a behavioral routine:

> At any time a firm's routines define a list of functions that determine . . . what a firm does as a function of various external variables (principally market conditions) and internal state variable (for example the firms prevailing stock of machinery or the average profit rate it earned in recent periods). (16)

> Organizational capabilities consist largely of the ability to perform and sustain a set of routines; such routines could be regarded as a highly structured set of "habitual reactions" linking organization members to one another and to the environment. The tendency for such routines to be maintained over time plays in our theory the role that genetic inheritance plays in the theory of biological evolution. (142)

The interactors are pretty clearly meant to be firms. Here is a typical expression of this commitment, as Nelson and Winter construct the parallels:

> The comparative fitness of genotypes (profitability of routines) determines which genotypes (routines) will tend to become predominant over time. However the fitness (profitability) clearly depends on the characteristics of the environment (market prices) confronting the species (collections of firms with similar routines). The environment (price vector) in turn depends, however, on the genotypes (routines) of all the individual organisms (firms) existing at a time – a dependency discussed in the subdiscipline called ecology (market theory). (160)

So replicator = behavioral routine, of which there are several different kinds; interactor = firm; fitness is measured in profits; and the environment is given by the price vector. But then what evolves? What is the lineage, what are the generations, what is the principle by which we individuate members of the lineage to establish intergenerational selection? Here, incoherence sets in, because Nelson and Winter also identify the unit of evolution as the firm – in other words, in their model the interactor is both the lineage of firms and its proper parts, the individual firms, for it is individual firms that grow in size and evolve, like populations. Nelson and Winter write, "Through the joint action of search [for routines] and selection, the firms evolve over time" (19). Thus, firms are both interactors and lineages. But if they are lineages, they must be composed of interactors as well.

At a minimum, the neatness of evolutionary arithmetic is destroyed by this complication. More likely, the result is the surrender of a Darwinian approach to economic evolution in favor of a Lamarckian one, in which anything can evolve into anything by any means. In the biological case to determine evolution within the lineage, one need only count the proportions of the distinct types of its component individual members. Changes that take place within an individual member of a lineage are matters of development. From a Darwinian perspective, these changes cannot count as evolution or even have a role in it. Only differential reproduction of the replicators – the genes or routines that give rise to them – can do this. The only way changes in interactors can themselves have an effect on evolution of the lineage is by Lamarckian means – the inheritance of acquired characteristics. Lamarckianism is, of course, not the label for an alternative evolutionary theory. It is just a label for the claim that change is not Darwinian. As such it sheds no special light on economic processes, or any other.

Might we preserve the Darwinian character of Nelson and Winter's theory by a little reorganization? Let's try. By the adoption of more adapted routines, a firm develops, grows in size, attains profitability, and the like. But if the firm also evolves, then it must at least be (one of) its own descendant(s), otherwise the analogy with evolutionary theory breaks down. For this sort of change to also count as evolution, the improved adaptation must be transmitted to the firm's descendants, successor, subsidiaries, and so on. But what if the firm becomes so adapted that it swamps the competition, spins off no subsidiaries, and grows to become a natural monopoly? Are we to say that the lineage of which it is a member has evolved in the direction of greater adaptation? The number of members of the lineage continually decreases until there is just one member left, and it is now vulnerable to extinction in a sudden environmental change. A reasonable thing to say about this scenario is that the single firm left has shown itself to be the fittest. Reasonable, but not from the perspective of Darwinian evolution and not just because only one individual is left at the end of a period of evolution. This way of describing the outcome of the evolutionary process obscures a real Darwinian insight.

An evolutionarily, coherent version of Nelson and Winter makes routines be replicators and the organizational unit that employs the routines the interactor. If the routine is a marketing strategy, the interactor is the smallest marketing department that can execute it; if the routine is a production technique, the interactor is the smallest shop-floor team that employs it. Each of these will grow in size subject to the constraints of other interactors, whether in the same or other firms. Firms are sets of interactors that are coadapted, that work together to produce outcomes that increase their numbers, either within a firm, if it can keep the routines proprietary, or across an industry. On this view firms are not lineages either. Lineages are composed of the smallest organizational units that reproduce. Firms cut across lineages, bundling together varying numbers of varying organizational units. Changes in the size and profitability of firms will reflect adaptedness of their component units to one another and to the industrial environment. Adaptation of interactors to the environment may result in rapid increase of the number of firms in an industry, each of them composed of a small number of units, or a decrease in the number of firms, each bundling together a vast number of the same units. Compare the industry structure for PC clones with the industry structure for supercomputers. From the point of view of natural selection, tracking the fiscal growth or shrinkage of firms may reveal little about the way in which Nelson and Winter's replicators determine economic evolution. If this is in fact the way to apply evolutionary theory to the firm's behavior, the result will be a discipline more like organization theory than economics. Few economists (besides March, Cyert, and Simon) want this. The evolutionary biologist will not be surprised, for organization theory looks like something biologists do. One important component of the biologist's discipline is empirical work in the field – taxonomy to identify the interactors and ecology to establish the communities of coadapted interactors and to identify the environmental forces that shape them and their adaptations. The purely theoretical modeling comes much later and has little additional explanatory or predictive power. But this is a division of labor that few economists will volunteer for. After all, theirs is a discipline that prescinds from psychology, sociology, and other details.

Of course, if we don't like the turn that our evolutionary theory has taken, we can go back to the drawing board and select new replicators, which will give us firms as the desired interactors and reflect a parallel with evolutionary theory. But now the tail is wagging the dog. We are rearranging our theory so that it will look like one that works well elsewhere. But what is the point?

The role of metaphors in science is not well understood. Indeed, the role of metaphors is still controversial on its home ground in language. It should be no surprise that when we metaphorically or otherwise extend literary metaphor to scientific practice, matters become quickly obscure. Darwin's notion of blind variation and natural selection has been one of the most tempting of metaphors in the social sciences. Whether it has been a source of fruitful stimulation is debatable. Whether the theories cut to its pattern have been well confirmed or not seems to me to be the only interesting question for scientists in these disciplines to actually concern themselves with. All the rest is ad hominem argument or the genetic fallacy.

Notes

I am indebted to Bruce Caldwell, Wade Hands, and participants in the conference "Natural Images in Economics" for helpful comments on a previous version of this chapter.
1. For a discussion of the predictive weakness of the theory of natural selection and the charge that it is a grand tautology, see Rosenberg (1985).
2. Page references in the text are to Alchian (1950).

References

Alchian, Armen. 1950. "Uncertainty, Evolution and Economic Theory," *Journal of Political Economy* 58:211–21.
Arrow, Kenneth. 1984. *The Economics of Information.* Cambridge, MA: Belknap Press.
Dawkins, Richard. 1976. *The Selfish Gene.* Oxford University Press.
Friedman, Milton. 1953. "Methodology of Positive Economics," *Essays in Positive Economics.* Chicago: University of Chicago Press.
Hull, David. 1989. *Science as a Process.* Chicago: University of Chicago Press.
McCloskey, Donald. 1985. *The Rhetoric of Economics.* Madison: University of Wisconsin Press.
Nelson, Richard, and Sidney Winter. 1982. *An Evolutionary Theory of Economic Change.* Cambridge, MA: Belknap Press.
Rifkin, Jeremy. 1984. *Algeny.* New York: Penguin.
Rosenberg, Alexander. 1985. *The Structure of Biological Science.* Cambridge University Press.
Smith, John Maynard. 1984. *Evolution and the Theory of Games.* Cambridge University Press.

CHAPTER 16

Hayek, evolution, and spontaneous order

GEOFFREY M. HODGSON

Introduction

The writings of Friedrich Hayek (1899–1992) embody a notable attempt to apply evolutionary ideas from biology to social science. His conception of socioeconomic and cultural evolution is the centerpiece of his mature theory, and it relates to such topics as his theory of law, the structure of political institutions, the nature of markets, and the critique of socialism and "constructivism." It is the object of this chapter to examine Hayek's evolutionary thinking. Although it is one of the most developed applications of evolutionary biology to socioeconomic theory, it reveals many problems.

The chapter commences by addressing some fundamental evolutionary concepts and issues, namely, Hayek's attitude to Darwin, social Darwinism and sociobiology, as well as the question of the chosen analogy to the gene and its relation to his methodological individualism. Subsequently we focus on Hayek's theory of group selection, his notion of "spontaneous order," his conception of the market, and his policy conclusions.

A number of questions hang over Hayek's characterization of the nature and processes of evolution. For instance, he repeatedly and proudly displays his own intellectual genealogy through Carl Menger, back to Adam Smith, David Hume, and Bernard de Mandeville. However, he does not seem to realize that their work is not equivalent to Darwinian evolution or natural selection in a fully specified sense. This search for genealogical roots in the works of Mandeville and the Scottish school thus leads to an attempt to diminish the significance of the Darwinian revolution and even the novelty of Darwin's own contribution to evolutionary theory.

This problem manifests itself at the theoretical level in terms of a tension between phylogenetic and ontogenetic conceptions of change. The distinction between ontogeny and phylogeny is borrowed from biology. Ontogeny involves the development of a particular organism from a set of given and unchanging genes. In contrast, phylogeny is the complete and ongoing evolution of a population, including changes in its composition and that of the gene pool. It involves changes in the genetic potentialities of the population, as well as their individual phenotypic development. The distinction between ontogenetic and phylogenetic evolution can be used to make distinctions between differing conceptions of "economic evolution." It is important to stress that such conceptions are applied for the purposes of analogy, not to imply that human behavior is necessarily determined by the genes.

Aware of the modern prestige awarded to Darwinism, Hayek admits some kind of selection process and phylogeny in his evolutionary theory. But insofar as his theory is still rooted in methodological individualism and the ideas of the Scottish school, it shall be argued that it largely remains in the confines of ontogeny.[1]

It will be suggested here that Hayek's evolutionary theory, while containing important insights, is sketchy and sometimes ambiguous. And finally, it does not support the kind of political and policy conclusions that Hayek wishes to sustain. Nevertheless, it stands alongside the work of Thorstein Veblen and Herbert Spencer as one of the more developed and most important applications of the evolutionary analogy in the socioeconomic sphere.[2]

Given the importance of the comparison undertaken here between Hayek's evolutionism and his methodological individualism, the following section addresses this latter idea. Methodological individualism may claim some priority because of its explicit longevity in Hayek's work. Subsequently we return to a discussion of Hayek's evolutionism, as presented more prominently in his mature writings.

Methodological individualism

The term "methodological individualism" was adopted by thinkers of the Austrian school, including Hayek, and classically defended by Ludwig von Mises (1949). A clear and useful definition of methodological individualism is provided by Jon Elster (1982, 453): "the doctrine that all social phenomena (their structure and their change) are in principle explicable only in terms of individuals – their properties, goals, and beliefs." Note the unqualified key words "all" and "only" and the appropriate focus on explanation in this definition. It is consistent with the definition of von Mises.

Methodological individualists in a sense take the individual "for granted." The individual, along with his or her assumed behavioral characteristics, is taken as the elemental building block in the theory of the social or economic system. As Steven Lukes (1973, 73) puts it, "Individuals are pictured abstractly as given, with given interests, wants, purposes, needs, etc." In short, according to the methodological individualist, individuals do not evolve. Clearly, assumptions of this type are typical of neoclassical economics, as well as the economics of Hayek.

The obvious question to be raised is the legitimacy of stopping short at the individual in the process of explanation. If individuals are affected by their circumstances, then why not in turn attempt to explain the causes acting on individual "goals, and beliefs"? Why should the process of scientific inquiry be arrested as soon as the individual is reached?

After all, if "the scientific practice is to seek an explanation at a lower level than the explandum," as Elster (1983, 23) puts it, then why stop with the individual? Why not delve into the psyche and, further, observe the firing of the neurons and the electrochemistry of the brain? Hayek's own way out of these difficulties seems to be presented in quotations such as the following: If "conscious action can be 'explained,' " he writes, "this is a task for psychology but not for economics . . . or any other social science" (1948, 67).

This amounts to a dogmatic statement that economists and other social scientists should not concern themselves with "psychology" and explanations of purpose and preference. The idea that such explanations, if pursued, have to be purely in psychological terms is called 'psychologism' and is rebutted by Karl Popper (1945), Lawrence Boland (1982), and others. Arguably, however, it is impossible to exclude psychology – especially social psychology – from the domain of social science.

In sum, the methodological individualists have provided us with no good reason why explanations of social phenomena should stop short with the individual. We cannot exclude the idea that at least some human intentions have causes that are worthy of investigation. This conclusion is fatal for methodological individualism, at least as the term has been defined here.

If there are determinate influences on individuals and their goals, then these are worthy of explanation. In turn, the explanation of those may be in terms of other purposeful individuals. But where should the analysis stop? The purposes of an individual could be partly explained by relevant institutions, culture, and so on. These, in their turn, would be partly explained in terms of other individuals. But these individual purposes and actions could then be partly explained by cultural and institutional factors, and so on, indefinitely. We are involved in an apparently infinite regress, similar to the puzzle "Which came first, the chicken or the egg?" Such an analysis never reaches an end point. It is simply arbitrary to stop at one particular stage in the explanation and say "It is all reducible to individuals" just as much as to say it is "all social and institutional." The key point is that in this infinite regress, neither individual nor social factors have legitimate explanatory primacy. The idea that all explanations have to be in terms of individuals is thus unfounded. Accordingly, methodological individualism is fatally flawed.

Methodological individualism implies a rigid and dogmatic compartmentalization of study. It may be legitimate in some limited types of analysis to take individuals as given and examine the consequences of the interactions of their activities. This particular type of analysis, be it called "situational logic" or whatever, has a worthy place, alongside other approaches, in social science. But it does not legitimate methodological individualism because the latter involves the further statement that *all* social explanations should be of this or a similar type.

In contradistinction, it may reasonably be argued that there are external influences molding the purposes and actions of individuals, but that action is not entirely determined by them. The environment is influential but it does not completely determine either what the individual aims to do or what he or she may achieve. This approach involves a rejection of the extremes of both determinism and individualistic indeterminacy.

Culture and methodological individualism

Notably, Hayek's emphasis on the concept of culture does not itself imply a departure from methodological individualism. Indeed, there is an alternative tradition within anthropology that proselytizes an individualistic conception of culture. Likewise, sociobiologists such as Charles Lumsden and Edward Wilson (1981) offer a theory of culture that is redolent of methodological individualism. They write, "Culture is in fact the product of vast numbers of choices by individual members of the society" (206).[3]

In a critique of individualistic conceptions of culture, Anne Mayhew (1987) explains that there is a difference between regarding culture "as a consequence of the way in which people act" and of seeing behavior, in part at least, as a consequence of culture. If the individual is to be taken as given, as Hayek and other methodological individualists seem to insist, then culture can be embraced only in the former sense and not fully in the latter.

This line of argument is of even greater relevance with the move to an analysis of an evolutionary kind. With investigations into short-run processes, or partial equilibria, tastes and preference functions could be taken as given. But in an unfolding and evolutionary perspective involving long-run changes and developments in a social context, this compartmentalization is arguably out of place.

Biotic evolution involves natural selection of genes, which may themselves be taken as virtually invariant. However, the composition of the gene pool changes and it is necessary to explain this change. Moving to the socioeconomic sphere, individuals are clearly not as invariant as genes: Our attitudes and beliefs often change dramatically during the course of our lives. Yet even if particular individuals were wrongly regarded as invariant and akin to the genes, then the population of individuals would change through time. As selection takes place, the overall set of individual preference functions will change. These, in turn, would have to be explained.

It is thus necessary to take all possible changes into account and treat change itself, as Veblen argued, as "cumulative" in scope. In contrast to both Austrian and neoclassical theory, Veblen (1919, 75) saw "both the agent and his environment being at any point the outcome of the last process."

Thus, there is an inconsistency in Hayek's work between, on the one hand, the ideas emanating from his individualist roots, and, on the other, his growing commitment to an evolutionary perspective. In an evolutionary context, methodological individualism has to be either redefined or abandoned. There have been some shifts in Hayek's work over the years, and it may be that he "is by no means the champion of methodological individualism that he claims to be," as Stephan Böhm (1989, 221) alleges.

Hence, the development of Hayek's thought has not been continuous or free of major internal contradictions. In particular, the kind of evolutionary notions that he tries to embrace imply a conflict with many of his original presuppositions. This point is reinforced by a consideration of other aspects of Hayek's thought.

Evolution and purposeful behavior

A notable difficulty is created in his mature theory. On the one hand, there is the typical emphasis of the Austrian school on purposeful behavior, guided by expectations of an uncertain future. On the other, there is the modern biological idea of evolution in which intention plays no explicit part, and his unremitting emphasis of the concept of "tacit knowledge" derived from the work of Michael Polanyi (1957, 1967).

Consequently, if socioeconomic development is determined by some process of natural selection, then what role remains for the notions of intentionality, purposefulness, or choice, which economists in Hayek's tradition have held so dear? As John Gray (1984, 53) remarks, "The problem with the natural-selection approach is that in accounting for individual character traits, dispositions, and so on by reference to their survival values, it deprives individual choices and purposes of their place at the terminal level of social explanation."

Clearly, if Hayek's notion of cultural evolution is to retain the notion of purposeful action, it must be distanced from an evolutionary process of a strictly Darwinian kind. However, Hayek does not seem to recognize the full gravity of this problem. It is not until his work of the late 1980s that he describes cultural evolution as being specifically Lamarckian rather than Darwinian.[4] Even then it is without mention of the opening thus created for a notion of truly purposeful behavior, in contrast to the orthodox Darwinian scheme within which purpose is regarded merely as programmed or goal-seeking activity.

The emergence of Hayek's evolutionism

The delay in the emergence of the biological metaphor in Hayek's writings may stem in part from his earlier critique of "scientism" in social theory (Hayek 1952). There he denounces social theory for a "slavish imitation of the method and language of science" (15). Later, however, in the preface to his *Studies in Philosophy, Politics and Economics*, Hayek (1967, viii) notes a change in "tone" in his attitude to scientism, attributed to the influence of Popper. This is not, needless to say, a matter of mere tone, and as the door is progressively opened for the entry of the biological analogues, the row with the allegedly scientistic neighbors diminishes nearly to the point of insignificance. Insofar as the polemic against scientism remains, it changes its form as well as its tone, but still poses an inconsistency with the evolutionism of his later works.

Although the idea had been raised earlier, suggestions of a more prominent "evolutionary" approach in Hayek's work are found in a few passages of a collection of essays published in the 1960s (1967, 31–4, 66–81, 103–4, 111, 119). The bulkiest of these extracts refers to "the evolution of systems of rules of conduct," but direct references to the biological analogy therein are slight. The 1960s also saw the original publication of his important essay on Bernard de Mandeville, wherein there are few further references to evolutionary biology (Hayek 1978, 265).

In the 1970s the main exposition of Hayek's evolutionary theory is found in his three-volume *Law, Legislation and Liberty*. Once again, however, the references to the biological literature and biological conceptions of evolution are patchy (1982, 1:9, 23–4, 152–3, 3:154–9, 199–202). In fact, by far the longest discussion of the concept of evolution is in the epilogue to that work and its footnotes.

Strangely, we have to wait until the late 1980s to receive the fullest explicit statement of Hayek's evolutionary conception, in a few pages of *The Fatal Conceit* (1988, 9, 11–28). Given the significance of an idea of the "evolution" of social institutions in Hayek's mature work, it is odd that it receives so little elaboration.

The underestimation of Darwin

Despite this reticence, Hayek repeats in several places a rather curious account of the nature and origin of evolutionary theory. Hayek's omission of the role of Thomas Robert Malthus is particularly significant. Even more seriously, however, there is a tendency to underestimate the role of Charles Darwin in the development of evolutionary theory and both the originality and significance of his scientific work. For Hayek (1967, 32), the "basic conception" of the theory of evolution by natural selection is "exceedingly simple." Clearly these appraisals are likely to some extent to reflect on the nature and content of Hayek's own evolutionary theory.

The trouble seems to have started quite early on, when Hayek (1967, 103–4 n.) approvingly quotes a very outdated passage by the legal theorist – not biologist – Sir Frederick Pollock (1890, 41–2) to the effect that, "the doctrine of evolution is nothing else than the historical method applied to the facts of nature. . . . Savigny . . . [and] Burke . . . were Darwinians before Darwin." Pollock's trivializing estimation of Darwin's importance stems from a period when the influence of the famous biologist was at a low ebb (Bowler 1983, 1988), yet it seems to have affected Hayek adversely ever since.[5]

Hayek (1978, 265) further argues that writers like Johann von Herder, Wilhelm von Humboldt, and Friedrich von Savigny "made the idea of evolution a commonplace in the social sciences of the

nineteenth century long before Darwin." Repeating this theme elsewhere, Hayek writes:

> It was in the discussion of such social formations as language and
> morals, law and money, that in the eighteenth century the twin con-
> ceptions of evolution and the spontaneous formation of an order
> were at last clearly formulated, and provided the intellectual tools
> which Darwin and his contemporaries were able to apply to biologi-
> cal evolution. . . . A nineteenth-century social theorist who needed
> Darwin to teach him the idea of evolution was not worth his salt.
> (1982, 1:23)

Although in a later work Hayek (1988, 26) concedes that Darwin's
theory "is one of the great intellectual achievements of modern
times," he still continues to deprive the great biologist of much of his
glory. He writes that "Darwin's work was preceded by decades, indeed
by a century, of research concerning the rise of highly spontaneous
orders through a process of evolution" (24).

Note the imprecise use of the word "evolution" here. Hayek slurs
over the fact that the typical story of the emergence of "spontaneous
orders," as found in the works of the Scottish school, is ontogenetic in
character, and is not strictly analogous either to a Darwinian process
of natural selection or even to evolution of a Lamarckian kind. Hayek
(1988, 23) also writes that Darwin's

> painstaking efforts to illustrate how the process of evolution oper-
> ated in living organisms convinced the scientific community of what
> had long been a commonplace in the humanities – at least since Sir
> William Jones in 1787 recognised the striking resemblance of Latin
> and Greek to Sanskrit, and the descent of all "Indo-Germanic" lan-
> guages from the latter.

However, insofar as Herder, Jones, and Savigny introduced an idea
of evolution in their writings on the development of language and law,
it was one merely of lineal descent. The Darwinian idea of natural
selection is not therein to be found. Insofar as "the idea of evolution"
and "a commonplace in the social sciences in the nineteenth century,"
its main proselytizer was Spencer, who was not truly a Darwinian and
whom, incidentally, Hayek fails to mention in this context.[6] Unfortunately, these are not unique cases of a casual attitude to sources and
scholarship in Hayek's work.[7]

In regard to the alleged forerunners of Darwin's theory, Ernst Mayr
(1985, 769) argues that "virtually all of these so-called prior cases of
natural selection turn out to be a rather different phenomenon, which
is only superficially similar to selection."[8] Hayek's attempt to belittle

the importance of the Darwinian revolution by claiming multiple precedence is thus without foundation in the modern history of biology. It betrays both a misreading of the sources and some misunderstanding on Hayek's part.

Let us illustrate the kind of problem thus created. Note that, on the one hand, Hayek (1982, 1:24) mentions some kind of process of selection and rejects the old definition of evolution as *evolvere*, that is, as unfolding or unwinding. On the other hand, these statements sit uneasily with the slurred account of the development of evolutionary theory in Hayek's work. In fact, the most prominent idea of social evolution that was "a commonplace in the social sciences of the nineteenth century long before Darwin" was not one of selection in the Darwinian sense but simply of *evolvere*. Furthermore, in tracing his own intellectual pedigree from Hume and Smith, Hayek fails to notice that there is no developed idea of natural selection in their works.

When Hayek (1967, 72) writes that "the whole of economic theory . . . may be interpreted as nothing else but an endeavour to reconstruct from regularities of the individual actions the character of the resulting order," he is letting the cat out of the bag. Biological ontogeny is precisely the endeavor to explain the development of organisms from the regularities of their genetic endowment, in contrast to phylogeny, which considers the sifting and changing of the gene pool through natural selection or drift. Hayek's statement thus clearly suggests ontogeny rather than phylogeny.

Thus, in implicitly comparing his theory to the kind of economic ontogeny found in the writings of Walras or Smith, Hayek makes the addition of the idea of natural selection a mere appendage. Darwin is then reduced in stature because he is not significant for the Hayekian theory. Without further clarification, the latter can easily be reduced to the post-Humean ontogeny of the emergence of the coherent social order. With the epigenesis of Karl Ernst von Baer, for example, ontogeny was well established before Darwin. It is thus no accident that Hayek simultaneously upgrades ontogenesis and downgrades Darwin's contribution.

The rejection of biologism and social Darwinism

We now turn to a more positive aspect of Hayek's evolutionism. A strong and repeated aspect of Hayek's account of cultural evolution is his rejection of biological reductionism and social Darwinism, and his related critique of sociobiology. Hayek (1982, 3:154) convincingly argues that the social Darwinists spoiled their case by wrongly "concentrating on the selection of congenitally more fit individuals, the slowness of which makes it comparatively unimportant for cultural evolution, and at the same time neglecting the decisively important selective evolution of rules and practices." Since cultural evolution "differs from genetic evolution by relying on the transmission of acquired properties, it is very fast, and once it dominates, it swamps genetic evolution" (3:156).

In short, social Darwinism wrongly "concentrated on the selection of individuals rather than that of institutions and practices, and on the selection of innate rather than on culturally transmitted capacities of the individuals" (Hayek 1982, 1:23). A similar error, Hayek argues, is found in the modern "sociobiology" of Edward Wilson (1975) and others: "Perhaps the chief error of contemporary 'sociobiology' is to suppose that language, morals, law, and such like, are transmitted by the 'genetic' processes that molecular biology is now illuminating, rather than being the products of selective evolution transmitted by imitative learning" (Hayek, 1988, 24).

In this respect Hayek's conception of evolution is clearly different from that of, for example, Herbert Spencer and William Graham Sumner in the nineteenth century, as well as that of Edward Wilson in the twentieth. Hayek puts much more emphasis on the autonomy of culture, and of the evolution of institutions and rules themselves. In this manner, therefore, he continues in the direction that Veblen had taken many decades before.

The selection of rules

We now turn to Hayek's account of the mechanism of socioeconomic evolution. It will be argued that he fails to clarify many crucial aspects of the processes involved. For instance, Hayek repeatedly associates evolution with the existence of some kind of selection mechanism, although its specification, along with that of the unit(s) of selection and the criteria of fitness, are somewhat vague.[9]

The possible ambiguity in the term "selection" should be noted. For example, with Menger's theory of the "evolution" of money, the medium of exchange is "selected," but through cumulative reinforcement, not necessarily through the sifting and winnowing of competing alternatives (Hodgson, 1993, ch. 8). Neither does it necessarily involve the natural selection of the individual agents who are regarded as the genetic elements driving the system. The process here is the selection of a path of ontogenetic development, not the full natural selection observed in phylogeny.

Hayek does not resolve this ambiguity. When he writes of the "selective evolution of rules and practices," it is not clear whether rules are being selected in an ontogenetic or a phylogenetic sense. If it is ontogenetic selection, then Hayek's conception of evolution is limited. In contrast, if it is phylogenetic selection, then, as will be argued, there is a contradiction between Hayek's methodological individualism and the idea of the selection of rules.

Furthermore, as Norman Barry (1979, 82) has pointed out, Hayek is unclear as to the criteria on which evolutionary selection takes place. Jim Tomlinson (1990, 47) has elaborated the same point, noting:

> Hayek . . . for example, suggests that religions which encourage strong families (undefined) provide favourable evolutionary conditions, but never spells out this point in any detail. This is a large hole in the argument, because he suggests that certain characteristics are crucial to evolutionary progress, but does little to identify what these characteristics are.

Hayek states that selection is not of individuals themselves but of "institutions and practices" (1982, 1:23) and "rules" related to individuals. However, the identification of what is being selected does not itself involve the specification of a selection mechanism. While he makes it clear that the objects of selection are institutions or rules, this stance creates problems for Hayek's continuing adherence to methodological individualism, as explained further in the next section.

Are rules or individuals analogous to genes?

Biological genes have a number of significant features. They are "replicators," in that they pass on their information with some degree of fidelity. This information itself consists of coded instructions programming or directing behavior or growth. Hence, the gene could be described as an "instructor" as well as a replicator.

If rules are seen as analogous objects of selection then they are attributed with both the functions of replicator and of instructor. When Hayek (1982, 3:199) writes of the "genetic primacy of rules of conduct" he seems to be suggesting that the rule is analogous to the gene. This is, prima facie, a reasonable proposal because the rule does have the dual functions of replicator and of instructor.

However, Hayek's own standpoint, although vague and rarely elaborated, is more complicated. The first problem arises from the definition of the concept of "rule." Hayek (1967, 66–7) writes, "It should be clearly understood that the term 'rule' is used for a statement by which a regularity of the conduct of individuals can be described, irrespective of whether such a rule is 'known' to the individuals in any other sense than they normally act in accordance with it."[10] This is an important clarification, as the word "rule" is often associated by other authors with the idea of an explicit instruction or prescribed pattern of behavior. In contrast, Hayek seems to have in mind the notion of a rule as a behavioral disposition or habit.

Despite his long-standing opposition to this philosophy, it should be noted that Hayek's definition of a rule is behaviorist, because of its exclusion of intent or design. To define a rule merely as a phenomenal "regularity of conduct" is behaviorism pure and simple and creates many problems for Hayek's theory, as we shall see.

What sustains the rule and gives it some durability through time? Once again, Hayek does not give us a sufficiently clear answer, but in discussing the process of cultural transmission he puts emphasis on the role of imitation.[11] The possibility of rule replication through imitation plausibly accounts for the much faster rate of cultural evolution, compared with the sluggish biotic processes of genetic change and selection. Genetic evolution, Hayek (1988, 16) rightly argues, is "far too slow" to account for the rapid development of civilization. Instead, new practices were spread by imitation and acquired habit. "This gradual replacement of innate responses by learnt rules increasingly distinguished man from other animals."[12]

However, if the rule is simply an existing regularity of conduct, then it is not entirely clear how other agents imitate existing rules. We could assume that humans act as if programmed to blindly follow others; but this would rob them of choice and the purposive ability to break rules, which Hayek is rightly keen to retain. Furthermore, do we follow rules simply as rules or because they are embodiments of the wills of others? The mechanisms of rule replication are not clarified or explained. The mere suggestion of imitation is not enough.

Further, if the rule is simply an existing regularity of conduct, and need not take a prescriptive or codified form, as Hayek insists, then it is not entirely clear how it acts as an instructor for the human actor. What are the mechanisms involved in the genesis of action: the transformation of a rule into an act? Hayek (1967, 69) writes vaguely of the "external stimulus" and the "internal drive," without giving us much more to go on. Here there is another unfilled gap in his theory, and it is necessary to interpolate and conjecture in an attempt to understand his theoretical system as a whole.

Are rules instructors in themselves or only because they reflect the decisions and actions of individuals? Perhaps a methodological individualist should deny the capacity of rules to "instruct" behavior by themselves and see them as the intended or unintended outcomes of individual and purposeful behavior. Yet this is to remove the instructor function of the rule and to undermine its analogy with the gene. The instructor thereby becomes the individual rather than the rule.

Individual genes replicate biologically. Individual actions and thoughts are sustained by habit. Rules replicate by conformism, obedience, and imitation. However, as Hayek himself would agree, human choices are potentially novel. We may choose between existing rules, and there is always the possibility of novelty and creativity that is not mirrored in existing rules. Thus, the replicative fidelity of rules can be undermined by real choices, even if choices are themselves replicated through their establishment as rules. While rules are clearly objects of replication in socioeconomic evolution, humans are not "instructed" by rules alone; they also make choices. If choice is made supreme in the human sphere, then the analogy between the rule and the gene becomes imperfect.

Hence, the question of whether rules can be endowed with the qualities of an instructor depends on the general methodological and ontological position that is taken. For this and other reasons, Hayek's own explicit adherence to choice, purposeful behavior, and methodological individualism would seem to be inconsistent with his own supreme emphasis on the object of selection being rules.

In sum, in the social context, neither rules nor individuals provide exact parallels to the biological gene. Both individuals and rules, and perhaps additional entities as suggested in the following section, are units of selection in socioeconomic evolution. Individuals, individual acts, and rules both replicate and are "selected" in different ways, making the exact analogy with conventional biology problematic.

Despite having written on cultural evolution for over twenty years, Hayek not only fails to present an adequate solution to these problems, but also fails to articulate them clearly. Without a satisfactory solution, his evolutionary theory remains incomplete. As noted, part of the problem is the juxtaposition in Hayek's writings of methodological individualism with evolutionary ideas. For instance, the retention of methodological individualism would seem to require a solution with all its weight on individual purposefulness and choice, to the neglect of conditioning and structure,[13] in which case the notion of the rule takes second place, and much of Hayek's emphasis on rule following would have to be removed.

Should a reductionist choose the individual or the gene?

As will be discussed in more detail later, Viktor Vanberg (1986) has attacked Hayek's version of cultural evolution precisely because it is inconsistent with methodological individualism. Appealing for support for his view, Vanberg cites the works of biologists such as John Maynard Smith, Robert L. Trivers, and Edward O. Wilson. There is also the seminal work of George C. Williams (1966) and the popular books of Richard Dawkins (1976, 1982, 1986, 1989).

It should be emphasized that the "genetic reductionist" mode of explanation that is developed by Dawkins, Maynard Smith, G. C. Williams, and others relies on the important fact that the gene is not only a replicator and an instructor, but that its features are also much more stable and potentially long lasting than those of the individual, the group, or the population. It is the stability of the gene and of the information within it, as well as its particular role in the evolutionary process, that is an important element in their case for regarding the gene as the unit of selection. If we are to regard individuals or rules as analogous to genes, then we have to authenticate a sufficient degree of stability in these terms as well.

In social science, however, reductionist explanations typically focus on the individual, as in the case of methodological individualism (Lukes 1973; Hodgson 1988, ch. 3). Given that individuals are much more malleable than genes, this makes an appeal to "genetic reductionist" biology in support of methodological individualism somewhat dubious.

There is a further problem in Vanberg's attempt to rescue Hayek by making him a consistent methodological individualist. If the impetus for a methodological individualist account is a reductionist attempt to explain the whole in terms of its parts, then the true reductionist should embrace the gene rather than the individual as the basic unit of explanation.

Accordingly, David Sloan Wilson and Elliott Sober (1989) go so far as to argue that to settle on the individual as the unit of selection involves an inconsistency. The same arguments concerning explanatory reduction from groups to individuals apply equally to explanatory reduction from individual to gene. If we can reduce explanations to individual terms, why not further reduce them to the terms of genes? This argument would seem especially apposite for one who appeals to the biological works of Maynard Smith, Trivers, and E. O. Wilson. Or can these two alternatives – individuals and genes – be somehow reconciled?

One possible means of reconciliation, it would seem, would be to adopt Dawkins's (1982) distinction between replicators and "vehicles" in the natural selection process. Dawkins sees the genes as replicators, and the individuals or groups are vehicles in which the genes are always carried. Natural selection works directly on the phenotypical vehicles; some are selected and others are not. This affects the genotypes only indirectly, through an extended period of time in which different genes are selected.

Hayek (1967, 67–8) says that the selection of rules will operate on the bases of the greater or lesser efficiency of the resulting order or system to which they relate. He could be loosely interpreted as saying that "the selection of rules will operate on the basis or the fitness of the resulting individuals and groups." In this particular formulation, the rules are clearly analogous to the genes, and the individuals or groups are analogous to organism (or possibly group) phenotypes. The rules are thus the replicators, and individuals (or groups) are the vehicles.

At first sight, this reformation of Hayek's theory would seem to neutralize some of the features of Vanberg's (1986) critique and within the terms of a genetic reductionist biology. However, there is a serious problem in this reformulation. In biological evolution, the genes of a given organism do not change; they endure as long as that organism remains alive, and may even be passed on to its offspring. This is clearly not the case with the rule in socioeconomic evolution; both individuals and groups can change rules. In consequence, these vehicles can alter the replicating material they are carrying.

This is not normally the case in the biotic sphere. Here it is not necessary to explain further why a given vehicle sustains its genetic material, because at least in modern evolutionary theory it is imprinted in the DNA and cannot easily be altered. In contrast, in cultural evolution the maintenance of given rules by a given individual or group vehicle is not automatic.

This important difference between biological and cultural evolution provides a source of serious error. While in biology it can be assumed that the genes have considerable stability and may maintain themselves with fidelity through time, we cannot assume the same in cultural evolution. This has an important implication for the patterns of explanation involved. In biology we can sometimes assume that the known contribution of a gene to the overall fitness of an organism helps to explain its very existence. This is not the case in cultural evolution, because if a trait or rule is selected because of its contribution to the fitness of an individual or group then we have to explain further why that trait or rule sustains itself beyond the instant of its selection.

Consequently, Vanberg (1986, 83) is right to suggest that Hayek's argument has a functionalist quality; it assumes that the contribution of a rule to the maintenance of a system is sufficient to explain the existence of that rule. Absent in Hayek's argument is the specification of a process by which a rule that is advantageous to the system is sustained in operation within that system.

Hayek is rightly criticized for assuming that the contribution of a rule to the maintenance of a system is sufficient to explain the existence of that rule. But note that this argument applies to individuals as well as to groups. An individual could be regarded as a kind of system, as could a group. Do we assume that the contribution of a rule to the welfare of an individual is sufficient to explain the adoption of that rule? Absent in such an argument is the specification of a process by which a rule that benefits a number of individuals is sustained in operation by those individuals.

If such antifunctionalism is combined with the kind of reductionist approach that Vanberg seems to prefer, then we encounter once more the problem of finding a sufficiently stable and enduring unit. Both individuals and rules have a transient quality, so the reductionist is impelled, once more, to turn to the gene. Hence, Vanberg's strong critique of functionalism, combined with an incautiously reductionist thrust, erodes his own chosen reliance on the individual as the basic explanatory unit.

The fatal conflict

It has been shown that it is not enough to follow Hayek and simply assume that a rule is a manifest behavioral regularity in individuals, without examining the procedures and mechanisms involved in its adoption by each individual. Clearly, such an explanation would have to delve into psychology, habit formation, and the nature of individual choice, among other factors. The endurance, or rules, should not be taken for granted; it has to be explained by detailed examination of both the cultural and psychological processes involved.

However, in line with his methodological individualism, Hayek (1948, 67; 1952, 39) suggests that in social science the given individual should be taken as the irreducible unit of explanation, excluding psychology in explanations of social phenomena. Yet these rigid statements specifically exclude an examination into some of the processes involved in the sustenance and replication of rules. Once again, the methodological individualist perspective that Hayek adopts from his Austrian heritage would seem to block the development of his evolutionary thinking.

It is in assuming that the benefits of a rule are sufficient to explain its continuing adoption by an individual that Hayek is posing too direct a connection between individuals and rules. Either the explanation rests on the rule rather than the individual, or it has to explain the adoption of rules by individuals. In the former case rules, not individuals, become the ultimate elements of explanation. The latter explanation involves psychology and other matters. In both cases there is a clash with methodological individualism – at least the kind that Hayek has advocated.

Group selection and the concept of an order

We now focus on his central concept of "spontaneous order." This is associated with the idea of group selection, which Hayek has taken from biology. Despite prominent criticism of group selection, here a defense is presented of this notion in regard to both biotic and socio-economic evolution. However, this defense leads to rejection rather than vindication of Hayek's policy stance.

Hayek makes an important distinction between an *order* of actions and the set of *rules* of action through which it emerges: "A particular order of actions can be observed and described without knowledge of the rules of conduct of the individuals which bring it about: and it is at least conceivable that the same overall order of actions may be produced by different sets of rules of individual conduct" (1967, 68). Although individual actions are governed by rules, orders are the unintended outcome of interactions, not the product of a single will.[14]

Hayek (1988, 20) states that rules are selected "on the basis of their human survival-value." In attempting to clarify what this might mean, Hayek (1967, 70; 1982, 1:164; 1982, 3:202) embraces the notion of "group selection" as advanced by Vero C. Wynne-Edwards (1962) in biology. He argues that habits and rules are indirectly selected, through their association with a particular type of group:

> Such new rules would spread not because men understood that they were more effective, or could calculate that they would lead to expansion, but simply because they enabled those groups practising them to procreate more successfully and to include outsiders. (1988, 16)

While the "*transmission* of rules of conduct takes place *from individual to individual,* the natural *selection* of rules will operate on the basis of the greater or less efficiency of the resulting *order of the group*" (Hayek 1967, 67). More particularly, "The evolutionary selection of different rules of individual conduct operates through the viability of the order it will produce" (68). Thus, "institutions and practices" which had first "been adopted for other reasons, or even purely accidentally, were preserved because they enable the group in which they had arisen to prevail over others" (1982, 1:9).

As noted, such passages have a distinct functionalist quality. Hayek's argument assumes that the contribution of a rule to the maintenance of the group is sufficient to explain the existence of that rule. He fails to specify a process by which a rule that is advantageous to a group is sustained in operation and not, for instance, replaced by other rules.

For similar reasons, the group selection idea has been the subject of a number of critiques from biology (G. C. Williams 1966; Maynard Smith 1976, 1980; Trivers 1985). These works explain the survival of specific group behaviors in terms of mechanisms involving the natural selection of the related genes, not in terms of the selection of the group as a whole.[15]

A prominent argument against group and cultural selection, allied to the critique of functionalism already noted, is that there is no clear mechanism to ensure that an advantageous pattern of behavior for the group will be sustained in operation within that system or replicated by the actions of the individuals concerned. In particular, such a mechanism must ensure that "free riders" do not become dominant in the groups that exhibit socially useful altruistic behaviors. Free riders would have the benefits of being members of a group whose other members perform socially useful and self-sacrificial acts, but would bear no personal costs or risks in terms of self-sacrificial behavior themselves. Consequently, in the absence of any compensating mechanism, it is likely that free riders within the group will expand in numbers, crowd out the others, and alter the typical behavior of the group as a whole.[16]

Thus, despite the possible benefits to the group of self-sacrificial behavior, Hayek indicates no mechanism that will ensure that groups with these characteristics will prosper above others. What therefore seems crucial is the selection of the constituent individuals and not the groups as a whole. Accepting this rationale, Viktor Vanberg further argues that Hayek's idea of group selection and his theory of socioeconomic evolution is inconsistent with methodological individualism. He thus concludes that the "notion of cultural group selection is theoretically vague, inconsistent with the basic thrust of Hayek's individualistic approach, and faulty judged on its own grounds" (1986, 97).

However, Vanberg is wrong to dismiss group selection so easily. It is shown elsewhere (Hodgson, 1991a) that a number of biologists now argue with good reason that there are levels of selection other than the gene, including group selection. Furthermore, apart from biology, there are additional reasons to assume that group selection may operate in cultural evolution. Some of these reasons will be discussed later.

As already noted, the idea of group selection does seem to conflict with a thoroughgoing methodological individualism, and there is a major internal inconsistency in Hayek's work. There seem at first to be two ways out of the difficulty: either to abandon group selection or to at least modify the individualistic thrust. Vanberg suggests the former, claiming an accord with both methodological individualism and attempts in biology to explain group phenomena in genetic terms.

The possibility of group selection

Biologists who argue the case for the possibility of group selection do not suggest that group selection will always operate; it depends on the processes and structures involved. Essentially, group selection is seen to act if all organisms in the same group are "bound together by a common fate" (Sober 1981, 107). A population of (diverse) units is so interlinked, with spillover effects and externalities, that it is selected upon as an entity.[17]

But what if the behavior of this interlinked group could somehow be explained in terms of the genes or individuals involved? Philosophers of biology such as Elliott Sober (1981) point out that a reductionist explanation in terms of genes – if one were possible – leaves open the question of what causes the gene frequencies themselves to alter. Although all information about ostensible group selection may be reduced to and represented by selection coefficients of organisms or genes, such a formal reduction to the genic or individual level leaves the question unanswered as to what causes the frequency of genes in the gene pool to change. Likewise, methodological individualist explanations leave open the questions of the origin or molding or composition of a population of individuals with their preferences and purposes.

In turn, the response to this argument from the genetic reductionist may be that the gene is the single unit of replication. However, while biological objects pass on their characteristics via their genes, this leaves open the question as to what causes their differential transmission. Just as individuals may be regarded as groups of genes that have become functionally organized by natural selection to perpetuate themselves, groups can be seen as groups of individuals similarly functionally organized.

Given the possibility of group selection in biology, it can be conjectured that the same phenomenon occurs in the socioeconomic sphere. Considerations of institutions, rules, norms, and culture are apposite. Assume that a particular characteristic affects all members of a group to a similar degree, such as the enforcement of different modes of diet, dress, or behavior. Assume further that this characteristic affects the future growth and prosperity of the group. Then there may be grounds for considering that group selection is at work. Thus, for example, the Shakers as a religious sect have approached demise because of their internal law of celibacy. In earlier times, as Max Weber argues, Protestant communities or nations prospered relative to the Catholics, partly because of their relatively individualistic culture and their disposition to accumulate worldly wealth.

Note that these examples are not straightforward cases of individual selection; it is not simply individuals with given behavioral propensities that are being selected. Although there was selection in favor of individuals who did not join Shaker sects, the preferences and behaviors of individuals were themselves changed, by indoctrination or cultural pressure, by becoming part of that group. Accordingly, groups and group cultures were being selected, or selected against, as well as were individuals.

Indeed, it could be argued that group selection is more likely with cultural inheritance in human society than with genetic transmission in the biotic sphere. Hence, although the parallel argument in biology is informative, the idea of cultural group selection does not depend on it. Cultural transmission is more collective and conformist than genetic transmission. As Robert Boyd and Peter Richerson (1985, 204–40) have shown, conformism provides a compensating mechanism to overcome the free-rider problem. Consequently, the potential free rider is under strong pressure not to free ride but to conform to the group. The different nature of the transmission process establishes a strong case for cultural group selection.

Organizational knowledge and group selection

There is another important reason for group selection that seems to be barred by Hayek's individualistic outlook. Following Michael Polanyi (1957, 1967), he stresses the importance of tacit knowledge. Like Polanyi, he relates this exclusively to individuals. However, experience suggests that it may in some sense reside in groups as well. An example is suggested by Sidney Winter (1982), who argues that the capabilities of an organization such as a firm are not generally reducible to the capabilities of individual members:

> The coordination displayed in the performance of organizational routines is, like that displayed in the exercise of individual skills, the fruit of practice. What requires emphasis is that . . . the learning experience is a shared experience of organization members. . . . Thus, even if the contents of the organizational memory are stored only in the form of memory traces in the memories of individual members, it is still an organizational knowledge in the sense that the fragment stored by each individual member is not fully meaningful or effective except in the context provided by the fragments stored by other members. (1982, 76)

Clearly, there is an important question here concerning the possibility of collective knowledge.[18] Hayek is not the only theorist to deny this and take an individualist position. For instance, Ward Goodenough (1981, 54) writes that "people learn as individuals. Therefore, if culture is learned, its ultimate locus must be in individuals rather than in groups." In taking an individualistic view of knowledge, Hayek is thus a member of an eminent collective.

In contrast, there is the "collectivist" position of anthropologists such as Marvin Harris (1971, 136), a stance more in accord with that of Winter: "Cultures are patterns of behavior, thought and feeling that are acquired or influenced through learning and that are characteristic of groups of people rather than of individuals." Arguably, culture is not simply "information affecting individuals" (Boyd and Richerson 1985, 33); it consists not merely of beliefs and assumptions, but also behavior patterns, habits, language, and signs, even rituals and patterns of behavior (Keesing 1974). Furthermore, the kind of information that is used and transmitted in a culture is embedded in social structures and organizations, in the sense that its existence and transmission depends on them. Even the kind of information held by a single individual is typically context dependent; information and structure are mutually intertwined. It is thus difficult to locate culture in individual persons. Culture and institutions transcend the individuals to whom they relate. By seeing culture as a structured and interactive belief–action system, its collective quality can be appreciated.

Winter's own argument suggests that although tacit or other knowledge must reside in the nerve or brain cells of a set of human beings, its enactment depends crucially on the existence of a structured context in which individuals interact with each other. Otherwise, no such knowledge can become operational. Furthermore, because organizational knowledge is tacit knowledge, by definition it cannot be expressed in a codified form. The knowledge becomes manifest only through the interactive practice of the members of the group. It is both learned and transmitted in a group context only.

There are many cases where the organizational knowledge is maintained within a structure, perhaps even for long periods of time, despite the turnover of its individual members. Just as our personal memory of past events is retained, despite the loss and renewal of our brain cells, organizational knowledge may survive the gradual but complete replacement of the individuals comprising the organization.

Clearly both individual and organizational outcomes depend on the nature of any such organizational knowledge. Here is a clear case of the fates of a number of individuals being bound together in a single group. Such organizational learning is thus feasibly associated with group selection.

Organizational knowledge can relate to a subset of the workers within a firm. If the knowledge relates to all the workers in a firm, or crucial aspects of its management, then the organization in which that particular organizational knowledge resides is the firm as a whole.

Selection may thus operate on a subset of the firm's routines, as in the selection process modeled by Richard Nelson and Sidney Winter (1982). If in contrast some aspects of "organizational learning" are inextricably related to the firm as a whole, then this implies the selection of firms and not simply the capabilities or routines that may reside within them.

We have noted that for Hayek it is the individual rather than the organization that is the carrier of the rule. But if there is such a thing as organizational knowledge, as just discussed, it would be a mistake to attempt an account of this wholly in terms of the interaction of individuals. As Hayek (1967, 71) himself puts it, "The existence of the whole cannot be accounted for wholly by the interaction of the parts but only in their interaction with an outside world both of the individual parts and the whole." In the present context this would suggest that the existence of collective knowledge can be accounted for only by the interaction of individuals and by their interactions with the environment and the group. But this interpretation seems to conflict with Hayek's proposition that rules are carried by individuals alone. Once again, there seems to be a contradiction in Hayek's thought.

Organizational knowledge involves externalities and spillovers of a significant kind. More generally, whenever a behavioral rule or attribute has strong positive externalities, thus affecting other individuals or rules, then the possibility of group selection may arise. The operation of such strong externalities implies that the benefits of one positively affect the welfare of others, and thereby a number of units are again "bound together by a common fate." In sum, the existence of some kinds of strong positive externality can create the basis for group or other levels of selection.

Markets and still-higher levels of selection

As already noted, the possibility of multiple and higher levels of selection is now accepted by a number of modern biological theorists, including the possibility of selection by species and even ecosystems. There is no apparent reason why multiple levels of selection should not also exist within the socioeconomic world as well.

Hayek sees selection as operating on a plurality of different groups or agencies, but seemingly always within a given (market) structure. Thus, he ignores the possibility that selection may also be working at the level of structure and substructure, creating a diversity not simply of groups and agencies but also of types of economic system or subsystem (Hodgson 1984), as well as a variety of market forms.

Hayek's very conception of the market is part of the difficulty here. In fact, Hayek is remarkably vague on how his image of the market fits into his picture of group selection and the spontaneous order. The fundamental dilemma here is this: Does the market correspond to a particular type of *order,* or does it correspond to the general *context* in which the evolutionary selection of (all) orders takes place?[19] This unresolved dilemma is of vital importance, in both theoretical and policy terms.

In one passage, Hayek (1988, 38–47) proposes the former interpretation. He sketches a history of the emergence of the market, suggesting that it is not itself the context of evolution but an evolved order: a specific outcome of evolution itself. However, this interpretation leaves open the nature of the context in which the selection of the market takes place. To assume that the market is itself selected in a market environment is either incoherent or suggests the important but unacknowledged possibility of a nested set of market structures in which selection occurs: a market for markets.

Furthermore, such a formulation does not imply that the particular evolved market is necessarily optimal or ideal. It is a general but common mistake to regard evolution in such terms (Hodgson, 1991b, 1993).

In contrast, in an earlier work, Hayek (1982, 3:162) supports the interpretation of the market as the general context of selection. The problem with this, however, is that Hayek does not explain how the specific rules and property rights associated with the market themselves emerge. The crucial question is left open as to how this long-standing general context of selection itself originally evolved.

Criticizing Hayek on this point, Vanberg (1986, 75) points out that the market "is always a system of social interaction characterized by a specific *institutional framework,* that is, by a *set of rules* defining certain restrictions on the behavior of market participants." Whether these rules are formal or informal, the result is that there is no such thing as the "true, unhampered market" operating in an institutional vacuum. "This raises the issue of what rules can be considered 'appropriate' in the sense of allowing for a beneficial working of the market mechanism" (97).[20]

Notably, the market itself is not a natural datum or ether, but is itself a *social institution,* governed by sets of rules defining restrictions on some, and legitimating other, behaviors. Furthermore, the market is necessarily embedded in other social institutions such as the state and is promoted or even in some cases created by conscious design.[21] Given that markets are themselves institutions, then they must all constitute objects of evolutionary selection, alongside other institutions of various types.

Given that the idea of supraindividual levels of selection is justified – an idea accepted by Hayek but not by Vanberg – then Hayek should be criticized, not for embracing group selection and eschewing a consistent individualism, but for failing to incorporate additional processes of selection above the group level.

This point, however, has embarrassing consequences for Hayek's theory. Clearly, such supraindividual selection must involve the selection of different types of institution, including varieties of both market and nonmarket forms. To work at such higher levels, evolutionary selection must involve different types of ownership structure and resource allocation mechanisms, all coexisting in a mixed economy.

It is thus important to emphasize that evolutionary theory does not justify the purified and ubiquitous market system that Hayek endorses. If the market is the *context* of selection, then the origin of this framework is itself unexplained. If the market is an *object* of selection, then for its selection to be real it must exist alongside other nonmarket forms. The rehabilitation of group selection, based on modern work in biology, thus rebounds on Hayek himself. His work presents multiple dilemmas from which there is no apparent escape.

Spontaneous order and evolution

Hayek writes repeatedly of the coupling of the "twin ideas of evolution and spontaneous order,"[22] implying that they are two facets of a single conception. But as Ellen Paul (1988, 261) argues, "The relationship between Hayek's concept of spontaneous order and his evolutionism is unclear."[23]

Nevertheless, to bolster his central idea, he linked the concept of spontaneous order together with "autopoiesis, cybernetics, homeostasis, spontaneous order, self-organisation, synergetics, systems theory" (Hayek 1988, 9) as supposedly allied and similar ideas and cited works by Ilya Prigogine and others (Hayek 1982, 3:200) in their support. However, this list of topics is not itself conceptually or theoretically homogeneous. It further betrays a serious shortcoming of Hayek's work: a lack of clarity about the crucial concept of spontaneous order.

It should be noted at the outset, however, that the ideas listed are developments of cybernetics and systems theory, and the latter very much owes its development to biological theorists such as Ludwig von Bertalanffy and Paul Weiss.[24] Nevertheless, a key point of the development of these "sciences of complexity" is their synthesis in the 1960s with nonequilibrium dynamics. This led to the distinctive ideas of autopoiesis and self-organization.[25] A crucial feature of autopoietic or self-organizing systems is the emergence of order from apparent chaos in a far-from-equilibrium state. In contrast, simpler systems are typically presented as being in equilibrium, or close to it.

The most charitable interpretation would be to associate Hayek's idea of a spontaneous order with the more sophisticated ideas of autopoiesis or self-organization. It is not clear, however, if he would want to take all the related baggage on board. For instance, a central idea in the literature on complex and evolving systems is that the occurrence of smooth economic growth over a long period is no guarantee that such a felicitous trajectory will continue. There is always the possibility of abrupt morphogenetic change. Interestingly, such structural disruptions do not need to come from exogenous sources. Working latently during the periods of peaceful development, built-in mechanisms can prepare for eventual catastrophic change.

Accordingly, Ervin Laszlo (1987, 46) argues: "As no autopoietic reaction cycle is entirely immune to disruption, constant changes in the environment sooner or later produce conditions under which certain cycles can no longer operate. The systems encounter a point known in dynamic systems theory as bifurcation." Unlike the intervening periods of relative macrostability, at the point of bifurcation the system is highly sensitive to minute changes. Small variations can affect the entire course and trajectory of development (Prigogine and Stengers 1984). In sum, the notion of spontaneous order, if conceived in these terms, should embrace the twin idea of spontaneous disorder as well.

However, in particular contrast to the evolutionary thought of Veblen, there is no discussion of the possible breakdown of a spontaneous order in Hayek's work. The entire emphasis is on the emergence and stabilization of the order, as an unintended consequence of individual actors. He invests the idea of spontaneous order with a hallowed and inviolable mystery, suggesting that in general it should not be tampered with. Yet if the possibility of spontaneous *dis*order was accepted, then perhaps some grounds for interventionist policies could be readily sustained.

The idea of a self-organizing, "dissipative structure" developed by Prigogine and his collaborators involves the emergence of order through the interaction of continuous fluctuations at the elemental level. Although such fluctuations introduce a limited type of variety into the system, they are kept within limits. Accordingly, Prigogine's work has been criticized by Peter Corning (1983, 75) for putting too much emphasis on the emergence of order: "If there has been order through fluctuations, there has also been disorder through fluctuations." Notably, Corning (70–6) also dwells at length on the similarities between the work of Prigogine and Spencer. Hayek seems to be willingly in the same boat.

In sum, Hayek takes on board a one-sided view of evolution that stresses the emergence of order rather than the possibility of disorder. He even gives relatively little attention to the clash of rival orders in turmoil and war, reassuring us continuously that spontaneous order can and will emerge. With evolution, however, there is no guarantee that it will always be directed toward an ordered state: Chaos and collapse are always possible.

Phylogeny approaching ontogeny

Nevertheless, Hayek seems to want to relate the idea of a spontaneous order to a phylogenetic concept of evolution in which selection is taking place. In this case an important question emerges: Are there major sources of renewed variety and diversity in the system, and if so, from where? We can see novelty as emerging from the creativity of the inventor or the entrepreneur, and potential variety in microscopic fluctuations or in the chaotic forces of nonlinear development. These are plausible sources of variety, but none is made explicit in Hayek's presentation.

In one passage Hayek (1967, 32) writes of "a mechanism of redupli-cation with transmissible variations." Vanberg (1986, 81) sees this as a process of variation in which "continuously new" transmittable vari-ants are "generated." This is something, but not much, to go on. Notably, this remark of Hayek's is in the very same paragraph where he refers to the theory of evolution by natural selection as being "exceedingly simple." However, even quite complex accounts of evolu-tionary process may largely ignore the question of the ongoing source of variety. Although Hayek finds the idea of evolution to be simple, he has left a gaping hole in his account of it. Precisely how is variety generated and renewed? Here, clearly, Hayek's omission of Malthus is telling. It is only in a few places elsewhere (1982, 3:161, 167) where Hayek cautiously talks both of rule breaking and the evolution of new rules.

In fact, Hayek's conception of evolution converges to that of Spencer at this crucial point. With the emphasis on the emergence of a stable order, and the corresponding neglect of the possibility of spontaneous disorder, Hayek's theory strongly resembles that of his nineteenth-century predecessor. Both theories are strictly phylogenetic in char-acter, but with an outcome that converges to a near-stable state.

As in the case of Spencer, the spontaneous order could involve growth and change, just as the ontogenetic development of an organ-ism with fixed genes involves growth. Ontogeny does not imply an equilibrium in a mechanical sense, but it does involve a degree of stability and continuity of form. Thus, it is indeed an equilibrium of a different kind. As Marina Colonna (1990, 64) notes, there is an as-sumption in Hayek's economic writings that "whatever the disturbing factors may be, in a free market economy the inherent tendency to-wards equilibrium finally will prevail, or at least it is always at work."

The movement toward such a well-formed outcome narrows the gap between phylogeny and ontogeny. With no further source of renewal or variety, the former converges on the latter. In this case, Hayek's theory of socioeconomic evolution again resembles Spencer's; it is asymptotic to ontogeny as the kind of variety that is introduced into the system becomes confined, or even progressively dries up. We find in Hayek's theory a case where phylogeny approaches ontogeny: the reverse of Haeckel's famous and controversial law.[26] Although strictly phylogenetic, Hayek's idea of evolution reduces essentially to an ontogenetic metaphor.

In view of this similarity with Spencer, it is uncanny that Hayek

(1982, 3:158) approvingly quotes the following statement of Gregoire Nicolis and Ilya Prigogine: "Wherever we look, we discover evolutionary processes leading to diversification and increasing complexity." This strongly Spencerian idea of evolution creating increasing variety is also suggested elsewhere in his work (Hayek 1988, 26, 126–7), but without acknowledgment of its source in Spencer.

Hayek clearly differs from Spencer in regarding individual rules, rather than individuals or genes, as the units of selection. Also, unlike Spencer, he rejects the idea of explicit laws of evolution (Hayek 1982, 1:23–4, 1982, 3:198). However, in suggesting that evolution involves greater and greater complexity, Hayek has precisely and inadvertently reproduced the alleged "law" of the "transition from something homogeneous and general to something heterogeneous and special" originally found in the work of Karl Ernst von Baer and embraced and popularized by Spencer.

Consequently, spontaneous order and evolution are not necessarily twin ideas at all. If evolution is phylogeny, then it conflicts with the more plausible ontogenetic interpretation of the emergence of a relatively durable and stable order. Phylogeny involves disorder as well as order, and chaos as well as equilibrium. It has been argued here that the greater interpretative weight should be put on the idea that Hayek has a concept of evolution in which there is an ongoing selection process, but in which the process of development, as in Spencer's theory, is asymptotic to ontogeny. The twin ideas are not of spontaneous order and evolution in general, but of spontaneous order and ontogeny.

Hayek and the perfectability of society

This comparison of Hayek and Spencer suggests a further examination of their work for possible similarities. Spencer (1855, 492) proposed that "life attains more and more perfect forms" and that evolution in general meant increasing progress and efficiency.

At first sight Hayek would seem to take a different view. For instance, he insists that there are no grounds to presume that any particular outcome of the evolutionary process is morally superior or necessarily just. As Hayek (1988, 27) puts it, "I do not claim that the results of group selection of traditions are necessarily 'good' – any more than I claim that other things that have long survived in the course of evolution, such as cockroaches, have moral value."

Unlike Spencer, and with the benefit of the hindsight of the totalitarian horrors of the twentieth century, Hayek does not hold the view that evolution is automatically leading in the direction desired by the classic liberal. He acknowledges and bemoans the fact that history evinces far more examples of illiberal than liberal societies. Accordingly, he does not believe that society, left alone, will evolve toward perfection.

With these qualifications, however, there is still a similarity with Spencer on this point. Both Spencer and Hayek call for eternal vigilance in the name of liberty and have similar visions of the better future that is its reward. Both propose a "Great Society" emanating from the strong traditions of classic liberalism, manifest in a set of political and social institutions involving supposedly minimal government and maximum individual liberty, and resting squarely on a constitution protecting well-defined property rights and extensive free markets.

So while Hayek rejects the suggestion that evolution automatically leads to progress, he also has a clear criterion by which advance may be judged: To the extent that rules consistent with the Great Society emerge, function, and overcome the assumed atavistic and collectivist instincts of humankind, then progress is deemed to be made.

Although Hayek has less faith than Spencer in the felicitous outcome of the evolutionary process, he has a clear preference for a particular kind of socioeconomic system and he believes that such a system is attainable. Most of his written output is directly related to the investigation of the principles governing the operation of the Great Society. This utopian strain in his thinking is somewhat underestimated by some other commentators. Notably, Hayek (1933, 123) himself wrote, "It is probably no exaggeration to say that economics developed mainly as the outcome of the investigation and refutation of successive Utopian proposals." Just as there are utopians proposing planned and collectivist solutions, there are those, like Hayek, suggesting an alternative utopia based on private property and markets.[27]

Here the double similarity with Spencer is obvious; both writers are utopians and propose utopias of a very similar variety. Both writers reject socialism, partly because of its apparent denial of diversity. However, while Hayek (1988, 80) quotes Wilhelm von Humbolt's celebration of "human development in its richest diversity," for him, as for Spencer, diversity is to be limited. Both visions are based on the single and ubiquitous economic arrangements of markets and private ownership. They embrace a competitive plurality of economic agents but not a pluralistic diversity involving quite different structural forms. While the pluralism of individuals and entrepreneurs is endorsed, true structural pluralism is shunned.

Although in detail they have different conceptions of the evolutionary process, implicit in the ideas of both Spencer and Hayek is the
common assumption of the eventual perfectibility of society. Strikingly, therefore, both thinkers are vulnerable to the Malthusian critique of the notion of such perfectibility. For Malthus, diversity itself
was essential to progress, and for this reason alone the system could
never take a perfect or purified form. To remain consistent with this
view, the idea of a Great Society based on a single type of structure or
economic arrangement has to be rejected. Arguably, any perfect society based on such a homogeneity of structure, even with an incorporated diversity of agents and cultures, is at risk. Stagnation and lack of
moral impulse may be its fate. Or there could be crises due to insufficient internal structural variety, such variety being necessary so that
novel responses may be generated to unanticipated change.[28]

This Malthusian line of argument finds in Hayek's kind of liberalism an Achilles' heel. Note the relevance here of the discussion of U.S.
liberalism by Louis Hartz (1955), as taken up by Albert Hirschman
(1982). Both Hartz and Hirschman see a problem of potential or
actual stagnation, of both a moral and an economic kind, in the kind
of developed capitalist individualism that is most advanced in the
United States: "Having been 'born equal,' without any sustained struggle against . . . the feudal past, America is deprived of what Europe
has in abundance: social and ideological diversity. *But such diversity is
one of the prime constituents of genuine liberty*" (Hirschman 1982, 1479).
Thus, in contrast to the fake diversity that is proclaimed by devotees
of the individualistic golden age, liberalism taken to extremes becomes its opposite: a monolithic order, embracing a species uniformity
of both ideology and structure, the tyranny of the like-thinking majority and a "colossal liberal absolutism" (Hartz 1955, 285).

The flaw in the kind of classic liberal utopia proposed by Hayek and
Spencer is both to conceive of a perfectible type of system based on a
ubiquitous kind of economic arrangement and to limit the indigenous
diversity to that of agency rather than structure. The Malthusian argument provides an antidote to this conception, even if Malthus himself
did not pursue it to the full. It is thus perhaps no accident that in
Hayek's accounts of the influences on Darwin, the name of Malthus is
omitted (Hodgson 1993, ch. 4).

Final remarks

There is much of great value in Hayek's writing that should not be
ignored. In particular, there is his (1935, 1948) argument that *complete*

central planning is not feasible. This is both correct in its main conclusion and appropriate in its focus on the problems of gathering and processing sufficient or meaningful knowledge about the economy. Furthermore, it has been explicitly or implicitly confirmed by writers less sympathetic to the unrestricted economics of the free market.[29]

While Hayek may go too far in his warnings of possible excesses of overrationalistic or "constructivist" ideas to reform society or transform the economy, his arguments concerning the inevitable decentralization and parcelization of knowledge must still act as powerful counters to those who believe that it is possible to reconstruct the system according to some comprehensive, rational blueprint or plan.

On the negative side, Hayek's evolutionary argument has a number of problems and flaws. While it counters any attachment to one hundred percent central planning, it does not support the policy of universal free markets either. Hayek's evolutionary argument has some resemblance to that of Spencer and social Darwinists such as William Graham Sumner because it still falls back on some strange, detached, and universal selective force emanating from the "free" market. In crucial respects the mechanisms of evolution are unclear. In some areas Hayek's theoretical structure has internal contradictions that are difficult to rectify without major change.

In sum, Hayek's corpus of writings in social science is an immense achievement. Yet his attachment to an evolutionary analysis of socioeconomic evolution creates problems for his enduring attachments both to methodological individualism and to classic liberal ideology.

Notes

The author wishes to thank Stephan Böhm, Philip Mirowski, and other colleagues for comments on earlier versions of this work. This chapter makes extensive use of material from the author's *Economics and Evolution*, chs. 11 and 12.

1. Later on, Hayek (1988, 26) does indeed mention the distinction between ontogeny and phylogeny. This is with a view to associating ontogeny, in contrast with phylogeny, with false and "historicist" notions of economic development. This is misleading because all organisms are open systems, and all ontogenetic development is context-dependent. With an unpredictable environment, and like phylogeny, ontogeny is neither predictable nor historicist.

2. For discussions of the "evolutionary" ideas in the works of Smith, Malthus, Marx, Spencer, Menger, Marshall, Veblen, and Schumpeter, see Hodgson (1993).

3. Some sociobiologists, such as Alexander Alland (1967), go even further,

promoting the unacceptable notion that culture is merely a kind of biological adaptation.

4. The idea of acquired character inheritance in socioeconomic evolution is somewhat tardily recognized by Hayek (1982, 3:156). We must wait even later, and after the influence of Karl Popper (1972), for an explicit description of the socioeconomic evolution as being Lamarckian rather than Darwinian (Hayek 1988, 25).

5. Pollock's quotation, with similar claims by Hayek, is repeated in Hayek (1982, 1:153). At the risk of protesting a little too much, in this same place Hayek (152–3) cites no less than fourteen sources, all in apparent support of Hayek's claim that there were many "Darwinians before Darwin" (23). Unfortunately, five of these references are pre-1900 and thus stem from a period when Darwin's theory was neither fully understood nor universally accepted. Another four stem from 1900 to 1930 when things were only slightly better.

In parading such inappropriate references, Hayek does not seem aware that it is only in the twentieth century that the distinctiveness of Darwin's theory has been widely understood and appreciated. One of the remaining and most recent references by Hayek is to the work by Bentley Glass et al., *Forerunners of Darwin* (1959). Yet Hayek fails to caution us with the words of Glass in the preface of this book, that certain of the alleged forerunners "were hardly evolutionists: others, in their own eyes, not evolutionists at all. Some, who lived in the period after 1859, even hated the Darwinian teaching and fought it vehemently" (vi).

6. Although Herbert Spencer does receive a few brief and rare mentions in Hayek's writings, there is no discussion of his evolutionary theory or that of other nineteenth-century theorists of social evolution, such as Ernst Haeckel, Lewis Henry Morgan, Albert Schäffle, William Graham Sumner, and Edward Tylor. For rather inadequate comparisons of Hayek's work with Sumner or Spencer, see Gray (1984) and Paul (1988).

7. Hayek's faulty account of the influences of and upon Darwin is paralleled by his inadequate examination of other evolutionary thinkers in social science. His failure to give Spencer and Graham Sumner anything more than a passing mention is particularly notable (Paul 1988). Furthermore, his dismissals of the U.S. institutionalists are brief and inaccurate (Leathers 1990, 164–5). Among other things, they are placed in the camp of the German historicists, ignoring not only the criticisms of that very school by Veblen (1919, 58, 252–78), but also the sustained appeal to Darwinian evolutionary theory in the economic thought of the latter theorist.

8. Mayr (1985, 769) goes on to explain that these earlier "evolutionary" theories concerned eliminations of "degradations of type," now referred to as "stabilizing selection." These ideas evinced typological essentialism, not the "population thinking" at the core of Darwin's theory: "Essentialism always had great difficulty in coping with the phenomenon of variation. One of its collateral concepts was that any deviation from the type that was too drastic

would be eliminated. But such a process is not natural selection in the Darwinian sense, a force that would permit directional change and an improvement of adaptation."

9. For mentions of evolutionary selection, see Hayek (1967, 32, 67, 71, 111; 1982, 1:9, 23; 1982, 3:155, 158, 202; 1988, 16, 20, 24, 26).

10. In this passage Hayek suggests that we can recognize a rule simply through the identification and description of its phenomenal form. However, this suggests an empiricist route to the knowledge of rules and ignores the fact that no rule can be known or described independently of concepts and other rules. As Hayek himself writes: "Rules which we cannot state thus do not govern only our actions. They also govern our perceptions, and particularly our perceptions of other people's actions" (1967, 45). Thus, there is a difference between rules governing perception and rules governing action, which is noted (56–7), but not brought out adequately, in his work.

11. See, e.g., Hayek (1967, 46–8; 1982, 3; 155–7; 1988, 21, 24).

12. However, the possibility of the existence of cultural traditions among birds and mammals is recognized by Hayek (1988, 16–17). Contrary to Hayek's earlier antiscientism, this usefully erodes a significant conceptual barrier between the social and the natural world, and suggests that some careful "imitation" of the life sciences by economics might not be so bad after all.

13. Recent attempts not only to combine but also to maintain the autonomy and reality of both structure and choice are provided by Anthony Giddens (1984) and Viktor Vanberg (1988). Although Vanberg's work expresses formal adherence to methodological individualism, while Giddens's does not, it is notable that the gap between them is not as great as it may appear at first sight. Lars Udéhn (1987) argues convincingly that many verbal attachments to methodological individualism are more formal than real and that the prescriptions of strict methodological individualist analysis cannot be fully implemented in practice. Recoiling against mechanistic versions of such a doctrine, G. B. Madison (1990, 91) asserts that Hayek "decidedly rejects the notion held by some methodological individualists that the only acceptable account of social phenomena is an analytic-reductive-empiricist one which is formulated entirely in terms of facts about individuals." However, this raises the question of the nature and viability of the kind of methodological individualism that may be left after the reductive and mechanistic varieties are exorcized.

14. There is a further distinction in Hayek's (1982, 3:140) work between an order and an organization. The state, for example, is an obvious example of the latter. Vanberg takes up this distinction in an interesting comparison of the theories of Menger and Commons; he sees "some kind of deliberate co-ordination of individual actions" as "the essential definitional attribute of what is commonly called an organization" (1989, 342). However, as argued elsewhere, the spontaneity of many real-world institu-

tions, in particular the market, is often overestimated (Hodgson 1988, 173–6).

15. In one passage, however, Dawkins accepts the possibility of an autonomous level of cultural evolution. He argues that because a bit of cultural information can "make copies of itself" (1976, 208), through imitation and learning, it is a viable unit of selection in addition to the gene. This seems to undermine the kind of genetic reductionism that is more prominent elsewhere in his writings and perhaps points to a "dual inheritance" model of the Boyd and Richerson (1985) kind.

16. Faced with arguments such as this, Wynne-Edwards (1978) subsequently accepted that he had failed to specify an adequate mechanism of group selection. More recently, however, he (1986, 316–26) has adopted D. S. Wilson's (1975, 1977, 1980) theoretical justification of the phenomenon, as discussed in Hodgson (1991a).

17. Sober (1985, 880) makes the important point that "group selection hypotheses are examples of population thinking *par excellence*."

18. See also the interesting discussion by Masahiko Aoki (1988) of the collective nature of employee knowledge in the firm. Since "learning and communication of employees take place only within the organizational framework, their knowledge, as well as their capacities to communicate with each other are not individually portable" (45).

19. Robert Sugden (1989, 86) writes that "the market itself is in important respects a spontaneous order," and he considers "the possibility that the institution of property itself may ultimately be a form of spontaneous order." But by extending the concept of spontaneous order to these elemental institutions, Sugden is leaving open the question of the nature of the selection process between different spontaneous orders. He does not describe the structural context in which such selection between (say) market and nonmarket orders takes place. A similar problem arises in a work by Douglass North (1978, 970), in which he suggests that the United States has adopted political regulation of economic transactions rather than pure markets because of the relative price of these two options. In response, Philip Mirowski (1981, 609) points out that this leaves unresolved the issue of "what structures organize this 'meta-market' to allow us to buy more or less market organization."

20. As Vanberg (1986, 99) and M. Prisching (1989) both note, and contrary to many other members of the Austrian school, Carl Menger did not take the suitability of "organic" institutions such as the market for granted.

21. For similar and related points, see Commons (1934, 713), Dosi (1988), Hodgson (1988, ch. 8), Lowry (1976), K. Polanyi (1944), Samuels (1966), and even Robbins (1952). It is also striking that modern experimental economists, in stimulating a market, have found that they have had also to face the unavoidable problem of setting up its institutional structure. As Vernon Smith (1982, 923) writes, "It is not possible to design a resource allocation experiment without designing an institution in all its detail."

22. See Hayek (1967, 77; 1978, 250; 1982, 1:23, 3:158).

23. Paul makes the even more general point that the survival of liberalism must involve the ditching of all evolutionist baggage. Clearly she would prefer the evolutionism, rather than the liberalism, to be thrown away. However, the understanding on which her hostility to evolutionism is based is defective. For instance, she does not note the arguments by modern evolutionary thinkers (such as Gould, 1978, 1980, 1989; Gould and Lewontin, 1979), who reject the idea that what happens to evolve is necessarily superior or just – or even fitter – than what does not. Her poor knowledge of the development of evolutionary theory is exemplified by her suggestion that "under the pressure of Darwinian influences, Spencer came to concede that the 'survival of the fittest' could play a role" (Paul 1988, 271). In fact it was Darwin who was persuaded, against his initial judgment, to adopt the "survival of the fittest" phrase that Spencer had first coined. Nevertheless, while there are several flaws in both her account of evolution and her understanding of Spencer, she is right to point out the tension between the Hayekian concept of a spontaneous order and a specifically Darwinian theory of evolution. In contrast, the allegation of general incompatibility between liberalism and some version of evolutionism remains unproven and unconvincing.

24. See, e.g., Bertalanffy (1952, 1971), Emery (1981), Laszlo (1972), Miller (1978), Weiss (1973), and Weiss et al. (1971).

25. See Benseler et al. (1980), Brooks and Wiley (1988), Jantsch (1975), Laszlo (1987), Nicolis and Prigogine (1977), Prigogine (1980), Prigogine and Stengers (1984), Salthe (1985), Varela et al. (1974), Wicken (1987), and Zeleny (1980, 1981).

26. For an excellent discussion of Haeckel's law – "ontogeny recapitulates phylogeny" – see Gould (1977).

27. In contrast, Commons (1950, 29) rejected fixed constitutions as reflecting the "individualistic devices of our founding fathers." Charles Leathers has made a useful comparison of the theories of Commons and Hayek, noting that "by interpreting the evolutionary changes in customs as a process of natural selection, Hayek was able to develop his concept of spontaneous orders and, hence, an argument against activist government. By interpreting the same evolutionary process as involving artificial selection guided by human purpose, Commons developed a much more activist view of government as a generally positive form of collective action that creates a workable mutuality which is sustainable even as economic and political conditions change" (Leathers 1989, 378).

28. For a further discussion of this concept of "insufficient variety" and the related "impurity principle," see Hodgson (1984, 108, 238; 1988, 257–8, 262–7, 303–4).

29. See, e.g., Hodgson (1984) and Nove (1983).

References

Alland, Jr., A. 1967. *Evolution and Human Behavior*. New York: Natural History Press.

Aoki, M. 1988. *Information, Incentives and Bargaining in the Japanese Economy*. Cambridge University Press.

Barry, N. 1979. *Hayek's Social and Economic Philosophy*. London: Macmillan.

Benseler, F., Hejl, P. M., and Koeck, W. K. (eds.) 1980. *Autopoiesis, Communication and Society*. Frankfurt: Campus.

Bertalanffy, L., von. 1952. *Problems of Life: An Evaluation of Modern Biological Thought*. New York: Wiley.

Bertalanffy, L., von. 1969. "Chance or Law," in Koestler and Smythies (1969, 56–84).

Bertalanffy, L. von. 1971. *General System Theory: Foundation Development Applications*. London: Allen Lane.

Böhm, S. 1989. "Hayek on Knowledge, Equilibrium and Prices: Context and Impact," *Wirtschaftspolitische Blatter*, 36(2): 201–13.

Boland, L. A. 1982. *The Foundations of Economic Method*. London: Allen & Unwin.

Bowler, P. J. 1983. *The Eclipse of Darwinism: Anti-Darwinism Evolution Theories in the Decades Around 1900*. Baltimore: Johns Hopkins University Press.

Bowler, P. J. 1988. *The Non-Darwinian Revolution: Reinterpreting a Historical Myth*. Baltimore: Johns Hopkins University Press.

Boyd, R., and Richerson, P. J. 1985. *Culture and the Evolutionary Process*. Chicago: University of Chicago Press.

Brooks, D. R., and Wiley, E. O. 1988. *Evolution as Entropy: Toward a Unified Theory of Biology*, 2d ed. Chicago: University of Chicago Press.

Colonna, M. 1990. "Hayek on Money and Equilibrium," *Contributions to Political Economy*, 9:43–68.

Commons, J. R. 1934. *Institutional Economics: Its Place in Political Economy*. New York: Macmillan. Reprinted 1990 with a new introduction by M. Rutherford, New Brunswick, NJ: Transaction.

Commons, J. R. 1950. *The Economics of Collective Action*. New York: Macmillan.

Corning, P. A. 1983. *The Synergism Hypothesis: A Theory of Progressive Evolution*. New York: McGraw-Hill.

Dawkins, R. 1976. *The Selfish Gene*. Oxford University Press.

Dawkins, R. 1982. *The Extended Phenotype: The Gene as the Unit of Selection*. Oxford University Press.

Dawkins, R. 1986. *The Blind Watchmaker*. Harlow: Longman.

Dawkins, R. 1989. *The Selfish Gene*, 2d ed. Oxford University Press.

Dosi, G. 1988. "Institutions and Markets in a Dynamic World," *Manchester School*, 56(2):119–46.

Elster, J. 1982. "Marxism, Functionalism and Game Theory," *Theory and Society* 11(4):453–82.

Elster, J. 1983. *Explaining Technical Change*. Cambridge University Press.

Emery, F. E. (ed.) 1981. *Systems Thinking*, 2 vols. Harmondsworth: Penguin.

Giddens, A. 1984. *The Constitution of Society: Outline of the Theory of Structuration*. Cambridge: Polity Press.

Glass, B., Temkin, O., and Strauss, W. L. Jr., (eds.) 1959. *Forerunners of Darwin, 1745–1859*. Baltimore: Johns Hopkins University Press.

Goodenough, W. H. 1981. *Culture, Language and Society*. Menlo Park, CA: Benjamin-Cummings.

Gould, S. J. 1977. *Ontogeny and Phylogeny*. Cambridge, MA: Harvard University Press.

Gould, S. J. 1978. *Ever Since Darwin: Reflections in Natural History*. London: Burnett Books.

Gould, S. J. 1980. *The Panda's Thumb: More Reflections in Natural History*. New York: Norton.

Gould, S. J. 1989. *Wonderful Life: The Burgess Shale and the Nature of History*. London: Hutchinson Radius.

Gould, S. J., and Lewontin, R. C. 1979. "The Spandrels of San Marco and the Panglossian Paradigm: A Critique of the Adaptationist Programme," *Proceedings of the Royal Society of London*, Ser. B, 205:581–98. Reprinted in Sober (1984).

Gray, J. 1984. *Hayek on Liberty*. Oxford: Blackwell.

Harris, M. 1971. *Culture, Man and Nature*. New York: Crowell.

Hartz, L. 1955. *The Liberal Tradition in America: An Interpretation of American Political Thought Since the Revolution*. New York: Harcourt, Brace, World.

Hayek, F. A. 1933. "The Trend of Economic Thinking," *Economica*, 1(2):121–37.

Hayek, F. A. (ed.) 1935. *Collectivist Economic Planning*. London: Routledge & Kegan Paul.

Hayek, F. A. 1948. *Individualism and Economic Order*. Chicago: University of Chicago Press.

Hayek, F. A. 1952. *The Counter-Revolution of Science: Studies on the Abuse of Reason*, 1st ed. Glencoe, IL: Free Press.

Hayek, F. A. 1967. *Studies in Philosophy, Politics and Economics*. London: Routledge & Kegan Paul.

Hayek, F. A. 1978. *New Studies in Philosophy, Politics, Economics and the History of Ideas*. London: Routledge & Kegan Paul.

Hayek, F. A. 1982. *Law, Legislation and Liberty*, 3-vol. combined ed. London: Routledge & Kegan Paul.

Hayek, F. A. 1988. *The Fatal Conceit: The Errors of Socialism – Collected Works of F. A. Hayek*, vol. 1. London: Routledge.

Hirschman, A. O. 1982. "Rival Interpretations of Market Society: Civilizing, Destructive, or Feeble?" *Journal of Economic Literature*, 20(4):1463–84. Reprinted in Hirschman (1986).

Hirschman. A. O. 1986. *Rival Views of Market Societies*. New York: Viking.

Hodgson, G. M. 1984. *The Democratic Economy: A New Look at Planning, Markets and Power*. Harmondsworth: Penguin.

Hodgson, G. M. 1988. *Economics and Institutions: A Manifesto for a Modern Institutional Economics.* Cambridge and Philadelphia: Polity Press and University of Pennsylvania Press.

Hodgson, G. M. 1991a. "Hayek's Theory of Cultural Evolution: An Evaluation in the Light of Vanberg's Critique," *Economics and Philosophy,* 7 (1):67–82.

Hodgson, G. M. 1991b. "Economic Evolution: Intervention Contra Pangloss," *Journal of Economic Issues,* 25(2):519–33.

Hodgson, G. M. 1993. *Economics and Evolution: Bringing Life Back into Economics.* Cambridge: Polity Press and Ann Arbor: University of Michigan Press.

Jantsch, E. 1975. *Design for Evolution: Self-Organization and Planning in the Life of Human Systems.* New York: Braziller.

Keesing, R. 1974. "Theories of Culture," *Annual Review of Anthropology,* 3:73–9.

Koestler, A., and Smythies, J. (eds.) 1969. *Beyond Reductionism.* Macmillan: London.

Kohn, D. (ed.) 1985. *The Darwinian Heritage.* Princeton, NJ: Princeton University Press.

Laszlo, E. 1972. *Introduction to Systems Philosophy: Toward a New Paradigm of Contemporary Thought.* New York: Harper & Row.

Laszlo, E. 1987. *Evolution: The Grand Synthesis.* Boston: New Science Library – Shambhala.

Leathers, C. G. 1989. "New and Old Institutionalists on Legal Rules: Hayek and Commons," *Review of Political Economy,* 1(3):361–80.

Leathers, C. G. 1990. "Veblen and Hayek on Instincts and Evolution," *Journal of the History of Economic Thought,* 12(2):162–78.

Lowry, S. T. 1976. "Bargain and Contract Theory in Law and Economics," *Journal of Economics Issues,* 10(1):1–22.

Lukes, S. 1973. *Individualism.* Oxford: Blackwell.

Lumsden, C. J., and Wilson, E. O. (1981). *Genes, Mind and Culture: The Co-Evolutionary Process.* Cambridge MA: Harvard University Press.

Madison, G. B. 1990. "Between Theory and Practice: Hayek on the Logic of Cultural Dynamics," *Cultural Dynamics,* 3(1):83–112.

Mayhew, A. 1987. "Culture: Core Concept Under Attack," *Journal of Economic Issues,* 21(2):587–603.

Maynard Smith, J. 1976. "Group Selection," *Quarterly Review of Biology,* 51:277–83.

Maynard Smith, J. 1980. "The Concepts of Sociobiology," in G. S. Stent (ed.), *Morality as a Biological Phenomenon,* 21–30. Berkeley and Los Angeles: University of California Press.

Mayr, E. 1985. "Darwin's Five Theories of Evolution," in Kohn (1985, 755–72).

Miller, J. G. 1978. *Living Systems.* New York: McGraw-Hill.

Mirowski, P. 1981. "Is There a Mathematical Neoinstitutional Economics?" *Journal of Economic Issues,* 15(3):593–613.

Mises, L. von. 1949. *Human Action: A Treatise on Economics.* London: William Hodge.

Nelson, R. R., and Winter, S. G. 1982. *An Evolutionary Theory of Economic Change*. Cambridge, MA: Harvard University Press.

Nicolis, G., and Prigogine, I. (1977). *Self-Organization in NonEquilibrium Systems: From Dissipative Structures to Order Through Fluctuations*. New York: Wiley.

North, D. C. 1978. "Structure and Performance: The Task of Economic History," *Journal of Economic Literature*, 16(3):963–78.

Nove, A. 1983. *The Economics of Feasible Socialism*. London: Allen & Unwin.

Paul, E. F. 1988. "Liberalism, Unintended Orders and Evolutionism," *Political Studies*, 36(2):251–72.

Polanyi, K. 1944. *The Great Transformation*. New York: Rinehart.

Polanyi, M. 1957. *Personal Knowledge: Towards a Post-Critical Philosophy*. London: Routledge & Kegan Paul.

Polanyi, M. 1967. *The Tacit Dimension*. London: Routledge & Kegan Paul.

Pollock, F. 1890. *Oxford Lectures and Other Discourses*. London: Macmillan.

Popper, K. R. 1945. *The Open Society and Its Enemies*, 2 vols. London: Routledge & Kegan Paul.

Popper, K. R. 1972. *Objective Knowledge: An Evolutionary Approach*. Oxford University Press.

Prigogine, I. 1980. *From Being to Becoming*. New York: Freeman.

Prigogine, I., and Stengers, I. 1984. *Order Out of Chaos: Man's New Dialogue With Nature*. London: Heinemann.

Prisching, M. 1989. "Evolution and Design of Social Institutions in Austrian Theory," *Journal of Economic Studies*, 16(2):47–62.

Robbins, L. 1952. *The Theory of Economic Policy*. London: Macmillan.

Salthe, S. N. 1985. *Evolving Hierarchical Systems*. New York: Columbia University Press.

Samuels, W. J. 1966. *The Classical Theory of Economic Policy*. Cleveland, OH: World.

Smith, V. L. 1982. "Microeconomic Systems as an Experimental Science," *American Economic Review*, 72(5):923–55.

Sober, E. 1981. "Holism, Individualism, and the Units of Selection," in P. D. Asquith and R. N. Giere (eds.), *Philosophy of Science Association: 1980*, 2:93–121. East Lansing, MI: Philosophy and Science Association.

Sober, E. (ed.) 1984. *Conceptual Issues in Evolutionary Biology: An Anthology*. Cambridge, MA: MIT Press.

Sober, E. 1985. "Darwin on Natural Selection: A Philosophical Perspective," in Kohn (1985, 867–99).

Spencer, H. 1855. *The Principles of Psychology*. London: Williams & Norgate.

Sugden, R. 1989. "Spontaneous Order," *Journal of Economic Perspectives*, 3(4):85–97.

Tomlinson, J. 1990. *Hayek and the Market*. London: Pluto Press.

Trivers, R. L. 1985. *Social Evolution*. Menlo Park, CA: Benjamin-Cummings.

Udéhn, L. 1987. *Methodological Individualism: A Critical Appraisal*. Uppsala: Uppsala University Reprographics Centre.

Vanberg, V. J. 1986. "Spontaneous Market Order and Social Rules: A Critique of F. A. Hayek's Theory of Cultural Evolution," *Economics and Philosophy*, 2(June):75–100.

Vanberg, V. J. 1988. "Rules and Choice in Economics and Sociology," *Jahrbuch für Neue Politische Ökonomie*, 7 (Tübingen: Mohr):1–2.

Vanberg, V. J. 1989. "Carl Menger's Evolutionary and John R. Commons' Collective Action Approach to Institutions: A Comparison," *Review of Political Economy*, 1(3):334–60.

Varela, F. J., Maturana, H. R., and Uribe, R. 1974. "Autopoiesis: The Organization of Living Systems, Its Characterization and a Model," *Bio-Systems*, 5:187–96.

Veblen, T. B. 1919. *The Place of Science in Modern Civilisation and Other Essays.* New York: Huebsch. Reprinted 1990 with a new introduction by W. J. Samuels, New Brunswick, NJ: Transaction.

Weiss, P. A. 1973. *The Science of Life.* Mt. Kisco, NY: Futura.

Weiss, P. A., et al. 1971. *Hierarchically Organized Systems in Theory and Practice.* New York: Hafner.

Wicken, J. S. 1987. *Evolution, Thermodynamics, and Information: Extending the Darwinian Paradigm.* Oxford University Press.

Williams, G. C. 1966. *Adaptation and Natural Selection.* Princeton, NJ: Princeton University Press.

Wilson, D. S. 1975. "A General Theory of Group Selection," *Proceedings of the National Academy of Sciences, U.S.A.*, 72:143–6.

Wilson, D. S. 1977. "Structured Demes and the Evolution of Group Advantageous Traits," *American Naturalist*, 111:157–85.

Wilson, D. S. 1980. *The Natural Selection of Populations and Communities.* Menlo Park, CA: Benjamin-Cummings.

Wilson, D. S., and Sober, E. 1989. "Reviving the Superorganism," *Journal of Theoretical Biology*, 136:337–56.

Wilson, E. O. 1975. *Sociobiology.* Cambridge, MA: Harvard University Press.

Winter, Jr., S. G. 1982. "An Essay on the Theory of Production," in S. H. Hymans (ed.), *Economics and the World Around It*, 55–91. Ann Arbor, MI: University of Michigan Press.

Wynne-Edwards, V. C. 1962. *Animal Dispersion in Relation to Social Behaviour.* Edinburgh: Oliver & Boyd.

Wynne-Edwards, V. C. 1978. "Intrinsic Population Control: An Introduction," in F. J. Ebling and D. M. Stoddart (eds.), *Population Control by Social Behaviour*, 1–22. London: Institute of Biology.

Wynne-Edwards, V. C. 1986. *Evolution Through Group Selection.* Oxford: Blackwell.

Zeleny, M. (ed.) 1980. *Autopoiesis, Dissipative Structures, and Spontaneous Social Orders.* Boulder, CO: Westview.

Zeleny, M. (ed.) 1981. *Autopoiesis: A Theory of Living Systems.* New York: North Holland.

PART V

Negotiating over Nature

CHAPTER 17

The realms of the Natural

PHILIP MIROWSKI

One major theme of the inquiry into the place of Natural metaphors in economics is the question of order and how we know whether we have it or whether it has slipped through our grasp. Because the notion of order is frequently treated as an undefined primitive, we find references made to it only obliquely or covertly, often through the use of analogy and metaphor. This volume is devoted to the excavation of metaphors of Natural Order in the history of economic thought, such as orderly ongoing barter compared to celestial mechanics, the orderly capitalist firm conceptualized as a living body, and the orderly profession of bankers as competent physicians. When I first embarked upon my Koch lecture, I thought I might attempt a systematic review of the literature on the role of metaphor and analogy in science, which has grown to enormous proportions in the past two decades.[1] However, a quick perusal of some of this literature convinced me that most writers there were striving to instill a little order of their own in metaphor itself, and I did not relish the prospect of using one fuzzy literature to drape a shroud of obscurity over a separate one. In any event, one of the great attractions of metaphorical discourse is precisely its intrinsic fuzziness, which comes from playing with the notion of identity of two disparate and dissimilar phenomena; and so there seems something willfully perverse about trying to reduce the effulgent effervescence of creative metaphorical confusion to a few simple cut-and-dried categories. Attempts to define and formalize metaphor are fun, but they won't be retailed as expert system programs for the PC in our lifetimes.

Thus I elected instead to concentrate on the process of constructing conceptions of order that undergirds and motivates many of the incidents discussed in this volume. I propose to explore the problem that the description of the Social in terms of the Natural does not automatically banish all dispute or dissension, nor does it invariably foster the conviction of order among social theorists or among the general populace. In other words, natural metaphor is not always naturally effective. I should like to ask, What could possibly account for its success when it does work? When does law and order reign in the realms of the natural?

There are a number of hallowed theoretical traditions in the human sciences that bear directly upon this topic, especially those dating from the Enlightenment and the nineteenth-century German reaction to it.[2] Although their discussions would still repay close attention, I shall not attempt a survey here, mainly because the very Germanic idea that the natural and the social require dichotomous realms has never been accorded much respect in English-speaking cultures throughout most of the twentieth century.[3] The predominant attitude in our little neck of the woods has been rather that the obvious successes of our versions of the natural sciences must transparently dictate that their methods and modalities should be eminently applicable to social questions, essentially consummating the Enlightenment project of their unification.

The other important literature that bears upon our topic is the modern trend towards a sociology or anthropology of science, which has sought to turn the Enlightenment project upon its head: Instead of accepting the overwhelming orientation of economists, political scientists, and psychologists that the Social is identical with the Natural, these sociologists, anthropologists, and literary theorists insist that the Natural is itself Social. Although they differ in various respects, the Edinburgh "Strong Programme" of David Bloor, Barry Barnes, and Steven Shapin, the philosophical anthropology of Mary Douglas by way of Emile Durkheim and Marcel Mauss, the archaeology of knowledge of Michel Foucault, and the participant ethnography of Bruno Latour and Harry Collins all tend to reduce the natural sciences to various norms, coalitions, and self-interested strategies. This, of course, can only discomfit those who hoped to endow social science with some rigor by appropriating natural science methods.

From the vantage point of metaphorical analysis, one of the most interesting theoretical developments of the social studies of science is probably the Durkheim–Mauss–Douglas thesis, which assumes increasingly more elaborate forms as we approach the present.[4] For Durkheim and Mauss in 1903, it was an assertion that "the classification of things reproduces the classification of men." For Mary Douglas

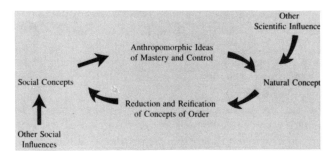

Figure 17.1. Durkheim–Mauss–Douglas thesis.

in 1973, it was "The social body constrains the way the physical body is perceived. The physical experience of the body, always modified by the social categories through which it is known, sustains a particular view of society" (93). I might wish to amend her version further to state that anthropomorphic ideas of mastery and control induce a bias in cultures to project their own social categories onto their explanations of the external world; but in an infinite regress, subsequent reification of notions of order prompt others in the same culture to appropriate those preceding Natural concepts and re-project them back into models and images of society. It seems to me that concrete examples of this game of metaphorical musical chairs in the history of Western science are legion; they grace so many narratives in the history of science that someone should produce a catalogue of them someday.[5]

It has been argued by many, including some of the contributors to this volume, that the Durkheim–Mauss–Douglas thesis, and indeed much of this recent literature in the sociology and anthropology of science, is fundamentally flawed, for two major reasons: (1) It is much too narrowly functionalist, in pretending that there is some coherent social theory of norms, interests, and coalitions lurking behind our Natural convictions, but which simply cannot be underwritten by any extant theoretical tradition; and (2) it treats any social order as if it were purely stipulative and conscious, ignoring the role of custom, habit, the unconscious, and brute historical contingency in buttressing social order. As someone schooled in neoclassical economics and therefore preternaturally suspicious of ahistorical explanations from transparent fixed self-interest, I must confess that these objections have gained in gravity over time what they perhaps lack in theoretical precision. Even in the social studies of science literature, one now begins to see trepidations broached here and there that the social constructivist program is really just another form of the modernist or Enlightenment project of the long-sought-after unity of the sciences, substituting an elusive metanarrative of the ineffable unity of Society for an equally elusive metanarrative of the unity of Nature.[6]

To avoid this impending gridlock, I would like to propose an alternative approach to the problem of the constitution of the Natural and the Social, an approach that attempts neither an Enlightenment-style reunification, nor a Germanic quarantine, nor a sociological inversion. I will not seek to categorize the Natural and the Social according to their putatively legitimate methods, since one of the hallmarks of the past quarter-century of the history and philosophy of science is a profound skepticism concerning the existence of a uniquely "scientific" method. Nor will I attempt to isolate their respective hegemonies in subject matters, since a historian of ideas is resigned to the fact that imperialist pretensions will always be a motive in any organized inquiry. I will, however, maintain that one is not free to dispense with the distinction between the Natural and the Social in Western culture; indeed, so important are those categories that their mere appearance is a sure sign of crisis somewhere in the polity.

I would like us to entertain the hypothesis that the Natural and the Social are merely provisional designations in our culture for where explanation will halt during a crisis. In other words, those concerned with problems in shoring up order conventionally deemed "social" will often repair to Nature for their resources, while those occupied with conceptual problems in their theories of nature will resort, tacitly or explicitly, to images of the Social. In this stance, there is absolutely nothing fixed about the respective capital-N capital-S definitions or their content, as we shall shortly witness. Furthermore, this hypothesis will be made operational by the corollary that the Natural–Social distinction is indispensable in Western culture, a tonic to render tolerable the inherent anthropomorphic character of every viable definition of order, and to create what Thomas Nagel has dubbed "the view from nowhere" (McFague, 1982; Nagel 1986; Daston 1992a, 1992b). In other words, we shall assume that every recent comprehensible order is irredeemably anthropomorphic, or as Charles Saunders Peirce put it, "I do not believe that man can have the idea of any cause or agency so stupendous that there is any more adequate way of conceiving it than as vaguely like a man" (1965, 5:536). In modern Western culture, this anthropomorphic theme is generally tidily disguised and repressed so that order can truly remain authoritative. What the Natural–Social distinction does in this view is to smooth the transfer of the metaphor of self by buffering the shock of recognition; fine-tuning the tedium of repeatedly encountering the same familiar protagonist in each new setting, or meeting the enemy and always finding it is us.

At this juncture, one might object that we have yet to escape the vague and unworkable functionalist arguments of Durkheim and Douglas, since the hypothesis still appears to posit that some shadowy unspecified actor or entity is rectifying some species of conceptual dilemma in the transcendental logic of the transpersonal arena. On the contrary, I will suggest that this is another way my hypothesis will diverge from all previous work on the definitions of the Social and the Natural. Far from accepting a vague functionalist explanation, I will argue that this dynamic of the Natural–Social distinction is most often played out on a very specific stage and within a very limited sphere, both of which will render the hypothesis amenable to further empirical elaboration. I assert that the boundaries of the Natural and the Social have been explicitly negotiated in the West, either in an actual judicial tribunal or upon a juridical model, and then only when the existing categories of order and disorder are threatened or in disarray. At any other time, the boundaries of the distinction simply lie dormant, much the way we can ignore our breathing or the sewage system or monetary unit when they are in good working order. (Hence, the social studies of science might be regarded as akin to an outbreak of cholera, an opinion often mooted by those revulsed by relativism.)

This periodic remission of consciousness of the Natural–Social distinction might be called "custom" or "habit." Explicit acknowledgment of the role of custom avoids a purely stipulative (or perhaps even rational choice) theory of the Natural–Social distinction, since this particular symbiosis of this cognitive process with the political-juridical model has been entirely arbitrary, thoroughly customary and historically specific to the West. In other words, the "rationality" of this set of practices is not particularly relevant to their theoretical description. The differential jurisdictions of the realms of the Natural and the Social have been free to shift and evolve, since there is no teleological imperative inherent in the juridical model. The major distinguishing characteristic of our juridical model is the central role of analogical reasoning: When is one situation sufficiently like another to sanction application of a particular configuration of existing rules? Hence, the actual deployment of the discourse of the Natural and the Social by any concrete science follows a long process of negotiation and adjudication, the testing and criticism of rival metaphors, the fruit of endless disappointments and shocks to our prior convictions about the orderliness of a universe that has room for us in it precisely because we insist that it looks so very much like us.

To illustrate this hypothesis, and with an eye to the movie option, I shall describe two animal stories and two crashes. In each, we shall observe our themes of the reconfiguration and recalibration of the Social and the Natural within a juridical context, responses to the erosion of order with anthropomorphic anxieties lurking just beneath the surface. For those wondering what all this has to do with economics, rest assured: Market theorists will someday learn that they can dispense with nature-talk only if pigs can fly and money grows on trees.

Animal trials

Figure 17.2 (from Evans 1906, 140–1) portrays an engraving of a fresco that is reported to have graced the transept in the Church of the Holy Trinity in Falaise in Normandy. It depicts the execution of a sow dressed in human attire in the public square in Falaise in 1386. The sow had eaten an infant, and therefore it was sentenced to be mangled in the same manner as the infant and then to be hanged until dead. While such portraits are now rare, the actual judicial proceeding against offending occupants of the animal kingdom was not. Some highlights in the genre are the trial in ecclesiastical court of rats in Autun in 1522, where the subtle legal maneuvers of the distinguished jurist and counsel for the defense Bartholomew Chassenée drew out the proceedings for weeks and weeks, with such arguments that the rats did not obey their summons to the courtroom because of fear of their mortal enemies, the cats (see Evans 1906, 18; Hyde 1916, 706). Another is the trial of a rooster in Basel, Switzerland, in 1474 for laying an egg (see Evans 1906, 162; Walter 1984). Far from being mere fowl play, it was the contention of the prosecution that the rooster was a threat to public order because such eggs might hatch a basilisk – a malignant winged reptile with the head of a cock, the tail of a serpent, and the capacity to destroy men with its glance. These are just a few examples of what appeared to be fairly frequent occurrences in Europe in the fourteenth through eighteenth centuries. Since the publication of E. P. Evans's book on animal trials in 1906, a considerable underground literature on the topic has developed that

Figure 17.2. Pig execution from the cover of Evans (1906).

has unearthed even more instances of such proceedings, extending even well into the twentieth century.[7]

Evans used his animal stories as a pretext to ridicule the Middle Ages as an era of muddled animism and unbridled superstition, but the modern literature has attempted to treat the phenomenon in somewhat more sympathetic terms. It has divided up the animal trials into four rough classes: (1) attacks by animals against individual humans, as with the sow of Falaise; (2) anathemas or excommunications pronounced against swarms or plagues, like the rats of Autun; (3) condemnations of *lusus naturae,* or monstrous freaks, like the rooster of Basel; and (4) prosecution of animals involved in sexual bestiality. Evans's tabulation most assuredly underestimates the prevalence of animal trials, since he primarily enumerates proceedings in the first two categories. Trials in the first and fourth categories seem to have been rather perfunctory, perhaps not even deserving the designation judicial proceeding, with the rare defense of the animal mounted only to preserve the economic interests of the owner. The second and third categories turn out to be much more interesting, often containing long, drawn-out disputes over the culpability and capability of the defendants in the proceeding. Far from being unaware of our more enlightened attitudes toward the place of animals in the larger scheme of things, those antediluvian counsels for the defense, citing such authorities as Thomas Aquinas, would regularly protest that the animals in the dock were insensate and irrational and could therefore suffer no guilt or culpability for their actions. Some have suggested that these trials were nothing more than cynical exercises in neglecting to kill the goose that laid the golden egg, in that jurists were loathe to quash meaningless charades that they found lucrative.[8] While such an explanation resonates with our own self-images as cunning mercantile creatures, it does not ring true for the transcripts of these trials that survive down to the present, with their extensive arguments concerning the merits and significance of the cases. While those suffering from pestilent infestations or freakish disasters might be gullible and easily hoodwinked, it would seem there might be better and more dignified ways to earn a *sou* than sitting beside a sow quoting Aquinas in some provincial courthouse.

What makes these litigations all the more significant is the difficulty of finding their equivalent outside of Europe. J. J. Finkelstein has provided a comparison of the Code of Hammurabi and the Code of Exodus in the Old Testament regarding an ox that gored a human and has shown only in the latter case is there the prescription that the ox must be stoned to death in punishment. Joseph Needham has gone so far as to regard animal trials as indicative of basic cultural differences between Chinese and Occidental conceptions of natural law: If a rooster laid an egg in pre-modern China, it would be the provincial governor or perhaps even the emperor who would be in trouble, not the rooster (see Needham 1969a, 1969b, 575; Finkelstein 1981). Other reports of punishment of animal transgressions in non-Western cultures appear to lack the element of judicial inquiry, which is the most striking characteristic of the European trials here cited. What seems to be relevant in all these cases is not merely the brute fact of revenge, which is of course present in all human culture, but the Western penchant for reestablishing order by means of formal relegation of the offensive beast to its appropriate natural or social category.

One of the more salient characteristics of all four categories of European animal trials was their constitution as an open public inquiry into the exact locus of the violation of prevalent notions of order. If, for instance, a sow killed an infant, it could be attributable to diabolical agency (the devil may have taken possession of the sow) or divine agency (the sow may have been sent to punish us for our sins) or human agency (here anything from the owner's carelessness to a history of a vile training regimen of human flesh), or else it could be attributed to ineffable Nature. One or more of these options could procedurally be ruled out of bounds beforehand, but such a tactic was never effectively foolproof, which accounts for the pervasive uncertainty over the correct venue for these trials, be they ecclesiastical, civil, or criminal courts. Rather than resolve this problem by fiat, always relegating the incident to a single category, as we moderns tend to do, the medieval mind instead subjected the boundaries of the natural and the social causes of animal misbehavior to public judicial inquiry. The judicial option was singularly apt because understanding in each of the categorizations required a different anthropomorphic perspective; yet the appropriateness of each version of anthropomorphism was itself at issue. The appearance of animal trials in the thirteenth century coincides with the revival of rhetoric and the rebirth of the modern legal tradition, all three predicated upon the efficacy of reasoning by analogy and metaphor.

This raises the issue of the possible connection between the aforementioned Western juridical inclination and the rise of modern science in roughly the same time period. It is a speculative conjuncture already broached by Joseph Needham (1969a) and E. V. Walter (1984) among others (e.g., Kelley 1990, 143). While many plausible links have been proposed to account for the temporal coincidence, such as the shared stress on a publicly demonstrative empiricism and a common openness to a conception of probabilistic reasoning, I shall dwell only upon a less-appreciated path from the courtroom to the laboratory described by Katherine Park and Lorraine Daston (1981). They claim that attitudes toward monsters, freaks, and prodigies, such as that found in Figure 17.3, underwent substantial transformation over this period, with the legalistic training of natural philosophers such as Francis Bacon providing the catalyst. Whereas aberrant phenomena had previously been treated as frightening omens fundamentally impervious to human understanding, in the new juridical attitude, "monsters provided both the key to understanding more regular phenomena and the inspiration for human invention. As prodigies, monsters had straddled the boundaries between the natural and the supernatural; as natural history, they bridged the natural and the artificial" (Park and Daston 1981, 25). Thus, the anthologies of grotesqueries and teratologies of the early modern era that contained illustrations like this one were derivative of the judicial mentality of Western Europe and, in fact, constituted the preliminary assays of what ultimately became the laboratory, which finally reduced all those bumptious oddi-

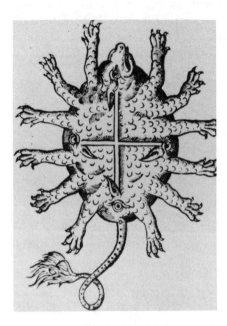

Figure 17.3. Monster from Park and Daston (1981).

ties to a strict Natural regularity. Once the jurisdiction of Nature had been extended, then the monsters would all be banished, as Adam Smith so trenchantly observed:

> Every class of things has its own particular conformation. . . . It is the form which Nature seems to have aimed at in all of them, which, however, she deviates from in a great variety of ways, and very seldom hits exactly; but to which all the deviations bear a strong resemblance . . . Monsters, or what is perfectly deformed, are always most singular and odd, and have the least resemblance to the generality of that species to which they belong. . . . The most customary form is the most beautiful. (1976, 324–5)

The forcible confinement of monsters for the preservation of public order is not so very unlike the confinement of any Natural phenomenon in an artificial setting for the purpose of interrogating it. Since the monster could rarely talk back, it must have an advocate in the ritual proceeding to speak for it; and here the obvious model was the courtroom.

This conjectured similarity between the courthouse and the laboratory is essential for my next example of animal trials. Although the

Figure 17.4. Rat in Skinner box.

inquisitions I shall describe take place before a different kind of bar, I will suggest that it is functionally the same. Figure 17.4 shows a rat in a Skinner box, the very paradigm of a style of behavioralist psychology now largely discredited. But the rat is not illustrating standard behavioralist claims about operant conditioning; the picture exemplifies an experiment run by a group of economists associated in various ways with Texas A&M University and concerned to discover, in their own words, "demand curves for animal consumers." This group, with generous financial support from the National Science Foundation, has been subjecting animals to trials in Skinner boxes since 1975 and has managed to publish the results in all the major journals of the neoclassical economics profession.[9] This development has not escaped controversy. For instance, the respected economist Nicholas Georgescu-Roegen resigned from the American Economics Association in disgust when "Animals' Choices Over Uncertain Outcomes" was published as the lead article in the house journal in 1985. Nevertheless, on the whole it has met with surprisingly little resistance and has even been endorsed by such leading orthodox economists as Robert Lucas (in Hogarth and Reder 1986, esp. 224–7).

It is of profound importance for a comprehension of modern economic attitudes toward the Social and the Natural to reach some preliminary perspective on what this research program does and does not do. First and foremost, it is not an exercise in animal ethology, since the causes and consequences of specific animal behavior patterns are not vigorously pursued. The ethology literature is mostly neglected, and with only one apparent exception, no work of the Texas A&M group appears in those venues. Furthermore, it is hard to regard this research as a serious contribution to the psychological literature, since it neglects all relevant issues of interpretation, conditioning, and learning, instead replicating the type of experiments carried out by a previous generation of behaviorist lab apprentices a half-century ago. Nor is it an attempt to bring animal ecology models over into economics, unlike, say, Kirman (1993). It does not even really legitimately belong in the sociobiology literature, which is far and away more sophisticated about the role of environment and genetic factors in the behavior of specific species. Close examination of the entire sequence of papers demonstrates that the only intended audience of this work is economists, and neoclassical economists, at that. What is going on here?

I want to argue that these animal trials closely resemble the trials of the sow of Falaise or the rats of Autun, although the mise-en-scène has definitely shifted from the courtroom to the laboratory. What provoked the trials in both instances was a transgression of existing notions of order, which then elicited the standard Western response of a judicial inquiry intended to shore up the ragged battlements between the Social and the Natural. The social order at risk, perhaps so transparent to most of us in the case of the sow of Falaise, has to be teased patiently out of the context in this latter case, if only because the anthropomorphic component has grown ever more opaque in modern economics. It takes a broader perspective to see how the exclusiveness and reclusiveness of the laboratory has helped to mask the terrors of a world turned upside down.

The society under stress in the modern animal trials is not the captive pack of rats, but rather the imperiled nursery of neoclassical economists. Notwithstanding their outward trappings of success in the groves of academe, the intellectual roots of their enterprise are being nibbled away by some new organisms in the larger culture. I will dispense here with a rehearsal of its peculiar immediate problems as a latter-day bowdlerization of nineteenth-century physics, which I have discussed in detail elsewhere (Mirowski 1988, 1989, 1992, 1994). Nonetheless, this attempted appropriation of the legitimacy of physics has had further dire implications well beyond the upheavals of the 1870s or the 1930s. First, their imitation of mathematical formalisms has never yet managed the concomitant mimesis of the strong experimental tradition also found in physics; and in the interim it had be-

come a tiresome cliché to bemoan the inability to experiment in economics. This, in turn, has resulted in a widespread impression that
neoclassical theory has been exposed as empirically empty, in the
sense that the Walrasian variant neither rules out nor sanctions any
specific economic phenomenon.[10] When the neoclassical tenets are
augmented by some auxiliary hypotheses that do allow direct empirical access to the central doctrines concerning preferences, the results
have been almost uniformly hostile toward the neoclassical program
(Hogarth and Reder 1986; Sugden 1991). It should go without saying
that these developments have been a severe disappointment to the
scientific pretenses of the program fixated upon establishing the identity of the Social and the Natural.

Second, while neoclassical theory has been nominally based upon
the lawlike structure of individual preferences, the actual relationship
of neoclassical economics to psychology, at least since its salad days
(Mirowski 1994; White, Chapter 8, this volume) has been ambivalent
to the point of disdain. The mathematical dictates of the theory insist
that preferences be regarded as innate and invariant with respect to
the social processes of the market, but few practitioners can bring
themselves to testify wholeheartedly to such a belief. These preferences and the logic of maximization that organize them must also be
self-transparent; so since Freud, any psychological theory that has
made some allowance for a modicum of self-deception has been intrinsically hostile to neoclassical doctrine. Indeed, the only school of psychology in which neoclassicals have shown any sustained interest has
been the most mechanical Fechnerian–Skinnerian behavioralism, and
that is mostly because it is so easily reconciled with their prior mechanical image of human nature. Of course, since behavioralism has lost
much of its luster in psychology, the neoclassicals have been at sixes
and sevens to defend their supposedly individualist and psychologistic
underpinnings.

Third, there has been the rise of sociobiology as a cultural phenomenon. This brute-force attempt to reduce most social formations to
mere excrescences of genetic codes would seem to present a direct
threat to the legitimacy of neoclassical theory, since it would displace
both the physics analogy and the spurious mentalist orientation by a
more palpably direct form of materialism, one firmly rooted in a
biological metaphor. In fact, the actual situation has been a bit more
clouded than that, since E. O. Wilson's 1975 book was chock-full of
simple Marshallian neoclassical models describing insect behavior, although little notice was accorded to that fact at the time. Thus, the
shape of the neoclassical reaction to the challenge was underde-

termined: Had the sociobiologists built a better mousetrap? Total oblivion was one possibility, but some subtle form of accommodation was also equally in the cards.

The Texas A&M animal trials constituted one possible response to this crisis in the standard configuration of the Natural and the Social, and judging by their increasingly warm reception in the neoclassical journals, they have been reasonably effective in restoring some sense of law and order in the neoclassical nest. The Texans' perceptive innovation with respect to the problems of experimentalism, psychology, and sociobiology was to mimic the procedures and literary forms of the behavioral psychologists, so as to counter the criticisms of neoclassicism as devoid of legitimate psychology in a subtle and nonstrident manner. By this, I do not mean to suggest that the authors affiliated with Texas A&M were so cold-bloodedly calculating as to have had this strategy of prudent circumlocution in mind from the very beginning of their project. Indeed, I think a case can be made that the first 1975 paper could have been as much a joke as anything else, with rats expressing their "preferences" between Tom Collins mix and stale root beer (why were the rats assumed not to be connoisseurs of carbonation?) with the putative "income" being a limited number of level presses and putative "prices" being the size of the cup of liquid. But in the subsequent papers, the tone and presentation lose their levity, and the project of "verifying" the core propositions of neoclassical theory becomes prosaic and proleptic to the point of tedium, especially as others hop heedlessly on the treadmill. It would not be the first instance of a *jeu d'esprit* turning into its antithesis.

The analogy with earlier animal trials is apt because the Texas A&M authors are fully aware that they are reconfiguring the conventional boundaries of the Social and the Natural in order to solve some pressing problems. I offer a sampling of quotes: "Ever since Darwin it has been widely recognized that behavior and structure vary continuously across species and that behavioral principles do not stop suddenly at the boundary separating humans from animals" (Kagel et al. 1975, 22). "The fact that the straightforward interpretation of the theory employed yields consistent results in a new domain of application provides renewed scientific evidence for the theoretical concepts of consumer demand theory" (Kagel et al. 1981, 13). "Data allowing straightforward tests of standard microeconomic theories of choice are rare" (Morgan and Tustin 1992, 1134). "Whether or not pigeons or humans have consciously thought out their behavior is irrelevant to characterizing that behavior as a solution to a constrained optimization problem" (Battalio et al. 1981, 88). For these researchers and their audience, animals unproblematically epitomize Nature, and Nature can speak in an unimpeded and *straightforward* manner, if only we can learn to listen: to submit our inquiry to the Court of Legitimation, to speak our questions out loud in a laboratory.

But what is more relevant to our hypothesis is the fact that their papers explicitly cite the challenges or crisis points for which their exercise is a neoclassical response. Kagel et al. (1981) explicitly cite E. O. Wilson's work on sociobiology, as well as discuss the perennial problems of experimentation in neoclassical economics; Battalio et al. (1981) claim to refute the results of Kahneman and Tversky on preference reversals and other disconfirming evidence with regard to neoclassical preferences; Battalio et al. (1985) rejoice in the fact that since rats also display the "Allais paradox," it should be seen as a natural law of psychology and not a direct refutation of expected utility theory. Of course, it must be acknowledged that "a simple myopic gradient learning process will not lead to the optimization solution" (Morgan and Tustin, 1992, 1146), and maybe it seems a little odd to claim that Nature speaks with a pristine voice when all learning effects must somehow be abstracted away by only dealing with "seasoned subjects," but these are the sorts of little internal contradictions and anomalies that can keep an academic research program rolling well into the next century.

When a rooster laid an egg in Basel in the fifteenth century, the rooster went on trial and life went on as before. When a modern research program in economics lays an egg in the twentieth century, pigeons and rats go on trial and life goes on as before.

Big crashes

We turn now to a brace of much more disturbing events, which because of their tragic consequences have each provoked quasi-juridic inquiries into their causes. Figure 17.5 shows a computer-enhanced photograph of the space shuttle *Challenger* on January 28, 1986, immediately after solid rocket motor ignition and just before the takeoff that would end in an explosion and crash just seventy-three seconds later. The crash resulted not only in the loss of five astronauts' and two civilians' lives, but in a collective loss of confidence in the U.S. space program and the ability of the National Aeronautics and Space Administration to manage it. The arrows in the photographs point to a puff of black smoke between the field joint of the right-hand solid rocket booster and the external fuel tank, which rapidly became a prime suspect in the search for the cause of the crash, although it was perplex-

Figure 17.5. Shuttle *Challenger* before takeoff (PCSS 1986; 1:23).

ing in that telemetry and computer monitors did not relay any exceptionally abnormal phenomena right up to the explosion, and subsequent visual reconstructions of the event only detected a plume of
flame on the outside of the booster fifty-eight seconds into the flight,
followed by the rupture of the external tank at seventy-one seconds.

Most people who got their information about this event from the
news media believe that solving the mystery was simply a matter of
scientific and engineering inquiry, and specifically (as in Figure 17.6)
Richard Feynman's widely publicized "experiment" with a C-clamp and
an O-ring dunked in ice water, which finally isolated the culprit as a
defective O-ring seal exacerbated by the abnormally cold weather on
the day of the launch. The published conclusion of the presidential
commission on the accident was actually less specific: "The cause of the
Challenger accident was the failure of the pressure seal in the aft field
joint of the right Solid Rocket Motor. The failure was due to a faulty
design unacceptably sensitive to a number of factors. These factors

Figure 17.6. News photograph of Richard Feynman and O-ring.

were the effects of temperature, physical dimensions, the character of the materials, the effects of reusability, processing and the reaction of the joint to dynamic loading" (Presidential Commission on the Space Shuttle Challenger [PCSS] 1986, 1:72). The reason for this rather less than precise indictment was, quite simply, that the evidence was less unequivocal than it had been made out to be by the news media. The photographic evidence on the black smoke was less than optimal because the two cameras that should have recorded the precise location of the smoke were inoperative on the day of the launch. The visual flame evidence was more solid, but still had to be reconciled with the fact that it was the external tank which ruptured and actually caused the final explosion. The third class of evidence, the recovered wreckage of the solid booster and external tank, was also less than optimal both because the booster and tank were further damaged by the subsequent autodestruct order issued by ground control in the interests of the safety of the populated areas near the Cape and because some critical parts of the solid booster immediately around the suspected burn area were never recovered (PCSS 1986, 1:19, 69).

My intention here is not to second-guess the conclusions of the shuttle accident commission, but rather to point out that even after an intensive search for evidence, the cause of the shuttle disaster remains uncertain and that the need to reach closure on the interpretation of the accident could not be satisfied by some uncontentious and impersonal scientific method. In the course of the testimony, Richard Feynman admitted as much: "We have the same thing in physics experiments. The theorists sit on top of the experiment and as the data starts to come out, when it still has errors in it that haven't been checked out, they are already making theories to explain the bumps in the curve which turn out to be nothing" (PCSS 1986, 4:227).

But there was a significant difference between your average particle experiment at Brookhaven and the explosion of the space shuttle *Challenger*. The explosion was a catastrophe for all sorts of people, to the extent that it challenged notions of a stable and just order in the U.S. polity; this violation of order called forth the usual jurisdictional response, in the format of an appointed presidential commission to settle the matter once and for all. Unlike experiments at Brookhaven or CERN, the idea was to forestall the entry of other interested parties who would want to bring their own interpretations and evidence to bear upon the final evaluation of the causes of the disaster. There was an explicit arrangement that Congress would not institute any inquiry into the accident until the commission issued its report; and the chairman of the commission fought a running battle with the newspapers to prevent the inquest from being conducted in their pages.[11]

The purpose of this special quasi-juridical body was not to bring the scientific method to bear on the problem, but rather to reconfigure the threatened boundaries of the Social and the Natural by relegating the offending phenomenon to its correct category. Was the culprit to be Nature in the guise of the freak cold weather, or the wind shear that occurred between thirty-seven and sixty-four seconds into the flight, or nearly imperceptible hairline fractures in the solid booster? Or was the culprit the Social in the guise of greedy subcontractors of the solid booster pressure seals, or harried officials of NASA driven to meet a grueling launch schedule at the expense of prudent safety guidelines, or a Congress unwilling to appropriate scarce funds to redesign a jerry-built solid fuel booster system, or indeed even Libyan terrorists out to embarrass and shame the United States? (The entire testimony on physical security of the site was omitted from the published report on the grounds of – what else? – national security [PCSS 1986, 4:193].)

The fact that the juridical restoration of a sense of order tended to predominate over a commitment to explore every possible malfunction and apparent failure, no matter where it might lead, is illustrated by a few neglected aspects of the proceedings. After the commission was constituted, a letter to the editor of the *New York Times* by a professor emeritus of engineering with more than four decades in rocketry claimed that all the committee members were known to him personally and that "none seem ever to have been responsible for engineering of a rocket of any kind, and definitely none have had any involvement in the engineering of solid-propellant rocket boosters" (Summerfeld 1986). The inclusion of such luminaries as Chuck Yeager and Neil Armstrong on the panel seemed to have been motivated more by star quality than their ability to ask relevant questions. Furthermore, everyone tends to remember Nobel physicist Richard Feynman as the key member of the commission, but as he himself admitted, he was baffled by NASA's jargon, and he did not really do an "experiment" in any legitimate sense when he dunked a bit of rubber in ice water before the television cameras, and much of what he did do on the commission came under the scientific and unsavory rubric of assigning blame and guilt (Gieryn and Figert 1990). After Feynman's lunchtime recess demonstration before the television cameras, the commission chairman William Rogers said the episode "amounted to grandstanding by Feynman," an interpretation that gains a modicum of credibility when one learns that it came in the wake of a prior leak of some memos expressing doubts about the O-ring seals to the *New York Times* by unidentified parties, which forced the commission to turn its attention to the seams of the solid rocket boosters to the exclusion of other potential problem areas off schedule and out of agenda order.

Consider the following scenario. The space shuttle is an incredibly complex engineering feat, which means that there are myriad questions and controversies about the reliability of many of its component systems at any one time. If and when a catastrophic failure of obscure origins does occur (as in the case of the animal trials), everyone immediately clamors for an ascription of the outlines of the incident to its proper category as Social or Natural, and its attendant anthropomorphic assignment of blame and guilt. The engineers know that such ascriptions will not be straightforward or clear-cut, but they are themselves suspect due to their personal involvement and, in any event, are restricted to occupying the wrong side of the table at the tribunal. Someone then leaks a memo to the news media expressing alarm over some subsystem of the shuttle, which is of course just one more memo in a ream of memos on a whole list of suspects in the failure. Then a Nobel laureate physicist on the judicial panel who has always considered himself a bit of a rebel anyway, prompted by an unnamed informant through a third party, reduces the whole mind-numbing complexity of the crash in front of the TV cameras outside the hearing room during a luncheon recess to the simple anthropomorphic phenomenon of something flexible getting stiff when it is cold.[12] Suddenly every little inconvenient fact is forgotten, like the fact that the only other serious O-ring erosion occurred during the warmest launch of the sequence of shuttles. All public efforts are abruptly turned to finding corroborating evidence for the cold weather/O-ring theory, which is of course easy to find, since both NASA and Morton Thiokol (the manufacturers) had openly worried about both it and a raft of other serious flaws and engineering anomalies in an endless stream of paper and phone conversations.[13] Given the situations of cost-plus contracts and shrinking NASA budgets, a certain modicum of vulnerability surrounds all the players. Some middle-management scapegoats at both NASA and Morton Thiokol are then belatedly identified, and thus sufficiently sated, public attention is rapidly diverted to the next clamoring crisis (PCSS 1986, 1:88–103).

For all I know, the O-rings were ultimately responsible for the shuttle disaster.[14] Certainly the track record of previous economists pronouncing upon the causes of this disaster should evoke vertigo, and not just garden-variety skepticism (Kremer 1993). Nevertheless, reading the transcripts of the proceedings of the presidential commission does not fill one with confidence that the quasi-judicial procedure was the best or even the most methodical way of arriving at an understanding of the causes of the accident. But then, that would be mistaking the main function of the commission, which was never qualified to deconstruct and reengineer the solid rocket booster or, indeed, the shuttle itself. The purpose of the commission was to hold a public trial of the booster of Utah, and just as with the rooster of Basel, to reconcile all parties to the conclusion that the Natural Order was not at risk.

I will conclude with the story of one more crash and one more presidential commission that followed close on the heels of a disaster, but a narrative perhaps more germane to the interests of many economists. Figure 17.7 shows a graph of the stock market crash of October 19 and 20, 1987, popularly known as Black Monday and Terrible Tuesday. Just as with the *Challenger* commission, most people possess some vague recollection of the report of the Brady Commission, which they believe somehow identified computerized trading as the culprit. It is true that there was no theatrical cathartic moment commensurate with Feynman's paper cup of ice water, and one might make the case that this is symptomatic of a problem endemic to economics. In any event, it seems to have been primarily the absence of long-term fallout from this particular crash rather than the compelling deliberations of the Brady Commission that accounts for the fact that attention has now shifted elsewhere, although I cannot resist pointing out that as this chapter was written, in the midst of a widely acknowledged anemic economy, the Standard and Poor's 500 Stock Index was substantially higher than its

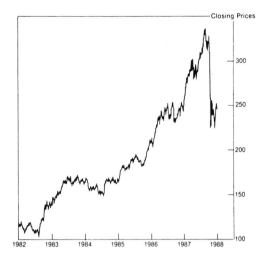

Figure 17.7. Standard and Poor 500 Index, January 1982 to November 1987.

peak in late 1987, when many insisted that it was wildly out of line with any rational valuation of the underlying assets. For this reason alone, an instance of a failure of a juridical proceeding to stabilize the Social and the Natural can be as significant for our thesis as a success.

The drop in prices on October 19 was by far the worst in the modern history of the U.S. stock market: the Dow-Jones Industrial Index fell 508 points, or 23 percent, while the Standard and Poor's 500 Stock Index on our graph fell 29 percent. Though the only loss of life attributable to this crash was the murder of a Merrill-Lynch broker by a disgruntled customer on October 20, the immediate loss in pecuniary terms qualified the event as an unmitigated disaster. Although predisposed to ignore the crash altogether, cooler heads prevailed upon then-president Reagan to convene on November 5 a "task force," if not indeed a full-blown judicial commission, to seek out the true causes of the crash and thus preempt the building clamor for retribution. His hesitation was reflected in the composition of the task force, which possessed neither star quality nor a clear juridical mandate nor a broad base in the various constituencies that were sure to push their own explanations of the crash.[15] There were no Nobel Prize–winning economists, no advocates for the Chicago exchanges (although the New York Stock Exchange was well represented), no vengeful movie stars (how could they not have seen that Martin Sheen would have been an inspired choice?), no public-interest lawyers, and no one from the Securities and Exchange Commission. The big brokerage houses were, if anything, overrepresented. There were no public hearings as such, no mysterious leaks to the press building suspense, and no good photo opportunities, although there was a questionnaire mailed to market participants and, as an afterthought, all Nobel Prize winners in economics since 1973.

One fundamental flaw in the constitution of the task force was clear lack of appreciation for the different constituencies that would have to be mollified if order was to be restored. First, there was the general populace, which lived in mortal fear of a repeat of 1929 and the Great Depression. Then there was the mass of individual investors, or what was left of them, who were suspicious of being hoodwinked by insider trading and the institutional investors, and convinced they had been slighted by specialist floor traders and the electronic order system. Then there were the partisans of the Chicago exchanges, who trembled at the thought of curtailment of their burgeoning profitable markets in "derivative instruments" like futures options on various stock indices. Finally, we musn't forget the orthodox neoclassical economists, who had much to lose from an inquest into markets that were generally perceived to have gone haywire.

The depth of distress that was experienced by economists that October has largely gone unnoticed. It was they, more than any other group, who felt the Natural world turned upside down by the crash. The sources of the vertigo were many and deep-seated. By 1987, Keynesian economics had largely been superseded within the higher reaches of the profession by a neoclassical version of macroeconomics retailed under the banner of "rational expectations" theory (Sargent 1987; Hoover 1988). This school essentially espoused the position that government intervention at the macro level to prevent a repeat of the 1930s was unnecessary and counterproductive and that something like the Great Depression could not happen again. An important component of this new doctrine was the "efficient markets hypothesis," which, stated crudely, said that market prices continuously embodied all the necessary information relevant to the correct understanding of an economic phenomenon like asset pricing, representing in an optimal fashion the underlying fundamentals. The efficient markets hypothesis was itself intimately bound up with a long tradition in neoclassical economics attempting to reconcile the rigid determinism inherent in its model of equilibrium appropriated from nineteenth-century physics with the apparent stochastic character of asset prices, and stock prices in particular.[16] Finally, there was the recent phenomenon of neoclassical economists producing complex mathematical theories of the correct prices of options, warrants, and various synthetic instruments and then retailing them in the form of computerized trading packages to brokerage houses and large institutions under the rubric of "portfolio insurance" or program trading. The logic of these developments was intimately interconnected, and all were severely threatened by the October 19 crash.

The Brady Commission, probably due to the composition of its members, ultimately adopted a bureaucratic-policing stance toward the problem, instead of the more broad-based juridical approach described in our previous three cases. The first flaw was to presume that if order had broken down, as the Brady Commission said, the solution was to give the police more resources rather than dwell on the causes. Although the report did include a laundry list of possible precipitating factors in the timing of the downturn, they were presented without any weighting or analytical emphasis, essentially because none was even remotely commensurate with the magnitude and scale of the collapse (Presidential Task Force on Market Mechanisms 1988, I-11 to I-14). Rather than adopt some explicit theoretical stance, the Brady Report trumpeted the discovery that the New York Stock Exchange and the Chicago exchanges were really "one market," and thus there should be only one regulatory agency and one set of rules for things like clearing systems, margin requirements, circuit breaker mechanisms, and transaction monitoring. What had precipitated the unified market, it was claimed, was the combination of new computer technologies and new derivative instruments, notably index futures and options. Thus, the narrative structure of the report, insofar as one could have been said to exist, took the format of an old genre in Western art, the theme of technics out of control (Winner 1977). To blame the machine seemed both politically expedient and intellectually acceptable to the Brady Commission, since none of the nervous supporters of the Reagan administration within the financial community could be corraled as scapegoats under this scenario.

I would like to suggest that this was the second fundamental flaw of the operation of the Brady Commission and that our revised hypothesis concerning the Social and the Natural can help us understand why this was so. To have blamed the *Challenger* crash on technical change gone mad would never have been an appropriate response to that tragedy, because society required reassurance that order could be readily restored and that the universe had not undertaken to punish humankind for the hubris of leaving our natural home. By attributing to Nature the things deemed Natural, the things deemed Social became truly tangible, with real names and faces, somewhere someone's responsibility. Likewise, the attempt of the Brady Commission to attribute the possible destruction of macroeconomic harmony to technical change gone mad did not banish our fears or reassure us that our fortified and revigilated police could reinstate order, since it opened up the possibility that the universe itself was hostile to our little schemes to make money. Everyone knows the moral of Mary Shelley's *Frankenstein*, and it is not an injunction to go back to the castle parapet and try again. The problem with most narratives of technics out of control is that they do not shore up our categories of the Social and the Natural; on the contrary, they poke holes in the boundaries, and nothing is more inclined to render the Western mind uneasy than not knowing where the Natural is located, which is precisely why *Frankenstein* is one of the greatest horror stories in the Western canon.

The failure of the Brady Commission can be demonstrated by the raft of further "reports" on Black Monday by the Chicago Mercantile Exchange, the Commodity Futures Trading Commission, the U.S. General Accounting Office, the Working Group on Financial Markets, the Security and Exchange Commission, and various others, none of which agreed upon the cause and all of which took the Brady Report to task (U.S. Securities and Exchange Commission 1988; Working Group on Financing Markets 1988; Kamphuis et al. 1989). That failure can also be read in the response of neoclassical economists, not one of whom has had a nice word to say for the Brady Report (Fischer 1988; Kamphuis et al. 1989; Lucas and Schwartz 1989; Shiller 1989). Finally, the recommendations of the Brady Commission have been allowed to molder in peaceful neglect, to the extent that there is no substantial difference between the structure of the securities markets today and back in October 1987. It is as if the entire disaster had never happened.

I do not wish to advocate that the Brady Commission's findings should or should not have been taken more seriously; instead, I wish to ask why the symbiotic juridical relationship between the laws of physics and the *Challenger* inquiry was not likewise achieved between economics and the Brady Commission, and therefore why the outcome did not result in some substantive stabilization of our notions of the Natural and the Social. I should like to suggest that the final failure lay in the inability of commission members and the orthodox neoclassical economists to cooperate in effectively anthropomorphizing the designated villain – namely, the computer – and the further failure of the orthodox economists in providing a coherent alternative scenario of the Natural and the Social. We have already explained why pinning the crash on computer trading didn't work from the vantage point of social narrative; but there is another reason why neoclassical economists could not bring themselves to wholeheartedly support that indictment.

Since the 1930s, it has been a source of irritation for the neoclassical program that while it could prove the mathematical existence of a Walrasian general equilibrium, it seemed incapable of providing a satisfactory account of the process by which those equilibrium prices were arrived at. In the nineteenth century, Walras himself imagined an ideal supervisor or auctioneer who never traded on his own account and whose job it was to prevent everyone else from trading until just the right set of equilibrium prices that eliminated all excess supply and demand had been discovered. This story was implausible in the extreme when it was invented; but worse, all the modern attempts to remedy it have their own drawbacks (Fisher 1983; Ingrao and Israel 1990; Weintraub 1991). Nevertheless, from the 1940s onward the Walrasian auctioneer tended to be replaced in the minds of many neoclassicals by the image of a machine, a supercomputer that would calculate those equilibrium prices in real time and disseminate them to the waiting transactors, a natural embodiment of the rationality that would vindicate their model. The machine would never trade on its own account, would never lie, and would speak guilelessly in the unmediated language of inanimate Nature. The upshot was that the computer became a metaphor for what the market really was like in the neoclassical worldview; indeed, it embodied their very image of social order.[17] Hence, there was no way that neoclassicals could bear the cognitive dissonance of a judicial verdict that blamed a market crash on the evolution of computer technology, a technology some of their very own number had pioneered.

Alas, rejection of the Brady Commission narrative did not mean that the neoclassicals had a better narrative with which to replace it. It was not for lack of ingenuity that candidates were not forthcoming: Every possible permutation of the Natural and the Social in the neoclassical toolbox was floated at one time or another. One proposal was that the share market remained rational and efficient, even on October 19 and 20: In other words, the 500-point drop just meant people had revised their estimation of the fundamentals over the weekend; or in cruder terms, market crashes are Natural. Another option resonant with the roaring 1980s was that the crash was somehow the government's fault, even if the precise mechanism was obscure; this was the ever-popular scenario of the Social frustrating the Natural. Another variant on the Unnatural (or Preternatural?) thwarting the

Natural was Robert Shiller's widely quoted claim that a vast wave of mob psychology, a weekend crisis of confidence, had swept over the investing populace (in Fischer 1988; Shiller 1989). Finally, in a desperate resort to epicycles, some liberal economists attempted to temper the Natural with the Social by maintaining that if the market were left to the professionals, it would be as efficient as the neoclassical model maintained, but the presence of "noise traders" – that is, humble, simple individual investors – kept inducing Unnatural disturbances in the rational prices (de Long et al. 1990, 1991). None of these options, with the possible exception of the first, was rigorously consistent with the neoclassical model of general equilibrium, and therefore none of them ever constituted a serious challenge by the orthodox economists to preempt the narrative of the Brady Report. Even the bestowal of the Nobel Prize in 1990 to three of the progenitors of the construction of computer models of neoclassical stock pricing could belie the fact that the rational expectations doctrine was in tatters.

The third and final flaw traceable to the Brady Commission and its contretemps with the economics community was their joint lack of appreciation for the role and functions of a juridical inquiry into violations of natural order. In such instances, people do not want to be told that risk and danger can be mathematically formalized, packaged, and sold like some sort of dog food, and that they had unwittingly though voluntarily bought into this commodity and therefore had to suffer the consequences of their purchase. The role of the juridical inquiry in a crisis is rather to determine which calamitous transgressions were Natural and which were Social, to reduce the complexity of the transgression to an anthropomorphically comprehensible phenomenon, the better to mete out blame and punishment accordingly. Apparently economists and corporate executives are not as cognizant of this pattern as are lawyers, physicists, and engineers, and therefore they often end up looking stumble-footed and inept vis-à-vis their scientific cousins.

Reprise

While these narratives do illustrate my hypothesis concerning the Natural and the Social, some may feel that the examples are too eccentric or perhaps too outlandish to justify a general hypothesis. Although this is not the place to launch into an extended treatise, I do want to stress that the phenomenon of the legal stabilization of the Social and the Natural through metaphorical construction is much more widespread than my examples show; yet the ideal of a naturalis-tic social science has stifled examination of this phenomenon. The prevalence of metaphorical reasoning in legal history is staggeringly ubiquitous. For instance, British tort law in the nineteenth century explicitly compared water that escaped from a reservoir to a dangerous animal that had escaped from its cage in order to extend the law of damages.[18] Or in another case, German and Swiss jurists explicitly decided early in this century that the theft of electricity was not covered under the existing penal code because it could not be considered a "mobile material object," and in any case, the judges decided that the physicists were as yet incapable of settling the real nature of electricity.[19] These are the kinds of phenomena that we simply presume without second thought to have been exclusively settled by "science" but which were actually relegated to their Natural categories by historical juridical proceedings. Communities in crisis can rarely wait for the scientists single-handedly to recapture their sense of equilibrium.

One of the liberating aspects of history – or at least a history that is not a retrodiction of present common sense – is that it opens up pathways to the past as a disarmingly foreign country. Only a historian can imagine a world where no one has an "occupation": just as the U.S. Congress blocked a question on occupations in the 1790 census because too many Americans couldn't answer it (Starr 1992, 279). The problem of categorization is one major preoccupation of the modern liberal state, because disorder lurks in the interstices of every distinction that makes a difference. Order means a place for everything, and everything in its place.

Notes

1. Luckily, I was able to persuade Arjo Klamer and Thomas Leonard to do it instead, as a specially commissioned chapter for this volume (see Chapter 2). The literature obliquely cited here includes Hesse (1966), Leatherdale (1974), Sapir and Crocker (1977), Ortony (1979), Sacks (1979), Masterman (1980), and McFague (1982).
2. In rough chronological sequence, first there was the Reformation attack on the supposed vulgar error of religious anthropomorphism. Then there were various Enlightenment figures who asserted that the Social and the Natural were identical in subject matter and epistemological import and, after that, the Counter-Enlightenment writers beginning with Vico who asserted the contrary, predicated upon a distinct and incommensurate set of laws of history. The Enlightenment project to banish anthropomorphism while at the same time subjecting nature and society to the identical set of regulative principles resulted in some severe cognitive dissonance, as we shall shortly witness. Then in the nineteenth century, there was the

protracted debate over the similarities and differences between the *Naturwissenschaften* and the *Geisteswissenschaften*, with the neo-Kantians stressing an *a priori* logical distinction in terms of methods, whereas the followers of Dilthey insisted that the subject matter of the human sciences was incommensurate with those of the natural sciences. On this, see Berlin (1977) and Brown (1984).

3. On this, see Ermarth (1978), Rickert (1986), and Dilthey (1989).

4. Beginning with Durkheim and Mauss (1963 [1903]), continuing with Douglas (1973) and Bloor (1982); it is discussed further in Mirowski (1988, 109–11). This strain of social studies of science is itself situated in a larger context of Western attitudes toward the categories of the Natural and the Social outlined in my Chapter 1, this volume.

5. Some examples are discussed in Chapter 1, this volume. Perhaps the most extended exemplar in economics is the energetics–neoclassicism connection detailed in Mirowski (1989).

6. See, e.g., Rouse (1991), Bruno Latour's "One More Turn after the Social Turn" in McMullin (1992), and a number of the authors in Pickering (1992).

7. Compare Evans (1906, 265–86) with Hyde (1916), Finkelstein (1981), Cohen (1986), and Vartier (1970).

8. This is the opinion of Cohen (1986).

9. An incomplete list of papers includes Kagel et al. (1975, 1980, 1981), Battalio, Kagel, and Green (1981), Battalio, Kagel, Rachlin, and Green (1981), Battalio et al. (1985, 1986, 1991), and MacDonald et al. (1991).

10. This has been clarified by the recent Sonnenschein–Mantel–Debreu results. See Rizvi (1991).

11. "Now we're talking about the documents you produced, lets forget the New York Times. . . . I mean, we're not here to decide whether the New York Times writes good stories or not" (PCSS 1986, 4:264–5). "SUTTER: I would rather help you guys investigate this rather than have the Goddamned New York Times or Washington Post do it. MOORE: We are with you 100% on that, and if we can stay ahead of the press, we are a lot better off" (PCSS 1986, 4:493).

12. "Any moron knows that pliable things get brittle when cold, even your editor, but the belief becomes all the more credible when we are told it is so by a Nobel physicist who has no obvious stake in the outcome" (Gieryn and Figert 1990, 90).

13. "CULBERTSON: . . . but you must expect that you probably haven't seen the last of these memos where somebody says hey, don't do it. You will probably come across many" (PCSS 1986, 4:326).

14. Doubt persists, however, when one remembers that the shuttles were plagued by fuel leaks throughout 1990, even after the solid boosters were re-engineered, causing some to speculate that the space shuttle was inherently unreliable. See Eliot Marshall (1990, 499–500).

15. The members of the Brady Commission were Nicholas Brady, James C.

Cotting of Navistar and the New York Stock Exchange, Robert G. Kirby, John R. Opel of IBM, and Howard M. Stein of the Dreyfus Fund.

16. This history will be documented in a forthcoming work entitled *Who's Afraid of Random Trade?*

17. This was made manifest in numerous ways throughout the history of neoclassicism, from the "socialist calculation controversy" to the genesis of such econometric consulting firms as DRI to the work on artificial intelligence by Herbert Simon and the interplay between the design of the computer and the invention of game theory. On the last incident, see Mirowski (1992).

18. *Rylands v. Fletcher*, 1868, discussed by Bernard Jackson in Nerhot (1991, 148).

19. *Cees Maris* in Nerhot (1991, 77).

References

Barnes, Barry, and Shapin, Steven, eds. 1979. *Natural Order*. London: Sage.

Battalio, R. 1986. "Risk Aversion in Rats Under Varying Levels of Resource Availability," *Journal of Comparative Psychology*, 100:95–100.

Battalio, R.; Kagel, J; Winkler, R.; Basmann, R.; and Krasner, L. 1973. "A Test of Consumer Demand Theory Using Observations of Individual Consumer Purchases," *Western Economic Journal*, 11:411–28.

Battalio, R.; Kagel, J.; and Green, L. 1981. "Income–Leisure Tradeoffs of Animal Workers," *American Economic Review*, 71:621–32.

Battalio, R.; Kagel, J.; and Kohut, C. 1991. "Experimental Confirmation of the Existence of a Giffen Good," *American Economic Review*, 81:961–70.

Battalio, R.; Kagel, J.; and MacDonald, D. 1985. "Animals Choices over Uncertain Outcomes," *American Economic Review*, 75:597–613.

Battalio, R.; Kagel, J.; and Phillips, O. 1986. "Optimal Prices and Animal Consumers in Contested Markets," *Economic Inquiry*, 24:181–93.

Battalio, R.; Kagel, J.; Rachlin, H.; and Green, L. 1981. "Commodity Choice Behavior with Pigeons as Subjects," *Journal of Political Economy*, 81:67–91.

Berlin, Isaiah. 1977. *Vico and Herder*. New York: Vintage.

Bijker, W.; Hughes, T.; and Pinch, T., eds. 1987. *The Social Construction of Technological Systems*. Cambridge, MA: MIT Press.

Bloor, David. 1976. *Knowledge and Social Imagery*. London: Routledge.

Bloor, David. 1982. "Durkheim and Mauss Revisited," *Studies in the History and Philosophy of Science*, 13:267–97.

Brown, Robert. 1984. *The Nature of Social Laws*. Cambridge University Press.

Canguilhem, Georges. 1989. *The Normal and the Pathological*. New York: Zone Books.

Cohen, Esther. 1986. "Law, Folklore and Animal Lore," *Past and Present*, 110:6–37.

Daston, Lorraine. 1989. *Classical Probability in the Age of the Enlightenment*. Princeton, NJ: Princeton University Press.

Daston, Lorraine. 1992a. "Objectivity and the Escape from Perspective," *Social Studies of Science*, 22:597–618.

Daston, Lorraine. 1992b. "Baconian Facts, Academic Civility, and the Prehistory of Objectivity," *Annals of Scholarship*, 8:337–63.

de Long, B.; Schleifer, A.; Summers, L.; and Waldmann, R. 1990. "Noise Trader Risk in Financial Markets," *Journal of Political Economy*, 98:703–35.

de Long, B.; Schleifer, A.; Summers, L.; and Waldmann, R. 1991. "The Survival of Noise Traders in Financial Markets," *Journal of Business*, (64): 1–19.

Dilthey, Wilhelm. 1989. *Introduction to the Human Sciences*. Princeton, NJ: Princeton University Press.

Douglas, Mary. 1973. *Natural Symbols*. London: Barrie & Jenkins.

Douglas, Mary. 1986. *How Institutions Think*. Syracuse, NY: Syracuse University Press.

Durkheim, Emile, and Mauss, Marcel. 1963. *Primitive Classification*. Chicago: University of Chicago Press.

Ermarth, Michael. 1978. *Wilhelm Dilthey: The Critique of Historical Reason*. Chicago: University of Chicago Press.

Evans, E. P. 1906. *The Criminal Prosecution and Capital Punishment of Animals*. New York: Dutton.

Finkelstein, J. J. 1981. "The Ox That Gored," *Transactions of the American Philosophical Society*. (71):part 2.

Fischer, Stanley, ed. 1988. *NBER Macroeconomic Annual 1988*. Cambridge, MA: MIT Press.

Fisher, Franklin. 1983. *Disequilibrium Foundations of Equilibrium Economics*. Cambridge University Press.

Gieryn, Thomas, and Figert, Anne. 1990. "Ingredients for a Theory of Science in Society," in S. Cozzens and T. Gieryn, eds., *Theories of Science in Society*. Bloomington: Indiana University Press.

Goodman, Nelson. 1978. *Ways of Worldmaking*. Indianapolis, IN: Hackett.

Hesse, Mary. 1966. *Models and Analogies in Science*. Notre Dame, IN: University of Notre Dame Press.

Hogarth, R., and Reder, M., eds. 1986. *Rational Choice*. Chicago: University of Chicago Press.

Hoover, Kevin. 1988. *The New Classical Macroeconomics*. Oxford: Blackwell.

Huber, Peter. 1991. *Galileo's Revenge: Junk Science in the Courtroom*. New York: Basic.

Hyde, W. W. 1916. "The Prosecution and Punishment of Animals and Lifeless Things in the Middle Ages and Modern Times," *University of Pennsylvania Law Review*, 64:696–730.

Ingrao, B., and Israel, G. 1990. *The Invisible Hand*. Cambridge, MA: MIT Press.

Kagel, J., and Battalio, R. 1980. "Token Economy and Animal Models for the Experimental Analysis of Economic Behavior," in J. Kmenta and J. Ramsey, eds., *Evaluation of Economic Models*. New York: Academic Press.

Kagel, J.; Battalio, R.; Rachlin, H.; and Green, L. 1981. "Demand Curves for Animal Consumers," *Quarterly Journal of Economics*, 96:1–15.

Kagel, J.; Rachlin, H.; Green, L; Battalio, R.; Basmann, R.; and Klemm, W. 1975. "Experimental Studies of Consumer Demand Behavior Using Laboratory Animals," *Economic Inquiry*, 23:22–38.

Kamphuis, Robert, et al., eds. 1989. *Black Monday and the Future of Financial Markets.* Homewood, IL: Dow Jones-Irwin.

Kelley, Donald. 1990. *The Human Measure.* Cambridge, MA: Harvard University Press.

Kirman, Alan. 1993. "Ants, Rationality and Recruitment," *Quarterly Journal of Economics,* 108:137–56.

Kremer, Michael. 1993. "The O-Ring Theory of Economic Development," *Quarterly Journal of Economics,* 108:551–72.

Latour, Bruno. 1987. *Science in Action.* Cambridge, MA: Harvard University Press.

Leatherdale, W.H. 1974. *The Role of Analogy, Model and Metaphor in Science.* Amsterdam: North Holland.

MacDonald, D.; Kagel, J.; and Battalio, R. 1991. "Animals' Choices over Uncertain Outcomes," *Economic Journal,* 101:1067–84.

Malkiel, Burton. 1989. "Is the Stock Market Efficient?" *Science,* 243:1313–17.

Marshall, Eliot. 1990. "The Shuttle: Whistling Past the Graveyard?" *Science,* 26(October)244: 499–500.

Masterman, Margaret. 1980. "Braithwaite and Kuhn: Analogy-clusters within and without hypothetico-deductive systems," in D. H. Mellor, ed., *Science, Belief and Behavior.* Cambridge University Press.

McFague, Sallie. 1982. *Metaphorical Theology.* Philadelphia: Fortress Press.

McMullin, Ernan, ed. 1992. *The Social Dimension of Science.* Notre Dame, IN: University of Notre Dame Press.

Mirowski, Philip. 1988. *Against Mechanism.* Totawa, NJ: Rowman & Littlefield.

Mirowski, Philip. 1989. *More Heat Than Light: Economics as Social Physics, Physics as Nature's Economics.* Cambridge University Press.

Mirowski, Philip. 1992. "What Were von Neumann and Morgenstern Trying to Accomplish?" in E. R. Weintraub, ed., *Towards a History of Game Theory.* Durham, NC: Duke University Press.

Mirowski, Philip. 1994. "Marshalling the Unruly Atoms," in P. Mirowski, ed., *Ysidro Ycheued.* Savage, MD: Rowman & Littlefield.

Morgan, P., and Tustin, D. 1992. "The Perception and Efficiency of Labor Supply Choices by Pigeons," *Economic Journal,* 102:1134–48.

Murphy, James. 1993. *Foundations of an Aristotelian Social Theory.* New Haven, CT: Yale University Press.

Nagel, Thomas. 1986. *The View from Nowhere.* Oxford University Press.

Needham, Joseph. 1969a. "Human Laws and Natural Laws," in *The Grand Tradition.* Toronto: University of Toronto Press.

Needham, Joseph. 1969b. *Science and Civilization in China,* vol. 2. Cambridge University Press.

Nerhot, Patrick, ed. 1991. *Legal Knowledge and Analogy.* Dordrecht: Kluwer.

Ortony, Anthony, ed. 1979. *Metaphor and Thought.* Cambridge University Press.

Park, Katherine, and Daston, Lorraine. 1981. "Unnatural Conceptions: The Study of Monsters in France and England," *Past and Present,* 92:20–54.

Peirce, Charles Sanders. 1965. *The Collected Works,* vol. 5. Cambridge, MA: Harvard University Press.

Pickering, Andrew, ed. 1992. *Science as Practice and Culture.* Chicago: University of Chicago Press.

Presidential Commission on the Space Shuttle Challenger Accident. 1986. *Report to the President.* 5 vols. Washington DC: U.S. Government Printing Office.

Presidential Task Force on Market Mechanisms. 1988. *Report (Brady Commission).* Washington DC: U.S. Government Printing Office.

Rickert, Heinrich. 1986. *The Limits of Concept Formation in Natural Science* (1902). Cambridge University Press.

Ritvo, Harriet. 1990. "New Presbyter or Old Priest?" *History of the Human Sciences,* 3:259–76.

Rizvi, Abu. 1991. "The Microfoundations Project in General Equilibrium Theory," University of Vermont, Department of Economics, working paper.

Rouse, Joseph. 1991. "Philosophy of Science and the Persistent Narratives of Modernity," *Studies in the History and Philosophy of Science,* 22:141–62.

Ruby, Jane. 1986. "The Origins of Scientific Law," *Journal of the History of Ideas,* 47:341–59.

Sacks, Sheldon, ed. 1979. *On Metaphor.* Chicago: University of Chicago Press.

Sapir, J., and Crocker, J., eds. 1977. *The Social Uses of Metaphor.* Philadelphia: University of Pennsylvania Press.

Sargent, Thomas. 1987. *Macroeconomic Theory,* 2d ed. New York: Academic Press.

Schlanger, Judith. 1971. *Les métaphores de l'organisme.* Paris: Vrin.

Shiller, Robert. 1989. *Market Volatility.* Cambridge, MA: MIT Press.

Sloan, Allan, and Stern, Richard. 1988. "How $V_0 = V_sN(d_1) - E/e^{rt}N(d_2)$ Led to Black Monday," *Forbes,* 28:55–9.

Smith, Adam. 1976. *The Theory of Moral Sentiments.* Indianapolis, IN: Liberty.

Smith, John Maynard. 1990. "Triumphs of Colonialism," *New York Review of Books,* 27:36–37.

Starr, Paul. 1992. "Social Categories and Claims in the Liberal State," *Social Research,* 59:263–94.

Streuve, Pierre. 1921. "L'idée de loi naturelle dans la science économique," *Revue D'économie politique,* 38:294–307, 463–82.

Sugden, R. 1991. "Rational Choice: A Survey," *Economic Journal,* 101:751–83.

Summerfeld, Martin. 1986. "Challenger Questions," *New York Times,* Feb. 9.

Thomas, Keith. 1983. *Man and the Natural World.* New York: Pantheon.

Tiemersma, Douwe. 1989. *Body Schema and Body Image.* Amsterdam: Swets & Zeitlinger.

U.S. Securities and Exchange Commission. 1988. *The October 1987 Market Break.* Chicago: Commerce Clearing House.

Vartier, Jean. 1970. *Les procès d'animaux du moyen âge à nos jours.* Paris: Hachette.

Walter, E. V. 1984. "Nature on Trial: The Case of the Rooster that Laid an Egg," in R. Cohen and M. Wartofsky, eds., *Methodology, Metaphysics and the History of Science.* Boston: Reidel.

Weintraub, E. R. 1991. *Stabilizing Dynamics.* Cambridge University Press.

Winner, Langdon. 1977. *Autonomous Technology.* Cambridge, MA: MIT Press.

Working Group on Financial Markets. 1988. *Interim Report.* Washington, DC: U.S. Government Printing Office.

CHAPTER 18

The place of economics in the hierarchy of the sciences: Section F from Whewell to Edgeworth

JAMES P. HENDERSON

[Adam Smith] severed economic science from politics; he dealt with it as concerned with physical objects and natural laws. To his English predecessors it had been a department of politics or morals; while many of his English successors recognised that in his hands it had become more analogous to physics, and delighted to treat it by the methods of mechanical science.

Cunningham (1910, 2:594)

Introduction

At its 1833 meeting, the British Association for the Advancement of Science (BAAS) was taken over by

Cambridge and metropolitan savants, who preferred an ideology of science derived more from Newton than from Bacon. Naive inductivism was replaced by an ideology of method which gave more emphasis to theory, to deduction, and to mathematics. . . . The effects of these moves, due chiefly to [William] Whewell, were to legitimate the vested career and intellectual interests of certain Cambridge and London savants. . . . A hierarchy of sciences was proclaimed, with Newtonian astronomy at its head. Deductive and mathematical reasoning was given new importance. The Association's edicts on proper science came increasingly from Trinity College, Cambridge. (Morrell and Thackray 1981, 267)

The concept of a hierarchy of sciences stemmed from William Whewell's understanding of the developmental processes of science. "The central, and clearly the most intriguing, thesis of Whewell's philosophy of science is that science develops by becoming a more and more comprehensive system of laws that are both universal and

484

necessary, and that are, nevertheless, in some sense the result of induction" (Butts 1989, 4). The hierarchy of sciences reflected the different stages of development of the various sciences. Thus, when Morrell and Thackray (1981, 267) maintain that Whewell and his followers introduced "an ideology of method which gave more emphasis to deduction" and that "deductive reasoning was given new importance," it should be emphasized that deduction was deemed appropriate only for those highly developed disciplines that stood at the top of the hierarchy of sciences. In Whewell's view only astronomy had advanced to the point where "particulars are completely subjected to generals, effects to causes." For a discipline as underdeveloped as economics, adopting the deductive method was premature.

The founders of Section F, the new statistical section of the BAAS, "were engaged in an attempt to redefine the province of political economy through the incorporation of empirical material drawn from all areas of social existence" (Goldman 1983, 600). They intended to make political economy into a science, and "in the England of the 1830's, 'to be scientific' meant 'to be like physical astronomy'" (Cannon 1961, 238). The founders of Section F chose to make economics scientific by constructing it upon a statistical foundation:

> It seems clear that the advocacy of a mathematical statistical approach [to economics] was based on more than the 18th-century orthodoxy that probabilities were the best that could be arrived at in the "moral sciences." . . . One new factor in establishing the validity of a statistical approach was the prestige of the theory of probability in its role as trusted assistant to the queen of the sciences. It was the men of theoretical astronomy . . . who certified as to the validity of the statistical approach to knowledge. (Cannon 1978, 241)

At the 1833 meeting of the BAAS, Whewell proclaimed that astronomy "is not only the queen of sciences, but, in a stricter sense of the term, the only perfect science" (1833, xiii). An important theme of this study is the recurring notion that if political economy was to be scientific, it must be patterned after "the queen of sciences" – astronomy. Francis Y. Edgeworth stated the connection between economics and astronomy best when he declared that "the Newtonian astronomy is . . . the model of our science" (1909, 386). After a review of the "irregular" founding of Section F, attention is directed to the efforts to abolish it. In the chapter's final section, the triumph of the utilitarian image of science is considered.

The "irregular" founding of Section F

While the Rev. Thomas Robert Malthus was an early and persistent critic, it was William Whewell who led the methodological attack on Ricardian deductive economics. In Goldman's words,

> No economist would have agreed with [David] Ricardo on all or even a majority of points, but . . . only the "Cambridge inductivists" attacked the very method of political economy – its reliance on deduction from "self-evident truths" of human behavior and its restriction to the existing economic state of Britain. (Goldman 1983, 598–9)

In a letter to Richard Jones, Whewell summarized his critique of the Ricardians this way:

> They have begun indeed with some inference of facts; but, instead of working their way cautiously and patiently from there to the narrow principles which immediately inclose a limited experience, and of advancing to wider generalities of more scientific simplicity only as they become masters of more such intermediate truths – instead of this, the appointed aim of true and permanent science – they have been endeavouring to spring at once from the most limited and broken observations to the most general axioms. (Whewell to Jones, Whewell Papers, Add. Mss. c.51^{92})

Whewell declared that "political economy must be a science of *induction* and not of *deduction*. It must *obtain* its principles by reasoning upwards from facts, before it can *apply* them by reasoning downward from axioms" (1831, 52; italics in the original). The term "induction" meant more than Baconian data gathering. "Proper science was to be based on slowly cumulating inductive observations and hard-won experimental results; only on this basis could true, mathematical generalizations be securely erected" (Morrell and Thackray 1981, 271). Menachem Fisch maintains that by 1831 Whewell had come to regard well-formed sciences "as combinations of two bodies of knowledge: a body of induced empirical knowledge on the one hand, *cast in terms* of . . . a well-formed 'pure' articulation of a Fundamental Idea on the other" (Fisch 1991b, 49).

Whewell did not restrict "the term 'science' to the sphere of physical phenomena" for he believed "that the intellectual processes which [science] involved could be extended to other areas" (Yeo 1991, 178). He was determined to correct the image of science that was developing. In his view, the "current associations between physical science, empiricist epistemology, and the principle of utility were producing an image of science hostile to moral and metaphysical enquiry" (178).

To correct the image of science, Whewell distinguished "between science and utilitarianism, by underlining the moral effects of scientific enquiry, and by stressing the metaphysical dimensions of scientific knowledge" (179):

> Whewell was hostile to utilitarianism for a number of reasons, the most important being that the utilitarians portrayed the world in a way which denied the existence of God. People were portrayed as governed entirely by selfish pleasure-seeking, society as divided by divergent class interests, and the misery of starvation as inevitable; the world of the utilitarians was materialistic and lacking in benevolent design. (Williams 1991, 133)

For Whewell, induction meant more than merely a method for avoiding logical fallacies:

> It was also a way of avoiding irreligion and intellectual conceitedness. True knowledge and its pursuit, he believed was necessarily concordant with Christian belief and Christian morality. . . . Whewell was not claiming that certain doctrines were false *because* they conflicted with Christian religion, but that such a conflict was an indication that they could be shown to be false *on independent grounds*. . . . Faced, then, with the manifold errors of the contemporary sciences, Whewell formed the conviction that to follow the proper method of inquiry was to be continually mindful of God, and to be humble and respectful of tradition. . . . If he could only make [others] understand Induction in the same way he did, then the creditability of utilitarianism, and other forms of atheistic radicalism, would be destroyed. (136–7)

In Richard Jones's inductive approach to political economy, Whewell saw the opportunity to extend the intellectual processes used in proper science into other areas. Yeo correctly maintains that "Whewell hoped to use the dispute on political economy as a means of establishing correct views about the nature of moral science and its analogy with physical science" (Yeo 1991, 182). Jones's work showed that Ricardian political economy clearly lacked "a body of induced empirical knowledge" at its foundation (Fisch, 1991b, 49). Thus, "the deductive character of Ricardo's system was not a mark of its scientific character but a symptom of its failure to appreciate the process by which sciences were established" (Yeo 1991, 183). The underlying utilitarian philosophy of the Ricardians further cloaked political economy with an image of science that conflicted with Whewell's embryonic theory of excellent science. "Whewell appealed to notions of a general inductive method, or to analogies in the history and construction of various sciences, in order to defend the scientific status of political economy" (184). Jones claimed that certain Ricardian doctrines " 'having been first insisted on with a dogmatical air of *scientific* superiority,' were then asserted as 'an apparent inconsistency between the permanence of human happiness, and the natural action of the laws established by Providence' " (184). Thus, the doctrines of the dominant school of political economy "threatened to associate the name of science not only with inappropriate modes of procedure, but with improper moral and religious attitudes" (184).

If the methodological attack on Ricardian economics was to succeed, it would need an institutional base of operation. Jones and Whewell explored launching both a periodical and a statistical organization. In 1831, Jones proposed to Whewell that they launch an inductivist periodical.[1] Jones's enthusiasm for the project convinced Whewell to set aside his initial misgivings. In an April 24, 1831, letter to Jones, Whewell declared:

> I have a very strong conviction that taking such [an inductive] line of moral philosophy, political economy, and science, as I suppose we should, we might partly find and partly form a school which would be considerable in influence of the best kind. (Todhunter 1876, 2:118)

Whewell made a failed effort to enlist Malthus into their campaign for the periodical (see the correspondence between Whewell and Malthus in de Marchi and Sturges 1973). With Malthus's rejection of the effort to recruit him and Whewell's interests far too encompassing to devote the necessary time and energy to this project, "Jones was confronted with the dual role of rounding off a system and publicising it. The task was too much for him" (Checkland 1949, 45).

Even though Malthus rejected the attempt to recruit him to write for the proposed inductivist review, he did join Jones and Whewell in launching the statistical organizations. In June 1833, at the third meeting of the BAAS, the three of them joined with Charles Babbage and Adolphe Quetelet, a prominent Belgian astronomer and statistician to organize the "Statistical Section" (later Section F).[2] Adam Sedgwick, Woodwardian Professor of Geology at Cambridge and president of the 1833 meeting, initially rejected "the prospectus of the new section during the 1833 meeting because we found it politically controversial" but was persuaded by Whewell and the others to approve it when assured that the investigations of the section would be limited to scientific matters (Goldman 1983, 591). Cannon's account of the formation of Section F emphasized the roles played by Malthus, Jones, Babbage, Quetelet, and Sedgwick, but Goldman, more accurately, downgrades Sedgwick's role and substitutes "William Whewell, who was in personal contact with the other founders" (see Cannon 1978, 240–4; Goldman

1983, 591). The importance of Whewell's role in launching Section F is better understood in light of Jones's personality and Whewell's personal and professional relationship with him. As Todhunter described Jones,

> public business and the fascinations of society absorbed his time; and thus he never effected what his friends had anticipated, and what he might have accomplished by greater concentration of his powers, and by a more ascetic discipline. (Todhunter 1876, 1:xxi)

Whewell's numerous letters to Jones are filled with exhortations urging him to concentrate his powers on his inductive studies of economics.[3] While Jones was gifted at proposing projects, sustained effort was not his forte.

Cannon points out that "Jones was the entrepreneur of the movement" and that the conjunction of the organizers at the 1833 meeting "was by no means accidental or uncaused" (Cannon 1978, 242). In February 1833, in his inaugural lecture as professor of political economy at King's College, London, Jones "advocated a statistical society for England," and he and Whewell "discussed strategy several months before the British Association meeting" (Cannon 1978, 242). Whewell wrote to Jones on March 24, 1833, that "I want to talk to you about getting statistical information, if the British Association is to be made subservient to that, . . . which I think would be well" (Todhunter 1876, 2:161). Cannon's narrative of the founding of Section F notes that Whewell

> collected the small group in his rooms at Cambridge in June during the meeting. A decision was reached; Babbage acted as spokesman to the general meeting; and Sedgwick knew how to carry off any situation in front of an early Victorian audience with his own mixture of humour, eloquence, and an affirmation of his belief in God and Truth. He assured the meeting that the section would be devoted to mathematics and facts, not social rabble-rousing. (Cannon 1978, 242–3)

The Drinkwater notes of the founders gathering at Cambridge on June 28, 1833, reveal that Jones "read to the meeting a sketch of the objects" of this new section:

> In its narrowest sense considered as a subordinate to the inquiries of the political economist alone, the science of statistics would have for its subject-matter such phenomena only as bear directly or indirectly upon the production or distribution of public wealth. It is with wider views that such an association as the present would approach the subject. It may be presumed that they would think foreign to the objects of their inquiries no classes of facts relating to communities of

men which promise when sufficiently multiplied to indicate general laws. (Quoted in Goldman 1983, 599)

This last sentence, in a slightly altered form, became the statement restricting the research activities of the new section. In a letter to Whewell, Jones outlined the four "divisions I propose" defining the scope of the inductions that would be undertaken in Section F and the Statistical Society:

> Economical Statistics: 1. Agriculture, 2. manufactures, 3. commerce & currency, 4. distribution of wealth, i.e. rent, wages, & profits. Political Statistics: 1. Statistics of elements of institutions, Jurors – electors – &c., 2. Legal Statistics number of national & local tribunals, nature of courses tried &c. &c., 3. Finance – taxes, expenditures, public establishments &c. &c. Medical Statistics: 1. general medical statistics, 2. Population (the doctors say they shall want subdivisions). Moral & Intellectual Statistics: 1. Crime, 2. education & *literature*, 3. *ecclesiastical* statistics. (Jones to Whewell, Whewell Papers, Add. Mss. c.52^{60})[4]

The 1833 meeting of the BAAS at Cambridge is crucial to understanding Whewell's vision of the place of economics in the hierarchy of sciences. At the general meeting on the afternoon of Tuesday, June 25, Sedgwick took over the presidency and the British Association came under the dominance of what Cannon named the "Cambridge Network of Scientists" (Cannon 1978, ch. 2). Sedgwick called upon Whewell to address the members. Whewell made clear his concept of the hierarchy of sciences:

> Astronomy, which stands first on the list, is not only the queen of sciences, but, in a stricter sense of the term, the only perfect science; – the only branch of human knowledge in which particulars are completely subjugated to generals, effects to causes . . .
>
> Such is Astronomy: but in proceeding to other sciences, our condition and our task are of a far different kind. Instead of developing our theories, we have to establish them; instead of determining our data and rules with the last accuracy, we have to obtain first approximations of them. (Whewell 1833, xiii, xiv)

To obtain "first approximations" of the data of economics, the founders of Section F sought to construct it upon a statistical foundation. This approach was authenticated by "the prestige of the theory of probability in its role as trusted assistant to the queen of the sciences" – astronomy (Cannon 1978, 241).[5] Arguments of this nature seem to have overcome Sedgwick's initial hostility to the formation of the statistical section. Confirming the existence of a hierarchy of the sciences, Sedgwick announced that the association's governing committee authorized the division of the meeting into six sections. These six "Sections" or "Committees of Sciences" were numbered and arranged in hierarchical order: 1. mathematics and general physics; 2. chemistry, mineralogy, and so on; 3. geology and geography; 4. natural history; 5. anatomy, medicine, and so on; and 6. statistics (Anonymous 1833a, xxxix–xl).[6] On Friday, June 28, in his presidential address, Sedgwick admitted "an irregularity which had occurred in the formation of a new [Statistical] Section" (Sedgwick, 1833, xxvii),[7] the "irregularity" being that sessions were held and papers delivered for a Statistical Section that did not yet exist. New sections could be created only after formal proposals were approved and the section authorized by the General Committee. No such proposal had been submitted and no formal approval had been given to the new section, which simply "had come into operation, the object of which was to promote *statistical* inquiries" (1833, xxviii). Sedgwick explained the "irregularity" in the section's formation:

> He had the day previous announced the formation of a new Section, for the promotion of Statistical Inquiries; which had originated with the distinguished Professors Malthus, Babbage, Jones, and Quetelet. From the first, he had no doubt that Statistical inquiries might be legitimately embraced by the Association; and when he was made acquainted with the combination of such eminent men, he could only say to them, Go on and prosper – he could only do his best to have this new branch engrafted on the stem of the Association. He acknowledged, however, that the announcement by himself yesterday was altogether out of order; and had been made, partly because he had been taken by surprise, but chiefly out of respect to the great names he had just mentioned. But when the Report of this new self-formed Section was put in his hands this morning in the Senate House, in order to its being read before the assembled Association, he found it a difficult task to perform – and he resolved not to receive it; lest by doing so he should establish a very bad precedent, and risk the integrity of the consultation he had just heartily recommended. . . . He had little doubt that the new Section (perhaps after some limitation as to the specific objects of its inquiries) would be recognized by the Committee, and in that case it would become a legitimate member of their body, and its proceedings would appear as a matter of course in their Annual Report. (Anonymous 1833a, xxxvii)

To assuage the members' fears regarding its legitimacy, the Statistical Section was indeed saddled with "some limitation as to the specific objects of its inquiries." The formal approval for the new section was passed by the General Committee only after it was resolved that the inquiries of this Section should be restricted to those classes of facts relating to communities of men *which are capable of being expressed by numbers, and which promise, when sufficiently multiplied, to indicate general laws.* (Anonymous 1833b, 484)

Drafted originally by Jones, this limitation made the Statistical Section the only section in the BAAS with formal restrictions imposed on its field of inquiry.[8]

To reassure his audience further, Sedgwick pronounced his definition of science:

By science, then, I understand the consideration of all subjects, whether of a pure or mixed nature, capable of being reduced to measurement and calculation. All things comprehended under the categories of space, time and number properly belong to our investigations; and all phænomena capable of being brought under the semblance of a law are legitimate objects of our inquiries. (Sedgwick 1833, xxviii)

He asserted that the new section's statistical inquiries, properly pursued, fit his definition of science. "Considered in that light they give what may be called the raw material of political economy and political philosophy; and by their help the lasting foundations of those sciences may be ultimately laid" (xxviii).[9] Sedgwick's public pronouncements carried the day. "The *coup* was accepted; the new section prospered" (Cannon 1978, 243).

The creation of section F did not complete the formation of the inductivists' institutional base. The permanent committee of the Statistical Section made the following announcement in its "Recommendations":

In a Report since addressed to the Council [of the British Association] by this Committee, it is stated, that the Committee having deemed it expedient to promote the formation of a Statistical Society in London, a public meeting was held on the 15th of March, 1834, at which it was resolved to establish such an institution. (Anonymous 1833, 483–4)[10]

In a letter to Whewell, Jones reviewed the decision to approach that committee to seek their "authority" to form the Statistical Society of London:

I prevailed on Babbage (who was not reluctant) to call a general meeting of the Committee of the Association for next week and to get an authority for them to set about forming a society as the best means of carrying the spirit of the Cambridge Inductions into effect. (Jones to Whewell, Whewell Papers, Add. Mss. c.52[60])

This justification for seeking the approval of the BAAS to institute the Statistical Society differs from the reasons that the economists had when they went to Section F for approval of launching the British Economic Society. At the founding of the Statistical Society of London, "again Babbage was the public arranger, with Malthus and Jones as principal supporters" (Cannon 1978, 243).[11]

Section F and the Statistical Society formed the institutional base for an organized inductive assault on Ricardian deductive economics. Like the Whewell Group of Mathematical Economists, this Statistical Group was part of the Cambridge Network of Scientists (see Henderson 1985). Goldman notes that the "real bond" between the members of this Statistical Group "came from an intellectual contempt for the method of Ricardian economics as it was developed in the 1820s and 1830s and a related desire to base economic and social analysis on inductive procedures" (1983, 594). Not only was induction a way of avoiding logical errors; in Whewell's view "it was also a way of avoiding irreligion and intellectual conceitedness" (Williams 1991, 136).

Throughout the 1830s, Whewell's conception of induction was changing and maturing (see Fisch 1991b). He was working out his philosophy of science based on a sophisticated conception that science combines "two bodies of knowledge: a body of induced empirical knowledge on the one hand, *cast in terms* of . . . a well-formed 'pure' articulation of a Fundamental Idea on the other" (Fisch, 1991b, 49). Yet induction meant different things to different people. To many unsophisticated participants in both the Statistical Society and Section F, induction meant merely fact gathering. H. L. Moore described the issue in terms of the differing research interests of "practical men" and "philosophers":

> One road, travelled chiefly by practical men intent upon the exigent business of the day, has led through a dreary region directly to practical, but unrelated results; the other road, followed mainly by philosophers with primary interest in causes and relations, has ascended to picturesque heights affording distant views of the ensemble of economic activity, but has stopped short amid the enchanting scene and left the explorers in doubt as to what might be the real destination of so promising a beginning. (Moore 1929, 1)

Moore's "practical men" found easy access to the meetings of the London Statistical Society and Section F. Their intellectual wanderings, which "led through a dreary region directly to practical, but unrelated results" combined with the violations of the limitations imposed upon its research activities, soon raised the question of the legitimacy of Section F in the British Association.

The effort to abolish Section F

A mere four years after he played such an instrumental role in launching it, William Whewell declared that "the statistical Section ought never to have been admitted into the Association" (Morrell and Thackray 1981, 294). Instead of restricting its efforts to "those classes of facts relating to communities of men which are capable of being expressed by numbers, and which promise, when sufficiently multiplied, to indicate general laws," the section had become "an ambulatory body, composed partly of men of reputation, and partly of a miscellaneous crowd, [who] go round year by year, from town to town, and at each place . . . discuss the most inflammatory and agitating questions of the day" (Morrell and Thackray 1981, 294; Todhunter 1876, 2:291). At the 1839 meeting in Birmingham, a local committee "was appointed expressly to collect . . . information to be presented to the Association" (Anonymous 1839, 290). Applauding this innovation, the Statistical Section made this seemingly innocent suggestion:

> It is to be hoped that the example thus set in Birmingham will be followed in all the towns which the Association may in future visit, and that the announcement of its approach may serve as a signal for the appointment of a Committee to collect such information, to be laid at its meeting before the Statistical Section. The Association will thus both sow and reap knowledge at each of its visits. (290)

Two events at the 1840 meeting in Glasgow raised a storm of controversy. The first was H. J. Porter's paper, "On the Mont de Piété System of Pawnbroking in Ireland," which gave "rise to a public meeting, and to the nomination of a committee, for the purpose of establishing a Mont de Piété at Glasgow" (Anonymous 1840a, 210). This exposed the association to the charge of stirring up local political controversy. Even more controversial was the action taken by the section following papers given by W. P. Alison, M.D., and Rev. Thomas Chalmers "upon the important subject of Pauperism in Scotland, which afforded . . . [these] two rival authorities . . . an opportunity of bringing forward the facts upon which their opinions are founded" (Anonymous 1840a, 210–11). Afterwards:

> A resolution was passed by the Committee of the Section, recommending that the Council of the Association should take steps to urge upon the Government the expediency of extending the system of registration of births, deaths, and marriages, now operating in England, to Scotland. (211)

In the *Report of the British Association*, only the titles of the Chalmers and Alison papers were given, and this note was added: "The discourses of Dr. Chalmers and Dr. Alison contained frequent references to statistical data, but the enumeration of these would be of little service without a full statement of the arguments they were intended to support" (Anonymous 1840b, 186). Whewell was exasperated by the unscientific behavior of the Statistical Section which allowed the discussion of these "most inflammatory and agitating questions of the day."

Whewell was elected president of the BAAS in 1841.[12] His exasperation with such behavior provoked the first public rebuke of Section F. In his presidential address, he warned that there are "subjects which our constitution directs us to avoid" (Whewell 1841, xxxiv). Whewell still believed "that there is ample employment for this section, in subjects which can be dealt with in the same calm speculative spirit as the other sciences which we here cultivate" (xxxiii). He warned, however, "that in many statistical subjects, the discussion, and even the collection of facts, is rather the office of a legislative than of a scientific body" (xxxiii). In his view, topics "where the information is such as almost necessarily suggests legislation, or discussions having legislation for their natural end, and involving the deepest political and moral considerations" is best left to the government and not to Section F (xxxiii). Whewell continued:

> There may very fitly be voluntary associations, which aim directly at improving the intellectual, or moral, or social condition of our population; but we must ever remember that we are an association for a different purpose, namely, the advancement of science; and we are bound alike by our regard to the prosperity of our body, and by our most solemn and repeated declarations, to avoid the storm of opinions which is always raised when the parties which aim at social permanence and social progress are brought into conflict. The pursuit of scientific truth is, no doubt, a means of *indirectly* elevating man's intellectual and social condition; but we assemble in order to promote the *direct* pursuit of scientific truth; and we must not turn aside into the more wide and tangled paths of those who make its collateral effects their main object. Knowledge is power, we are told. Knowledge *is* power; but for us, it is to be dealt with as the power of interpreting nature and using her forces; not as the power of exciting the feelings of mankind, and providing remedies for social evils, on matters where the wisest men have doubted and differed. (xxxiii–xxxiv)[13]

On at least two other occasions before 1877, presidents of Section F had used the opportunity of their presidential addresses to complain about the quality of papers presented at its meetings. In 1860, four years after the name of Section F had been revised to "The Section of

Economic Science and Statistics," Nassau Senior declared that he had "looked through the papers" presented since then and declared that he was "struck by the unscientific character of many of them" (Senior 1860, 182).[14] Then in 1873, T. E. Cliffe Leslie criticized the quality of the papers presented at Section F.[15]

Finding fault with the papers read at the Section F meetings, Whewell, Senior, and Leslie sought to reform it. The situation was beyond reforming in the view of Francis Galton.[16] At the 1877 meeting of the BAAS, Galton submitted a paper demanding the abolition of Section F to a committee that "was appointed to consider and report to the Council on the possibility of excluding unscientific or otherwise unsuitable papers and discussions from the Sectional Proceedings of the Association" (Anonymous 1877, xlix). The Council of the BAAS adopted two of the committee's recommendations.[17] The issue of the suitability of the continued existence of Section F remained unresolved:

> The Committee in their Report further considered that some of the subjects brought before Section F could not be considered scientific in the ordinary sense of that word, and that the question of the discontinuance of Section F deserved the serious consideration of the Council. The Council have requested the Committee to report more fully the reasons which had induced them to come to this conclusion, but the Committee have not yet made a further report. (xlix)

Galton asserted that "this Section . . . occupies a peculiar position of isolation, being neither sufficiently scientific in itself, nor receiving help from other Sections" (Galton 1877, 471). He "freely conceded that Section F deals with numerous and important matters of human knowledge," but that did not give it title to be part of the BAAS (471). Galton drew a careful distinction between general knowledge and science. Science was confined "in the strictest sense to precise measurement and definite laws, which lead by such exact processes of reasoning to their results, that all minds are obliged to accept the latter as true" (471). He examined all seventy-two of the papers read before Section F during the years from 1873 through 1875 and found only four of these that he classified as "scientific."[18] As further evidence that Section F was unscientific, he noted that "in the 112 lectures that have been given since the system of two annual lectures to the Association generally was first established in 1842, not a single one has been either a statistical or an economic subject" (472). Moreover, few of the "Committees appointed by the General Committee to make investigations, and who receive grants of money to defray the cost of making them" have examined Section F topics (472); see Table 18.1). This assertion is somewhat surprising since Galton himself was then an active member of the Anthropometric Committee, which was sponsored by Section F from 1875 until 1884 and had already received appropriations of £266 by 1877. This particular committee received total appropriations of £456 and was paid grants amounting to £303 15s during its lifetime. Next Galton claimed that, from 1867 to 1875,

> there have been upwards of 250 reports, referring to perhaps 220 different subjects. Only four of these appear to be strictly appropriate to Section F, namely: – Pressure of Taxation on Real Property; Sewage; on Arrangements with the approaching Census; and on combinations of Capital and Labour. (472)

Galton also alleged that since Section F "is isolated and avowedly attracts much more than its share of persons of both sexes who have had no scientific training, its discussions are apt to become even less scientific than they otherwise would have been" (472). He raised the old fear of rabble-rousing, warning that "any public discredit which may be the result of its unscientific proceedings has to be borne by the whole Association" (472). Next he asserted that the BAAS needed "to keep the number of Sections as small as possible" in order to be able to accommodate the existing sections and to meet the "pressing claims" for new sections brought on by "the rapid extension of science" (472).[19] He concluded his demand for the abolition of Section F by assuring the BAAS that its removal would not hinder "the progress of Economic Science and Statistics, because those subjects now find a more congenial and appropriate home in the Social Science Congress" which provides "a larger gathering of experts in these subjects . . . than can ever be assembled at the British Association" (472).

Galton's proposal to dissolve Section F was brought to the attention of the Statistical Society of London at its "Forty-Third Anniversary Meeting" held on June 26, 1877, nearly two months before the annual meeting of the BAAS. Dr. W. Farr, president of Section F in 1877, informed the members of the Statistical Society of the challenge raised by Galton. He had managed to get the Council of the BAAS to postpone any decision on the matter on the grounds that "he was not prepared to discuss the subject then, but wished to consult the Statistical Society, which had always taken a deep interest in the section" (Anonymous September, 1877b, p. 343). Farr maintained that "it would be undesirable to break off the connection" between the Statistical Society and the BAAS (343). He identified two benefits arising from this connection. First, the Statistical Society benefited because "the object of the British Association was to give a stronger impulse in a more systematic direction to scientific inquiry" (343). By bringing men of science together and "promoting intercourse between them," scientists from other fields can better "appreciate the work of the Statistical Society" (343). A second "object of the Association was to draw attention to scientific matters in the country" (343). Here, Farr asserted that numerous papers presented at Section F by "some of the most eminent and distinguished Fellows of this Society . . . would bear comparison with any read before other sections" (343). In the discussion that followed, Mr. F. P. G. Neison asked if the proposed abolition of Section F was not prompted

> by the fact that the Statistical Society already thoroughly occupied the ground, and that therefore there was not the same necessity for papers on statistical research and economic science as formerly. If that were so, the proposed abolition was rather a compliment to the Society. (344)

Farr, anxious to save Section F, answered Neison by saying "there are other societies in a similar position, such as the Chemical Society, and Linnaeen Society, but it was not therefore suggested that it was unnecessary to have a Chemical or a Biological Section" (344). Sir Rawson Rawson put forth several arguments that would later be elaborated by other defenders of Section F. The BAAS would feel a "material loss" by the abolition of the Economic Section for the following reasons:

> There was a certain number of distinguished visitors who were attracted chiefly by this section, and in each place of meeting were a large number of persons who took little or no interest in pure physical science, but who did take an interest in statistical science, and who were led to inquire into local questions for the purpose of bringing the subject before the Economic Section, and it would be a serious loss to the inhabitants generally of the towns where the meetings were held, if the section were abolished. (344–5)

The "material loss" argument would be developed more fully by Edwin Chadwick and others to show the revenue that the British Association would lose by abolishing Section F. Rawson's other argument in defense of Section F, that it provided a place where "large number of persons who took little or no interest in pure physical science" could "inquire into local questions" reversed Whewell's major objection in 1840 that the section had become "an ambulatory body, composed partly of men of reputation, and partly of a miscellaneous crowd, [who] go round year by year, from town to town, and at each place . . . discuss the most inflammatory and agitating questions of the day"

(Todhunter 1876, 2:291).[20] Finally, William Guy argued for more careful screening of the papers proposed for Section F:

> There were some people, purists in science, who denied to statistics the name science; but if all statistics were not scientific, there were some statistical essays which were purely and eminently scientific. Science was many sided, and the members of the Statistical Society cultivated one particular branch to the best of their ability. If papers were offered to the British Association which were undeserving of the name of science (papers relating to subjects not tested by experience, or properly supported by numerical details), they ought to be excluded, but if they were worthy of the name they should be accepted. (Anonymous 1877b, 346)[21]

Any number of the early arguments defending the continued existence of Section F are curious and fail to confront directly Galton's primary argument that the section dealt with unscientific matters.[22] Farr wrote a rejoinder to Galton's charges in the September issue of the *Journal of the Statistical Society.* He listed the names of the most distinguished persons who had served as president of the section.[23] His most interesting appeal proclaimed that "the Association, in advance of some other scientific bodies, admits members of both sexes, and the number of ladies has latterly ranged from 600 to 1,058. Among the 856 papers read in this section since its origin, 21 have been by ladies" (Farr, 1877, 473–4). Farr then quoted a letter from Robert Giffen and Hammond Chubb, the secretaries of the Statistical Society, who defended the existence of Section F on two grounds: First, it is "a conspicuous advertisement to men to different sciences" that scientific knowledge can be applied beyond the physical sciences and is indispensable to the study of mankind, and second, in exchange for the "evil" of a few unscientific discussions, this section because of its popularity, communicates "some notion of scientific method and its value, and of the conclusions of scientific study, to the unscientific multitude" (474–5). Finally, Farr referred to a letter from Edwin Chadwick who noted that the open meetings of Section F had always attracted large, *paying* audiences, while "it has taken out very little from the funds of the Association" (476; see Tables 18.1 and 18.2).[24] Chadwick also claimed that the section's appeal to the working classes had positive effects. In fact, at the meeting held in Belfast, "the papers and discussions in Section F were so fortunate as to put an end to a disastrous strike" (476).[25] Notice, in all of this, that there was very little effort (other than William Guy's remarks) to counter Galton's most important accusations that the activities in Section F, however important and interesting, were unscientific.

In the December 1877 issue of the *Journal of the Statistical Society*, was a reprint of a defense of Section F from the *Economist*.[26] This writer identified two issues which needed to be resolved. The first was easily settled and involved matters of screening papers and timing. The officers of the sections who approved the papers to be presented, "are nominated privately by the general committee only a few weeks, sometimes not so long, before the actual date of meeting; and the secretaries and committee are left, to a large extent, to the chances of the first day of the meeting itself" (Anonymous 1877c, 631). To resolve this problem, the writer suggested that the section president, the local and one other secretary, and two of the three vice-presidents be "*publically* nominated" no less than six months nor more than twelve months prior to the meeting. Public nominations would assure both that all members of the British Association would know the names of those nominated and "that the reputation and character of these persons may become pledged, as it were, to the success of their" sections (632). Moreover, Section F would again face special conditions not imposed on the other sections:

> I would suggest that the Statistical Society of London should constitute, from among its members, a standing committee, charged with the duty of assisting and co-operating with the office-bearers-elect of Section F. In this manner it would be possible to settle beforehand a programme of papers, and arrange for the presence at the meeting itself of persons competent to sustain scientific discussion. (632)

The writer wished to impose this additional restraint on the section because recently Section F was "invaded by the miscellaneous and meandering class of papers, which in later years have unhappily become far too frequent in the proceedings of the section" (631).

This anonymous writer also recommended another change, which would be more difficult to agree upon and implement. He argued that statistical studies were of increasing importance and therefore needed scientific direction like that offered by the British Association:

> The necessities of Government, the competition of commerce, and the labours of individual inquirers have amassed statistical materials, which are in a great degree useless, because not yet dealt with on scientific principles of reduction and classification. In this respect statistics closely resembles meteorology, and the remedy is precisely the same in both cases, viz., controversy and discussion – rival explanations and antagonistic theories – carried on with all the excitement of discovery and contest until the truth be made plain. (633)

This proposal supported the initial argument that these studies should be conducted scientifically and private opinions excluded from their discussions.

In 1878, John K. Ingram, the new president of Section F, defended its existence from the attacks of Galton and the special committee. In his presidential address, "The Present Position and Prospects of Political Economy," Ingram expressed his fear that the effort to abolish Section F could not have received a hearing "unless supported by a considerable weight of opinion amongst those within the body who are regarded as competent judges" (Ingram 1878, 5). Ingram's fears confirm Ted Porter's claim:

> It is far from clear that the natural scientists who led the BAAS preferred abstruse economic theory to determined efforts at counting and measuring. Scientists took practical issues of instrumentation and measurement very seriously, and the BAAS in its institutional capacity perhaps even more so. (Porter 1991a, 3)

Ingram said that economics "has the most momentous influence of all on human welfare" (Ingram 1878, 7). Contrary to Galton's claim that Section F "occupies a peculiar position of isolation, being neither sufficiently scientific itself, nor receiving help from other Sections," Ingram replied:

> It receives contributions from all other departments of research – whether in the ascertainment of results to be used for its purposes, or in the elaboration of methods to be applied in its inquiries. It presides, in fact, over the whole intellectual system – an office which some, mistaking the foundation for the crown of the edifice, have claimed for mathematics. It is the most difficult of all the sciences, because it is that in which the phenomena dealt with are most complex and dependent on the greatest variety of conditions, and in which, accordingly, appearances are most deceitful, and error takes the most plausible forms. (1878, 7)

Ingram distinguished between two beliefs held by those in favor of abolition of the section. First, "that economic facts do not admit of scientific investigation," he dismissed as unfounded (6). To hold such a position was "doubly disastrous – first, by leaving the scientific system without its necessary completion in a true theory of the highest and most important class of [social] phenomena accessible to our research" (7). Second, removing Section F from the British Association, would be "to hand over to minds of insufficient power, and destitute of the necessary preparation, studies which, more than any others, require a strong intelligence, disciplined in the methods and furnished with the results of the sciences" (7). Outside of Section F, "the mode in which the study of these phenomena has been conceived and prosecuted in the hitherto reigning school is open to serious objections" (8).

The belief that the "prevailing mode of studying those facts is unsatisfactory, and many of the current generalizations respecting them unsound," led Ingram to attack deductive political economy on four grounds (6):

> first, to the attempt to isolate the study of the facts of wealth from that of the other social phenomena; secondly to the metaphysical or viciously abstract character of many of the conceptions of the economists; thirdly, to the abusive preponderance of deduction in their processes of research; and fourthly, to the too absolute way in which their conclusions are conceived and enunciated. (10)

Regarding the second one, Ingram aimed two accusations at the reigning deductive school. First, they based their entire system "on the hypothesis that the sole human passion or motive which has economic effects is the desire of wealth," and second, they treated labor "exclusively as an agent . . . an instrument of production" while disregarding that workers are individuals, as well as members of families, of society, and of political systems (17–18).

Concerning his third charge, he admitted that "deduction has indisputably a real and not inconsiderable place" in economics (19). However,

> the office of deduction is . . . to verify and control inductions which have been arrived at, using for this purpose considerations founded on the qualities of human nature and the external conditions to which society is subjected. Results which could not have been elicited by *a priori* reasoning from the latter data, may, when inductively obtained, be in this way checked and rationalized. . . . This method, in which inductive research preponderates, and deduction takes a secondary place as a means of verification, is the really normal and fruitful method of [economic] inquiry. (20)

Agreeing with Richard Jones, Ingram also insisted that "the nature of a social fact of any degree of complexity cannot be understood apart from its history" (21).

Rather than removing Section F from the BAAS, Ingram suggested that "the field of the section should be enlarged, so as to comprehend the whole of sociology" (28). While there were other organizations devoted to the study of the social sciences, Ingram insisted that the advantage of affiliation with the BAAS was "to aim at a genuinely scientific character in our work" (29). He concluded his speech with this comment on statistics: "It is impossible to vindicate for statistics the character of a science; they constitute only one of the aids or adminicula of science" (29). However, by returning economic analysis to "the true nature and conditions," which "should prevail, the importance of statistical inquiries will rise, as the abstract and deductive method declines in estimation" (30).[27]

Robert Lowe (1878) reponded to Ingram's speech. In his defense of deductive economics, he accused Ingram of "fortify[ing] himself with four dicta out of Comte" (Lowe 1878, 859). Lowe offered this definition of science: "Science means knowledge in its clearest and most absolute form, and there is but one crucial test of the existence of such knowledge, and that test is prediction" (860). Clearly Lowe's definition coincides with Whewell's emphasis on the predictive capacity of the hypothesis, both men anticipating in a sense Milton Friedman's position.[28] For Lowe, "The difference between political economy and the other moral sciences consists in this, that it admits of that prediction which . . . is the true test of science" (864).

T. E. Cliff Leslie (1879) published his rejoinder to Lowe's attack on Ingram. In Leslie's view, the primary problem with Lowe's approach to economics was his deductive methodology. He objected, in particular, to Lowe's assertion that Adam Smith based the whole science of political economy on two pecuniary motives: "the desire for wealth and aversion from labour" (Leslie 1879, 194). This "is contrary not only to the spirit but to the letter of Adam Smith's 'Wealth of Nations' " (194). To Lowe's contention "that the scientific character and the complete success of the method of eliminating all other motives, is demonstrated by its enabling the economist to predict," Cliffe Leslie answered that "just the opposite is the truth" (197). In his view, Lowe and his deductive colleagues "nominally concede a place" to the "other motives and forces" that operate on human behavior, but immediately set these

> . . . aside as "disturbing causes" in a manner without precedent or analogy in physical science. The last thing an astronomer would dream of is, that having admitted in general terms the existence of other forces besides those taken account of by the earliest observers, he need not concern himself with them further, and may calculate the movements of the heavenly bodies without reference to them. (198)

Since "the last thing an astronomer would dream of" would be routinely to set aside disturbing forces in the manner of Lowe and the other deductivists, Cliffe Leslie looked to astronomy as the proper model for economics. He believed that "before predicting the future, . . . we should learn to predict the present, by studying the forces at work in the world around us, the conditions under which they operate, and their actual results" (203). If Lowe's definition that "science means knowledge in its clearest and most absolute form, the test of which is prediction" were true, said Cliffe Leslie, then "no science could have a beginning or a youth: it must spring into life fully grown and armed . . . and only a science founded, like deductive political economy, on fiction, could do so" (213). Instead, he argued, in keeping with Whewell's convictions, that "science is patient and progressive, never, therefore, reaching perfection; its essence consists in a right method of investigation more than in the extent of its progress" (214).

Cliffe Leslie's article brought forth responses from two utilitarians – William Stanley Jevons (1879) and Henry Sidgwick (1879). These two utilitarians and F. Y. Edgeworth destroyed Whewell's and Jones's effort to create a scientific economics and settled instead for establishing a scientific image for economics.

The triumph of the utilitarian image of science

Fisch gives the best short summary of Whewell's mature theory of scientific truth:

> Since . . . all knowledge comprises two antithetical elements, one factual and one conceptual, [Whewell's] theory of scientific truth is correspondingly two-fold. "Ideas are the *Form*, facts are the *Material*, of our structure. Knowledge does not consist in the empty mould, or in the brute mass of matter, but in the right moulded substance."

> Therefore, continues Whewell: "our knowledge is then most complete, then most truly deserves the name Science, when both its elements are most perfect; – when the Ideas which have been concerned in its formation have, at every step, been clear and consistent; and when they have, at every step also, been employed in bonding together real certain facts." (Fisch 1991a, 290–1; quotations from Whewell 1858, 70, 72)

During the "1830s and 1840s, the extension of the method of natural science to social and political questions was still a contentious issue" (Yeo 1986, 283). While Whewell advocated that political economy adopt the method of natural science, induction, he was also "critical of hasty transfers of concepts and methods from physical to moral sciences. By the end of the century, however, the analogies between natural and social inquiries were pursued with enthusiasm" (283). There developed a growing "dichotomy between the content and method of science" (285). In economics the three utilitarians, Jevons,

Sidgwick, and Edgeworth, contributed to this dichotomy. They down-graded the importance of the empirical element ("content") in economics and elevated mathematical theorizing ("method"). Ted Porter makes this clear:

> Mathematization implies theoretical formulation in the language of mathematics, emphasizing derivations involving the manipulation of terms to reach new results. Quantification . . . refers first of all to purely or partly empirical operations, such as measurement, counting, and statistical analysis. High neoclassical economics assigns a distinctly subordinate place to these forms of quantification, and worships at the alter of mathematization. Physics and engineering are, to say the least, far more ambivalent about the priority of theoretical mathematics. (Porter, 1991b, 3)

Porter points out that "physicists regarded theory as important, but almost never in isolation from experiment, and their customary rhetoric emphasized experimental fact, not mathematical rigor" (3–4). In contrast, what the neoclassical economists created

> was very much a program of mathematization, one that did not condemn quantification, but was willing to defer it indefinitely. Though patterned in important ways afte · physical statics, this was not the economics of choice for physicists, and it permitted theory a degree of autonomy from measurement that went well beyond what is normally condoned even by twentieth century physicists. (5)

Thus, the victory of the neoclassical school of economics was a "triumph of the utilitarian image of science" rather than the creation of an economic science as physicists and their colleagues understand science. The "utilitarian image of science" was an image founded upon the developing dichotomy of the content and method of science. The utilitarians were "willing to defer [quantification – content] indefinitely" (5) while they "worship[ed] at the alter of mathematization" (3) (method). The mathematical method created an image of economics as a science while economists "deferred indefinitely" the "purely or partly empirical operations, such as measurement, counting, and statistical analysis" that genuine science required.

In the preface to the second edition of his *Theory of Political Economy*, Jevons responded to Cliffe Leslie's charges. Of particular importance is Jevons's proposal for the separation of "abstract theory" ("mathematization") from "the empirical element" ("quantification"):

> Mr. Cliffe Leslie . . . would reconstruct the science in a purely inductive or empirical manner. Either it would then be a congeries of miscellaneous disconnected facts, or else it must fall in as one branch

of Mr. Spencer's Sociology. In any case, I hold that *there must arise a science of the development of economic forms and relations.*

But as regards the fate of the deductive method, I disagree altogether with my friend Mr. Leslie; he is in favour of simple deletion; I am for thorough reform and reconstruction. . . . the present chaotic state of Economics arises from confusing together several branches of knowledge. Subdivision is the remedy. We must distinguish the empirical element from the abstract theory, from the applied theory, and from the more detailed art of finance and administration. Thus will arise various sciences, such as commercial statistics, the mathematical theory of economics, systematic and descriptive economics, economic sociology, and fiscal science. (Jevons 1879, xvi–xvii)

For Jevons, abstract theory must be distinguished from the empirical element, and there must arise a separate science – "the mathematical theory of economics." This Jevonian conception of economic science differs dramatically from the Whewell's conception of scientific economics. Where Jevons asserted that "subdivision is the remedy," Whewell insisted that "science at its best . . . comprises, in its finished form, an entire body of fact perfectly colligated by means of a well-formed Euclidian conceptual scheme" (quoted in Fisch 1991a, 291). Just how far Jevons was prepared to go in the subdivision of economics is made most clear in this statement, in the Preface to the second edition of his *Theory*, where he noted that several readers of the first edition

have pointed out that a little manipulation of the symbols, in accordance with the simple rules of differential calculus, would give results which I have laboriously argued out. The whole question is one of maxima and minima, the mathematical conditions are familiar to mathematicians. But . . . I do not write for mathematicians, nor as a mathematician, but as an economist wishing to convince other economists that their science can be treated on an explicitly mathematical basis. When mathematicians recognise the subject as one with which they may usefully deal, I shall gladly resign it to their hands. (Jevons 1879, xiii–xiv)

All that was required for Jevons to "resign" economics to the hands of the mathematicians was that they "recognise the subject as one with which they may usefully deal." Mathematicians need not make any effort to engage in "quantification . . . [the] purely or partly empirical operations" of the kind that Whewell and Jones sought to establish, "such as measurement, counting, and statistical analysis."

Jevons's second contribution to the triumph of the utilitarian image of science was his suggestion that in addition to the alleged parallels between astronomy and economics, a mathematical economics could be built by taking over the mathematical models of mechanics. In Mirowski's words:

> Jevons wrote that his equation of exchange does ". . . not differ in general character from those which are really treated in many branches of physical science." He then proceeds to compare the equality ratios of marginal utility of two goods and their inverted trading ratio to the law of the lever, where in equilibrium the point masses at each end are inversely proportional to the ratio of the respective distances from the fulcrum. Note at this stage that Jevons' exposition does not adequately support his statements in the text: since he does not derive the equilibrium of the lever from consider-ations of potential and kinetic energy, he fails to justify the parallel between the expression of physical equilibrium and his differential equations in his own equations of exchange. (Mirowski 1988, 13)

Jevons went beyond the earlier efforts simply to draw parallels be-tween scientific economics and physical astronomy, where models are derived from observations of the phenomena explored. Instead, he tried to force economics into existing mathematical mechanics mod-els, ignoring the empirical basis to justify such an endeavor. Henry Sidgwick added another key element to this utilitarian campaign.

Sidgwick argued: "The controversy on economic method which has now been carried through three stages by Mr. Ingram, Mr. Lowe, and Mr. Cliffe Leslie, involves two distinct issues; one historical and one purely theoretical" (1879, 301). By separating these two issues and focusing attention on the second one, Sidgwick laid the groundwork for Edgeworth's "resolution" of the debate over method:

> I am inclined to think that the most important progress in theoretical economics has been and will be derived from an exercise of thought which is not strictly deductive or inductive, as these terms are com-monly used; and which the antithesis between deduction and induc-tion . . . has an unfortunate tendency to obscure. I mean the process which is sometimes called Analysis, sometimes Interpretation, of facts; that is, the application to concrete facts of such general concep-tions, in a condition of adequate clearness and definiteness, as may fix the most important characteristics of the facts, and present them permanently to the mind in true relations. (308)

That Sidgwick meant to diminish the importance of the empirical foundations of economics can be seen clearly in his statement elevat-ing the importance of analysis above the functions of " 'observation,' 'generalisation,' and 'induction' " (308):

> It is tacitly supposed to be easy to observe and collect the facts on which economical conclusions have to be based. . . . But the truth is,

that in dealing with a subject-matter of which the scientifically important characteristics are not directly presented to the mind through
the senses, it is very difficult for any one to see clearly what others
have not seen before him, however plain it may appear when it has
once been pointed out; such "seeing" is the fruit either of prolonged
and patient reflection, or of an intellectual originality that amounts
to genius. (308)

If economics was to progress, economists must sharpen "the process
which is sometimes called Analysis, sometimes Interpretation, of
facts." Here is the solution put forth by Sidgwick:

> There is still much scope for the exercise of analytical penetration in
> the more difficult and complicated departments of economics; but it
> is a gift which cannot be got by merely seeing the need for it. Mean-
> while in default of any special gift, something may be gained by a
> more thorough reflection on the fundamental notions by means of
> which we think and reason about economic facts; by considering
> more carefully the characteristics of things already known and famil-
> iar, even without any more extensive or accurate information than
> we already possess. In short, I desire a reform in the department of
> Economic Definition, before we come to demonstration. (308–9)

Sidgwick's "desire [for] a reform in the department of Economic Definition" was meant to sharpen economic analysis. He emphasized "the
importance of making our thought precise" and in doing so eluci-
dated Porter's distinction between scientific quantification and neoclassical mathematization (310):

> I have spoken once or twice of the importance of making our
> thought precise. I do not mean that we should necessarily aim at
> quantitative exactness in our statements of economic laws. I quite
> agree with the writers (such as Cairnes) who have warned us against
> the futility of such attempts. But the more inevitable it is that our
> conclusions should be rough and approximate, the more important
> it becomes that we should be thoroughly aware when and how far
> they are wanting in exactness; and in order that we may be aware of
> this, we should make our *conceptions* as precise as possible, even when
> we cannot make our *statements* so. (310–11)

Thus, what Sidgwick intended precise thinking to bring to economics
was not "purely or partly empirical operations, such as measurement,
counting, and statistical analysis." Sidgwick's call for precise thinking
and his reformulation and reduction of the role that quantitative
analysis ought to play in economics anticipated Edgeworth's ideas.

The crucial role played by Francis Ysidro Edgeworth in the transition from classical to neoclassical economics, in particular the adop-

tion of the image of natural science methodology, was significant. The vital function he performed is revealed in his 1889 presidential address to Section F, "Points at Which Mathematical Reasoning is Applicable to Political Economy." Of particular importance was Edgeworth's explicit statement of the contribution that mathematization can make to building abstract economic theory.[29] Edgeworth asserted:

> The idea of reducing human actions to mathematical rule may present itself to common sense as absurd. . . . It should be understood, however, that the new method of economical reasoning does not claim more precision than what has long been conceded to another department of science applied to human affairs, namely, Statistics. . . . But, indeed, even the limited degree of arithmetical precision which is proper to statistical generalisations need not be claimed by our mathematical method rightly understood. It is concerned with quantity, indeed, but not necessarily with number. It is not so much a political arithmetic as a sort of economical algebra, in which the problem is not to find x and y in terms of given quantities, but rather to discover loose quantitative relations of the form: x is greater or less than y; and increases or decreases with the increase of z. (Edgeworth 1889, 274)

Edgeworth's idea that economics "is not so much a political arithmetic as a sort of economical algebra" by which we can "discover loose quantitative relations" clearly "assigns a distinctly subordinate place to [the empirical] forms of quantification, and worships at the alter of mathematization" (274). The parallels between Edgeworth call for mathematization and Sidgwick's earlier call for precise thinking are evident. For Sidgwick, economists need not "necessarily aim at quantitative exactness in our statements of economic laws" (1879, 310); for Edgeworth, economics "is concerned with quantity, indeed, but not necessarily with number. . . . the problem is not to find . . . given quantities, but rather to discover loose quantitative relations" (1889, 274).

Edgeworth declared that this approach to economic issues drew heavily on the mathematical tools employed in astronomy, and it was particularly enlightening when analyzing systems of markets that are mutually dependent. Once economists

> obtain the idea of a system of markets mutually dependent . . . it is not necessary to distinguish whether the state of one part is connected as cause or effect with other parts of the system. As Professor Marshall says: "Just as the motion of every body in the solar system affects and is affected by the motion of every other, so it is with the elements of the problem of political economy." This conception of mutually dependent positions is one in which minds disciplined in mathematical physics seem particularly apt to acquiesce. . . . [This

enables us to develop] a correct view of the [system of markets], the principle of mutual dependence – what may be called the Copernican theory of distribution, in which one variable is not more determined by another than the other is by that one. (1889, 276–7)[30]

Edgeworth also took up Jevons's efforts to mold economics into the energy equations of mathematical physics. He maintained that, once account is taken of all of the aspects of economic problems, their exposition becomes extremely complex:

> When Gossen, the predecessor of Jevons as exponent of the law of final utility, compares that principle to the law of gravitation, and the character of our science to that of astronomy, he betrays a parental partiality. A truer, though still too flattering, comparison would be afforded by some immature and imperfect specimens of physics, say the theory of fluid motion applied to the problems of house ventilation. (280)

Mirowski cites Edgeworth's most explicit statement of "the wellsprings of the neoclassical movement" (Mirowski 1988, 15):

> The application of mathematics to the world of the soul is countenanced by the hypothesis (agreeable to the general hypothesis that every physical phenomenon is the concomitant, and in some sense the other side of a physical phenomenon), the particular hypothesis adopted on these pages, that Pleasure is the concomitant of Energy. *Energy* may be regarded as the central idea of Mathematical Physics: *Maximum energy* the object of the principle investigations in that science . . . "Mécanique Sociale" may one day take her place along with "Mécanique Celeste," throned each upon the double-sided height of one maximum principle, the supreme pinnacle of moral as of physical science. As the movements of each particle, constrained or loose, in a material cosmos are continually subordinated to one maximum sub-total of accumulated energy, so the movements of each soul whether selfishly isolated or linked sympathetically, may continually be realising the maximum of pleasure. (Edgeworth 1881, 9, 12, quoted in Mirowski 1988, 15)

Though Marshall spoke of introducing the methods of biology into economics, he did not actually do so. Edgeworth proclaimed that physics, not biology, offered the appropriate methodological model for giving economics a scientific image. As he put it in his "Introductory Lecture on Political Economy," delivered at Oxford in 1891 on the occasion of his appointment to the Drummond Chair of Economics:

> There is a certain affinity between the mathematical physics and the one social science which is largely occupied with measurable quantities. The nature of things which has involved the knowledge of physics

in the mysteries of mathematics has not wished the way of cultivating economics to be altogether free from that difficulty. In the memorable words of Malthus, "Many of the questions both in morals and politics seem to be of the nature of problems *de maximus et minimus* in fluxions." The differential calculus, the master-key of the physical sciences, unlocks the treasure-chamber of the pure theory of economics. (Edgeworth 1891, 6)[31]

Several years later, in the paper "Application of the Differential Calculus to Economics," published in *Scientia,* a journal that was "born of the desire to co-ordinate the work carried on in different fields of knowledge" (Edgeworth 1909, 367) Edgeworth declared:

> The Newtonian astronomy is rather the model of our Science; but we can only follow it at a great distance owing to the multiplicity of variables in Social Science and the want of a unit for measuring advantage in a subjective sense. Often we must be content with knowing that knowledge is unattainable without more data than we possess – the Socratic lesson of modesty which was taught by Cournot and Jevons. (368)

This "want of a unit for measuring advantage in a subjective sense" was a pretext for assigning "a distinctly subordinate place to quantification," and worshiping instead "at the alter of mathematization." Edgeworth developed a new definition of the limited territory of economics that he sought to analyze mathematically – with "the master-key of the physical sciences [which] unlocks the treasure-chamber of the pure theory of economics":

> . . . if we understand "Economics" in its largest sense, almost coincident with – only slightly narrower than – the field which is covered by the well-known dictum of Malthus: "Many of the questions, both in morals and politics, seem to be of the nature of the problems *de maximis et minimis* in fluxions." Such is the little territory, on the borderland between Physics and Psychology, which I attempt here to survey. (368)

The divorce of quantification, as it was practiced in Section F and the Statistical Society, and mathematization, as it was practiced by the neoclassical economists, also took an institutional form. The neoclassicals used Section F as a surrogate mother to give birth to their own organization, the British, (later Royal) Economic Society. In April 1890, the founders of the BEA approached the "committee members of Section F of the British Association . . . [seeking] approval of the scheme for an *Economic Journal* and/or an English Economic Association" (Coats 1968, 356). When Richard Jones had "prevailed on Babbage (who was not reluctant) to call a general meeting of the Committee" of the BAAS, he sought "to get an authority" from it to create the Statistical Society because he believed that this was "the best means of carrying the spirit of the Cambridge Inductions into effect" (Jones to Whewell, Whewell Papers, Add. Mss. c.52[60], quoted earlier). Those who sought "approval of the scheme for an *Economic Journal* and/or an English Economic Association" went only to "Committee members of Section F," rather than to the governing body of the British BAAS itself. Since Edgeworth had been president of Section F in 1889 and Marshall was president in 1890, it was unlikely that serious opposition would develop among the "committee members of Section F." Their approval would give the new association and its journal the proper image of science without having to face the scientists who governed the parent organization, the BAAS. Edgeworth himself was named editor of the new *Economic Journal,* which was seen as the "first fully professional journal" in Britain, whereas the *Journal of the (Royal) Statistical Society* was merely a "semi-professional journal" for economists (Stigler 1964, 40). For neoclassical economists, the new British Economic Association quickly eclipsed in importance the older organizations. In his 1889 presidential address to Section F, Edgeworth declared that mathematization offered economists an alternative way out of the apparent impasse created by the debate over methodology:

> With reference to the heated controversy between the Historical and the Deductive schools, the mathematical economist as such is not committed to any side. It may be dangerous to take wide general views; it may be better to creep from one particular to another rather than ascend to speculative heights. Our only question here is whether, if that ascent is to be made, it is better to proceed by the steep but solid steps of mathematical reasoning, or to beguile the severity of the ascent by the zigzag-windings of the flowery path of literature. It is tenable that the former course is safest, as not allowing us to forget at what a dangerous height of abstraction we proceed. As Professor Foxwell has well said, with reference to the mathematical methods in the hands of Jevons and Marshall, "It has made it impossible for the educated economist to mistake the limits of theory and practice, or to repeat the confusions which brought the study into discredit and almost arrested its growth." (Edgeworth 1889, 288)

Appendix

At the "Natural Images in Economics" conference at the University of Notre Dame, Professor Ted Porter and Professor Timothy Alborn raised the issue of assessing the scientists' estimation of the standing of Section F within the British Association. In Porter's words:

It might give a more faithful picture of the actual place of economics in the sciences to see if there were other official reports in the BAAS on economic matters, and to ask what they were about, and what methods they used, and how they were received. (1991a, 4)

An analysis of the grants records of the BAAS generates such an assessment of the changing place of economics of section F in the hierarchy of the sciences in the BAAS, from Whewell's time to Edgeworth's era (see Tables 18.1 and 18.2). Using Table 18.1, a reasonable judgment can be formed of the scientific community's appraisal of the relative quality of the research projects sponsored by Section F in contrast to the projects sponsored by the other sections by comparing their success in obtaining the grant money dispensed by the BAAS. This table provides two measures of the standing of Section F in the opinion of these British scientists – money appropriated (A) and actual grants paid (P) – for specific Section F research proposals and for all of the research projects sponsored by the various sections of the BAAS. The money appropriated figures best measure the status of Section F, since these amounts were approved first by the specific scientific section submitting the grant request and then were voted on by the General Committee of the BAAS, which reviewed all grant proposals.

The early success of Section F during the period from 1836 to 1842 indicates support for the initial effort to put economics on a scientific footing. The controversies that arose in the early 1840s resulted in the BAAS shutting off grant money to Section F research proposals. It is apparent that Whewell exercised his influence to limit research grants coming from Section F. At the 1841 meeting, the committee of Section F passed five "resolutions relative to the recommendation of grants" (Anonymous 1841, 182). This committee decided not to recommend renewal of grants issued previously for two research projects – a study of the "British coal fields" and an inquiry "into the state of Schools" (182). Three other grant proposals were submitted – "an inquiry into Vital Statistics" (applying for £150), a committee "for the encouragement of inquiries into the condition of the population in one or more large towns, *considered merely as to numerical analysis*" (applying for £100), and a committee "to inquire into the operation of Loan Funds and Monts de Piété in Ireland" (applying for £50) – only the first of these was "sanctioned by the [BAAS] Committee of Recommendations" (182; emphasis added). Whewell's opposition to the last two proposals has been established. The BAAS Committee of Recommendations rejected an application for a £50 grant for a committee "for sanitary inquiries in the cities of Cork and Limerick" at the 1843

Table 18.1. *Money appropriated and grants paid: BAAS totals and Section F totals*

Year	BAAS (A)			BAAS (P)			Section F (A)	Section F (P)		
1834	£860			£20			0	0		
1835	£1760			£167			0	0		
1836	£2659	13s		£435			£150	0		
1837	£3057			£922	12s	6d	£250	0		
1838	£3742	10s		£932	2s	2d	£300	£50		
1839	£2789	14s	7d	£1595	11s		£100	£50		
1840	£2591	5s		£1546	16s	4d	£225	£150		
1841	£3033	9s	11d	£1235	10s	11d	£150	0		
1842	£3339	5s		£1449	17s	8d	£150	£70		
1843	£1877			£1565	10s	2d	0	£36	5s	8d
1844	£1421	11s	5d	£981	12s	8d	£40	0		
1845	£480	13s	8d	£831	9s	9d	£20	£20		
1846	£410			£685	16s		0	0		
1847	£290	10s	9d	£208	5s	4d	0	0		
1848	£213	10s		£275	1s	8d	0	0		
1849	£371			£159	19s	6d	0	0		
1850	£448			£345	18s		0	0		
1851	£441			£391	9s	7d	£20	0		
1852	£355	10s		£304	6s	7d	0	0		
1853	£379	12s		£205			0	0		
1854	£751			£380	19s	7d	0	0		
1855	£730			£480	16s	4d	0	0		
1856	£620			£734	13s	9d	0	0		
1857	£760	5s		£507	15s	4d	0	0		
1858	£1265			£618	18s	2d	0	0		
1859	£930			£684	11s	1d	0	0		
1860	£1395			£766	19s	6d	0	0		
1861	£2263			£1111	5s	10d	0	0		
1862	£1891			£1293	16s	6d	0	0		
1863	£1715			£1608	3s	10d	0	0		
1864	£2037	17s		£1289	15s	8d	£20	0		
1865	£2135			£1591	7s	10d	£50	0		
1866	£2270			£1750	13s	4d	£30	£50		
1867	£2200			£1739	4s		£50	£30		
1868	£1696			£1940			£25	£50		
1869	£1572			£1622			£25	£25		
1870	£1840			£1572			£25	£25		
1871	£1620			£1472	2s	6d	£75	£75		
1872	£2025			£1285			0	0		
1873	£1545			£1685			£25	0		

Table 18.1 *(cont.)*

Year	BAAS (A)			BAAS (P)			Section F (A)			Section F (P)		
1874	£1080			£1151	16s		£25			£25		
1875	£1489	4s	2d	£960			£100			0		
1876	£1620			£1092	4s	2d	£110			£13	15s	
1877	£1081			£1128	9s	7d	£66			£34		
1878	£1412			£725	16s	6d	£50			£66		
1879	£960			£1080	11s	11d	£50			£50		
1880	£1010			£731	7s	7d	£30			£50		
1881	£1280			£476	8s	1d	£50			£30		
1882	£1265			£1126	1s	11d	0			£50		
1883	£1445			£1083	3s	3d	£10			0		
1884	£1515			£1173	4s		0			£10		
1885	£1195			£1385			£10			0		
1886	£1300			£995	0s	6d	£10			£10		
1887	£1975			£1186	18s		£30			£10		
1888	£1645			£1511	0s	5d	£30			£30		
1889	£1265			£1417	0s	11d	£25			0		
1890	£1335			£789	16s	8d	0			0		
1891	£1013	15s	6d	£1029	10s		0			0		
1892	£1000			£864	10s		£5			0		
1893	£705			£907	15s	6d	£10			£3	7s	
1894	£1093			£583	15s	6d	0			£9	10s	
1895	£1160			£977	15s	5d	0			0		
1896	£1355			£1104	6s	1d	£25			0		
1897	£1350			£1059	10s	8d	£25			0		
1898	£1495			£1212			£18	13s	6d[a]	£15		
1899	£1115			£1430	14s	2d	£18	13s	6d[a]	0		
1900	£945			£1072	10s		£28	13s	6d[a]	£2	10s	
1901	£1015			£920	9s	11d	£30			£15		
1902	£960			£947			£25			£30		
1903	£900			£845	13s	2d	£25			£25		
1904	£1000			£887	18s	11d	£20			£25		
1905	£1047	8s	11d	£928	2s	2d	£20			£4	4s	8d
1906	£1061	12s	4d	£882	0s	9d	£25			0		
1907	£1288	9s	3d	£757	12s	10d	£6			£8	19s	7d
1908	£1191			£1157	18s	8d	£21			£3	7s	6d
1909	£1249			£1014	9s	9d	£21			0		
1910	£1090	13s		£963	17s		£5			£15		
1911	£1050			£922			0			0		
1912	£1036	18s	8d	£845	7s	6d	0			0		
1913	£1285	11s	9d	£978	17s	1d	0			0		
1914	£1634	16s	6d	£1086	16s	4d	£30			0		

Table 18.1 *(cont.)*

Year	BAAS (A)			BAAS (P)			Section F (A)	Section F (P)
1915	£986			£1159	2s	8d	£175	£30
1916	£602	6s	2d	£715	18s	10d	£70	£155
1917	£286	2s	10d	£427	17s	2d	£20	£80[b]
1918	£268	4s	8d	£220	13s	3d	£20	£20
1919	£1127			£160			£135	0
1920	£1011	13s		£959	13s	9d	£50	£135
Payments made from the Caird Fund[c]								
1913				£327	3s			0
1914				£775				0
1915				£410				£100
1916				£270				0
1917				£250				0
1918				£106				0
1919				£250				0
1920				£240				0

Note: A denotes money appropriated; P, money paid.
[a]Total includes "£13 13s 6d in hand" from a £15 grant paid in 1898.
[b]Total includes two £10 grants attributed to 1917 reported in 1918.
[c]Beginning in 1913, with a £10,000 gift from J. K. Caird, a special fund (the Caird Fund) was established to finance additional research projects.

meeting (Heywood 1843, 282). At the 1845 meeting, "it was not deemed advisable to make any appeal to the Council for funds to carry out specific investigations" (Anonymous 1845, 290). Note on Table 18.1 the decline in appropriations and payments beginning around 1843, and from 1846 until 1863 no payments were made and only one £20 appropriation was approved. Modest financial support resumes in the mid-1860s, but no actual payments were made until after Whewell's death (March 6, 1866). Smith notes:

> J. D. Morrell and Arnold Thackray point out in their *Gentlemen of Science* that the Cambridge network used the platform of the British Association for the Advancement of Science to secure funds and publicity. . . . But in the case of the Neptune discovery we see the Cambridge network could be used to restrict access to information as well as to disseminate it. (1989, 418)

In the case of Section F, it is evident that the "Cambridge network could be used to restrict access" to funding for its research proposals

Table 18.2. *Approved Section F research projects "Involving Grants of Money"*

1. 1836–42. "State of the Schools in England" (aka "Inquiries into the State of Education in the Schools in England," "Statistical Inquiries in Schools for the Working Classes," "Inquiries into the Actual State of Education," and "Statistics of Education"). Chaired by Col. Sykes (1836 and 1838), Lord Sandon (1837), and Sir Charles Lemon (1839 and 1840). Funding: in 1836, A = £150, P = 0; in 1837, A = £150, P = 0; in 1838, A = £150, P = £50; in 1839, A = £100, P = 0. "Mining Statistics," A = 0, P = £50; in 1840, A = £100, P = £50; and in 1842, A = 0, P = £20.

2. 1837–40. "Condition of the Working Population" (aka "Inquiries into the State of the Working Population" and "Working Population"). Chaired by Lord Sandon (1837) and Sir C. Lemon (1838). Funding: in 1837, A = £100, P = 0; in 1838, A = £100, P = 0; in 1840, A = 0, P = £100.

3. 1838–40. "Inquiries into the Statistics of the Collieries of the Tyne and Wear" (aka "Mining Statistics"). Chaired by Mr. Cargill (1838 and 1839) and Prof. Johnson (1840). Funding: in 1838, A = £50, P = 0; in 1839, A = 0, P = £50; in 1840, A = £25, P = 0.

4. 1840–3. "Vital Statistics." Chaired by Col. Sykes. Funding: in 1840, A = £100, P = 0; in 1841, A = £150, P = 0; in 1842, A = £150, P = £50; in 1843, A = 0, P = £36 5s 8d.

5. 1844–6. "For Statistics of Sickness and Mortality in York." Chaired by Dr. Laycock. Funding: in 1844, A = £40, P = 0; in 1845, A = 0, P = £20; in 1846, A = 0, P = £12.

6. 1851. "Report on the Census of the United Kingdom." Chaired by Lord Monteagle. Funding: A = £20, P = 0.

7. 1864–72. "Metrical Committee." Chaired by Lord Wrottesley (1864) and Sir J. Bowring (1865–72). Funding: in 1864, A = £20, P = 0; in 1865, A = £50, P = 0; in 1866, A = £30, P = £50; in 1867, A = £50, P = £30; in 1868, A = £25, P = £50; in 1869, A = £25, P = £25; in 1870, A = £25, P = £25; in 1871, A = £75, P = £25; in 1872, A = 0, P = £75.

8. 1873–4. "Economic Effects of Trade Unions" (aka "Economic Effects of Combinations of Labourers or Capitalists" and "Trade Unions"). Chaired by Lord Houghton. Funding: in 1873, A = £25, P = 0; in 1874, A = £25, P = £25.

9. 1875–84. "Systematic Examination of Heights, Weights of Inhabitants of the British Isles" (aka "Anthropometric Committee," "Physical Characteristics of Inhabitants of the British Isles," "Anthropometry," and "Estimation of Weights and Heights of Human Beings"). Chaired by Dr. Beddoe (1875), Dr. Farr (1876–9), F. Galton (1880–2), and E. W. Brabrook (1883–4). Funding: in 1875, A = £100, P = 0; in 1876, A = £100, P = £13 15s; in 1877, A = £66, P = £34; in 1878, A = £50, P = £66; in 1879, A = £50, P = £50; in 1880, A = £30, P = £50; in 1881, A

Table 18.2 *(cont.)*

= £50, P = £30; in 1882, A = 0, P = £50; in 1883, A = £10, P = 0; in 1884, Λ − 0, P = £10.

10. 1876. "Common Measure of the Value of Direct Taxation." Chaired by Rt. Hon. J. G. Hubbard. Funding: A = £10, P = 0.

11. 1885–7. "Regulation of Wages Under Sliding Scales" (aka "Regulation of Wages"). Chaired by Prof. H. Sidgwick. Funding: in 1885, A = £10, P = 0; in 1886, A = £10, P = £10; in 1887, A = 0, P = £10.

12. 1887–9. "Precious Metals in Circulation." Chaired by Mr. S. Bourne (1887) and Mr. R. Giffen (1888–9). Funding: in 1887, A = £20, P = 0; in 1888, A = £20, P = £20; in 1889, A = £15, P = 0.

13. 1887–9. "Variations in the Value of the Monetary Standard." Chaired by Mr. R. Giffen. Funding: in 1887, A = £10, P = 0; in 1888, A = £10, P = £10; in 1889, A = £10, P = 0.

14. 1892–4. "Methods of Economic Training." Chaired by Prof. W. Cunningham. Funding: in 1892, A = £5, P = 0; in 1893, A = £10, P = £3 7s; in 1894, A = 0, P = £9 10s.

15. 1896–1900. "State Monopolies in Other Countries." Chaired by Prof. H. Sidgwick (probably 1896 and 1897–9) and Sir R. Giffen (1900). Funding: in 1896, A = £15, P = 0; in 1897, A = £15, P = 0; in 1898, A = 0 ("£13 13s 6d in hand"), P = £15; in 1899, A = 0 ("£13 13s 6d in hand"), P = 0; in 1900, A = 0 ("£13 13s 6d in hand"), P = 0.

16. 1896–1900. "Future Dealings in Raw Produce." Chaired by L. L. Price. Funding: in 1896, A = £10, P = 0; in 1897, A = £10, P = 0; in 1898, A = £5, P = 0; in 1899, A = £5, P = 0; in 1900, A = 0, P = £2 10s.

17. 1900–3. "Legislation Regulating Women's Labour." Chaired by E. W. Brabrook. Funding: in 1900, A = £15, P = 0; in 1901, A = £30, P = £15; in 1902, A = £25, P = £30; in 1903, A = 0, P = £25.

18. 1903–6. "British and Foreign Statistics of International Trade" (aka "International Trade Statistics"). Chaired by Dr. E. Cannan. Funding: in 1903, A = £25, P = 0; in 1904, A = £20, P = £25; in 1905, A = £20, P = £4 4s 8d; in 1906, A = £15, P = 0.

19. 1906–9. "Gold Coinage in Circulation in the United Kingdom." Chaired by R. H. Inglis Palgrave. Funding: in 1906, A = £10, P = 0; in 1907, A = £6, P = £8 19s 7d; in 1908, A = £6, P = £3 7s 6d; in 1909, A = £6, P = 0.

20. 1908–10. "Amount and Distribution of Income Below the Income-Tax Exemption Limit." Chaired by Prof. E. Cannan. Funding: in 1908, A = £15, P = 0; in 1909, A = £15, P = 0; in 1910, A = £5, P = £15.

21. 1914–16. "Fatigue from an Economic Standpoint." Chaired by Prof. J. H. Muirhead. Funding: in 1914, A = £30, P = 0; in 1915, A = £40, P = £20; in 1916, A = £40, P = £40.

22. 1915. "Enquiry into Outlets of Labour After the War." Chaired by W. R. Scott. Funded by a £100 grant from the Caird Fund.

Table 18.2 *(cont.)*

23.	1915–16. "Industrial Unrest." Chaired by Prof. A. W. Kirkaldy. Funding: in 1915, A = £20, P = £20; in 1916, A = £20, P = 0.
24.	1915–20. "Women in Industry." Chaired by Prof. W. R. Scott. Funding: in 1915, A = £90, P = £90; in 1916, A = £20, P = 0; in 1917, A = £10, P = £10 0s 11d; in 1918, A = £10, P = £10; in 1919, A = £30, P = £30; in 1920, A = 0, P = £30.
25.	1915–20. "Effects of War on Credit &c." Chaired by Prof. W. R. Scott. Funding: in 1915, A = £25, P = £25; in 1916, A = £10, P = £10; in 1917, A = £10, P = £10; in 1918, A = £10, P = £10; in 1919, A = £100, P = £100; in 1920, A = £50, P = £100.
26.	1919–20. "Railway Travel," Mr. E. Brabrook. Funding: in 1919 A = £5, P = £5; in 1920, A = 0, P = £5.

Note: A denotes appropriated; P, paid.

(Anonymous 1833a, xxxvii). No doubt Whewell resolved to "restrict access to information" and its dissemination when it went beyond "those classes of facts relating to communities of men which are capable of being expressed by numbers, and which promise, when sufficiently multiplied, to indicate general laws" – the initial restriction imposed on that section's researches (Anonymous 1833b, 484).

There is some indication of the dwindling importance of Section F to the economists beginning in 1890 when the BAAS and the *Economic Journal* were launched. At the outbreak of World War I, the scientific community turned to the economists to identify, investigate, analyze, and recommend solutions to the pressing economic problems confronting the nation. Thus, a significant share of both the money appropriated and grants paid went to Section F projects. Table 18.2 identifies all of the Section F research projects "Involving Grants of Money," from its founding until 1920, when all of the World War I research activities were completed. Both tables were developed using various issues of both *Reports of the Meetings of the British Association for the Advancement of Science* and the *Journal of the [Royal] Statistical Society.*

Notes

I would like to thank the master and fellows of Trinity College, Cambridge, for permission to publish items from the Whewell Papers Collection. Thanks also are due to Professor James A. Gherity of Northern Illinois University, Professor John B. Davis of Marquette University, Professor

Timothy Alborn of Harvard University, and Professor Ted Porter of UCLA for a number of helpful suggestions.

1. In January 1830, Whewell rejected a proposal from the Rev. H. J. Rose to launch a periodical that had a similar intent as Jones's project. See Whewell to Rose in Todhunter (1876 2:105–6).

2. Adolphe Quetelet's presence at the 1833 meeting of the British association was not some "fortunate accident" as Babbage implied, for "Mr. Whewell induced M. Quetelet . . . to attend the meeting" (Smyth 1971, 157; Todhunter 1876, 1:63). In the published "Recommendations of the Committees," the Statistical Committee recognized "the distinguished foreigner (M. Quetelet) who contributed so materially to the formation of the Statistical Section" (Anonymous 1833b, 484). Of the organizers of the Statistical Section, Quetelet was the only statistician. "Placing statistics under the domain of mathematical probability was [Quetelet's] highest aim" (Porter 1986, 45). He proposed establishing the scientific study of society, "social physics," based upon statistical regularities. In his presidential address to Section F in 1856, Lord Stanley quoted what he labeled "the dictum of Quetelet": "All observation tends to confirm the truth of this proposition, that which concerns the human race, considered collectively, is of the order of physical facts: the greater the number of individuals, the more completely does the will of individuals disappear, and allow the series of general facts, which depend upon the causes by which society exists and is preserved, to predominate. . . . We must admit, that on submitting to careful experiment unorganized bodies, and the social system, we are unable to say on which side causes act in their effects with the greatest regularity" (Stanley 1856, 123).

   Quetelet's work in astronomy led him to conclude that the forces governing social activity paralleled similar forces governing celestial mechanics. He distinguished between the constant force of nature and perturbational forces, generated by conscious decisions of man. Goldman shows that Quetelet's objective was to construct "predictive laws of social behavior" (Goldman 1983, 601). By highlighting prediction, Quetelet agreed with Whewell's emphasis. The parallels between this view of social order and planetary activity is obvious (see Porter 1986, 47). Quetelet's support of the establishment of Section F, as well as his support of the Statistical Society, was important to this movement in Britain and to his own career, for he aspired to become "the Newton of statistics" (Porter 1986, 46).

3. Whewell and Jones were frequently in contact plotting various strategies for overthrowing Ricardian deductive economics. Whewell attacked the deductive work of Ricardo and J. S. Mill in his four mathematical economics papers published in the *Transactions of the Cambridge Philosophical Society* (see Henderson 1985, 1990). Their effort to develop an inductive alternative brought forth Jones's *Essay on the Distribution of Wealth, and on the Sources of Taxation. Part I. – Rent,* the first and only book of a projected three- or four-volume study of income distribution; Whewell's *Six Lectures on Political*

Economy; and *Literary Remains Consisting of Lecture and Tracts on Political Economy, of the Late Rev. Richard Jones,* edited by Whewell.

4. Though Jones's letter is undated, it was clearly written just before the 1833 meeting of the British Association. A companion letter written shortly after this one, on the same general topics, has been dated by an unknown hand as either 1833 or 1836. In the first of the two companion letters, Jones refers to a meeting that included Malthus. Since Malthus died in 1834, the 1836 tentative dating of these two letters is clearly mistaken.

Jones's "divisions" were adopted and elaborated in the "Prospectus" of the Statistical Society of London:

> The whole subject [of subdivisions] was considered, by the Statistical Section of the British Associations at Cambridge, as admitting a division into four great classes:
>
> 1. Economical statistics
> 2. Political statistics
> 3. Medical statistics
> 4. Moral and intellectual statistics
>
> If these four classes are taken as the basis of a further analysis, it will be found that the class of *Economical Statistics* comprehend, 1st, the statistics of natural productions and the agricultural nations; 2ndly, of manufactures; 3rdly, of commerce and currency; 4thly, of the distribution of wealth, or all facts relating to rent, wages, profits, &c.
>
> *Political Statistics* furnish three subdivisions: 1st, the facts relating to the elements of political institutions, the number of electors, jurors, &c.; 2ndly, legal statistics; 3rdly, the statistics of finance and of national expenditure, and of civil and military establishments.
>
> *Medical Statistics,* strictly so called, will require at least two subdivisions; and the great subject of population, although it might be classed elsewhere, yet touches medical statistics on so many points, that it would be placed most conveniently, perhaps, in this division, and would constitute a third subdivision.
>
> *Moral and Intellectual Statistics* comprehend, 1st, the statistics of literature; 2ndly, of education, 3rdly, of religious instruction and ecclesiastical institutions; 4thly, of crime. Although fourteen subdivisions have now been enumerated, it is probable that more will be required. (*Report of the Third Meeting of the British Association,* 1833, 492–3)

See Table 18.2 for a summary of research projects sponsored by Section F for which grant support was provided by the BAAS.

5. The *Journal of the Statistical Society of London* was quick to point out the relationship between statistics, political economy, and the sciences in a report "An Address Explanatory of the Objects and Advantages of Statistical Enquiries" given by Capt. J. E. Portlock at the second meeting of the Statistical Society of Ulster. Portlock asserted: "In truth, the systems of Statistics, as well as the Theories of Political Economy which ought to be founded on them, although of very recent origin, have been hitherto little known and little studied, and in them as in all other sciences, reasoning or

theory has preceded the collection of facts, and produced in consequence conjectural results as wild as they are often contradictory. We need not wonder at this, since every science has gone through the same course; the time being only yesterday since astronomy, zoology, botany, chemistry, and geology, have been cultivated on statistical principles, and thereby established on the sure basis of correct facts. Nor need we doubt that the study of Statistics will, ere long, rescue Political Economy from all the uncertainty in which it is now enveloped" (Portlock 1838, 317).

6. The ordering of these six sections follows closely the hierarchy laid out in Whewell's speech to the general meeting of the BAAS. In the two meetings before 1833, there had been separate structures. At the 1831 meeting, there were six subcommittees (mathematical and physical science, chemistry, mineralogy, geology and geography, zoology and botany, and mechanical arts) with no number or letter assigned and no sections. At the 1832 meeting, there were four sections and four committees of science (1, pure mathematics, mechanics, hydrostatics, hydraulics, plane and physical astronomy, meteorology, magnetism, philosophy of heat, light, and sound; 2, chemistry, mineralogy, electricity, magnetism; 3, geology and geography; and 4, zoology, botany, physiology, anatomy) with each section having a designated chairman and secretary. The sections established at the 1833 meeting kept their numbers until 1835, when the numbers were simply replaced with letters. The hierarchical structure of the sciences established within the association at its 1833 meeting was retained with only minor changes thereafter (see Morrell and Thackray 1981, Table 11, 453–4).

Morrell and Thackray give these names for the six sections established at the 1833 meeting and also list these subsections: 1, mathematical and physiomathematical sciences (astronomy, mechanics, hydrostatics, hydraulics, light, sound, heat, meteorology, and mechanical arts); 2, chemistry, electricity, galvanism, magnetism, mineralogy, chemical arts and manufactures; 3, geology and geography; 4, natural history (botany and zoology); 5, anatomy, and medicine; and 6, statistics (Table 11, 453–4).

7. Like the other sections of the BAAS, the Statistical Section had its "Committee of Science." At its founding, that committee included the following members:

> *Chairman.* – Professor Babbage.
> *Secretary.* – J. E. Drinkwater, M.A.
> H. Elphinstone, F.R.S. W. Empson, M.A. Earl Fitzwilliam, F.R.S. H. Hallam, F.R.S. E. Halswell, F.R.S. Rev. Professor Jones. Sir C. Lemon, Bart. F.R.S. J. W. Lubbock, Treas. R.S. Professor Malthus. Capt. Pringle. M. Quetelet. Rev. E. Stanley, F.L.S. G.S. Colonel Sykes, F.R.S. F.L.S. G.S. Richard Taylor, F.L.S. G.S. (Anonymous 1833b, xl)

8. In the "Prospectus of the Objects and Plan of the Statistical Society of London," a similar limitation was adopted. The "Prospectus" announced: "The Statistical Society will consider it to be the first and most essential rule of its conduct to exclude carefully all *opinions* from its transactions and

publications, – to confine its attention rigorously to facts, – and, as so far as it may be found possible, to facts that can be stated numerically and arranged in tables" (Anonymous 1833b, 492).

In 1838, when the Statistical Society published its first *Transactions*, John Robertson attacked "the first and most essential rule of its conduct to exclude carefully all *opinions*." Writing in the *London and Westminster Review*, he listed four objections to this rule: "It prevents the discovery of new truths; – it deprives the labours of the Society of definite purposes; – the facts of which it causes the collection and arrangement are those which are useless and irrelevant as evidence; – and lastly, the observance of this rule is irreconcilable not merely with the progress of science and knowledge, but with the actions and operations of the Society itself" (R. [John Robertson] 1838, 47–8).

In 1865, Dr. William A. Guy maintained that these limitations adopted by both Section F and the Statistical Society indicated that "*statistics* had already come to mean rather the materials of science than the science itself" (Guy 1865, 483). He went on to note that very early "in the history of this [Statistical] Society, . . . we find its very founders and office-bearers, men of whom we are justly proud, breaking through the narrow bounds within which it was sought to confine them, and setting at nought the self-denying ordinance which, had it been narrowly observed, would have made the Statistical Society of London a very bye word for contented dulness and senseless drudgery" (484). It was the violation of the limitation on the inquiries of Section F that led Whewell to declare that "the statistical Section ought never to have been admitted into the Association" (Morrell and Thackray 1981, 294).

9. Sedgwick went on to distinguish between the "physical truth" and the "moral and political reasonings" aspects of the social sciences. In the social sciences, he declared:

> These inquiries are . . . most intimately connected with moral phaenomena and economical speculations, – they touch the mainsprings of passion and feeling, – they blend themselves with generalizations of political science; but when we enter on these higher generalizations, that moment they are dissevered from the objects of the Association, and must be abandoned by it, if it means not to desert the secure ground which it has now taken. . . .
>
> In physical truth, whatever may be our difference of opinion, there is an ultimate appeal to experiment and observation, against which passion and prejudice have not a single plea to urge. But in moral and political reasoning, we have ever to do with questions, in which the waywardness of man's will and the turbulence of man's passions are among the strongest elements. . . . Our Meetings have been essentially harmonious, only because we have kept within our proper boundaries, confined ourselves to the laws of nature, and steered clear of all questions in the decision of which bad passions could have any play. But if we transgress our proper boundaries, go into provinces not belonging to us, and open a door of communication with the dreary wild of politics, that instant will the foul Demon of discord find his way into our Eden of Philosophy. (Sedgwick 1833, xxviii–xxix)

These remarks help explain why the inquiries of the new section were restricted.

Sedgwick's position that statistical inquiries provide "the raw material of political economy" was echoed in Portlock's "Address" and would be repeated in later meetings of Section F. In his paper, "On the Connexion Between Statistics and Political Economy," presented at the 1843 meeting, Professor Lawson said: "Political economy, though a mixed science, yet has its abstract part, and the application of the principles thence derived to facts leads us on to new truths. Statistics afford at once the materials and the test of political economy" (1843, 94).

10. The "statement of the objects and regulations" of the Statistical Society of London appears on pp. 492–5. The "Recommendation" of the permanent Committee of the Statistical Section continues: "The Committee remark, that 'though the want of such a society has been long felt and acknowledged, the successful establishment of it, after every previous attempt had failed, has been due altogether to the impulse given by the last meeting of the Association. The distinguished foreigner (M. Quetelet) who contributed so materially to the formation of the Statistical Section, was attracted to England principally with a view of attending that meeting; and the Committee hail this as a significant instance of the beneficial results to be expected from that personal intercourse among the enlightened men of all countries, which it is a principal object of the British Association to encourage and facilitate'" (Anonymous 1833b, 484).

The officers of the Statistical Society included the following: president – the Marquis of Lansdowne; treasurer – Henry Hallam; honorary secretaries – Woronzow Greg, Charles Hope Macleat, and E. Carleton Tufnell; council – Charles Babbage, William Burge, Rev. George D'Oyley, John Elliot Drinkwater, Howard Elphinstone, Earl Fitzwilliam, Rt. Hon. Henry Goulburn, Joseph Henry Green, Edmund Halswell, F. Bisset Hawkins, Rt. Hon. Francis Jeffrey (MP), Rev. Richard Jones, John Shaw Lefevre, Sir Charles Lemon (MP), the Lord Bishop of London, Samuel Jones Loyd, Rev. T. R. Malthus, G. R. Porter, Viscount Sandon (MP), G. Poulett Scrope (MP), Nassau Senior, John Sims, Lt.-Col. W. H. Sykes, Thomas Tooke, Thomas Vardon, and Rev. William Whewell; and trustees – John Bonham Carter (MP) and the Hon. Mountstuart Elphinstone (*Annals of the Royal Statistical Society*, 1834, 16–17).

11. Jones's dominating role in organizing Section F and the Statistical Society is best seen in his comment to Whewell just quoted in text. Thus, while "Babbage was the public arranger," Jones was more than merely a "principle supporter"; he was an initiator. The historical association between the new Statistical Society and the earlier inductive tradition of political arithmetic was emphasized by having the Marquis of Lansdowne chair its first public meeting and by electing him as its first president. Lansdowne had edited a collection of William Petty's writings on political arithmetic.

12. A year earlier, shortly after the 1840 meeting of the BAAS, Whewell had

complained in private to Sir Roderick Impey Murchison, in a letter dated September 25, 1840: "It was impossible to listen to the proceedings of the Statistical Section on Friday without perceiving that they involved exactly what it was most necessary and most desired to exclude from our proceedings. Is there any objection to the President declaring in his place, in the most emphatic manner, that the mode in which this Section has been conducted is inconsistent with the objects and character of the Association?" (Todhunter 1876, 2:289).

Whewell raised the question of "the President declaring in his place" because Murchison had proposed that he serve as president of the BAAS for the next meeting. So annoyed was Whewell with the activities of Section F that he made the following declaration in a letter to Murchison dated October 2, 1840: "As to the Statistical Section scruple, I cannot get over the utter incongruity of its proceedings with all our professions and all our principles. Who would venture to propose (I put it to Chalmers, and he allowed the proposal to be intolerable) an ambulatory body, composed partly of men of reputation, and partly of a miscellaneous crowd, to go round year by year, from town to town, and at each place to discuss the most inflammatory and agitating questions of the day? Yet this is exactly what we have been doing for several years. I must say plainly, that rather than be concerned in such wild and dangerous absurdity, in defiance of solemn professions to the contrary, I would utterly renounce the Association with all its advantages. You have made me your President, with no good will of mine; in everything else I will be instructed by you, and labour, as well as I know how, for the advantage of the Association, in any way in which I can aid it: but I will make no agreement with you that I will not denounce, in the most public and emphatic manner, this gross violation of our fundamental constitution. If we offend people by recurring to our professed principles, I cannot help it. If our Association does not suit them, when conducted on its only rational grounds, let them make one of their own" (Todhunter 1876, 2:289).

On October 5, 1840, Whewell laid out the exact nature of his quarrel with Chalmers in a letter to Lord Northampton: "If such discussions be allowed, there is nothing in legislation or politics which can be consistently excluded. Dr. Chalmers made an attempt to justify or mask this impropriety by saying that it was an example of the value of *numbers*. . . . The absurdity of such a plea is, I think, undeniable, and the inconsistency of such discussions with our fundamental constitution. And this is not a question of form merely. For what kind of institution do we become, if we allow ourselves to be made an ambulatory meeting for agitating in assemblies, when both *eminent* and *notorious* men (Dr. Chalmers and Robert Owen) address a miscellaneous crowd on the sorest and angriest subjects which occur among the topics of the day? If we cannot get rid of this character, most assuredly I shall be disposed to make my connection with the Association as brief as I can do" (Todhunter 1876, 2:294).

13. It is apparent that Whewell exercised his influence to limit research grants for proposals coming from Section F. Tables 18.1 and 18.2 in the Appendix show the money appropriated and grants paid to research projects sponsored by Section F.

14. The "Science of Economics" was defined by Senior as "the Science which states the laws regulating the production and distribution of wealth, so far as they depend on the action of the human mind" (1860, 182). For Senior, science was divided into "two great genera," the "Material, or, as they are usually called, the Physical, and the Mental, or, as they are frequently called the Moral, Sciences" (182). In his view, the political economist took "the facts supplied by physical science" as given and looked for "his proofs, as far as he can, in the human mind" (183). However, the science of statistics is much broader in scope: "It applies to all phenomena which can be counted and recorded. It deals equally with matter and with mind. Perhaps the most remarkable results of the statistician's labours are those which show that the human will obeys laws nearly as certain as those which regulate matter" (183).

In keeping with the intentions of the founders of Section F, Senior insisted that "the observation, the recording and the arranging facts, which is the science of statistics, and the ascertaining, from observation and from consciousness, the general laws which regulate men's actions with respect to production and exchange, which is the science of political economy, are distinct from the arts to which these sciences are subservient. We cease to be scientific as soon as we advise or dissuade, or even approve or censure" (184).

Nassau Senior's distinction between the science of economics and the art of policy is remarkably similar to Adam Sedgwick's discrimination between "physical truth" and "moral and political reasonings," in his assurances to the association members when Section F was founded (see note 9 above).

15. In an article in the *Athenaeum*, Cliffe Leslie identified three definitions of statistics: "One follows the popular view of statistics; the etymological and original meaning almost disappearing in the notion merely of tables of figures, or numbers of facts, of which the chief significance lies in their numerical statement. According to another conception, statistics, following etymology and the signification given to Statistik by the famous Göttingen school, should be regarded as equivalent to the science of States, or political science, but nevertheless, as confining itself to the ascertainment and collection of facts indicative of the condition and prospects of society, without inquiring into causes or reasoning on probable effects, and carefully discarding hypothesis, theory, and speculation in its investigations. A third conception is, that statistical science aims at the discovery, not only of the phenomena of society, but also their laws, and by no means discards either inquiry into causes and effects or theoretical reasoning" (Leslie 1873, 155).

Both statisticians and economists benefited from the meetings of Section F, since such contact "tends to correct the errors" to which both were prone (157). Statisticians "have been apt to think only of facts," while economists tended "to neglect facts altogether" (157–8). Moreover, statisticians "have often been content to collect phenomena without heed to their laws," while economists often jump "to laws without heed to the phenomena" (158). Leslie believed that statisticians too often abide "in the region of dry figures and numerical tables," while economists "have dwelt chiefly in that region of assumption, conjecture, and provisional generalization" (158). Finally, he complained of "the defective character of the kind of statistical inquiry which confines itself to the collection of a multitude of instances of facts, without reference to causes" (161). This particular error tended to be fostered by "the principles laid down by the illustrious Quetelet" (161). Where Quetelet had "assumed that by enlarging the number of instances" investigated by the statistician, "we eliminate chance, and arrive at general and stable laws or conditions," Leslie contended that "a great number of instances" does not necessarily reveal either the laws governing society or "justify us in any positive conclusion respecting the future" (161–2). Too many new conditions and disturbing causes can arise in the future to alter the outcome of one's observations.

16. Galton was the originator of the concepts of regression and correlation in statistics. Foremost in his life was a belief that virtually anything is quantifiable. Some of his exercises in this direction are now merely amusing – a statistical inquiry into the efficacy of prayer, a study of the body weights of three generations of British peers, and a solemn assessment of womanly beauty on a pocket scale are examples. When I mentioned this to our professor of classics at Valparaiso, he informed me that the people in his discipline had done some work on the last topic and had developed the "MilliHelen – a unit of womanly beauty sufficient to launch one ship."

17. The Council of the BAAS took the following action:

> The Committee recommended that papers which have been reported on unfavourable by the Organizing Committees shall not be brought before the Sectional Committees, and that, in the rules for conducting the business of the Sectional Committees, the following rules shall be inserted, viz.: –
>
> 1. The President shall call on the Secretary to read the minutes of the previous Meeting of the Committee.
> 2. No paper shall be read until it has been formally accepted by the Committee of the Section, and entered on the minutes accordingly.
>
> The Council propose that this alteration of rules shall be carried into effect. (Anonymous 1877a, xlix)

The whole controversy is reviewed in the September and December 1877 issues of the *Journal of the Statistical Society.*

18. These four "scientific" papers were: Jevons's (1875) "Influence of the Sun-spot Period upon the Price of Corn," Hyde Clarke's (1873) "Influ-

ence of Large Centres of Population on Intellectual Manifestation," C. O. Groom Napier's study "Legislative Protection to the Birds of Europe," and Dr. John Beddoe's "Need of Systematic Observations on Physical Characteristics of Man in Britain." It was Galton's contention that Jevons's paper could have been read before Section A (mathematics and physics) and the other three could have been presented in the Anthropological Department of Section D (biology). This was brought to my attention by Professor Royall Brandis, University of Illinois at Urbana-Champaign. He claims that Jevons's paper was the only "scientific" paper of the four cited because Galton suggested that the other three be placed in the Anthropological Department, which failed Galton's definition of science in its strictest sense. Galton maintained that the Anthropological Department might be "open to the same charge" as Section F, except that "the leading anthropologists are physiologists, geologists, or geographers, and the proceedings of the department are largely indebted to their special knowledge" (Galton 1877, 472). Yet Galton's views regarding the Anthropological Department seem more supportive of its scientific position for he was involved in changing its status from that of a subsection or department of the Biology Section into a separate Section H (see note 19 below).

19. This assertion may well reveal Galton's motivation for demanding the abolition of Section F as he was interested in creating a new section. From 1880 through 1882, Galton chaired the Anthropometric Committee, and at the 1883 meeting of the British Association it was reported that "the Council have considered the question of amalgamating the Departments of Zoology and Botany and Anatomy and Physiology for the present year, and have decided to amalgamate them under the designation of the Section of Biology, retaining the Department of Anthropology" (Anonymous 1883, lix). This set the stage for the action taken at the next meeting. In 1884, this resolution was passed by the General Committee: "That the Council be empowered, if they think fit, to form a separate section of Anthropology, and to give to the section of Biology the title 'Section D. – Biology (Zoology, Botany, and Physiology).' The Council, after consideration, resolved to form a separate section of Anthropology, with the title 'Section H. – Anthropology,' but considered that it was better to continue to designate the section of Biology by the simpler title 'Section D. – Biology' " (Anonymous 1884, lxiv). The next year, Galton was elected president of Section H, and he also chaired a research committee whose projects were funded under the auspices of the new section for several years thereafter. Galton may have been concerned in 1877 that a proposal to create a new "Section H. – Anthropology" would fail on grounds that there were already too many sections and that Anthropology must remain merely a department of the Biology Section.

20. The president of the Statistical Society, George Shaw-Lefevre, argued that the reporters who attended the meetings of the British Association, were more familiar with the subjects dealt with in the Statistical Section

than with those discussed in other sections. The consequence was that the reports of that section [usually] occupied a larger portion of the daily press, than . . . the reports of other sections. There was therefore some difficulty; he did not want to use the word jealousy. The proper way to meet it was for gentlemen of the press to be sent who could describe subjects of physical science in a popular way" (Anonymous 1877b, 345).

21. In the December 1865 issue of the *Journal of the (Royal) Statistical Society,* Guy published a paper, "On the Original and Acquired Meaning of the Term 'Statistics,' and on the Proper Functions of a Statistical Society: Also on the Question of Whether There Be a Science of Statistics; and, If So, What Are Its Nature and Objects, and What Is Its Relation to Political Economy and 'Social Science' " (478–93; see also note 7 above). In December, 1870 he published another paper in the *Journal,* "On the Claims of Science to Public Recognition and Support; with Special Reference to the so-called 'Social Sciences' " (pp. 433–451). So these questions were of ongoing interest to him.

22. It may well be that Jevons published his "Bibliography of Works on the Mathematical Theory of Political Economy" partly in response to Galton's charges. Jevons's "Bibliography" appeared in the June 1878 issue of the *Journal of the (Royal) Statistical Society,* which had published Galton's charges the previous September (see Jevons 1878). In any case, among the list of papers that "the Council [of the Statistical Society] have reason to expect" would be "communicated to the Society" during the "1877–78 Session" was one titled " 'The Position and Prospects of the Statistical Section of the British Association' by Professor W. Stanley Jevons, M.A., LL.D., F.R.S." (5).

23. Farr's "complete list of the Presidents of the Section" included these names: "Babbage, Sandon (Earl of Harrowby), Sykes, Hallam, Wood (Lord Halifax), Earl Fitzwilliam, G. R. Porter, Lyttleton, Boileau, Whately, Heywood, Tooke, Houghton, Lord Stanley, Nassau Senior, Newmarch, Chadwick, Farr, Professor Rogers, Brown, Sir Stafford Northcote, Stanley Jevons, Lord Neaves, Professor Fawcett, W. E. Forster, M.P., and Sir George Campbell" (Farr 1877, 473).

24. Henry Sidgwick, president of Section F in 1885, noting in his diary that the officers of the BAAS distributed over £1,300 to various researchers, commented that "The British Ass. is a Golden Ass" (A.S. and E.M.S. 1906, 425).

25. At the 1868 meeting of the BAAS, Leone Levi had read a paper titled "On the Progress of Learned Societies, Illustrative of the Advancement of Science in the United Kingdom During the Last Thirty Years" (Levi 1868). At the 1879 meeting, largely in response to the attack on Section F, he updated that study in his paper, "The Scientific Societies in Relation to the Advancement of Science in the United Kingdom." Levi compared membership figures for various scientific societies, noting the large number and rapid growth in the membership of the London Statistical Soci-

ety. He supported Chadwick's position that the popular interest in Section F attracted large funds to the BAAS, while little was spent on research projects related to topics of concern to that section. Finally, Levi, echoing the earlier position of both Adam Sedgwick and Prof. Lawson, declared that "the Statistical Society subjects the real worth of economic doctrine to the close test of numbers, the great corrective of experience, using the inductive rather than the deductive method in its researches for the guidance of the philosopher and statesman" (Levi 1879, 467).

26. This article, "The Proposed Discontinuance of Section F, Economic Science and Statistics, at the British Association," was authored by an anonymous writer, who identified himself only as one who had recently served "in an official capacity with Section F, and also in an official capacity with the Statistical Society" and who signed himself a Fellow of the Royal Society ("F.R.S.") (Anonymous 1877c, 631).

27. Ingram's arguments in his 1878 presidential address to Section F, delivered on Thursday, August 15, may have been aired earlier at the meeting of the General Committee or the meeting of the Council. If so, he must have swayed the BAAS. Galton's proposal to abolish Section F was officially resolved at the Wednesday, August 14, meeting of the General Committee when it adopted the recommendation of the Council to add this rule: "That no paper received after commencement of the Meeting shall be read, unless recommended by the Committee of the Section, after it has been referred and reported upon" (Anonymous 1878, lvi). This rule change was deemed "a sufficient guarantee for the exclusion of unscientific and unsuitable papers" (lvi). While this action ended the formal controversy in the British Association, the debate over methodology continued among the economists.

28. Important to Whewell's method were three tests used to verify hypotheses: First, the hypothesis must explain all of the observed phenomena; second, the hypothesis must possess the ability to predict phenomena that have not yet been observed; and third, the hypothesis must have the capacity to predict cases of different kinds, such that it explains more than it was originally intended to because it coincides with other inductions derived from other sets of facts (see Henderson 1990, 10; Ducasse 1951, 229–30).

29. Edgeworth (1889, 671) considered the following "points at which mathematical reasoning is applicable to political economy":

    A. – Perfect Competition –
      1. Simplest type of market.
      2. Complex system of markets; simplified by certain abstractions.
      3. The more concrete problem of an Exchange and Distribution.
    B. – Monopoly –
      1. Transactions between a single monopolist and a competing public.
      2. Transactions between two monopolists or combinations.

This introductory statement does not appear in the reprinted version (1909, 2:273–312) of Edgeworth's speech.

30. Edgeworth's quotation is from Marshall's remarkable review of Jevons's *Theory* (see Marshall 1872, 94–5).
31. Edgeworth's position on the proper role of mathematics as a tool for economic analysis was hinted at earlier by Jevons. In the case of the theory of value, mathematics could do for economists what it had long done for astronomers. In the Preface to the second edition of his *Theory of Political Economy*, Jevons noted that the most important changes in the new edition "are those treating of the *dimensions of economic quantities*. . . . The subject, of course, is one which lies at the basis of all clear thought about economic science. . . . Imagine the mental state of astronomers if they could not agree among themselves whether *Right Ascension* was the name of a heavenly body, or a force or an angular magnitude. Yet this would not be worse than the failing to ascertain whether by value we mean a numerical ratio, or a mental state, or a mass of commodity" (Jevons 1879, xi).

References

Annals of the Royal Statistical Society, 1834–1934. 1934. London.

Anonymous. 1833a. "Proceedings of the Meeting," *Report of the Third Meeting of the British Association for the Advancement of Science,* i–xl.

Anonymous. 1833b. "Recommendations of the Committees," *Report of the Third Meeting of the British Association for the Advancement of Science,* 469–84.

Anonymous. 1839. "Ninth Meeting of the British Association for the Advancement of Science – August, 1839." *Journal of the Statistical Society of London,* 2 (October): 287–90.

Anonymous. 1840a. "Tenth Meeting of the British Association for the Advancement of Science – September, 1840." *Journal of the Statistical Society of London,* 3 (October): 209–11.

Anonymous. 1840b. "Transactions of the Sections – Statistics." *Report of the Third Meeting of the British Association for the Advancement of Science,* 169–86.

Anonymous. 1841. "Eleventh Meeting of the British Association for the Advancement of Science. Held at Plymouth, July, 1841." *Journal of the Statistical Society of London,* 4 (October): 181–2.

Anonymous. 1845. "Fifteenth Meeting of the British Association for the Advancement of Science at Cambridge, June 18th–25th, 1841. Proceedings of the Statistical Section." *Journal of the Statistical Society of London,* 8 (December): 289–90.

Anonymous. 1877a. "Report of the Council for the Year 1876–77, presented to the General Committee at Plymouth on Wednesday, August 15th, 1877." *Report of the Forty-Seventh Meeting of the British Association for the Advancement of Science,* xlix–l.

Anonymous. 1877b. "Proceedings of the Forty-Third Anniversary Meeting." *Journal of the Statistical Society,* 40 (September): 342–6.

Anonymous. 1877c. "Miscellanea: – I. Economic Science and Statistics at the British Association." *Journal of the Statistical Society,* 40 (December): 631–3.

Anonymous. 1878. "Report of the Council for the Year 1877–78, presented to the General Committee at Dublin on Wednesday, August 14th, 1878." *Report of the Forty-Eighth Meeting of the British Association for the Advancement of Science*, lvi–lvii.

Anonymous. 1883. "Report of the Council for the year 1882 – 83, presented to the General Committee at Southport, on Wednesday, September 19, 1883." *Report of the Fifty-Third Meeting of the British Association for the Advancement of Science*, lviii – lx.

Anonymous. 1884. "Report of the Council for the year 1883–84, presented to the General Committee at Montreal, on Wednesday, August 27, 1884." *Report of the Fifty-Fourth Meeting of the British Association for the Advancement of Science*, lxiii–lxviii.

Butts, Robert E. (ed.). 1989. *William Whewell's Theory of Scientific Method*. Pittsburgh: University of Pittsburgh Press.

Cannon, Susan Faye. 1978. *Science in Culture: The Early Victorian Period*. New York: Science History Publications.

Cannon, Walter F. [Susan Faye Cannon]. 1961. "John Herschel and the Idea of Science." *Journal of the History of Ideas*, 22:215–39.

Cannon, Walter F. [Susan Faye Cannon]. 1964. "History in Depth: The Early Victorian Period." *History of Science*, 3:20–38.

Checkland, S. G. 1949. "The Propagation of Ricardian Economics in England." *Economica*, n.s. 16, no. 61 (February): 40–52.

Checkland, S. G. 1951. "The Advent of Academic Economics in England." *Manchester School*, 19, no. 1 (January): 43–70.

Coats, A. W. 1968. "The Origins and Early Development of the Royal Economic Society." *Economic Journal*, 78, no. 310 (June): 349–71.

Cunningham, William. 1910. *The Growth of English Industry and Commerce*. Rpt. New York: Kelley, 1968.

de Marchi, N. B., and R. P. Sturges. 1973. "Malthus and Ricardo's Inductivist Critics: Four Letters to William Whewell." *Economica*, n.s. 40 (November): 379–93.

Ducasse, C. J. 1951. "Whewell's Philosophy of Scientific Discovery." *Philosophical Review*, 40 (January, April): 55–69, 213–34.

Edgeworth, F. Y. 1881. *Mathematical Psychics*. London.

Edgeworth, F. Y. 1889. "Points at Which Mathematical Reasoning Is Applicable to Political Economy," in *Report of the Fifty-ninth Meeting of the British Association for the Advancement of Science*, 671–96, and partially reprinted in *Papers Relating to Political Economy*, 2: 273–312. Rpt. New York: Burt Franklin, 1970.

Edgeworth, F. Y. 1891. "The Objects and Methods of Political Economy." *Papers Relating to Political Economy*, 1: 3–12. Rpt. New York: Burt Franklin, 1970.

Edgeworth, F. Y. 1909. "Application of the Differential Calculus to Economics," rpt. in *Papers Relating to Political Economy*, 2: 367–86. Rpt. New York: Burt Franklin, 1970.

Farr, W. 1877. "Considerations, in the Form of a Draft Report, Submitted to

Committee, Favourable to the Maintenance of Section F." *Journal of the (Royal) Statistical Society,* 40, pt. 3 (September): 473–6.

Fisch, Menachem. 1991a. "Antithetical Knowledge," in Menachem Fisch and Simon Schaffer, eds., *William Whewell: A Composite Portrait,* 289–310. Oxford: Clarendon Press.

Fisch, Menachem. 1991b. "A Philosopher's Coming of Age: A Study in Erotetic Intellectual History," in Menachem Fisch and Simon Schaffer, eds. *William Whewell: A Composite Portrait,* 31–66. Oxford: Clarendon Press.

Foxwell, H. S. 1887. "The Economic Movement in England." *Quarterly Journal of Economics,* 2 (October): 84–103.

Galton, Francis. 1877. "Considerations Adverse to the Maintenance of Section F (Economic Science and Statistics), Submitted by Mr. Francis Galton to the Committee Appointed by the Council to Consider and Report on the Possibility of Excluding Unscientific or Otherwise Unsuitable Papers and Discussions from the Sectional Proceedings of the Association." *Journal of the (Royal) Statistical Society,* 40, pt. 3 (September): 468–73.

Goldman, Lawrence. 1983. "The Origins of British 'Social Science': Political Economy, Natural Science and Statistics, 1830–1835." *Historical Journal,* 26, no. 3: 587–616.

Guy, William A. 1865. "On the Origin and Acquired Meaning of the Term 'Statistics,' and on the Proper Functions of a Statistical Society: also on the Question Whether There Be a Science of Statistics; and, If So, What Are Its Nature and Objects, and What is Its Relation to Political Economy and 'Social Science.' " *Journal of the (Royal) Statistical Society,* 28, pt. 4 (December): 478–93.

Guy, William A. 1870. "On the Claims of Science to Public Recognition and Support; with Special Reference to the So-called 'Social Sciences.' " *Journal of the (Royal) Statistical Society,* 33, pt. 4 (December): 433–51.

Henderson, James P. 1985. "The Whewell Group of Mathematical Economists." *Manchester School,* 53, no. 4 (December): 404–31.

Henderson, James P. 1990. "Induction, Deduction and the Role of Mathematics: The Whewell Group vs. the Ricardian Economists." *Research in the History of Economic Thought and Methodology,* 7: 1–36.

Heywood, James. 1843. "Thirteenth Meeting of the British Association for the Advancement of Science at Cork, August 17–23, 1843: Account of the Proceedings of the Statistical Section." *Journal of the Statistical Society of London,* 6 (December): 2181–2.

Ingram, John K. 1878. *The Present Position and Prospects of Political Economy.* London: Longmans.

Jevons, William Stanley. 1878. "Bibliography of Works on the Mathematical Theory of Political Economy." *Journal of the (Royal) Statistical Society,* 47 (June): 398–401.

Jevons, William Stanley. 1879. Preface to *Theory of Political Economy,* 2d cd. Rpt. New York, 1965.

Lawson, 1843. "On the Connexion Between Statistics and Political Economy," in *Report of the Tenth Meeting of the British Association for the Advancement of Science*, 94–5.

Leslie, T. E. Cliffe. 1873. "Economic Science and Statistics," in *Essays in Political Economy*, 155–62. Rpt. New York: Kelley, 1969.

Leslie, T. E. Cliffe. 1879. "Political Economy and Sociology," in *Essays in Political Economy*, 191–220. Rpt. New York: Kelley, 1969.

Levi, Leone 1868. "On the Progress of Learned Societies, Illustrative of the Advancement of Science in the United Kingdom During the Last Thirty Years," in *Report of the Thirty-eighth Meeting of the British Association for the Advancement of Science*, 169–73.

Levi, Leone. 1879. "The Scientific Societies in Relation to the Advancement of Science in the United Kingdom," in *Report of the Forty-ninth Meeting of the British Association for the Advancement of Science*, 458–68.

Lithographed Signatures of the Members of the British Association. 1833. Cambridge University Press.

Lowe, Robert. 1878. "Recent Attacks on Political Economy." *Nineteenth Century*, no. 21 (November): 858–68.

Marshall, Alfred. 1872. "Mr. Jevons' *Theory of Political Economy.*" *Academy* (April 1). Rpt. in A. C. Pigou (ed.), *Memorials of Alfred Marshall*, 93–100. London: Macmillan, 1925.

Mirowski, Philip. 1988. *Against Mechanism: Protecting Economics from Science.* Totowa, NJ: Rowman & Littlefield.

Moore, Henry Ludwell. 1929. *Synthetic Economics.* Rpt. New York: Kelley, 1967.

Morrell, Jack, and Arnold Thackray. 1981. *Gentlemen of Science: Early Years of the British Association for the Advancement of Science.* Oxford: Clarendon Press.

Porter, Theodore M. 1986. *The Rise of Statistical Thinking, 1820–1900.* Princeton, Princeton University Press.

Porter, Theodore M. 1991a. "Comment on James Henderson, 'Economics in the Hierarchy of the Sciences.' " Unpublished comments read at the conference "Natural Images in Economics," University of Notre Dame, September 26–9.

Porter, Theodore M. 1991b. "Rigor and Practicality: Rival Ideals of Quantification in Nineteenth-Century Economics." Paper read at the conference "Natural Images in Economics," University of Notre Dame, September 26–9.

Portlock, J. E. 1838. "An Address Explanatory of the Objects and Advantages of Statistical Enquiries." *Journal of the (Royal) Statistical Society*, 1 (October): 316–17.

R. [John Robertson]. 1838. "Transactions of the Statistical Society of London. Vol. I. Part I. London, Charles Knight and Co. 1837." *London and Westminster Review*, 31, no. 1 (April): 45–72.

Sedgwick, Adam. 1833. *Report of the Third Meeting of the British Association for the Advancement of Science*, xxvii–xxxii.

Senior, Nassau. 1860. "Opening Address," in *Report of the Thirtieth Meeting of the British Association for the Advancement of Science*, 182–4.

S[idgwick], A[rthur], and E. M. S[idgwick]. 1906. *Henry Sidgwick: A Memoir.* London: Macmillan.

Sidgwick, Henry. 1879. "Economic Method." *Fortnightly Review,* n.s. 25, no. 146 (February 1): 301–18.

Smith, Robert W. 1989. "The Cambridge Network in Action: The Discovery of Neptune." *Isis,* 80, no. 303 (September): 395–422.

Smyth, R. L. (1971). "The History of Section F of the British Association 1835–1970," in Nicholas Kalder, ed. *Conflicts in Policy Objectives,* 156–75. Oxford: Basil Blackwell.

Stanley, Lord. 1856. "Opening Address," in *Report of the Twenty-sixth Meeting of the British Association for the Advancement of Science,* 122–8.

Stigler, George. 1964. "Statistical Studies in the History of Economic Thought," in *Essays in the History of Economics,* 31–50. Chicago: University of Chicago Press.

Todhunter, Isaac. 1876. *William Whewell, D.D., Master of Trinity College, Cambridge: An Account of His Writings,* 2 vols. London: Parker.

Whewell, William. 1831. "Jones – on the Distribution of Wealth," *The British Critic, Quarterly Theological Review, and Ecclesiastical Record,* 10 (July): 41–61.

Whewell, William. 1833. *Report of the Third Meeting of the British Association for the Advancement of Science,* xi–xxvi.

Whewell, William. 1841. "Address," in *Report of the Eleventh Meeting of the British Association for the Advancement of Science,* xxvii–xxxv.

Whewell, William. 1858. *Novum Organum Renovatum.* London: Parker.

Whewell Papers Collection. Trinity College Library, Cambridge.

Williams, Perry. 1991. "Passing the Torch: Whewell's Philosophy and the Principles of English University Education," in Menachem Fisch and Simon Schaffer, eds., *William Whewell: A Composite Portrait,* 117–48. Oxford: Clarendon Press.

Yeo, Richard R. 1986. "Scientific Method and the Rhetoric of Science in Britain, 1830–1917," in J. A. Schuster and R. R. Yeo, eds., *The Politics and Rhetoric of Scientific Method,* 259–97. Dordrecht: Kluwer.

Yeo, Richard R. 1991. "William Whewell's Philosophy of Knowledge and Its Reception," in Menachem Fisch and Simon Schaffer, eds., *William Whewell: A Composite Portrait,* 175–200. Oxford: Clarendon Press.

CHAPTER 19

The kinds of order in society

JAMES BERNARD MURPHY

Introduction: from Hayek to Aristotle

Philip Mirowski has shown us that neoclassical economic theory has incorporated some very dubious analogies to nineteenth-century energy physics; in addition, we have seen that economic theory of various schools has employed many analogies to biology. Indeed, the rhetoric of economics is highly promiscuous in its liaisons with the various natural sciences; my favorite example of this promiscuity is from the "Preface to the First German Edition" of *Capital*, where Marx makes a wanton metaphorical appeal to physics, chemistry, and biology in one breadth: He proposes to "lay bare the economic law of motion of modern society" and to prove "that the present society is no solid crystal, but an organism capable of change."

The chapters in this volume have shown that few metaphorical appeals to nature will bear critical scrutiny and that all analogies will break down if pushed far enough. I hope to advance this deconstructive project by showing that there is an important logical difference between metaphor and analogy – a difference that makes metaphors obscure in a way that analogies are not. But my chief concern is not with demolition but with construction, for I believe that the ubiquitous appeals to nature in social theory suggest some important truths: If, as ecologists insist, human society is only a part of the whole of nature and if, as hermeneutics insists, all understanding moves in a circle from part to whole, then it follows that our knowledge of nature will play an important role in our knowledge of society, just as our knowledge of society will play a role in our knowledge of nature. Not all circles are vicious. What we need is to find a role for nature in social theory without reducing social life to nature. Aristotle suggests such a role for nature when he argues that to explain human morality we must take into account our natural dispositions, our habits or customs, and finally our stipulated ideals. In this complex, nonreductionist model of social theory, social customs presuppose human nature but are not reduced to it, just as our stipulated rational ideals presuppose our customs but are not reduced to them. In my Aristotelian model of social theory, then, nature, custom, and stipulation are the three kinds of order in society.

Friedrich von Hayek seems to have had something like this in mind when he distinguished three species of social order in his seminal essay "Kinds of Order in Society": "Much of what we call culture is just such a spontaneously grown order [custom], which arose neither altogether independently of human action [nature] nor by design [stipulation], but by a process that stands between these two possibilities, which were long considered as exclusive alternatives" (1964/1979, 509). Hayek credits Adam Ferguson with the distinction here between the spontaneous order of custom and the designed order of stipulation: "Nations stumble upon establishments, which are indeed the result of human action, but not the execution of any human design" (Ferguson 1767, 187).

It is both surprising and unfortunate that Hayek never refers to Aristotle's nature, custom, and stipulation trichotomy: surprising because Hayek was (for an economist) a formidable scholar, and unfortunate because Aristotle's theory of social order is far superior to Hayek's. Hayek's apparent ignorance of Aristotle's trichotomy is especially surprising because this trichotomy recurs, in various guises, throughout the history of social thought. Let us begin with Aristotle: "There are three things which make men good and excellent; these are nature (*physis*), habit (*ethos*), and reason (*logis*)" (*Pol.* 1332a 40). Aristotle is saying that morality has three dimensions: We start with our natural dispositions, we cultivate these dispositions into habits, and we reflect on our habits in order to stipulate new moral ideals for ourselves. Over time, Aristotle's trichotomy was employed by jurisprudence to define the kinds of laws and by semiotics to define the kinds of signs. Thomas Aquinas latinized Aristotle's trichotomy as "*natura, consuetudo, ratio,*" and these three terms became the basis of Thomistic jurisprudence as natural law, customary law, and positive law. John Poinsot (John of St. Thomas) in his seventeenth-century treatise on semiotics, considers "whether the division of signs into natural (*naturale*), stipulated (*ad placitum*), and customary (*ex consuetudine*) is a sound division?" By natural signs he means those signs that relate to their objects independently of human activity: Smoke is a sign of fire; by customary signs he means those signs that arise from the collective and nonreflective practices of human communities: Napkins on a table are a sign that dinner is imminent; by stipulated signs he means those signs whose meaning is deliberately appointed by an individual, as when a new word is introduced (Poinsot 1632/1985).[1] Poinsot's trichotomy in turn became the basis for Condillac's eighteenth-century division of signs into natural signs, accidental signs, and instituted signs (Condillac 1971).

Both Aristotle and Hayek developed their trichotomies as a way of transcending the Sophistic dichotomy between nature and convention. They agree that the polar opposition of nature and convention is a disaster for social thought. The natural became the necessary, the universal, the real; the conventional became the arbitrary, the local, the ephemeral. Only the natural is intelligible: To explain something we give an account of its "nature." The distinction between nature and convention became the distinction between the true and the false, *ens reale* and *ens fictum*. But how satisfactory is a theory of social life that denigrates custom and stipulation as arbitrary, ephemeral, and illusory? It is no wonder that European social thought is characterized by the recurrent effort to reduce custom and stipulation to nature – witness natural right, natural law, the state of nature, natural liberty, natural reason, natural prices and wages, and the natural level of unemployment.

Hayek rightly finds it odd that "we still cling to a division, deeply embedded in Western thought since classical antiquity, between things that owe their order to 'nature' and those that owe it to 'convention.' " Hayek agrees with Aristotle that the term "convention" collapses the important distinction between the collective, habitual order of custom and the individually designed order of stipulation. Sometimes Aristotle unfortunately reverts to the vague concept of convention: He tells us, for example, that money exists not by nature but by convention (*nomos*). Eric Roll (1956, 34) points out that this comment led the medieval schoolmen to a confused doctrine of money: They were not able to distinguish the stipulation of money as legal tender from money as a customary medium of exchange. Nonetheless, in general, Hayek, like the Sophists, treats his concepts as mutually exclusive alternatives (nature or custom or stipulation), whereas Aristotle treats his concepts as complementary and mutually inclusive (nature and custom and stipulation).

Hayek's tendency to treat the kinds of social order as mutually exclusive is evident in his treatment of market order: The market, he says, is an example of a "spontaneous order" that arose neither by nature nor by deliberate stipulation. "That division of labor on which our economic system rests is the best example of such a daily renewed order." Like Adam Smith, Hayek takes the phenomenon of the division of labor to be the paradigm of "the order created by the market." How, then, are we to account for this complex example of social order? Hayek bases his commitment to laissez-faire economic policy on the view that because the division of labor embodies the "spontaneous order" of custom, if we attempt to transform the division of labor through legal stipulation, "we destroy the forces making for a spontaneous overall order." Where my Aristotelian model of social order will treat the capitalist division of labor as the joint product of nature, custom, and stipulation, Hayek tends to see a given institution as the exemplar of only one kind of social order – the capitalist division of labor is the exemplar of the spontaneous order of custom just as the state is the exemplar of the stipulated order of law. I will use Hayek's example of the division of labor to test the explanatory power of my Aristotelian model of the kinds of order in society. Not surprisingly, an Aristotelian model has very different policy implications from those of Hayek's model.

In my Aristotelian model, there is the natural order of physical, chemical, and biological processes; there is the customary order of habitual social practices; and there is the stipulated order of deliberate design. Every human institution is the joint product of all three: Human language, for example, evolves due to natural physiology (ease of pronunciation), customary usage (the unconscious formation of grammatical analogies), and stipulation (the rules of grammarians and academies).

What I intend to establish, in short, is the claim that nature, custom, and stipulation represent the three fundamental concepts of order in the sense that all other concepts of order can be shown to be derivative. Perhaps the most profound challenge to my claim for the logical priority of Aristotle's trichotomy comes from the pervasive appeal to the distinction between organic and mechanical order in social and economic theory. Hayek's key distinction between "organism" and "organization" is based on the contrast between the organic and the mechanical – for which Hayek (1964/1979, 506–7) credits Karl Menger. Thus, Nicholas Georgescu-Roegen is not being fair in his assertion: "Yet, among economists of distinction, only Alfred Marshall intuited that biology, not mechanics, is the true Mecca of the economist."[2]

R. G. Collingwood sees a profound contrast between the views of nature as organism and nature as mechanism:

> The Greek view of nature as an intelligent organism was based on an analogy: an analogy between the world of nature and the individual human being. . . . The Renaissance view of nature as a machine is equally analogical in origin, but it presupposes a quite different order of ideas. (1945/1976, 8)

The question is whether organism and mechanism do presuppose in fact a quite different order of ideas. Obviously a machine and an organism differ in genesis: A machine is deliberately designed by an individual, while an organism is generated from the genetic material of another organism. But do mechanism and organism differ as types of order? Ever since Plato's natural teleology, the order of an organism has been understood as if it were a machine designed by an individual. Indeed, since *organa* is Greek for tools, to say that an organism is made up of organs, is identical to saying that an organism is a machine.

Plato was the first to use the order of mechanical design to explain the order of natural organism: Plato's demiurge is a craftsman who uses his mechanical art to impose order on nature. Just as Aristotle makes Plato's forms immanent in matter, so Aristotle makes the demiurge immanent in nature: The craftsmanship, which in Plato supervened from outside, is now an immanent characteristic of nature's own operations. Thus, Aristotle insists that nature designs animals to fit their environment optimally: "In all this Nature acts like an intelligent workman." Aristotle is not claiming that an intelligent being actually designed natural organisms, but only that the order of organisms should be explained as if they were deliberately designed. The structure of a machine is explained by its function; similarly, the structure of an organism is typically explained by its function. Biologists Oster and Wilson see mechanical and organic order as isomorphic: "The crucial difference between engineering and evolutionary theory is that the former seeks to design a machine or an operation in the most efficient form, while the latter seeks to infer 'nature's design' already created by natural selection" (1984, 272). In short, the order of both machines and organisms are explained in terms of stipulated design: Insofar as we account for organic structure and behavior in terms of function, or efficiency, or adaptiveness, we have assimilated organism to mechanism.

None of the attempts to sharply distinguish the mechanical order from the organic is adequate. First, many have argued that the self-regulating quality of an organism, the interactions between part and whole, is what separates an organism from a mechanism. According to Thoben, "So in contrast to the mechanistic approach in economics the modern organistic (or cybernetic) approach, which is based on systems thinking, emphasizes the property of integrativity" (1982, 293). Here Thoben's use of the term "cybernetic" undermines his attempt to distinguish the mechanical from the organic: Like organisms, sophisticated mechanisms are self-regulating. Second, many have contrasted the teleological structure of biological explanation with the mechanistic structure of physical theory. But teleology is pervasive in classical physics: The physics of constrained maximization based on the extremal properties of motion, the principle of least action, the principle of the conservation of energy, all presuppose that the universe exhibits efficient design. Ernest Nagel (1979) shows how any teleological explanation can be translated into an equivalent mechanistic explanation (see also Schumpeter 1954). Collingwood states: "Bergson puts this by saying that teleology is only mechanism turned upside down – *un méchanisme au rebours*" (1945/1976, 138). Organism and mechanism are but two variations on the same theme of stipulated order: The attempt to explain structure as if it were deliberately designed for its function. Customary order, by contrast, is best exhibited where structure does not correspond to function: A customary structure is the product of historical inheritance, not of current function.

The logic of nature, custom, and stipulation: as interdefinable

There is a profound tendency in European thought to treat nature, custom, and stipulation as a circle of interdefinability. That is, we tend to define each of our concepts in terms of one or both of the other concepts. "Cases are known where there is a set of concepts such that any member of that set may be defined in terms of one or more other members of the set, but no member can be defined otherwise."[3] In Aristotle and the Aristotelian tradition, nature, custom, and stipulation are not formally interdefined, but they are described through a circle of metaphors. For example, the order of nature is often described in terms of the order of legal stipulation, "the laws of physics"; while law is often described in terms of nature, "natural law" and "natural right." And custom is typically described both in terms of nature as "second nature" and in terms of stipulation as "unwritten law." What is the meaning of this circle of metaphors? Is this a vicious circle?

The use of these expressions to define nature, custom, and law is so ubiquitous that they have lost their metaphorical force; the notion of the "laws of physics," for example, has become so cliché that it is now taken literally. These are dormant metaphors and we cannot interrogate them until they are awakened; and since a metaphor is a condensed analogy, we awaken it by making explicit the implicit analogy.[4] The metaphor of "the laws of physics" is a condensed analogy of the form: Human laws are to social order what physical laws are to natural order. The metaphor describing custom as unwritten law implies the analogy that custom is to law what the unwritten is to the written. What we find in this way is that these metaphorical descriptions of nature, custom, and law are merely abbreviations for rather elaborate analogies. The first step, then, in making sense of a metaphor is to unpack the implicit analogy.

If a metaphor is a condensed analogy, then our circle of metaphors is actually a circle of analogies. Nature is analogous to custom, custom is analogous to law, and law is analogous to nature. What, then, is the meaning of this circle of analogies? An analogy is often described as a relation of resemblance, but analogy is more precisely described as a resemblance of relationship: A: B :: C: D (Perelman and Olbrechts-Tyteca 1969). Our circle of analogies reflects the Aristotelian insight that there are important logical similarities between natural, customary, and stipulated order. In response to Antiphon's influential claim that nature and convention are antithetical, Aristotle employed a variety of analogies to bridge the presumed chasm between the natural and the social. His favorite analogy compares rational teleology to natural teleology: Just as the craftsman rationally orders his means to his end, so nature orders its means to its ends. Aristotle's insight that natural organs, like human artifacts, can be explained by their functions laid the basis for the fruitful scientific program of natural teleology. Similarly, Aristotle's metaphor of custom as "second nature" is an important corrective to the Sophistic view that customs are merely arbitrary; and the metaphor of custom as "unwritten law" rightly conveys the normative force of custom. The later Aristotelian-Thomistic doctrine of natural law and the laws of nature presuppose an analogy between the legal order and the natural order. Juristic natural law rightly emphasized the universality of certain moral norms in human society; physical natural law rightly emphasized the generality and necessity of many natural processes.

The frequent treatment of nature, custom, and stipulation as a circle of interdefinability has undoubtedly generated many fruitful analogies: The history of science shows that theoretical innovation is usually a matter of seeing analogical resemblance between different phenomena.[5] The dormant metaphor "electric current" abbreviates a complex analogy between electricity and hydrodynamics; and the metaphor "consuming inputs" abbreviates a complex analogy between production and consumption in neoclassical economics. Yet all analogies have implications that can distort theory if the analogies are not subjected to criticism. Niels Bohr, for example, conceived his theory of atomic structure by analogy to the solar system, but physicists soon dropped this analogy as misleading. As Philip Mirowski rightly says: "Scientific metaphors [i.e., analogies] should set in motion research programs which strive to make explicit all of the attendant submetaphors of the original. They should provoke inquiry as to whether the implications are consistent one with another, as well as consistent with the background tacit knowledge" (1989, 278–9). Mirowski's critique of neoclassical economics is precisely a critical inquiry into the complex analogies that underlie the energy metaphor in the theory of value. In the same way, we must subject our circle of analogies to critical scrutiny: Are natural organs really designed for a specific function? Who does the designing? When were they designed? If customs are second nature, then why do they differ so much over time and place? Do customs differ from laws only by being unwritten? Were the laws of nature stipulated all at once or did they evolve over time like habits?

Our Aristotelian circle of interdefinability is only a special case of a more general phenomenon: In every human society we find myriad analogies drawn between natural order and social order, between the classification of natural things and the classification of social things. Anthropologists have long speculated on the meaning of these analogies. James Frazer, for example, argued that the social classification of castes among primitive peoples reflects the natural classification of totemic animals. Durkheim and Mauss, however, argued against Frazer that actually the classification of nature is a reflection of the social structure: "According to him, men were divided into clans by a preexisting classification of things; but, quite on the contrary, they classify things because they were divided by clans" (Durkheim and Mauss 1903, 82). Mary Douglas accepts the Durkheim–Mauss thesis that concepts of the natural order reflect the social order; in addition, she argues that these concepts of natural order often originate in the desire to legitimate the social order. Therefore, to justify a given set of social relations, "there needs to be an analogy by which the formal structure of a crucial set of social relations is found in the physical world (Douglas 1986, 48).[6] Mary Douglas extends this sociology of knowledge from primitive to modern society: Everywhere, she says, our concepts of natural order reflect a desire to legitimate the existing social order.

What are we to make of these explanations? They all suffer from bad anthropology and worse logic. To begin with, it is anachronistic to describe primitive classification as a rhetorical device for creating analogies between natural order and social order, since the distinction between nature and social convention was the invention of Greek philosophy. Claude Lévi-Strauss rightly points out that primitive classification is designed to articulate both nature and society as an organized whole: Castes naturalize society while totemic groups socialize nature.[7] Lévi-Strauss criticizes the attempt to see primitive classification as either a projection of nature on society or of society on nature: "In fact, however, it is pre-eminently the means (or the hope) of transcending the opposition between them" (Lévi-Strauss 1962, 91).

That primitive classification cannot be explained as a rhetorical strategy for legitimating social relations can be shown by an analysis of the logic of analogy. Analogies have argumentative force only if they assimilate the less known to the better known: Thus, economists compare the circulation of goods with the circulation of blood. This analogy has force only if it is asymmetrical, that is, if we know more about the circulation of blood than about the circulation of goods. What we find in primitive classification, however, are not such asymmetrical analogies grounding social order in natural order, but symmetrical homologies between nature and society. Lévi-Strauss illustrates this symmetry by showing that sometimes castes are patterned after nature and sometimes totemic groups are patterned after society.

Douglas (1986, 49) argues, however, that the analogy "female is to male as left hand is to right" is a rhetorical device often used to justify the sexual division of labor. Unfortunately, the use of a thing tells us little about its origin and purpose; hammers are used for murder, but this fact tells us little about the origin and function of hammers. Indeed, the symmetrical structure of her example shows that it functions to socialize nature as much as naturalize society. The relation of the right to the left hand cannot ground social relations in nature because the very notion that the right hand is good and superior, while the left hand is evil and inferior, derives from social categories. This analogy was clearly not designed to ground social relations in nature, because the definition of the natural body already presupposes those social relations. Because of their symmetrical structure, most analogies between nature and society lack the rhetorical force of true asymmetrical analogies. They must be explained by a deeper proclivity of the human spirit to articulate the natural and the social universe as an organized whole. Such analogies reflect the universal human desire to make sense of the cosmos more than the desire for rhetorical weapons. The historic mission of philosophical speculation, says John Dewey, is to bring our knowledge of nature into relation with our knowledge of human conduct (Dewey 1929/1960; Lévi-Strauss 1962). The construction of an analogy is precisely the effort – at once poetic and philosophical – to make sense of the place of human activity in the context of the cosmos as a whole.

Douglas is forced to see analogies as strategies for social legitimation because she is blind to the profound role of custom in social life. Because she defines institutions as conventional, rather than customary, she sees social stability as contingent on rational consent: "The shared analogy is a device for legitimating a set of fragile institutions" (1986, 49). She tells us that the social division of labor is "likely to be challenged all the time" unless it is grounded through an analogy to nature. To those who have ever attempted to change an institution, the notion that it is fragile and ready to dissolve must come as a surprise. In reality, of course, it is the inertia of social custom, grounded in individual habit, that gives institutions stability. What keeps the miner in his mine, the secretary at her desk, is custom, not some analogical rationale. William James proves himself a far superior anthropologist by seeing that "habit is thus the enormous fly-wheel of society, its most precious conservative agent" (1890/1981, 125). As we shall see, explicit justification of an institution is required only in rare moments of crisis. And finally, if appeal to natural order is a strategy for legitimating existing institutions, then why is natural order invoked by radicals as much as by conservatives: "Natural law" and "natural right," for example, were the weapons of American and French revolutionaries.

The logic of nature, custom, and stipulation: as a progressive hierarchy

A great deal of the history of social theory has consisted in the elaboration of this handful of Aristotelian metaphors. Nonetheless, as an account of nature, custom, and stipulation this circle of metaphors is radically defective. To begin with, metaphors are obscure in a way that analogies are not: Because a metaphor fuses terms A and C but leaves terms B and D unexpressed, there are always several possible analogies implied by any one metaphor. A metaphor is not simply an abbreviated analogy; it is an abbreviation that may stand for many different analogies. Even if we know the context of the metaphor, the choice of the appropriate analogy is never unambiguous. To cite Perelman's example, the metaphor "an ocean of false learning" may imply the analogy: ocean: swimmer:: false learning: scientist; or the analogy: ocean: terra firma:: false learning: truth (Perelman and Olbrechts-Tyteca 1969,

410). As we shall see, the metaphor "natural law" has been interpreted by Aristotelian, Christian, and Newtonian analogies. Moreover, in the fusion of a metaphor, the underlying analogy is not presented as a hypothesis for inspection but as a datum; indeed, the analogy functions as the concealed presupposition for grasping the metaphor. The rhetorical power of metaphor is precisely this ability of getting us to accept an implied analogy without knowing that we have.[8]

The capacity of a single metaphor to imply many different analogies helps to account for the paradox of identity and difference in intellectual history. Certain pervasive metaphors give continuity to intellectual history, while the underlying analogies create radical differences. If we focus only on the continuity of metaphor, then, we are forced to agree with Borges's ironic dictum that "universal history is the history of different intonations given a handful of metaphors" (quoted in Mirowski 1989, 1). Nonetheless, beneath this smooth continuity of metaphor are the profound ruptures marking radically different underlying analogies. Plato's metaphor of the "body politic" becomes interpreted by the analogy of Christ to his church in St. Paul and by the analogy of artificial to natural man in Hobbes; the metaphor of "natural law" becomes interpreted by Aristotelian, Thomist, and Newtonian analogies. The pervasive use of our Aristotelian metaphors by various intellectual traditions does not mean that history is the eternal return of the same, nor does it mean that diverse traditions are essentially incommensurable. The employment of the metaphor of natural law by Aristotelians, Thomists, and Newtonians is neither univocal nor equivocal, but analogous: The various modes of analogy are themselves mutually analogous.

Even if we translate our circle of metaphors into a circle of analogies, we are still a long way from giving an account of nature, custom, and stipulation. Analogy, like definition, has argumentative force only if the less familiar is assimilated to the more familiar: Analogy and definition must be asymmetrical relations. Our circle of analogies lacks this asymmetry for the simple reason that none of our concepts is intrinsically more familiar than any other. Calling custom "second nature" is no more plausible than calling nature "first custom"; calling custom "unwritten law" is no more plausible than calling law "written custom"; calling laws "natural" is no more plausible than calling nature "lawful."[9] Moreover, even where Aristotle constructs a true asymmetrical analogy, it still is vulnerable to the fallacy of *petitio principii*: For example, Aristotle's analogy between the teleology of art and nature assimilates nature as the less familiar to art as the more familiar. Yet Aristotle's doctrine that art is governed by hypothetical necessity, meaning that there is only one right way to make something, shows that he has understood art by analogy to natural necessity. He cannot, therefore, explain nature by analogy to art since his account of art already presupposes his account of nature. Or conversely Aristotle can define art as the imitation of nature only because he has already assumed that nature is the imitation of art.

If the role of analogies in the history of science is to generate theoretical hypotheses, then the nature, custom, and stipulation circle of analogies should generate a theory of our trichotomy. The circle of analogies embodies the important insight that nature, custom, and stipulation are essentially interrelated. We cannot give an account of any one concept without a theory of the trichotomy as a whole. A more adequate grasp of nature, custom, and stipulation is impossible unless we escape the circle of metaphorical interdefinability; piecemeal attempts to reform the circle are never adequate. For example, when it became clear to eighteenth-century thinkers that the customary order is not a function of stipulated design, customs were assimilated to nature – witness the Burkean adage that "constitutions are not made, but grow." If we are to escape the circle, rather than simply tour through it, we must develop a theory of the whole trichotomy.

In accordance with Aristotle's explicit logic of classification, I have treated nature, custom, and stipulation as the three and only three species of the genus "order." One shortcoming of this genus–species logic is that the genus "order" is more or less empty and does not add any information to the *differentiae* "nature, custom, and stipulation." More importantly, the genus–species logic does not indicate the serial and hierarchical relations of nature, custom, and stipulation. I will argue, in other words, that nature is prior to custom and that custom is prior to stipulation – in both cases the priority is logical and causal.

Aristotle, however, offers an alternative logic of classification, which is most clearly illustrated by his analysis of the kinds of souls. Here, instead of defining the genus "soul" and the species of plant, animal, and human souls, Aristotle says that the plant soul is living, the animal soul is living plus sensitive, and the human soul is living and sensitive plus rational (*On the Soul* 414a 29–415a 13). I will argue that nature, custom, and stipulation form such a hierarchy: "In every case the lower faculty can exist apart from the higher, but the higher presupposes those below it" (Hicks 1907, 335). Nature represents the physical, chemical, and biological processes of the created universe; nature can and did exist apart from human custom and stipulation. Human custom is rooted in the physiology of habit, but transcends individual habit by becoming a collective system of normative behavior. Custom presupposes nature, but custom can exist without being the object of reflective stipulation by an individual mind (language can and did exist apart from grammarians). Stipulation is the synoptic order deliberately imposed upon the prereflective materials of custom; stipulation always presupposes custom: Philosophy, law, engineering, and grammar never arise ex nihilo.

What does it mean to say that custom presupposes nature and that stipulation presupposes custom? First, it suggests that certain natural processes (like habit formation) are necessary but not sufficient causes for the emergence of social customs; and, for example, if human biology were not sexually bimorphic, then human customs defining gender would not arise. Second, custom is a necessary but not sufficient cause for the emergence of deliberate stipulation; reflective stipulation of a new definition for a term, for example, presupposes the existing customary definition. If nature were a sufficient condition for custom, then custom could be reduced to nature; if custom were a sufficient condition for stipulation, then stipulation could be reduced to custom. In Aristotle's terms, nature is potentially custom and custom is potentially stipulation; yet for potentiality to become actuality, other causal factors must be present. Our model of nature, custom, and stipulation thus creates the theoretical framework for testing empirical hypotheses about what biological conditions are necessary for the emergence of social customs and about what customary practices lead to the emergence of stipulation.

Our progressive hierarchy has a descending as well as an ascending moment. We have just seen the ascent from nature to custom to stipulation; now we shall briefly describe the descent from stipulation to custom to nature. Legal stipulation presupposes custom but is often intended to reform and even to negate custom; managers of factories and offices, for example, stipulate work rules intended to replace traditional customs and to create new customs. Stipulated laws for conscription create social customs of military service in some regions. Stipulation, then, can create new customs, which in turn will create the need over time for new stipulations. We must, then, consider the question, If customs are increasingly the product of legal stipulation, does it still make sense to argue that custom is logically prior to stipulation? The answer is that although stipulation can influence the question of which customs will be formed, stipulation cannot alter the fundamental customary processes of habit and imitation whereby social practices are learned. The stipulations of grammarians have more influence on speech behavior now than they did in the past, but language remains a habitual social practice learned by imitation. Human behavior will always be rooted more in habit and imitation than in deliberate stipulations. What has changed historically is not the role of custom so much as the source of customs.

Similarly, over time custom and stipulation have transformed nature: How, then, can nature (at least this corner of nature called earth) be said to be logically prior to custom and stipulation if nature is increasingly the product of human activity? The answer is that although we can transform pristine nature into a human environment, we cannot transform the basic processes or "laws" of nature. We transform pristine nature only by conforming to the processes of nature: If we destroy nature it will be through the laws of nature. The early evolution of man reveals the power of custom to transform human nature: Physical anthropology has revealed the far-reaching role of custom in the transformation of the small-brained protohuman Australopithecus into the large-brained, fully human *Homo sapiens*. Through the development of customs, "man determined, if unwittingly, the culminating stages of his own biological destiny. Quite literally, though quite inadvertently, he created himself."[10] Still, custom was able to shape human nature only because of natural selection: Those individuals with greater social and technical skills had a selective advantage. With genetic engineering, we are now able for the first time to shape human nature through deliberate stipulation; whether we can predict the outcome of such manipulation is another question. The priority of natural order is evident: Custom made use of natural selection; stipulation makes use of biochemical processes.

Traditionalists, like Burke and Oakeshott, emphasize the ascent from custom to stipulation; they insist that rational stipulation ought not wander far from its moorings in custom. Rationalists, like Paine and Ungar, emphasize the descent from stipulation to custom: They insist on the power of reason to transform custom. Both perspectives are equally one-sided. Sociobiologists, like Wilson and Tiger, emphasize the role of nature in social life to the neglect of custom and stipulation. In short, viewing nature, custom, and stipulation as a progressive hierarchy with ascending and descending moments offers the most comprehensive and logically rigorous framework for social theory. We are now ready to consider the role of nature, custom, and stipulation in the constitution of the social division of labor.

The natural division of labor

Labor is the unity of conception and execution, which, for most of human history, has meant the unity of the mind and the hand. Since the human brain and the human hand evolved in part through an interaction with custom, there can be no human nature and, *a fortiori*, no human labor apart from custom. We lack the appropriate instincts to divide and to coordinate social labor, so without customary norms we are lost. Yet from Plato to E. O. Wilson, we find the pervasive attempt to describe the division of labor as natural. In part, this ubiquitous naturalism derives from the etymological fact that "nature" means "essence" so that when we define something we describe its "nature"; thus, if we seek the "nature," that is, the essence, of the division of labor, it seems only logical to look to "nature." In short, the ambiguity of the term "nature" has created the universal prejudice that the natural dimension of a social institution must be its essence.

I call "naturalism" all attempts to reduce custom and stipulation to nature – a reduction that often reflects the confusion between what is natural and what is essential. To add to the confusion, there are two distinct species of naturalism that are themselves usually conflated. Something may be termed natural because it is causally determined by nature, or something may be termed natural because it is formally analogous to nature. The conflation of these two distinct senses of "natural" vitiates most of what has been written about the role of nature in social and political philosophy. Analogies should lead to the search for causes rather than serve as a substitute for genuine causal explanation, because arguments from an analogy to nature are not empirically falsifiable, while arguments from natural causation are. In social theory, however, all too often arguments from analogy and arguments from causation are simply confounded.

Plato, for example, says that the division of labor is natural because different individuals have different innate aptitudes; yet Plato also says that the division of labor is natural because the specialization of workers is analogous to the specialization of organs of the body: the metaphor of the body politic (*Republic* 370A and 462C). In the first case, the division of labor is causally determined by nature, and in the second, the division of labor is analogous to nature. Plato's elaborate analogy between the three parts of the soul and the three classes of the ideal city makes use of both senses of natural. Each person is psychologically suited by nature to his social caste; and there is an analogy of proportionality between the hierarchy of classes and the hierarchy of the parts of the soul. The guardian rules by nature because his rational soul causes him to be fit to rule; and the guardian rules by nature because the dominance of reason in the ideal city is analogous to the dominance of reason in his soul.

According to Aristotle, the division of labor is natural in both

senses. Within the household, roles are specialized according to biological differences in aptitude:

> The freeman rules over the slave after another manner from that in
> which the male rules over the female, or the man over the child;
> although the parts of the soul are present in all of them, they are
> present in different degrees. For the slave has no deliberative faculty
> at all; the woman has, but it is without authority, and the child has,
> but it is immature. (*Pol.* 1260a 7)

Slavery is natural both because slaves have deficient minds and because the master–slave relation is analogous to the mind–body relation (*Pol.* 1254a 31).

Adam Smith describes the division of labor as natural in both of
these senses. In Smith's view, all scientific explanation has two parts:
The first refers to the specific causal mechanisms involved – for example, the laws of motion; the second refers to the harmonious order
that Providence creates out of these mechanisms. According to O. H.
Taylor:

> Psychological and social science has to explain the operation of the
> mechanisms by which the Divine purpose is achieved. This argument
> makes it clear that Smith's references to the purposes of Nature, the
> "guiding hand," etc., were not substitutes for scientific explanations
> of social phenomena but an appendage to them. (1955, 91)

The division of labor, says Smith, stems from the natural psychological
propensity to truck, barter, and exchange. An invisible hand ensures
that these individual propensities lead to an optimal division of labor.
The division of labor – and the market economy as a whole – is natural both because it is rooted in causal psychological propensities and
because the spontaneous order of the market is analogous to the
spontaneous order of nature (Smith 1776/1979, 1:2, 25; 4:2, 456; 4:5,
530). Smith, therefore, not only makes use of these two senses of
natural, but with his "invisible hand" he provides a means of ensuring
that causal determinism leads to a social order whose harmony is
analogous to the harmony of the natural order.

Edmund Burke develops an elaborate analogy between natural and
social hierarchy in his version of the great chain of being:

> For in all things whatever, the mind is the most valuable and the most
> important; and in this scale the whole of agriculture is in a natural
> and just order; the beast is as an informing principle to the plough
> and cart; the labourer is as reason to the beast; and the farmer is as a
> thinking and presiding principle to the labourer. An attempt to

> break this chain of subordination in any part is equally absurd. (1795/1839, 4:256)

Here the causal role of the mind in directing the body is merged with the analogy between the subordination of a beast to a man and the subordination of a laborer to a capitalist.

Karl Marx claims that the division of labor within a family "springs up naturally" and is a "purely physiological" division based on the "differences of age and sex" (1867/1967, 1:iv, 14, 332). This is a fairly straightforward example of an argument from natural causal determinism. But Marx goes on to describe the division of labor as natural in a different sense:

> Castes and guilds arise from the action of the same natural law that regulates the differentiation of plants and animals into species and varieties, except that, when a certain degree of development has been reached, the heredity of castes and the exclusiveness of guilds are ordained as a law of society. (321)

Marx is clearly developing an analogy between the speciation of organisms and the specialization of trades; yet he also means to suggest that this is more than an analogy. He does not specify what "natural law" is responsible for the social division of labor, but the language suggests that he is referring to Darwin's natural selection.[11] Since there is no evidence that the division of labor is caused by natural selection, Marx must trade on the ambiguity of the term "nature": He suggests that if a social institution is analogous to nature, then it must be causally determined by nature. Actually, of course, such analogies prove nothing about causal determination: Analogies may serve as hypotheses for the empirical investigation of causation, but they do not constitute evidence of any causal relation. Alfred Marshall argues quite explicitly that the analogy between the social division of labor in a factory and the natural division of functions in an organism proves that the division of labor is causally determined by natural laws. Marshall writes of "the many profound analogies which have been discovered between social and especially industrial organization on the one side and the physical organization of the higher animals on the other." These analogies "have at last established their claim to illustrate a fundamental unity of action between the laws of nature in the physical and in the moral world":

> This central unity is set forth in the general rule, to which there are not very many exceptions, that the development of the organism, whether social or physical, involves an increasing subdivision of func-

tions between its separate parts on the one hand, and on the other a more intimate connection between them. (1920/1982, 200)

Marshall thus makes explicit Marx's implicit argument from analogy to causation.

The complete collapse of the distinction between natural analogy and natural causation is found in the sociobiology of E. O. Wilson: "A single strong thread does indeed run from the conduct of termite colonies and turkey brotherhoods to the social behavior of man" (1975, 129). Is this "strong thread" a causal link between species or merely an analogy between species?

> Specialization of members of a group is a hallmark of advance in social evolution. One of the theorems of ergonomic theory is that for each species (or genotype) in a particular environment there exists an optimal mix of coordinated specialists that performs more efficiently than groups of equal size consisting wholly of generalists. (17)

Just as Smith saw an invisible hand guiding individuals into a socially optimal division of labor, so Wilson sees natural selection guiding individual organisms into a division of labor optimal for the species. Yet where Smith treated the invisible hand as an analogy, Wilson treats his "optimizing" natural selection as a causal principle. Wilson sees an analogy between the division of labor among insects and the human division of labor; he then concludes the human division of labor must be natural: "My own guess is that the genetic bias is intense enough to cause a substantial division of labor even in the most free and most egalitarian of future societies" (1975a, 48).[12]

From Plato to E. O. Wilson virtually every social theorist has described the division of labor as natural. None of our authors has thematized the distinction between these two senses of "natural"; indeed, most theorists have traded on the ambiguity of "natural" for rhetorical effect. The problem confronting any theory of the social division of labor is this: There are undeniable resemblances between the human division of labor and various infrahuman divisions of labor. What are we to make of these resemblances? To begin with, if our account is to be compatible with modern biology, then we must carefully distinguish between a resemblance due to homology and a resemblance due to analogy. Humans' arms and whales' fins are homologous because both derive from the limbs of our common ancestor; bats' wings and birds' wings, by contrast, are merely analogous because their common ancestor was wingless. Homologous structures are genetically inherited from a common ancestor; analogous structures are genetically created by natural selection because of a common functional need.

In both cases, an initial analogy or resemblance led to the search for a causal explanation; once the initial resemblance is explained by homology or by analogy, then it ceases to be an analogy; rather, the two structures become illustrations of a general biological process. Sociobiology thus manages to conflate three distinct senses of "natural": analogy to nature, cause by homology, and cause by analogy.

The naturalism of Wilson's sociobiology, then, is the attempt to reduce the customary and stipulated dimensions of a human institution to nature; the conventionalism of B. F. Skinner, by contrast, reduces nature to cultural conditioning. Social theory is still trapped in the Sophistic antithesis between nature and convention. If we are to transcend this sterile opposition, we need a concept of nature that does not exclude custom and stipulation; indeed, we need a concept of nature that makes custom and stipulation possible.

Such a concept of nature is implicit in Aristotle's doctrine that to become a morally good person we need nature, custom, and reason. What does Aristotle mean by nature in this trichotomy? He means that by nature we receive a set of potentialities that are made actual by habit and reason: "Neither by nature, then, nor contrary to nature do excellences arise in us: rather we are adapted by nature to receive them, and are made perfect by habit" (NE 1103a 23). Nature provides the potentialities for us to become good or bad, depending on whether we form good or bad habits. Clifford Geertz rightly says that man is to be defined not by his innate capacities nor by his learned behavior "but rather by the link between them, by the way in which the first is transformed into the second, his generic potentialities focused into his specific performances" (1973, 52). In this view, nature does not determine human institutions; nature simply provides the powers employed by custom and stipulation. In one sense, every human activity is natural because humans are a part of nature; in another sense, however, nothing humans do is natural because custom and stipulation have shaped not only the most basic human behavior such as eating, sleeping, and sex, but also human anatomy, physiology, and psychology. This paradox vanishes as soon as we see that any given social institution is at once natural, customary, and stipulated.

Moreover, we need a concept of nature in social theory that is compatible with modern natural science; the nature at work in morality, in economics, and in politics is the same nature studied by physicists, chemists, and biologists. The explosion of knowledge in the life sciences makes it clear that progress in the understanding of human social institutions will depend, in part, on a dialogue between natural scientists and social theorists; such a dialogue is impossible unless social theorists employ a concept of nature compatible with the findings of natural science. The theory of nature and the concept of nature are philosophical, not scientific, matters; the philosophical concept of nature need not be the concept used by all natural scientists, since some scientists have a mechanistic and reductionist view of nature that is not in fact required by contemporary natural science; we must not confuse the findings of modern natural science with the bad metaphysics of some scientists.

I therefore propose to develop an extended analogy between the social hierarchy of nature, custom, and stipulation and the biological hierarchy of emergent complexity. The theory of emergence, like our theory of social order, is a nonreductionist account of complex phenomena. According to Lloyd Morgan (1894), "At various grades of organization, material configurations display new and unexpected phenomena." Just as the properties of water cannot be deduced from the properties of hydrogen and oxygen, so the properties of custom cannot be deduced from the properties of nature. The notion that from complexity emerges new phenomena that cannot be reduced to simpler parts is at the center of modern biology, which is another way of saying that modern biology is nonreductionist. Theory reductionism, says Ernst Mayr, is a fallacy because it confuses processes and concepts: "Such biological processes as meiosis, gastrulation, and predation are also chemical and physical processes, but they are only biological concepts and cannot be reduced to physicochemical concepts." Customary and stipulated human behavior is also biological, chemical, and physical behavior, but custom and stipulation cannot be reduced to nature. Complex systems very often have a hierarchical structure, and the hierarchical structure of living systems shares some important features with our hierarchy, one being that higher levels can affect properties of components at lower levels. We observed this "downward causation" in the descent from stipulation to nature. Our theory of nature, like that of modern biology, is neither vitalist nor reductionist.[13]

The plasticity of nature is a function of how we selectively use these natural powers; the constraint of nature is a function of the limits of compossibility in our selection of a set of powers. J. S. Mill defines the laws of nature as a set of such powers:

> Though we cannot emancipate ourselves from the laws of nature as a whole, we can escape from any particular law of nature, if we are able to withdraw ourselves from the circumstances in which it acts. Though we can do nothing except through laws of nature, we can use one law to counter-act another. (1874/1969, 7)

All human activities are subject to natural causal laws, but to a considerable extent, custom and stipulation select which causal laws govern a
particular activity. All forms of linguistic behavior, for example, make
use of natural processes, but different forms of language select different natural laws: Vocalization uses one process, writing another, sign
language another, computer language still another.

Nature's role in the social division of labor is always mediated by
custom and stipulation. E. O. Wilson says that the sexual division of
labor "appears to have a genetic origin." This is quite true, not in the
sense that specific genes determine the sexual division of labor, but in
the sense that the sexual division of labor makes use of genetic differences between the sexes. Whether a person is male or female has a
genetic origin; custom and stipulation divide tasks by sex; thus, the
sexual division of labor has a genetic origin – but only because custom
selects sex as the basis of social function. Every division of labor selects
among various natural differences among people: differences of sex,
age, race, strength, or intelligence. As a general rule, traditional societies based the social division of labor on natural differences between
social groups defined by sex, age, and clan; modern societies, by contrast, base the social division of labor increasingly on natural differences between individuals. This contrast could be interpreted as a
transition from an emphasis on the qualitative differences between
groups to an emphasis on the quantitative differences between individuals. Nature plays many roles in the division of labor, but custom
and stipulation determine which roles nature plays.

The customary division of labor

Although the concepts of habit and custom were once central to social
and political philosophy, they have been jettisoned from large parts of
contemporary social science. The current *International Encyclopedia of
the Social Sciences* (1968) no longer includes articles on habit and custom as it did in the previous edition (1930). Habit and custom were
dropped from sociology during the transition from Max Weber to
Talcott Parsons. Weber defines rational action as either the pursuit of
explicit ultimate values or as the deliberate selection of means to pursue explicit ends. For Weber, habitual or customary action is not only
nonrational – it is not even meaningful. Parsons then proceeded to
excise habit and custom from his typology of social action.[14] And John
Rawls constructed his theory of justice by removing all influence of
habit and custom from the agents who deliberate behind the veil of
ignorance. However, dissatisfaction with functionalist and Kantian

modes of social theory has led to a renewed interest in tradition, interpretation, community, and history. Unfortunately, this general "hermeneutic turn" in social theory makes use of many vague concepts like tradition, community, convention, and culture instead of the more precise notions of habit, custom, and stipulation.

Similarly, while habit and custom once played a significant role in classical political economy, in the historical school of economics, and in American institutionalist economics, they have been jettisoned from neoclassical economics. When habit or custom is treated by neoclassicism, the results are ludicrous. Von Mises (1949/1966), for example, argues that habits are always deliberately acquired and changed to conform with explicit criteria.[15] In short, habit and custom do not exist for neoclassicism. However, there is an important current in recent economic theorizing, as well shall see, that has attempted to introduce historicity into economic processes in a way that implicitly acknowledges the role of habit and custom.

The reasons for the excision of habit and custom go to the heart of the theoretical logic of much of modern social theory. We can only touch on the two most basic grounds for the absence of habit and custom. First, Kant posited a radical dichotomy between the causally determined realm of nature and the morally free realm of human action. Since Kant defined the moral realm as the locus of the free and deliberate stipulation of rules, habitual or customary action is incompatible with moral action. This explains why Kant banished habit and custom from the realm of moral action.[16] Kant's dichotomy between nature and morality, between facts and values, was the basis of Dilthey's dichotomy between the natural sciences and the cultural sciences (*Naturwissenschaften* and *Geisteswissenschaften*). Weber and Parsons accepted this dichotomy: Social science studies normative action while natural science studies factual regularities. Since they defined social action in terms of the reflective choice of ends and means, habitual action was banished to the sciences of nature. Clifford Geertz accepts Dilthey's dichotomy when he says that the analysis of culture should be "not an experimental science in search of law but an interpretative one in search of meaning" (1973, 5). The upshot of this story is that any attempt to create a dichotomy between natural facts and moral values will exclude habit and custom, for customary habit is precisely the indissoluble unity of factual regularity and normative value. Since habit is a bridge from nature to custom, the existence of habit is incompatible with the view that nature and custom are antithetical.

The second ground for the excision of habit and custom is that modern economics modeled itself on the mechanics of physical forces where causal relations are independent of time. Neoclassical economics, by adopting the constrained maximization techniques of preentropic physics, presupposes that economic processes do not depend on time: Market equilibrium is independent of any historical path and all transactions are reversible.[17] Economic coordination is a function of individual preferences that are given *a priori* and are independent of prior acts of choice. "The process of coordinating economic activity is explicitly removed to a timeless epoch *prior* to the operation of the economy: to production, trade, and consumption. No dynamic process of learning and adaptation, of ongoing organization and planning enters this picture of economic evolution" (Bausor 1986, 98). Rational economic action maximizes the preferences of an individual, excluding collective customary action; and economic action maximizes current preferences, excluding actions based on prior habits. The extension of the neoclassical theory of rational choice to social and political theory renders any accommodation of habit and custom impossible.

I will argue that, contrary to modern social theory, habit and custom are fundamental concepts for any adequate theory of social institutions. Habits form a bridge from the simplest animal behavior to the most complex human semiotics of custom. The existence of habits presupposes the plasticity of nature: If nature were not a field of possibilities, habits could not arise.[18] If, in other words, genotype determined phenotype, if instinct determined behavior, then there would be no place for habit. Actually, the concept of instinct has been jettisoned by most ethologists due to the recognition that all behavior is, at least in part, learned.[19]

Habits have three dimensions of importance to social theory: They are the foundation of all learned behavior, are always general rules or concepts, and are constituted by history. Ironically, just when habit was jettisoned from social theory, the study of habit became central to neural physiology, ethology, and cognitive psychology. The area of the most substantial achievement and consensus concerns the basic substrate of habit known as "habituation." If a moderate stimulus to which an organism initially responds is repeated, the organism gradually ceases to respond. In other words, when an organism becomes habituated (or "accustomed") to its environment, it gradually ceases to respond to its environment. "It is perhaps the simplest form of learning – learning not to respond" (Thompson 1976, 49). According to ethologist John Bonner, habituation is the first form of learning to have evolved: The ability of even the simplest organisms to learn to ignore mild disturbances through habituation, while avoiding those that are potentially dangerous, is adaptive behavior in the evolutionary sense (1980, 113). The human ability to become habituated to the most stressful environments has considerable adaptive and social significance: Through the physiology of habituation, our social and natural environments become invisible to us.[20] Similarly, we become habituated to our own routine activities. It is of the essence of our habits and customs that they become invisible to us – every society depends on foreigners to describe its customs. Habituation is the first form of learning both in the evolution of organisms and in the development of the individual.[21]

Habituation begins as a response to a particular stimulus but generalizes to other related stimuli. Similarly, learning is a process of generalizing our habits of thought from one area to other related domains. According to C. S. Peirce, all habits are general rules of response; a habit is not a particular response to a particular stimulus; the habits of even the simplest mollusks are inductive generalizations. "Induction proceeds from Case and Result to Rule; it is the formula of the formation of a habit or general conception – a process which, psychologically as well as logically, depends on the repetition of instances or sensations" (in Hartshorne and Weiss 1960, 2.712).[22] There is thus a significant continuity between the habits of the simplest organisms and the most sophisticated of our inductive generalizations. Indeed, a concept has often been defined as a cognitive habit.[23] Of course, most organisms are not reflectively aware of their habitual concepts; but then most human habits of thought – beliefs, concepts, and prejudices – are not conscious either.

Habits are much more radically dependent on historical time than are most of the causal relations of physics. All causal relations take place in time, but habits are constituted by time. Classical mechanics and classical energy physics concern locomotion and position: The physical equilibrium is defined independently of the historical path of the particle. Within a system of locomotion, time is in principle reversible: If a falling body strikes a perfectly elastic surface, it returns to equilibrium as if time were reversed. History emerges in physics as the phenomenon of hysteresis: Any causal relation that is dependent on prior history exhibits hysteresis. The behavior of a magnet, for example, depends on its prior uses. Yet although the behavior of a magnet depends on its history, the magnet's behavior is not habitual because it is neither general nor plastic, but specific and rigid. Moreover, a magnet can be demagnetized and remagnetized, so its behavior, though nonreversible, is not irrevocable. The second law of thermodynamics (the entropy law) introduces a more profound dimension of time into physical processes: "The entropic degradation of the universe as conceived by classical thermodynamics is an irrevocable process: the free energy once transformed into latent energy can never be recuperated."[24]

C. S. Peirce argues that the phenomenon of habit taking presupposes the action of the entropy law: first, because entropic processes are irrevocable; and second, because entropic processes are indeterminate and have the requisite plasticity for habit taking.[25] William James emphasizes the irrevocable nature of habits: "Nothing we ever do is, in strict scientific literalness, wiped out" (1890/1981, 131). Habits and customs are constituted by a unique historical path. To explain a customary order, we must tell a narrative about how the custom or habit was formed and modified in the course of time. If habits bear the imprint of individual history, then customs bear the imprint of social history. Ever since Laplace, the ideal of natural science has been to predict the future from knowledge of the present alone; but the phenomenon of hysteresis shows that, even in physics, knowledge of past history is necessary to predict future changes. Thus, the social sciences, ironically trying to become more "scientific," eliminated history just when history was restored to physics.

Although Paul Samuelson says that to acknowledge hysteresis would be to take economics out of the realm of science and place it in the realm of history, Jon Elster, in his discussion of Georgescu-Roegen's *Entropy Law and the Economic Process*, shows that hysteresis plays an important role in the theory of capital, the theory of consumer behavior, the interpretation of historical materialism, and the mathematical theory of social mobility. The sociological distinction between old money and new money, for example, shows that predicting behavior depends on knowing not only the amount of wealth but the history of that wealth (Elster 1976, 371–2). James Duesenberry was the first to show that one cannot predict current spending patterns on the basis of current income alone: "Past income has an influence on current consumption and saving" (1952, 85). Although it may seem obvious that people attempt to maintain the standard of living to which they have become accustomed, this fact was regarded as a revelation in economic theory. Consumer behavior exhibits a truly habitual hysteresis, as opposed to a reversible magnetic hysteresis, because consumption patterns are not readily reversed: "The irreversibility of income consumption relations produces a sort of 'ratchet effect.' "[26] A rising standard of living threatens one's habits much less than does a falling standard of living.

We have thus far tended to use the terms "habit" and "custom" interchangeably. Yet to grasp the centrality of custom and habit to social theory, we must be careful to distinguish social custom from individual habit. Customs are social patterns of behavior with norma-tive import; customs are rooted in individual habit, but they reside in the collectivity. Customs cannot exist apart from habits, but idiosyn-cratic habits can exist apart from customs:

> The mores [i.e., customs] come down to us from the past. Each individual is born into them as he is born into the atmosphere, and he does not reflect on them, or criticize them any more than a baby analyzes the atmosphere before he begins to breathe it. Each one is subjected to the influence of the mores, and formed by them, before he is capable of reasoning about them. (Sumner 1906, 76)

Customs are an indissoluble unity of empirical facts and normative values; customs demand conformity simply by being customs.[27] Two aspects of this unity can be distinguished though not separated. First, customs are binding due to force of habit: "It is the essence of routine to insist upon its own continuation" (Dewey 1922/1957, 71). Second, customs are binding because they signify membership in a commu-nity: Since even the most trivial activities can signify community, they are experienced as binding.

Many organisms have individual habits without having any social customs. From an evolutionary point of view, the question emerges: What causes habits to become customs in certain species? The an-swer seems to be the proclivity to imitative behavior: Where habits are learned through social imitation, we have the beginnings of cus-tom. Aristotle traced the origin of drama to the innate human pro-pensity to imitation: "Imitation is natural to man from childhood, one of his advantages over the lower animals being this, that he is the most imitative creature in the world, and learns at first by imita-tion" (*Poet.* 1448b 6). After several decades of behaviorist research asserting that the child's capacity for imitation must be learned, many developmental psychologists were astounded by Meltzoff and Moore's demonstration that newborn infants can imitate facial ex-pressions.[28] Psychology and human ethology are returning to the Aristotelian view that imitation, like habit formation, is a key part of our biological inheritance. Jerome Bruner (1972) has adopted an evolutionary perspective and argues that since imitation is pervasive among the higher primates, it must have evolved along with human communication skills as an adaptation to an existence increasingly dominated by culture. Since, as we have observed, human physiol-ogy evolved in part due to the selective advantages of his culture, imitation is of great adaptive importance in a species whose pro-longed immaturity makes possible a great deal of observation of the behavior of adults. The imitative behavior of children can be seen as a type of play that facilitates the transmission of cultural skills from one generation to the next.

Imitation is at the center of the mother–infant relationship in all primates, especially humans. Developmental psychologists have discovered a complex nonverbal communication of great subtlety between mothers and two-month-old infants. Through mutual imitation, mother and infant learn to sequence and to coordinate their facial gestures to elicit the desired responses. Not only is this communicative activity the most complex activity of an infant, but many ethologists and psychologists believe that the developmental mastery of language and of tool skills depends on the arena of mother–child interaction.[29] From both a phylogenetic and an ontogenetic perspective, then, imitation emerges as a mechanism for learning social skills; and yet, as a by-product, imitation is conveniently preadapted for learning productive skills. Just as feathers evolved for warmth but were preadapted for flight, so imitation evolved for social skills but is preadapted for productive skills (see Clementson-Mohr 1982, 67).

When one considers the human species over time and place, it is clear that little of what we know is learned by deliberate instruction when compared to what we learn by observation and imitation. Indeed, even in the context of formal instruction, it has long been known that students learn in part by treating their teachers as role models. Among all primates, adults teach by example and children learn by imitation – or what is aptly called "aping." Scientific study of primates has shown how protocustoms emerge among primates. In one laboratory, a chimp learned how to use a drinking fountain; what began as an individual habit became a social custom when the other chimps learned this skill by imitation; drinking from a fountain is now a permanent tradition for this colony of chimps. But the most remarkable example of the rise of customs among primates comes from the work of the Japanese Monkey Center, where groups of macaques have been isolated on small islands to study the emergence of different customs. On one island, a young female macaque began to wash the sand off sweet potatoes before eating them; in addition, she discovered how to separate wheat from sand by throwing the mixture on the water and skimming off the wheat from the surface. These discoveries quickly spread by imitation and they are now the established customs of this island colony.[30] As Aristotle suggests in his discussion of the origins of dramatic art, imitation plays many roles in human social life in addition to its central role in education. The phenomenon of cultural and technological diffusion, the behavior of crowds, the ease with which people are indoctrinated, the disposition to conformity, all presuppose the proclivity to imitate.

Customs have two dimensions which are separable in thought but not in reality – the synchronic and the diachronic. At the synchronic level, there are in turn two primary features: Customs reside in the collectivity, and customs are sign-systems. Individuals do not have customs; individuals participate in customs.[31] Although individual habits can, if imitated, create social customs, in general social customs create individual habits because we form our habits within the context of social customs. Nonetheless, by learning customs we modify and distort them; by imitating social customs we introduce variation: Our linguistic habits, for example, modify our customary language leading to the dramatic transformations of languages over time.[32] Weber rightly terms custom "a collective way of acting (*Massenhandeln*)" (1925/1978, 25). What Saussure says of language is true of all customs:

> It is a fund accumulated by the members of the community through the practice of speech, a grammatical system existing potentially in every brain, or more exactly in the brains of a group of individuals; for the language is never complete in any single individual, but exists perfectly only in the collectivity. (1916/1986, 13)

All customs are signs that convey meaning to the community. Weber thought that many of the customs that constitute everyday life are devoid of meaning, but every custom, no matter how trivial, is still a sign of membership in a community.[33] Linguistic customs – like ritual greetings – convey no information, but function to signify inclusion in a community. Indeed, knowing the local custom is like knowing the local language: Without such knowledge, we would not know how to express affection, concern, anger, or gratitude. Customs are more than mere social uniformities of habit; customs are organized into complex systems of meaning as, for example, Lévi-Strauss has shown with customs of naming plants and animals.

Customs are fundamentally constituted by history. The structure of our institutions, our behavior, our language, cannot be explained in terms of its current function. Our institutions are the sediment of thousands of years of human practices; the sheer inertia of this historical inheritance resists adaptation to current functional needs.[34] There is an analogy between the evolution of cutoms and the evolution of species. Organisms inherit a bodily architecture that constrains the possible future paths of development. "In many cases, evolutionary pathways reflect inherited patterns more than current environmental demands" (Gould 1983, 156). Humans, for example, suffer chronic backaches and hernias because our spinal vertebrae are the product of a long line of four-footed ancestors; we are not well designed for walking upright. "Evolution cannot achieve engineering perfection because it must work with inherited parts available from previous histories in different contexts" (Gould 1985, 210). We can compare this view of natural evolution with Lévi-Strauss's view of the historical construction of myth: He calls the patchwork of myth a "bricolage," because the "bricoleur" uses whatever has been inherited:

> His universe of instruments is closed and the rules of the game are always to make do with "whatever is at hand," that is to say with a set of tools and materials which is always finite and is also heterogeneous because what it contains bears no relation to the current project, or indeed to any particular project, but is the contingent result of all the occasions there have been to renew or enrich the stock or to maintain it with the remains of previous constructions or destructions. (1962, 17)

Like Gould, Lévi-Strauss contrasts the customary order of history to the stipulated order of the engineer.

The role of history in natural or customary evolution is most evident in cases where structure and function do not correspond. This lack of correspondence can be due either to inherited architectural constraints or to the presence of vestigial elements.[35] Indeed, the founder of modern anthropology, E. B. Tylor, illustrates the distant historical origin of customs by offering examples of vestigial customs, which he terms "survivals" (1871/1958, 16). He describes these survivals as "meaningless customs" (94). But here is where the analogy between biological and customary evolution misleads us: Vestigial organs can indeed lose their function and become meaningless, but customs are never meaningless. Customs that lose their original function can easily take on a new function: Thus, the useless buttons on clothes become fashionable. And customs, unlike organs, are always signs of membership in a community.

Yet even where structure is perfectly adapted to function, we cannot assume that a structure is the product of its function. The feathers of birds seem ideally suited to flight, but feathers evolved for warmth not flight. "In short, the principle of preadaptation simply asserts that a structure can change its function radically without altering its form as much" (Gould 1977, 108). The absence of a one-to-one correspondence between a structure and its functions undermines the attempt to account for a structure simply in terms of its current function. Social institutions like the division of labor are the product of a long historical inheritance; yet from Plato to E. O. Wilson, the division of labor is explained only in terms of its supposed efficiency. Studies of alternative job designs cast considerable doubt on the view that the prevailing social division of labor in the factory and the office is especially efficient; but even if one were to grant that the division of labor in a modern factory is uniquely efficient, we still have not shown that it can be explained by its efficiency. The social division of labor in a typical office between male professionals and female clericals is the product of ancient domestic customs; even if it were shown that this sexual division of labor is uniquely efficient, we still could not explain it by that efficiency. Only knowledge of the particular historical path of an institution can determine whether a structure is the product of inherited patterns or current utility. Is the pervasive division of labor between those who plan and those who execute required for current efficiency? Or is it simply the persistence of traditional relations between masters and servants?

We are now in a position to grasp the synchronic logic of the customary division of labor. The one universally valid rule governing the division of labor is that every human society divides labor by sex. This rule is purely formal: It does not specify how tasks are divided; it states only that tasks are in fact divided. At the synchronic level, then, we can say two things about the customary division of labor: The first is that there tends to be a binary opposition so that tasks performed by men are forbidden to women, while tasks performed by women are forbidden to men; the second is that male tasks – no matter what the content – will be more highly valued than female tasks. As the structuralists have rightly emphasized, what is most important in customary patterns of behavior is the opposition of meaning: What is crucial, in other words, is the hierarchical division of tasks into male and female tasks; how the tasks are divided is much less important. The division of even the most mundane human activities into male and female tasks endows them with the rich symbolic connotations associated with sexual difference. The Jibaros of Ecuador, for example, "attribute to every plant either male or female sex . . . the male plants must be cultivated by men and the female by women" (Thurnwald 1932, 65). It would be ludicrous to suggest that such a division of labor is determined by the natural differences between the sexes; rather, these Indians have made use of sexual difference to create a binary system of meaning. Customary patterns of the division of labor convey symbolic meaning just as does art, religion, and poetry; indeed, anthropologists have shown that even the most allegedly natural human activities, such as cooking, eating, drinking, and bathing, are full of symbolic and speculative meaning. We tend to look to such elemental production and consumption as natural in contrast to the higher cultural activities of art, religion, and poetry. But this is an unfounded prejudice. Custom creates systems of metaphor, analogy, and allegory in every realm of human activity; and these customary patterns of meaning are not reducible to natural causes.[36]

All attempts to account for the sexual division of labor solely on the basis of innate natural capacities have failed. Malinowski, for example, commenting on the sexual division of labor among Australian aborigines, says "heavier work ought naturally to be performed by the man, [though] the contrary obtains"; therefore, he concludes, "compulsion is the chief basis of this division of labor" (cited in Herskovits 1952, 128). Malinowski, like Aristotle, contrasts here what is natural with what is compulsory; however, if men are by nature stronger than women, then it is just as natural for men to compel women to do the heavy work as it is for men to do it themselves. Whether male strength is used to dominate women or to perform heavy labor is determined, then, by custom. Natural strength cannot be the basis for the sexual division of labor because some women are stronger than some men. If natural strength were the basis for the division of labor, then we would expect to see the heaviest work performed by the strongest men and the strongest women, while the lightest work would be performed by the weakest women and the weakest men; yet we never see this pattern: Work is divided not by strength but by sex. Phyllis Kaberry correctly notes that the sexual division of labor among the aborigines has nothing to do with the strength requirements of tasks; rather "the men go out to hunt, the women to forage" (cited in Herskovits 1952, 128). The contrast between hunting and foraging is full of symbolic meaning that has little to do with physiological requirements.

In those societies without agriculture, both past and present, it seems to be a universal pattern that men hunt and women forage. Is this division of labor natural? E. O. Wilson asserts that this primitive division of labor "appears to have a genetic origin"; Wilson believes that men have a genetic disposition to hunt and women to forage (1975a, 48). But this division of labor may simply be an accidental by-product of women's reproductive role. Childbearing periodically keeps women at home, so they tend to specialize in tasks that can be done at home. Since "practice makes perfect," it is often efficient for people to specialize even when they have identical aptitudes. We can, therefore, explain this primitive sexual division of labor without recourse to genetic speculation – except insofar as childbearing is genetically restricted to women.

Diachronic analysis reveals how custom creates analogies between activities over time. To explain how specific tasks are sexually divided, for example, we must know the particular historical genealogy whereby each sex becomes symbolically linked to specific tasks. In some societies pottery is made by women, while in other societies it is made by men. Melville Herskovits describes how the pattern of historical inheritance can produce either form of this customary division of labor: Men who hunted or kept herds became associated with large animals, just as women who foraged became associated with plants. When beasts of burden became attached to a plow, tilling the soil could become associated either with men (due to their links to animals) or with women (due to their links with plants). Next, when these beasts were used to pull a cart, the wheel became associated with the sex linked to tilling the soil. Finally, when pottery was turned on a wheel, it became associated with the sex linked to the wheel (Herskovitz 1952, 129–30).[37]

This genealogy nicely illustrates the historical order of custom: There is a distinct causal pattern, but no rigid determinism. One could apply a similar analysis to show why women, for example, tend to enter some professions (medicine) rather than others and even learn some languages (French) rather than others – there is usually some customary association at work. The conventions of custom may be initially arbitrary, but over time they develop associations that are far from arbitrary. As Lévi-Strauss observes, there is no necessary relation between the color red and the concept of danger; but over time, red has become associated with danger. When traffic lights were introduced, the use of red for "stop" was not arbitrary, but the product of history. "To simplify my argument, I will say that the linguistic sign is arbitrary *a priori*, but ceases to be arbitrary *a posteriori*" (Lévi-Strauss 1963, 91).[38] The customary division of labor makes use of natural differences between the sexes, but the order of custom certainly cannot be explained by these natural differences.

The stipulated division of labor

Customs are rooted in habit; customary thought and practice are unreflective routines. How then does thought become reflective and practice become deliberate? The pragmatists insist that obstacles to routine create the occasion for reflection: If my key will not turn the bolt, I begin to reflect on the nature of locks.[39] Peirce argues that we reflect on our customary modes of thought – our prejudices – only when an anomaly disconfirms our tacit beliefs: "Thus, surprise is very efficient in breaking up associations of ideas" (in Hartshorne and

Weiss 1960, 5.478). Just as obstacles in habitual routines generate individual reflection, so conflicts over customary practices generate social reflection. Legal stipulation is the attempt to resolve conflict that arises within the realm of custom: "Custom begins to be law when it is brought into dispute and some means is provided for declaring or recognizing its obligatory character" (Lobingier 1930). In the same way, the conflict between capitalists and workers brought customary work routines into contention; managers stipulated ever new divisions of labor in the attempt to reduce industrial conflict.[40]

The transition from custom to stipulation has two related features: The habitual becomes the object of reflection; and the social system of custom becomes reduced to a synoptic perspective. A stipulated order is designed by an individual author or by a collective body acting as an individual.[41] The process of reflection or deliberation is always a conversation: either the internal conversation of thought (*in foro interno*) or the external conversation of politics (*in foro externo*).[42] But the product of reflection always aspires to the synoptic perspective of an individual author. The linguist stipulates a grammar both by reflecting on the habitual use of language and by reducing the social system of language to a synoptic perspective. The grammarian, the legislator, the philosopher, the engineer, all strive to impose a synoptic unity to the social system of custom.

The view that stipulation always presupposes custom, even as it modifies custom, avoids two common misunderstandings about the relation of custom to stipulation. The first misunderstanding is the pervasive traditional claim that social institutions may be attributed simply to the stipulation of an individual. In this way, the ancient Greeks ascribed virtually all social institutions – morals, constitutions, money, even language – to individual authors. Similarly, Cartesian method illustrates the reduction of philosophical reason to individual stipulation: We first set aside all habits of thought through systematic doubt, and we then construct our knowledge from a strictly synoptic perspective.[43] Against this view, Dewey insists that reflection expresses a conflict of custom and that the duty of reflection is to reorganize custom (1922/1957, 73).[44]

The second common misunderstanding arose in response to the first: Ever since the importance of custom was rediscovered in the eighteenth century, many theorists have asserted that language and other social institutions are the product of custom alone, that individual stipulation plays no role at all. Savigny, for example, argued that legal stipulation could no more modify custom than a grammarian could modify language. Saussure shares this view: "No individual is able, even if he wished, to modify in any way a choice already established in the language. Nor can the linguistic community exercise its authority to change even a single word" (1916/1986, 71).[45] Modern structuralists often describe the individual mind as simply the unwitting vehicle for customary sign systems: Customs have reasons unknown to individuals (see Lévi-Strauss 1962, 252). Within this all-powerful social system of custom, the individual is "decentered" or even "dissolved." Peirce anticipated this line of thought when he observed that it is more just to say that we are in thought, than to say that thoughts are in us (in Hartshorne and Weiss 1960, 5.289n). Neither extreme position is plausible: In the realm of custom, we are vehicles for language and ritual; but in the realm of stipulation, we turn language and ritual into vehicles for the synoptic projects of an agent.

From an epistemic point of view, the distinction between custom and stipulation is the distinction between what Gilbert Ryle calls "knowing how" and "knowing that," or "learning how" and "learning that." And just as custom is logically prior to stipulation, so knowing how is prior to knowing that. We learn how to do something through imitation and habit; we learn that something is the case by an explicit set of rules. Ryle shows that knowing how is logically prior to knowing that because the rules or principles governing an activity presupposes the exhibition of those rules in practice. "Rules, like birds, must live before they can be stuffed." Knowing how to do something exhibits the implicit knowledge of its principles, canons, and rules; but knowing the rules and principles certainly does not imply knowing how to do something. Only by knowing how to cook can one write a cookbook, just as only by knowing how to conduct experiments can one formulate hypotheses. The stipulation of rules, principles, and canons does not generate habitual practices; rather, habitual practices generate stipulated knowledge. What, then, is the use of stipulated rules and principles if they are not required for knowing how to do something? Ryle suggests that stipulated rules, though not necessary, may help the novice acquire the proper habits of action; too much attention to the rules of knowing that, however, actually becomes an impediment to knowing how – reflection interferes with the smooth operation of habit.[46]

Any theory of education must find the appropriate mix of customary learning how and stipulated knowing that. Although rationalist educators believe that we should cultivate reflective awareness of our activities, Whitehead insisted that it is much more efficient to operate from unthinking habit. "Civilization advances by extending the number of operations which we can perform without thinking about them." But

Aristotle insists that reflective stipulation plays a crucial role in learning how to adjust, subdue, and redirect our habits; in the words of Peter Medawar, "Civilization also advances by bringing instinctive [i.e., habitual] activities within the domain of rational thought, by making them reasonable, proper and co-operative." Learning, says Medawar, is thus a twofold process: We learn to make deliberate thought habitual, and we learn to make our habitual operations the subject of deliberate thought (1976, 500–1).

The logic of stipulation is especially evident in the case of law. Law is the deliberate stipulation of an individual or of a legislature acting as an individual; as such, law stands in sharp contrast to the habitual and collective order of custom. Yet one often hears of "customary law." The expression "customary law" usually refers simply to law stipulated by a judge, as opposed to law stipulated by the sovereign. The metaphor "customary law" implies an analogy between legal norms and customary norms, which serves only to blur the distinction between the two. Legal officials stipulate laws to reinforce, reform, alter, or abolish customary norms; in every case, law presupposes custom. Legal stipulation has a double relation to custom: First, substantive law resolves conflicts that arise in the customs and practices of nonlegal institutions; second, procedural law resolves conflicts that arise in the customs of specifically legal institutions (see Bohannan 1965).

Aristotle described custom both as "second nature" and as "unwritten law." We find the same metaphorical assimilation of custom to nature and to stipulation in the doctrines of natural law theorists and positivist legal theorists. The legal positivists Bentham and Austin, for example, argued that all social norms, including customs, are in principle sovereign commands: "For this purpose they invoked the idea of a 'tacit,' or 'indirect,' command resting on the principle that whatever the sovereign permits he commands" (Hart 1967). This effort to incorporate custom into the realm of stipulation completely effaces all that is distinctive of custom. By contrast, advocates of natural law subsume custom into the order of nature. Natural law has long been invoked to account for the phenomenon of norms outside of stipulated law. These norms include the standards for judging the justice of positive law, the rules that govern behavior where there is no law (law between nations), and the reasons why people obey the law even when sanctions are improbable. The existence of such norms is undeniable; but why should we call these norms "natural"? Custom is a much more accurate description of the origin and character of such norms. Indeed, natural law (*ius naturale*) in Roman jurisprudence is derived from the law of nations (*ius gentium*); the law of nations was simply the codification of the customs of the various Italian tribes and other non-Roman peoples. The metaphor of the "natural law" implied an analogy between the universality of nature and the universality of certain customary norms – so what was common to the various Italian and foreign customs became defined as natural law.

The historical derivation of the *ius natural* from the *ius gentium* reflects a deep confusion about the origin and character of social norms that are not explicitly stipulated. As Suarez points out, that a set of customs is universal does not make them natural – they could be diffused by imitation. Here Aristotle's progressive hierarchy serves to sort out the competing claims made for natural law, customary law, and positive law. I suggest that we distinguish law as a species of social order from jurisprudence as the explanation of law. Thus, law is essentially stipulated, but the jurisprudential explanation of law requires us to make use of our nature, custom, and stipulation trichotomy. Law, like any form of stipulation, presupposes natural order and customary order; but nature and custom cannot stipulate law – only a rational will can stipulate law. There is no such thing, in short, as a natural or a customary law; rather, nature and custom are categories belonging to the jurisprudential explanation of law.[47]

How, then, does the customary division of labor become the object of reflections? Adam Smith tells us that he discovered the importance of the division of labor in society by studying the division of labor within a firm (1776/1979, 1:1, 14). Indeed, the capitalist factory led not just Smith, but a host of managers and workers to reflect on the division of labor. The earliest factories were simply agglomerations of traditional crafts organized by a customary division of labor (see Braverman 1974, 59; Marglin 1976, 28). Gradually, managers began to break up customary modes of production and then reconstitute them on a new basis. At first, managers assumed control over the acquisition of raw materials and the marketing of the product; then, managers assumed control over the productive process itself and stipulated both the technical and the social division of labor. Marx was the first economist to thematize the role of deliberate stipulation in the design of the division of labor within a factory. According to Marx, the assignment of workers to tasks in manufacturing follows "a fixed mathematical relation" that "has been experimentally established" (1867/1967, 1:327). There is no doubt that the industrial conflict between owners and workers is a fundamental reason why customary modes of production became the object of deliberate stipulation; managers found that highly detailed divisions of labor reduced the autonomy and power of workers.

The stipulated social division of labor in the modern factory or office is based on the principle of the separation of conception from execution: Managers plan and workers execute. According to the classical political economists, including Marx, this division of labor is the product simply of the rational quest for maximum profit. There is, thus, considerable agreement that the stipulated division of labor is simply a function of rational economic calculation. Yet it is easy to show that the capitalist division of labor is not simply the product of profit maximization: It also reflects various historical customs. The contrast between Marx and Burke is instructive on this point. Marx saw a radical discontinuity between the rationally stipulated relations of capitalist production and the customary relations of feudal production:

> The bourgeoisie, wherever it has got the upper hand, has put an end to all feudal, patriarchal, idyllic relations. It has pitilessly torn asunder the motley feudal ties that bound men to his "natural superiors," and has left remaining no other nexus between man and man than naked self-interest, than callous "cash payment." (Marx and Engels 1848/1976, 486–7)

Burke, by contrast, saw considerable continuity between the feudal relations of masters and servants and the capitalist relations of employer and employee.[48] This fact helps to explain the apparent paradox that Burke could simultaneously champion traditional feudal hierarchy and the capitalist market economy. Far from being paradoxical, Burke insisted not only that capitalism needed feudal hierarchy, but that capitalism is the best way to preserve hierarchy in a changing world.[49] Burke, in short, defended legislation promoting capitalist relations of production because he believed that they embodied traditional customs of class dominance and subordination.

Burke's emphasis on the role of custom in the capitalist division of labor is well justified by the historical evidence. The separation of conception from execution in the modern firm is directly derived from the customs governing the relation of master and servant. The traditional master, like the modern employer, has the right to specify not only what shall be done, but how it shall be done.[50] Similarly, the capitalist employer owns the produce of labor just as did the slave employer. James Mill noted the similarity between slave production and capitalist production: "The only difference is, in the mode of purchasing [labor]."[51] Many early factories were associated with prisons, orphanages, and workhouses so that the division of factory labor assimilated customs derived from forced labor. The principle of unity of command and the separation of line from staff functions in the modern firm derive from military practices.[52] Marx often remarked on the analogy between the factory regime and the army; but he usually failed to mention that there is a direct causal relation (1867/ 1967, 1:314). The capitalist division of labor turns out to embody many feudal customs, just as any form of stipulation presupposes customary norms.

Although the factory regime has antecedents in the deployment of slaves and the deployment of soldiers, the deliberately stipulated division of labor did not become general until the rise of modern industrial firms. According to Adam Smith, the division of labor is "more easily understood" if we see the firm as a microcosm of society. The firm generates reflection in the same way that all miniaturization generates reflection: by making relations more perspicuous to the mind. Lévi-Strauss sees the miniature as the universal type of the work of art, because it reveals the structural relations obscured by size: "In other words, the intrinsic value of a small-scale model is that it compensates for the renunciation of sensible dimensions by the acquisition of intelligible dimensions" (1962, 24). Before the factory, the production of a complex product involved the cooperative efforts of many spatially dispersed tradesmen; it was only when their disparate efforts were concentrated within a factory that the logic of the customary division of labor became apparent. Perspicuity has long been known as an aid to comprehension and reflection: The development of writing makes language more perspicuous and leads to reflection on the grammatical structure of language; law existed before writing, but writing clearly aided the rise of legal stipulation out of custom; and the development of perspicuous notation was crucial to the development of formal logic. The firm, as a miniature version of social production, is where stipulation shapes the customary division of labor.

Notes

This chapter develops themes found in my book, *The Moral Economy of Labor: Aristotelian Themes in Economic Theory* (New Haven, CT: Yale University Press, 1993), ch. 2.

1. For a critique and reconstruction of Poinsot's doctrine of signs, see Murphy (1991, 33–68).
2. Karl Menger's seminal use of this distinction is in *Problems of Economics and Sociology* (1883/1963, 130). For Georgescu-Roegen's claim, see *The Entropy Law and the Economic Process* (1971, 11).
3. "Example: In logic, 'or' can be defined in terms of 'not' and 'and'; also, 'and' can be defined in terms of 'not' and 'or' " (Wells 1977, 8).

4. On the logical structure of metaphor and analogy, see Perelman and Olbrechts-Tyteca (1969, 370–410).

5. Pierre Duhem says, "The history of physics shows us that the search for analogies between two distinct categories of phenomena has perhaps been the surest and most fruitful method of all the procedures put into play in the construction of physical theories." Cited in Mirowski (1989, 277–8).

6. David Bloor agrees that our concepts of natural order derive in part "because of their assumed utility for purposes of justification, legitimation, and social persuasion" (1982, 283).

7. "Simplifying a great deal, it may be said that castes picture themselves as natural species while totemic groups picture natural species as castes" Lévi-Strauss (1962, 127).

8. On the compatibility of several analogies with a single metaphor, see Perelman and Olbrechts-Tyteca (1969, 400–1).

9. Pascal actually performed such a reversal: "Custom is a second nature which destroys the former. But what is nature? For is custom not natural? I am much afraid that nature is itself only a first custom as custom is a second nature" (in Trotter 1958, par. 93).

10. "Without men, no culture, certainly; but equally, and more significantly, without culture, no men" (Geertz 1973, 48–9).

11. "My standpoint," wrote Marx, is that "from which the evolution of the economic formation of society is viewed as a process of natural history" (Feuer 1978, 111).

12. This comment is confused because Wilson neglects the fundamental fact that humans would find it efficient to specialize even if all persons had identical aptitudes.

13. On the theory of emergence and its importance for a nonreductionist biology, see Mayr (1982, 59–67).

14. For the story of how habit was jettisoned from sociology, see Camic (1986). See also Weber (1925/1978, 24–5) and Parsons (1937/1949, 44–8, 762–5).

15. For a contemporary neoclassical argument that habits are optimizing strategies, see Ault and Ekelund (1988).

16. Nowhere is Kant's radical departure from Aristotelian philosophy more evident than in his resolute opposition to habit and custom: "Customary habit (*assuetudo*), however, is a physical and inner compulsion to proceed farther in the very same way in which we have been traveling. Acquired habit deprives good actions of their moral value because it undermines mental freedom. . . . Generally, all acquired habits are objectionable." Habit, adds Kant, places us "in the same class as the beast" (1800/1978, 35). "The more habits a man allows himself to form, the less free and independent he becomes; for it is the same with man as with all other animals; whatever he has been accustomed to early in life always retains a certain attraction for him in later-life. Children, therefore, must be prevented from forming any habits, nor should habits be fostered in them" (1803/1960, 45).

17. On the origin of neoclassical economics in classical energy physics see Mirowski (1989). "The mathematics of pre-entropic physics was the pinnacle of the development of static mechanism, where all physical phenomena are portrayed as being perfectly reversible in time, and no system exhibits hysteresis. Nineteenth-century physical laws were thought, by definition, to possess no history" (Mirowski 1986, 189).

18. According to Thomas Aquinas, there are two necessary conditions for the possibility of habit: "First, the possessor of the state (*dispositio*) must be distinct from the realization of the capacity, and must stand to it in the relation of potentiality to actuality. . . . Second, it must be possible for the unactualized subject to actualize its potentialities in more than one way, and with regard to more than one object." *Summa Theologiae*, I–II, Q. 49, art. 4. C. S. Peirce interprets this field of potentialities as indeterminacy: "For without such fortuitous variation, habit-taking would be impossible; and intellect consists in a plasticity of habit" (in Hartshorne and Weiss 1960, 6.86). "Plasticity, then, in the wide sense of the word, means the possession of a structure weak enough to yield to an influence, but strong enough not to yield all at once. Each relatively stable phase of equilibrium is marked by what we may call a new set of habits" (James 1890/1991, 110).

19. See Gregory (1987, s.v. 'Instinct') and Thompson (1977).

20. As Thomas Jefferson observed, "All experience hath shewn, that mankind are more disposed to suffer, while evils are sufferable, than to right themselves by abolishing the forms to which they are accustomed" (United States Declaration of Independence).

21. According to William Estes: "Investigations ranging over the entire phylogenetic scale, and often using similar or even identical stimuli, demonstrate very similar properties for habituation from one-celled organisms to man. There is, however, no reason to think that the neural basis is the same in organisms at very different levels. Rather, functional properties appear to be those demanded by requirements of adaptation" (1978, 245–6).

22. "For every habit has, or is, a general law" (Peirce, in Hartshorne and Weiss 1960, 2.148). "Habituation of response to a given stimulus exhibits stimulus generalization to other stimuli" (Tighe and Leaton 1976, 331).

23. Richard Robinson defines a concept as a habit of thinking in *Definition* (1950, 187–88). In a handbook of psychology we find this definition: "Concept: Any perceptual or representational habit, because all [habits] are more or less abstract or generalized or conceptual" (M. Marx 1970, 3:325). Learning is the transfer to habits from one situation to others: "The principal mechanism assumed to underlie the transfer of learning to new situations is stimulus generalization. This notion is represented in the theory by the assumption that, when a habit has been acquired relating a particular stimulus to a given response, the habit strength is automatically generalized to other stimuli which are similar to the given one" (Estes 1970, 99).

24. "The first category of 'nonreversibility' consists of all processes which, though not reversible, can return to any previously attained phase. . . .

Processes such as these are nonreversible but not irrevocable" (Georgescu-Roegen 1971, 197).

25. On irreversible nature of entropy (what Peirce calls "nonconservative forces") and on the plasticity of entropy, see Peirce (in Hartshorne and Weiss 1960, 7.471, 6.2). "The thermodynamic principles, therefore, leave some substantial freedom to the actual path and the time schedule of an entropic process" (Georgescu-Roegen 1971, 12).

26. "The fundamental psychological postulate underlying our argument is that it is harder for a family to reduce its expenditures from a high level than for a family to refrain from making high expenditures in the first place" (Duesenberry 1952, 114).

27. "The notion of right is in the folkways. It is not outside of them, of independent origin, and brought to them to test them. In the folkways, whatever is, is right" (Sumner 1906, 28). As John Dewey says, "Customs in any case constitute moral standards" (1922/1957, 70).

28. For a behaviorist argument that imitation is learned, see Miller and Dollard (1941). For the view that imitation is caused by an "innate releasing mechanism," see Eibl-Eibesfeldt (1989, 55–6). Meltzoff and Moore, however, did not conclude that imitation is innate: "In brief, we hypothesize that the imitative responses observed are not innately organized and 'released,' but are accomplished through an active matching process and mediated by an abstract representational system" (1987, 78).

29. Judy Dunn describes these interactions: "She [the mother] watches, subdues her own responses, follows and supports the baby's animated mood by imitating his expressions, holding back when it is his 'turn,' uses rhythmic touching, calling, and moving to keep him interested and sociable. . . . Through these joint games and through his mother's responses to his actions, the baby begins to understand what his actions and expressions 'mean' for other people, and begins to use them with intention in a social context" (1976, 482).

30. For these and other examples of the evolution of custom, see Bonner (1980, 166–77).

31. "The mores are social rituals in which we all participate unconsciously" (Sumner 1906, 62).

32. "In this educative process customs may be thought of as preceding habits, but if this were the whole story the weight of the past would repress all innovation, all readjustment, all development" (MacIver and Page 1950, 196).

33. "Custom ever signifies community" (Toennies, 1909/1961, 98).

34. This is not to deny that customs are subject to adaptive pressures: "The folkways are, therefore, 1) subject to a strain of improvement towards better adaptation of means to ends, as long as the [prior] adaptation is so imperfect that pain is produced. They are also 2) subject to a strain of consistency with each other, because they all answer their several purposes with less friction and antagonism when they cooperate and support each other" (Sumner 1906, 5).

35. "The best illustrations of adaptation by evolution are the ones that strike our intuition as peculiar or bizarre" (Gould 1977, 91).

36. Kinship terminologies, for example, are based not on biological relations, but on metaphors of engendering and rearing; animals are taboo not because of gastronomic analogies, but because of symbolic analogies; rituals of purification are not based on hygiene. See Douglas and Isherwood (1979, 60–1).

37. A similar genealogy is described by Richard Thurnwald: "We have, therefore, two branches of progress from the hunter stage. The one, roughly speaking, leads from the hunting activity of the men to pastoral life, the other, from the collecting activity of the women to the tilling of the soil. Plough cultivation, where they meet, represents the fusion of these two main branches" (1932, 7).

38. Aristotle makes the same point: He defines legal justice as "that which is originally indifferent, but when it has been laid down is not indifferent" (*Nicomachean Ethics* 1134b 20).

39. "Reflection," says Dewey, is the "painful effort of disturbed habits to readjust themselves" (1922/1957, 71). According to Martin Heidegger, it is only when the hammer breaks that one reflects on the nature of tools: "When its unusability is thus discovered, equipment becomes conspicuous" (1927/1962, par. 16).

40. On the role of industrial conflict in generating new forms of the division of labor, see Edwards (1979).

41. Thus, we speak of the "will of the Congress"; legislation that is the product of collective debate is usually attributed to an individual author.

42. Thus, for Aristotle, moral wisdom (*phronesis*) is identical to political wisdom (*politike*) (*Nicomachean Ethics* 1141b 22).

43. As Descartes says, "There is very often less perfection in works composed of several portions, and carried out by the hands of various masters, than in those on which one individual alone has worked" (in Haldane and Ross 1931, 1:87). Karl Popper, however, seeks to show "the social character of reasonableness, as opposed to intellectual gifts, or cleverness. Reason, like language, can be said to be a product of social life" (1966, 2:225).

44. According to Peirce, philosophy arises out of custom: "We cannot begin with complete doubt. We must begin with all the prejudices which we actually have when we enter upon the study of philosophy" (in Hartshorne and Weiss 1960, 5.264).

45. Saussure is wrong on both counts: Languages have been profoundly altered both by individual authors (like Chaucer, Dante, and Luther) and by public authorities (like the French and Prussian academies).

46. "In short the propositional acknowledgement of rules, reasons, or principles is not the parent of the intelligent application of them; it is a stepchild of that application" (Ryle 1945–6, 9).

47. For a more expansive effort to make sense of the conflicting claims made for natural law, customary law, and positive law, see Murphy (1990).

48. "No slave was ever so beneficial to the master as a freeman that deals with him on an equal footing by convention, formed on the rules and principles of contending interests and comprised advantages" (Burke 1795, 262).
49. See MacPherson (1980, 63). J. G. A. Pocock concurs with MacPherson on this point: "Burke declared that manners [which Pocock terms *consuetudines*] must precede commerce, rather than the other way round, and that modern European society need and must not sever its roots in a chivalric and ecclesiastical past" (1985, 209–10).
50. In *Black's Law Dictionary*, under "employee" we read, "Employee" is synonymous with "servant." The standard work on employer–employee law is Batt, *The Law of Master and Servant* (1929).
51. "He [employer of wage labor] is equally therefore the owner of the labour, with the manufacturer who operates with slaves" (Mill 1826, 21).
52. "It was unfortunate for society at large that a large power–organization like the army, rather than the more human and cooperative craft-guild, presided over the birth of the modern forms of the machine" (Mumford 1934, 96).

References

Ault, Richard, and Ekelund, Robert. 1988. "Habits in Economic Analysis: Veblen and the Neoclassicals," *History of Political Economy* 20:431–45.

Batt, Francis. 1929. *The Law of Master and Servant*. New York: Pitman.

Bausor, Randall. 1986. "Time and Equilibrium," in P. Mirowski, ed., *The Reconstruction of Economic Theory*, 93–135. Boston: Kluwer-Nijhoff.

Black, Henry. 1979. *Black's Law Dictionary*, 6th ed. St. Paul, MN: West.

Bloor, David. 1982. "Durkheim and Mauss Revisited: Classification and the Sociology of Knowledge," *Studies in the History and Philosophy of Science* 13:267–97.

Bohannan, Paul. 1965. "The Differing Realms of the Law," in Laura Nader, ed., *The Ethnography of Law*, American Anthropologist 67:33–42.

Bonner, John Tyler. 1980. *The Evolution of Culture in Animals*. Princeton, NJ: Princeton University Press.

Braverman, Harry. 1974. *Labor and Monopoly Capital*. New York: Monthly Review Press.

Bruner, Jerome. 1972. "Nature and Uses of Immaturity," *American Psychologist* 27:687–708.

Burke, Edmund. 1839. "Thoughts and Details on Scarcity" (1795), *The Works of Edmund Burke*, vol. 4. Boston: Little Brown.

Camic, Charles. 1986. "The Matter of Habit," *American Journal of Sociology* 91: 1039–87.

Clementson-Mohr, Donald. 1982. "Towards a Social-Cognitive Explanation of Imitation Development," in George Butterworth and Paul Light, eds., *Social Cognition*, 53–74. Chicago: University of Chicago Press.

Collingwood, R. G. 1976. *The Idea of Nature* (1945). Oxford: Oxford University Press.

Condillac, E. B. 1971. *An Essay on the Origin of Human Knowledge,* translated by Thomas Nugent. Gainesville FL: Scholars' Facsimiles & Reprints.

Dewey, John. 1957. *Human Nature and Conduct* (1922). New York: Modern Library.

Dewey, John. 1960. *The Quest for Certainty* (1929). New York: Capricorn Books.

Douglas, Mary. 1986. *How Institutions Think.* Syracuse, NY: Syracuse University Press.

Douglas, Mary, and Isherwood, Baron. 1979. *The World of Goods.* New York: Basic.

Duesenberry, James. 1952. *Income, Saving and the Theory of Consumer Behavior.* Cambridge, MA: Harvard University Press.

Dunn, Judy. 1976. "How Far Do Early Differences in Mother–Child Relations Affect Later Development?" in P. P. G. Bateson and R. A. Hinde, eds., *Growing Points in Ethology,* 481–96. Cambridge University Press.

Durkheim, Emile, and Mauss, Marcel. 1903. *Primitive Classification,* translated and edited by Rodney Needham. London: Cohen & West.

Edwards, Richard. 1979. *Contested Terrain.* New York: Basic.

Eibl-Eibesfeldt, Irenaus. 1989. *Human Ethology.* New York: De Gruyter.

Elster, Jon. 1976. "A Note on Hysteresis in the Social Sciences," *Synthese* 33:371–91.

Estes, William. 1970. *Learning Theory and Mental Development.* New York: Academic Press.

Estes, William, ed. 1978. *Handbook of Learning and Cognitive Processes,* vol. 6. New York: Wiley.

Ferguson, Adam. 1767. *An Essay on the History of Civil Society.* Edinburgh: A. Miller & T. Caddel.

Feuer, Lewis. 1978. "Marx and Engels as Sociobiologists," *Survey* 23:109–36.

Geertz, Clifford. 1973. *The Interpretation of Cultures.* New York: Basic.

Georgescu-Roegen, Nicholas. 1971. *The Entropy Law and the Economic Process.* Cambridge, MA: Harvard University Press.

Gould, S. J. 1977. *Ever Since Darwin.* New York: Norton.

Gould, S. J. 1983. *Hen's Teeth and Horse's Toes.* New York: Norton.

Gould, S. J. 1985. *The Flamingo's Smile.* New York: Norton.

Gregory, Richard, ed. 1987. *The Oxford Companion to the Mind.* Oxford University Press.

Haldane, E. S., and Ross, G. R. T., eds. 1931. *Philosophical Works of Descartes,* vol. 1. Cambridge University Press.

Hart, H. L. A. 1967. "Legal Positivism," *Encyclopedia of Philosophy.* New York: Macmillan.

Hartshorne, Charles, and Weiss, Paul, eds. 1960. *The Collected Papers of Charles Sanders Peirce.* Cambridge, MA: Harvard University Press.

Hayek, F. A. 1979. "Kinds of Order in Society" (1964), in Kenneth Templeton, Jr., ed., *The Politicization of Society,* 501–23. Indianapolis, IN: Liberty Press.

580   **James Bernard Murphy**

Heidegger, Martin. 1962. *Being and Time* (1927), translated by John Macquarrie and Edward Robinson. New York: Harper & Row.

Herskovits, M. 1952. *Economic Anthropology*. New York: Knopf.

Hicks, R. D. 1907. *Aristotle: De Anima*. Cambridge University Press.

James, William. 1981/1890. *The Principles of Psychology*. Cambridge, MA: Harvard University Press.

Kant, Immanuel. 1978/1800. *Anthropology from a Pragmatic Point of View*, translated by Victor Dowdell. Carbondale: Southern Illinois University Press.

Kant, Immanuel. 1960/1803. *Education*, translated by Annette Churton. Ann Arbor: University of Michigan Press.

Lévi-Strauss, Claude. 1962.*The Savage Mind*. Chicago: University of Chicago Press.

Lévi-Strauss, Claude. 1963. *Structural Anthropology*. New York: Basic.

Lobingier, C. S. 1930. "Customary Law," *Encyclopedia of the Social Sciences*, 4:662–7. New York: Macmillan.

MacIver, R., and Page, C. 1950. *Society*. London: Macmillan.

MacPherson, C. B. 1980. *Burke*. New York: Hill & Wang.

Marglin, Steven. 1976. "What Do Bosses Do?" in Andre Gorz, ed., *The Division of Labor*. Sussex: Harvester.

Marshall, Alfred. 1982. *Principles of Economics* (1920). Philadelphia: Porcupine Press.

Marx, Karl. 1967/1867. *Capital*, vol. 1. New York: International.

Marx, Karl, and Engels, Frederick. 1976. "Manifesto of the Communist Party" (1848). *Collected Works*, vol. 6. New York: International.

Marx, Melvin. 1970. *Learning*, vol. 3. London: Macmillan.

Mayr, Ernst. 1982. *The Growth of Biological Thought*. Cambridge, MA: Harvard University Press.

Medawar, Peter B. 1976. "Does Ethology Throw Any Light on Human Behavior?" in P. P. G. Bateson and R. A. Hinde, eds., *Growing Points in Ethology*, 497–506. Cambridge University Press.

Meltzoff, Z., and Moore, M. 1977. "Imitation of Facial and Manual Gestures by Human Neonates," *Science* 198:75–8.

Menger, Karl. 1963. *Problems of Economics and Sociology* (1883), translated and edited by Louis Schneider. Urbana: University of Illinois Press.

Mill, James. 1826. *Elements of Political Economy*. London: Baldwin, Cradock & Joy.

Mill, J. S. 1874. "Nature," *Three Essays on Religion*. New York: Greenwood.

Miller, Neal, and Dollard, John. 1941. *Social Learning and Imitation*. New Haven, CT: Yale University Press.

Mirowski, Philip. 1986. "Mathematical Formalism and Economic Explanation," in Philip Mirowski, ed., *The Reconstruction of Economic Theory*, 179–240. Boston: Kluwer-Nijhoff.

Mirowski, Philip. 1989. *More Heat Than Light: Economics as Social Physics, Physics as Nature's Economics*. Cambridge University Press.

Mumford, Lewis. 1934. *Technics and Civilization*. New York: Harcourt Brace.

Murphy, James Bernard. 1990. "Nature, Custom, and Stipulation in Law and Jurisprudence," *Review of Metaphysics* 43:751–90.

Murphy, James Bernard. 1991. "Nature, Custom, and Stipulation in the Semiotic of John Poinsot," *Semiotica* 83(1/2):33–68.

Nagel, Ernest. 1979. *The Structure of Science*. Indianapolis, IN: Hackett.

Oster, G. F., and Wilson, E. O. 1984. "A Critique of Optimization Theory in Evolutionary Biology," in Elliott Sober, ed., *Conceptual Issues in Evolutionary Biology*. Cambridge, MA: MIT Press.

Parsons, Talcott. 1949. *The Structure of Social Action* (1937). New York: Free Press.

Perelman, Ch., and Olbrechts-Tyteca, L. 1969. *The New Rhetoric*. Notre Dame, IN: University of Notre Dame Press.

Pocock, J. G. A. 1985. *Virtue, Commerce, and History*. Cambridge University Press.

Poinsot, John (John of St. Thomas). 1985. *Tractatus de Signis* (1632), edited and translated by John Deely. Berkeley and Los Angeles: University of California Press.

Popper, Karl. 1966. *The Open Society and Its Enemies*, vol. 2. Princeton, NJ: Princeton University Press.

Robinson, Richard. 1950. *Definition*. Oxford University Press.

Roll, Eric. 1956. *A History of Economic Thought*. Englewood Cliffs, NJ: Prentice Hall.

Ryle, Gilbert. 1945–6. "Knowing How and Knowing That," *Proceedings of the Aristotelian Society* 46.

Saussure, Ferdinand. 1986. *Course in General Linguistics* (1916), translated by Roy Harris. LaSalle, IL: Open Court.

Schumpeter, Joseph A. 1954. *History of Economic Analysis*. New York: Oxford University Press.

Smith, Adam. 1979. *The Wealth of Nations* (1776), edited by R. H. Campbell, A. S. Skinner, and W. B. Todd. Oxford University Press.

Sumner, W. G. 1906. *Folkways*. Boston: Ginn.

Taylor, O. H. 1955. *Economics and Liberalism*. Cambridge, MA: Harvard University Press.

Thoben, H. 1982. "Mechanistic and Organistic Analogies in Economics Reconsidered," *Kyklos* 35:292–306.

Thompson, Nicholas. 1977. "Instinctive Behavior," *International Encyclopedia of Psychiatry, Psychology, Psychoanalysis, and Neurology*. New York: Van Nostrand.

Thompson, R. F. 1976. "Neural and Behavioral Mechanisms of Habituation and Sensitization," in Thomas Tighe and Robert Leaton, eds., *Habituation*, 49–93. New York: Wiley.

Thurnwald, Richard. 1932. *Economics in Primitive Communities*. Oxford University Press.

Tighe, Thomas, and Leaton, Robert. 1976. "Comparisons Between Habituation Research at the Developmental and Animal-Neurophysiological Levels," in Thomas Tighe and Robert Leaton, eds., *Habituation*, 321–40. New York: Wiley.

Toennies, Ferdinand. 1961. *Custom* (1909), translated by A. F. Bornstein. New York: Free Press.

Trotter, W. F., trans. 1958. *Pascal's Pensées*. New York: Dutton.

Tylor, E. B. 1958. *The Origins of Culture* (1871). New York: Harper & Brothers.

von Mises, Ludwig. 1966. *Human Action* (1949). Chicago: Henry Regnery.

Weber, Max. 1978. *Economy and Society* (1925), edited by Guenther Roth and Claus Wittich. Berkeley and Los Angeles: University of California Press.

Wells, Rulon S. 1977. *A Perfusion of Signs*, edited by Thomas A. Sebeok. Bloomington: Indiana University Press.

Wilson, E. O. 1975a. "Human Decency Is Animal," *New York Times Magazine*.

Wilson, E. O. 1956. *Sociobiology*. Cambridge, MA: Harvard University Press.

CHAPTER 20

Feminist accounting theory as a critique of what's "natural" in economics

DAVID CHIONI MOORE

Toute position inscrite est une position conquise.
(Every inscribed position is a conquered position.)
Marcel Griaule, Les Saô légendaires, 66.

I suppose I could do worse than to begin by answering the following question: Why is a feminist literary theorist discussing accounting in a book written by economists interrogating the natural? In August 1991, I had the dubious honor of being present in a room full of two thousand academic accountants at the Opryland Hotel in Nashville, Tennessee, listening, not to Johnny Cash or Waylon Jennings, but to the distinguished economist Rudiger Dornbusch and his keynote speech to the American Accounting Association on the future of the global economy. Though Dornbusch understandably left out the feminist literary angle, he too felt compelled to address the accounting–economics relationship at the beginning of his talk, and did so by saying, essentially, that the only thing factual that economists talked about was accounting information – everything past that was mere theory.

A ripple of unease with the speaker's ignorance filtered through the large audience as, theoretically aware or not, the assembled accountants noted to themselves how wrong he was, since every accounting number ever produced has been, to say the least, highly contestable. What Dornbusch revealed in his off-the-cuff remark was that accounting had achieved, at least in the eyes of certain major economists, the ultimate goal of the rhetorician's art: to be perceived as not rhetoric at all. Economists may have their disputes, Dornbusch was saying, but when accountants send them the word that the labor force worked W hours, inventories expanded by X, total investment declined by Y, or the dog food market amounted to Z – economists can safely talk, measurement errors aside, about the facts, the real, the truth, or the *natural*.

583

The purpose of this volume is to interrogate the natural image in economics, and I would propose as a supplement to that overall project to begin the critique at Dornbusch's bedrock level of facts, by interrogating economics' natural credentials via *accounting,* that first-order naming discipline that underlies economics, if you will permit me a natural image, insofar as it is the ore-body from which economists traditionally mine their nonsocially constituted facts.[1] Further, I would propose a *feminist* critique of the naturalness of accounting – a critique based on the advances of feminist literary criticism since 1971.

Literary theory may strike readers as an odd hunting ground for accounting or economics research models, and so I will explain what feminist literary criticism has to do with accounting. The deeply rooted and currently burgeoning (if not colonizing) field of literary criticism is related to accounting insofar as two central questions in both disciplines are the same: *representation* and *interpretation.* First, writers and accountants represent a certain world or set of facts in text, and then novel-readers or users of accounting statements interpret, according to certain canons of judgment, those texts. Of course, some may object that crucial differences still exist, for literature concerns *fiction,* while accounting is about *fact.* But what does it mean, after all, to differentiate fact from fiction? Robert Scholes (1981, 3) puts it as follows:

> Fact and fiction are old acquaintances. . . . Fact comes from *facere* – to make or do. Fiction comes from *fingere* – to make or shape. Fact still means for us quite literally "a thing done." And fiction has never lost its meaning of "a thing made." But in what sense do things done or things made partake of truth or reality? A thing done has no real existence once it has been done. A thing made, on the other hand, exists until it decays or is destroyed. Fact, finally, has no real existence, while fiction may last for centuries.

In Scholes's strict sense – that fictions are "a thing made," a human product – accounting is absolutely fictional, since accountants produce not truth but *texts:* texts that do not so much reflect reality as *construct* particular versions of complex realities; versions constructed according to historical genres, or conventions; accounting conventions neither absolute nor universal but that vary across epochs and cultures; conventions that each embody (in both their in- and their exclusions) the various social, economic, and political interests of the specific race, gender, and class group that produce the accounts in the first place. And accounting is *irremediably* that way.[2]

Within literary criticism, a specifically *feminist* approach is chosen to critique accounting because the breadth of recent feminist theory constitutes perhaps the single most corrosive attack on naturalness by Western scholarship since the cultural and linguistic relativism of Herskovitz and Whorf began some sixty years ago. While feminist theory has occurred virtually not at all in the calculative disciplines, it has been positively explosive in literary studies.[3]

Enough, then, of the economics-natural-accounting-lit crit-feminism linkages. At this point we move on to our theorizing proper, which will take place as follows: The history of Anglo-American and French feminist literary criticism since 1970 will be sketched out as a roughly chronological six-part progression, borrowing heavily from Toril Moi's important if overly francophilic *Sexual/Textual Politics: Feminist Literary Theory* (1985).[4] Though I will reference Moi (1985) only for direct quotations, my debt is much greater than those citations will indicate. At each point in the progression, the beginnings of a parallel feminist accounting critique will be sketched out – beginnings upon which future critical accountings or economics may (or may not) wish to be based. The chapter will close with reflections on the six platforms presented and will speculate further on whether the natural can be said to exist at all.

Two final notes before we begin. First, though I will use the past tense in the main, this should not imply that the research programs described in this chapter are dead and gone. Second, though it may be tempting to read the following review of successive theories as an Enlightenment tale of progress to better thinking, I wish not to endorse such a view of intellectual history. Rather, following Gould (1986, 1989), I would instead account for these successive theories as nonteleological adaptations to changing conditions, and as Gould would put it, if the tape of feminist literary theory were to be rewound and played again under different circumstances, the new winners at tape's end would likely (though not necessarily) be quite different. And so I will make no recommendations about which of the following six theoretical platforms should undergird a future feminist accounting, for they can be chosen only in the context of local conditions, specific goals (e.g., "tenure or political fame?"), cognitive tastes, and so on.

Platform One: arraignment and indictment

As Alice Echols (1989) vigorously documents, the modern "second wave" U.S. women's movement (if the first wave stretches from Seneca Falls in 1848 to the early-twentieth-century suffragists) grew out of a disaffection with black and white male domination of the civil rights and antiwar movements of the late 1960s (serving coffee at the freedom rally rightly seemed a paradox) and a concomitant realization that a *separate* struggle would have to be pursued to secure the then-termed "liberation" of women.[5] Feminist literary criticism – which virtually did not exist before 1970[6] – was a direct outgrowth of the explosiveness and politicization of this movement. It is generally acknowledged that Kate Millett's spectacular *Sexual Politics* (1969) – which created a sensation when it was published (Moi [1985, 24] calls it "surely the world's best-selling Ph.D. thesis") – was the great precursor to all of the feminist literary criticism that followed: the powerful opening volley in the feminist literary wars that followed, to use a masculine metaphor.

The first two sections of *Sexual Politics* describe Millett's view of power relations between the sexes and sketch a history of nineteenth- and twentieth-century feminist activism; its final section focuses on literature. There Millett angrily surveys the fantasy-ridden and misogynistic portrayal of women by a legion of twentieth-century male authors from D. H. Lawrence to Norman Mailer, and shows how domination of women is enacted and reenacted in these male works of fiction. Millett's fierce analyses have since been faulted on a variety of grounds (avoidance of women authors, exclusive focus on content over formal analysis, reductionism in favor of the main point, etc.), and as a result she has not had an enduring influence on literary theory per se. Yet Millett's work must emphatically be included in any feminist theory review because theories and intellectual traditions are inseparable from their particular social and political situations. One often thinks of politics suppressing research, such as with optimization work in the Soviet Union in decades past,[7] but I believe analysis shows that politics is as frequently *constitutive* as it is repressive of intellectual programs.

Thus, the first stage of a feminist accounting critique might have to take the same form as did Millet's in literary studies: as an angry, eloquent, sensation-causing exposé of the gender-based power imbalances in applied and academic accounting – how women have been under-, mis-, and nonpresented throughout the modern Western history of purportedly objective accounting, and how this has worked to their enduring disadvantage. Though feminist research is today accorded vastly greater general credibility than it was in 1970, still-extant barriers to feminist work in the calculative disciplines may require a forceful, space-clearing effort such as Millet's to spark a feminist blaze in the cold, wet forests of quantitative or "formal" research. Such a study wouldn't be hard to write, but perhaps the historical conditions for such a monograph are wrong; I can only hope I am proved false on this point.

Platform Two: "Images of Women" criticism

Once Millett's *Sexual Politics* had cleared some space for feminist literary research, the predominant criticism in the years immediately following became known as "Images of Women" criticism (Moi 1985, 42); the name comes from a similarly titled collection of essays, *Images of Women in Fiction: Feminist Perspectives* (Cornillon 1972). The interpretive paradigm underlying "Images of Women" criticism is a familiar one, variously and loosely termed realism, objectivism, positivism, or the correspondence theory of knowledge. The epistemological stance of "Images" criticism posited a world existing "out there," independent of its observers, and that through various bias-free or transparent languages (e.g., good-faith natural languages, perfected accounting) this world (or parts of it) could be accurately represented. "Images" criticism took its objectivism seriously by calling for a strong form of literary realism, which, at its extreme, adopted an almost accounting-like quality. Cheri Register, for example, while recognizing the difficulty critics would have in measuring "the authenticity of a single female protagonist's inner turmoil," noted that it would be "useful to compile statistical data on a collection of works from a limited time period to see how accurately they mirror female employment, educational attainment, marital status, birthrate, and the like" (1975, 13). "Images" critics also detailed and decried, in a more sophisticated manner than did Kate Millett, the negative and incorrect "natural image" of women in Western literature over the centuries: how female literary characters were (and are) disproportionately premenopausal, either virgins or whores, useless or monstrous, diabolic or powerless, and so on.

The translation of an "Images" model to a feminist accounting is clear: Where traditional accounting has always worn a just-the-facts, mirror-of-nature mien, a feminist accounting would seek to expose the historical biases in the representations of women by accountings of all kinds: corporate, municipal, familial, and so on. *Non*portrayal would be one major area of research. One could imagine, for example, studies documenting the exclusion or nonvaluation of traditional women's work (such as family raising) in accounts of gross national product, or the historical omission from internal corporate accounts of the burdensome and economically significant home entertainment contributions of unpaid executive wives.

*Mis*portrayal could be a second major area of research, and analyses there might include the historical bias in management accounting wherein traditionally male labor is described as "real," "essential," or especially "direct" product cost, while traditionally female labor in selling, general, and administration is more frequently characterized as "overhead" or "indirect," somehow superfluous or "exterior" to the product "itself," whatever that means. Indeed, from an "Images" perspective, even a basic cost-accounting text, such as Davidson et al., *Managerial Accounting* (1988), seems a nonstop exercise in underrecognition as regards the contributions traditionally made by women to firms.

There is little doubt that an "Images of Women" research program could bear much fruit for a feminist accounting, and still less doubt that such a successful program would effect substantial changes in the discipline itself. Beyond the purely accounting domain, were such a program to succeed, economists would be forced to deal with a significantly different collection of facts. Indeed, on the margins of disciplinary economics, "Images" efforts have been undertaken by, among others, Nancy Folbre and Heidi Hartmann (see Hartmann and Treiman 1983; Wagman and Folbre 1988).

Yet at the same time, the eventual decline of "Images" efforts in literary studies should give pause to critical accountants or economists considering taking it up in the first place. "Images of Women" was eventually eclipsed in literary studies for two reasons. The first and most obvious defect of its realist approach was that most literature could not be held responsible for "accurate" portrayals of anything. Mary Shelley's horror, Ursula LeGuin's science fiction, and Gabriel García Márquez's magical realism name only three examples of literary genres that do not take as their goal any "realistic" portrayal whatsoever. In this regard, Moi (1985, 79) points out that "it is not accidental that ["Images of Women"] criticism has dealt overwhelmingly with fiction written in the great period of [literary] realism between 1750 and 1930" and has ignored in contrast the great sweep of literary history in which "realism" was not the dominant value. Of course, it is arguable that nonrealism is also a permanent if not cardinal feature of *accounting* – what with the science fiction of U.S. defense contract costings, the horror of modern product liability amortizations, and the fantasy in so many savings and loan asset valuations – but I suspect that the calculative professions will never be as enamored of these genres as my colleagues are of Cervantes or Poe.

Critical accounting and economics readers will instead find a second weakness in the realist approach of "Images" criticism much more germane to a potential feminist accounting; this weakness is centered on a critique of realism itself – literary, accounting, or otherwise. As is pointed out elsewhere (Moore 1991, 1993), academic accounting has tenaciously held on to its objectivist epistemological stance despite evidence provided every day (on the front page of the *Wall Street Journal,* in conversation with practicing accountants, etc.) that accounting systems construct rather than reflect reality. Amazingly enough, according to stubbornly objectivist accounting scholars, the numerous, indeed countless, counterexamples to accounting's purported objectivity do not compromise the underlying objective potential of accounting "itself" (whatever that means); rather, nonrealist counterexamples provide added impetus for accounting scholars to understand and eliminate these biases so as to render the system more perfect.

While an extended discussion of objectivism versus constructivism in accounting or elsewhere is beyond the scope of the present chapter, it must be noted that beyond the rich relevant philosophical literature (e.g., Nietzsche 1873; Kuhn 1962; Derrida 1967, 1972; Feyerabend 1975; Hollis and Lukes 1982; Lakoff 1987), there exists an important body of critical accounting research (e.g., Belkaoui 1978; Chua 1986; Hines 1988; Morgan 1988) that argues persuasively that our accounts fabricate rather than reflect reality; this literature indeed *accepts* bias as a basic condition of human knowledge. Such "constructivist" critiques – which we will return to in our conclusion – may prove more satisfactory than objectivism for a potential feminist accounting. But this can, once again, be decided only in particular contexts, with particular objectives in mind.

Platform Three: woman-centered criticism I – canon revision

The next three stages of feminist literary scholarship first flowered in the second half of the 1970s and remain today extremely rich sources of feminist criticism. Shifting the focus away from male authors' "correct or incorrect" portrayals of women, this next phase was distinctly a "woman-centered" criticism, a revisionism or, following Showalter (1979), a "gynocriticism." In woman-centered criticism, feminist scholars focused on reading, valorizing, privileging, and interpreting literature written *by* women, quite explicitly as a counterweight to the centuries of masculinist criticism that preceded. Often revisionism involved burnishing the literary reputations of established writers such as Charlotte Brontë or Jane Austen, who had been subject to chauvinist barbs as long as they had been read. Vladimir Nabokov's famous Cornell lectures on Dickens, for example, began as follows:

> We are now ready to tackle Dickens. We are now ready to embrace Dickens. We are now ready to bask in Dickens. In our dealings with Jane Austen we had to make a certain effort in order to join the ladies in the drawing room. In the case of Dickens we remain at table

with our tawny port. . . . Here there is no problem of approach as
with Jane Austen, no courtship, no dillydallying. We just surrender
ourselves to Dickens's voice – that is all. (1948, ix)

We'll leave the subversive reading of that text aside for the moment
and note that, just as frequently, revisionist criticism necessitated pains-
taking archival work to unearth long-forgotten novels that were immensely popular in their day, but had over time been ignored into
oblivion by a wholly male community of scholars, publishing executives, and archivists who controlled the processes of literary transmission. In many cases it was not so much a question of glorifying these
works as of rediscovering their existence in the first place. These
initial revisionist efforts had as their principal goal the elevation of
major women authors into the so-called canon of great literature, and
considering the enormous weight of the precedents to overcome, to a
large extent these efforts have succeeded.

Today fewer and fewer literature survey courses are offered in U.S.
universities without a strong representation of women authors on the
syllabus; and dissertations, academic papers, and conferences all frequently focus on the works that comprise the rich woman-authored
canon. As a critique of a historically male-privileging, "mirror-of-
nature" accounting, a similar woman-centered intervention is not hard
to imagine: It would consist of a systematic upward reappraisal, both
historically and in present-day terms, of the value assigned to women in
the economy. Woman-centered revisionist accounting would differ
from an "Images" accounting in that while the latter would focus on
exposing the historical *misrepresentation* of women, canon revision
would direct its efforts toward the upward *revaluation,* along more
woman-centric lines, of women's formerly mis- or nonvalued contributions to the total economy.

What would this mean in practical terms? Well, all good management
accountants know, for example, that a company's books often radically
misidentify where value is created within the firm: Product A may be
said to be more profitable than B, but the opposite might in fact be true;
or the factory may seem a big profit contributor while the direct-
marketing staff only breaks even, but this too may be an accounting
illusion. A woman-centered accounting would begin with the research
hypothesis that women's economic work has been as systematically un-
dervalued as women's literary achievements, and then would test this
hypothesis in as many gender-marked situations as possible: the relative contributions of homemakers versus go-to-work husbands; flight
attendants versus baggage handlers; financial controllers versus hu-

man resources staff; and so on. Recommendations for dollar revaluation both historically and prospectively would result. Theoretical work as well as field studies would take place, all with the goal of reorienting the canons of value in less phallocentric ways. Aspects of such cost-accounting work are also well within the domain of a disciplinary economics, as evidenced by the recent historical and comparable worth studies by, among others, Heidi Hartmann and Jane Humphries (see Hartmann and Donovan 1987; Humphries 1987).

Platform Four: woman-centered criticism II – canon deconstruction

Still, despite the clear successes of canon revision on the part of feminist literati, and despite the obvious potential for such an approach in accounting research as well, we should note that feminist criticism eventually moved away from revision and on to an even more theoretically powerful canon *deconstruction*. For what was the point, after all, of women's gaining access to evaluative categories defined by and for *men*? It would be an odd liberation, it was argued, whose mere goal was but a mimicry of the declining and discredited colonial power. With this in mind, feminist criticism began to question the male-produced canon itself: Why should great *novels* (or plays or poems) be the privileged definitions of "literature" when women's writing had historically focused on other forms, such as the letter, the journal, and the family diary? How could women be expected to measure up except exceptionally, since only rarely had they been accorded the time or resources to engage in traditionally male literary pursuits? Who had decided that the novel was the acme of literary value, and what was the inherent superiority of it over the epistle? The point, finally, was to reject as God-given and then revolutionize entirely the always already gendered standards, "take," or view on which the total literary universe was judged.

On the disciplinary accounting front, such deconstructions should give pause to the writers of the largest body of woman-oriented accounting literature today: the papers, found in both academic and practitioner journals (such as *CPA Journal* or *Woman CPA*), which empirically investigate the barriers to entry and advancement for women in the accounting profession. This literature is, in one sense, a masculinist literature, insofar as it privileges assimilation into the existing male-defined world of public accounting.[8] Should assimilation (with perhaps moderate modifications for child leaves and business entertainment choices) be the goal of feminists in accounting, or is a more radical institutional critique in order? Would feminism be satisfied with a military once 50 percent of its generals were women, if its armies went on behaving as they had for centuries? Or would a feminist program instead explore entirely new approaches to resolving conflict? What types of accounting have been historically done *by* women, and how have they been done? Have they occurred in household budgets, family firms, journals, and diaries, or elsewhere? These are among the central questions for a feminist accounting.

Put in more concrete academic terms (if that is not an oxymoron), a deconstructionist feminist accounting would interrogate the natural-category privileges that accounting accords to, for example, individuals and firms – for perhaps these categories themselves are too phallocentric: As we know from anthropology and paleontology, even the taxonomy of animals is not "natural" (see Bulmer 1967; Gould 1990). Let us take, for example, a hypothetical if not classic case of seemingly male-generated value in a small neighborhood delicatessen, circa 1952, run by the hard-working father of a middle-class family. While Father put in twelve-hour days and realized modest gains for twenty-six years, Mother stayed home, kept house, prepared meals, and raised the children single-handedly, paying particular attention to their schooling and social skills. By 1978, Junior had developed into a talented young Manhattan-based Harvard MBA, while all of his old neighborhood friends, whose families had not emphasized education and culture, did not seem to have progressed nearly as far. One day, while back on a weekend visit to his parents' modest apartment, Junior realized that his mother's tasty dishes were both simple and freezable. Junior resigned his position with Citicorp just after bonus time and joined his father's delicatessen, and by 1983 the business was grossing several million dollars per year marketing frozen home-style ready-to-heat specialties in upscale Manhattan groceries.[9]

The accounting question is, of course, What was the source of the increase in value? How do we account for the delicatessen's growth? *Let us admit in the very first instance that there is no "natural" way to answer these questions:* Long gone are the prelapsarian days when Adam could directly read the names of the beasts, which were visibly inscribed (by a male God) on their bodies. The accounting choices we make at this point will instead be conditioned by social and cultural values (which we may perceive as natural) and by inertia; in the cases when more than one set of values or versions exists (which is to say, in every case), the "correct" version will be that of the group with the power to impose its will by force, expressed or implied.

A standard accounting solution to our delicatessen problem would tell us that the *business* created the value, principally as a result of the *son*'s marketing efforts from 1978 to 1983. But this clearly makes no sense, for it ignores, among other things, the mother's central contribution to Junior's analytical and social skills, and ignores also Mother's unrelenting years of culinary research and development that provided the highly successful recipes. A *revisionist* accounting corrective to this misrecognition might now account for the mother as part of the firm and revise the books retroactively, assigning her the dual titles of R&D consultant and executive-succession director. Values would be calculated for the mother's efforts using shadow-pricing or cost-avoidance techniques, and these values would be scaled by the open-market price of equivalent management training or culinary research services.

But does this really make sense? Isn't our problem more fundamental than any set of technical adjustments can handle? Why should the mother be inscribed within individualist, corporatist, traditionally masculine economic canons, which might not be how *she* would characterize her efforts at all? From a feminist perspective beyond revisionism, what is needed may be a total deconstruction and reconstruction of the masculinist privileging of the individual subject, firm, and "growth" in the first place. The family (and not the delicatessen, or the firm) might become the privileged locus of total economic output – or the neighborhood, or the town.

To properly account for the intergenerational value creation so frequently a result of women's efforts, accounting horizons might need to be stretched from one year to decades, though intermediate reporting technologies would need to be developed along the way. As with women's beginningless, endless writings such as journals or letters, static or begin–end states would become less important than continuous processes. In addition, the notion of the individual subject as the basic productive unit might need to be deemphasized, since this may arbitrarily privilege a historically masculine form of value generation.[10] And finally, the notion of economic "growth" itself and how it is constituted might need to be challenged as well. It is perhaps ironic that the natural economic value of the West has taken the individualist, corporatist, and nationalist turns that it has, in light of the origin of the word "economic," from the Greek οικος + νεμειν (oikos + nemein), or "extended household management."

It is here more than anywhere else that the crucial role of accounting in producing "natural" objects of study for economists is demonstrated. Though pioneering work has been done by, again, Nancy

Folbre (questioning family-unit accounting in developing economies
[1984, 1986], and Folbre et al. [1984]), one can easily see how the
shape and bias of the accounting-produced "facts" for study (records
of men's work, revenues of corporate entities or nation-states in single
years), must strongly influence the economic truths thence derived.
Alone, a dissenting, accounting-rejecting economist has only a few
thousand dollars with which to produce the alternative facts necessary
to survival. Alone he or she cannot long compete with the mainstream
theorist already standing on a pile of accounting facts some millions of
dollars deep. We will return to this point in our discussion of Bruno
Latour.

Platform Five: woman-centered criticism III – canon *re*construction

To recap, from a feminist historical perspective a deconstruction of
accounting's basic "natural" elements – firms, individuals, years – is indicated; and familial, intergenerational, or some other types of accountings might provide more satisfying descriptions of the total human
economy, or parts thereof. Going forward, yet other aggregations
might be necessitated by the changing composition of the Western
family, and different accountings would be indicated for different cultures. Among other things, culturally more nuanced approaches to
"accounting" might put an end to the myopic frustrations of often
astute financial newsmagazines such as the *Economist,* which often predict that the Japanese economy will eventually stagnate if its women
don't get out of the house and begin to "work" and which, steeped in
individualist traditions dating back at least to Adam Smith, declare the
Japanese system of cooperating "families" of companies to be somehow
damaging to the "total economy." And you'd think that twenty-four
years (1950–73) averaging 10.5 percent real annual GDP growth (see
Kennedy 1987, 417) (assuming one privileges this sort of growth)
would make one reconsider one's basic assumptions about women's
"work" and "nonmarket" collaboration!

The biggest obstacles to such revolutionary reconstructions of accounting are, of course, not theoretical but material, for the inertia of
existing accounting systems is huge, and the cash cost of completely
reworking them would be enormous. If the billions of dollars annually
expended on the calculation and policing of corporate- and individual-
centered notions of value were instead devoted to some future agreed-
upon feminist accounting, then a workable, usable, acceptably self-
consistent system of value would no doubt result. The traditionalist

may say, "But our current accounting system is *proven*." But to this I can only respond, "Give *me* a few billion a year and I can prove that *kindergarten* drives the world economy, your truths are only illusions about which you have forgotten that that is what they are."[11] Unfortunately for kids, however, kindergarten teachers do not control the massive and self-confirming apparatus of value recognition. And absent this apparatus, the most sophisticated deconstructed and reconstructed feminist accounting theories we could imagine would have little chance at escaping the theory journals, at generating facts believable in the current context. As Bruno Latour points out about "hard" science, profound intellectual dissent is no simple matter:

> It is not only words that are now lined up to confront the dissenter, not only graphs to support the words and references to support the whole assembly of allies, not only instruments to generate endless numbers of newer and clearer inscriptions, but, behind the instruments, new objects are lined up. . . . Dissenters have now done all they can do to disbelieve, disaggregate and disassociate what is mustered behind the claim. . . . At this point . . . there is no other way open to the dissenters than to *build another laboratory*. The price of dissent increases dramatically and the number of people able to continue decreases accordingly. (1987, 79)

Later in his book Latour tells us again that

> shaping reality . . . is not within everybody's reach. . . . Since the proof race is so expensive that only a few people, nations, institutions or professions are able to sustain it, this means that the production of facts and artifacts will not occur everywhere and for free, but will occur only at restricted places at particular times. (179)

No doubt Latour's observations are important for all of the six platforms presented in this chapter, but nowhere would Latour's points be more pertinent than for a thoroughly deconstructed-reconstructed feminist accounting, which would require the largest material commitment of all. This in mind, it is perhaps no accident that, in the modern academy, deconstruction of traditional value systems has fared best in departments of literature – not because existing literary values were initially shakier, more inherently susceptible to de- and reconstruction, but because the material barriers to alternative fact production were (and still are) much lower there. Should dissenting accountants and economists, for want of material backing, then despair? Or, what strategy should they pursue in the face of such obstacles? Latour's important study on Louis Pasteur (1984) demonstrates well how some early, sketchy results on sheep bacteriology could be rapidly transformed into a colossal international health movement: Pasteur allied himself from the very start with an army of hygienists and military physicians who had been desperate to wash France but lacked a good reason why; Pasteur provided them one. In a separate work, Latour (1987, 173) lays bare the general strategy of such a Pasteurian move (the reader may substitute "critical accountants and economists" for "budding scientists"): "The problem of finding resources to pursue the proof race has been historically solved when budding scientists have linked their fate to that of people whose general goal was seen as being approximately the same: mobilising others." Offhand, as regards a reconstructed accounting or economics, I can think of at least 2.5 billion people (maybe more) whose goals might be seen as being congruent to a feminist version thereof. Their mobilization will be crucial to its success.

Platform Six: Hélène Cixous, the Gift, and the Proper

At this point we move east across the Atlantic to examine one last theoretical platform for a potential feminist accounting, one that engages the question of the natural in quite a different way. Here I will pause briefly to explain a bit of theoretical geography. "Women's studies" has engaged quite different sets of intellectual traditions in various Western regions, and to grossly oversimplify, one could put U.S. criticism in a pragmatic tradition, place British and Scandinavian feminisms among more socialist or Marxist cultural critiques, and locate the important French feminists in "poststructural" and psychoanalytical traditions whose luminaries include Derrida, Foucault, and Lacan.[12]

Here we will focus on the works of the French feminist theorist Hélène Cixous, whose dense, rapturous writings of the 1970s (including her 1975a, 1975b, 1976) have exercised considerable influence on both sides of the Atlantic in the decade or more since. In the first instance, Cixous rejects any notion of a feminist "equality" with men: "Are we going to be the equal of men, are we going to be as phallic as they are? Or do we want to save something else, something more positive, more archaic, much more on the side of *jouissance,* of pleasure, less socializable? If so, how and at what price?" (1975a, 308). From that point Cixous embarks on a remarkable and often mystical, contradictory, even (perhaps intentionally) undecipherable project to explore an "écriture féminine," or feminine writing – not necessarily writing by women, but writing that avoids the controlling, hierarchizing, systematizing style she identifies as masculine. This literature could include James Joyce as well as Clarice Lispector. Cixous's writings come to describe the masculine and feminine domains as the

"Realm of the Proper" and the "Realm of the Gift." The masculine, hierarchizing Realm of the Proper (as in "belonging to one," or property) is for Cixous a result of that classic overwhelming masculine fear identified by Freud, the fear of castration:

> Unlike man, who holds so dearly to his title and his titles, his pouches of value, his cap, crown, and everything connected with his head, woman couldn't care less about the fear of decapitation (or castration), adventuring, without the masculine temerity, into anonymity, which she can merge with, without annihilating herself: because she's a giver. (1975a, 317)

Cixous's Gift/Proper analysis profoundly troubles any neutral, neuter, or natural accounting, for it implies that, in a Gift/Proper world, the writing practice called accounting (hierarchizing, categorizing, classifying) that underlies modern quantitative and formal economics is essentially (perhaps even biologically) a masculine endeavor. Could this possibly be true? Could accounting be a catharsis or compensation for men's fear of castration? Two buttressing points are worth mentioning in this regard; the first is etymological, and the second is social.

On the etymological front, it is interesting to trace the history of the verb "to account," which according to Webster comes to us by way of the Middle English *accounten,* itself a descendant of the Middle French *acompter,* which crossed the English Channel in the company of many other Latinate words after the Norman conquest of 1066. The Middle French *acompter* is a composite of the Latin words *ad* + *com* + *putare,* or "to + with + consider," and here, in *putare* and its older Sanskrit cousin *pu,* we have the historical essence of "to account." The etymologist W. W. Skeat (1879, 126, 487) tells us that "the primary notion of *putare* was to make clean, then to bring to cleanliness" (this is no doubt an accounting quality), and Barnhart (1979, 1534) also ascribes to *putare* the meanings of cleanse, trim, and importantly, *to prune.* This is crucial to us, for from these ancient common roots of *pu* and *putare* were descended accounting's first cousins: the modern English verb "to amputate" and the Old High German *arfûrian,* "to castrate"! Thus, it seems that Cixous is right and that somewhere deep in our common (Indo-European) history – French *compter,* German *Konto,* Spanish *cuenta,* Norwegian *konto,* and so on – accounting and castration are somehow inextricably linked. Accounting, like landscaping, may indeed be an essentially masculine activity.

There is also what I will call "sociohistorical" evidence for Cixous's division of genders into the realms of Proper and Gift, and for a connection of Gift/Proper to historical accounting as well. It will be noted that the great bulk of women's labor in modern Western history – child-bearing, breast feeding, childcare, housekeeping, clothes making, food preparation, marital consort, and so on – has been labor for which no specific monetary, indeed no categorizable, recompense was given. Men, on the other hand, have been historically linked in the West not with Gift but rather with exchange economies (including the exchange of women) – economies in which uncompensated loss (as with decapitation, castration, or woman-initiated divorce) was not accepted willingly. Cixous writes (1975a, 320):

> Wherever history still unfolds as the history of death, she does not tread. Opposition, hierarchizing exchange, the struggle for mastery which can end only in at least one death . . . all that comes from a period in time governed by phallocentric values. The fact that this period extends into the present day doesn't prevent woman from starting the history of life somewhere else. Elsewhere, she gives. She doesn't "know" what she's giving, she doesn't measure it; she gives, though, neither a counterfeit impression nor something she hasn't got. She gives more, with no assurance that she'll get back even some unexpected profit from what she puts out. She gives that there may be life, thought, transformation. This is an "economy" that can no longer be put in economic terms.

What then can we do with Cixous's quite shocking ruminations – assuming, of course, we find them plausible in the first place? What *accounting* research programs can we develop from her theories? The case is far less clear when it was in regard to the application of, for example, our canon revision platform, and indeed it should be noted that in literary studies Cixous's writings have generated not so much practical criticism as more theorizing – theorizing about natural versus artificial genders and cultures, about the relationship between psychoanalysis and textual representation, and so on.

If one were to continue theorizing Cixous in accounting, a few questions might be near the top of the agenda. Would a feminist accounting wish to accept the troubling biological determinism that Cixous seems sometimes to imply, but that she elsewhere denies? Would a feminist accounting accept woman's "giver" status as essential, or should it be seen as a social construct that may be rejected if so desired? Though there is great value in Cixous's at-the-roots identification of supposedly neut(e)/natu/ral accounting with the masculine, there is perhaps also danger in her reinscribing a new, different, now feminine biological natural, linked as it is to childbearing and so on, for a new type of writing that would include history, literature, and arguably, accounting as well. One of the great obstacles in feminist scholarship to date has been to overcome the previously accepted belief that the existing, perhaps patriarchal status quo has been some-how the genetic way of things. Should the goal of a feminist account-ing be to replace one human-made construction of "the natural" with another, as Cixous seems at times to do? And if one were to link women to Gift, how would a feminist accounting account for gifts, or account in a gift economy[13] – or would it account at all?

Conclusion: accounting and the construction of gender

Ordinarily, in the conclusion of a chapter one summarizes the points presented and makes recommendations as to their use, but that would make little sense here, since the essay is itself a summary of other work and since, as an outsider to the fields to which these theories might be applied, I am ill qualified to recommend applications of any of what I have here presented. Instead I will briefly critique my own work to this point. First, this chapter's various calls for a revolutionized femi-nist accounting may have been contradicted by the highly reductive, classificatory, hierarchizing way in which it is presented. "Feminist theory" is a continuum without borders, and each of the six platforms I "identified" I in fact *constructed* – constructed in ways that are them-selves highly contestable. While I must of course plead guilty to this charge, I should also point out that these six reductions may be useful to certain interests and that the reductions show, if nothing else, the need to organize the world in *some* fashion. The feminist question is, Who's fashioning?[14]

Second, my six-plank presentation has neglected many other impor-tant feminisms, those that offer their own gender troubles in account-ing and elsewhere, those whose insights would no doubt be of use to potential feminist accountings. These unaccounted-for feminisms in-clude, first, a U.K.-centered socialist feminism that revolves around a more general cultural (as opposed to literary) critique and that sees the feminist struggle as part of a wider commitment to justice across class lines; no doubt its version of accounting would be of use to a more traditional Marxist critique of economics.[15] A second omission is gay-lesbian feminism, which among other things goes further to deconstruct our traditional binary notions of gender. Third comes a black or African-American feminism, which has found traditional white middle-class feminist analysis only partly responsive to the con-cerns of women of color; what's "natural" in accounting may turn out to be masculine, but likely it can be shown to be European as well. Fourth comes an "eco-feminism," which views gender justice as part and parcel of a wider call to species or environmental justice. There is, indeed, a substantial literature on environmental or total social costs, such as those of burning high-sulfur coal or producing chlorofluoro-carbons (see Cairncross 1991), and this is perhaps another area for a "Latourian" alliance. And even this list of excluded feminisms has excluded still others.

My third autocritique is that I have paid insufficient attention, in this all-too-brief survey, to the social and academic context of these theories, specifically to their highly political nature: how they have declared their politics, how they have been resisted, and how, even if they professed no politicization, they were politicized by the context of their reception. (This is not to say, of course, that mainstream account-ing research is therefore *not* political; quite the contrary.)

My fourth and final self-criticism regards a clear *limitation* of literary theory for feminist accountings, in that it theorizes *representation* far better than it does social power. It has been pointed out to me, for example, that as regards the "Images of Women" platform, women on factory floors may well feel less misrepresented than *controlled* by ac-countants and economists – and indeed, literary theory is of little use here. More fertile sources for feminist accounting theories of power might instead come from close readings "against the grain" of the massive traditional accounting literature on control, or from the im-portant, often Foucauldian, but as yet unfeminized critical accounting literature on representation and control (e.g., Hoskin and Macve 1986; Boland 1987; Knights and Collinson 1987; Miller and O'Leary 1987; Moore 1991 [section on Foucault]). One might also wish to consult Foucault (1977, 1978) or Said (1989). It is interesting to note that etymologically, "control" comes from the Middle French "contre-roller": to check the faithfulness of a hand-copied text by reviewing the double columns.[16]

My point, finally, or my final point, is this: Feminist accounting to date, including the present meager effort, has only scratched the sur-face of both its theoretical and applied research potential; its existing form, dominated by empirical gender-in-the-practitioner-ranks stud-ies, leaves many more questions unasked than answered. Feminist accounting's diverse agenda can hardly be called parochial – at least not when it concerns some 2.5 billion people (maybe more); at least not when no mainstream accounting can explain why the world's sec-ond largest national economy, whose wealth is distributed more evenly than in all but a few nations, was developed by a nation in which half the population didn't "work"; and at least not in the context of a stunted discipline that considers dividend-signaling mechanisms to be a major area of research. In sum, feminist literary theory – and the theoretical constructs of many other academic feminisms as well – can be highly effective tools for all variety of interventions against the natural.[17] Beyond that, as to whether or not accounting will eventually and rightfully surpass a derivative economics as the science of material truth – as literature may have already rightfully surpassed a derivative history as the science of textual truth – this is a question upon which I dare not hazard a guess.

The first question in this chapter asked how we have historically accounted for gender and speculated on how we might wish to do so differently in the future. Next we moved to the question of whether accounting as we know it is gendered (i.e., gendered masculine) and queried, too briefly, if differently gendered accountings are even theoretically possible. The question we have *not* asked, that we can only brush near in a virtually postscriptural fashion, and that we will have to defer to another time and place, is Doesn't accounting actually *produce* gender?

Recent feminist theory (e.g., Riley 1988; Spelman 1988; Butler 1990) has differentiated between "sex," which may be a function of biology (itself perhaps socially constructed), and "gender," that enormous overlay of differentiated clothing, manners of speech, taste in sports, relationships to one's body, hairstyles, family life, career patterns, and more, which have nothing to do with biology and, instead, are socially produced by a variety of "technologies of gender," including television, magazines, parental expectations, schools, courts of law, and no doubt, accounting. In feminist theory, this is termed the question of "essentialism": Is the category "woman" essential, or is it socially produced?

Consider for a moment the twentieth-century Western woman whose child-rearing efforts, we argued earlier, were misrepresented by accounting. Isn't, however, the deeper feminist truth about her situation that she was *produced* as a child rearer, an education monitor, and a cook in part *by accounting*? Likely, given the state of accounting and gender, her husband's job was more highly valued than hers, and when the baby came it was only "natural" that she stay home. Thus, perhaps we may not speak, primarily, of accounting "misportraying" women, for before it misportrays them, it may in fact *create* them, as "women" (and men as men) in the first place.

Thus, in this final stage beyond stages, to our earlier question – "Isn't our problem more fundamental than any set of *technical* adjustments can handle?" – accounting's answer must unfortunately be no.[18] No because there is nothing natural at all, anywhere or ever, to be represented or misrepresented: All objects, including ourselves, *are* technical – as in τεχνη, or *technē,* art, craft, a thing made – and one must eventually concur with Nietzsche that our consciousness of our own significance "hardly differs from that which the soldiers painted on canvas have of the battle depicted upon it" (1872, 41). Economics then becomes, like all other disciplines, a science of manipulations of always already textual objects, objects produced mainly by accounting but also by other naming disciplines such as cartography, demography, and taxonomy. Economics produces in its turn yet more textual objects for other disciplines, such as law, sociology, and military science, which in their turn constitute such disciplines as cartography, demography, taxonomy, and accounting.

The natural, if it exists at all, is surely not available in this endless network.

Notes

The author would like to thank Kathleen Biddick, Michael Chorost, Keith Hoskin, Samira Kawash, Cheryl Lehman, Philip Mirowski, Roberta Chioni Moore, Valerie Moore, Janice Radway, an exacting anonymous reader, and participants at the Third Interdisciplinary Conference on Accounting, University of Manchester, July 1991, who heard this chapter in an earlier formulation.

1. I mean a "dangerous supplement" in the Derridean sense: the add-on that reveals a lack. See Derrida (1967).
2. As many "critical" economists know, the notion that writing technologies construct rather than reflect reality has partially unnerved two major disciplines that also have deep (and in some cases statistical) objectivist traditions: history (see White 1973, 1987), and anthropology (see Geertz 1980; Marcus and Cushman 1982; Clifford and Marcus 1986; Clifford 1988; Said 1989). We will return to the constructivist view of accounting, and its elaborations in the critical accounting literature, several times.
3. Since 1970 feminism has significantly refashioned many disciplines in the humanities and history, made strong but fewer interventions in several social sciences, and had only uncertain, marginalized effects on those disciplines that considered themselves most "objective," namely, the sciences, their wanna-be cousins such as economics, and economics' wanna-be, academic accounting.

    Between 1971 and 1990, four of the leading accounting journals – the *Accounting Review,* the *Journal of Accounting Research,* the *Journal of Accountancy,* and *Accounting, Organizations and Society* – published 3,460 indexible articles among them, and not once did the words "feminist" or "feminism" appear in any title or abstract. In dramatic contrast, in the authoritative literary studies bibliography (MLA 1990) the number of scholarly articles classified yearly as "feminist" or "feminism" (a far narrower measure than word occurrence in abstracts) has climbed steadily from one in 1971. Since 1985 three to four hundred articles have been published each year in literary studies on feminism. Today no fewer than twenty-two North American academic journals classified under "feminism" or "women's studies" (MLA 1990–1) attest to the field's size and complexity.

Still, these figures do not imply that there has been no modern accounting for "women," only that there have been no explicitly feminist efforts in mainstream journals. Declared feminist accounting inquiries have occurred either in more marginalized literature (e.g., Lehman 1988; Shearer and Arrington 1989) or altogether outside of "accounting" (e.g., Waring 1988; *BEA* 1990). Thus, the question is not the noetic "Why hasn't feminist accounting been thought," but the sociopolitical "Why hasn't existing feminist accounting appeared, as such, in the mainstream literature?"

Recently there have occurred inexplicit types of accounting feminism, feminism that for academic-political reasons may have been, as Heidegger put it, "written under erasure." In the practitioners' literature, substantial attention has been paid to subjects such as comparative gender stress and relative barriers to professional advancement, but these have not gone under the name "feminist." In the more academic literature, important recent articles in *Accounting, Organizations and Society* (e.g., Burrell 1987; Crompton 1987; Hopwood 1987; Tinker & Neimark 1987; Lehman 1991) have opted for "gender" over feminist. While these articles may in fact be feminist, and while their choice of the heading gender over feminism may reflect a more catholic approach, the choices on the part of authors or journal may also reflect a reluctance, conscious or not, about adopting the highly charged, inevitably political, always contested label feminism. Feminism has ranged from assimilationism to terrorism over the past two decades. This paper employs feminism over gender out of deference to the historical self-identification of the six theories here elaborated.

Needless to say, the dearth of feminist accounting has not been for any lack of subject matter: Traditional women's work has been systematically under-, mis-, and nonaccounted for in textbooks, research, and financial statements; a scanty 3.7 percent of Big Six partners are women (Pillsbury et al., 1989), while excuses for this imbalance wear thin; and a recent issue of the American Accounting Associations' *Accounting Education News* (AAA 1991) regales us with 19 photographs of 111 accounting notables, only 7 of whom are women, all of whom are white.

Nonetheless, this chapter's task is not to investigate the marginalization of feminist accounting, though accounting's (oxy)moronic claim to be value-free (see Jensen 1983, 320) clearly deters feminist studies in mainstream accounting journals: "Value-free" is a possibility that feminism will always deny.

4. "Anglo-American" in this context means largely American scholars theorizing in regards to both English and American literature.

5. Echols's history is an enlightening read, though it leaves underdeveloped the question of the larger social conditions of possibility for this movement – its material underpinnings, how and why millions of women could suddenly be mobilized, those it left out, and more.

6. Robin Morgan's highly detailed 1970 bibliography of *Writings from the Women's Liberation Movement*, for example, lists "only five works wholly or partly concerned with literature" (Moi 1985, 22); the five works were Virginia Woolf's *A Room of One's Own* (1929), Simone de Beauvoir's *The Second Sex* (1949), Katherine M. Rogers's *The Troublesome Helpmate* (1966), Mary Ellmann's *Thinking About Women* (1968), and Kate Millett's *Sexual Politics* (1969). This, of course, refers only to *academic* literary criticism, which is itself barely a century old. An extensive Western feminist theory has been documented since at least 1399. See Kelly (1982) and Gilbert and Gubar (1985).

7. As noted by Ivor Grattan-Guinness, Chapter 4, this volume.

8. In a similar vein, one observes that lists of "notable women" generally focus on those, like Amelia Earhart and Marie Curie, who succeeded in what have been traditionally male pursuits.

9. Though my scenario is hypothetical, I am told that it resembles the story of the New York–based Celentano family and company. Accounting histories of this and other firms might well be on the agenda of a future feminist accounting. I thank Keith Hoskin for pointing out that this story can be read in ways differently from the way I propose here – the Oedipal interpretation, for example, can be quite successfully pursued.

10. It is just such individualist notions that permit the inscription of my name (and my name only) at the beginning of this chapter – despite the fact that, in many important ways, this chapter can be traced back to, among other people, my grandmothers, and beyond.

11. The latter half of this sentence is taken from Nietzsche (1873).

12. For those unfamiliar with these traditions, for Foucault, go first to his (1977) and (1980); see (1978) specifically on gender. Foucault has also been deployed in *Accounting, Organizations and Society* frequently since 1983. For Derrida, go first to Culler (1982) or Norris (1982); in the accounting literature see the highly important Arrington and Francis (1989). For Derrida himself, go to the three selections in Adams and Searle (1986). For Lacan, go first to Freud (1900 and 1917).

13. There is a rich and decades-long anthropological literature on the gift, beginning with Marcel Mauss. Among the recent flurry of interdisciplinary articles on the gift, one may wish to consult Marilyn Strathern (1988).

14. Which I take from Michel Foucault's (1966, 305; 1969, 68) celebrated Nietzschean "Première question: qui parle?" or "first question: Who's speaking?"

15. A 1970s British and Scandinavian literature on "social accounting," and many 1980s articles written by the aggressively Marxist accounting scholar Tony Tinker would also fit in this vein.

16. My thanks to Michael Hutter for clarifying this.
17. Among many disciplines' feminisms, of recent U.S. work one may wish to examine, among others, Enloe (1990) in political science, Hubbard (1990) or Fausto-Sterling (1985) or the more high-theoretical Haraway (1989, 1991) in biology and medicine, Minow (1990) in legal studies, Scott (1988) or DuBois and Ruiz (1990) in history, the prestigious interdisciplinary feminist journal *Signs: Journal of Women in Culture and Society* (1975 to present), and/or the *Women's Review of Books* (1983 to present).
18. My thanks to Keith Hoskin (1991) for this answer.

References

Adams, Hazard, and Leroy Searle, eds. 1986. *Critical Theory Since 1965.* Tallahassee: Florida State University Press.

American Accounting Association (AAA). 1991. *Accounting Education News.* January.

Arrington, C. Edward, and Jere Francis. 1989. "Letting the Chat out of the Bag: Deconstruction, Privilege and Accounting Research. *Accounting, Organizations and Society,* 1–28.

Barnhart, Robert R., ed. 1988. *The Barnhart Dictionary of Etymology.* New York: Wilson.

Belkaoui, A., 1978. "Linguistic Relativity in Accounting," *Accounting, Organizations and Society,* 97–104.

Boland, Richard J., Jr. 1987. "Discussion of 'Accounting and the Construction of the Governable Person,' " *Accounting, Organizations and Society,* 267–72.

Building Economic Alternatives (BEA). 1990. Special double issue, "Measuring the Economy: People, Pollution and Politics." Fall.

Bulmer, R. 1967. Why Is the Cassowary Not a Bird? *Man,* n.s. 2: 5–25.

Burrell, Gibson. 1987. "No Accounting for Sexuality," *Accounting, Organizations and Society,* 89–101.

Butler, Judith. 1990. *Gender Trouble: Feminism and the Subversion of Identity.* New York: Routledge.

Cairncross, Frances. 1991. *Costing the Earth.* London: Economist Books.

Chua, Wai Fong. 1986. "Radical Developments in Accounting Thought," *Accounting Review,* 601–32.

Cixous, Hélène. 1975a. "Le rire de la Méduse," *L'Arc* 61:39–64. Trans. Keith Cohen and Paula Cohen, "The Laugh of the Medusa," *Signs* 1 (1976):875–99. Version referenced here from Adams and Searle, eds. 1986, 308–20.

Cixous, Hélène (in collaboration with Catherine Clément). 1975b. *La jeune née.* Paris: Union Générale d'Éditions 10/18. English edition trans. Betsy Wing, *The Newly Born Woman.* Minneapolis: University of Minnesota Press, 1986, and chapter excerpted in Marks and Courtivron, eds. (1980).

Cixous, Hélène. 1976. Le sexe ou la tête? *Les Cahiers du GRIF* 13, 5–15. Reprinted as "Castration or Decapitation?" Annette Kuhn, trans. *Signs,* 7 (1983):41–55.

Clifford, James. 1988. *The Predicament of Culture: Twentieth-Century Ethnography, Literature, and Art.* Cambridge, MA: Harvard University Press.

Clifford, James, and George Marcus, eds. 1986. *Writing Culture.* Berkeley and Los Angeles: University of California Press.

Cornillon, Susan Koppelman, ed. 1972. *Images of Women in Fiction: Feminist Perspectives.* Bowling Green, OH: Bowling Green University Popular Press.

Crompton, R. 1987. "Gender and Accountancy: A Response to Tinker and Neimark." *Accounting, Organizations and Society,* 12(1):103–7.

Culler, Jonathan. 1982. *On Deconstruction: Theory and Criticism After Structuralism.* Ithaca, NY: Cornell University Press.

Davidson, Donald. 1973–4. "On the Very Idea of a Conceptual Scheme," *Proceedings and Addresses of the American Philosophical Association,* 47:5–20.

Davidson, Sidney, Michael W. Maher, Clyde P. Stickney, and Roman L. Weil. 1988. *Managerial Accounting: An Introduction to Concepts, Methods, and Uses,* 3d ed. Chicago: Dryden.

de Beauvoir, Simone. 1952. *The Second Sex* (1949), trans. H. H. Parshley. New York: Knopf.

Derrida, Jacques. 1967. *De la grammatologie.* Paris: Editions de Minuit. Translated and excerpted in Adams and Searle, eds. (1986).

Derrida, Jacques. 1982. "Différance." In *Margins of Philosophy* (1972), trans. Alan Bass. Chicago: University of Chicago Press. Collected in Adams and Searle, eds. (1986).

DuBois, Ellen Carol, and Vicki L. Ruiz, eds. 1990. *Unequal Sisters: A Multi-Cultural Reader in U.S. Women's History.* New York: Routledge.

Echols, Alice. 1989. *Daring to be Bad: Radical Feminism in America, 1967–1975.* Minneapolis: University of Minnesota Press.

Ellmann, Mary. 1979. *Thinking About Women* (1968). London: Virago.

Enloe, Cynthia. 1990. *Bananas, Beaches and Bases: Making Feminist Sense of International Politics.* Berkeley and Los Angeles: University of California Press.

Fausto-Sterling, Anne. 1985. *Myths of Gender: Biological Theories About Women and Men.* New York: Basic.

Feyerabend, Paul. 1975. *Against Method.* London: Verso (rev. ed. 1988).

Folbre, Nancy. 1984. "Household Production in the Philippines: A Non-Neoclassical Approach," *Economic Development and Cultural Change,* 32:303–30.

Folbre, Nancy. 1986. "Cleaning House: New Perspectives on Households and Economic Development," *Journal of Development Economics,* 39:5–40.

Folbre, Nancy R., Mark R. Rosenzweig, and T. Paul Schultz. 1984. "Market Opportunities, Genetic Endowments, and Intrafamily Resource Distribution: Comment/Reply," *American Economic Review,* 74:518–22.

Foucault, Michel. 1969. *L'archéologie du savoir.* Paris: Editions Gallimard.

Foucault, Michel. 1971. *The Order of Things: An Archaeology of the Human Sciences* (1966). New York: Random House.

Foucault, Michel. 1977. *Discipline and Punish: The Birth of the Prison.* New York: Vintage.

Foucault, Michel. 1978. *The History of Sexuality*, Vol. 1: *An Introduction*. New York: Pantheon.

Foucault, Michel. 1980. *Power/Knowledge: Selected Interviews and Other Writings, 1972–1977*, ed. Colin Gordon. New York: Pantheon.

Freud, Sigmund. 1965. *The Interpretation of Dreams* (1900). New York: Avon.

Freud, Sigmund. 1966. *Introductory Lectures on Psychoanalysis* (1917). New York: Norton.

Geertz, Clifford. 1980. "Blurred Genres: The Refiguration of Social Thought," *American Scholar* 49: 165–79, and collected in Adams and Searle, eds., (1986).

Gilbert, Sandra and Susan Gubar, eds. 1985. *The Norton Anthology of Literature by Women*. New York: Norton.

Gould, Stephen Jay. 1986. "Evolution and the Triumph of Homology, or Why History Matters." *American Scientist*, 74(Jan.–Feb.):60–9.

Gould, Stephen Jay. 1989. *Wonderful Life: The Burgess Shale and the Nature of History*. New York: Norton.

Gould, Stephen Jay. 1990. "Taxonomy as Politics: The Harm of False Classification," *Dissent*, 37(Winter):73–78.

Griaule, Marcel. 1943. *Les saô légendaires*. Paris: Gallimard.

Haraway, Donna. 1989. *Primate Visions: Gender, Race, and Nature in the World of Modern Science*. New York: Routledge.

Haraway, Donna. 1991. *Simians, Cyborgs, and Women: The Reinvention of Nature*. New York: Routledge.

Hartmann, Heidi I., and Suzanne Donovan. 1987. "The Economics of Comparable Worth," *Journal of Economic Literature*, 25(Sept.).

Hartmann, Heidi I., and Donald J. Treiman. 1983. Notes on the NAS Study on Equal Pay for Jobs of Equal Value," *Public Personnel Management*, 12(Winter):404–17.

Hines, Ruth D. 1988. "Financial Accounting: In Communicating Reality, We Construct Reality," *Accounting, Organizations and Society*, 13:251–62.

Hollis, Martin, and Steven Lukes, eds. 1982. *Rationality and Relativism*. Cambridge, MA: MIT Press.

Hopwood, Anthony. 1987. "Accounting and Gender: An Introduction," *Accounting, Organizations and Society*, 65–9.

Hoskin, Keith. 1991. "Comments on David Chioni Moore's 'Notes Towards Feminist Theories of Accounting: A View From Literary Studies.'" Presented at the Third Interdisciplinary Perspectives on Accounting Conference, Manchester, U.K., July.

Hoskin, K. W., and R. H. Macve, 1986. "Accounting and the Examination: A Genealogy of Disciplinary Power," *Accounting, Organizations and Society*, 105–36.

Hubbard, Ruth. 1990. *The Politics of Women's Biology*. New Brunswick, NJ: Rutgers University Press.

Humphries, Jane. 1987. "'The Most Free from Objection . . .': The Sexual Division of Labor and Women's Work in Nineteenth-Century England," *Journal of Economic History* 47(Dec.):929–49.

Jensen, Michael C. 1983. "Organization Theory and Methodology," *Accounting Review*, 319–39.

Kelly, Joan. 1982. "Early Feminist Theory and the Querelle des femmes, 1400–1789," *Signs*, 7:4–28.

Kennedy, Paul. 1987. *The Rise and Fall of the Great Powers: Economic Change and Military Conflict from 1500 to 2000*. New York: Random House.

Knights, D., and D. Collinson. 1987. "Disciplining the Shopfloor: A Comparison of the Disciplinary Effects of Managerial Psychology and Financial Accounting," *Accounting, Organizations and Society*, 457–78.

Kuhn, Thomas. 1962. *The Structure of Scientific Revolutions*. Chicago: University of Chicago Press.

Lakoff, George. 1987. *Women, Fire, and Dangerous Things: What Categories Reveal About the Mind*. Chicago: University of Chicago Press.

Latour, Bruno. 1987. *Science in Action: How to Follow Scientists and Engineers Through Society*. Cambridge, MA: Harvard University Press.

Latour, Bruno. 1988. *The Pasteurization of France* (1984), trans. A. Sheridan and John Law. Cambridge, MA: Harvard University Press.

Lehman, Cheryl. 1988. "Single-Entry Accounting: A Feminist Critique." Paper presented at the American Accounting Association annual meeting, Orlando, Florida, August.

Lehman, Cheryl. In press. " 'Herstory' in Accounting: The First Eighty Years," *Accounting, Organizations and Society*.

Marcus, George, and Dick Cushman. 1982. "Ethnographies as Texts," *American Review of Anthropology*, 2:25–69.

Marks, Elaine, and Isabelle de Courtivron, eds. 1980. *New French Feminisms: An Anthology*. Amherst: University of Massachusetts Press.

Miller, P., and T. O'Leary. 1987. "Accounting and the Construction of the Governable Person," *Accounting, Organizations and Society*, 235–66.

Millett, Kate. 1969. *Sexual Politics*. Garden City, NY: Doubleday.

Minow, Martha. 1990. *Making All the Difference: Inclusion, Exclusion, and American Law*. Ithaca, NY: Cornell University Press.

Modern Language Association. 1990. *M.L.A. International Bibliography*. New York: Modern Language Association (issued annually).

Modern Language Association. 1990–1. *M.L.A. Directory of Periodicals*. New York: Modern Language Association.

Moi, Toril. 1985. *Sexual/Textual Politics: Feminist Literary Theory*. London: Routledge.

Moore, David Chioni. 1991. "Accounting on Trial: The Critical Legal Studies Movement and Its Lessons for Radical Accounting," *Accounting, Organizations and Society*, 16(8):763–91.

Moore, David Chioni. 1993. "Fear of Rhetoric, Denial of Force; or, Does Positive Accounting Exist?" Delivered at the Third Critical Perspectives on Accounting Symposium, New York, April.

Morgan, Gareth. 1988. "Accounting as Reality Construction: Towards a New Epistemology for Accounting Practice," *Accounting, Organizations and Society*, 477–86.

Nabokov, Vladimir. 1980. *Lectures on Literature* (1948). New York: Harcourt, Brace, Jovanovich. Cited in this chapter from the preface to Charles Dickens, *Bleak House* (1853). Toronto: Bantam, 1983.

Nietzsche, Friedrich. 1954. "On Truth and Lie in an Extra-Moral Sense" (1873). In *The Portable Nietzsche,* trans. and ed. Walter Kaufmann. New York: Penguin/Viking.

Nietzsche, Friedrich. 1956. *The Birth of Tragedy from the Spirit of Music* (1872), trans. Francis Golffing. New York: Doubleday.

Norris, Christopher. 1982. *Deconstruction: Theory and Practice.* New York: Methuen.

Pillsbury, Ceil Moran, Liza Capozzoli, and Amy Ciampa. 1989. "A Synthesis of Research Studies Regarding the Upward Mobility of Women in Public Accounting," *Accounting Horizons,* 3(Mar.):63–70.

Register, Cheri. 1975. "American Feminist Literary Criticism: A Bibliographic Introduction," in Josephine Donovan, ed., *Feminist Literary Criticism: Explorations in Theory,* 1–28. Lexington: University Press of Kentucky.

Rogers, Katherine M. 1966. *The Troublesome Helpmate: A History of Misogyny in Literature.* Seattle: University of Washington Press.

Said, Edward. 1989. "Representing the Colonized: Anthropology's Interlocutors," *Critical Inquiry,* 15:205–25.

Scholes, Robert. 1981. *Elements of Fiction.* New York: Oxford University Press.

Scott, Joan Wallach. 1988. *Gender and the Politics of History.* New York: Columbia University Press.

Shearer, Teri and Ed Arrington. 1989. "Accounting in Other Wor(l)ds: A Feminism Without Reserve." Paper delivered at conference "Accounting and the Humanities – the Appeal of Other Voices," University of Iowa, September.

Showalter, Elaine. 1979. "Towards a Feminist Poetics," in Mary Jacobus, ed., *Women Writing and Writing About Women.* London: Croom Helm; Totowa, NJ: Barnes & Noble.

Signs: Journal of Women in Culture and Society. 1975–. Chicago: University of Chicago Press.

Skeat, Walter W., Rev. 1879. *An Etymological Dictionary of the English Language.* Oxford: Clarendon Press.

Spelman, Elizabeth V. 1988. *Inessential Woman: Problems of Exclusion in Feminist Thought.* Boston: Beacon.

Strathern, Marilyn. 1988. *The Gender of the Gift: Problems with Women and Problems with Society in Melanesia.* Berkeley and Los Angeles: University of California Press.

Riley, Denise. 1988. *Am I That Name? Feminism and the Category of "Women" in History.* Minneapolis: University of Minnesota Press.

Tinker, Tony, and Marilyn Neimark. 1987. "The Role of Annual Reports in Gender and Class Contradictions at General Motors, 1917–1976," *Accounting, Organizations and Society,* 71–88.

Wagman, Barnet, and Nancy Folbre. 1988. "The Feminization of Inequality: Some New Patterns," *Challenge* (Nov.–Dec.):56–9.

Waring, Marilyn. 1988. *If Women Counted: A New Feminist Economics.* New York: Harper/Collins.

White, Hayden V. 1973. *Metahistory: The Historical Imagination in Nineteenth-Century Europe.* Baltimore: Johns Hopkins University Press.

White, Hayden V. 1987. *The Content of the Form: Narrative Discourse and Historical Representation.* Baltimore: Johns Hopkins University Press.

Women's Review of Books. 1983–. Wellesley, MA: Wellesley College Center for Research on Women.

Woolf, Virginia. 1929. *A Room of One's Own.* London: Hogarth.

Index

611